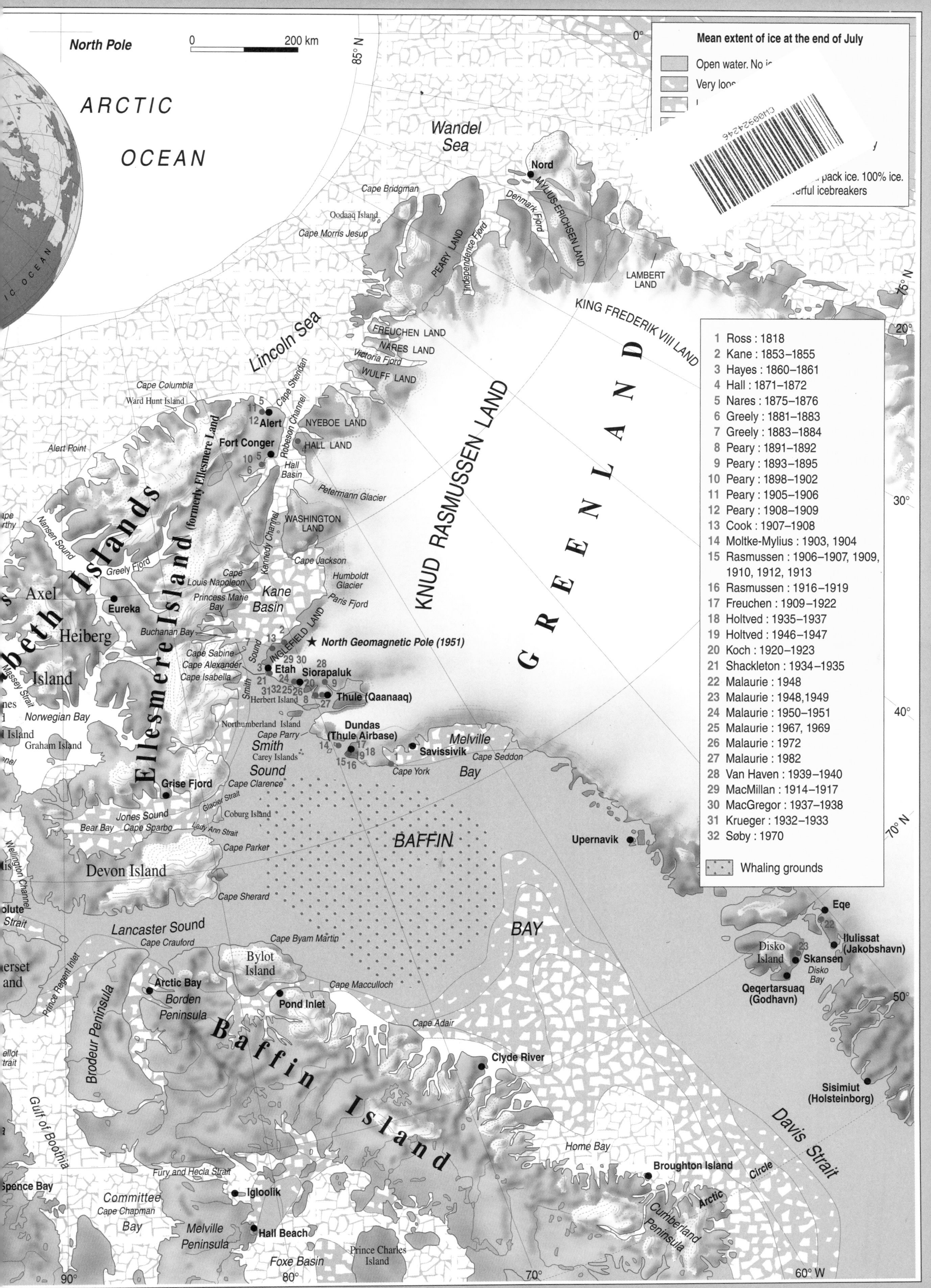

North Pole
0
200 km
85° N
0°
Mean extent of ice at the end of July
Open water. No i
Very loos
pack ice. 100% ice.
rerful icebreakers
ARCTIC
OCEAN
Wandel
Sea
Nord
Cape Bridgman
Oodaaq Island
Cape Morris Jesup
PEARY LAND
Independence Fjord
Denmark Fjord
MYLIUS-ERICHSEN LAND
LAMBERT
LAND
75° N
KING FREDERIK VIII LAND
Lincoln Sea
FREUCHEN LAND
NARES LAND
Victoria Fjord
WULFF LAND
Cape Columbia
Ward Hunt Island
Cape Sheridan
Robeson Channel
Alert
NYEBOE LAND
Fort Conger
HALL LAND
Alert Point
Hall
Basin
KNUD RASMUSSEN LAND
G R E E N L A N D
Petermann Glacier
WASHINGTON
LAND
Kennedy Channel
Nansen Sound
Ellesmere Island (formerly Ellesmere Land)
Greely Fjord
Cape Jackson
Humboldt
Glacier
Cape
Louis Napoleon
Princess Marie
Bay
Kane
Basin
Paris Fjord
Axel
Heiberg
Island
Eureka
Buchanan Bay
INGLEFIELD LAND
North Geomagnetic Pole (1951)
Cape Sabine
Cape Alexander
Cape Isabella
Sound
Smith
Etah
Siorapaluk
Thule (Qaanaaq)
Herbert Island
Massey Strait
Norwegian Bay
Graham Island
Northumberland Island
Cape Parry
Dundas
(Thule Airbase)
Smith
Sound
Carey Islands
Savissivik
Melville
Cape Seddon
Bay
Cape York
Grise Fjord
Cape Clarence
Glacier Strait
Coburg Island
Jones Sound
Bear Bay
Cape Sparbo
Lady Ann Strait
Cape Parker
BAFFIN
Upernavik
70° N
Wellington Channel
Devon Island
Cape Sherard
Lancaster Sound
Cape Crauford
Cape Byam Martin
BAY
Bylot
Island
Prince Regent Inlet
Arctic Bay
Borden
Peninsula
Pond Inlet
Cape Macculloch
Brodeur Peninsula
Baffin Island
Cape Adair
Clyde River
Gulf of Boothia
Eqe
Ilulissat
(Jakobshavn)
Disko
Island
Skansen
Disko
Bay
Qeqertarsuaq
(Godhavn)
Sisimiut
(Holsteinborg)
Davis Strait
Home Bay
Broughton Island
Circle
Arctic
Cumberland
Peninsula
Fury and Hecla Strait
Spence Bay
Committee
Cape Chapman
Bay
Igloolik
Melville
Peninsula
Hall Beach
Foxe Basin
Prince Charles
Island
90°
80°
70°
60° W
20°
30°
40°
50°
1 Ross : 1818
2 Kane : 1853–1855
3 Hayes : 1860–1861
4 Hall : 1871–1872
5 Nares : 1875–1876
6 Greely : 1881–1883
7 Greely : 1883–1884
8 Peary : 1891–1892
9 Peary : 1893–1895
10 Peary : 1898–1902
11 Peary : 1905–1906
12 Peary : 1908–1909
13 Cook : 1907–1908
14 Moltke-Mylius : 1903, 1904
15 Rasmussen : 1906–1907, 1909, 1910, 1912, 1913
16 Rasmussen : 1916–1919
17 Freuchen : 1909–1922
18 Holtved : 1935–1937
19 Holtved : 1946–1947
20 Koch : 1920–1923
21 Shackleton : 1934–1935
22 Malaurie : 1948
23 Malaurie : 1948,1949
24 Malaurie : 1950–1951
25 Malaurie : 1967, 1969
26 Malaurie : 1972
27 Malaurie : 1982
28 Van Haven : 1939–1940
29 MacMillan : 1914–1917
30 MacGregor : 1937–1938
31 Krueger : 1932–1933
32 Søby : 1970
Whaling grounds

JEAN MALAURIE

ULTIMA THULE

EXPLORERS AND NATIVES IN THE POLAR NORTH

TRANSLATED FROM THE FRENCH
BY WILLARD WOOD AND ANTHONY ROBERTS

W. W. NORTON & COMPANY • NEW YORK • LONDON

First U.S. Edition:
W. W. Norton&Company, New York, © 2003
ISBN: 0-393-05150-1

First French edition:
Editions Bordas, Paris, 1990
Editor: Thierry Foulc

The work was overseen by
Jean Castel/Tract. for Editions Bordas.
Picture research by the author, in collaboration with
Henri Froissard and Mathilde Majorel.

Translations: Raymond Ahlbeck (from the Danish)
Geneviève Doze (from the English)

Managing Editor
PHILIPPE PIERRELÉE

Editor
AUDE LE PICHON

Art Direction
SABINE HOUPLAIN

Design and composition
SOPHIE CLÉMENT
JEAN-CHRISTOPHE HUSSON
JEAN-PHILIPPE ROUSSILHE
DECEBEL SCRIBA

Proofreading
FABIENNE VASLET

Maps
PATRICK MÉRIENNE

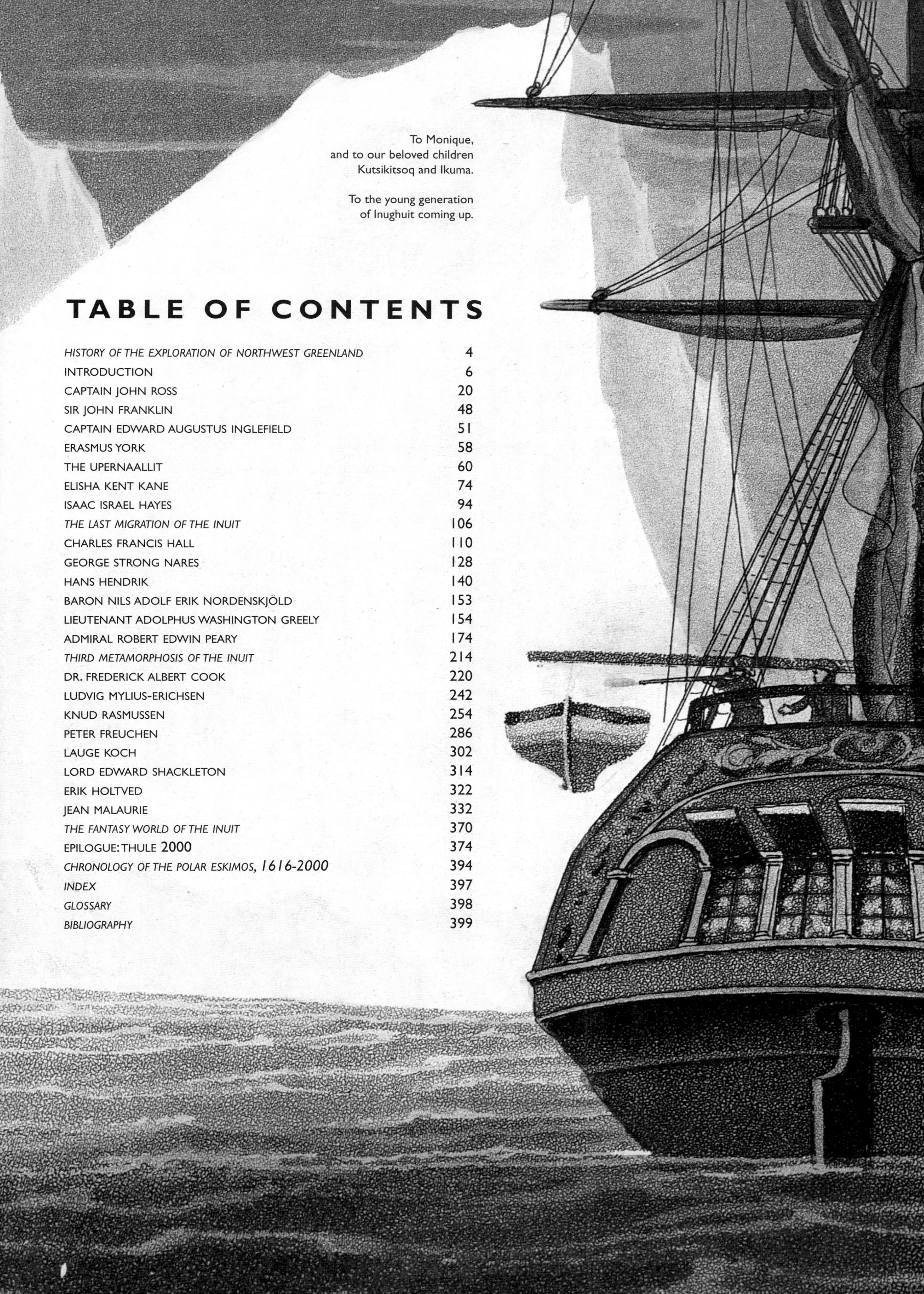

To Monique,
and to our beloved children
Kutsikitsoq and Ikuma.

To the young generation
of Inughuit coming up.

TABLE OF CONTENTS

HISTORY OF THE EXPLORATION AND C

EXPLORERS OR EVENTS Ship or means of locomotion	**AREA OF EXPLORATION** * Northenmost latitude ** Latitude of winter base *** Main summer-autumn base	**GOAL OF EXPEDITION**
W. BAFFIN R. BYLOT **England** *Discovery* (sailing vessel)	5 July1616 * 77° 45' N (Smith sound) 72° W (Cape Alexander)	Search for the Northwest Passage or route to Cathay and the Indies; discovery, not credited at the time, of Thomas Smith Sound.
JOHN ROSS W. E. PARRY **Great Britain** *Isabella* et *Alexander* (sailing vessels)	15 August 1818 * 76° 54' N (northwest of Carey Islands) Naming of Prince Regent Bay Cape York sector Savissivik	Search for the Northwest Passage. After discovering the Polar Eskimos, an uncontacted people, on 10 August 1818, Ross was unable in the following days to tell at a distance whether Smith Sound (78° N) was a bay or a channel toward the north. On his maps, Ross calls it "Smith Bay."
BRITISH WHALERS, PRIMARILY SCOTSMEN	1819-1900 76° N (approx.) Melville Bay, North Walesa, Pond Inlet	Whale fishery (occasional brief contact with the Polar Eskimos of Cape York and the Carey Islands).
J. FRANKLIN **Great Britain** *Erebus* and *Terror* (sailing vessels)	May 1845-1848 ** 70° 5' N, 98° 23' W ** 74° 47' N, 91° 39' W (Beechey Island)	The Admiralty's most massive expedition. Franklin dies aboard the Erebus, which was beset in the ice, on 11 June 1847. Captain Crozier and the other survivors disappear without a trace in 1849.
J. SAUNDERS **Great Britain** *North Star* (sailing vessel)	1849-1850 * 76° 43' N, 73° 00' W (Carey Islands) et 76° 34' N, 68° 49' W (Uummannaq) Uummannaq (Thule), Cape York, Carey Islands	Whaler sent to resupply James Clark Ross's expedition (Barrow Strait). First overwintering on Polar Eskimo territory. The North Star, J. Saunders commander, winters in Wolstenholme Sound, in the middle of the territory of the Uummannaq Eskimos. Visit of several Eskimo families. Successive epidemics.
H.T. AUSTIN W. PENNY CAPT. OMMANEY **Great Britain** *Lady Franklin, Assistance, Sophia* (sailing vessels)	August 1850 * 76° 34' N, 68° 49' W ** Wolstenholme Sound (Uummannaq, 76° 34' N) Cape York, Wolstenholme Sound (Uummannaq)	Two large English expeditions led by H. Austin and W. Penny. Communication with four Eskimos from Cape York. Danish interpreter: Carl Petersen.
E.A. INGLEFIELD **Great Britain** *Isabel* (steam-auxiliary sailing vessel)	27 August 1852 * 78° 21' N, 74° W From Cape York to Cape Alexander, rapid visits to Inuit camps.	Search for Franklin. A week spent north of Cape York, even entering Smith Sound. Inglefield visits most of the Eskimo settlements except Etah. Maps coast from Cape York to Cape Alexander (Greenland coast, coast of Ellesmere Island, and southwest coast of Inglefield Land).
E. K. KANE **United States** *Advance* (sailing vessel)	1853-1855 (24 June1854) * 80° 10' N, 67° W ** Rensselaer 78° 37' N, 71° W Kane Basin and territory of the Polar Eskimos	Search for Franklin, and search for the open polar sea. First overwintering of an official scientific expedition in Polar Eskimo territory, Rensselaer Harbor (Aannartoq). Dog sleds.
I. I. HAYES **United States** *United States* (sailing steamship)	1860-1861 (19 May1861) * 81° 35' N 70°30' W ** 78° 18' N, 72° 43' W (Port Foulke) Kane Basin and territory of the Polar Eskimos	Search for the open polar sea, whose discovery is claimed. "No land to the east" from Ellesmere Island (dog sleds), after his supposed (and contested) journey to Cape Lieber. Overwinters at Port Foulke (Etah).
C. F. HALL **United States** *Polaris* *ex-Periwinkle* (sail-assisted steamship)	1871-1873 (30 August1870) * 82° 11' N, 61° W (1870) * 81° 37' N, 62° W (1871) ** 78° 20' N, 72° 30' W Hall Basin, Inglefield Land (south)	First official American attempt on the Pole. Winter base 1871-1872: Thank God Harbor (Hall Land). Murder of Hall. Part of the group winters in 1872-1873 in Life Boat Cove or Qallunaalik (Inglefield Land). Dog sleds. Another part of the expedition drifts on an ice floe to Labrador.
G. S. NARES **Great Britain** *Alert, Discovery, Valourous* (sailing steamships)	1875-1876 (12 May 1876) * 83° 20' 26" N 65° W (with sleds) ** 82° 25' N 62° W	Last British attempt on the Pole from Greenland and Canada. Sleds hauled by men. Discovery winters in Discovery Harbor: 81° 41' N. Alert winters at Floeberg Beach: 82° 15' N.
A.W. GREELY **United States** *Proteus* (sail and steam)	1881-1884 (13 May 1882) * Lockwood Island 83° 24' N, 42° 45' W ** 81° 44' N, 64° 45'W ** 78° 43' N, 74° 97' W Fort Conger (north Ellesmere Island) and North Greenland	1st International Polar Year. Winter 1881-1882: Fort Conger (81° 44' N, 64° 45' W) Winter 1883-1884: Cape Sabine (Pim Island), 78° 43' N, 74° 07' W (Cape Sabine). Dog sleds.
A.E. NORDENSKJOLD **Sweden** *Sofia* (steam and sail)	26 July 1883 * 76° 07' N, 68° 37' W (Parker Snow Point) Ivsugissoq, north of Cape York. Brief visit of Inuit settlement.	Cape York, Ivsugissoq. Meteorite: failure.
R. E. PEARY **United States** *Kite* (sail-assisted steamship) *Hope* *Hope* *Windward* (sail-assisted steamship) *Roosevelt* *Roosevelt* (sail-assisted steamship)	(6 April 1909) 1891-1892 ** 77° 35' N 1893-1895 ** 77° 40' N 1896 (summer) 1897 (summer) 1898-1902 * 83° 50' N (1899) * 84° 17' N (1902) 1905-1906 * 87° 6' N 1908-1909 * 90°(?) N	McCormick (77° 35' N) Bowdoin Fjord (77° 40' N) excursion to Navy Cliff, Thule district, North Greenland (glacier). Meteorites taken from Savissivik (Cape York). 1898-1899: Cape d'Urville, Grinnell Land. 1899-1900: Etah (78° 20' N). 1900-1901: Fort Conger (81° 20' N) 1901-1902: Cape Sabine (78° 45' N). Cape Sheridan, Ellesmere Island (82° 28' N). Cape Sheridan, Ellesmere Island (82° 29' N, 61° 26' W). Dog sled, following Eskimo techniques. Use of Eskimo labor. Partial ethnographic study by Cook, then sporadically by other expedition members, finally by Kroeber with Eskimos brought to New York.
F.A. COOK **United States** *Kite* (steam) *Erik* (steam) *John H. Bradley* (sail/steam)	21 April 1908 1891-1892 (Peary exp.) ** 77° 35' N McCormick Bay, Inglefield Bay, Cape Sabine 1902 *78° 35' N 1907-1909 ** Anoritooq 78° 33' N, 72° 30' W * 90°(?) N ** Cape Sparbo. 65° 49' N, 83° 48' W (Cape Hardy). Anoritooq (Thule Strait), Ellesmere Island, Arctic Ocean, Axel Heiberg Island, North Devon, Ellesmere Island, Melville Bay	Cook was volunteer doctor and ethnographer on Peary's first expedition. Summer expedition sent by the Peary Arctic Club to bring supplies to Peary. Dr. Cook was the volunteer doctor. Expedition to the North Pole by dog sled with Eskimos and return by Ellesmere Island and Jones Sound with Ittukusuk and Aapilaq, then crossing of Melville Bay by dog sled to Tasiusaq (north Upernavik), then Danish ship to Copenhagen.

ONQUEST OF NORTHWEST GREENLAND

L. MYLIUS-ERICHSEN H. MOLTKE K. RASMUSSEN **Denmark** By dog sled from Jakobshavn across Melville Bay	April 1903-January 1904 ** Saunders Island 76° 32' N. From Cape York to North Star Bay and Etah, Thule Strait (having come from Upernavik)	Danish Literary Expedition to the west coast. Mylius-Erichsen, Rasmussen, Moltke: first studies of the Polar Eskimos, collecting of myths and legends. Dog sleds.
K. RASMUSSEN H.P. STEENSBY First (1912) and Second (1917) Thule Expeditions **Denmark** *Godhaab* (steam) *Danemark* (steam/sail)	1907-1909 1909 (summer) ** 76° 34' N (Thule) 1912 * 83° (Peary Land) 1917 Thule and Cape York From Thule to Peary Land	Rasmussen lives as an Eskimo among the Polar Eskimos. Steensby: first Danish ethnographic studies (summer) after Rasmussen. First Thule Expedition: cartographic and geographic surveys. Second Thule Expedition: (1916-1918) multidisciplinary, in Peary Land. Dog sleds, following Eskimo usage and with help of the population.
C. LEDEN **Norway** *Godhaab* (steam)	1909 (summer) 76° 34' N North Star Bay	Musicology research. 31 phonographic recordings (in cooperation with Knud Rasmussen).
Expedition of the Danish Missionary Society **Copenhagen** *Godhaab* (steam)	July-August 1909 First 76° 34' N (Thule) * 76° 34' N From Cape York to Thule and Etah	First evangelical mission (Gustav Olsen); Uummannaq (summer 1909), Thule (1910) Kangerlussuaq: 1915
"KAP YORK STATIONEN THULE" private company directed by Knud Rasmussen **Denmark** *Sea Kongen* (motor)	1910-1933 76° 34' N Thule North Star Bay	First trading post in Northwest Greenland. Privately held from 1910-1937. Taken over by authorities after death of Knud Rasmussen, its director, in 1933.
D. B. MCMILLAN **United States** *Bowdoin* (sail/steam)	1914-1917 1923-1924 ** 78° 20' N (Etah) ** 78° 29' N, 72° 27' W (Refuge Harbor) Thule District, Ellesmere Island, Arctic Ocean	Dog sleds. Meteorology, map-making, geography. The 1917 expedition was intended to find Crocker Land, described by Peary (nonexistent). Dog sleds.
L. KOCH **Denmark** *Louise* (motor/sail) *Fylla* (sailboat with motor)	1920-1923 * 83° (Peary Land, 1922) ** 77° 46' N Illulorsuit, (north of Siorapaluk) Northwest Greenland (from Cape Saddon to Peary Land)	Overwinters alone at Illulorsuit. Official Danish expedition: "Jubilaeum Ekspedition": Koch and 4 Eskimos. Mapping, glaciology, and geology of northwest Greenland, from Melville Bay to Peary Land. Fundamental research. Dog sleds.
H. K. E. KRUEGER **Germany**	1932-1933 ** 77° 51' N Neqi (Cape Saumarez) Ellesmere Island	Mapping, geology: Krueger, a young Dane (Bjare), and an Eskimo hunter (Ajaku), with only one dog sled. They disappear entirely (May 1933?) in western Ellesmere Island (south of Meighen Island), having left in March 1933.
COPENHAGEN Court of The Hague	1933	Greenland in its entirety, from north to south and from east to west, is recognized as a territory under Danish sovereignty.
E. SHACKLETON, N. HUMPHREYS, D. HAIG-THOMAS Oxford Ellesmere Island Expedition **Great Britain** *Signal Horn* (steam/sail)	1934-1935 * 82° 25' N, 70° W ** 78° 20' N Etah Ellesmere Island	Mapping and geology on Ellesmere Island, to Grant Land (reconnaissance of Mt. Oxford). Eskimos take part, including: Inuterssuaq, Kutsikitsoq, Qaaqqutsiaq. Dog sleds.
E. HOLTVED **Denmark** *Dannebrog* (ship)	1935-1937 * 79° 10' N 1946-1947 ** 76° 34' N Thule Thule District Inglefield Land	Philology, ethnography, and archaeology (120,000 artifacts). Fundamental research. Dog sleds.

MCGREGOR **United States**	1937-1938 ** 76° 34' N	American meteorological station in Foulke Fjord. Overwinters.
GRONLANDS STYRELSDE **Copenhagen**	1937	Assumption of the property of "Kap York Stationen Thule" by the Danish government, after compensation of the company's shareholders. Territory administered directly by the Gronlands Styrelsde, with observance of local laws.
J. VAN HAUEN **Denmark** *Svaerdfisken* (motor)	1939-1941 ** 77° 51' N Neqi (Cape Saumarez) Ellesmere Island and Inglefield Land, Thule district.	Mapping and geology on Ellesmere Island (J. C. Trodsen). Geological research in Inglefield Land: study of marine mammals in the Thule district (Ch. Vibe). The expedition's photographer was Knud Rasmussen's son, now a photographer in New York. Dog sleds.
J. MALAURIE **France** *Disko* (steam) to Jakobshavn, *Tikerak* (motor) to Thule, *Fylla* (sailboat with motor) to Etah	1950-1951 (21 May 1951) * 80° 03' N, 67° 06' W ** 77° 47' N, 70° 42' W (Siorapaluk) (Robertson Fjord) Winter: from Savissivik to Etah Spring: Inglefield Land, Washington Land (south coast), Ellesmere Island (east) Summer: Thule region (Wolstenholme Fjord, Uvdle)	Dog sleds, with Eskimo squads. Geographic expedition. Overwintered alone in Siorapaluk (genealogical, socio-economic, and psycho-sociological research). Tests administered in winter, including Rorschach and Zazzo, to school children and adults. Geomorphological expedition in spring (March-June) in Inglefield Land, south coast of Washington Land, and Ellesmere Island (east coast, Alexander Fjord) with three sleds, four Eskimos, 43 dogs. Survey for geomorphological map at 1:100,000 to 4 km inland. Twelve new names in Inglefield and Washington lands. First Frenchman to travel in area of Geomagnetic North Pole, with two dog sleds (with Kutsikitsoq) on 29 May 1951 (78° 29' N, 68° 54' W).
US AIR FORCE, US NAVY **United States** Operation "Arctic Blue Jay" Landing of 5000 men, with 100 ships, massive air operations.	June-July 1951 76° 34' N Thule (Dundas Bay) North Star Bay 1953	Establishment of the so-called Thule nuclear military base; artificial port, airport. Base ultra-secret for several years. Eskimos displaced from Thule territory in June 1953. Founding of Qaanaaq-Thule: 77° 28' N, Murchison Sound. One fifth of Polar Eskimo territory taken away. Base expanded.
J. MALAURIE* **France** Airplane	1967 *** 77° 47' N (Siorapaluk) Summer-fall: Siorapaluk and entire central district 1969 *** 77° 47' N (Siorapaluk) Spring: from Etah to Savissivik 1972 *** 77° 47' N (Siorapaluk) Summer-fall: Etah to Thule-Dundas 1982 *** 77° 28' N (Qaanaaq) Summer: Qaanaaq-Siorapaluk-Qeqertaq-Thule-Dundas 1995. August: Savissivik, Qaanaaq, Siorapaluk, Etah, Ellesmere (Alexandra Fjord), Cape Sparbo (Jones Fjord)	Consulting expedition for the Greenland Ministry (Copenhagen). Filming of Last Kings of Thule. Natsilivik and Siorapaluk-Neqi (Thule-Dundas) area in April-May 1969. Dog sleds (six). Study of paleoclimate: Siorapaluk, Savissivik (two dog sleds). Ecological atlas (microeconomic research in all of district) and checking of genealogical data, family by family. Community motor boat, then Inuterssuaq's. Recording of songs, legends, interviews for a compact disk. Finish of ecological project and study of the social crisis following on massive Danish immigration and accelerated modernization. Quick trip aboard the ice-breaker Kapitan Khlebnikov with W. Herbert and P. Schledermann.

* Numerous foreign and Danish expeditions were made after 1951. In particular we should note the overwintering of two explorers of the North Pole: the Briton Wally Herbert (1967), at Qeqertarsuaq (Herbert Island)), and Guido Monzino, Italian, who reached the Pole by dog sled, in the company of many Eskimos led by Peary's grandson (Talilanguaq) on 17 May 1971. Prior stays: 1969, 1970.
Mention also goes to the important anthropological work of Regitze Margrethe Søby, my colleague and friend (Denmark): Savissivik, 1973-1975; 1979-1980; 1982; 1987; and to Vagn F. Buchwald, the eminent Danish mineralogist, who searched for new meteorites and in 1963 found a 20-ton fragment called Agpalilik, the largest found in Europe to that time and the fifth largest in the world. Expeditions: 1961, 1963, 1964, 1965, 1966.

INTRODUCTION

Beyond the North, the ice, the everyday,
Beyond death, at a remove
Our life, our happiness
Neither on land, nor on sea
Will you find the hunter who leads
To us, Hyperboreans,
About whom also
A wise mouth has prophesied.

FRIEDRICH NIETZSCHE, POEMS.

This book sets out to retrace—taking the fabled ground of Thule as its reference—one hundred and eighty-two years of relations between the northernmost native people on the planet and their discoverers, who voyaged in search of the North Pole and its myths.

Since the dawn of time the North Pole, that sacred space, the presumed seat of paradise, has been the focus of the oddest speculations, imagined as an open, ice-free sea, and as an island of black rock.

The new historiography reminds us of the great influence of mental realities on the course of civilizations. This work examines the close relations—whether admitted or not—between the Inuit and their conquerors and shows the technological and psychological ascendance very quickly assumed by the former—these anarcho-communist "primitives"—over the latter—these whites with their so-called advanced civilization. The British and American expeditions were forced willy nilly—and after what disasters!—to admit their powerlessness beside the experience of these "savages," whom they described as "human animals." The terrible accounts we are about to read provide evidence of two fatal blights on our time: the overlooking of minorities, and the ignorance of the Other.

It is the story of resistance as well, on the part of a small people whose specific genius was never recognized until the advent of the visionary Danish-Eskimo Knud Rasmussen, who at the start of the twentieth century organized a close collaboration between himself and this people, after a hundred years of non-communication and contempt.

The history of this coexistence shows that a civilization can advance only by complementarity, or else run the risk of sterility and repetition. And this complementarity must favor the weaker society. In June 1951, in Thule, an ultrasecret nuclear base was built under my eyes, a figurehead of the all-powerful atomic era . . .

This book is the chronological study of a fabled site, seen from opposing perspectives: the accounts of a few of the greatest adventurers to travel among the Inuit, and the indifferent return gaze of a group of one hundred fifty to two hundred hunters, willing all the same to accept innovations they deemed useful. From 1818 to 2000, turning the pages, time accelerates, until, at the dawn of the third millennium, close to a thousand men and women make up the quiet force of this millennial tradition, confronting the crushing advance of "progress"—a "progress" that is hostage to common accidents, as when an airplane crashed on 21 January 1968 carrying four hydrogen bombs, threatening to destroy for all time the fragile equilibrium of the high latitudes.

Under our eyes, a new people therefore is seeking its destiny at the crossroads of tradition and modernity—a modernity so advanced that the Community of the Polar Inuit in Thule might be in a position, ironically enough, to repossess the land of the military base, which was decommissioned in 1990 at the end of the Cold War and returned to the civil authorities. From the civilization of the seal to the electronic civilization . . .

This book is intended as a call to attention, which could be summed up in two simple questions: what purpose do the social sciences serve? and what has become of the mission and morality of the West?

This hybrid of a man and a woman has its head in what appears to be the pillory. Its body, tensed in defiance, and the cry it seemingly hurls into the depths of time might serve as the painful symbol of the Inuit people's entry into the world (Walrus ivory, A.D. 700-900, Inuarfigssuaq Thule).

"Es war ein König in Thule"

In 1808, ten years before the Scottish captain Sir John Ross discovered the men of the North, till then lost in the ice and mist, the first part of Goethe's *Faust* was published in Germany. In Scene viii of the tragedy, Marguerite prepares for the night by singing: "Es war ein König in Thule . . ." There was a king in Thule, faithful to the grave, to whom his dying lover gave a golden chalice. When he knew himself on the point of dying, he left all his belongings to his heirs except the chalice, which he threw into the sea from the top of his castle. If, in the context of the play, this song prefigures a faithfulness to love that transcends the lover, even the divine love that Marguerite will pay for with her life, it also shows the faithfulness of European culture to the more than two-thousand-year-old myth of Thule.

It was the European faithfulness of the Dane Knud Rasmussen that caused him to name the northernmost trading post on earth "Thule" when he founded it in 1910 on the age-old site of Uummannaq. The name is of unknown origin—is it from the Greek *tele*, meaning "distant"? or the Celtic *tuah*, meaning "north"? According to one of the esoteric traditions it is the distant Earth, the White Island, the pole of light, the sanctuary of the world, the capital of the priests of

The first man, at the dawn of Inuit history, as carved for me by the shaman Pualuna (b. 1874) in the image of his dreams. Siorapaluk, 1950.

the Sun-god. Thule, in North Star Bay (so called because a Scots whaler, the *North Star*, was trapped in pack ice and forced to winter there in 1849), has become the capital of the Polar Inuit and of the legendary Hyperboreans. For us Frenchmen, the place is very real. Of all the early navigators who searched for these Immortals, the best known is the Marseillan Pytheas. At the end of the fourth century B.C., he came upon a land called Thule, beyond which there extended "a sea congealed by the cold."

But why "Ultima Thule"? The phrase comes from a prophecy made in Seneca's *Medea*. The scene takes place in Corinth. Medea, the daughter of Aeëtes, king of Colchis, rails against Jason, who is cheating on her, but the chorus reminds her of the great deeds of the Argonauts and in so doing opens a door into the future: "Later, when the world is older, a time will come when the Ocean will loose the bonds between things. An enormous land will open up, and Thetis will discover new continents. Then Thule will no longer be the last of lands (*Detegat orbes nec sit terris ultima Thule*)."

The men of Greco-Roman antiquity believed that in the north there existed a place beyond the last land, named if still unvisited. Tradition made the Pole the center of a paradisal country and also an open ocean. Might the Arctic explorers have been the faithful of legend, those through whom the promise was kept? History is more complex. The motive for all exploration is certainly imagination, fed by myths and stories, inspired by the blank areas on the map, the vacuum that attracts.

But myth, the archetype of thought, has its own life. Steeped in the Bible, from which they heard verses every Sunday, the conquerors of the North saw the Arctic through their own dream-shrouded eyes. Whether allegorical expressions of a lived experience or fabulous attempts at explanation, the ancient myths rise from their collective unconscious at unpredictable moments and enter the thoughts of individual men, changing the course of their lives. Their power—as we will see—is immense.

Apollo, god of the North

First among these myths: Hyperborea. It reflects a nostalgia deep within Greek thought for a virginal land of uniform whiteness, the symbolic color of purity and peace. So strong is the power of myth that, despite the testimony brought back by travelers of cold, ice, and the long polar night, the Greeks continued to identify the boreal lands with happiness. Belonging to a golden age, the Hyperboreans lived in fraternal closeness with the gods and at peace with the neighboring peoples: a Nordic society of strong, powerful, and pious men. It is to the north, Plato tells us, that souls rise. Boreas, says Homer, is the generative wind, taking and bringing souls.

The god of the North is the handsomest, youngest, and most mysterious in Greek mythology. In memory of his childhood voyage to Hyperborea (carried by swans, birds of the north that sing only to die, according to Callimachus, Alexandrian poet of the third century B.C.), Apollo, son of Zeus and Leto, was born in Delos, where seals and sea monsters bring forth their young on hidden rocks. Apollo, god of the hunt, wolf god, archer god, musician god (he plays the lyre at Zeus's table), returns every autumn to the Far North "beyond the North Wind" to restore himself and to exercise his great prophetic powers in the spring at Delphi—like a shaman from the north with his mediumistic abilities.

He is more than anything *Alexikakos*, the god who shields from evil, the wonder-worker god, the healer, the divine. Sun-like, Apollo stands in opposition to the forces of night and earth. Eternally young, always naked, beardless, his hair unshorn and sometimes gathered in a knot at the neck, with delicate feminine traits, Apollo is the god of spirit who inspires and orders matter. He rules over the harmony of the world. He soothes and brings together. According to Plato, he develops the fundamental laws of the Republic—he is the very spirit of the laws that bind man to god and form the initial alliance. "This god, who came from the north," said Plato, "established himself at the center and umbilicus of the earth to guide Mankind." From the North, the Hyperboreans sent him messengers every year, young virgins who presented him an offering at Delos. During certain rituals, the priests of Apollo dressed the initiate in crow feathers, to remind him of his heavenly and boreal origin. Aristaeus (sixth century B.C.), the author of a tragedy that has come down to us in fragments, who was called the "Possessed of Apollo," identified Apollo with the crow: black as the polar night, long-lived, and vast-memoried. The crow is the tutelary bird of certain Siberian peoples, namely the Koriaks. He inspired omens.

The knowledge of this Apollonian territory is geographic as well as poetic. Herodotus wrote in the fifth century B.C. that "the country of the Hyperboreans is farther from Greece than Egypt or Cyprus." Diodorus of Sicily (first century B.C.) situates this people beyond the northern Celtic lands, where the Moon is only a short distance from the Earth. The ancient Greek geographer imagined that there existed a mountain chain north of Europe, the Hyperborean Mountains, that separated the primordial people from other men. The details that appear in the writings of Greek geographers and historians are even more astounding.

One of the most illustrious Greek philosophers, Pythagoras (sixth century B.C.), is said to have studied with a sage or shaman who came from the east or the Far North, from a place where "day lasts uninterruptedly for half a year." Pomponius Mela (first century) is more specific: "They do not see the Sun rise and set every day as we do but enjoy its presence above the horizon from the spring equinox to the autumn equinox. Their day therefore lasts six months, and their night also."

East Asia: pole and paradise

What civilization has not given thought to this sacred spot, as axis of the Earth, land of the dead, paradise . . . ? Its importance is such that the Chinese emperor, the Son of Heaven, who believed himself always directly under the celestial pole, laid claim to being the "North Pole." Where the emperor is, there is the Pole, was reiterated to the subjects of the Middle Kingdom. He was the "germ," and the pivot, around which everything turned. As Paul Mus liked to say, the compass on the emperor's chariot only pointed south, for "in East Asia the king is conceived as the priest of a heavenly religion, serving as an intermediary between men and God, who lives at the North Pole, the Heavenly Pole."

In the most ancient Brahmanic texts, the earthly world is represented by the four cardinal points. Brahma has four heads; there are four classes, and four directions open to the religious man in India. In the north is Siddhapura, the paradise-city. The vulgar lot of humanity live in the plains to the south. The initiate, for his part, lives at altitude, in the north, in the mountains, near the legendary Mount Meru, India's North Pole; through asceticism he can experience the highest spirituality there. The Vedas describe this primordial time, the "Arctic," where, "under a sky that turns" overhead like a hat and where the night lasts for six months, a race of initiates lives in the Far North.

The North is thus sacred; the gods live beyond the northern mountains. In all the mythology of the Indian epics, one approaches the gods by going north. The North is the land of the Brahmans. The Far North, beyond the Himalayas, is the land of deliverance, where, no longer condemned to be reborn, the initiate lives in Shiva's domain.

North of Mount Meru, at the extremities of the Earth, is the country of Uttarakuru. It is surrounded by a river that becomes petrified (frozen?) when a man touches it. Farther north, in the Northern Ocean, rises Mount Somarigi, "barely accessible to the gods."

The Uttarakuru (from *uttara*, "north"; and *kuru*, "men, heroes") are born twins, but of opposite sexes. They live in couples. And all men exchange women. Sexual life, and the life of the senses and feelings, is so intense for these men who are not bound by material contingencies that a simple touch, smile, or look is enough to give the body internal sensations of pleasure. There is no private property, there are no restrictions or rules. These men, finally, can die, but they are reborn as mortals or gods.

In pre-Islamic Iran, the cradle of mankind is north of the Albordj, the pole and center of the world. This sacred place rises to the sky. A celestial spring brings water to the Tree of Life, and, as in the Book of Genesis, four rivers flow from it. Avicenna, the great Iranian philosopher, wrote these visionary words in the eleventh century: "You will have heard of the darkness that rules the regions of the Pole. He who challenges this darkness will attain a vast and unbounded space filled with light. The first sight to greet him will be a spring, whose waters flow like a river. . . . Whoever bathes in this spring will become light, light enough to walk on the waters . . ."

Note that this written mythology is resolutely ignorant of the people of the antipodes and their philosophies.

Zophane, the hidden

The Biblical tradition intimately inspired the first British, North American, and Danish explorers—the chaplains read chapters from the Bible to their assembled shipmates, and men and officers joined together in singing hymns—the word "north" (*zophane*) is related to the Hebrew *zophune*, "hidden," or "dark." Literally, it is the "promontory," and therefore the sacred. The references to the north are eloquent: "And thou shalt put the table on the north side" (Exod. 26:35); "And he shall kill it on the side of the altar northward before the Lord" (Lev. 1:11); "Mount Zion, on the sides of the north, the city of the great King" (Ps. 48); "Then he said unto me, Son of Man, lift up thine eyes now the way toward the north. So I lifted up mine eyes the way toward the north (Ezek. 8:5). The Book of Enoch in particular describes this cardinal geography: "And the four quarters which are called North are divided into three parts. The first is the place of man's habitation, the second is the oceans and gorges and forests and rivers, darkness and fog. The

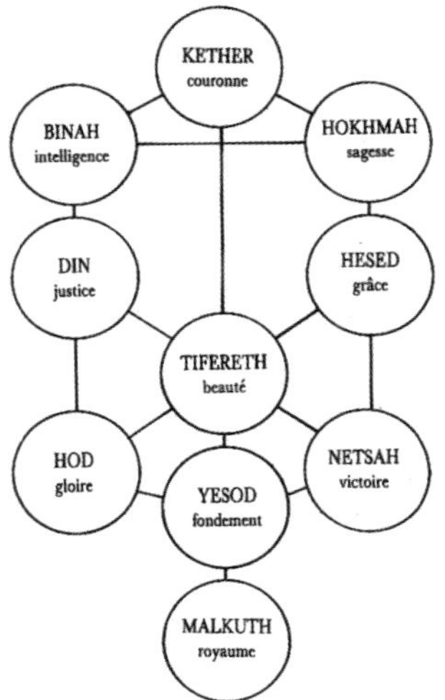

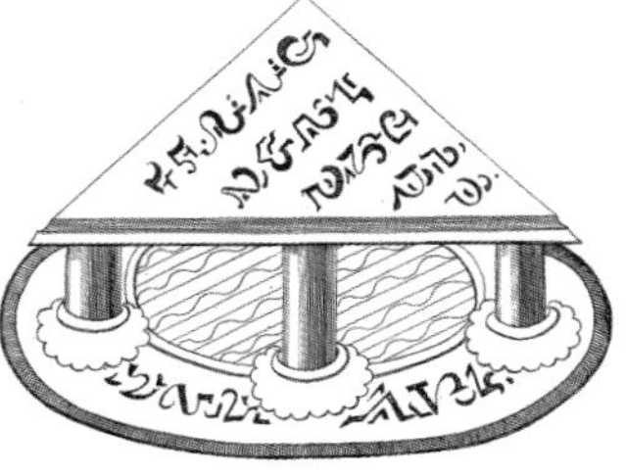

Relation of a voyage from the North to the South Pole through the Center of the World (anonymous, Amsterdam, 1721).

68 *Paſſage du Pole*

d'une eau très-claire ſerpentoit vers le milieu, nous apperçûmes à l'extrêmité d'un enfoncement quelque choſe de blanc à travers de grandes herbes, nous en étans aprochez nous y vîmes avec la derniére ſurpriſe, un petit Edifice † d'une ſinguliére ſtructure, il étoit tout de pierre blanche, ſa partie ſupérieure, étoit une grande pierre plate de figure triangulaire, poſée ſur ſix colonnes hautes d'environ trois pieds, ſur une baſe en ovale qui s'élevoit de

† Voyez la figure D.

Arctique & Antarctique. 69

de terre à la hauteur de quatre ou cinq poûces, ſur la pierre à trois angles on voyoit une Inſcription de caractéres bizares, qui n'étoient connus d'aucun de nôtre troupe, & en bas ſur la circonférence de la baze, paroiſſoient encore d'eſpace en eſpace les mêmes caractéres, mais preſque effacez; ce Monument fit naître entre nous une infinité de raiſonnemens, car nous voyions très-bien que ce n'étoit pas-là un Ouvrage du hazard, mais j'en laiſſe la déciſion à de plus habi-

E 3 les

The arrival of the Vikings in Greenland (engraving on polychrome wood, late nineteenth century).

third part is the Garden of Justice" (77:3). If intelligence and Justice are to the West, Wisdom, Grace, and Eternity are to the East, and the North is the crown of God (Kether), according to the Kabbala. Presumably it is the Pole—although the Kabbala's import is always hidden, only the profane being clear.

Ever since Noah, the Hebrew people have walked backwards toward the future, their faces turned toward the past. In the Christian tradition with its Biblical roots, the primary axes of a sacred geography are variously repeated: the Jordan flows north-south. And Jesus, the Galilean, goes south to Jerusalem, where he will declare himself God. The cross, in its mystical symbolism, represents the cardinal points, with Christ's dolorous head to the north. In cathedrals with a cruciform plan, the north transept often has a small, low door that one ducks one's head to pass through (north representing the Night before the creation): it is the door of light leading to the sanctuary. Finally, in the Masonic tradition (and the American explorers Kane, Hayes, and Peary were Masons and celebrated Masonic rituals before the Inuit), the temple, which is oriented west-east with the door to the west, receives the initiate to the northeast. In that position, the initiate represents the cornerstone of the Temple; once a companion, he rotates in position toward the south.

Along the white trail, the meeting of two world views

This book proposes to be the encounter between two visions of the world, an interface between two apparently hermetic civilizations: that of the West and that of the Inuit. Chapter after chapter, it follows the silent discourse between men of vastly alien races and mentalities, swinging from one outlook to another.

Face to face in conversation, elbow to elbow on sleds and in igloos, after the hardships of the day's travels, two understandings of the world took each other's measure. To the surface came unspoken thoughts, private feelings, presuppositions, areas of complicity, confessions, hurts. The Inuit, in their extreme material poverty, quickly established their distance, their moral ascendancy over the white sailors and officers, fragile in their sumptuous wealth. And in these western minds, tormented by the visceral fear of never returning south (their ships were trapped in ice), the anguish was aggravated by the group's internal tensions, by the blizzard howling in the polar night. It is in such moral solitude that childhood stories resurface. Each man questioned himself, according to his education. Among the officers, graduated from the universities of Oxford and Cambridge, the gods of a humanist education—Apollo, or the gods who stormed heaven to overthrow Zeus, or Hespera, the

daughter of twilight, who lived among the Hyperboreans, the primordial people—rose through the subconscious, along with national legends: Saint Brendan, the Isle of Avalon . . . Many first encounters with this lunar country took on an initiatory significance. And on the ships, in their cold, dank quarters, after painful excursions over the floe, during the anxious vigils of their months of voluntary asceticism, the officers and men experienced the sometimes suicidal impulses of their deepest selves. The darkest traditions crowded into their minds, particularly as some of them read the Bible night and day, all the more fervently for being triply confined: by night, by the ship, and by their shipmates. On Sunday, psalms were sung, and the prophecies were recalled. The Scots Presbyterians prayed in an atmosphere of sacred fright, their ears singed by the terrors of the Apocalypse, spoken in the chaplain's craggy Gaelic tones: "For I testify unto every man that heareth the words of the prophecy of this book, If any man shall add unto these things, God shall add unto him the plagues that are written in this book." (Rev. 22:18). In the damp and cold belowdecks, on the icy trail, under the Aurora borealis, the voyage became fraught with primal meaning.

And the sky? The whites had learned the nostalgia for beatitude, that inner aspiration to live in the eternal, from the tympanum of a cathedral when, as children, they stepped into the narthex, on the threshold of that sacred space where the spirit of God stirs. The childhood vision came back to them in this gigantic cathedral of ice, without walls, without a roof except the starry sky, a vast nave made even bigger by the solemn silence. Psalms, prophecies, apocalypse . . . when all is said, is it not at the very heights, in the highest part of the Earth, closest to the sky, the celestial pole, that our Great Judge lives? The sailors, who were often illiterate, preserved the last thoughts of the dying. "Don't leave us, friend, in the accursed country of Gog and Magog." Such were their last wishes. Gog and Magog, the horrible Satanic forces announced by Ezekiel at the end of the world, but where were they? On their dog sled trips over the unfamiliar floe, the men dreaded rounding an iceberg to meet one of these northern monsters, whose presence could be imagined in the cracking of the ice, the moaning of the wind. If there were any skeptics among the officers, they were reminded of the exhortations of Sir Francis Bacon, a chancellor of England and the father of modern philosophy and the experimental method, who was convinced of the existence of Gog and Magog, and constantly urged that the exploration of the world should be hastened so that the habitation of these evil forces might be identified, and he urged the building of a wall at the northern end of the civilized world so as to forestall their invasion at the time of the Second Coming. Who could doubt such statements? Was the Church not under the personal authority of the King of England?

Atheists, agnostics, and believers all join in a procession of images that form an orderly pattern. Kane, a Mason from the Great Lodge of Philadelphia, engaged before his departure to a spirit medium, believed in 1853-1854 that he recognized in the iceberg landscape the Utopia celebrated by the poets. The hallucination was so strong that after glimpsing—on the say-so of a Greenlander and a quartermaster—a stretch of open water, which I myself saw in May 1951 for the limited pool that it was, he was convinced that the North Pole was an ice-free sea and not a paradisal continent, as tradition had it. So, at any rate, was it conceived by the mystic poet Guillaume Postel, who in 1569 drew the first map centered on the Pole, and by the cartographer Mercator, who in 1595 showed the Pole as a high black rock, *"rupes nigra et altissima,"* from which flowed outward the four rivers of Paradise, in accordance with Genesis. Kane, swayed by the arguments of the geographers, particularly the greatest among them, the German Johan Justhus Perthes, declared to his sober and prudent crew that Sir John Franklin, the object of his search, though he had disappeared without a trace seven years before with 140 sailors, was waiting a few tens or hundreds of miles away on the edge of the floe, looking out over an ocean furrowed with mighty waves, holding a fishing line, and fully confident that the British Admiralty would rescue him. The frozen environment, the mountains of hummocks, the cold that grew more implacable every winter—nothing could shake his conviction: the Pole equaled an open sea. Hayes, an eminent American explorer, a doctor who followed Kane into the Arctic, even published a book on his return from his second great expedi-

Earliest man from Thule: this is the oldest carved head found to date (Nudglit Phase, A.D. 950-1100, Ruin Island, Inglefield Fjord).

tion to the Pole in 1862 with the eloquent title: *The Open Polar Sea.* Not only did he claim to have seen it, but he had planted the Stars and Stripes on its wave-battered shores.

A race of giants, predecessors of the Eskimos

And the Inuit? They were indifferent to these intruders and their torments. But they too were thinking and living . . . What reading did they give the world? A different one, unquestionably. But there were areas of convergence. They too believed in a people farther to the north, a mythic race of giants, who preceded them. The Polar Eskimos preserve the memory of a strong and conquering pre-Eskimo people, the Tornit, or Tunit. Remarkably, the South Greenlanders were still vividly aware of this unknown people in the nineteenth century. European expeditions had a difficult time recruiting South Greenlandic hunters because the natives were terrified of meeting this sometimes cannibalistic race of giants. In the Canadian Central Arctic in 1961, on Boothia Peninsula, the Inuit respectfully showed me the huge stones used by the Tunit to build their oversized igloos. At Thule, among the Polar Eskimos in 1950-1951, I had repeated to me several words from the speech of this people, who are now lost in the mists of previous centuries. Several fleeting—and tragic—encounters between the Inuit and the Tunit were related to me with every assurance of their truth. And eyewitness accounts of murderous raids by the powerful and warlike Tunit against their Inuit neighbors were transmitted to me, several of which I have published.

The four cardinal points have a specific symbolic value in all cultures, in the West as among the Inuit. The North (*ava-avannaa*: "to the north") signifies elevation—it is the land of souls and of the dead—while the South is hot and bright. This cardinal geography reflects a bisexual view of the universe. The Inuk believe that the incestuous union of a sister and a brother presided over the creation of the sister sun (*Seqineq*) and the brother moon (*Anningaaq*) . . . The sun is feminine, and the moon masculine, as in Old Norse and German.

This geography of space is not without an origin. In China, the cradle (with Central Asia) of American Indian and Inuit cultures, the topology of the directions was and remains fundamental. The yin, which is female, is the west and the north: it corresponds to darkness, winter, humidity, the occult (as opposed to the manifest), the seed. The yang, on the other hand, is masculine and corresponds to the east and the south: it is heat and dryness, the center of being, fire, the color red, blossoming. Feng-shui is the expression of this sacred geography, whose roots are so ancient and alive in the Middle Kingdom, as in contemporary Japan, that its philosophy permeates all minds, from the statesman's to the humblest citizen's.

To better grasp these complex facts, let us turn toward the cradle of the Inuit peoples: the coast of the Siberian Chukotka region, whose hunters set out ten thousand years ago toward America, then still partially glaciated and, in the north, unpeopled. In 1976, on the shores of the Bering Strait, in Yupik territory, two remarkable Soviet archaeologists, Arutyonov and Clenov, discovered an important site of the Early Punuk. Corresponding in time to the European Middle Ages, it shows evidence of a an ancient esoteric tradition, which remained unchanged in the Inuit mind until the dawn of the contemporary era, so conservative is religious belief among these isolated peoples. And it is worth noting that Chukotka was the cradle of the Inuit peoples, who, having set off from Asia, migrated to the extreme east of Greenland while maintaining considerable cultural unity.

Siberia's Chukotka Peninsula, cradle of the Inuit

I am on the deserted island of Ittygran (Sikluk, in the Eskimo language), off Chaplino (Chukotka), in August 1990; I discover, the first Westerner on this high and lonely spot, two lines of posts made from the jawbones of whales, their bleached color standing out almost aggressively against the summer green of the bay. A row of whale skulls extends for 400 meters, comprising thirteen groups of skulls in a precise order. Two groups have two skulls, three groups have four skulls. Groups 2, 3, 4, 5, 6, and 7 are spaced at regular intervals of 20 to 22 meters, in strict alternation. The total number of skulls in this row is 47. Each skull is 2.2 to 2.4 meters in diameter. Two solitary posts made from the lower jaw of the whale mark the end points of the alley. One of them, which is well preserved, is five meters high. In the middle of the alley, 5 groups of 3 to 5 posts stand a few meters from one another: 13 columns are standing, and 21 are in ruins. In the geometric center of the alley, a flat surface forms an amphitheater 4.5 meters in diameter, its perimeter marked by solid blocks of stone. A hearth of calcified whale and walrus bones has been excavated in the northwest sector. In the nearby jumble of rocks, there are 120 funnel-shaped ditches 1 to

2 meters deep and .5 to 1.5 meters in diameter, where pieces of walrus and whale bones were piled. Finally, the center of the rocky area is occupied by a circular structure 4 to 4.5 meters in diameter called the "main shrine" by the two Soviet archaeologists, from whom I have borrowed almost word for word the numerical data and the partial description. This structure is linked to the solitary post by an almost straight stone-lined path one meter wide and 50 meters long. Along the length of the neighboring island extends a series of eleven columns at intervals of 3 to 5 kilometers, "so that from each column one can see the preceding and the following columns. This series of columns stops across from the alley of whales."

This vast cultural site has no equivalent anywhere on the Alaska coast or anywhere else in the Arctic. Think of the extraordinary effort it must have taken to bring whales 18 to 20 meters long, weighing 80 tons, to this deserted shore and build monumental lines reminiscent of Carthage in this solitary place. A single skull weighs two and a half tons . . . Landmarks, these posts must be understood in the light of the Eskimos' religious rites during large-scale seasonal gatherings. As the whale hunt was a strictly masculine operation, the Soviet archaeologists are inclined to believe that this was the work of a secret and local male organization with about a hundred men. Might these arrangements have been inspired by ancient China or Central Asia? Charles Morazé, author of *The Sacred Origins of Modern Science*, has recently wondered whether the Cape Chaplino site might not be related to the I Ching, "for which we have no prehistoric precedent," providing us with "the evidence that such precedents may have existed."

The Inuit creation

In their legends and in their imaginative life, the Inuit are pragmatic. Their myths of creation appeared in ancient times, several thousand years ago in the great Yuit and Inupiat cultures. What touches on the creation of the world is factual, precise. The two hundred legends of the Inuit of Northwest Greenland—of which extracts appear in this book, as if in answer to their conquerors—testify to an understanding of the era of creation. They are told with almost geological precision. In the beginning the earth was one, and man witnessed its fragmentation. The ancestors of the Inuit were present at the Flood, when great seas advanced over the shores of the continents. When the water was high, the ancients were afraid. Shells have been gathered from the soil of the high plateaus. The sky—paradise—is above. Two men tried to lift themselves up to it, one pushing the other; and the one who saw immense herds of caribou there did not return.

The Sun and the Moon were created by the Inuit *allanik*, "long, long ago." The Sun/Moon pair re-enact the horror of incest: the Sun is a young girl who is pursued by her brother after they have made love unknowingly at night in the igloo, when the seal blubber lamps were extinguished so that men and women could be exchanged, according to custom. During the summer, the young woman Sun lives outside the igloo; it is hot both day and night. And the young boy Moon stays at home. During the winter, it is the opposite, with the young woman Sun remaining in the igloo while the young boy Moon stays outdoors. The moon disappears only to bring back the animals that the men hunt. Thus, when the men see the new moon they cry out: "Thank you, thank you, you bring us food!"

Thunder and the stars are humans who were transformed when they became immortal. All of the tales are similarly concerned with the problem of man's relations to the generative forces of nature. The tutelary father of the Inuit is a man-animal made of dog excrement, in a cocoon of intestines. At the start of Inuit life, an agreement was made. It has not always been respected. Thus Nirrivik, the wife of a gull, became frightened when she discovered her spouse's horrible eyes, which he hid behind goggles. Nirrivik fled by boat with her parents. The gull, furious, pursued her and, flying very close to the boat, threatened to overturn it. The blind father threw Nirrivik into the water, and, when she held on to the boat's side, he cut off all her fingers one by one. Nirrivik sank to the bottom of the sea and became a water spirit. No hunt can be undertaken without the *angakkuq* or shaman going to the depths of the seas first to speak to her, comb her hair, and clean her igloo.

In their eschatological view, the Inuit divide the world into levels. Through trance, the Inuk can voyage cosmically to different levels and in particular to the Moon, looking for souls that have fled or been stolen. The Inuk can speed healing by combating bad spirits who assume animal form. The *angakkuq* predicts the future and regulates social life, retelling the great mythological tales, which are each family's book of hours.

History and amnesia

The memory of a people always has its pockets of repression and forgetting, which are more or less deliberate. Essential moments and facts in the long history of the Inuit are missing, as though time and the Inuit themselves had wanted to occlude them.

People are the architects of their own memory and invent their past so as to project themselves better into the future. Jung forcefully reminds us: "The great events in the history of the world are in the

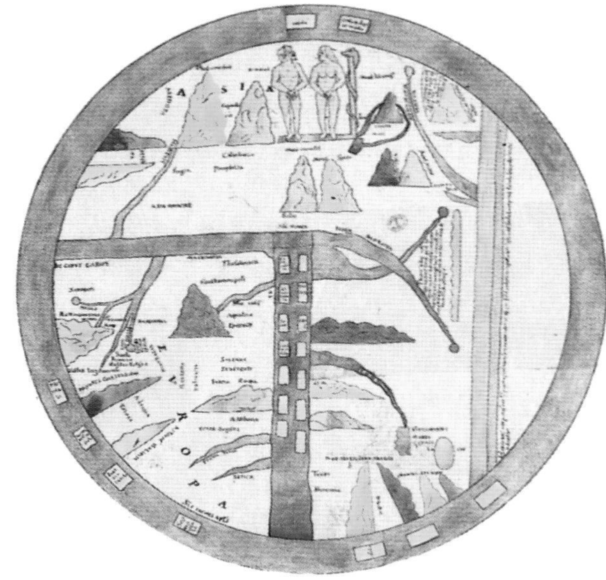

Map of the world (ascribed to the eleventh century), from a twelfth-century manuscript, Turin Royal Library. The globe is surrounded by a crown of water. Adam and Eve stand between the mountains of Armenia and the mountains of Lebanon, above Sinai and Carmel. An island near their heads is named "Croca Algure Insula." Note the place (top left) named "Tilé."

end of little significance. All that is essential, in the final analysis, is the subjective life of the individual. It alone makes history. And all the great changes are first reflected in it.

The history of an oral culture is in fact built on a base of erratic words and on a mythology that dissolves and reforms, that is reinterpreted again and again by an isolated group of twenty or thirty families, whose average life expectancy is twenty to thirty years. Entire segments of history are from time to time deliberately obscured. Dreams, fears, passions, and the subjective life of these hunters and their wives in their igloos are responsible for these "lapses of memory." The motivation for them we will never know. Yet let us examine a few of these major refusals of memory.

First example of a deliberate obscuring of the past: the Vikings. They were the first to colonize Greenland in the tenth century. After they arrived from Iceland with Erik the Red in 985, they settled—some 3000 of them—on the southwest coast of Greenland where, for five centuries, they maintained trading relations with the Inuit. They were farmers, but they remained hardy explorers, and their progress northward—for the purpose of trading—is evidenced by a rune-covered stone left in Upernavik on a certain 25 April by three Vikings.

An example of their boldness has recently come to light. In the twelfth or thirteenth century, a Viking longboat—a longboat!—wintered on the east coast of Ellesmere Island at Bache Peninsula, northwest of Thule. The Scandinavians were therefore the first discoverers

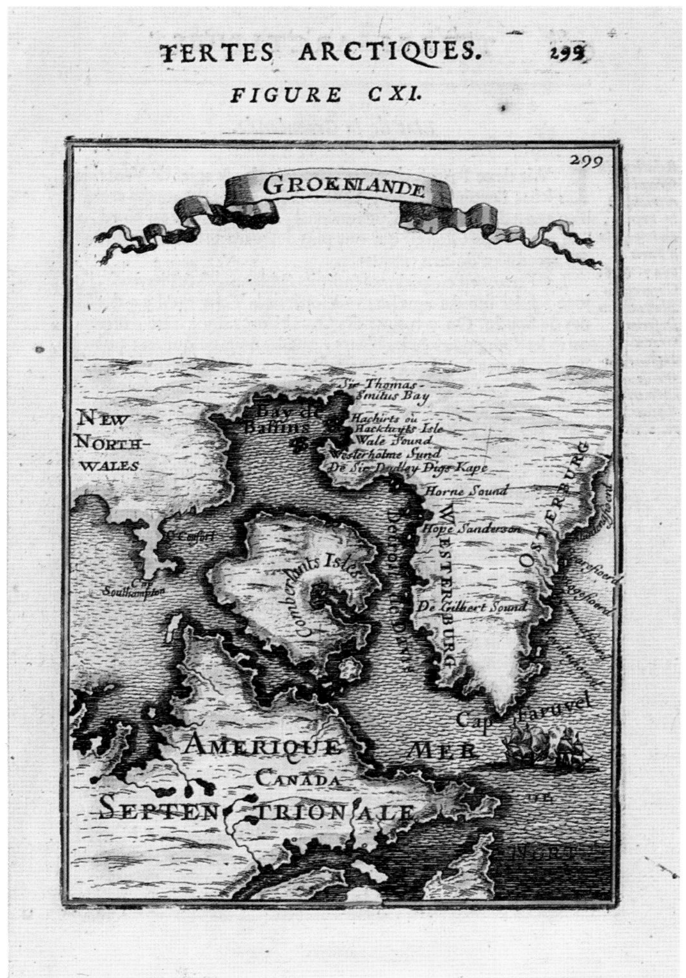

A map of Greenland and Baffin Island in the eighteenth century. The Polar Eskimos in the north of Baffin Bay were still undiscovered.

of the New World, before Christopher Columbus. Entering storied Smith Sound, Vikings overwintered on the island that would later be called Skraelling Island. Extraordinary excavations by Canadian archaeologist Peter Schledermann in 1977 have proved it beyond doubt. He discovered objects, statuettes, nails, boat rivets, pieces of cloth: an ivory Eskimo figurine depicts one of these Vikings. This voyage of exploration could not have escaped the Inuit, who have inhabited Skraelling Island for 4000 years, hunting walrus, narwhal, seal, fox, and birds there, and yet no Inuit legend tells the story. The longboat has been erased from Inuit memory. And the contemporary Inughuit of Thule do not know this important part of their heritage.

Another discovery of Schledermann's is even more surprising: on beaches raised thirty or thirty-five meters above sea level there have been found camp sites (communal igloos forty-five meters long and five meters wide, with cooking hearths in a row outside them) dating from between 2500 to 600 B.C. On beaches raised 3 to 14 meters, more recent sites have been found (600 B.C. to 1000 A.D.). The most recent sites date from 100 to 1700 A.D., on beaches raised 2 to 8 meters above sea level. After 1650, at the beginning of the Little Ice Age, these Inuit left Ellesmere Island, for 4000 years the cradle of their history, and went to northwest Greenland sixty miles to the southwest. There, forgetting the art of pottery, they merged with their cousins, who had been living in Greenland since at least the twelfth century.

Traditional peoples are peoples who rely on memory . . . but a people's memory can leave out important moments of its history, as though practicing self-censorship. This second example of collective amnesia is in fact eloquent: 4000 years of their ancestral history had been erased from the memories of the Inuit of Northwest Greenland by the nineteenth and twentieth centuries. The proof of their ignorance: if these Inuit of northwest Greenland, who were without wood or iron, had known that there were nails and barrel hoops under the Skraelling ruins near Ellesmere Island, the land of their forefathers (from 4000 B.C. to 1600 A.D.), the site would have become a precious iron mine—more precious even than the four lumps of meteoric iron in the Savissivik area (northern Melville Bay), from which they had been laboriously chipping flakes the size of a finger nail since time immemorial, and for two centuries at least (1600-1860). Pottery was unknown to them? The Polar Eskimos preciously preserve the memory of the fabled era of their beginnings, yet they neglect 4000 years of their own history and ignore even the place where their people came into being. Why? We have only contradictory hypotheses for how the collective unconscious works. When my Inuit companions and I were in Alexandra Fjord on 1 and 5 June 1951, bivouacking a few dozen meters from Skraelling Island, we were totally ignorant of this cradle of Inuit history, which was revealed by Peter Schledermann.

Third example: "We are alone in the world," said the Polar Eskimos when they were discovered on a sunny morning in August 1818 by Sir John Ross. Is it true that they were never visited before? Were the Eskimos questioned by Ross and his officers correctly understood when translated into the pidgin of the South Greenlander John Sacheuse (Hans Zakaeus)? Or did the interpreter introduce his interpretation unawares, and the commentator provide his own gloss? The question is a valid one, because there was a persistent rumor, from

Upernavik 300 miles to the south, originating with Materaq, an old hunter, that his great-grandmother Lisa had told him of a south-north migration by the Greenlanders. They were fleeing a terrible epidemic—it is on record—that decimated Greenland north of Disko Bay at the end of the eighteenth century, and traveled north with their leader Tulugaq in a *umiak* (skin boat with oars). We know that they never returned. According to rumor they were absorbed by the Polar Eskimos. The custom in Greenland is for women and children to travel by umiak, while men follow by kayak, hunting so as to feed their families. The Eskimo Meqru, wife of Hans Hendrik and grandmother of my companion Sakaeunnguaq, confirmed when she lived in Upernavik in 1864 (having come from among the Polar Eskimos) that the migration took place, stating that some of her ancestors were from Upernavik.

Did this fabulous voyage take place before 1818 or immediately after? It is impossible to know precisely, particularly as there is no story or legend describing it.

The isolation of this people is therefore relative; we are now certain of it. In 1902, in a little-known article, the geographer Rudolph Stein published his research on place names among the Polar Eskimos, showing that this fragile and adventurous people knew the geography of the entire coast of Melville Bay, from the northern bay (Cape York) to Holms Island, and that the bear hunters even had a vague notion of the settlement of Upernavik, called Upengawiig. A legend collected by Knud Rasmussen gives evidence of a tradition of bartering expeditions and a silent north-south trade, concluded without direct encounters. This was confirmed to me by my companion Kutsikitsoq, as something he might have experienced firsthand, in February 1951. Pastor Oestergaad wrote in 1833-1841 that the Greenlanders of Upernavik still remembered sporadic contacts between the peoples from the north end of the bay and those of the south. On the other hand, no myth or tale told by the Polar Eskimos gives any evidence of north-south voyages across Melville Bay, or of any umbilical link with the South on the part of the twenty or thirty families isolated on the roof of the world.

The memory of a people is thus a product of self-censorship and borrowing. So much so that portions of the traditional legends and tales of the Polar Eskimos were replaced by legends belonging to Eskimos who immigrated from Igloolik in 1862-1863, as if each wave of immigration superimposed its collective memory on the heritage of the people whom they come to join. The memory of a people therefore does not offer a simple geologic perspective, with history laying down its sediment horizontally, layer by layer, century after century. Selection is at work, its rules uncertain, eliminating strata here, mixing others there, according to an unknown alchemy. A coherent whole in the end re-emerges, its existence more or less independent.

Fourth and last example: the historic encounter in 1818 with other men (Captain John Ross), with whalers, with colorful explorers (Peary, Cook); the conversion to the worship of a man-god who is crucified and whose body is eaten in the form of bread and wine by the Eskimos, themselves converted in 1920—all these major events and revelations are absent from traditional stories.

These lapses in memory are not confined to traditional societies.

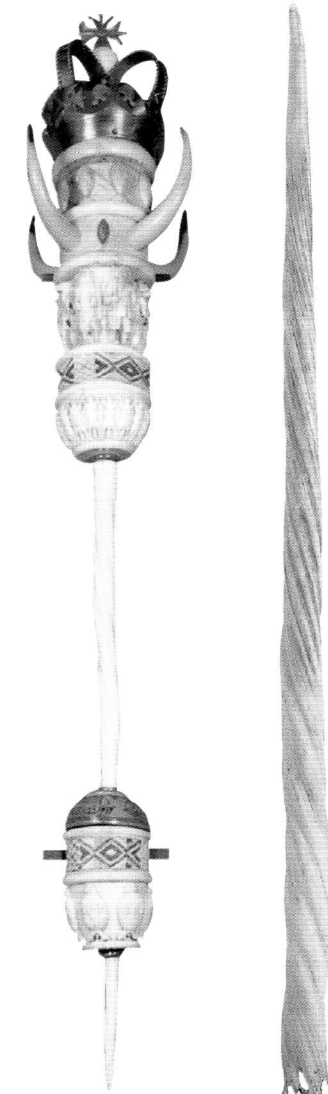

The mace of the government of the Canadian Northwest Territories, the symbol of Arctic authority, is a narwhal tusk surmounted by a crown and a cross. Yellowknife, 1987. This original mace was used for 43 years. In January 2000, a new mace for the Northwest Territories was inaugurated.

Tusk of the male narwhal. Some attain ten feet in length and weigh almost nine pounds.

An extraordinary discovery was hidden away by the West for two centuries: William Baffin of London, one of the greatest explorers in Arctic history, discovered the Northwest Passage and Smith Sound in 1616. It was he who named them. Yet London gave no credence to the results of this exceptional voyage—Baffin did not belong to the British establishment!—and his map was lost by the Admiralty. The arrogance of the authorities set back Arctic exploration by 200 years.

It allowed the Inuit (history has its occasional mercies) to regroup themselves in preparation for entering the modern world.

It is revealing that the Eskimos of North Greenland, to whom the West wanted to assign a destiny by naming Thule their capital, have wisely kept their distance from Europe and its ancient heritage since the construction of the American airbase at Thule, turning their backs on this legendary universe. They have reclaimed the ancient name of Qaanaaq, placing their history under the protection of this tutelary animal, which has never failed its annual rendezvous: the narwhal, the extraordinary "sea-unicorn," which reproduces every three years not far from Qeqertaq, at Nulioqqaarfik, where, according to legend, the first men—the Inuit—were born. I first saw a narwhal while traveling by dog sled, one winter morning in the darkness of November 1950. *Qilaluaq . . .* [unicorn], my Eskimo companion reminded me in his cracked voice, as he sat before me at the front of our modest sled. To the Inuit, the narwhal is the symbol of woman: its tusk is the twisted braid of an Eskimo crone, who has been dragged underwater while trying to pull the narwhal ashore to feed her hungry children.

Horn, unicorn, and narwhal

All through the Middle Ages, the unicorn (the narwhal's tusk, or ox horn) was the animal symbolizing the incarnation and death of Christ. "But my horn shalt thou exalt like the horn of a unicorn" (Ps. 92:10). In the Vulgate, Christianity had conflated the horn of the Biblical *re-em* (ox?) and the mythical unicorn. The unicorn, which arose in India (*eka-sanga* in Sanskrit, "one-horn," which is also one of the names of Vishnu) or in China, was imagined as a timid animal, which according to Confucianist tradition only appeared in times of good government and also represented the Buddha in an earlier life. With the white body of a horse, the head of a deer, red eyes, "the cloven hoof of a goat," the unicorn appeared in the mythology of the twelfth century as the incarnation of Christ and the Virgin.

One of the many medieval bestiaries, based on the fourth-century Greek *Physiologus*, states: "It is thus that Our Savior Jesus Christ, who is spiritually the tooth of a unicorn, descends into the womb of the Virgin."

The Church strongly affirmed the unicorn's existence. Saint Bonaventure equated the unicorn with the Tree of Life. According to the tradition of the priest John, the unicorn stood at the gates of Heaven. The tooth of a narwhal was sometimes placed to the right of the altar in medieval churches—there was one at the church of Strasbourg and another at Saint-Denis. In the sixteenth century, Ambroise Paré bravely opposed these fables from antiquity and medieval times, which carelessly mixed myth and reality.

But myth pursued its subterranean course. In the fifteenth century—as the Cluny tapestries show—the unicorn's tooth had already become boreal: it twisted like the narwhal's. "Monoceros is it called, and lives in the highest places. Monoceros is the unicorn, because it has but one horn. Such is its nature that only a maid may capture it . . ." How avoid confusion when, in British churches and on the decks of Scots ships in the Arctic, the voice of the prophets was evoked in English? In that language, the "Unicorn" or sacred beast is confused with the "sea-unicorn," as the British explorers called the narwhal, with its elongated tooth, in that region of icy seas and contradictory symbolism: Heaven, Gog and Magog, the land of the dead and of rebirth, the ice-free sea, the route to China.

"Will the unicorn be willing to serve Thee . . ." (Job 39:9) "He hast it were the strength of the unicorn" (Num. 23:22).

The mythical unicorn, the confluence of five mutually unknown traditions—Inuit, Asiatic, Greco-Roman, Hebrew, and Christian—has dissolved and been reconfigured into a monster or an animal according to the local religion or mythology or reality and has become over the centuries a symbol of power, after having been a symbol of virginity.

Attached to the crown of Scotland, the unicorn has figured since the sixteenth century on the crest of John I, then on the crest of the British crown. The unicorn is seated, with a crown around its neck, a chain and a ring attached to it. The unicorn is on the left of the crest. In the later seventeenth century, the kings of Denmark built their sacred throne of narwhals' tusks, accompanied by three silver lions.

After the Second World War, the mace of the government of the Canadian Northwest Territories, the symbol of Ottawa's power over the "native" peoples, Indians and Inuit, was a narwhal tusk, topped by a crown with a cross.

The Second Coming

Thule (Greenland): I pace to and fro along the shore of North Star Bay, which is battered by the icy waters. Offshore are icebergs, drifting superbly and unconcernedly; in the background are the aggressive structures of the military base with its nuclear missiles.

I pace and, though my mind is naturally drawn to religious skepticism, I think of the inspired words inscribed across the front of the Polar Institute at Cambridge University: *Quaesivit arcana poli: videt Dei* ("He sought the mysteries of the Pole; he saw those of God"). I murmur verses from Isaiah, remembering the Apocalypse of Saint John, particularly the passages on the Second Coming: "For thou hast said in thine heart, I will ascend into heaven, I will exalt my throne above the stars of God: I will sit also upon the mount of the congregation, in the sides of the north: I will ascend above the heights of the clouds; I will be like the most High" (Isa. 14:13-14).

Dies irae, dies illa . . . "Now is the judgment of this world: now shall the prince of this world be cast out" (John 12:31). John describes Christ's glorious return. Great military and cosmic catastrophes will strike men, followed by inconceivable hardships: the Sun and the Moon will be blotted out. Stars will fall to Earth.

In an ultimate johannic vision, the sign of the Son of Man appears in the sky. Satan is momentarily released from his prison to seduce the nations. Christ in majesty advances through the clouds on a chariot, escorted by angels.

"And before the throne there was a sea of glass like unto crystal . . ." (Rev. 4:6).

"And I saw as it were a sea of glass mingled with fire: and them that had got the victory over the beast, and over his image, and over his mark, and over the number of his name, stand on the sea of glass, having the harps of God" (Rev 15:2).

A sea of crystal. A glassy sea . . . Ultima Thule, the North, center of the aurora borealis, the geomagnetic pole. The words of the Bible assume here a sacred force. At the end of all things, will these high latitudes, at the summit of the skies, be the seat of a final struggle between the supreme God and the Prince of Darkness? Is the Thule nuclear base its first intimation?

The searing rhetorical stab in Arthur Rimbaud's *Illuminations* has proved prophetic: "What witch will arise on the white setting?" ■

RIGHT: **Walrus ivory figure,** eleventh or twelfth century, representing a woman (excavated by Erik Holtved, Thule).

Ellesmere Island, ancestral land of Greenland's Polar Inuit.

A Viking ship discovered North America three centuries before Columbus, stopping at Ellesmere Island to meet with unknown Inuit. The waters off this coast, where Greely's expedition starved tragically, represent one of the Arctic's great coastal polynyas, or stretches of open water. In mid-June, seals and walruses abound, and the air teems with birds. It is the month of love.

The first immigrants were the Dorset-culture Eskimos, who arrived from Bering Strait. Makers of small stone tools, they maintained their strongly shamanistic culture for thirty-three centuries. Around one thousand years ago, the climate warmed and the Thule Inuit appeared. They hunted seal, walrus, and, to a lesser extent, whale. Ancestors of the North Greenlanders, they left Ellesmere for warmer Greenland in A.D. 1700, at the start of the Little Ice Age. Archaeological research has uncovered forty centuries of unknown history under the frozen ground of the tundra.

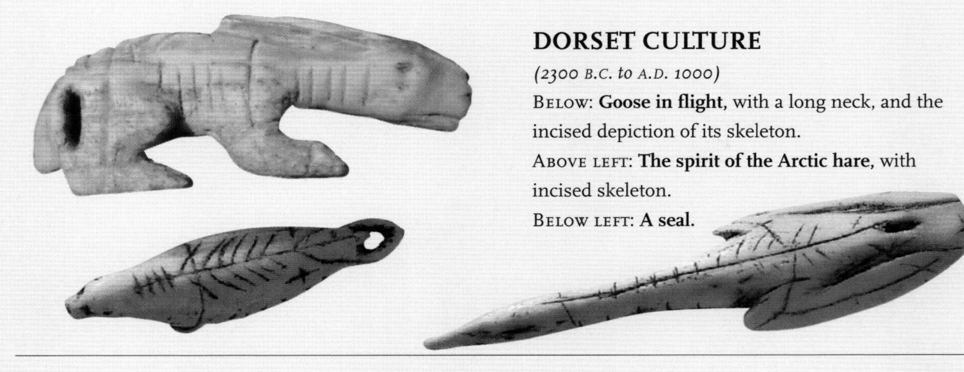

DORSET CULTURE

(2300 B.C. to A.D. 1000)

BELOW: **Goose in flight,** with a long neck, and the incised depiction of its skeleton.

ABOVE LEFT: **The spirit of the Arctic hare,** with incised skeleton.

BELOW LEFT: **A seal.**

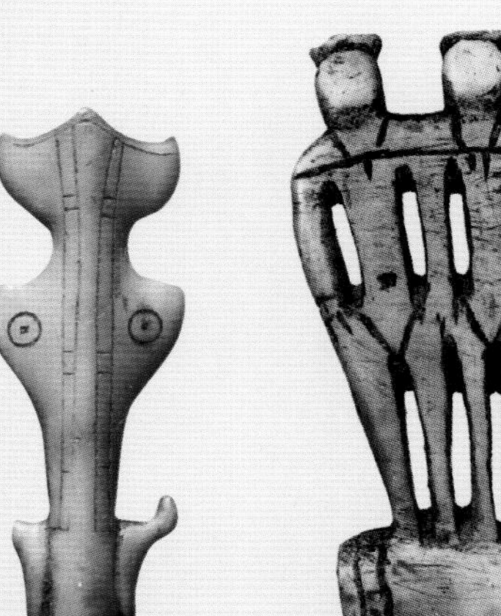

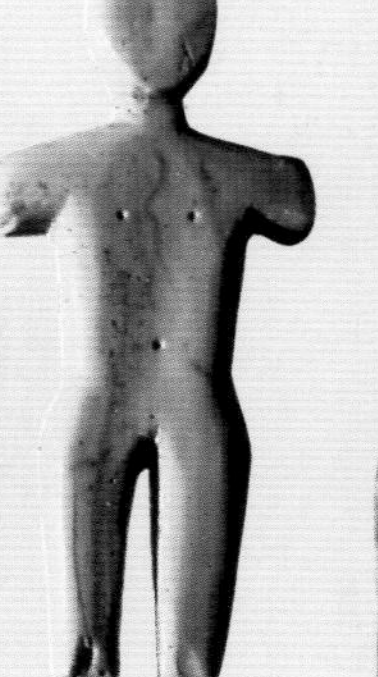

THULE

(A.D. 1000 to A.D. 1700)

FROM LEFT: **Needle case; ivory clasp** representing three joined women; **Thule woman,** made of wood, with sealskin trousers and a Dorset-culture hairbun (A.D. 1450); **two miniaturized women.**

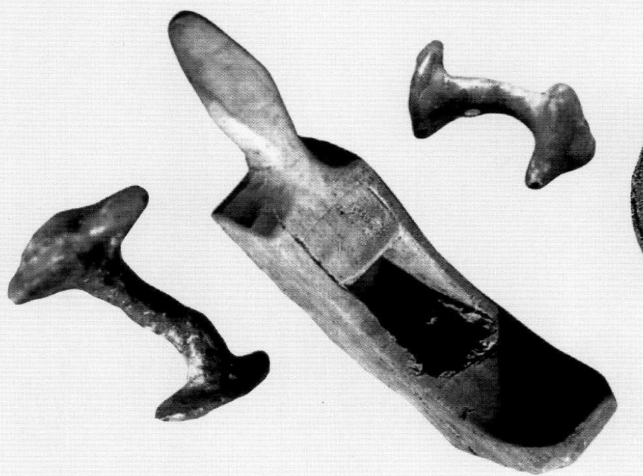

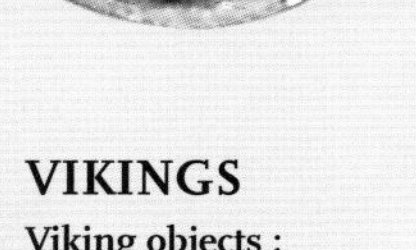

VIKINGS

Viking objects :

A plane, nails, cloth.

SMITH SOUND (4,000 YEARS OF HISTORY)

Smith Sound, between northern Greenland and Ellesmere Island (Bache Peninsula), was one of the centers of Arctic history. In 1977, over the course of a week, the archaeologist Peter Schledermann discovered more than 150 prehistoric sites, some dating back 4000 years. Groups of hunters from Bering Strait traveled east some 4000 years ago in search of game. Th ey advanced eastward in stages, from century to century.

Their descendants discovered an exceptional stretch of open water along Ellesmere Island, near Bache Peninsula, which was rich in plankton and afforded seals, walruses, beluga whales and right whales a place to surface and breathe. In summer, Arctic birds congregated there.

On the shelving slopes along the coast are raised beaches. At a height of 30-35 meters, Schledermann discovered Early Dorset-culture remains (2300 to 600 B.C.); at a height of 3-14 meters, traces of Dorset-culture communities (600 B.C.to A.D. 1000); and at a height of 2-8 meters, the multi-family culture of the hunters known as the Thule Inuit (A.D. 1000 to 1700). "Thule" designates a sea-going culture that flourished particularly on the northwest coast of Greenland in the nineteenth and twentieth centuries. The Canadian Inuit—ancestors of the Polar Inuit—left the coast of Ellesmere Island in the seventeenth century to rejoin their northwest Greenland cousins, who seemed hardly to know them.

VIKINGS AT LATITUDE 79° NORTH!

In 1977, feverishly excavating the Inuit past on Skraelling Island, off Ellesmere—not two steps away from a cairn I erected in 1951—Peter Schledermann discovered a trove of Viking artefacts. A Viking ship from South Greenland apparently deposited a group of Viking hunters on the island in A.D. 1100 to 1200, where they wintered. They left figurines, nails, and cloth. A statuette of these Vikings, made by the Inuit, shows that the two peoples coexisted. This was the first evidence that Viking exploration had reached such high latitudes—the Inuit preserved no memory of it.

SIX CENTURIES OF PRE-HISTORY

The North American peoples who settled the north, south, and east coasts of Greenland all migrated across Smith Sound and Kennedy Channel. Syncretic in nature, Greenland's northwest coast has been inhabited at least since the thirteenth century. The area of settlement between Washington Land and Melville Bay has expanded and contracted according to climatic conditions. The twelfth to the seventeenth century saw a demographic expansion, and the Inuit were spread over 500 miles of coast. During the Little Ice Age, from A.D. 1600 to 1800, the Inuit drew in to the center of the territory (the three islands of Northumberland, Herbert, and Hakluyt, and the Etah coast to Siorapaluk, Inglefield Fjord, and Cape York). The flat grounds below bird-nesting cliffs were highly prized settlement sites. The remarkable excavations conducted by Erik Holtved in 1936-1937 at Inuarfissuaq on the eastern shore of Kane Basin, at Nullit to the south on Melville Bay near Thule, and at Thule itself (Uummannaq) have brought to light an archaic and plural medieval society (twelfth to thirteenth centuries). On the Inglefield Plateau, these Eskimo hunted caribou and musk ox; on the floe in winter and the open water in summer, they hunted seal, walrus, and probably whale. These hunters used kayaks and dog sleds—perhaps even the *umiaq*, a large skin boat. Their tools were primitive, made of stone, bone, and ivory. In comparing these objects and those of the following period with

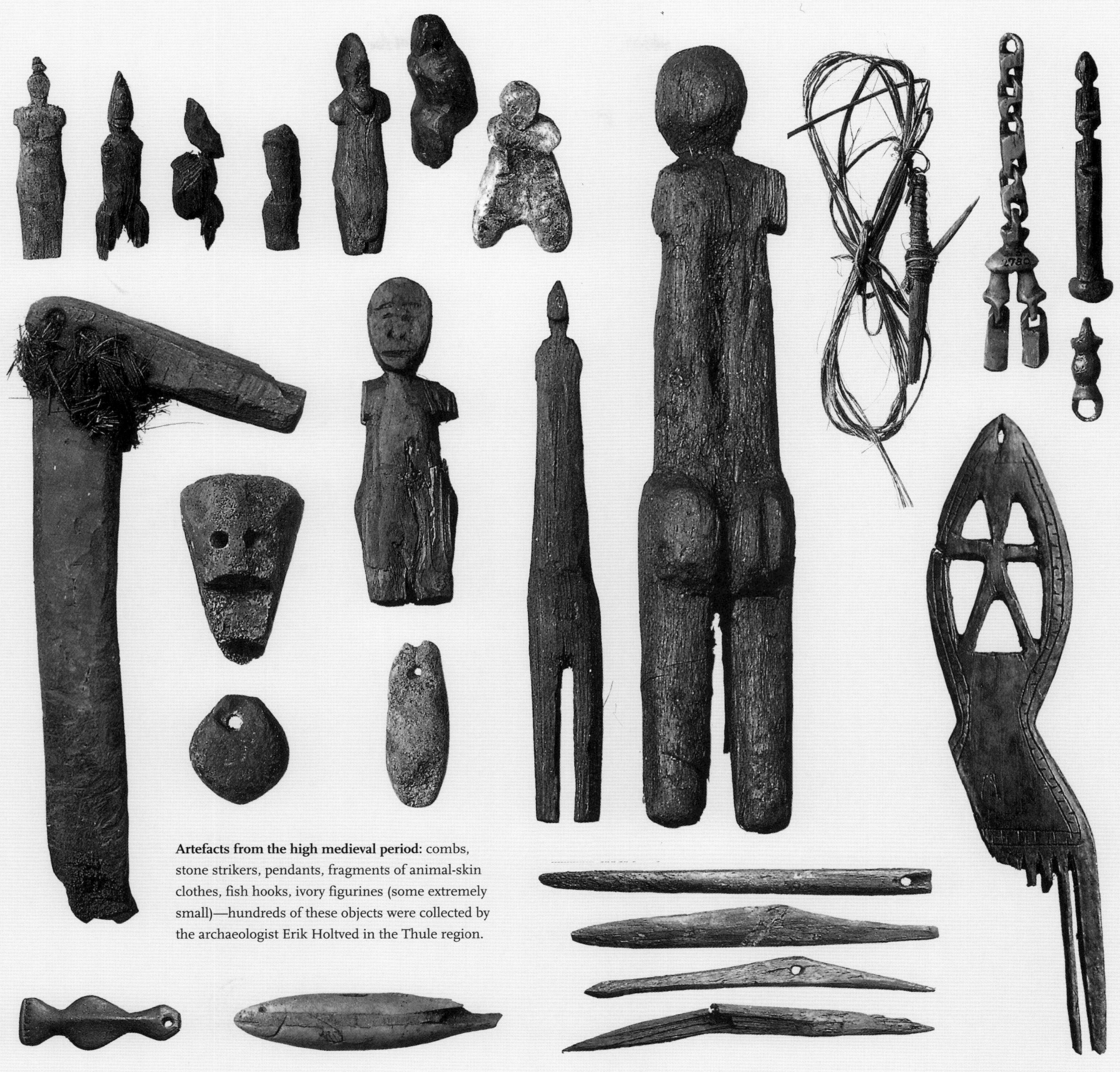

Artefacts from the high medieval period: combs, stone strikers, pendants, fragments of animal-skin clothes, fish hooks, ivory figurines (some extremely small)—hundreds of these objects were collected by the archaeologist Erik Holtved in the Thule region.

contemporary objects, one notices how similar they are in manufacture and shape: harpoon heads, harness rings for dogs, drying racks, blubber lamps, wound pins for seal, the *ulu* (women's knife), scrapers, whips. In the fourteenth century, the North Greenland Inuit benefited from the evolved technology of the western Canadian and Alaskan Inuit. They turned strongly toward hunting large whales, at least until the seventeenth century. The society expanded. Its ideas underwent renewal: men and women no longer buried their dead, they threw them into the sea. A large proportion of the artefacts found by archaeologists relate to whale-hunting—close to a quarter of all objects dating from the thirteenth and fourteenth centuries. This society, now rich, became concerned with luxury and started producing works of art. But in 1600 a blanket of fog descended on the area, then the cold, and the fjords were iced over for long periods: this was the Little Ice Age, a period of great cold that lasted two centuries. The pack ice was so thick that seals could no longer keep their breathing holes (*agluq*) open. Polar bears left the country for warmer areas to the south. The Polar Inuit, starving, devised a survival strategy that would keep the bare minimum of life from flickering out.

By means of sexual and dietary taboos, of euthanasia (voluntary suppression of the elderly), and of demographic controls (infanticide of girl children to the age of one or two in cases of hardship or death of a parent), the group voluntarily limited itself to about thirty families. Until 1862, the Inuit's diet was governed by strict taboos, such as the prohibition against eating salmon and caribou. The restrictions on technology were Malthusian: the use of the *umiaq* and the bow were forbidden. The throwing board, the leister, the fish hook, the bow drill, wood, and non-meteoric iron were no longer used. Bone and skin became once again the primary raw materials, whereas in the thirteenth and fourteenth centuries, whales and wood were the basic materials.

The Eskimos, corseted within an extremely severe system of social organization, survived mainly by using nets to hunt migrating auks, which they ate raw in summertime and rotten in winter. From being a people of the water and the ice, the Eskimos became a people of the air. Integrated as they were with nature and its least changes, they became cautious. The group became primitive once more and restricted itself, obliterating its past. The hunters discovered by Captain John Ross on 6 to 10 August 1818 had lost all memory of their past on the coast of Ellesmere Island and mislaid even the Eskimo terms for the caribou and the kayak. Few of their legends relate to their great medieval past. Their myths are rooted in the origins of the people, then leap tens of centuries to deal with the years since the Little Ice Age. Emerging diminished but alive from this terrible time of misfortune—two and a half centuries of fog and cold, ice fields, and isolation—the Polar Eskimos of August 1818 acted as though they refused to search their surroundings or their memory. Under their feet, literally, lay the wood, the iron, and the tools whose use they had lost. They had a confused awareness of coming from the west, but allowed themselves to search no farther in their memory, lest it imperil the strict Malthusian socio-economic rules they had made for themselves in order to survive. The Inuit of the 1818 encounter needed to forget this knowledge, or else the young would know their own poverty and, missing iron, wood, bows, kayaks, and *umiaqs* ever more keenly each morning, lose the taste for living.

Their happiness, like their survival, depended on this lobotomy.

J.M.

Captain John Ross 1777-1856

THE DISCOVERER OF THE POLAR ESKIMOS

One of the most unfortunate figures in the history of polar exploration—as though such strong personalities were drawn to these regions that they sometimes expressed themselves as much in baseness and violence as in greatness.

Like William Baffin, the daring British navigator who, in 1616, discovered the bay that bears his name and minutely explored the portals of the North Pole, Captain John Ross, the fourth son of the pastor Andrew Ross, was born in Scotland, on 24 June 1777, in Balsarroch, in the poor county of Wigtown. His mother died when he was two, and seven years later he enlisted in the navy. He quickly acquired the appearance of a corsair, somewhat moderated by his deep and kindly gray eyes. He was wounded thirteen times in bloody engagements against the French, and interned three times in French prisons. At forty, with Napoleon in exile on Saint Helena, tired of war, and despite commanding a naval unit that operated in the Baltic and along the Scottish coast, Ross decided to take a leave of absence from the Royal Navy. He married a young woman from Edinburgh.

On 11 December 1817, a letter from the Admiralty summoned him to London. At the suggestion of Sir George Hope, First Lord of the Admiralty, he was offered the command of a polar expedition. With thirty years of sailing experience, Ross had a considerable advantage over the many officers in his generation (nine tenths of the Royal Navy), who were equally eager for preferment and had been sidelined since the battle of Waterloo.[1] His health, the letter specified, must be sound, and his will indomitable. Ross replied by return mail that he could answer for both. On 30 December he was in London, waiting on Lord Melville. His first concern, in keeping with his Scots heritage, was to ascertain that this posting, so tangential to military concerns, would not prejudice his chances for promotion. Reassured on this score, he went to inspect the two ships under his command: the *Isabella*, a former whaler, 385 tons, and the *Alexander*, 252 tons. Both struck him as too large for polar exploration. Like William Baffin, he believed that the proper size for a ship sailing into the polar ice was between 100 and 200 tons. He asked for smaller ships, but in vain. The two vessels were sheathed in a second layer of oak three inches thick. The prow was armed with a steel spur.

In January 1818, Captain John Ross was officially appointed to command the expedition, at the request of the second secretary of the Admiralty, John Barrow, who was

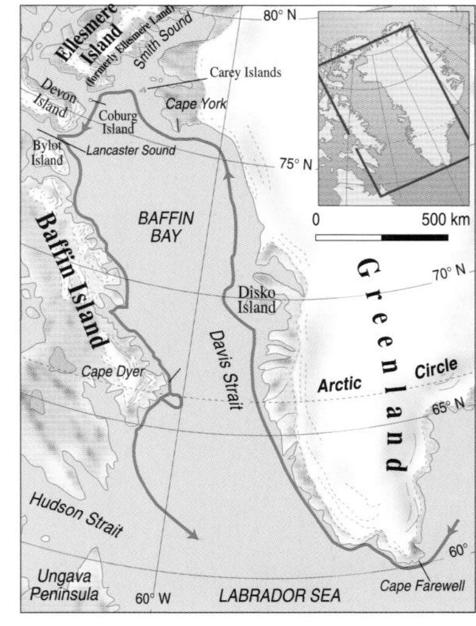

Above:
Route of the *Isabella* and the *Alexander* on Captain John Ross's first voyage. (1818)

Left: **Sir John Ross.** This portrait, by an anonymous British painter, dates from *circa* 1830. National Maritime Museum, London.

1) One hundred and twenty thousand soldiers were put on half-pay after Waterloo. The exploration of far-off places was the only opportunity that offered the navy's six thousand officers a chance to distinguish themselves, in the great tradition of captains Cook, James, La Pérouse, and Bougainville. The chosen officers, commanding expeditions that were partly political and partly scientific in nature, aroused great public interest, partly fueled by reports in the press and partly by their own published accounts. Fragile and ephemeral stars, they were subject to the laws of stardom and to the vagaries of public opinion.

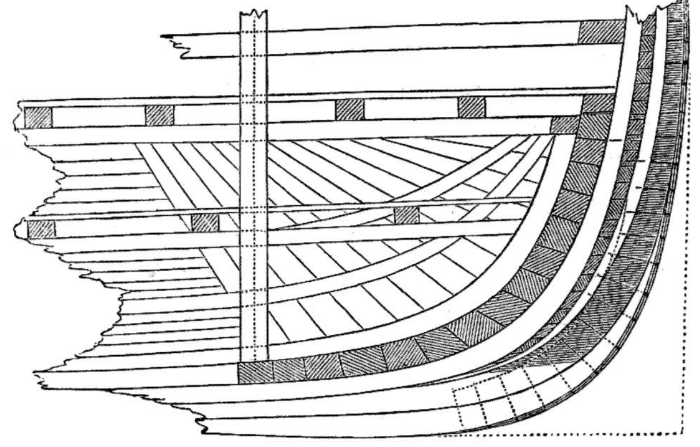
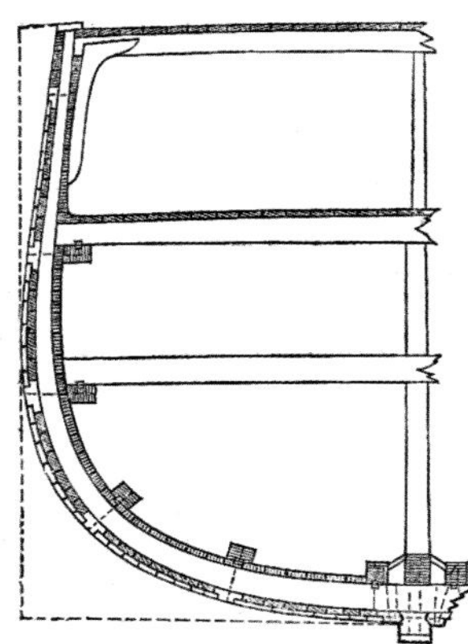

The *Isabella* and the *Alexander* were specially reinforced for this voyage to the polar seas. The pilot had to maneuver the ship through a channel in the pack ice, with the crew often towing the ship from a floe. The hulls were built of reinforced oak, rounded so that the pressure of the ice would lift rather than crush them.

convinced of the importance of polar exploration for Britain's maritime commerce and its industry generally. Captain Ross's stated mission was to discover the Northwest Passage and to gain China via the North Pole. The project was one of considerable scope. [2] The British Admiralty, after a century of inactivity in the higher latitudes, had decided to resume its patient search for a northern route to China: England would provide the brains, Scotland the arms and legs. The daring, fortitude, and imagination of its navy would see it through.

Ever active, the irascible John Barrow would provide inspiration and ardent advocacy for this quest over the course of forty years (1803-43). A farmer's son who rose to a prominent and strategic position through his skill at dealing with those in power, he appointed himself the geographer and historian of the polar regions. In fact, his polar experience went no farther than a summer voyage on a whaler to Baffin Bay. He was convinced, after an armchair study of the north-south currents in Davis and Bering straits, that Greenland was an island and the North Pole an ice-free ocean: the "Open Polar Sea."

The accounts of whaling captains, and particularly that of the celebrated William Scoresby, gave support to his project. Whalers claimed that the east coast of Greenland, which had been blocked with ice for four centuries, had warmed to an extraordinary degree in 1817. Scoresby, known as the pre-eminent Arctic sailor of his era, had noticed that some whales caught by his crews in the North Pacific carried harpoons in their hides from the North Atlantic and vice versa. The whales therefore traveled between the Pacific and the Atlantic: incontrovertible proof that there were open-water straits between the oceans. This observation was crucial in spurring on the obstinate attempts mounted all through the nineteenth century by British expeditions. [3]

Service record filled out by Sir John Ross, who was then sixty-three years of age. National Maritime Museum, London.

FORMULA

REQUESTED TO BE FILLED UP FOR MR. O'BYRNE'S

BIOGRAPHICAL DICTIONARY

OF

ALL LIVING NAVAL OFFICERS.

*** This truly national and important undertaking, which has long occupied the attention of the Author, will consist of authentic Details of the Life and Services of every Officer in her Majesty's Navy, from the rank of Admiral of the Fleet to that of Lieutenant inclusively, comprising, with a statement of his Family Connexions, minute particulars of his professional career,—the Ships in which he has served,—the Engagements in which he has taken part,—his Promotions, Appointments, and Rewards, all with their accurate Dates.

The Work will be published by Mr. Colburn, of 13, Great Marlborough Street.

Rank and Name in full? John Ross — Capt. RN. C.B. [illegible]

Dates of Birth and Marriage, name of Wife, and number of Children? If possessing any Relatives in the Service? Their names? *** These inquiries may be answered or not, according to the wish of the party addressed. Born 24 June 1777 [illegible]

Date of entering the Service? 1786 — [illegible]

Date of Passing? — 1802

Dates of Promotions? [illegible] 1812 — Captain [illegible] 1818

If holding, or having held, any Civil Appointment? Consul at Stockholm

Present Official Employment, (if any?) Consul at Stockholm

A Model of Preparedness

Two expeditions were launched together. One, with Captain Buchan and Lieutenant John Franklin, was to cross the polar sea via Spitsbergen (a complete failure); the second, commanded by Captain John Ross, with the twenty-eight-year-old Lieutenant William Parry as his second-in-command, was to follow the passage opened by William Baffin in 1616.

On 18 April 1818, Captain John Ross boarded the *Isabella* (fifty-seven men). William Edward Parry—who in 1819 would discover the Northwest Passage—rode the *Alexander* (thirty-seven men).

Preparations for the expedition were remarkably thorough. Captain Ross personally chose each member of the crew, notably the ship's interpreter, John Sacheuse, an imaginative, energetic, and talented South Greenlander recommended to Ross in Edinburgh. Sacheuse had left Pröven (South Greenland) as a stowaway aboard a Scottish ship, determined to get an education in theology, and now wanted only to return to his country to serve his people. In Edinburgh he immersed himself not only in theology but also in the fine arts, and was thus able to record in ink and watercolor the historic meeting of the Europeans and the Polar Eskimos. [4]

Aside from Bibles for his crew, Captain Ross brought along numerous presents for the unknown peoples he would meet along the way: knives, knick-knacks, snuff (102 lbs.), gin (129 gallons), and . . . 40 umbrellas! There were also foodstores enough for three years.

In keeping with nineteenth-century custom, the salaries on both ships reflected the steep hierarchy of authority. The captain received £56 per month, the cook £4, the able seamen £3 (a ration of 19 to 1). Sacheuse, whose presence on the expedition would prove crucial, was valued at a lower rate than the cook, receiving £3 per month.

In the north of Baffin Bay, at latitude 70° 43' north, near Hare Island, the expedition encountered forty-three British whaling ships. One of them, the *Bon Accord*—an omen that, please the northern gods, might prove propitious to the Eskimos!—was commanded by a Scotsman from Aberdeen and would accompany the two ships up the coast to latitude 75° 12' north and longitude 61° 22' west, only 75 miles from Cape York. On 24 July, between latitudes 75° 12' and 76° north, Captain John Ross discovered a large bay, naming it Melville Bay, in honor of the former First Lord of the Admiralty. Navigating north along the Greenland coast on the advice of the whalers through lanes of water opened in the pack ice by the tide and currents, the sailors hauled the ships along by hand, boldly but with mounting caution. These precarious and discontinuous channels were, when necessary, enlarged with handsaws. The *Isabella* and the *Alexander* made regular progress.

Whenever the ice closed in, threatening to break the ships in its jaws, Ross's tactic was to crowd on all sail and flee—but always forward. In times of dead calm, the crews would tow the ships from the floe with all speed, spurred on by the martial accents of a violin, pressing northward into ice and mist. On 7 August, the storm-tossed ships narrowly avoided a fatal collision that might have resulted in shipwreck. Then more ice and mist . . . Captain Ross navigated skillfully. On 8 August, the fog parted to reveal the first land north of an enormous glacier that stretched 185 miles along the Greenland coast. From Upernavik north, the continental ice cap spills into the upper end of Baffin Bay. Exploring a small island seaward of the narrow fringe of open water along the shore, artillery captain Edward Sabine, the astronomer and naturalist on board the *Alexander*, accompanied by second lieutenant Bushnan, discovered several graves as well as a piece of plant stem most likely used to trim the wick of an oil lamp. Had men become lost in this icy desert north of the last human settlement? Skeletons, traces of fire—those small flames testifying to the vitality of man—were hastily searched for. The tiny island was named Bushnan Island. Feelings ran high on both ships. Lively discussions arose on all sides. Caught up in the spirit of exploration, Captain John Ross and Lieutenant William Parry were more resolved than ever to go forward.

In the morning mists

On 9 August, the *Isabella* sighted some men through the early morning mists. [5] The ships were in the north-northeast of Melville Bay, at latitude 75° 55' north and longitude 65° 32' west, north of Bushnan Island, between Savissivik and the headland that Captain Ross would name Cape York, south of Baffin's Cape Dudley Digges. [6] They were on the floe at a distance of seven or eight miles. [7] Could it be the crew of a shipwrecked whaler? It was inconceivable that a group of Eskimos could live at such high latitudes. The ships advanced toward them. The eight men came forward, then retreated . . . As the sun rose higher, visibility improved. Dozens of sailors were posted in the rig-

On 7 August 1818, the *Isabella* and the *Alexander* were caught in a storm. The two ships would have been dashed to pieces against each other without the extremely skillful handling of Captain John Ross and his officers, who managed to stave off catastrophe.

2) The Royal Navy offered the following prizes: £ 5,000 to the first ship to reach longitude 130° W at a point north of the Arctic Circle; £ 10,000 for reaching 140° W; £ 15,000 for reaching 150° W; and £ 20,000 for transiting to the Pacific Ocean.

3) A true pioneer of British Arctic exploration, Scoresby was unfortunately kept from commanding a polar expedition by John Barrow, who grew ever more authoritarian and vindictive. As Scoresby was a whaling skipper, there was a perceived class issue, and his unequaled abilities as a seaman and observer were consequently lost to the British Arctic effort.

4) Sir John Ross was himself an excellent draftsman, as his final report, A Voyage of Discovery, would show. Paintings were also made by the midshipmen A. M. Skene and J. Bushnan. On the Alexander there was another painter of talent, Lieutenant H. H. Hoppner.

5) The following account draws on Ross's relation (1819).

6) William Baffin proceeded as far as Cape Alexander on 5 July 1616, a feat not repeated for several centuries. As his original map was lost, the truth of his claims was long in doubt. It was Captain John Ross who, in the account of his own voyage, would confirm the accuracy of Baffin's discoveries. The names given by Baffin to various capes and bays were kept: Wolstenholme and Whale fjords; Cape Dudley Digges; Smith, Jones, and Lancaster sounds; the Hakluyt and Carey islands.

7) One nautical mile equals 1,852 meters.

Dovekie (*Alle alle*): With its short wings, the dovekie can dive and swim underwater as well as fly long distances, from Virginia, U.S.A., to North Greenland.

The arctic tern flies the greatest distance of all migratory birds: 20,000 miles.

ging, like birds, their eyes trained on the ice. Sacheuse called out to the strange men, but they seemed not to understand his South-Greenland dialect. They stared intently at the two ships . . . then gave a simultaneous shout. Gesticulating strangely, they hurriedly climbed back onto their small sleds and fled toward shore . . . Had the arm and flag signals exchanged by the two ships frightened them?

After a mile, the natives stopped. Two hours went by. A boat was sent to them, containing an assortment of presents, largely knives and clothes. This gesture was met with seemingly sovereign indifference. A second boat was sent, this one carrying an Eskimo dog with several strands of blue beads around its neck. On an iceberg, the explorers raised a white flag with an image of the Sun and the Moon over a hand holding a sprig of heath, the only shrub discovered growing along the coast. To the flagstaff was attached a sack containing more presents, decorated with a hand pointing toward a ship. Leaving these signs and offerings behind, the ships sailed westward along the edge of the pack ice looking for a passage. Finding nothing, they returned that night to where they had met the Eskimos. On 10 August, the wind had dropped, and the sea was calm. The Eskimos appeared a second time. At the end of the morning, they approached the boat with eight sleds on a roundabout course. They stopped a mile from the pole, at whose foot the dog was sleeping; the presents were untouched. They climbed to the top of a small iceberg to survey the situation, consulting among themselves for half an hour. Finally, four of them walked toward the flag staff but stopped at a safe distance. Far off, the ships were flying the white flag.

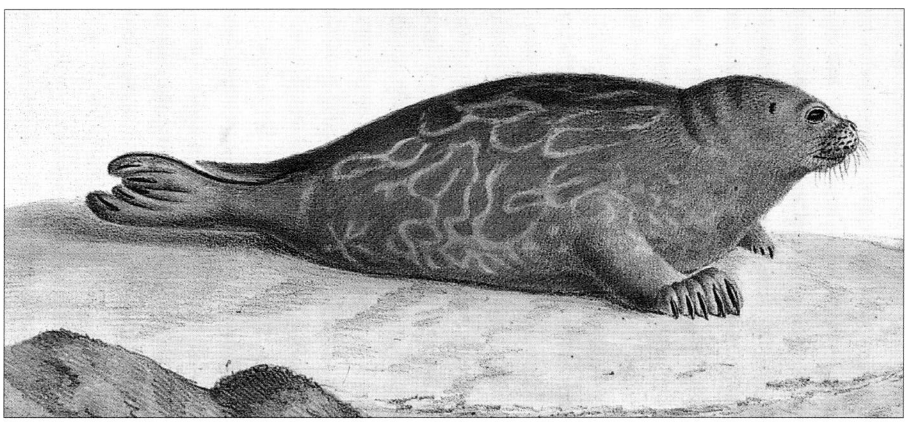

Seal, walrus, and narwhal. These species, which are numerous in the seas north and south of Upernavik, are the main ones hunted by the Polar Inuit. Above, the ringed seal (Phoca hispida), whose length varies from 3 to 5 feet, with a girth of about 4 feet, and a weight of 175 to 220 pounds. Born between mid-March and mid-April, they nurse for six weeks.

Seeing their indecision, Sacheuse volunteered to go toward them alone, armed only with a white flag. This showed considerable courage, at a time when the legends and traditions of the South Greenlanders depicted the inhabitants of the Far North as fierce giants and cannibals . . .

A lane of open water several yards wide separated him from these unknown humans. He planted the white flag at the edge of the floe, took off his hat and waved it in the air. But he backed away for fear that he might frighten the natives. The Eskimos were now about three hundred yards away. They dismounted from their sleds and gave a loud, deep cry: "Halloo! Halloo!" which Sacheuse answered by imitating it. They approached, carrying only their whips. Sacheuse held out the presents and called to them: "*Kahkeite!*" (Come!) But the Eskimos, trembling in their whole bodies, spoke fragments of sentences: "*Naakrie! Naakrieai-plaite!*" (No! No, go away!), miming that they were afraid of dying on the spot. Finally, the eldest of them strode forward a few steps to the edge of the channel and, pulling a small knife from his boot, shouted "Go away! I can kill you!" Sacheuse held his ground; he threw over a few beads and a checked shirt, which did nothing to reassure them. Then he threw them a large knife. This time, the group came forward, but with the greatest caution. One of them finally picked up the knife, shouting and pulling his nose. Sacheuse responded in kind. Then pointing to the shirt, which they had been fingering attentively, the Eskimos asked him of what animal it was made . . .

After several further questions that Sacheuse could not understand, they asked him whether he came from the sun or the moon. Sacheuse told them he was man like themselves, with a father and a mother, and that he came from the south. To which the Eskimos replied that it was impossible: "There is nothing but ice there." They then questioned Sacheuse about the two "birds" (the *Isabella* and the *Alexander*) whose wings were beating in the wind. Were they truly birds or some other flying creature? "They are made of wood," Sacheuse told them. "No," said the Eskimos, "they are alive. We saw their wings move!" When Sacheuse asked them who they were and where they came from, the men answered that they were Inuit (men) and lived in that direction (pointing north), where there was open, ice-free water. They had come here to hunt narwhal. Believing that a sufficient rapport had now been established between them, Sacheuse invited the Inuit to come meet the others of his party. He indicated that he was going to the ship to fetch a plank.

During this encounter, Captain Ross had been leaning against the ship's railing, watching the proceedings through his telescope. "I beheld the first man approach," he recounted, "with every mark of fear or distrust, looking frequently behind to the other two, and beckoning them to come on, as if for support. They occasionally retreated, then advanced again, with cautious steps, in the attitude of listening, generally keeping one hand down by their knees, in readiness to pull out a knife which they had in their boots; in the other hand they held their whips with the lash coiled up; their sledges remained at a little distance, and the fourth man being apparently stationed to keep them in readiness for escape.

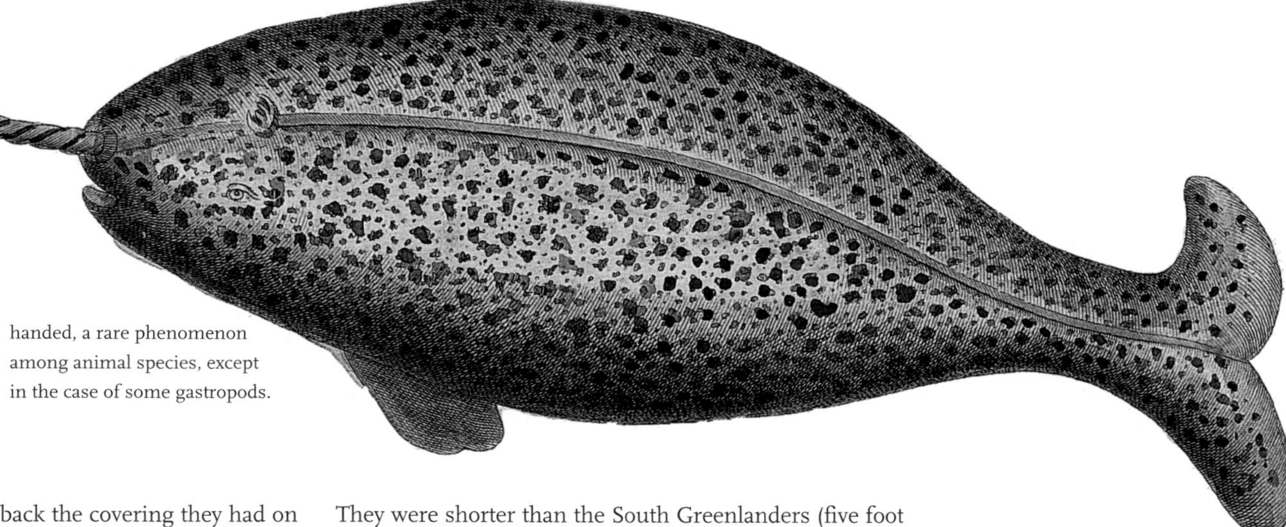

Narwhal (*Monodon monoceros*): 15 feet long and 9 feet in circumference, the male can weigh 3500 pounds. Male narwhals usually have a single tusk (and the females none) measuring some 6 feet in length. Its spiral is left-handed, a rare phenomenon among animal species, except in the case of some gastropods.

"Sometimes they drew back the covering they had on their heads, as if wishing to catch the most distant sounds; at which time I could discern their features, displaying extreme terror and amazement, while every limb appeared to tremble as they moved." [Ross, *A Voyage of Discovery*, p. 85]

But events now started moving faster. Two sailors arrived carrying a plank and laid it across the channel separating Sacheuse from the Eskimos. Still fearful, the Eskimos asked that only Sacheuse come across. He agreed and, having crossed the divide, found himself before them. The Eskimos begged him not to touch them, as they would "certainly die." When Sacheuse finally convinced them, after much arguing, that he was truly flesh and blood, an Eskimo resolved to touch him on the hand, after which he immediately pulled on his nose and shouted "*Heigh-yaw!*" Sacheuse did the same. The three other Eskimos also joined in shouting. Sacheuse offered them more beads and a few articles of clothing, which the Inuit shared out amongst themselves indifferently. Then Sacheuse exchanged his knife for a very small Eskimo knife. The Polar Inuit, for whom exchange is a way of life, thus engaged for the first time in barter with strangers. And barter was to be the basis of their material culture throughout the nineteenth century until the establishment of a trading post in 1910.

Ross, deciding that the time had come to discuss things directly with these men, went over to them accompanied by Lieutenant William Parry, both in full dress uniform and carrying presents. On reaching them, he ordered the flag of the Sun and Moon to be planted in the ice and personally offered them knives, mirrors, shirts, and caps. A first encounter informed by majesty and protocol . . .

The Inuits as British citizens

Captain Ross, Lieutenant Parry, John Sacheuse, and the two seamen thus found themselves face to face with eight Eskimos from the northernmost human group on earth. They were shorter than the South Greenlanders (five foot one and three quarters inches, according to the account of Lieutenant Hoppner) and wore long, sparse beards, quite unusual among the Inuit. Everything suggested that they were experiencing great fear, an ontological panic. The brightly colored uniforms of the two officers gave them particular anxiety. Sacheuse tried to reassure them. The Eskimos answered by rubbing their noses and shouting "*Heigh-haw!*" which the Britons chorused back to them. The dogs howled. The Eskimos silenced them with lordly ease, the tips of their whips flicking at the snow in front of the dogs' paws. A feeling of fellowship grew. The aborigines were given mirrors and, writes Captain Ross, discovered their own faces for the first time—with what surprise! First they examined themselves for a long time in silence. Then they started shouting and guffawing. [8] Before long they had brought out their own modest belongings: small knives of meteoric metal, bits of narwhal and walrus tusk. The Polar Eskimos—whom Sacheuse instructed to take off their hats before the British officers as a sign of good will and respect, like Friday before Robinson Crusoe—seemed astonished to see the two officers pulled on sleds by the seamen. Were those men then of no more worth than dogs? And in any case, where were their dogs? Such were no doubt a few of their many inner thoughts.

The Eskimos were invited to come aboard the ship. The entire crew was on deck or in the rigging. Five of the Eskimos, who had never before seen other men,

THEY EAT THEIR MEAT RAW

"We . . . had now an opportunity of discovering that [the Eskimaux] had no scruple of eating raw flesh in any state. One of them, who had a bag full of auks, took out one in our presence, and devoured it raw; but on being asked if this was a common practice, they informed us that they only ate them in this state when they had no convenience for cookery. (Captain John Ross)

Ross, John, *A Voyage of Discovery* (London: J. Murray, 1819), 146.

8) Knowing as I do the Inuit's penchant for play-acting, I suspect that they feigned surprise and exaggerated their wonder in order to please their visitors. They had certainly seen their own faces before, either mirrored in the ice, or reflected in the open water of summer, or in one of the mirrors of black mica whose existence has been confirmed by archaeologists.

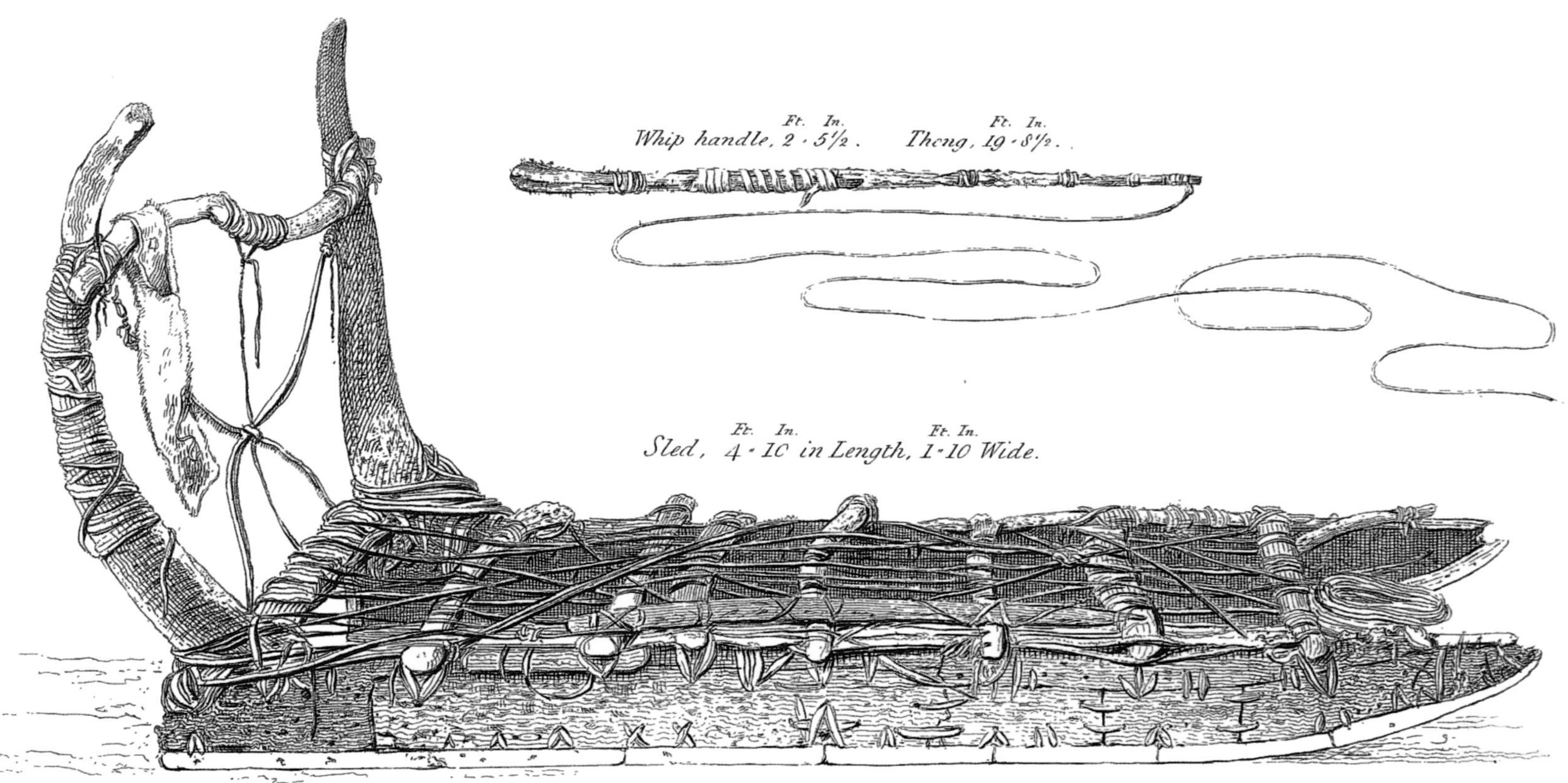

Sled and whip, Cape York. Lithograph published in Sir John Ross's report of 1819. The construction would remain unchanged until the 1950s or later. Only the dimensions would be altered, but proportionately.

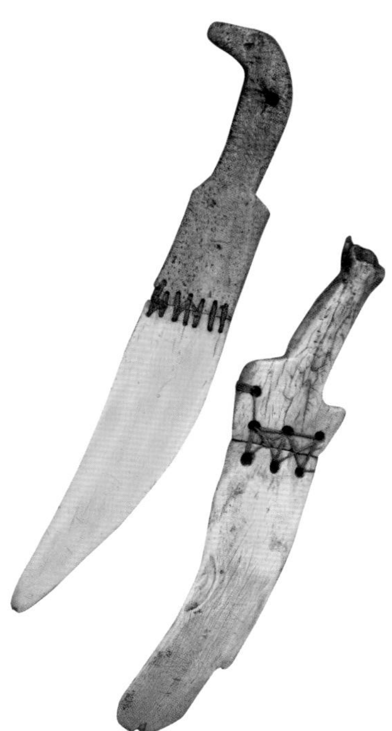

Bone knives of the Polar Eskimos. These are not established as having been collected by John Ross, and may be of later date.

walked toward the ship across the pack ice. They remained in a tight group. When the ships' sails flapped, the natives stopped in a panic. These enormous wooden houses seemed truly alive to them. One Eskimo addressed himself distinctly to the *Alexander*: "Who are you? What are you? Where do you come from? Is it from the Sun or the Moon?" With great reluctance, and after much persuasion, the Eskimos placed their small feet, shod in sealskin boots, on the rungs of the rope ladder. Once on the deck they panicked again at the sight of a pig and a little dog. Very quickly, however, they grew bolder, amused themselves by making faces in a large mirror, expressed surprise at the pallor of the Englishmen's skin. What is striking is the extreme rapidity with which these Inuit adapted to this extraordinary situation. They looked at everything with great attention: the blacksmith's anvil, the ship's anchor. The red uniform of a sergeant made them wonder. They were fascinated by the ticking of a watch. "Is it good to eat?" they asked. A sailor from the *Isabella* played the trumpet, to which they listened with surprise. The sound of the flute and the violin left them indifferent. One of them nonetheless brought the flute to his lips and blew, only to fling it down onto the deck in fright. They wanted to know what sort of sea-ice was used in glazing a porthole, and also in making the glass cover of the ship's compass. As one observer noted, they seemed to want to test all the objects they saw by touching and weighing them. Unused to our food, they spat out in disgust the biscuit and salt meat served to them.

At length, a shamanistic session was organized on the bridge. One of the men with more ability at conjuring than the others, the *angakkuq*, agreed to it immediately, as he could then use the opportunity to recite his incantations in a low voice. The song was taken up by the other men in skins who, before these invaders, conjured their familiar spirits. One of them struck up a regular beat on a small drum of translucent skin, whose sounds seemed to cross into the realm of the invisible. His eyes shining with the spirits of the dead, the drummer seemed to sway on his feet like the swell of the sea, his torso bent forward. The effect was so alarming that Ross almost called for the ship's surgeon.

On 12 August, claiming possession of the region for the British Crown, Ross named the bay "Prince Regent's Bay." Noble patronage! The entry of this unknown people into history did in fact coincide with the birthday of His Royal Highness . . .

Between 12 and 15 August, other Eskimos arrived. They now numbered eighteen. The newcomers stayed on the ice at a distance from the ships, playing with a kickball most likely made of sealskin.

After a first unsuccessful attempt by Sacheuse, Captain Ross and Lieutenant Parry managed to persuade the Eskimos to come aboard. They had clearly heard a report from the first group, and they set to pilfering with a will. They took nails and pieces of wood, and even tried to carry off the anvil. An Eskimo named Meigack was particularly bold. Although he was closely watched, he managed to abscond from Ross's cabin with the captain's best telescope, a case of razors, and a pair of scissors, hiding them under his long sealskin coat. He walked impassively

9) For want of an appropriate museum to house it, this fundamental collection was dispersed. Only one authentic sled, deposited in the British Museum, survives, along with five spears of narwhal ivory, one of which broke into several pieces, a knife, and a harpoon point of meteoric iron. It is not the sled described in Ross's official report, which should be in the Edinburgh Museum but has not been found despite my earnest entreaties. The Vienna Museum acquired a knife of meteoric iron from the John Ross Collection through exchange. The sum total of the material culture of this uncontacted people amounts to eleven objects. I investigated the matter in considerable detail in both London and Edinburgh.

10) If one attentively examines the sled brought back to London by John Ross, as curator Jonathan King and I did in 1981, one discovers that it contains a tiny piece of wood and a riveted nail.

past the seamen, but the steward had seen his game. He demanded that Meigack return the stolen objects, which he promptly did. Meigack then snatched up a hammer, which this time he threw overboard. He walked past the seamen nonchalantly and climbed down from the ship with a determined air. But again he had been seen by one of the crew. On orders from the captain, the crewman ran onto the ice after Meigack, calling him. On the point of being overtaken, Meigack artfully dropped the hammer into the snow and went imperturbably on his way.

Within a few days, the Eskimos had taken the measure of the newcomers. They knew just how far they could go. And on their side, the white men had noticed a thousand and one particulars. The Eskimos did not know how to sit on a chair. Sacheuse explained that these men ate only meat: seal, narwhal, fox, bird, and—in times of famine—dog. It was also noticed that the group was egalitarian: a teak board that had been given to them was immediately divided into as many pieces as there were Eskimos present. During the day, the explorers measured the Eskimos' sleds, and recorded on paper the extraordinary scenes they were witnessing. Among those sketching the Eskimos were Captain Ross, Lieutenant Hoppner, and midshipmen Skene and Bushnan, as well as John Sacheuse. Wanting documentary evidence, they traded with the natives: in exchange for knives, telescopes, and beads they obtained ivory spears, knives of bone, meteoric iron, and a sled. [9]

Captain Ross, ever mindful of the interests of his government, tried to find out where the Eskimos obtained their supply of meteoric iron. On the strength of a promise of further gifts, the Eskimos told him that they chipped flakes of iron the size of a fingernail from meteorites in "Sowallick" (Savissivik), only twenty-five miles away, using very hard stones. Their knives were examined by the expedition's armorer. He determined that some of the blades had been made from flattened nails, no doubt recovered from driftwood. Thus contrary to the common wisdom of ethnographers, wood was not unknown to them. [10]

Captain Ross's misconception

When the Eskimos refused to provide the British with any meteoric iron—they brought the basalt stones they used to chip the meteors instead—Ross stopped allowing them on board the ships. Then, on 16 August, heeding the Admiralty's instructions not to "linger along the coasts," and seeing that the pack had broken up somewhat, Ross pursued his route northward (Wolstenholme Fjord, Whale Sound), but not before augmenting his men's rations by shooting large numbers of auks with a few shots. At the height of Wolstenholme and Dalrymple Islands (at what

Brief respite on an iceberg, with its tremendous store of fresh water, before facing the dense ice of the frozen sea. The icebergs in Melville Bay are calved from the continental ice sheet along the shore as well as from the great Humboldt Glacier.

a. **Snow goose** (*Anser caerulescens*)
b. **Crested grebe** (*Podiceps cristatus*)
c. **Common loon** (*Gavia immer*)
d. **Arctic loon** (*Gavia arctica*)
e. **Great auk** (extinct) (*Pinguinus impennis*)
f. **Horned puffin** (*Fratercula corniculata*)
g. **Gentoo penguin** (*Pygoscelis papua*)

f
b
a
d
c

Winter camp in Felix Harbor. Captain Ross's second expedition spent three winters here and would claim the record for the longest Arctic expedition. Its twenty-three men included three officers who chose to serve, as Captain Ross did, without pay. The expedition importantly discovered the magnetic north pole and mapped the Gulf of Boothia and Boothia Peninsula, the northernmost tip of the North American mainland.

was to become North Star Bay), Ross sailed west. He passed to seaward of the Carey Islands, which William Baffin had described two centuries earlier, then once again steered north.

It was at this point that he committed one of the two errors that were to cost him so dearly for the rest of his life. Glimpsing Smith Sound on 20 August, he made note of the two splendid capes that mark its entrance, naming them Cape Alexander and Cape Isabella. [11] He proceeded no farther, remaining at a distance of 50 to 60 miles while a field of ice separated him from the coast, and estimated that this strait, surrounded by a fretwork of fjords, was no more than a bay. How is it possible to explain such a blunder? Weariness? The influence of Rousseauvian dreams after several days spent with men from another era? One thing is at any rate certain: the Admiralty had misinformed him on the cartography of his predecessor William Baffin, who had identified Smith Sound as a strait. But from the end of the seventeenth century to the beginning of the nineteenth British maps denied the existence of Smith Sound. Baffin's detractors cast doubt on its existence in atlas after atlas. Had not Baffin been a commoner? When Ross reached latitude 76° 46' north, he seems to have allowed himself to be persuaded. Yet his soundings brought up a gray mud, and the icebergs indicated a great depth of water. One of his officers, cited in Ross's own account of the expedition, wrote: "It is likely that the gap where I can make out no land is what Baffin called Smith Sound." If only Ross had questioned the Eskimos in Savissivik about the coastline to the north! Having hunted polar bear at Etah since time immemorial, they could have told him of the seaway that, thirty-six years later, would be named Kane Basin and Kennedy Channel. [12] Inexplicably, at the expedition's decisive moment, Ross ordered the ship to bear west, in search of a route to China via the so-called Northwest Passage.

Ross's second expedition. Route of the expedition in search of the magnetic north pole in the central Canadian Arctic (1831).

While Ross failed to push north into Smith Sound and thereby unwittingly missed an important landmark—the gateway to the Pole—he did, again unconsciously, make a fundamental discovery in the history of mankind by finding the Hyperboreans of Greenland. With these eighteen Eskimos from Savissivik, the northernmost people on the face of the Earth made their entrance into history.

"We are alone in the world"

Let us return, if only briefly, to the days from 9 to 15 August marking the discovery of an unknown Arctic people. The Polar Eskimos were cut off from southern Greenland by more than a hundred miles of barren ice, with the coastline buried under the continental ice cap. Their nearest Canadian cousins were some five hundred miles to the southwest, near Igloolik. Lacking good means of transport, the Polar Eskimos (who were so miserly with their dogs that it was only with the greatest difficulty that Ross was able to procure even one) were never able to go very far north, south, or west of Ellesmere Island, according to the geographer H. P. Steensby, writing in 1910. "We are alone in the world," they told Sacheuse. Yet they had a vague notion that there were people living to the south of them.

Eleven months of frozen seas, one month of open water, three months of polar night, and a temperature that drops below -60° C with wind: such are the harsh basic elements that this people have to deal with. Famines are frequent. The Polar Eskimos had practically no wood or telluric metal; no kayaks; no bows or spears (with the exception of narwhal tusks); no leisters (three-pronged spears) for catching salmon. Apparently the only tools they needed were small knives, and raw materials such as bone and stone. Lacking kayaks, they hunted seal only from the edge of the floe, pursued walrus along the shore, ate birds raw, and disdained to eat caribou or salmon . . . In ethnographic history, they would be known successively, depending on who happened upon them and where, as Arctic Highlanders, Cape York Eskimos, Ita Eskimos, Itanese, Smith Sound Eskimos, and finally Polar

THEY BECAME IMPERTINENT

"As they brought neither the iron nor the articles of dress they had promised, I gave orders that they should not be permitted to come on board, or to receive any presents. They said they had been at Inmallick (the headland to the northward), to procure stones for the purpose of cutting off the iron from the rock; and they gave us one of these, which appeared to be a basalt, together with a little dried moss, in a state ready for trimming their lamps. . . . Finding they were not permitted to come on board, they became noisy and impertinent: but Sacheuse having told them that our *angekok* would cause the ice to separate, and prevent their return if they did not go, they departed, promising to bring the iron without delay." (Captain John Ross)

Ross, John, ***A Voyage of Discovery*** (London: John Murray, 1819), 152-153.

The *Victory* in trouble. This sailing steamship was bought for Ross by his patron Felix Booth, a distiller. Ross was anxious to mount a new polar expedition to stem the insidious and unending flow of slurs issued from the Admiralty. The *Victory* had previously shuttled between Liverpool and the Isle of Man, then between Dover and Calais. Shallow of draft and displacing only 150 tons, it would allow Ross to navigate the shallow channels of the Central Canadian Arctic. This was a technological revolution. The *Victory* was the first polar ship to be equipped with a steam engine, but, as the engine worked only poorly and then not at all, it became a handicap.

Eskimos. They call themselves Avanersuarmiut or, more generally, Inuit, more properly Inughuit.

Ross, who was impressed by them, called them "Arctic Highlanders." This shows his Scotsman's respect and his admiration for these "primitives," a rare attitude in those times. A former informations officer, he made a careful record of all that he saw. (Almost a century would pass before reports and sketches were again composed with comparable care, by such men as Kroeber, Steensby, and Rasmussen.) Ross is to be admired all the more in that his orders were to never stop his progress toward the "Open Polar Sea" and the Northwest Passage to China. In fact, he did not disobey orders. It was only the pack ice that obliged him to linger among the Eskimos.

Self-interest on one side and the other

With the Crown's interests ever in mind, Ross noted in his remarkable account of the voyage that the country might prove to be of real economic benefit. "Besides the whale fisheries, it is more than probable, that a valuable fur trade might be established; numbers of black foxes were actually seen by the officers and men . . . The ivory of the sea-unicorn, the sea-horse's teeth, and the bear's teeth, may also be considered as articles of trade. All these could be procured for European commodities, such as knives, nails, small harpoon heads, pieces of iron, wood of any description, crockery ware, and various cheap and useful utensils and tools; both to the great benefit of the merchant, and to that of this secluded race of human beings."

If the British quickly sized up the region's economic interest, the Polar Eskimos—though still living in the prehistoric age—drew a truly political lesson from these six days of discovery, formulating to themselves the potential danger represented by Whites. And the impact of this initial encounter would remain indelible.

Physical danger was the first concern. "Don't kill us, we are truly alive!" they pleaded at the very beginning of the encounter. (Their families—the women and children and the elderly—had been taken into hiding in the mountains. The Eskimos had thus provided for their escape.) Yet they did not break off negotiations. Pilfering for all they were worth, they presented a smiling mask to the newcomers, the mask of haughty and indifferent collaborators. But they would never forget their first impression: on the one hand, the white men were ill-adapted to the Arctic, and their technology, ethics, and rules were

11) These would later be called the "pillars of Hercules on either side of the gateway to the North Pole."

12) Subsequent expeditions to Igloolik (Parry, 1821-1823, northeast Canada) and to Angmagsalik (Holm, 1883-1885, southeast Greenland) have established the Eskimos' remarkable ability to draw maps of their territory from memory. I had the same experience in 1950-1951 (Etah-Siorapaluk, Thule, Savissivik).

JOHN SAKEOUSE,
A Native of Jacob Sound, Greenland,
the first ESQUIMAUX known to have been in this Country.

John Sacheuse (here spelled Sakeouse). A South Greenlander, Sacheuse was the official interpreter on Ross's first expedition, present at the historic encounter with the Polar Eskimos. He was also an accomplished painter and sketcher. This is one of the rare portraits of Sacheuse that is known to be authentic. Copperplate engraving (Scotland).

John Sakeouse

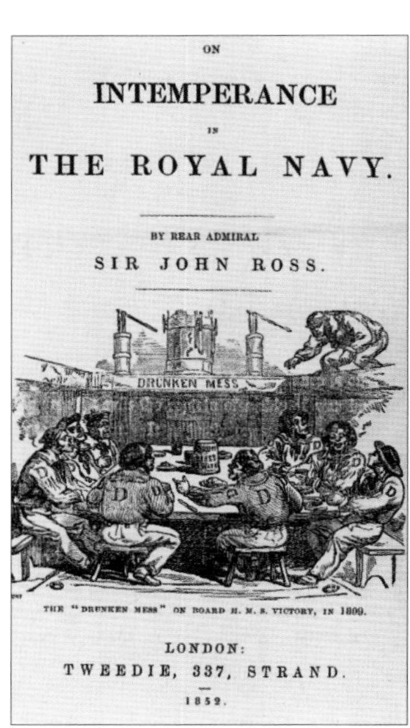

ON
INTEMPERANCE
IN
THE ROYAL NAVY.

BY REAR ADMIRAL
SIR JOHN ROSS.

THE "DRUNKEN MESS" ON BOARD H. M. S. VICTORY, IN 1809.

LONDON:
TWEEDIE, 337, STRAND.
1852.

Title page of a treatise by Sir John Ross on drunkenness (which is a problem in every navy) aboard British ships. Arguing against public corporal punishment, Ross proposes a method by which habitual drunkards would carry the letter D on their backs and remain segregated for a longer or shorter period in a separate part of the ship—to their great shame. Using this method, Ross reduced alcoholism significantly on his ships.

utterly alien; on the other hand, though white men might be dangerous, they could also be useful. The entrenched conservatism of the Eskimos with respect to their technology and culture over the following century, despite the onslaught of Western culture, thus finds some explanation . . .

Had the British government listened to Ross, North Greenland could have become a British colony at that time and been joined to Canada. A major route to the North Atlantic and the Arctic Ocean would have been assured. In ignoring John Ross and dismissing the discovery of the Polar Eskimos as unimportant, John Barrow served the Crown poorly. And the regular administration of the Polar Eskimos (which would only start with Knud Rasmussen in 1910 and become official in 1915) would have been set forward by a century.

For the Eskimos, the shock might have proved fatal, as they would not have had the time to adapt. These thirty or forty families, "primitive" and demographically fragile as they were, could well have been destroyed by the brutal impact of a dominant foreign culture.

A time of humiliation

On 31 August at 3:15 pm, Ross committed another error, this one even more serious than his error of 20 August. Having proceeded westward a miraculous fifty miles into Lancaster Sound, first discovered in 1616 by William Baffin, Ross observed no swell or current arriving from the west, nor any driftwood. By some magic of the atmosphere, some reflection on the water, he was convinced that he saw a mountain range barring the far end of the sound, which in fact measures 40 miles across and 126 miles in length. He named the illusory range (and illusions of this kind are far from uncommon in the Arctic) the Croker Mountains.[13] Ross drew the mountain, mapped it carefully, then turned around and sailed out of the sound, to the astonishment of all and against the advice of the commander of the *Alexander,* William Parry.[14] The expedition's return to England on 30 October 1818 caused some surprise, as it had carried provisions for overwintering in the north.

Once back in London, Ross met with Barrow, and sharp words were exchanged. Barrow, a geographer in a minister's armchair, was convinced that, the initial barrier once past, the Arctic Ocean would prove free of ice. Captain Ross, a capable and experienced navigator, tried calmly but with some asperity to argue the importance of his discoveries: the confirmation of Baffin's explorations (with the exception of the two "straits"), the mapping and charting of unknown regions, the encounter with a new people, and the finding of new whaling grounds. To no avail. "Incompetence," was Barrow's verdict. After drawing up a good report of every member of the expedition, Ross was promoted one grade on 7 December 1818. Imperturbable, he completed his remarkable official account of the expedition. The work was published in 1819 by John Murray and has become a classic of Arctic literature. Superb black-and-white plates appeared four months after the expedition's return! This elegant and accurate work has been an object of controversy ever since.

Only a few compatriots—Scotsmen—came to Ross's defense. The *Edinburgh Review* published a ringing en-

13) Ross christened the mountains after the first secretary of the Admiralty, while attaching Barrow's name to a small "bay" directly south of the "false" Lancaster Sound.

14) The two became engaged in a controversy. Parry claimed to have argued by semaphore for continuing on. Ross denied it. One year later, in August 1819, the newly promoted Captain Parry would enter this famous Northwest Passage aboard the Hecla.

15) The battle of Culloden (16 April 1746)—Scotland's Waterloo as a sovereign nation—was still present in all minds. Irritated, not to say exasperated, by Captain Ross's idiosyncrasy and his well-argued and critical studies, Barrow excluded him from the Polar Committee, thus sidelining one of Britain's greatest Arctic explorers. The order of the day in Admiralty circles was to bring down this marginal figure: his smallest errors were recorded, and he was treated like a peddlar. Certain officers, among them Captain Edward Sabine, who was jealous of Ross's reputation, took part in these sometimes defamatory campaigns, conducted through anonymous publications. It cannot be said too often how such great institutions as the navy, the army, and the university are prone to petty controversies. As Voltaire aptly wrote: "There are two monsters that consternate the earth: intolerance and calumny, and I'll combat them both until my death."

16) A strange manor house near Oban, Ross's home is now a small museum. Telescopes stand permanently at the windows for observing the passing ships, and a photography room faces the bay. Ross's bedroom is a replica of his cabin on the Victory. On the walls are relief maps, diagrams of the North Pole, model boats, and a coat of arms representing the Arctic. On it are the words: Arcilos numine files. Aspes aspera levant.

dorsement. But Barrow, in the *Quarterly Review,* publicly attacked the man he had himself chosen to test the truth of his polar theories. He accused Ross of "excessive timidity," of being a "captain for a summer outing." Ross's mapping errors would provide a source of humor to the Royal Navy for decades. To the end of his life, he would carry the nickname "Croker Mountain." He was reproached with spending too much time "rubbing noses with the Esquimaux"; and even his name for them, "Arctic Highlanders," was turned to ridicule by the English military establishment, which looked on the Scots with considerable contempt. [15]

One of his company, Royal Artillery captain Edward Sabine, an excellent geomagneticist and the expedition's astronomer and naturalist, attacked Ross in turn. He claimed that Ross's astronomical observations were inaccurate and that the Eskimo glossary Ross published had in fact been taken from him without permission. Ross answered Sabine's accusations in a pamphlet. Irritated by the uproar, the Admiralty opened an investigation, then decided to remove Ross from active command. Ross meanwhile demanded a military trial, a request the Admiralty refused. Ross's career was in ruins. In May 1919 a new Arctic expedition was organized by the Admiralty, assembling around Captain William Edward Parry all the shipmates he had personally chosen and trained in 1818. This was the outcome of Parry's quiet machinations against Ross. An ambitious man, Parry had sufficiently close ties to John Barrow to send him confidential reports about his expedition leader and the progress of Ross's mission. Also a mystic who prayed day and night, and a hero in Great Britain after his triumphant expedition in search of the Northwest Passage, Parry managed to put his career on the right track early on. It is easy to believe that Ross hastened his return to England on the dangerous expedition of 1818 because he sensed a cabal forming against him and further considered the two ships under his command unsuited to Arctic navigation. As a good sailor, he believed that his first responsibility was to return safe and sound with both ships.

Aboard the *Victory*

For ten years Ross held no command. He had been retired at half pay. From the windows of a large house he built for himself at the entrance to Loch Ryan in his childhood county, Ross glumly watched the comings and goings of ships, waiting for the summons to a new adventure. [16]

Unlike many polar explorers who quickly became depressed and defeated by the attacks on them, Ross kept his chin high. He applied his extraordinarily inventive mind to the futuristic project of steamships, an idea that captured all Europe's imagination and revolutionized polar exploration. Once again the Admiralty would attack him, this time for endangering the future of the Royal Navy, which relied entirely on sailpower. Ross wrote and published voluminously. His friendship with the wealthy distiller Felix Booth, who was incensed at the underhanded campaigns against his friend, allowed Ross to outfit a ship in 1828. It was a small vessel of 150 tons, as Ross wanted, for navigating in the shallow Arctic bays; he proudly named it the *Victory.* He assumed a sixth of the cost, drawing on his own fortune, and again chose his nephew Lieutenant James Ross for the expedition, though he was perfectly aware of his nephew's unsavory part in the campaign that had brought down his career in 1819. Ross had already introduced his nephew to ice navigation aboard the *Isabella* in 1818 and would perfect his training by taking him now as his second-in-command.

Thus was Ross's second expedition to the Arctic, organized in 1829, again aimed at discovering the magnetic north pole and the Northwest Passage. Having often dealt with newspapers and the publicity mill, Ross managed to arouse enormous popular interest in his new venture.

Ross was hailed for his courage and obstinacy in the face of official neglect, and the expedition set off from

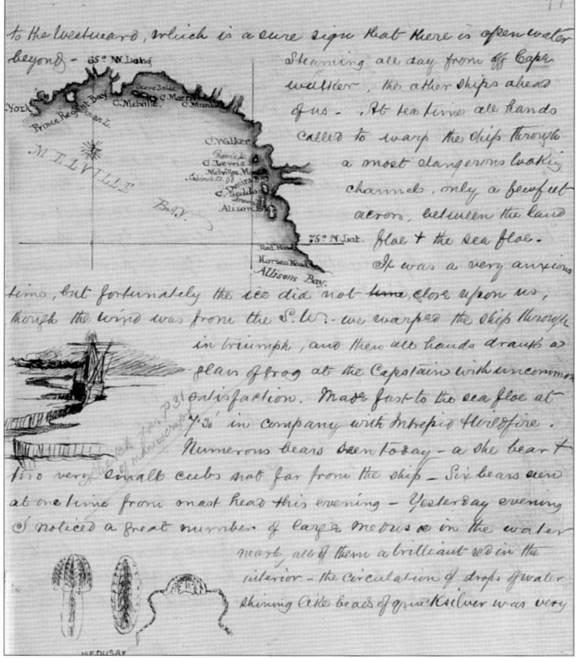

Page from the journal of the whaling skipper Smith. On 3 May, while sailing northward, Captain Ross met a fleet of 45 whaling ships trapped in the ice at latitude 70° 43' north and longitude 57° west (Hare Island). These ships would provide him valuable assistance. One of them, the Bon-Accord, would remain with him until 31 July 1818, at latitude 75° 32' north, longitude 60° 22' west, some 75 miles from Cape York, having caught five whales. (See transcript below.)

JOURNAL OF THE WHALING CAPTAIN SMITH

". . . to the Westward, which is a sure sign that there is open water beyond. Steaming all day from off Cape Walker, the other ships ahead of us. At tea time, all hands called to warp the ship through a most dangerous looking channel, only a few feet across, between the land floe and the sea floe. It was a very anxious time, but fortunately the ice did not close upon us, though the wind was from the S.W. We warped the ship through in triumph, and then all hands drank a glass of grog at the capstan with uncommon satisfaction. Made fast to the sea floe at 7:30 in company with Intrepid . . . Numerous bears seen today: a she-bear and two very small cubs not far from the ship. Six bears seen at one time from masthead this evening. Yesterday evening I noticed a great number of large medusae in the water, nearly all of them a brilliant red in the interior. The circulation of drops of water shining like beads of quicksilver was very . . ."

Sir James Clark Ross (1800-1862), nephew and rival, after 1818, of Sir John Ross. He was the discoverer of the North Magnetic Pole and would become the greatest hero of British Antarctic exploration.

England on 23 May 1829. The crew was small, as Ross had wanted, numbering only 23 men. During the four years of the expedition—three winters in Felix Harbor on Boothia Peninsula and another on the way to Lancaster Sound—Ross discovered the magnetic north pole, thanks to the enterprise of James Clark Ross, at latitude 70° 05' north and longitude 96° 44' west, on 1 June 1831. Finally, on 25 August 1833 Ross and his crew, having abandoned the ice-bound *Victory* and endured a thousand hardships, brought their ship's boats into Baffin Bay, where they were rescued by a whaler. As fate would have it, the ship was none other than the *Isabella!*

Ross had lost only one seaman to scurvy and hardship, and two to accidents. His triumph would be clouded somewhat by the accusations directed at him by the implacable Sir John Barrow—now eighty-two years old—and the even more insidious ones leveled at him by his nephew James Clark Ross (their relations are reminiscent of those described by Stevenson in *The Master of Ballantrae*). He lived an active life until the end. When Franklin's expedition disappeared without a word, Ross again offered the Admiralty his services for a rescue mission. At the recommendation of William Parry and his nephew, the Admiralty declined the offer, still believing that a rescue effort was premature. In fact, there was not a year to be lost: Franklin had provisions for only three years.

In 1850, exasperated with the Admiralty's coterie for Arctic affairs, Ross outfitted the *Felix* with funds from the Hudson Bay Company and sailed for Lancaster Sound in search of Franklin. He was then seventy-two years old.

On his return, harboring a premonition of where Franklin might be, Ross petitioned the Admiralty for a commission to resume his exploration but was refused. He then published a furious pamphlet accurately analyzing the failure of the fifty-three missions sent to rescue Franklin by the British government and others.

Wanting to keep informed of all domestic and foreign polar exploration, Ross was in London again in January 1856 to attend a speech at the Royal Geographic Society by the young doctor Elisha Kent Kane.

Sir John Ross died in London on 30 August 1856 at the age of seventy-nine. At the end of his life he had stopped responding to the many attacks of his detractors.

The following inscription might well have adorned his headstone: *Aquila non capit mergulas.* [17] ■

17) "The eagle pays no heed to birdlets."

CRITICAL ERROR: THE CROKER MOUNTAINS

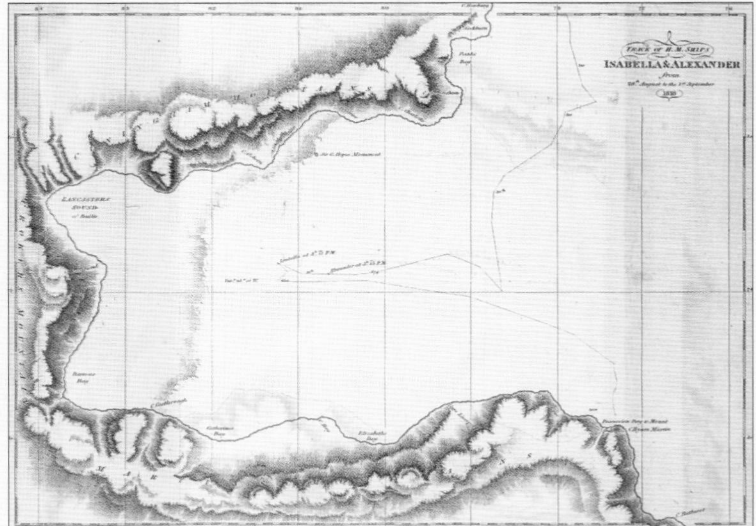

The mirage of Mount Croker. By identifying Lancaster Sound as a closed bay—without having penetrated far enough into it to make certain, and with no consultation of Lieutenant William Parry, who was following in the slower Alexander*—Ross fell short of the expedition's goal, namely, to discover the Northwest Passage. Another error: Smith Sound, as it had been named two centuries earlier, was mapped as an enclosed bay by Ross, who had again failed to examine it at close hand.*

Navigational Observations and Ships' Logs

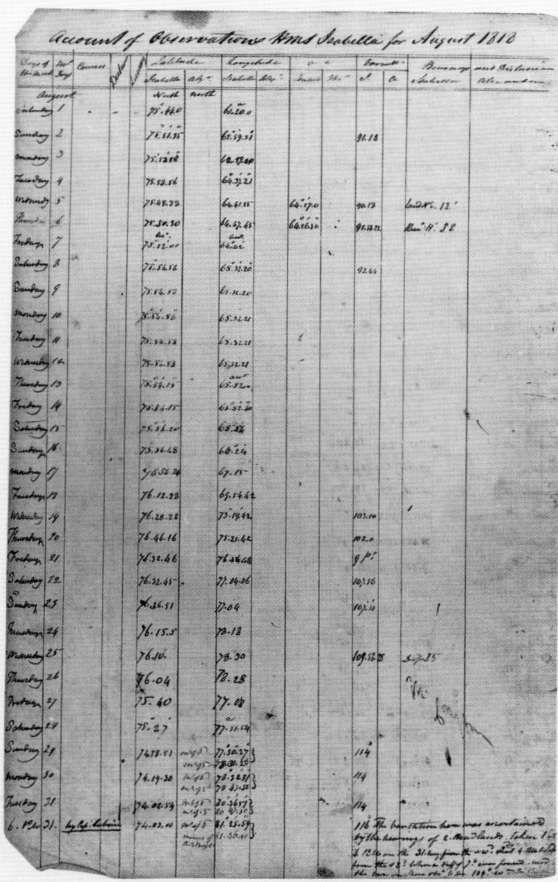
Account of Observations H.M.S. Isabella for August 1818

Meteorological observations for the month of August 1818 (from the logbook of the *Isabella*).

* The Alexander's position at this time was,
Latitude — — — 75. 54. 21
Longitude by Chro. — 65. 36. 30
Variation of the Compass 92. 16 Westerly

Position of the *Alexander* on the day the Eskimos were discovered.

THE DAY OF THE DISCOVERY OF THE POLAR ESKIMOS

Extract from the logbook of the *Alexander*: "10 August: 9:30 . . . Saw a group of natives coming toward the ship on sleds pulled by dogs. Sent forth our Esquimau with a white flag and presents to encourage them to come aboard. The Esquimau returned to fetch a board with which to cross a chasm of water. Captain Ross and Lieutenant Parry went out to meet the natives. 12 o'clock: mild and foggy. No sighting of the latitude."

117

1818 August 11th cont'd when a loose floe drifting on the iceberg (fortunately the opposite side to which the Isabella was made fast) produced such a violent concussion as to break off immense pieces from the Berg, which falling on the floe broke that up also — the noise made by this convulsion was like the sudden upsetting of a cart load of pebble stones, making the people who were below start from their seats in alarm and astonishment the ship immediately began to pitch heavy from the commotion in the water and the Isabella was surrounded with the broken fragments of ice.

Wed. 12th We did not fail to drink the Prince Regent's health on the anniversary of his birth, and Captain Ross further commemorated it by naming the deep bay in which we were then detained "Prince Regent's Bay." We made two or three efforts to proceed on this, and the following day, but without success. Thurs. 13th On the 13th however, we were in some measure consoled for our detention by the re-appearance of two sledges on the ice, from which the men were very soon induced to alight, and come to the Ship. They had

Page from the log of the *Alexander*, August 11, 12, and 13, 1818.

Augt 4th 1818
43.52.30 — 197.30
44.19.40 — 197.45
42.22.30 199.10

11.47.09 — 44.39.00 — 199.00
48.20 — 44.49.50 35
49.35 — 44.55.30 201.00

11.54.11 — 45.27.55
55.20 — 45.35.20
56.47 — 46.53.10
12.00.03 —

Northernmost Extt of the Bay — NBW½W
Southernmost Extt. of do — SSE½E
Cape or Highest Bluff — SE½ do
Pointed Bluff in the Middle of the bay — 26 N
Dist. Land to the North — N½ East
The Points of the Bay bearing each other N19°
Temperature on the Sea 42
These bearings were taken on the Ice at Noon
Lat 75.58.55 — Long by Chr. 64° 43' Var 90°

Observations recording the position of the *Isabella* on 4 August 1818.

Simultaneous views of the Polar Eskimos

"We measured a man: he was five feet one and three quarters inches tall, but he was among the smallest of the group. The average height was five feet four inches tall. Their hair was straight, long, thick, and black as jet. They had beards and mustaches. (W. H. Hooper, lieutenant aboard the *Isabella*)

Lithograph after a watercolor by John Sacheuse, in *A Voyage of Discovery*.

CAPTAIN JOHN ROSS

Being extremely anxious to communicate with the natives, I caused a pole to be prepared, on which a flag was fixed with a representation of the sun and moon painted over a hand holding a sprig of heath (the only shrub seen on the shore). This pole being carried to an iceberg, midway between the ships and the shore, was there erected, and a bag containing presents, with a device of a hand pointing to a ship, painted on it, was fastened to the pole within reach, and left there; the ships, in the mean time, being moored in a convenient situation for observing what might take place.

A canal and three hundred yards of ice between two peoples

August 10.— About ten o'clock this day, we were rejoiced to see eight sledges, driven by two natives, advancing by a circuitous route towards the place where we lay: they halted about a mile from us, and the people alighting, ascended a small iceberg, as if to reconnoitre. After remaining

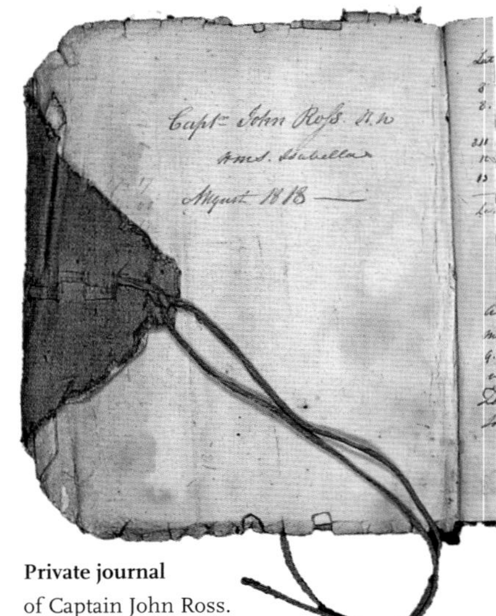

Private journal of Captain John Ross.

apparently in consultation for nearly half an hour, four of them descended, and came towards the flag-staff, which, however, they did not venture to approach. In the mean time a white flag was hoisted at the main in each ship.

A visceral fear

During the whole of this conversation I had been employed, with a good telescope, in observing their motions; and beheld the first man approach with every mark of fear or distrust, looking frequently behind to the other two, and beckoning them to come on, as if for support. They occasionally retreated, then advanced again, with cautious steps, in the attitude of listening, generally keeping one hand down by their knees, in readiness to pull out a knife which they had in their boots; in the other hand they held their whips with the lash coiled up.

Exchanges

Having now at length acquired confidence they advanced, offering in return for our knives, glasses, and beads, their knives, sea-unicorns' horns, and sea-horse teeth, which were accepted. They were then instructed by Sacheuse to uncover their heads, as a mark of good will and respect to us; and with this ceremonial, which they performed immediately, and of which they appeared to comprehend the meaning, our friendship became established.

One of them having enquired what was the use of a red cap, which I had given him, Sacheuse placed it on his head, to the great amusement of the rest, each of whom put it on his in turn. The colour of our skins became next a subject of much mirth, as also the ornaments on the frames of the looking-glasses. The eldest of them, who was also the one who acted as leader, addressing himself to me, now made a long speech, which being ended, he appeared to wait for a reply. I made signs that I did not understand him, and called for Sacheuse to interpret. He thus perceived that we used different languages, at which his astonishment appeared extreme, and he expressed it by a loud *Heigh, yaw!* . . .

A watch was also held to the ear of one, who supposing it alive, asked if it was good to eat.

An immense curiosity

[T]hey began to be very inquisitive, asking the use of everything in the cabin. We showed them papers, books, drawings, and various mathematical instruments, which produced only the usual effect of astonishing them, but on being shown the prints of Cook's voyage among the natives of Otaheite, they attempted to grasp them, evidently comprehending that they were representations of human beings. The sight of a writing desk, a bureau, and of the wooden furniture, also excited their astonishment, but apparently from the nature of the materials only, as they seemed to form no idea of their uses.

They were now conducted to the gun-room, and afterwards round the ship, but without appearing to distinguish anything particularly, except the wood, stamping on the deck, as if in evident surprise at the quantity of the valuable material.

In hopes of amusing them, the violin was sent for, and some tunes were played; they, however paid no attention to this, seeming quite unconcerned either about the sounds of the performer. . . . A flute was afterwards sounded for them, which seemed to exact somewhat more attention, probably from its resembling more neatly in shape the objects to which they were accustomed; one of them put it to his mouth and blew on it, but immediately threw it away. . . .

We then . . . , after some difficulty, succeeded in persuading two of the strangers, who, we were made to understand, were nephews of Ervik, to give us a specimen of their dancing. One of them accordingly began immediately to distort his face, and turn up his eyes in a manner so exactly resembling the appearance of a person in a fit of epilepsy, that we were convinced this accident had happened, and I was about to call for assistance from the surgeon. I was, however, soon undeceived, as he immediately began to execute, in succession, a variety of extraordinary gestures and attitudes, accompanied by the most hideous distortions of countenance. . . . After this had continued with increasing energy for ten minutes, the tune was suddenly changed to a shrill note, in which the words "*Weehee, weehee,*" were uttered with great rapidity. They then approached each other by slipping their feet forward, grinning, and in great agitation, until their noses touched, when a savage laugh ended this extraordinary performance. This exhibition was loudly applauded, and when it was explained that we wished them to repeat it they readily assented, with much good humour, Meigack, in the mean time, seeing the attention of every one engaged, took occasion to slip unobserved by us into the state room, and purloined my best telescope, a case of razors, and a pair of scissors, which he artfully concealed in his tunic; rejoining the party and the amusements as if nothing had happened. He, however, did not escape the vigilance of the steward, who followed him on deck, charged him with stealing the articles, and made him return them; which he did without hesitation.

(Extracts from John Ross, *A Voyage of Discovery* (London: J. Murray, 1819).

Conscious of the exceptional nature of the expedition, Ross gave the order two days before returning to port, on 9 November 1818, that every private journal, memorandum, and document composed during the voyage be given to him to read. In writing his report, *A Voyage of Discovery*, Ross could thus draw on all the information and personal impressions gathered by his officers. By announcing this at the last moment, Ross collected writings whose spontaneity is unmistakable.

When Captain John Ross was invited by Sir George Hope to take command of the expedition, he agreed without knowing that the Admiralty would take no account of his judicious criticisms. Royal Artillery Captain Edward Sabine was imposed on him by the Royal Society as a "supernumerary," a decision that was to give rise to conflict. If Ross chose not to overwinter, we may be justified in believing that the odious whisperings and rivalry of Lieutenant Parry and Captain Sabine played a part in his decision.

This makes it easier to understand the divergence in the accounts of three independent and rivalrous witnesses. Presented here are extracts from Captain Ross's report, from the unpublished journal of Captain Sabine, an officer aboard the Isabella, and from Alexander Fisher, assistant surgeon aboard the Alexander.

The interpreter, John Sacheuse, who was personally recruited by Ross and played a decisive role, has left only a painting of this historic encounter between the northernmost Eskimos on earth and their discoverer. His manuscripts, despite my researches, have not been unearthed. It was John Sacheuse who interpreted what these unknown Eskimos said, understanding them more or less—rather less than more. But it was his professional responsibility to understand their unfamiliar dialect, and he complied. A number of nonsensical utterances have thus been recorded: the Inuit are supposed to have said, "We are alone in the world," whereas we know that periodic contact occurred with Greenlanders south of Melville Bay. I would have preferred—for the sake of better knowledge of the Polar Eskimos, and for a comparative study of the accounts—if Lieutenant Fisher and Captain Sabine, for example, had relied on a different interpreter.

These accounts are nonetheless of exceptional value, especially as they are simultaneous descriptions, emanating from very different personalities. *J. M.*

CAPTAIN EDWARD SABINE

August 10th. This morning our flag was still in place, but toward ten o'clock we observed a group of men on sleds approaching the icebergs that lie between the ships and their dwellings; they dismounted from their sleds and climbed the icebergs, where they stayed to look at the ships. Jack Sackhouse (Sacheuse) was sent forth to them as an emissary, alone and unarmed, carrying presents and a small white flag, mounted on a staff.

Are these beings from the Moon?

Jack threw him his shirt saying that it was to keep him warm; that we came to give them clothes, not harm them. It was some time before he consented to touch the shirt: he asked if it would kill him, if the ships were

The Polar Eskimos (or Inughuit) had no wood at the time of first contact. Harpoon shafts were made of the tusk of the male narwhal.

gigantic beasts, but after he was told that they were houses, that they were full of people with many things to give, after colored beads and a mirror were thrown to him, he picked up the shirt; when he had shown it to his friends, they all burst into laughter; they responded the same way to the beads and the mirror. Once their fears had been calmed, they explained to Jack that this was their place of summer residence; that in winter they resided farther up on the coast, at a distance of several days' journey, where a large number of people were to be found; and that they lived farthest south of all that number, that they did not know that there existed other persons in the world in that direction; that they never ventured far in that direction, because it was all ice and snow, and that they thought there was no land to the south, no country, that there was always ice where we were presently, but that there would be none once we passed the headland visible to the west; it was all water and black earth (that is, not covered in snow), that they believed the ships to be great beasts come from the Moon to kill them; that they had been greatly terrified when they had fled on the evening of the 8th, to the point that a man had gone into the mountains and not returned. They asked of what skin his vest was made, of what skin his shirt, of what bone his buttons, and of what the houses (that is, the ships) were made. When they were told the ships were of wood, they answered immediately that they knew the Moon to have a great quantity of wood.

Opening and closing drawers

He looked attentively at Jack's canoe [kayak], asking many questions about it, and giving the greatest attention to the answers. He showed particular interest in the hole in the middle, in which one sits, and finally asked for the canoe in exchange for a great number of skins. Jack told him that it would be no use to him as he did not know how to handle it, and that he would drown. He was ushered into the captain's cabin and shown many things; he took great pleasure in opening and closing the drawer of a table, and in examining its contents, which were implements for letter-writing. Each in turn elicited a *hi-ya*, especially the pages of a small Johnson's *Dictionary*, but what most amazed him was a packet of goose feathers with their ends wrapped in blue paper, as one finds them at the bookseller's, and which it seemed to us that he took for a bird, as he lifted it in the air and laughed loudly. The drawer was removed entirely so that he could enjoy it better. When he put it back, it happened that the drawer was turned in the wrong direction, but he noticed the error and replaced it several times, as though he were happy to know the way of putting it back in place.

Always pilfering

We have received a third visit from the Eskimos today. They were the same who came on board the first time and, having sampled our generosity once, had apparently returned to partake of it again, bringing others with them, so that they now numbered nine. The individual who had tried to abscond with the hammer was among them, who showed great embarrassment when Parry reminded him of it. That it was wrong to steal, they were clearly aware, but just as clearly it was a practice they were accustomed to and highly adept at. Two of the natives offered to sing us a song in the cabin to divert our attention, and they had already concealed a

Ervick was the first Polar Eskimo encountered by Captain John Ross and his crew. "When Ervick was told that there was an omnipotent, omnipresent, and invisible Being, who had created the sea and the land, and all therein, he showed much surprise, and eagerly asked where he lived. When told that he was everywhere, he was much alarmed, and became very impatient to be on deck." (John Ross, *A Voyage of Discovery*, p. 129.) Lithograph from a watercolor by John Ross (in *A Voyage of Discovery*).

ARCTIC HIGHLANDER.

Captn. J. Ross. Del. D. Havell, Sculpt.

Ervick, a Native of Prince Regents Bay.

Lat. 76.12. N. — Long. 65. W.

London, Published Jany. 1819, by I. Murray, Albemarle Street.

Captain John Ross's book on his expedition of 1818 appeared in 1819 (it was partially written while on shipboard). It contains the ship's log, and all observations on hydrography, geography, zoology, ethnography, and the earth's magnetism.
Few expeditions had previously offered the public such a complete spectrum of research, and so luxuriously presented (with color plates, by John Sacheuse and Captain Ross among others).

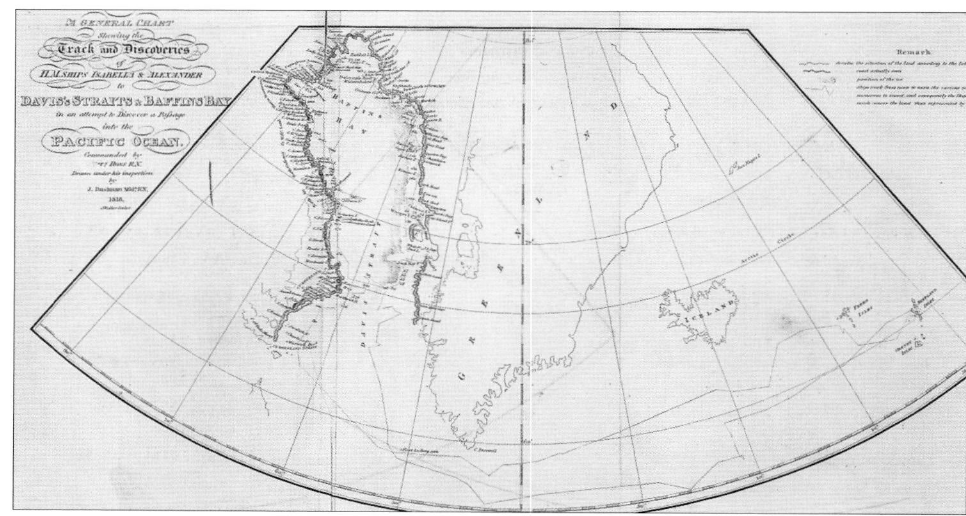

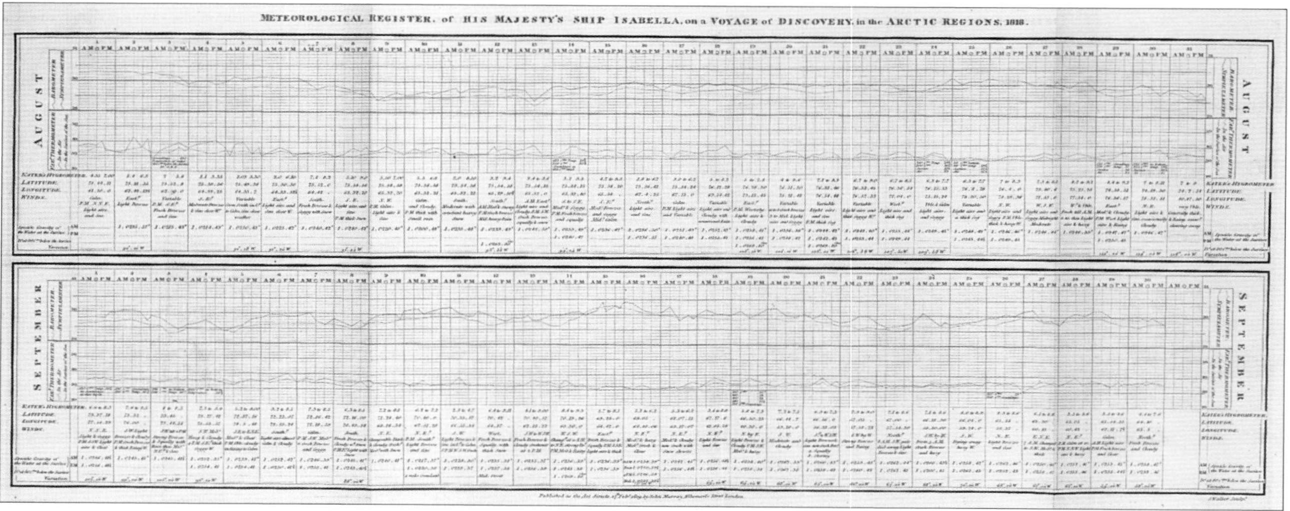

number of objects under their clothes before their game was discovered: razors, knives, and Captain Ross's large telescope. They show great skill at stealing, and are very little troubled when they are discovered in the act; we were very glad to be rid of them; they received the promise of a great many presents if they should bring us fragments of the stone from which they claim to extract their native iron.

Fear of the angakok

When one of the officers, pointing at Mr. Beverly, said "*angakok*" [*angakkuq*], which is the name given among them to persons having powers from the evil spirits, he rose in haste, followed by his son, and left the cabin in a state of extreme fear. Jack brought him back and persuaded him that we had no angakoks among us, that it was only a pleasantry. We succeeded in drawing his attention again, but it was clear that he was never afterwards at ease with Mr. Beverly, whom he constantly avoided, always accepting needles or any other small presents from Mr. Beverly with considerable mistrust.

LIEUTENANT ALEXANDER FISHER, ASSISTANT SURGEON

They were rather short: we measured one: he measured only five feet one inch and three quarters. Their features were noticeably broader than those of the natives from Jacob's Bight and farther to the south. They all wore long sparse beards.

Through the eyes of prehistoric men

We could add other anecdotes to reveal their complete ignorance of civilization: as we had offered a glass of wine to one of them, he seemed entirely amazed that it did not melt from the warmth of his hand, no doubt from his conception of first seeing it that the glass was made of ice. A mirror provoked equal amazement, when they saw their image reflected in it.

Their sleds were made entirely of bone, apparently whalebone.[18] Each of the natives carried a knife of sorts, composed of small slivers or plates of iron, inserted one next to the other in a groove, cut into a length of narwhal tusk; the last piece was riveted, but the others were held in place simply from being pushed forcibly into the groove. They had several other ridiculous ideas about our ships. When they saw us for the first time, they believed the masts to be a giant man who had come to kill them; they held so strongly to the idea that the ships were living creatures that among the first questions they asked Sacheuse was whether the ships flew, and if they swam.

Speaking to occult forces

Among the natives who came on board today was one who, according to Sacheuse, could speak like an *angakkuk*, although he did not claim to belong to that brotherhood. Our interpreter seemed to derive great pleasure from hearing him converse with the devil: he spoke in a soft muttering voice (the very opposite of the natives' usual way of speaking, which is extremely loud, as though they were addressing someone at a distance).

(Excerpt from Voyage vers le Pôle Arctique, *by Auguste Jean Baptiste Defauconpret, Librairie de Gide, Paris, 1819.)*

18) A mistake: in fact segments of walrus bone.

Captain John Ross is attacked by his peers. Public opinion supports him.

Letter by Commander William Parry (Norfolk, 25 May 1835). Parry denied that Captain Ross consulted him as the second-in-command when the decision was taken not to explore further into Lancaster Sound. The argument between the two officers became public after Sir John Barrow published a book critical of Ross. In this letter, Parry, a religious man (he prayed morning and evening) and the hero of British polar exploration, whose career was helped by his ties to the establishment and the sidelining of Ross in 1819, calls on his shipmate and subordinate aboard the *Alexander* in 1819 to support his testimony.

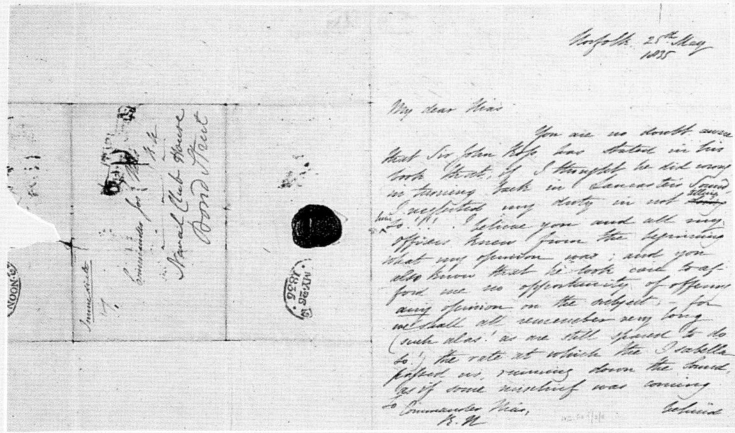
Norfolk. 25th May 1835

My dear [illegible]

You are no doubt aware that Sir John Ross has stated in his book that, if I thought he did wrong in turning back in Lancaster Sound I neglected my duty in not telling him so!! I believe you and all my officers knew from the beginning what my opinion was; and you also know that he took care to afford me no opportunity of offering any opinion on the subject; – for we shall all remember very long (such alas! as are still spared to do so,) the rate at which the Isabella passed us, running down the Sound, as if some mischief was coming [illegible]

Believe [illegible]

[illegible] Commander [illegible], R.N.

Caricature of the aging Sir John Ross.

PAMPHLET BY CAPTAIN EDWARD SABINE DENOUNCING ROSS

"On the appearance of Captain Ross's book I perceived that he had appropriated this paper; much of the information contained therein being published, not only without acknowledgment, but in the first person. Page 121, 122, 123, 132 are copied almost verbatim from this document; wherever he has ventured upon apparently even a trivial change of expression, he has fallen into error, which betrays the want of originality. I give an instance of this: — Where he is speaking of an animal called the *amarok* (mis-printed *ancarok*) he remarks, "I cannot find it to be *mentioned* by writers on Greenland." The original sentence was, "I have never seen a *description* of it by writers on Greenland." The change is unfortunate; it is mentioned both by Crantz and Egede, writers whose works were on board . . .

Captain John Ross responded with dignity to these accusations saying that, as head of the expedition, the responsibility fell to him to present all the findings.

On Ross's return to London, the press lampooned his supposed discovery of an unknown people (Arctic Highlanders!) and his efforts at fraternization, particularly his admission that he rubbed noses with the Eskimos . . . This caricature portrays all the members of the expedition . . . without their noses! The ship's scientist is portrayed as a starving savage carrying a narwhal tusk. James Clark Ross carries the flag, accompanying the barrel of "red snow" gathered on the north slopes of Cape York and caused by a unicellular plant that flowers in snowy terrain. The explorers' procession, with its Arctic animals (including a polar bear and an eider on the end of a bayonet), is urged on by a black fiddler (like the one who encouraged the towing party on the pack ice) and led by a paunchy and ridiculous Captain Ross, whose officers are nowhere to be seen. Among the first to stress the importance of a balanced life on shipboard, Captain John Ross was liked and respected by the crews of both his expeditions.

First ethnographic collection, partially mislaid by the Admiralty

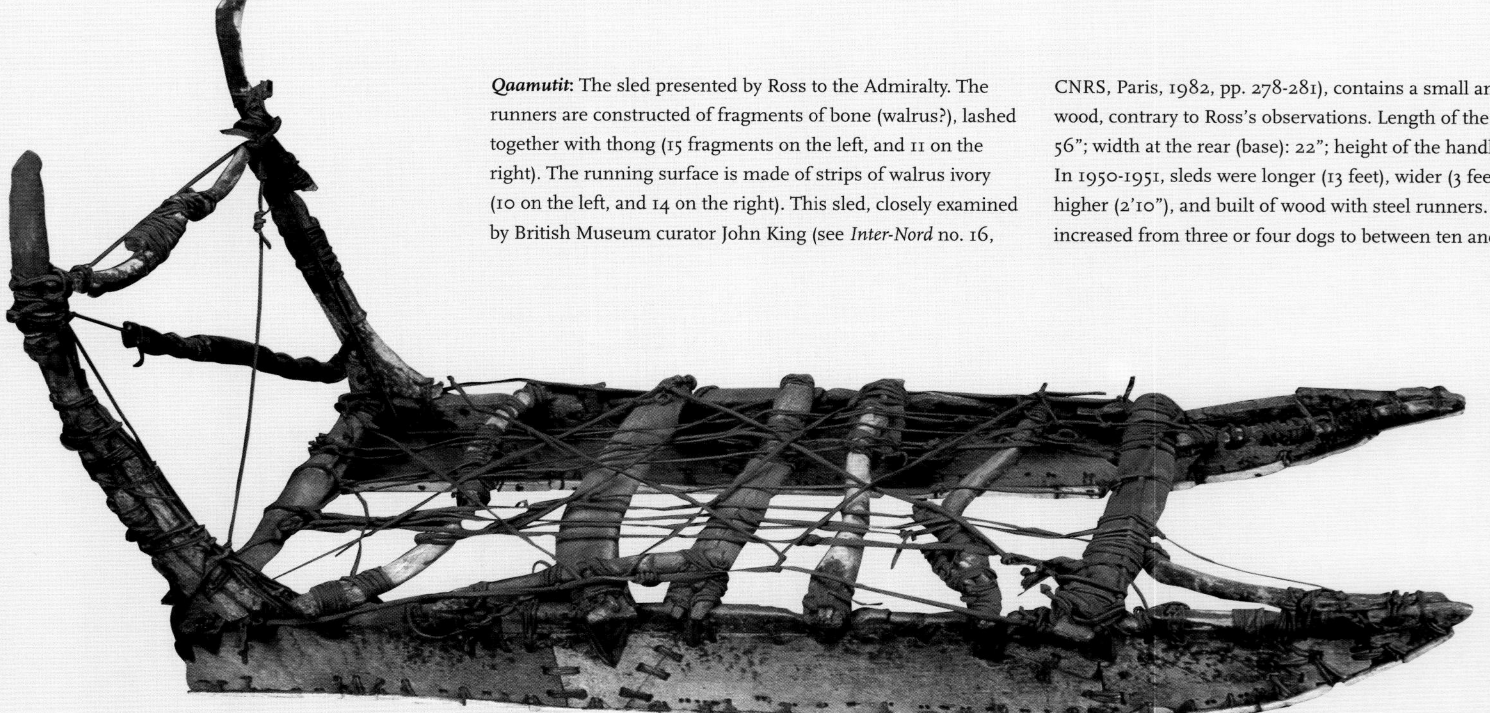

Qaamutit: The sled presented by Ross to the Admiralty. The runners are constructed of fragments of bone (walrus?), lashed together with thong (15 fragments on the left, and 11 on the right). The running surface is made of strips of walrus ivory (10 on the left, and 14 on the right). This sled, closely examined by British Museum curator John King (see *Inter-Nord* no. 16, CNRS, Paris, 1982, pp. 278-281), contains a small amount of wood, contrary to Ross's observations. Length of the runners: 56"; width at the rear (base): 22"; height of the handles: 27.5 ". In 1950-1951, sleds were longer (13 feet), wider (3 feet), and higher (2'10"), and built of wood with steel runners. Teams had increased from three or four dogs to between ten and fourteen.

Harpoon head, knives of ivory and meteoric iron. These are identified by the labels below as having been collected by Ross. A test conducted by the British Museum, after my visit there in 1986, determined that the "meteoric iron" of one of the blades was in fact of European origin. This would invalidate Ross's conclusion that this population was totally isolated. At the very least it had occasional access to drifting ship's timbers carrying nails and other iron.

BRITISH MUSEUM (MINERAL DEPT.)

An Eskimo knife tipped with Regd No. 87561

Native (Meteoric) Iron

("Ross's Iron")

Melville Bay, NW. Greenland

Collected by Capt. John Ross and presented by the Lords of the Admiralty, 1819.

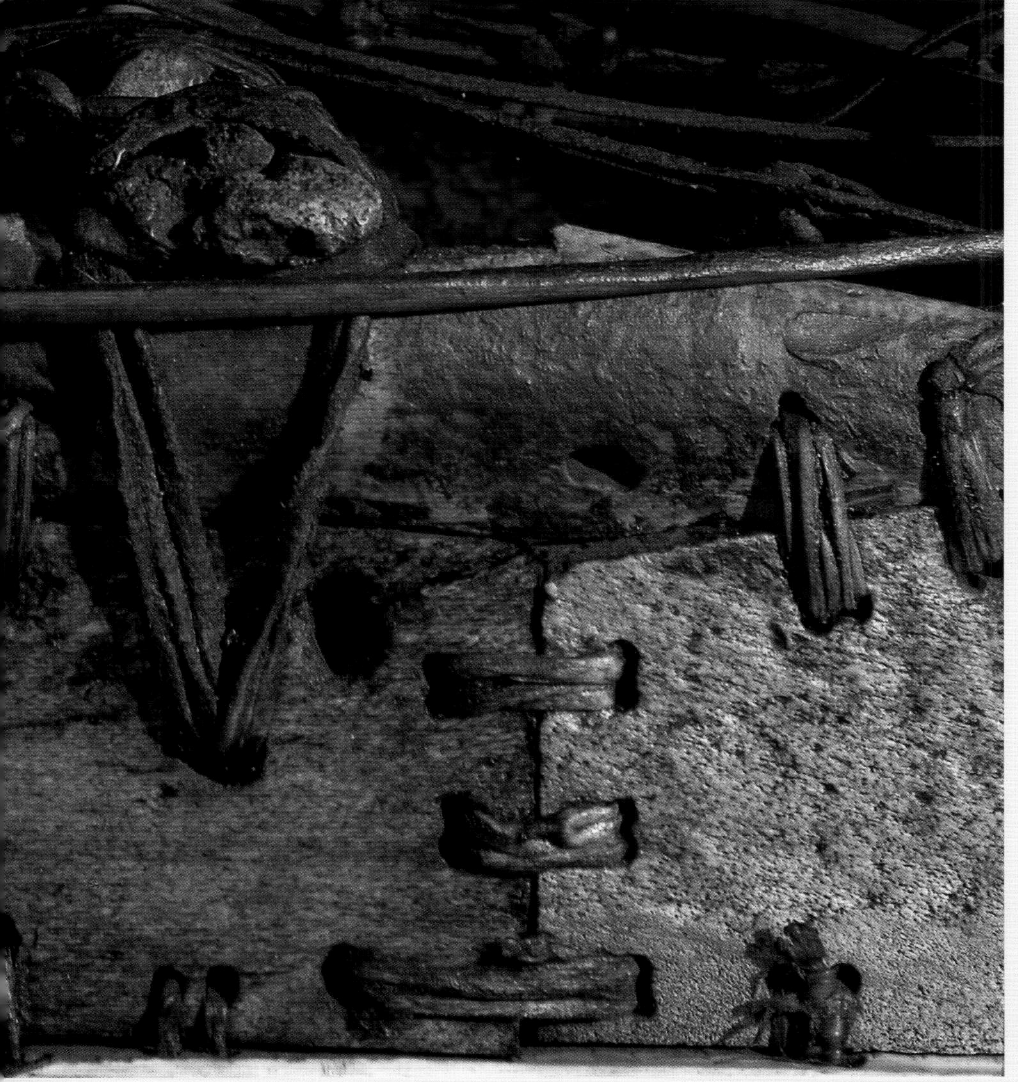

The John Ross Collection now consists of exactly eleven objects, "the others having been lost or given away by Sir Joseph Banks in 1819": a sled, identified as having come from the Polar Eskimos; a harpoon head; seven "sea-unicorn's horns," and some harpoon shafts. The Admiralty gave more importance to the cartographic data than to objects or ethnographic considerations. Original written records are lacking, and these objects are all attributed to Captain John Ross "by tradition," as it is commonly put, and preserved at the British Museum.

Captain John Ross's First Expedition
A first glimpse of North Star Bay

Unpublished letter by Captain John Ross: "Monsieur Le Ministre: The two cases of preserved meat about which I had the honor of addressing you not having arrived and being now obliged to leave Paris, I request that they may be forwarded to Monsieur Lomard de la Bibliothèque Royale who has my directions respecting their destination. I have the honor to be, with the highest respect, Monsieur le Ministre, your devoted and humble servant. Paris, 20th May. John Ross."

1923/841
à Monsieur le Secretaire de l'Etat des affaires Etrangeres. Hotel de

Monsieur Le Ministre

The two cases of preserved meats about which I had the honor of addressing you not having arrived and being now obliged to leave Paris, I request that they may be forwarded to Mons. Lomard de la Bib. Royale who has my directions respecting their destination

I have the honor to be with the highest respect
Monsieur le Ministre
your obedient & humble servt

Paris 20th May John Ross

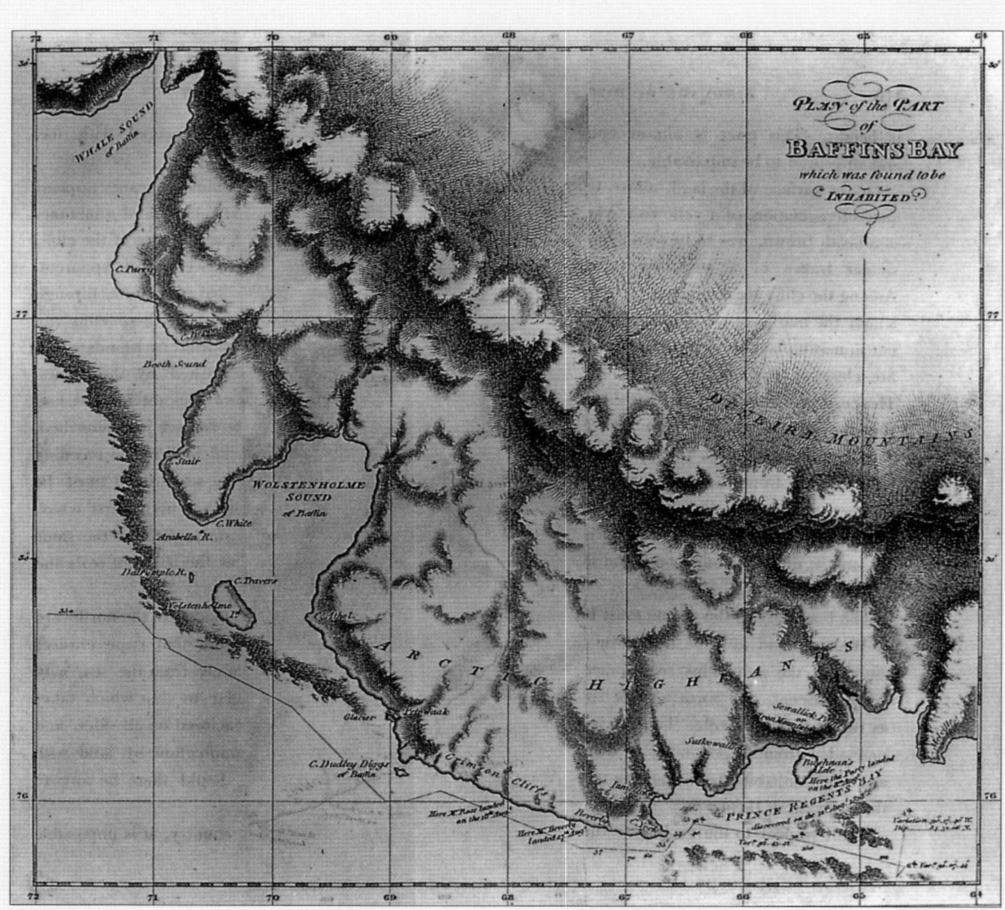

Map of the coast of northeastern Baffin Bay: Prince Regent's Bay, Whale and Wolstenholme sounds. (Map of Ross's expedition in *A Voyage of Discovery,* 1819.)

Wolstenholme Sound (Ross's first expedition, 1818). Lithograph after a drawing by Midshipman A. M. Skene. In Wolstenholme Sound (today's North Star Bay), one hundred thirty years later, the United States would build the port for the American airbase at Thule.

The North Magnetic Pole: Sir John Ross's second voyage

Boothia Peninsula: "January 9 (1830). Going on shore this morning . . . [I] saw some Esquimaux near a small iceberg . . . They retreated behind it as soon as they perceived me; but as I approached, the whole party came suddenly out of their shelter, forming in a body of ten in front and three deep, with one man detached on the land side who was apparently sitting in a sledge . . . Proceeding then alone to within a hundred yards, I found that each of the Esquimaux was armed with a spear and a knife . . . [W]e immediately found ourselves established in their unhesitating confidence." Ross received the Eskimos aboard the *Victory*, which was stuck fast in the sea ice, and presented them with thirty-one pieces of iron hoop, one for each hunter. The next day, Ross and his officers were received by the Eskimos in their nearby encampment. "The village consisted of twelve snow huts erected at the bottom of a little bight on the shore . . . When we prepared to make a drawing of this village, they appeared anxious . . . Each recognized his own house." "The ship's carpenter made a wooden leg for a hunter whose leg had been amputated in consequence of a bear hunt." In teaching Captain Ross and his companions how to live like Eskimos, how to eat salmon, seal, caribou, and musk ox, and how to travel by dog sled, the Inuit made it possible for the members of the expedition to live on the ice for four years without major difficulties. The Admiralty and Sir John Franklin failed, however, to analyze correctly the methods and spirit of this expedition, which was acclaimed by British public opinion.

SIR JOHN FRANKLIN 1786-1847

THE GREATEST DISASTER IN ARCTIC EXPLORATION

This officer of the Royal Navy would long embody the image of the tragically fated Romantic hero. In his heroism he never once considered abandoning his ice-bound ship or retreating on foot across the barren, frozen tundra. His expedition, the strongest ever sent by the British Admiralty into the Arctic, was lost with all hands.

Captain John Franklin left the Thames estuary on 19 May 1845 and died on 11 June 1847 at the age of sixty-one aboard his ship, the *Erebus,* which was trapped by pack ice north-northwest of Victoria Island. Having lost its leader and inspiration, the expedition came under the command of Captain F. R. M. Crozier. Two years later it had disappeared with all hands on its desperate quest for the famous Northwest Passage.

It took years to piece together an accurate picture of this tragedy. Lieutenant Inglefield played an important role in the process by conclusively proving that Franklin did not overwinter in Northwest Greenland. "Success is in our grasp. Our next port of call will be Hong Kong," was the last official message from the commander of the Admiralty's mission. That was on 12 July 1845, off Disko Island (latitude 69° north).

On 26 July, in Baffin Bay, the whaling captain Dannett invited the expedition's second-in-command on board. Franklin's ships, the *Erebus* (340 tons) and the *Terror* (370 tons), manned by 129 officers and men, were sailing in the direction of Lancaster Sound. Dannett would be the last to see any member of the expedition.

It is believed, from the statements made by the Eskimos of Pelly Bay (south of Boothia Peninsula) on 21 April 1854 to John Rae—one of the most extraordinary Arctic explorers—that the 105 members of the expedition still surviving after the unexplained death of Franklin abandoned their two ice-fast ships, most likely for want of food (the stock of food was intended to last three years). On 22 April 1848, they set off south across the ice, hauling heavy sledges. Weary and ill-equipped, they most likely died near the mouth of the Back River.[1] Parts of skeletons have turned up here and there . . . According to the Inuit, the men walked like ghosts and had resorted to cannibalism to survive.

The causes of this disaster remain obscure, given the vast equipment of these two large ships.[2] An analysis of Franklin's methods and an examination of his personality reveal only a few of the causes.[3] Franklin was religious in

Lady Jane Franklin, from a contemporary portrait (1816). The inspiration for some fifty expeditions launched in search of her husband, she financed four of them herself between 1850 and 1857.

OPPOSITE : **Sir John Franklin** in 1825 at the time of his second expedition, which set out westward from the mouth of the Mackenzie River toward Point Beechey, Alaska.

1) A note found under a cairn at Cape Felix establishes this fact. No other trace of them was ever found in this sector between western King William Island and the mouth of the Back River.
2) I inquired about this tragedy on the very site, in April 1963, from the Inuit and the sergeant of the Canadian Mounties who accompanied me. I was formally investigating the causes of a famine among the Utkuhikhalingmuit that had killed off 5 percent of their population.

Junius et Augustus, two Eskimo interpreters on Franklin's first expedition of 1819-1822. Tattannoeuck ("The Stomach") and Hoeootoerock ("The Ear") were recruited by Saint-Germain, a French Canadian. The voyageurs and *coureurs des bois,* of whom Saint-Germain was one, deserve our recognition for their legendary boldness and *joie de vivre.*

temperament (he examined his conscience every day to determine whether his actions were in accord with God's will), modest but concerned with glory, and haunted by the thought of being the first British officer to find the legendary Northwest Passage in the northern mists.

Disciplined, John Franklin was also stubborn and opinionated. He remained impervious to the dramatic lessons of his two earlier expeditions. The first was sent out to explore, on foot and by canoe, the coastline of Canada around the mouth of the Mackenzie River. Many lives were lost. Franklin was no walker, from the evidence. An officer of the Royal Navy, steeped in the caste system, he was incapable of pitching in to help with common tasks and refused to fish or hunt with the Franco-Canadian *coureurs des bois* and the Indians who accompanied them. The expedition, coming under the harsh law of the tundra, survived only thanks to the self-sacrifice of these remarkable men. The death of Gabriel Beauparlant, a Franco-Canadian member of the expedition, was one of the great but little-known heroic actions of the Arctic saga. This ill-conceived expedition cost eleven lives. The second expedition, in the same general area, was equally tragic. George Back wrote in a letter that "as to telling the truth . . . what happened should never be divulged."

On Franklin's third and fatal expedition, it is certain that the ships *Erebus* and the *Terror* were of too great displacement. The food unquestionably contributed to the disaster also: it contained too much salt, and was poorly preserved in containers sealed with lead. Scurvy and lead poisoning ruined the crew's health. The regulation dose of lemon juice was inadequate to take the place of fresh, healthy foods. The solution stared them in the face: to hunt seal, beluga whale, Arctic hare, and caribou—animals they disdained as being the staple food of the "savages" and not falling within their customs.

Having no experience of the Arctic, these men wore navy-issue clothing (wool and cotton, with leather shoes) that was totally unsuited to the environment. It would have paid to copy local adaptations, both those of men and of animals.[4] But these Westerners were so blinded by pride that they thought they could bend even the eternal laws to their volition. I might mention, finally, the tensions and violence

Storm at dawn on 23 August 1821 near Kent Peninsula and Bathurst Inlet: the two canoes are south of Victoria Island in what would come to be called Coronation Gulf. On this first adventurous expedition, Franklin led his men overland from the west shore of Hudson Bay to the Arctic Ocean, descending the Coppermine River, whose course he mapped to the sea. He charted 530 miles of coastline east of the river, logging some 5,500 miles on land and sea overall. The expeditions included a Scotsman, John Richardson, an intrepid navy surgeon; two young hopefuls, George Back and Robert Hood (the latter would be murdered, and his presumed killer, a French Canadian named Michel, in turn killed by Richardson); seventeen French Canadians; and several Indian guides with their wives.

of all sorts among the members of this overly large crew, confined to the cramped space of their respective living quarters. It was a textbook Royal Navy expedition, which is to say an aristocratic one: the ship's library counted 1200 volumes, the plates were pure porcelain, the cutlery in the officers' mess was silver . . . And it was conducted by a man "so sensitive that any fuss made him ill and paralyzed him to such an extent that when action was necessary, he seized up." And yet, what courage!

The search for the survivors, encouraged by the admirable Lady Franklin, the expedition leader's second wife, grew into an extraordinary international competition that extended from Alaska to northern Greenland. No fewer than fifty-two expeditions set off to find Franklin and his men, including the expeditions to northwest Greenland made by the distinguished British officer Inglefield and the American navy doctor Kane. While most were unsuccessful in discovering any traces of the lost men, they contributed to a greater knowledge of the Arctic. The maze of channels and islands in the Canadian Central Arctic, which John Barrow for one had imagined as an open sea, a pendant to the Great Polar Sea, became better known. It was during the expeditions mounted to rescue Franklin that King William, Victoria, and Banks islands were discovered. A transit of the Northwest Passage was made in 1851-1853, by the Scottish explorer Robert M'Clure. Sailing on the *Investigator*, then transferring to dog sled, M'Clure crossed from the Bering Strait to Lancaster Sound and was awarded the £10,000 prize for a successful traverse of the Northwest Passage.

Franklin's grave is unknown, but a stone was erected to the memory of this pioneer of the Northwest Passage in Westminster Abbey, with these lines from Tennyson as his epitaph:

NOT HERE: THE WHITE NORTH
HAS THY BONES; AND THOU HEROIC
SAILOR-SOUL, ART PASSING ON THINE HAPPIER
VOYAGE NOW TOWARD NO EARTHLY POLE.

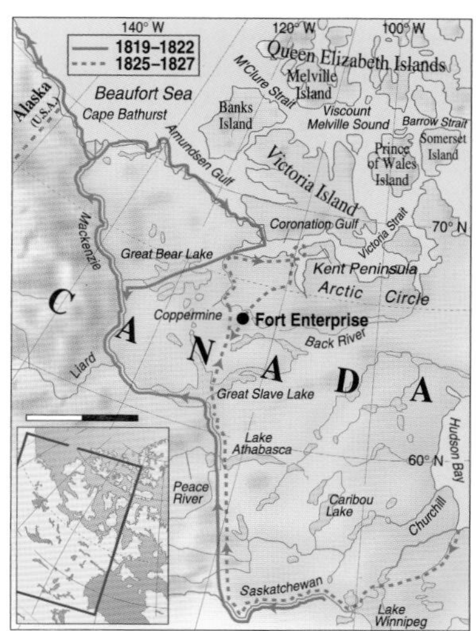

Franklin's first and second expeditions in the Canadian Arctic in search of the Northwest Passage (1819-1822 and 1825-1827).

SEARCHING FOR SIR JOHN FRANKLIN

CAPTAIN EDWARD AUGUSTUS INGLEFIELD, 1820-1894

Captain Edward Inglefield set sail in the spring of 1852, charged with investigating the rumors brought back by Adam Beck (Sir John Ross's interpreter on his second voyage in search of the magnetic north pole) that the Franklin expedition had been shipwrecked and murdered in Melville Bay. A place had even been designated as the spot where the bodies supposedly lay: North Omiak. The *Isabel*, Inglefield's ship, was the first sailing steamship to ply these northern waters.

Well-born and an excellent draftsman and painter, Captain Inglefield belonged to Sir John Franklin's circle and undertook his expedition at Lady Franklin's request, using private funds and drawing no salary.

Scouting Smith Sound

On 22 August 1852, the young captain sailed north from Cape York. With the competence of a trained information officer, he searched from settlement to settlement for the least clue, the least trace of his British comrades. In Uummannaq, a long-established village that was to become Thule in 1910, he dug up all the graves and examined them forensically, but in vain. He quickly became convinced that the rumors were absurd. Near Pitorarfik, a traditional crossroads for Polar Eskimos converging from the north and south to hunt walrus, he discovered a group of men going to and fro along the sandstone cliffs. Using sealskin nets on the ends of narwhal-tusk lances, they were catching auks as they wheeled through the air by the thousands. From all the evidence, the Inughuit he spoke to had neither metal nor wood, and they claimed never to have seen Whites. If they had looted the remains of Franklin's expedition, wouldn't it show in their equipment? Inglefield's observation also establishes that the whaling ships did not venture north of Cape York and the Carey Islands. It is nonetheless surprising that from north to south along this coast, where the natives, of anarcho-communist tradition, form one body, there should have been no wood. Yet the archaic technology of the camps visited by Inglefield in the Etah area prove that this was so. Eskimo sociology certainly eludes our models . . .

Farther south, on 25 August, in the village of Natsilivik, Inglefield suddenly discovered material evidence of dealings with the whalers: a metal knife blade with an English inscription, mounted on a narwhal ivory handle; a portion of an ax; a pewter box; and several pieces of steel, riveted to bone and used as knife blades. Evidence of barter, clearly, but on such a small scale!

Captain Edward Inglefield (1820-1894). Elegant and talented, he opened the route to the North Pole. His investigation cleared the Eskimos of the murder of Franklin and his crew. The first cartographer of the coast of Greenland north of Cape Alexander, Inglefield gave his name to a great Land. Painting by S. Peakoe (circa 1850-1856).

3) Born in Spilsby, Lincolnshire, a few miles from the coast, this steely, severe man hated literary language but could meditate for hours looking at the sea. He was married twice, both times to women very different from himself, who were exuberant, worldly, and passionate about literature.

4) Other than the second-in-command and the two Greenlandic ice pilots, none of the crew had any previous Arctic experience.

Port Leopold (northwest Canadian passage)northeast of Somerset Island, in the area around Cape Clarence, southeast of the Barrow strait.

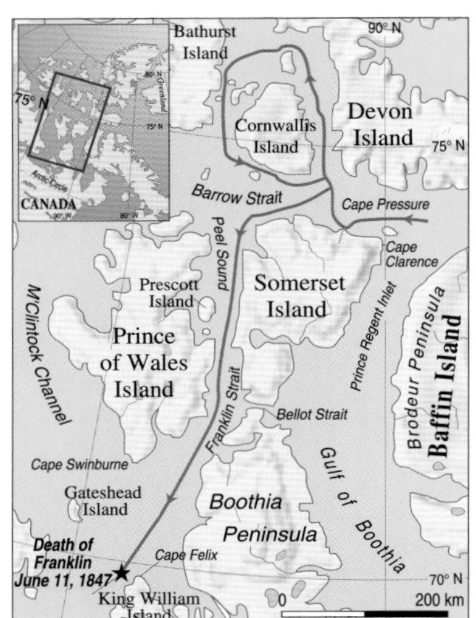

Sir John Franklin's tragic final expedition (1845-1847) aboard the *Terror* and the *Erebus*.

What Inglefield's voyage showed was that, thirty-four years after its discovery, Polar Eskimo society remained essentially in the age of bone and stone. The society so remarkably described by Sir John Ross in August 1818 resisted technological "progress," despite the annual opportunities for trade afforded by the dozens of whaling ships that anchored every summer off Cape York from 1819 onward. The effects of the whalers' visits—both changes in the Eskimos' outlook and interbreeding—have not been sufficiently studied.

The first to map Inglefield Land

Inglefield, favored by an unusually warm summer season, wanted to push on, and on 26-27 August he ventured into Smith Sound. This is certainly a significant date, as Inglefield established at that time that Smith Sound, the passage to the North Pole, was not a bay. This was the object of a long-standing controversy, arising from the discrepancies between the maps of the Baffin expedition (1616) and Sir John Ross's in 1818.

This strait certainly brought bad luck to explorers, since it served to darken Baffin's reputation and provoke false accusations against Ross. Inglefield, at any rate, was the first Westerner to enter Smith Sound, which leads, through a succession of channels and basins (those of Kane and Hall), to the Arctic Ocean.

On 26 August, Inglefield stood off Cape Alexander. On the 27th, he reached latitude 78° 21' north and, from the vantage of his ship, made the first map of the North Greenland coast from Cape York to Cape Alexander, which forms the Polar Eskimos' northern territory. Still ambitious, he mapped rapidly and from a distance the southwest coast of the land to which his own name would be given.

Four capes and bays on Inglefield Land, their positions fixed by sightings, still carry names that Inglefield gave them. [5] At last, hampered in his progress by ice and stormy weather, Inglefield retreated and sailed south.

This exceptionally short expedition was of great value from a geographical standpoint, although Inglefield, in keeping with the common beliefs of his time, claimed in his account of his explorations that an open polar sea existed north of Smith Sound.

In his official report to the Admiralty, dated 15 September 1852, he wrote: "We were no sooner engaged in the strait we had discovered than I exclaimed: 'This must open onto the great Russian polynia!'"

The Open Arctic Sea! "I cannot conceive of there not being a large sea beyond." This myth would resurface in various forms until 1908 and 1909, when the North Pole was "discovered" by F. A. Cook and R. E. Peary. Inglefield's report influenced the American Elisha Kent Kane to choose this route toward the Arctic Basin. Against all evidence and despite the opposition of his crew, Kane insisted on hauling his brig, the *Advance*, through channels and fractures toward the mythical sea his predecessor had depicted for him.

Captain Inglefield, whose short voyage was so fruitful, never returned to the Arctic. He would end his brilliant naval career bearing the rank of admiral. ■

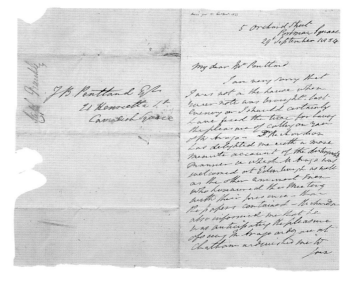

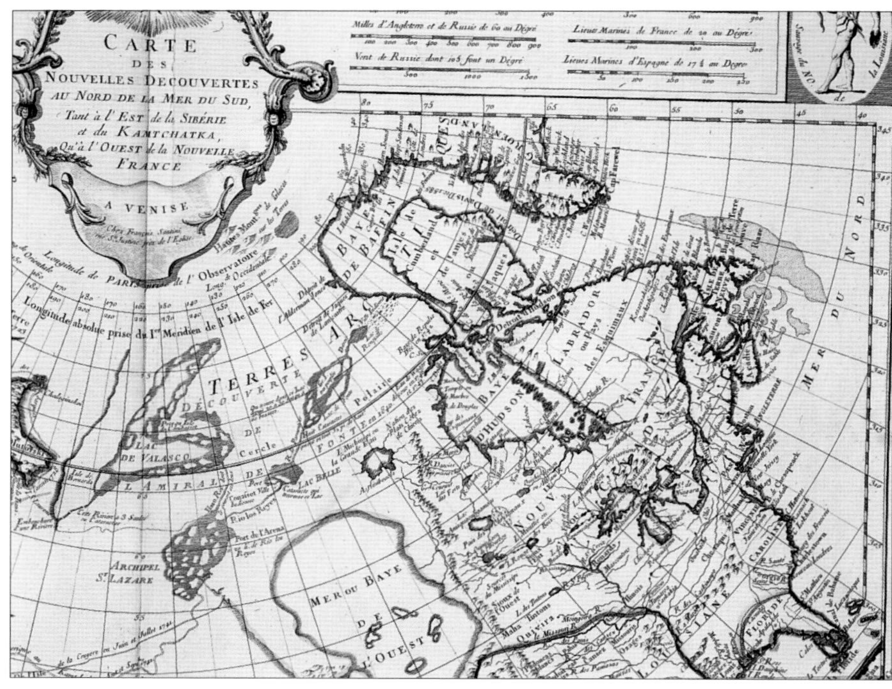

French map of the Canadian Arctic, dated 1824, before Sir John Ross's second expedition (1829-1833). Note that Greenland wazs not yet recognized as an island.

A long, friendly letter (unpublished) from Sir John Franklin to J. B. Penthand, dated 29 September 1834. Franklin had just published the account of his second expedition. In 1836 he would be appointed governor of Tasmania, a post he held until 1843.

5) I am drawn all the more to this explorer as I was the first geomorphologist to map the coastal section of Inglefield Land and southern Washington Land. I included in the published map the traditional Inuk toponymy, gathered through research among the local population. Inglefield named three features: Littleton Island (in Inuk, Pikiulleq), Cape Hatherton, and Cape Frederick VII. Baffin named only one: Smith Sound. Captain John Ross named Cape Alexander (Ulersuaq). I was permitted by the Danish authorities in 1951 to bestow eleven names, among them names derived from places (Paris), from historical figures (Martonne, Joset), from expeditions (Polaris), and from Inuit heroes unfeatured on maps (Uutaaq, who traveled with Peary to the pole in 1909; Aaqqiaq, who died with Krueger in 1931 on Ellesmere Island, having come from Neqe; Ajaku, Knud Rasmussen's favorite companion during the tragic expedition to Thule in 1917).

Smith Sound, off Cape Sabine, Ellesmere Island (August 1995).

The ***Isabel,*** caught in the pack ice of Smith Sound, August 1852.

The Franklin expedition: nowhere to be found. But unknown lands and peoples were discovered.

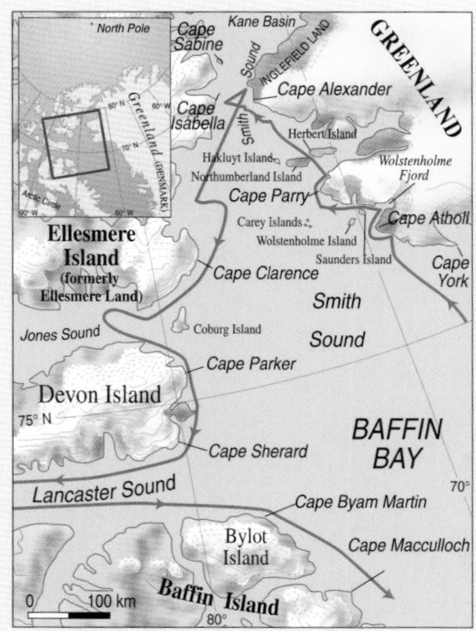

Route of Inglefield's rescue mission aboard the *Isabel* (1852) in search of Franklin and his crew, who disappeared off northwest Greenland.

Dramatic message left on 28 May 1847 in a tin box under a cairn near Point Victory (Victoria Island) by lieutenants Gore and Des Veaux. Discovered on 6 May 1859, and written on an Admiralty form in six languages, it relayed the following information: "H.M. ships *Erebus* and *Terror* wintered in the ice in lat. 70° 05' N.; long. 98° 23' W. Having wintered in 1846-7 at Beechey Island, in lat. 74° 43' 28" N.; long. 91° 39' 15" W., after having ascended Wellington Channel to lat. 77°, and returned to the west side of Cornwallis Island. Party consisting of 2 officers and 6 men left the ships on Monday 24th May 1847."

Scribbled around the margin of the form one year later were these terrible words: "April 25, 1848—H.M. ships *Terror* and *Erebus* were deserted on the 22nd April, 5 leagues N.N.W. of this, having been beset since 12th September, 1846. The officers and crews consisting of 105 souls, under the command of Captain F. R. M. Crozier, landed here in lat. 69° 37' 42" N., long. 98° 41' W. Sir John Franklin died on the 11 June, 1847; and the total loss by deaths in the expedition has been to this date 9 officers and 15 men. James Fitzjames, Captain H.M.S. *Erebus*. Crozier had added: "Start to-morrow, 26th, for Back's Fish River."

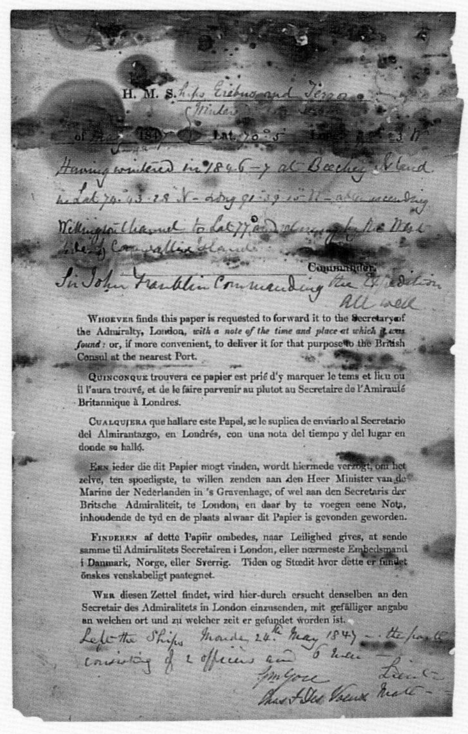

H. M. S.

Commander.

Sir John Franklin Commanding the Expedition

All well

WHOEVER finds this paper is requested to forward it to the Secretary of the Admiralty, London, *with a note of the time and place at which it was found*: or, if more convenient, to deliver it for that purpose to the British Consul at the nearest Port.

QUINCONQUE trouvera ce papier est prié d'y marquer le tems et lieu ou il l'aura trouvé, et de le faire parvenir au plutot au Secretaire de l'Amirauté Britannique à Londres.

CUALQUIERA que hallare este Papel, se le suplica de enviarlo al Secretario del Almirantazgo, en Londrés, con una nota del tiempo y del lugar en donde se halló.

EEN ieder die dit Papier mogt vinden, wordt hiermede verzogt, om het zelve, ten spoedigste, te willen zenden aan den Heer Minister van de Marine der Nederlanden in 's Gravenhage, of wel aan den Secretaris der Britsche Admiraliteit, te London, en daar by te voegen eene Nota, inhoudende de tyd en de plaats alwaar dit Papier is gevonden geworden.

FINDEREN af dette Papiir ombedes, naar Leilighed gives, at sende samme til Admiralitets Secretairen i London, eller nærmeste Embedsmand i Danmark, Norge, eller Sverrig. Tiden og Stædit hvor dette er fundet önskes venskabeligt paategnet.

WER diesen Zettel findet, wird hier-durch ersucht denselben an den Secretair des Admiralitets in London einzusenden, mit gefälliger angabe an welchen ort und zu welcher zeit er gefundet worden ist.

Left the Ships Monday 24th May 1847 — the party consisting of 2 officers and 6 men

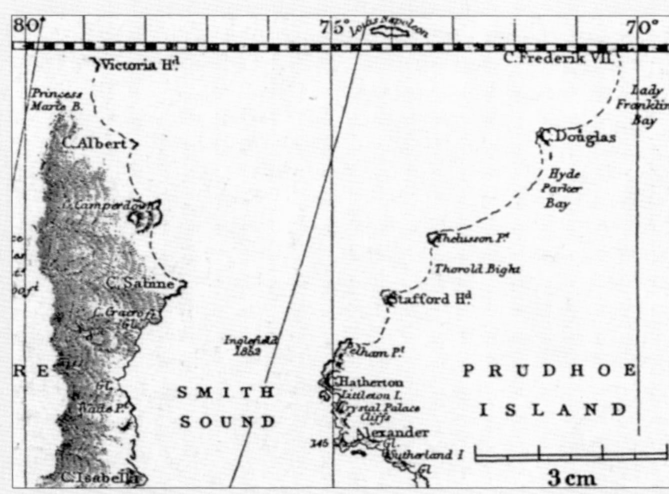

Survey map from the Inglefield expedition, published in London, 1853 (detail).

for many miles - lay in that direction - I then, sailing round the large island which I named after his Grace the Duke of Northumberland, proceeded to Smith Sound which I reached without difficulty and which I found to be about 36 miles across the entrance instead of the puny ten marked in the charts. It was a lovely morning the 27th of August when

Inglefield's official report, in which he confirmed that on 17 August 1852 he entered Smith Sound, a passage that, after being the center of much controversy, came to be called "the route to the North Pole."

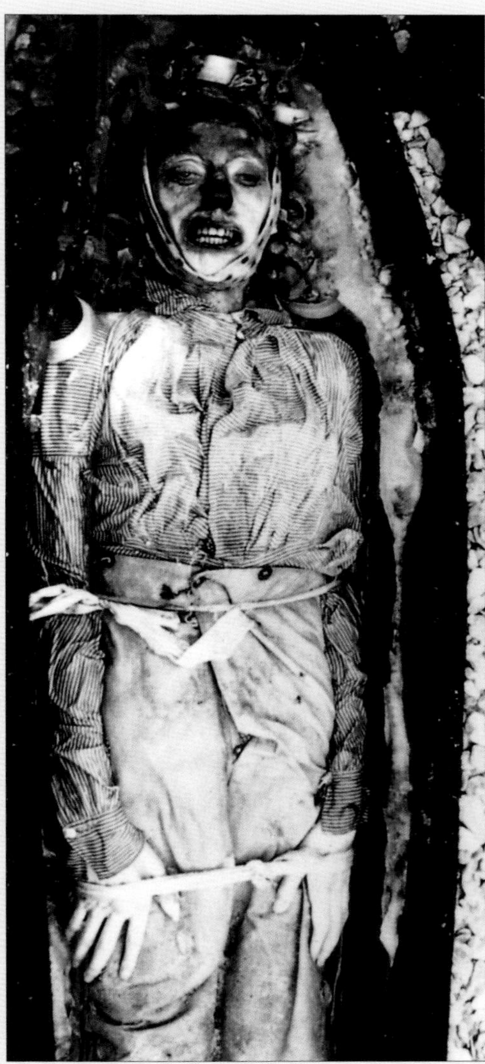

John Torrington Petty, died 1846, exhumed one hundred and thirty-eight years later. Petty was one of those who lost their lives during the thirty-six years of heroic exploration conducted by the British Admiralty in its stubborn search for the Northwest Passage. Analyses of the mummies, discovered in 1984, raised questions that are still unanswered.

Erasmus York

The first Polar Eskimo to be deported

QALASERSUAQ (THE "BIG NAVEL"), WHO WAS CHRISTENED ERASMUS AUGUSTINE YORK AT CANTERBURY, WAS THE HERO OF A PITIFUL TRAGEDY ENACTED IN THE NAME OF THE ADMIRALTY, PROGRESS, AND THE CHURCH.

On a peaceful day in the summer of 1850, Qalasersuaq—who was then seventeen years old—was netting auks at Cape York on the rockfall where they nest. Probably he was "hey-heying." [7] The sun and the birds had returned. It was the month of white nights, the time of love, of carefree days, of plenty. On that day, Her Majesty's ships *Assistance* and *Intrepid* steamed into view, commanded by captains Ommanney and Austin, and approached the coast. They were looking for Sir John Franklin and his two ships. Seeing an Inuit encampment on the plateau, they lowered a boat and invited the three families to visit the ships. But the attempt at seduction backfired. The large furnaces of the steam engine frightened the hunters, who ran back on deck and made for shore as fast as they could. Captain Ommanney then decided to visit the Inuit himself. Welcomed generously into their tents, he questioned them about the rumor that Captain Franklin and his men had been massacred north of Cape York in 1846 by men of their race. The Inuit denied "most emphatically" that they had ever done anything of the sort. "How can you accuse us?" they asked indignantly. "We have seen only a few whalers and one other ship (the *North Star*), which wintered in a bay to the north some six months ago (1849-1850)." The young hunter Qalasersuaq, himself indignant about the accusations against his people, offered to guide the two English ships to the bay, a traditional settlement site of the Inuit. Why should he doubt the good faith of these white men? He boarded the *Assistance* with perfect confidence and displayed much intelligence in piloting the ship toward Wolstenholme Fjord. Kalli (the familiar form of "Kallihirua," which was the English transcription of "Qalasersuaq") submitted to being washed and dressed in English clothes, then led the British to the small Inuit village of Uummannaq, where the *North Star* commanded by Captain Saunders had wintered six months earlier. He showed them his people's abandoned igloos, inside one of which were seven bodies heaped on top of one another, clad in their skin clothing. The dead were not buried under stones, as was the custom. The survivors had fled the spot in haste, terrified by the devastating illness. Yet now, under Kalli's very eyes, the sailors were searching through the nearby graves for any remnants of Captain Franklin and his crew. They discovered the skeletons of several seamen from the *North Star*, and disturbed the bones of several Inuit, which they examined minutely. In one of the Inuit graves lay a spear, probably a narwhal tusk. One of the officers took it, and Kalli ran up to the officer indignant and in tears, begging him to leave the spear where it had lain. Surprised, the officer assented and ordered a sergeant to build the graves up again and replace the spear. [8] It was the grave of Kalli's father, Kirshinguak. [9]

Portrait of Kallihirua, aged seventeen.

The abduction

Once back on board, Kalli was placed under the guard of a sergeant of Marines, who instructed him in the rudiments of English: no doubt they were already thinking how to use him.

The *Assistance* did not put in at Cape York on the return, contrary to the assurances given Kalli, and headed instead toward the Northwest Passage. Was the condition of the ice to blame? Kalli was desperate, crying constantly and calling out to his family. To cut off an Eskimo from his family and his home territory is to cut him off from his Ancestors, who are vital to him. Furthermore, he was a twin and had two sisters living with his mother, Sa-toorney. The ship wintered in Barrow Strait near Griffith Island. The following spring it was still impossible to return to Cape York in Greenland (the British once more invoked the condition of the ice). Despite Kalli's tears, they resolutely directed the helm south toward England. [10]

Here are two stanzas of a poem, "Kalli in the Ship," written on this occasion:

Poor lad, he strain'd his eyes in vain,
Till tears began to come,
To try if he could see again
His mother and his home.
O Kalli, fail not, day by day,
To kneel to God above;
Then He will hear you when you pray,
And guard you with his love.

But God, or British interests, decided otherwise. After landing on British soil, Kalli was brought in November 1851 to the Society for Promoting Christian Knowledge, then, on Admiralty orders, to the Missionary College of St. Augustine's, at Canterbury, where students were trained for Church of England missions to the colonies. He was a diligent student and learned to read and write, though not without difficulty. His vocabulary was at first limited to the words "ship," "sea," "very sick," "England, things very nice," and "captain very good." He expressed great delight on seeing drawings of ships in the ice and especially of Eskimos hunting seal, saying: "This one of my people! This Inuk!" He was often ill, yet he was asked to collaborate on revising one of the first English-Greenland Eskimo vocabularies (London, 1850). He was invited to London.

He showed little interest in the British Museum, the Crystal Palace, or Hyde Park, but was astonished at the vast multitude of white men around him: "So many men! So many men!"

A letter to a friend dated April 1853 shows his unhappy state of mind:

E. York. St. Augustine's College, April, 1853.

My dear Sir,

I am very glad to tell, How do you do, Sir? I been England, long time none very well. Long time none very well. Very bad weather. I know very well, very bad cough. I very sorry, very bad weather, dreadful. Country very difference. Another day cold. Another day wet, I miserable.

Another summer come. Very glad. Great many trees. Many wood. Summer beautiful, country Canterbury.[11]

Baptism

Qalasersuaq had only three years to live. His increasingly frequent coughing fits exhausted him. Asked if there was anything he would like, to make him better, he answered: "A little walrus." His cheerfulness was constant, if feigned. He prayed regularly, and uttered only words of gratitude: "Thank you, thank you . . . very happy . . . captain very kind . . . everyone very kind." He knew that he was being watched and that the white men had the power to repatriate him if they chose. An excellent actor, as are all Eskimos, he played a double game. He acted the part of extreme courtesy, reinforced by a false show of servility.[12]

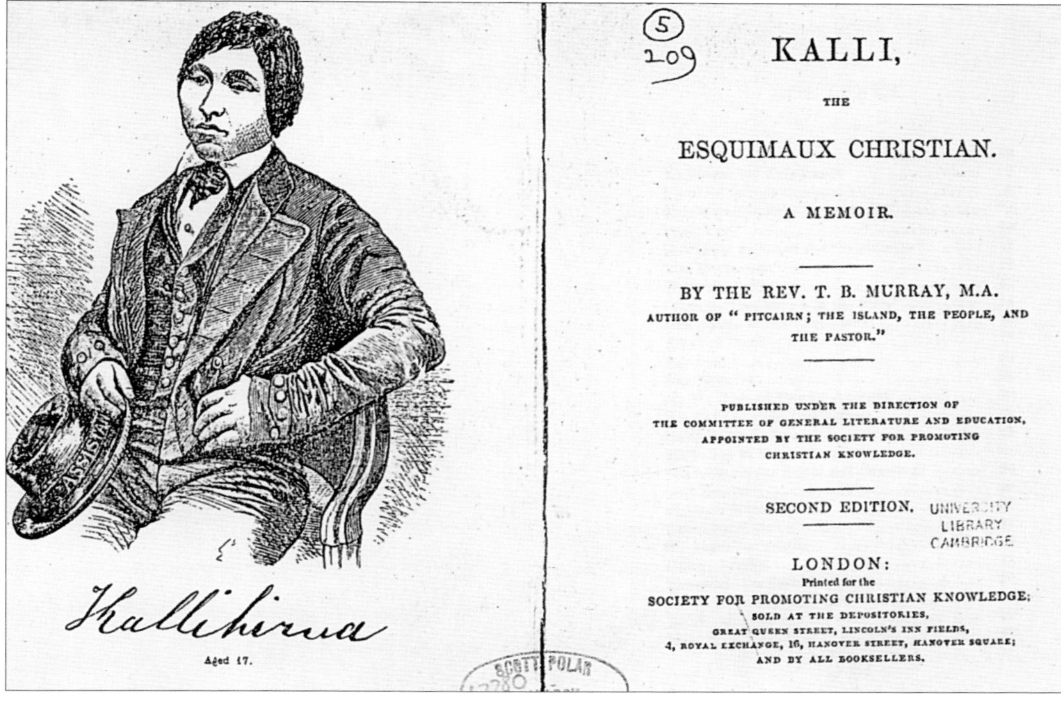

Kallihirua

Aged 17.

KALLI,

THE

ESQUIMAUX CHRISTIAN.

A MEMOIR.

BY THE REV. T. B. MURRAY, M.A.

AUTHOR OF "PITCAIRN; THE ISLAND, THE PEOPLE, AND THE PASTOR."

PUBLISHED UNDER THE DIRECTION OF THE COMMITTEE OF GENERAL LITERATURE AND EDUCATION, APPOINTED BY THE SOCIETY FOR PROMOTING CHRISTIAN KNOWLEDGE.

SECOND EDITION.

LONDON:

Printed for the

SOCIETY FOR PROMOTING CHRISTIAN KNOWLEDGE;

SOLD AT THE DEPOSITORIES,

GREAT QUEEN STREET, LINCOLN'S INN FIELDS,

4, ROYAL EXCHANGE, 16, HANOVER STREET, HANOVER SQUARE;

AND BY ALL BOOKSELLERS.

Frontispiece and title page of the book *Kalli, The Esquimaux Christian,* by the Reverend T. B. Murray, London.

For all repatriation, Kalli was given the honor of being the first Polar Eskimo to receive baptism. The ceremony, using water from the River Jordan, was performed on Advent Sunday, 27 November 1853, in the old St. Martin's Church, near Canterbury. Among those present were his abductor, Captain Ommanney, the daughter of Sir John Franklin, Eleonore Gell, and the secretary of the Society for Promoting Christian Knowledge. Kalli was christened Erasmus (after Captain Ommanney), Augustine (in remembrance of his college), and York (his place of origin).[13] The church warden wrote a poem for the occasion:

"I will take you one of a city, and two of a family, and I will bring you to Zion."—*Jer. 3:14*

But who so wild, so lost
In ignorance and sin!
No God they know, no Saviour own;
Is there a soul to win?

Warm is the Christian's heart,
Outstretch'd the Christian's hand,
"Assistance" lends her friendly aid
To reach a Christian land.

In this our calm retreat
He finds a peaceful home,
Is taught such learning as is meet,
In store for years to come.

Have pity on his race!
And bring them still to see
Their wretched state, and teach them all
The Father, Son, and Thee!

After helping with a Greenland Eskimo Vocabulary printed by direction of the Admiralty, young Erasmus was sent to Saint John's, Newfoundland, in the fall of 1855, with a view to his probable usefulness among the Eskimos of Labrador—a people who spoke an entirely different language. The Admiralty made him an allotment of £ 25 a year for three years. No document exists from which we can infer Qalasersuaq's private thoughts. His health declined precipitously in the winter of 1856. He coughed continuously and complained of being "colder than at Cape York." On 7 June he swam for a long time in cold water and caught a chill. He died on 14 June 1856, at the age of twenty-four. The diagnosis was "melanosis of the lungs," a disease in which the entire substance of the lungs turns completely black.[14]

Using conventional and cloying language, those who knew him extolled Kalli's extreme gentleness, his pious resignation and thankfulness, his acceptance of suffering in steadfast thought of Christ. During his last illness, he even babbled: "Mr. D. very kind, K. very kind. Sorry to give so much trouble." By way of a final irony to this sorry story, he gave instructions that the small credit remaining to him in the Canterbury Bank be left to Captain Ommanney!

Clear conscience

Thus all was in order. The Church and the Admiralty could have a clear conscience: the Eskimo had accepted his own fate. As in numerous prison systems, the authorities took good care to obtain the written consent of the victim. And had not Kalli served the course of progress and religion? At no time did the Admiralty consider repatriating him—than which nothing would have been easier, given the many departures of Scots whalers for Cape York, numbering ten to fifty ships annually. Nor did anyone think to send him as interpreter on the American expedition led by Kane, which left New York on 30 May 1852. The body of Erasmus York lies in the cemetery at St. John's, probably in the common grave.

7) Traditional song.

8) Presumably the men had received orders not to scare the young Inuk until he was safely back on board and in their power.

9) We can understand Kalli's indignation even more when we reflect that the Inuit believe in eternity. They leave the dead certain common objects, bring them food, and speak to them.

10) In 1893, Robert Peary would in turn deport six Eskimos, whom he presented at the American Museum of Natural History. When four of them died of tuberculosis within a few months, Peary sold or gave their skeletons to the Natural History Museum of New York. Minik, the fifth Eskimo, worked for a time as a taxi driver in New York before returning to his own country. The sixth, Uisaakassak, despite also having tuberculosis, was sent back to his tribe in North Greenland. Peary and the American authorities took not even the most elementary sanitary precautions, and Uisaakassak could easily have infected the entire remainder of his tribe, who had no immunity, triggering a fatal epidemic. In this period, and until 1920, epidemics did in fact sweep the Polar Inuit at intervals, reducing the population by one fifth.

11) Unlike his other letters, this one was not dictated by him.

12) In 1950 I saw proud, intrepid hunters act in the same way as soon as they were alone with white men in the white man's house or on his ship.

13) The name was given to that prominent headland by Captain John Ross in 1818, whereas its Inuk name, from time immemorial, had been "Innaanganeq."

14) Tuberculosis was still endemic among the Polar Eskimos in 1950, and certain men over the age of fifty knew that they had contracted it. Pualuna, visiting me during our work on a genealogy of the Polar Eskimos, always brought with him a small empty tin, into which he spat, covering his mouth with his forearm. I could easily see that he was tubercular: his sputum was bloody. He would say, his good Eskimo eyes already somewhat clouded: "Puak! my lungs . . ."

WHALERS, THE UNKNOWN HEROES

The very first discoverers of the Far North, who braved tremendous dangers, were the whalers (*upernaallit* in the Inuit language).[1] The Inughuit's contact with them was marked by brutality, epidemics, and interbreeding.

"I discovered in the Greenland Sea at the time of my last voyage approximately 18,000 square miles of water totally devoid of ice, between latitudes 74° and 80° north . . . Had I been commanding an expedition of discovery, rather than fishing for whales, I have not the slightest doubt that the mystery attached to the Northwest Passage would have been resolved."[2] This report by a Scottish whaleman, the famous William Scoresby, of an unmistakable warming trend along the southeast and west coasts of Greenland had great consequences, the first being the launching of many ships, for the most part Scottish, toward Melville Bay. William Baffin's discoveries of July 1616 had not been exploited to any great extent, for reasons I have already mentioned, but it should be added that a mantle of ice covered the Far North in the seventeenth century and that the shores of Baffin Bay were inaccessible because a permanent and solid field of ice obstructed them.

There is no doubt that Sir John Ross's account of his expedition, published in London in February 1819, influenced shipowners to concentrate their efforts in this quarter, the more so as the indomitable Dutch, who had long been masters of the whaling grounds off Spitsbergen and the southwest coast of Greenland, had not yet ventured there.[3]

Drawn by the profits to be made hunting whales, dozens of Scottish whalers would ply the waters of northern Melville Bay each year from 1819 to 1900.[4] But there were good and bad years, with fluctuations in the climate. The risks were great. In 1819 alone, fourteen whaling ships were crushed by the ice.

The pillage of the Arctic seas

In the sixteenth, seventeenth, and eighteenth centuries, it was mainly the Dutch who hunted whales around Spitsbergen and off the southwest coast of Greenland. Profits were high, and whales plentiful: from 1699 to 1778, more than 57,000 whales were taken, 8,500 in Spitsbergen alone—and from 1699 to 1709, 850 whales a year. A rich whale population in the coastal waters of southwest Greenland was thus decimated in three centuries.

Logbook. The tails of the Greenland whale illustrate the success of the hunt: sightings and kills.

OPPOSITE, **whaling ships** sailing through loose ice in Melville Bay (16 June 1818).

1) *Upernaallit* means "men of the spring" in Greenlandic. The whalers traveled north each spring.

2) Letter from William Scoresby to Sir Joseph Banks, London, September 1817.

3) 1816: 45 ships. 1817: 53. 1819: 63. 1821: 79. 1822: 60. 1823: 62. 1824: 79. 1825: 85. 1826: 90. 1826-1836: 90 ships per year. 1836: 58. 1837: 37. 1838: 8. 1839: 12. 1840: 20. 1841: 81. 1842: In 1821, the fleet represented an aggregate tonnage of 50,709 tons. One thousand four hundred and five whales were taken, for 16,853 tons of oil and 923 tons of baleen.

4) We should distinguish two periods: the era of sailing ships, from 1819 to 1850, and the era of steam, from 1850 to 1900, with the industrial consequences arising from the greater frequency of the ships.

The Greenland or right whale. Length: 80 feet; weight: 80 to 150 tons; equivalent in blubber to 2,000 seals or 200 walruses. One right whale can provide 40 tons of blubber, 20 tons of whale oil, and 10-foot lengths of baleen (300 on each side)—in all 90 tons of usable raw materials. The right whale is said to have little fear of man.

The British had vainly tried to keep the Dutch out of large areas of the cod fishery. They also tried to keep the Dutch from hunting whale off Spitsbergen, where they had long been established. This too was in vain. The British fishing enterprises of the time ended in bankruptcy. The Fishing Company of Great Britain and Ireland, founded in 1632, was ruined within two years. The Free Company of British Fishing, chartered in 1750 to harvest "the gold of the seas," met with early bankruptcy. Bad management and the Dutch superiority at sea were the causes. Great Britain did not yet have the tools that in time would make it powerful in the north: experienced crews, numerous ships, and especially naval dominance.

Melville Bay, whose very name inspired terror all through the nineteenth century, offered phenomenal dangers: fog and ice, not to mention the whales themselves, which could overturn or break the frail skiffs that carried the seamen to within a harpoon's throw of them. [5] Protected from the north wind by the great cliff at Cape York as well as by the high ice cliffs of the Greenland ice cap to the east, the sea ice might appear relatively stable to an inexperienced eye. And there were certainly years when the sea was open, but they were rare. Most of the time, a ship had to navigate through dense pack ice, following the narrow leads opened in early June along the Greenland coast by tides and warm south-north currents. This was the only route available to ships making for mythical Cape York, which the lookout in the crow's nest strained to see through snow storms and fog. At the latitude of Cape York, the whaling ships would drop anchor briefly, then proceed due west toward Pond Inlet (Baffin Island, Canada).

The northwest coast of Greenland and Ellesmere Island, showing the extent of the pack ice at the beginning of June.

Life on shipboard

A whaling ship of 150 to 400 tons carried a crew of fifty to one hundred men. The day started with prayers; service was celebrated every Sunday, and psalms were sung. And it was the captain, sole master on board (after the God of Ice), who officiated. The captain's wife sometimes came along on the voyage. The ship carried no doctor, unless it was a first-year medical student, who held the title of "surgeon."

Each whaler carried six to eight whale boats (25 feet long), crewed by six men and equipped with two harpoons attached to a hemp line 1400 yards in length. A lookout was kept in the crow's nest high atop the mast day and night. On the cry of "A fish!" or "She blows!" the boats would be lowered. The sleepy, half-naked men would hurriedly take their places in them, dressing with one hand along the way and pulling hard with the other. The slender boats skimmed over the waves. Once the whale was spotted, the steersman made sure not to lose sight of it, sensing intuitively what direction the whale would take under the ice from one pool of open water to another. At the first opportunity, the whale was harpooned in the back and behind the eye. The prick of this foreign object, hideously painful, made the beast react with great violence. Attached by the harpoon head in its flesh and the harpoon line to the whale boat, the whale would pull the small craft along on a wild ride. The harpooner had to have uncommon strength and energy. It was essential to tire the whale, to draw up to it, and to pierce it repeatedly, as in a bullring. What finished the whale off was plunging the lance into its vital organs. [6] In its final spasms, the whale thrashed desperately with its tail. It then rolled over and floated belly up. Three cheers would go up at the giant's death. The carcass was then laboriously towed back to the ship by the boats all in a line and lashed to the ship's side. In calm weather, the animal was cut up by men standing on its very body. [7] Let us recall the whale's great size: 65 feet in length, and a weight of 125 tons (its skeleton alone weighed 22 tons). [8] Working hip-deep in blubber, blood, and meat, and surrounded by crying birds, the seamen had to remain vigilant. Whales are social creatures, and if another appeared the hunt would be resumed immediately.

The seamen accepted the hard life aboard these ships because of the high returns of the whale hunt. From 1818 to 1900, eighty to one hundred and fifty ships appeared each year off the coasts where the Polar Eskimo lived, particularly in the area of Cape York and Pond Inlet on the north coast of Baffin Island. The main ports outfitting ships for Melville Bay were Hull, Dundee, Peterhead, and Aberdeen. Some sailors were "shanghaied," or brought on board after being made drunk. But otherwise the men and officers were all volunteers. From Cape York, after trading for a few days with the Eskimos, the whalers sped to Pond Inlet, the meeting place of all the whaling fleet. This was the famous North Water, which was ice-free even in the winter thanks to the convergence of water currents of different temperatures and profiles.

The men were paid shares and depended on their captain to fish actively and successfully. [9] A captain who knew where to find whales was greatly respected. And each captain had his "territories" and his "customs"; the logbooks were for this reason kept secret. Some of the whaling skippers, Captain Adam Smith among them, remained famous among the Polar Eskimos until as late as 1950. [10]

The Carey Islands north of Melville Bay served as a post office. The ships put ashore at intervals to collect fresh water. The great fear of the crews was obviously that their ship might be destroyed by an iceberg coming on unnoticed in a thick fog, or that the ship would be caught in pack ice as it sailed through a lead. [11]

The main foodstuffs—pork, beef, and mutton—were salty and pickled in brine. Scurvy was a constant threat. An invalid, lying weakly in his berth, was subject to terrible depression. Life on board ship was extremely trying. Living in damp quarters never more than five feet high, the sailors could not stand up. They slept in narrow bunks, whose straw was often wet. A Charles Dickens or a Victor Hugo would be needed to describe their life. These sailors, Scotsmen for the most part, were illiterate, crude, and brutal. Their captains were violent, not to say cruel, men. Discipline on board was harsh, and corporal punishment (flogging the bare buttocks) was common—it was even a regulation in the navy. Withholding from a man's pay was the most feared threat: the sailor's family, whose circumstances were extremely reduced, depended for its subsistence entirely on the pay of the husband, or son, or father, always supposing he had not spent his pay at the ship's store during low moments.

Harsh physical demands were made on the crew. A man had to climb into the rigging in all weather to raise and reef the frozen sails in glacial winds, often barehanded. Dense fogs were common in the summer. The seaman might be on watch for ten to fifteen hours, his feet in the icy water that filled the bottom of the boat, at a distance from the ghostly form of the mother ship.

A man might be tempted to flee, but where to? Onto the ice, that white desert stretching as far as the eye can

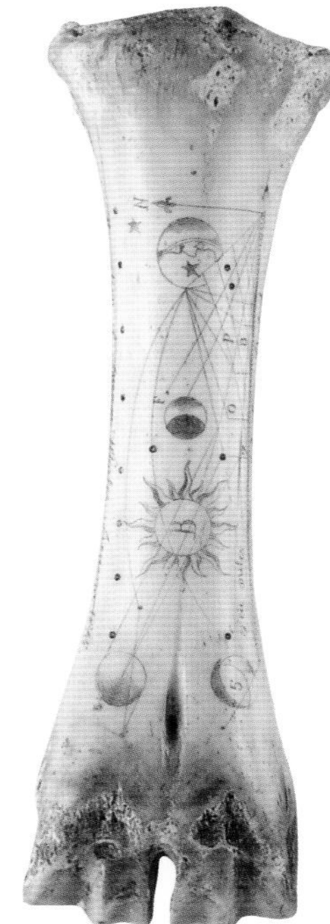

Scrimshaw, a sailor' engraving on the front leg bone of a walrus, showing a diagram of the sperm whale migration.

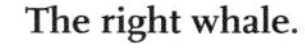

The right whale.
Its head comprises a third of its total length. The tail flukes, notched in the middle, are seven and a half yards wide. The whale rises to the surface at regular intervals to breathe. If frightened, it can dive for almost 40 minutes and to a depth of 400 meters. The population worldwide is estimated at 4,000.

5) In 1821, eleven ships were crushed in the ice; in 1822, seven; in 1830, nineteen.
6) After 1900, whales would be killed with explosive charges.
7) The blubber, cut off in long strips, was melted in enormous pots, then stored in barrels. Blubber consists of 63% oil, 13% protein, 24% water, and 1% minerals.
8) Baleen fetched a high price: £540 per ton. Oil was worth £40 per ton.
9) A seaman on a whaler earned the same wage as a worker in a jute factory: £2 per month. But the whaling companies recruited without much difficulty by tacking on a bonus that amounted to a quarter or a half of the fixed wage. A harpooner received twice the salary of an ordinary seaman, and an officer four times that salary. The captain received, in addition to his salary, anywhere from 1.5% to 10% of total profits.
10) The exploits of Alamisi (Adam Smith) and Ittupaluk (the Little Old Man) were recounted to me in 1950 by Pualuna, the focal individual in the genealogy I was constructing, and by my daily companion, Kutsikitsoq. Their memories were factual, with no friendly connotations. The elders remembered their names and their general aspect, and some could caricature their gestures, even reproducing their accents and their way of spitting.
11) The ship opened a lead with its prow and pushed back the edges with its cradle-shaped hull.

Break-up of the pack ice around the *Terror* (July 1837) in Hudson Bay, off Southampton Island. Painting by William Smyth.

Cutting up a whale. The flensers have cut a strip of blubber 1.5 to 2 feet in thickness. They also look for ambergris, used in making perfumes.

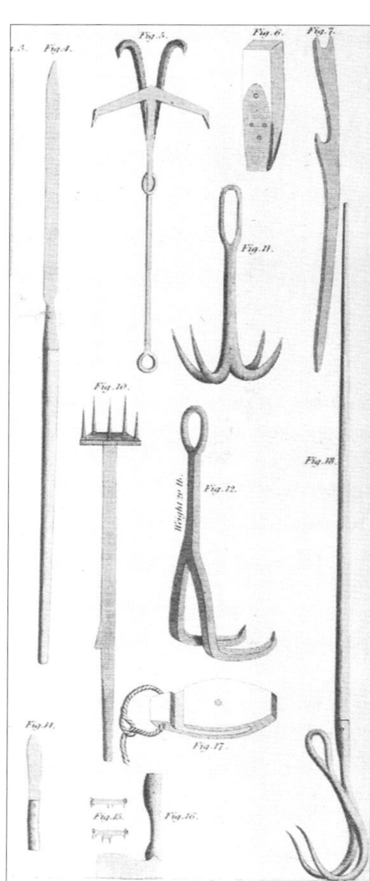

Hooks and grapnels used aboard whale boats (open boats 30 feet long and 6 feet wide).

see? Or onto the hostile shore? The general desolation and harshness of the country, along with the supposed hostility of the Eskimos, who were "savages, pagans, and cannibals," forced any mutineers to return on board, where they were put in irons.

There is no account, nor any legend, that tells of sailors deserting to live among the Inughuit. Yet one of my companions, Kutsikitsoq, told me in December 1950 that in his childhood he had heard tell of whites and a young boy wandering near Qeqertarsuaq. Lost sailors? Nothing is known for certain.

The poor man's habitual contempt for the native

Though the whalers were poor devils who left behind wretched and grief-stricken families, they looked with contempt at the men of the polar north whom Captain John Ross had recently discovered. Contemporary caricatures of these savages are telling. [12]

The whaling ships made only brief stopovers near the encampments in the south of the Polar Inuits' range (Cape York, Savissivik), 250 miles south of Etah (Cape Alexander). Families were invited on board to trade, while the ships remained at anchor off the ice field. Unlike the Eskimos of southern Greenland, the Polar Eskimos put up no resistance to the whalers. There was passive acceptance at first, followed by collaboration, as the native hunters hurriedly tried to get some basic tools from the whites on their rare visits: iron barrel hoops, wood, hammers, knives, axes, needles, and tin boxes, which were of considerable use to them in their daily lives—and also, before long, tobacco. The lawless and unprincipled seamen established a trade based on shameless practices. Tens of fox skins were exchanged for a single board or a metal box; sometimes the Eskimo women were even prostituted, to the extent that their men allowed it. Logbooks naturally kept silence on this subject. But we should note that the Eskimos are lax in sexual matters.

It is certain that the sight of these violent and female-deprived seamen could only encourage the Eskimos—who were ever pragmatists—to resort to the ultimate bargaining chip: lending their wives (made easier by the fact that their wives possessed a lively curiosity). Furthermore, the Eskimos were well aware of the dangers of inbreeding among a group of twenty to forty families isolated for two centuries (16% of couples in 1950 were sterile) and wished, as they told me more than once, to regenerate their race by interbreeding with other peoples. They acquired their knowledge of the effects of inbreeding from their experience of raising sled dogs.

The *North Star* overwinters

In 1849-1850, a 500-ton whaler overwintered among the Inughuit for the first time. This was the *North Star*, whose mission was to find the lost Franklin party and

12) The major newspapers looked ironically at the British explorers' willingness to rub noses with the Inuit. The caricatures are explicit: from pulling on their noses, they have pulled them off! We should note that this is a custom invented by the seamen. The Inuit have never pulled their noses; they rub them delicately against the nose of another. Thus in Igloolik in 1962, along the coast, during a brief stopover in a camp of seal and caribou hunters, I saw a couple rub their noses sensually one against the other, taking their time. Political issues also contributed to the public satire. Ross and his companions were always reproached for having in some sense ennobled the Inuit by calling them "Arctic Highlanders." The Admiralty and the British establishment generally may have been irked at Ross for extending the majesty of Scotland to these hyperborean savages.

13) On this subject, I quote Ivalu ("The Needle"), an aged Polar Eskimo woman and the wife of my friend Qalaseq ("The Navel"), whose mother told her not to accept invitations from sailors. She confessed to me, in the winter of 1950, that her disobedience had earned her only the happiest memories . . .

bring provisions to Captain James Clark Ross's rescue expedition operating somewhere in Barrow Strait. Trapped by ice, the ship's officers searched in vain for the meteorites reported by Ross in 1818. The ship was trapped in the ice of Melville Bay on 30 July 1849 and drifted north until 26 September, when it was freed, for a few short days. Because of its northward drift the ship was forced to lay over in Wolstenholme Fjord, first discovered by John Ross, near the old village of Uummannaq, a veritable capital of the Hyperboreans, at the heart of the territory included between Etah in the north and Savissivik (Cape York) in the south. The bay of Uummannaq, known in Altaic legend as the hub of the universe, would be christened North Star Bay. The luck of expeditions was certainly at work in giving a name of mythological significance to the site of a village that would later bear the legendary name of Thule—the country of the northern gods.

The captain of the *North Star,* John Saunders, remained famous in subsequent memoirs. He wrote that caribou and game generally were exceedingly rare during the winter: only fifty hares were caught. Few native families visited the ship, and only one Eskimo was treated for frostbite to his legs. He died after six weeks on board from "pulmonary disorders," a detail that confirms the fragility of the Inughuit hunters during their first contacts with whites. The consequences of the ship's wintering at Uummannaq were in fact tragic. Three Eskimo families in the area died of the "grippe" in the space of a few days. The Austin expedition, guided by the future Erasmus York, the first deportee in Inuit history, would discover a few months later in August 1850 three mortuary tents where the bodies had been piled. The abundance of food surrounding the dead showed that hunger could not have been the cause of death. The Inughuit were the first victims of "civilization" at these high latitudes. According to custom, the local population fled the area. The spot is all the more tragic for being also the burial site of several Scottish sailors, whose gravestones lie only yards from the dead Inughuit.

The *qallunaat* (or "whites" in the Eskimo tongue) were held to be curiously "short-legged" by their hosts. They inspired terror, as much for their violence as for the epidemics that follow even their briefest stay. Knud Rasmussen reported that in 1905, "fear was still so strong that when a child saw an iceberg in the form of a ship, he would immediately cry out: '*Qaaqqatsor suakkut!*' and everyone would flee to the mountains." The sailors did in fact make men and women come on board the ships at their whim. Yet it seems that unlike their cousins on Baffin Island, none of the Inughuit were ever talked into joining a whaling expedition. [13]

In 1902, at Cape Sabine, at the time of Peary's third expedition, many Eskimos who had had contact with the famous explorer's American companions died of influenza. *Nauak!* The few who escaped death became bald. In 1920, the outbreak of Spanish influenza after World War I made such inroads among this isolated people that a fifth of the population died. Tuberculosis was endemic. This was still the case in 1950: Pualuna would visit me, according to the custom, carrying his spitting box, and his sputum was often bloody. It is no surprise that these populations, threatened in their physiology as well as in their society, should prove culturally conservative. Their conservatism became second nature to them. Ross experienced it when he discovered them in 1818, and the population remained impervious to all introduced technologies until the last migration from the Canadian Arctic in 1862. Innovation equaled danger.

Selective memory: Eskimo stories make no mention of the presence of whites—or very little—as though to repress the memory of them and find protection from their harmful powers.

The contemptuous Royal Navy

Linked neither to the navy nor to the universities, whalers (*upernaallit*) were sovereignly neglected by the Admiralty. What a mistake! Were not the Scottish whaling captains ex-

Whale hunt in Melville Bay.

Wage slips for Charles Mayers, a seaman from Dundee, Scotland, aboard the whaler *Alexander*. The expedition, which lasted seven months and nine days, earned Mayers £17 17s. 10d. (oil and baleen included), figured on a share basis and paid to his wife, Agnes, in five installments during the expedition.

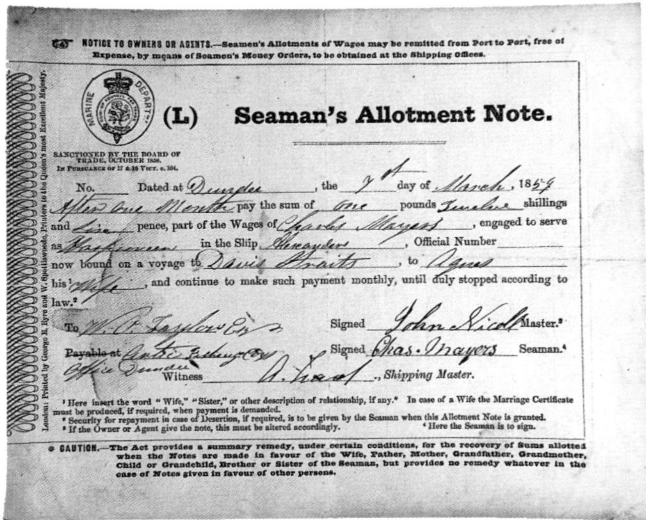

NOTICE TO OWNERS OR AGENTS.—Seamen's Allotments of Wages may be remitted from Port to Port, free of Expense, by means of Seamen's Money Orders, to be obtained at the Shipping Offices.

(L) Seaman's Allotment Note.

SANCTIONED BY THE BOARD OF TRADE, OCTOBER 1858. In Pursuance of 17 & 18 Vict. c. 104.

No. ___ Dated at Dundee, the 7th day of March, 1859

After One Month pay the sum of One pounds Twelve shillings and Six pence, part of the Wages of Charles Mayers, engaged to serve as [illegible] in the Ship Alexander, Official Number ___ now bound on a voyage to Davis Straits, to Agnes his[1] Wife, and continue to make such payment monthly, until duly stopped according to law.[2]

To W. [illegible] Esq. Signed John Nicol Master.[3]

Payable at [illegible] Office Dundee Signed Chas. Mayers Seaman.[4]

Witness [illegible], Shipping Master.

[1] Here insert the word "Wife," "Sister," or other description of relationship, if any.* In case of a Wife the Marriage Certificate must be produced, if required, when payment is demanded.
[2] Security for repayment in case of Desertion, if required, is to be given by the Seaman when this Allotment Note is granted.
[3] If the Owner or Agent give the note, this must be altered accordingly. [4] Here the Seaman is to sign.

* CAUTION.—The Act provides a summary remedy, under certain conditions, for the recovery of Sums allotted when the Notes are made in favour of the Wife, Father, Mother, Grandfather, Grandmother, Child or Grandchild, Brother or Sister of the Seaman, but provides no remedy whatever in the case of Notes given in favour of other persons.

London: Printed by George E. Eyre and W. Spottiswoode, Printers to the Queen's most Excellent Majesty.

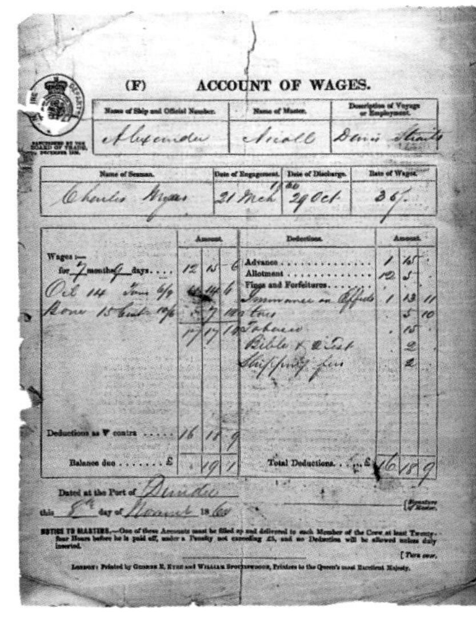

(F) ACCOUNT OF WAGES.

Name of Ship and Official Number.	Name of Master.	Description of Voyage or Employment.
Alexander	Nicoll	Davis Straits

Name of Seaman.	Date of Engagement.	Date of Discharge.	Rate of Wages.
Charles Mayers	21 Mch	29 Oct	36/.

	Amount			Deductions.	Amount		
Wages:— for 7 months 9 days	12	15	6	Advance	1	15	
Oil 14 Tuns 6/9	[illegible]	14	6	Allotment	12	5	
Bone 15 Cwt 19/6	[illegible]	7	[illegible]	Fines and Forfeitures			
	17	17	10	Insurance on Effects	1	13	11
				[illegible]		5	10
				Tobacco		15	
				Bible & [illegible]		2	
				Shipping fee		2	
Deductions as ♥ contra	16	18	9				
Balance due £		19	1	Total Deductions £	16	18	9

Dated at the Port of Dundee this 8th day of [illegible] 1859 (Signature of Master.)

NOTICE TO MASTERS.—One of these Accounts must be filled up and delivered to each Member of the Crew at least Twenty-four Hours before he is paid off, under a Penalty not exceeding £5, and no Deduction will be allowed unless duly inserted. [Turn over.

London: Printed by George E. Eyre and William Spottiswoode, Printers to the Queen's most Excellent Majesty.

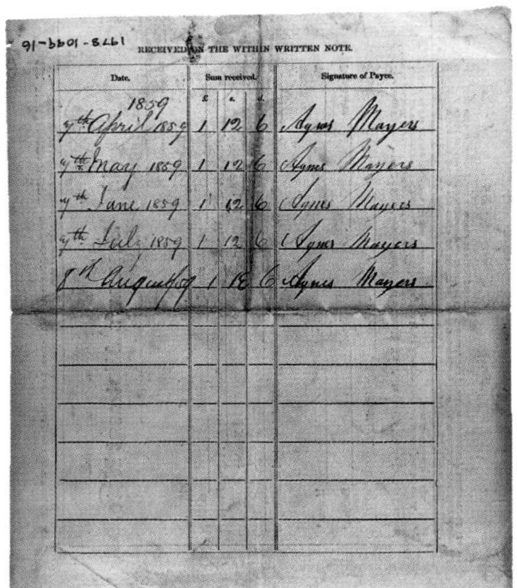

1978-1044-16

RECEIVED ON THE WITHIN WRITTEN NOTE.

Date.	£	s.	d.	Signature of Payee.
1859 9th April 1859	1	12	6	Agnes Mayers
9th May 1859	1	12	6	Agnes Mayers
9th June 1859	1	12	6	Agnes Mayers
9th July 1859	1	12	6	Agnes Mayers
8th August 59	1	12	6	Agnes Mayers

With the ship trapped, the crew try to break up the pack ice using explosives.

The crow's nest.

traordinary explorers of the high latitudes throughout the centuries? Nonfactual history, the history of minds, draws mainly on the whalers and their relations with the native populations. The arrogance of the navy officers and their never-ending antagonisms left bad memories on all sides. Who can forget the Penny scandal?

Penny was a brave whaling captain, hired by the Admiralty in 1850 to search for John Franklin, at Lady Franklin's urging. He was odiously slandered and judged to be incompetent by the establishment. A cabal formed by Royal Navy captain Austin brought him down. An Arctic Committee was convened to arbitrate his case. Despite the support of Lady Franklin, the verdict went against Penny. If, instead of constantly attacking commercial whalers, the authorities had managed to use these rough but competent men, the exploration of the high latitudes would have been set forward by a century and numerous tragic deaths could have been avoided. One famous example of an under-used talent is William Scoresby, an exceptional Arctic navigator, who offered his services to the Admiralty with the backing of Sir Joseph Banks. He was quickly informed that only officers of the Royal Navy had the honor of commanding Admiralty missions.

Better observation and an accurate understanding of the Inuit genius would have allowed the explorers, at the very least, to have better-adapted clothing. In all Admiralty expeditions, furs were scorned; boots were made of cowhide and canvas. Winter camps were European-style. Sleds were pulled by men, as honor demanded (this would become a British specialty). And finally let us remember that on their travels over the ice the men ate salt beef and pork along with ship's biscuit—after hours of exhausting work. Lying weakly in their bunks on their return, overcome with lethargy, suffering from scurvy (and taking an ineffectual astringent gargle by way of treatment), the men died slowly—when they could have been saved if they had eaten the fresh meat available on all sides of the ship: whale, seal, narwhal . . . They could even have eaten kelp from time to time, Japanese-style. But eating like a native would have been degrading and against regulations. There was also a strong belief in the Anglo-Saxon and Judaeo-Christian idea (amply fostered in British schools) that one must suffer to attain one's goals.

If it had been acknowledged, finally, that geographic exploration has the duty not only to study but to protect the peoples and cultural heritage it discovers, the government might have issued instructions and granted subsidies to shipowners so that the objects brought back from their expeditions could be properly gathered and preserved. An invaluable collection would thus have been built, of universal benefit to human thought. But this is no more than a dream: ethnography would become a reality only a century later.

The town of Dundee, despite a creditable effort to reorganize its great Whaling Museum, counts only about seventy-five Inuit objects, after a century of collecting. Each year, "souvenirs" must have been brought back by whalers, but as their worth passed unnoticed, they were divided up, dispersed, and sold at auction. Such is life. ■

A whale hunt using traditional harpoons, engraved on a plaquet from a whale's jawbone. The word "scrimshaw," which applies to this form of engraving, is of unknown origin.

The lines are inked with soot or tobacco juice. The whalebone is prepared by leaving the whale's jaw exposed on the ship's deck or trailing in the water astern until the flesh is gone. In the case of toothed whales, the teeth were distributed by the second or third mate to certain members of the crew, according to a ritual hierarchy.

Aaveqmiut, the "men of the whale."

WHALERS HAVE PLAYED A CRUCIAL BUT LARGELY IGNORED ROLE IN THE HISTORY OF THE ESKIMO PEOPLE

Putting in year after year along inhabited coastlines, the whaling crews—Scottish for the most part—convinced the Inuit people that they were no longer alone in the world.

The help that might be expected from these spring visitors (*upernaallit*) could hardly be formulated in Inuit thought. Before long whaling ships were perceived as a menace. Potentially an inexhaustible source of wood and iron, the whalers should have provided the Inuit a great wealth of material by 1830, 12 years after first contact.

Yet in 1852-1855 and 1860-1861, Kane and Hayes separately observed that wood and iron remained as scarce as ever among the Inuit. Given their harsh and precarious way of life, the Inuit refused to veer drastically from their known technologico-cultural system—a material culture based on bone, ivory, and stone, and an egalitarian society built on exchange and rigor—in favor of another culture, which was opaque and uncertain since it depended on the random comings and goings of foreigners, over whom the Eskimo had no power.

It was only in 1890-1900 that Eskimo society started to adopt elements of foreign culture that seemed useful to it, all the while retaining its dual nature. Peary's eight expeditions, by their regularity, their size, and their intimacy with the Eskimos, encouraged this rapprochement.

Short-lived sexual relationships occurred, mainly at Cape York, on board ship. The high level of inbreeding that had occurred among the Eskimos during the previous two centuries was thus lowered. No instances of whaling men who took up residence among the Eskimo are known. Seen as savages, as primitive men, the Eskimos inspired a vague fear. The Inughuit were equally afraid of the arrival of these ships driven by powerful, brutal, and unpredictable men.

It was through the whalers that the Eskimos were introduced to tobacco, which has become a passion among them. "Good for the Eskimo, bad for you," they liked to tell white men, while sucking on the feathers used by the sailors to ream their pipes. The same words were repeated to me identically in 1950 by Eskimos chewing the ash in their pipes, the black dottle, which they would swallow at a gulp.

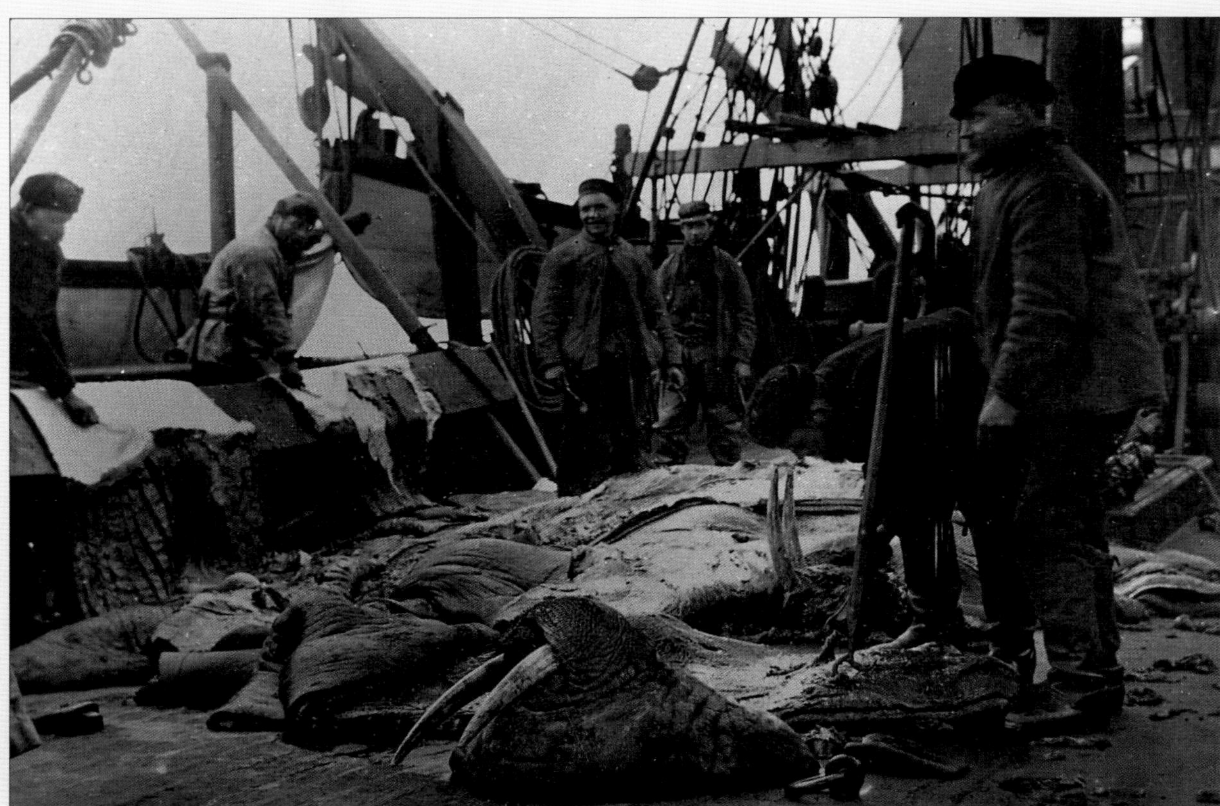

Walrus being cut up on the deck of a whaling ship. Only the tusks were kept.

Women, both young girls and married women, were invited aboard ship. The young woman in the hood is under taboo, either having recently aborted or lost a close relative. The sexual fraternization is unmistakable.

Baleen, 8 to 10 feet in length, hanging on deck. A right whale provided 300 barrels of oil and blubber, worth about $12,000. Whalers at the end of the nineteenth century also hunted walrus, harvesting only the ivory. When walrus hunting proved relatively unprofitable, it was left to the Eskimos.

Scottish sailor prying the strands of a rope apart with a wooden marlinespike. The crew slept belowdecks. The seamen's berths were damp and dirty. Their food was salt meat and biscuit, often spoilt. As on the codfishing boats of Iceland and Greenland, the captain often doubled as the ship's doctor.

Right, **an Eskimo child** posing on the deck of a whaler. For the boorish men, the Inuit were simple objects of curiosity, of which a "souvenir" was kept by means of a photograph. (Pond Inlet, 1889)

ELISHA KENT KANE 1820-1857

THE FIRST SIGNATORY OF AN INTERNATIONAL AGREEMENT WITH THE INUIT

Kane, who commanded the first American expedition to the Arctic, believed that he had found the Open Polar Sea. His account established the stereotype of the "crude, primitive, but endearing Eskimo." Yet it was this very people, "on the verge of disappearing," who saved the American explorers from scurvy and despair.

He was handsome, well-bred, and elegant. With his curly hair, he almost seems effeminate. He had striking brown eyes; was small and thin (5'3" and 110 lbs.), and suffered from an enlarged heart and rheumatoid arthritis. His "heartbeat made the sound of a bellows." He could not sleep lying down without running the risk of suffocation. And going to sea was unbearable to him. The least wave shattered his whole body. Yet he was a navy doctor and spent the greater part of his life on board ship.

"If you must die, Elisha, let it be standing!" his father had instructed him. The elder Kane was one of the most powerful judges in Philadelphia, descended from an old Irish-Scottish family—fairly posh gentry. On the eve of his departure for his last Arctic expedition, on 30 May 1853, Elisha Kane was so sick he was thought to be dying.

Elisha was the eldest of seven children. He was close to his mother, a woman of great beauty, and from an early age he defied his father, a possessive and authoritarian man who never understood his fascination with the desolate Far North and the inhuman ice of the Arctic. By nature wild, sensitive, and rebellious toward authority, Kane had a difficult time in school, but he nonetheless made a conscientious study of the classics and became a navy doctor, traveling all over the world: China, the Philippines, India, Brazil, the Middle East, and Africa. He visited Thermopylae, and dreamed of Sparta. Everywhere he left the memory of a man of great charm and lively curiosity, which might explain his explorer's temperament. In Mexico he fought with a sword and received a lance wound in the abdomen from guerrillas.

Religious in upbringing and outlook, he belonged to his parents' congregation, the Second Presbyterian Church of Philadelphia. On returning from his expedition in the fall of 1855, he asked his pastor to celebrate a service of thanksgiving. A Presbyterian and a Mason, he entered the Benjamin Franklin Masonic Lodge in Philadelphia in May 1852. On the eve of his second and last departure for Greenland, he was initiated into the Arcana Lodge of New York.

For forty years, the British Admiralty had dominated Arctic exploration with its expeditions. The energy of John Barrow had opened the way. In 1848, no fewer than ten expeditions were chartered from London to search for Sir John Franklin. [1]

1) Franklin was himself a Freemason.

Elisha Kent Kane in his cabin on the *Advance* (painting by Thomas Hicks). On the wall is a portrait of Sir John Franklin. Kane also brought the portrait of the young Margaret Fox, painted in New York before the ship sailed on 16 May 1853. Kane's officers, led by Hayes, constantly disparaged him. Not wanting to air his private life to his shipmates (who were sufficiently unpleasant to him in their daily criticism), Kane would occasionally hang the portrait on the wall, gaze intensely at Margaret, and speak to her.

The *Advance* north of Smith Sound, near the "great river," Kosoak. Sketch by Kane.

Taking up the British challenge

Five years had now passed since any word had reached Britain of the Franklin expedition, which left London on 19 May 1845 with stores for three years. Were the men still alive? Lady Franklin, who had commissioned prayers to be said in every church, was growing weary of the inertia of the English authorities and their way of conducting the search. She made an appeal to the American president, Zachary Taylor, and even to Tsar Nicholas I. Washington listened with respect and concern but kept its distance: this was a matter that regarded Great Britain. At this time, the United States had not yet grasped its own power. Only in 1867, when it purchased Alaska, did the United States assume responsibilities in the Arctic.

But Elisha Kent Kane heard the desperate call of this woman. He was touched to the depths of his soul. The grandson of a Revolutionary War hero and a citizen of haughty Philadelphia, he wanted, he wrote, "to save Captain Franklin, bring honor to the American flag, and carry it to the Pole; to carry it farther north than the Union Jack." His determination to live out his dreams was all the stronger for knowing that, owing to his poor health, his life would be a short one.

Bear hunt. The hunters are on their guard, watchful of the bear's powerful paws, which can tear anything in their path with one swipe. Bears are left-handed. Here, the hunters must plunge a knife into the bear's heart. In 1900, Inuit had their backs lacerated by a polar bear's claws.

Kane was named assistant surgeon and historian of the first Arctic expedition organized by the United States in 1850 to search for Franklin. Two ships, the *Advance* and the *Rescue*, were outfitted. Kane was then thirty years old.

The *Advance* overwintered in Wellington Channel in 1850-1851, providing Kane a harsh and (as he thought) unnecessary experience. Furious at the organization of the search by Edwin DeHaven, the expedition's leader (who was funded by the shipping magnate Henry Grinnell), Kane decided on his return to New York on 30 September 1851 to lead a search of his own, partly at his own expense. In 1852 he wrote an account of this first expedition, in the meantime mobilizing friends and acquaintances for the next.[2] He persuaded Henry Grinnell and a Mr. George Peabody of London to outfit the *Advance*, that excellent 140-ton brig that he knew so well, lightly reinforced in the bow to protect it. Kane made his first direct contribution to the expedition by forgoing his salary. Lacking official credentials, Kane could not obtain financial backing from the secretary of the navy, yet ten navy seamen and officers were allocated to the expedition, along with their wages and provisions.

For weeks, starting in December 1852, Kane feverishly assembled the equipment and provisions (pemmican, salt meat and fish, biscuit, dried potatoes, fruit) necessary for a year in the Arctic. As a doctor he gave special attention to the food. He thought of everything, except laying in enough! Naively, Kane refused to consider that his ship could be trapped by ice for several years, and we will see that in October 1854 the expedition was indeed starving.

Kane read every available book and article on the geography of the Arctic but, like so many others, retained only what coincided with his subconscious thoughts. The still unvisited poles, which had inspired medieval mystics, were

2) Kane's book, *The First Grinnell Expedition*, was published in New York in 1854 (while the second expedition was under way). This helped bring about a congressional resolution allocating $150,000 to outfit two rescue ships under the command of Captain Hartstene.

The two volumes of *The Second Grinnell Expedition* were published in Philadelphia in 1856, less than a year after Kane's return. Ross's record for publishing an account only months after his return has never been broken.

the subject of a book that had recently attracted popular attention in the United States, Edgar Allan Poe's *The Narrative of Arthur Gordon Pym* (1838). It is at the South Pole that Poe situates the country where there arose in the traveler's pathway "a shrouded human figure, very far larger in its proportions than any dweller among men. And the hue of the skin of the figure was the perfect whiteness of the snow. . . . A high range of light gray vapor appeared constantly in the southern horizon. . . . The temperature of the sea seemed to be increasing momentarily, and there was a very perceptible alteration in its color." Poe had been struck by Mercator's maps, "in which one sees the oceans plunge through four openings into the polar chasm and disappear into the bowels of the earth."

Kane's stated purpose was to rescue Franklin, but his secret ambition was to reach the open polar sea, on whose shores, as he believed, Franklin was detained with his one hundred and twenty-nine shipmates. He imagined the British explorer hunting for birds and fishing for cod from the edge of the floe, confident of being rescued; the British Admiralty never abandons its men.

A warm, open sea. The old myth of an ice-free boreal sea was believed at that time by all who studied the high latitudes. The famous German geographer Augustus Petermann (1822-1878) gave new life to the hypothesis. His learned theoretical studies—of the runoff of Eurasian and North American rivers toward the north, and of the northern migration of whales, narwhals, caribou, and birds—proved that the pole must be surrounded by open water. It is thus possible to be a great geographer and an ignoramus, even in Germany. Kane accepted Petermann's analyses and was convinced he would find Franklin by surmounting the girdle of ice that encircled the Polar Sea to latitude 80° north.

A controversial leader

On 30 May 1853, Kane sailed for Greenland. He was captain of the ship and commander of the expedition. It was rare for a man to hold both titles, but it gave him an authority he would have to use more than once—and with what determination! On board with him were nineteen companions, all volunteers: sixteen Americans, two Danes, and a French-Canadian. The crew, some of whom were hastily chosen (Godfrey and Blake on the Brooklyn waterfront on the eve of departure), was disparate, inexperienced, and divided. The two Danish seamen in the group (the second was recruited in Greenland) constantly made impertinent comments about the abilities of their leader and his pretensions of being an Arctic expert. Godfrey and Blake quarreled with the second-in-command Brooks, and mutinied only a week after leaving port. They were placed under arrest.

With a crew such as this, anyone else might have been hesitatant to proceed. But nothing could obstruct Kane's will, which had been tempered by long illness. This man who was always on the verge of dying, and an insomniac to boot, found new life in the face of danger. The *Advance* sailed north into the Atlantic, putting in at Fiskenaesset, where the South Greenlander Hans Hendrik was recruited; and on 20 July in Upernavik, the Danish-Greenlander Carl Petersen, after some hesitation, joined the expedition as its interpreter. He would lead the chorus of disparagement against Kane.

With reckless boldness, the ship sailed ahead into the ice. It passed capes Alexander and Isabella in the night of 6 to 7 August 1853. Kane refused to overwinter in Etah, though it was near a large expanse of open water (reported in 1852 by Inglefield, whose account Kane had read). He entered Smith Sound, and after depositing a boat and provisions on Littleton Island (also on 7 August) in case of a forced retreat, Kane pressed northward. The ship was nipped by closing ice and almost sank. Godfrey committed a further act of insubordination on 11 August and was again arrested. "North, ever northward," Kane kept repeating, irritated by the mutterings of the men, who were starting to balk. He refused to accept his officers' advice to show caution. Wanting to bring the *Advance* close to the North Pole and Captain Franklin, he deliberately ignored the dangers of advancing into an unknown pack. Showing excessive caution, he believed, was the equivalent to giving up. And he repeated to all hearers that exploration was synonymous with boldness. This voyage was not only a rescue mission but an exploration of unknown coasts, including those of the Arctic Ocean, with all the considerable but necessary risks this entailed.

The ice grew denser. On 22 August, Kane had the crew tow the *Advance* north through a channel that was opened along shore by the tides, while the ice closed in solidly behind the ship. A few days later the *Advance* met with a terrible storm and moored at the head of Aungnartoq Bay (latitude 78°37′ north and longitude 71° west, where my own

Route of the expedition to northwest Greenland commanded by Kane (1853-1855), showing the course of the *Advance* and the exploration by dog sled.

First meeting with eight Eskimos from Etah, 7 April 1854. The natives came to examine the whites of the "great ship." The expedition was in trouble but, distrusting their visitors, the men and officers hid their distress. Engraving after a drawing and notes by Kane.

The crew of the *Advance* fraternizes with South Greenlanders in Julianehaab.

depot of stores was located during the expedition I led to Inglefield and Washington lands and Ellesmere Island in April-June 1951). Kane named this inlet Rensselaer Bay, after a small woods near his family home.

10 September 1853: start of the northernmost overwintering ever undertaken by a scientific expedition. The *Advance* could have moored in the bay, but the hyper-energetic Kane decided to investigate the entire coast to the north without losing a day, to find the best site for overwintering. Afraid of an early winter, he set off in the ship's boat *Forlorn Hope* with seven men. He left the *Advance* under the command of the carpenter, Christian Ohlsen, with whom he had only a distant relationship. Why Ohlsen and not Wilson, his first lieutenant, whom he trusted fully? Because Ohlsen had previous Arctic experience, and competence always came before emotion with Kane. The reconnaissance mission by boat was quickly abandoned, as the pack was already too compact, but Kane refused to be thwarted and continued on foot toward Humboldt Glacier. This daring expedition convinced him that there was no better overwintering site than Rensselaer Bay. Then too, the state of the ice left him little choice.

Aquiluktuq. Hunting seal with a harpoon (lying at the hunter's feet) at the breathing hole kept open by the seal in the ice, which can be six feet thick. The wait may last an hour or two. The Inuk lives outside of time.

The men set about preparing their winter quarters. The stern was turned to the southeast to take full advantage of the sun, and the *Advance* was anchored near the mouth of a river to benefit as early as possible from the spring break-up. The ship's high masts stood out elegantly against the vast and desolate expanses of ice. In a few days, the *Advance* would be truly trapped by ice. The crew, overcome with fear, bemoaned their fate at all hours of the day. Why had they not stayed at Etah? Why had they hauled the ship so far north? Petersen reproached Kane for his preoccupation with setting records, which, on the pretext of beating the British, had brought them to this extreme pass with no guarantee of returning home. Kane listened, silent and scornful. He was there to conquer the inner, inaccessible North.

Unmoved by his men's grumbling, Kane decided to send out a five-man dog sled party to make food depots in preparation for the work of the following spring. They explored and mapped Inglefield Land for twenty days. As the party was still not back by 10 October, Kane set out to look for them.[3] He managed to find his men on 15 October. On 28 October, the moon was full. On 7 November, the dark became more daunting, with the start of the polar night. Tensions mounted correspondingly. The Greenlander Hans Hendrik seems to have been the only person on whom Kane could still count; he felt an almost paternal affection toward him.

Kane imposed regulations of puritan severity that stressed the importance of discipline and courtesy, while forbidding all alcohol. The Bible was read aloud, as was *David Copperfield* (published in 1850). Daily prayers were the rule, punctuated by thanksgiving services. Navy regulations were observed in their strictest form: corporal punishment, imprisonment (on board ship), and even hanging could be meted out according to the severity of the infraction. First Lieutenant Wilson expressed growing concern in his journal: "Kane? A peevish, coarse, and sometimes insulting man." He also reproached Kane with gadding on at the officers' table about his society life and his numerous voyages, interspersing his words with French and Latin expressions.[4]

I traveled in the same area in April 1951, and the cruel cold of March and April occasioned no major difficulties. It is true that: 1) I was on the trail all winter with the Inuit going from igloo to igloo, from one hunting area to another, in order to establish the genealogy of 70 families. I had five months to grow used to the cold, while Kane and his men were quartered within the brig. 2) My equipment and food were entirely native. The same applies to Knud Rasmussen (1903-1917), Peter Freuchen (1910-1920), and Lauge Koch (1921-1922). 3) I was alone, adopted by the native group.

August Sonntag studies magnetism in a small hut built on land and named the "Observatory." This scientist, an American of German ancestry, was the target of antisemitic remarks, the sentiment having been fairly common in nineteenth-century America. He died in December 1860 in Pitorarfik (south of Cape Alexander) after a suspicious fall into a fracture in the ice. Did the Eskimo who accompanied him, Hans Hendrik, abandon him? Hayes suspected as much, but without proof.

Hallucinatory expeditions

On 19 May 1854, Kane organized a new expedition of eight men to prepare the next stage of the assault on the open polar sea. At Cape Lieber, latitude 78° 43' north, the expedition took a turn toward tragedy. Conducted American-style, that is, without the slightest attention to what the Inuit could teach, the expedition had barely progressed half a dozen miles when two of its men died, and two more became ill. Downhearted, paralyzed with cold and fear, their faces blackened by the intense cold, the men showed clear signs of delirium and madness. Some cried or burst out laughing for no reason, and growled like animals. The expedition's astronomer and surveyor, August Sonntag, walked numbly like a sleepwalker.

Kane, who had remained on the *Advance*, was sick himself but nonetheless set off on a rescue mission with William Godfrey, who showed magnificent energy. They traveled through a blizzard and, after many mishaps, reached their stricken shipmates. Once back on the *Advance,* the men lay helplessly in their sick-beds. Hayes, the young surgeon, amputated a leg and some frozen toes—notably those of Ohlsen, the expedition's most experienced member (along with Hendrik and Petersen). "The ship is like a madhouse," he wrote in his memoirs. On the ship, tensions increased. Some officers refused to speak to Kane. Conditions were exacerbated by the confinement of the party to a few square yards of the ship. It was a prison, whose walls consisted of an unending field of ice. And how could one live on a ship infested with rats? Every method of extermination failed: the rats were fumigated with burning rubber and arsenic, forcing the crew to sleep on deck to avoid being poisoned in turn. But the rats survived these extreme measures. They made inroads into the remaining food stores. Again the rats were fumigated, but the ship nearly caught fire. They were everywhere, in the sleeping bags, in clothes: Kane was bitten to the bone one morning by a mother rat who had installed her litter in one of his gloves. Yet the daily gathering of scientific information (meteorological observations, research on magnetism) continued. Kane never wavered. He was the motor and the axle of this microsociety in disarray.

Kane issues orders at gunpoint

Ever determined, Kane, at gunpoint, forced the Eskimos who had started visiting the ship in greater and greater numbers to give back the little objects they had stolen. As they continued to pilfer, Kane took hostage several Eskimo women from a neighboring village (Anoritooq, Cape Inglefield). He drove them back to the ship with their hands bound and, ignoring their piteous cries, their songs, or *ayaya,* of despair, locked them up for five days—the Eskimo period of mourning—in the dark hold. Kane maintained that this was a necessary show of force, as the troubled expedition was in fact at the mercy of these "primitive" hunters. They were clearly only waiting for the death of the ship's occupants to take possession of its vast trove of wood and iron. Kane was equally resolute when it came to his own men. He hid his face in his fur clothing so as not to be recognized and, having reached the igloos, suddenly pulled a gun from his sleeve to arrest Godfrey, who had deserted to Etah, and handcuffed him in front of the terrified Inuit.

But how were they to hide the distress of the party aboard the *Advance* from the inquisitive Eskimos? It was clear that the matter of provisions had been mishandled. Yet by whom if not by Kane himself? Within a few months (in fact, starting the first winter), the men's gums had started to bleed, their bodies to weaken, and their joints to ache. The first to die was Baker, on 7 April 1854. A short time later the cook Pierre Schubert, a French-Canadian, died following the amputation of his foot, complicated by a deplorable state of health. He was heard to hum popular airs by Béranger up to his last hour. Curiously, the Americans proved to be poor hunters, though the country is full of game. In two years, these twenty men managed to kill only four bears, one walrus, and six seals. Their diet was otherwise one of scarcity and famine: "Better organized hunting could have augmented these figures by an untold amount," wrote Kane afterward. In the meantime, the members of the expedition grew weak and lost all their reserves of energy. Unable to shake off their Western dietary habits, they refused to eat even the Arctic hare, which they fed to their dogs. The daily ration for ten men, in November 1854, was reduced to six pounds of flour, six ounces of dried fruit, three pints of molasses, five pints of rice, and one ounce of butter; the sick also received four ounces of fox meat. Kane was the only man to eat the rats that infested the depths of the hold. Who would have imagined? The rats that Hendrik shot with a bow in the bottom of the hold proved excellent for his health: despite his generally weak constitution, Kane was the fittest of them all. "The rats saved my life," he said.

His sense of justice, and the authority he managed to retain over the Eskimos, allowed him, on 15 September 1854, to negotiate the first treaty ever made with the Inuit in their long history. "We concluded a veritable treaty with these Esquimaux—a race of the greatest interest," he wrote in his official report to the U.S. Secretary of the Navy.[5]

Igloo discovered three miles from the *Advance*. The entrance to these sandstone and sod constructions consists of a long corridor in two sections, thinner toward the outside.

3) Before setting out by sled, he looked for a long time at the portrait of Franklin, even (according to his officers) holding conversation with it.

4) This is a good moment to denounce the inappropriate use of journal entries. It would be horribly wrong to enshrine this caricature of Kane. Phrases from private journals should only be used with extreme care. Unfortunately, the history of the Arctic is too often written with sprinklings of little anecdotes, lifted out of context in a spirit of denigration.

5) A strong memory of this treaty was retained. "Good doctor Kane," said Pualuna, Imina, and Sakaeunnguaq, my Eskimo companions during the winter of 1950. Pualuna, the eldest of the three, was born in 1872.

Pullat, a traditional Inuit fox trap. The heaviest stone, which topples when the fox tries to grab the meat inside, falls on the animal. It blocks the entrance, imprisoning the fox, who dies of cold and hunger if it is not already crushed. In April 1969, the Inuit encouraged me to film a trap that was possibly still in use (Herbert Island, north coast). Steel traps came in during Peary's last expeditions (1892-1895).

The open polar sea

Kane continued to follow his dream, though the ice held his ship fast. Contrary to his expectations, the water from the nearby river did not make the sea melt in July 1854. He continued to believe that farther north, beyond the anarchic barriers of hummocked ice, an ice-free ocean surrounded the north pole. A boat was always carried on his sledding expeditions. With four dogs bought from the Eskimos at Etah (those he had brought from Southern Greenland had died suddenly and unexpectedly of an epidemic disease—as sometimes happens), and despite the scurvy that kept half his crew in their sick-beds, despite the death of three shipmates, the amputations suffered by several others, the general fear and anxiety, he organized a new excursion toward the north on 25 April 1854. To show its importance, he joined it himself. New setback. He returned on 4 May with a frozen foot. Then, from 14 to 20 May, he was struck down with typhoid fever and lay at death's door. Barely recovered, on 20 May, he organized another sortie to the west, with Hayes and Godfrey. They returned after making the first exploration of Ellesmere Island as far north as Cape Frazer (79° 43' north). Failure again. This time it was not the cold that defeated his men but the intense light; unequipped with the slitted snow goggles of the Inuit, his men had burned their eyes in the bright glare. In June 1854, Kane sent out a third two-man expedition of William Morton and Hans Hendrik to make directly for the north pole. "It is my last arrow," wrote Kane. This excursion explored the south of Washington Land as far as Cape Jackson in late June. Morton discovered an area of open water at the cape he named Cape Jefferson. On 24 June, the two men reached the northernmost point yet reached by an expedition (latitude 80° 35' north), near Cape Constitution, where they found a new polynya, or area of open water.

At their return on 10 July, Kane exulted: "I can say that I have led an expedition whose results will remain eternally in the memories of men . . . The proof of an iceless polar sea? Here it is!" A romantic representation of it would appear in the sketches and illustration of Kane's second book, *Arctic Explorations* (1856): an open sea furrowed with powerful waves, free of ice as far as the horizon—a lake on which one might sail to the North Pole.

How the Inuit supply themselves with fresh water in the igloo. The oil is made from seal blubber, and the wick from plant matter. The slab is of stone, and the container of seal skin, with a bone rim.

Hans Hendrik, Morton's travel companion and fellow eyewitness, tried to moderate these hasty conclusions: "*Sikou, sikou suak!*" ("Ice, much ice, everywhere!"). But what weight did a native's word carry? Kane paid so little attention to Hendrik's testimony that he and his companions, Hayes in particular, long spoke of the "open polar sea." Petermann, the German, could only corroborate the discovery. An armchair geographer, he wrote magisterially that it confirmed his own theory of a warm sea surrounding the North Pole. [6]

A scientific station

A good observer and draftsman, capable and alert, Kane also proved a geographer and acute observer. He recorded everything every day: ice, vegetation, weather, native houses, customs . . . The *Advance* had become a scientific station, the northernmost of its time. Data from the observatory near the ship were collected several times a day with great precision. The measurements and daily observations of the environment (meteorological, magnetic, oceanographic, botanical, and ornithological) would supply the material for three large volumes published by the Smithsonian Institution and the U.S. Navy. The first census of the Polar Eskimo group was summarily conducted: eight villages, one hundred and forty souls. Yet the numbers are not certain: Carl Petersen, the interpreter, counted the population from Cape York to Etah at one hundred and twenty-four. The discrepancy is hard to account for. Did not Kane's party live in close relations with this isolated people for two years? They depended on them for their survival. And among the Inuit, everyone knows everyone from Cape York to Etah. The Eskimos provided the whites with meat, dog sled teams, and furs, according to the terms of their treaty. But Kane was neither an ethnographer nor a demographer, and his records are no more than the exact formulation of his impressions. The "social sciences" were not yet conducted with the rigor evident in his studies of weather and magnetism. Why bother to make precise observations when there was as yet no methodology or certainty in the study of "primitive man"? Though a doctor and a cultivated man, Kane was never very precise as an ethnographer. Nor were the other members of his expedition. Observations were derived from anecdotes. The reports of the navy officers accompanying Captain John Ross were infinitely more accurate and credible.

Kane records that the Eskimos had virtually no wood or iron, no bows and no kayaks. This is surprising, since this egalitarian and communitarian group had been in contact, at least through intermediaries, with Cape York and its whalers since 1818-1819. True, the Inuit are governed by taboos. Conservative and cautious, they kept their distance from any innovation not sanctioned by tradition. They basically lived off seal, walrus, bear, and especially birds, either fresh or gamy. The millions of auks that nested in the Precambrian sandstone cliffs formed the basis of their diet. Hunting caribou and fishing for salmon remained under taboo. Kane's notes concern Etah, the village farthest (four to six days' sled journey) from Cape York, where wood and iron had been obtained from whalers for thirty years, though never in great quantities. [7]. However, Kane records that harpoon shafts were starting to be made of pieces of wood placed side by side and laced together, and that some knife blades were made from the barrel hoops used on ships. The tips of certain harpoon heads were made of imported steel, cunningly riveted.

Though Kane was a medical doctor, he conducted no medical examinations. There are no remarks on the physiology or the pathology of the Eskimos, no analysis of the native pharmacopoeia, no mention of hibernal amenorrhea. [8] Nor did he make any study of the nocturnal vision of the Inuit. Kane was blind and deaf in this area, as were many of his contemporaries; he collected no legends, gathered no sociocultural data. He ignored the realm of the sacred. His eye was profoundly subjective and selective. Like his companions, he was immediately struck by the material poverty of the Eskimo and their skill as hunters, but he never went beyond superficial observations: they were "dirty"; they gesticulated constantly; they thought "together." He made much of their larcenous habits, their ability to eat raw meat. He admired the Inuit but did not "get" them. Yet he came after James Cook, La Pérouse, Bougainville, Darwin, and Diderot's *Supplement to the Voyage of Bougainville,* a dissertation on cultural differences and the civilization of savage peoples. The accounts and works of Kane's fellow expedition members show similar lacunae. The Dane Carl Petersen, who lived for a long time in Upernavik, south of Melville Bay, confused the customs of southern and northern Greenland and believed that all these peoples were fairly inconsistent in their beliefs.

As the year 1854 progressed, further misfortunes befell the expedition. But Kane would not give up: he believed the

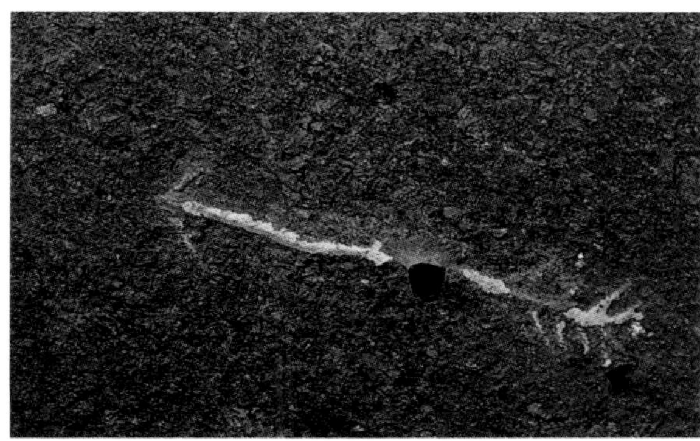

A message drop, drilled into the rock and signposted by Kane, at the spot where he abandoned his ship. In April 1951, I was able to ascertain that it contained no message. A white among the Inuits, I was carried by this society—unlike Kane. Kane saw his energy sapped by the "prison aspect" of communal life. His group, with its white man's clothes and food, with its domineering certainty, was grafted onto the environment and could only be rejected by it.

expedition would simply have to transcend its difficulties. Not a sailor, he put the goal of the expedition ahead of the safety of the ship; yet as captain (if a jumped-up one), he long hesitated over whether to abandon the ship he was responsible for. In 1855 his thinking became more complex: the expedition was wherever the expedition leader was, with the ship or without it.

Mutiny on the *Advance*

Before the second winter (1854-1855), Kane himself made a difficult and courageous voyage to the south with Hans Hendrik and six men to get help from the whaling ships in Melville Bay. He knew the area for having explored it with DeHaven in 1851 on the *Advance,* a ship whose fate was certainly intertwined with his. This voyage—which represented their last chance, and was a failure—was accomplished by hauling a boat along the ice with great effort and launching it wherever open channels appeared along the coast. He wanted to reach Beechey Island, where he might find the expedition's auxiliary ship, the *Belcher.* But he got no farther than the Cape Parry area. The ice in this year of early cold—Kane saw a return of the Little Ice Age—had already turned into an impassable barrier.

They faced the prospect of another winter in the north.

The hazards of the trail: hummocks and ice barriers.

ON THE FRAILTY OF TESTIMONY

Extract from an interview given to the New York Times on 27 October 1855 by William Morton, steward on the *Advance.*

"The ship was abundantly provisioned. The menu was varied. . . . The food was not only nourishing but tasty. We often hunted walrus . . . the animals were killed when they came up to their breathing holes . . . we killed a great number of them. No alcohol, except in cases of illness . . . we never had scurvy . . . only a small number of deaths on board. Esquimaux men and women frequently came aboard the ship, where we fed and boarded them . . ."

6) I can only be surprised at such exaggerations. I visited the spot in May 1951 and saw the "polynya" at Cape Jackson. The open water looked to me at that season to be no more than what one might expect to find near a large cape due to the action of the currents. Kennedy Channel was entirely iced over as far as the eye could see. Nonetheless, Kane named this pool of open water the Kennedy "channel," convinced that it was the open polar sea.

7) This according to Inglefield's observations in 1852.

8) Women of the Polar Eskimo group menstruate little or not at all during the winter, according to studies done in 1893. Given the group's isolation, these observations would also hold good for earlier times; they were verified again in 1951. Possible causes might include: lack of sunlight, the predominantly meat diet, and demographic isolation.

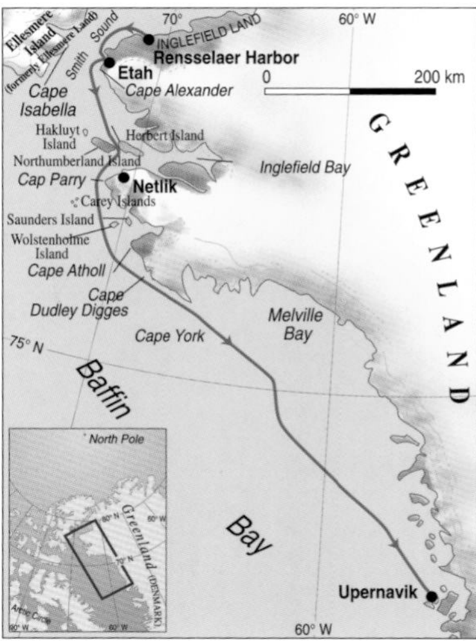

August 1854. Most of the officers and a portion of the crew deserted the ship. Their southward flight would end in failure.

The expedition's return in two ship's boats. The operation was masterfully conducted by Kane (19 June to 6 August 1855).

"It is horrible—yes, that is the word—to look forward to another year of disease and darkness to be met without fresh food and fuel," he wrote.

But he was to experience worse than the hardships of winter: when he returned to the ship on 10 August 1854 he was humiliated to find that all the scientists and officers, tired of his authoritarianism and terrified at the prospect of a second winter, were proposing to leave the ship. This quasi-mutiny, aggravated by the failure of his mission to get help, resolved itself on 28 August with the "flight" of half his men toward the south in hopes of finding a whaling ship to rescue them in Melville Bay. Actually Kane had held a secret vote (only five of his men chose to stand by him) and agreed to let the others go so as to avoid an open rebellion and maintain some semblance of authority over his mutinous men. He negotiated with certain of his men to stay, sometimes using amiable words and sometimes threats, while communicating with others only through the written word . . .

The ringleader of the mutiny, according to Kane, seems to have been the Dane Christian Ohlsen. Kane required him to sign a document saying that from the moment he left the ship his fate was no longer in the hands of the expedition. Suddenly cautious, Ohlsen refused to sign this document testifying to his desertion, preferring the lesser evil: staying with the *Advance*. In all, eight men—only one an officer, Henry Brooks—remained on board. And the other eight men? "They have left the expedition, and may God's blessing go with them, for they carry not the respect of good men. . . . They are deserters in act and in thought. . . . To argue with such base and surly spirits would be to abase oneself," he confided to his private journal. And it proved that, despite a solemn vow to the contrary, they raided the emergency stores left on the trip north at Littleton Island.

Millions of auks, *Uria lomvia* and *Plautus alle*. With these the Eskimos made birdskin anoraks and *kiviaks* for the winter.

Four months later, the prudent and energetic Kane was to have his victory. The eight desperate deserters had asked the Eskimos of Natsilivik, some two hundred miles south of the *Advance*, to lead them back to the ship.

Starving, the deserters had for weeks been eating mosses scraped from rocks and scraps of meat and blubber obtained through barter from the Eskimos of a neighboring camp. And though the Eskimos had been shamefully deceived and robbed by them earlier, they led the deserters back to their ship. [9] Kane greeted the mutineers, who arrived dazed by suffering and humiliation, with contempt.

The two groups would now live side by side for weeks. According to the regulations laid down by Doctor Kane, the scientists and officers who had deserted could no longer take part in research activities. They were henceforth only guests of the expedition. Kane nobly performed the bulk of the daily work—what health in this invalid!—and helped the men who had remained loyal so that all the scientific programs could continue without disruption. He attempted to dispel the anguish felt by his men. How would they return to the United States? He proposed evacuating the ship in July 1855.

In fact, the *Advance* was evacuated earlier, on 20 May, because another misfortune had struck it: Hans Hendrik, good and loyal Hendrik, had himself deserted. In love with a young Eskimo woman, Meqru, he fled by dog sled when Kane sent him out to buy fresh meat in Etah. Far from this group in moral limbo, he wanted finally to live freely, intensely, with his Great Ancestors, the Polar Inuit, the Inughuit.

20 May: Kane, whose sense of theater was well developed, assembled the crew in front of the ship, now a ghost ship trapped by ice whose superstructure had been used for fuel during the coldest winter months. Solemnly, Kane read a passage from the Bible. A prayer was spoken. Franklin's portrait was removed from its frame and wrapped in a piece of canvas. Then Kane made a speech, and every man signed the document stating the decision to abandon the ship. The flag was hauled and lowered, and a procession marched around the ship. "Augusta," the painted mermaid on the prow, was detached and set in the bow of one of the boats, the *Hope*. The retreat began. The two boats, *Hope* and *Faith*, were hauled with great effort over the ice to Etah. This forty-mile portage from Rensselaer Bay to Etah with two boats carrying more than 1500 pounds of food and four sick men was masterfully handled by Kane. Dog sleds shuttled back and forth to carry the loads forward. During this time Christian Ohlsen died, his bladder pierced by a sled runner. When the explorers reached Etah on 18 June, the Eskimos greeted them with joy, and Kane gave them the *Advance*.

Life on board the *Advance.* From left to right: Amos Bonsall, farmer and simple seaman, who, though he had ties to Kane's family, abandoned him tearfully on 18 August 1854; Henry Brooks, carrying a gun, the ship's first mate, who remained loyal to Kane and would die in New York of exhaustion and scurvy fifteen months after the expedition's leader; Kane, in a thoughtful mood; Doctor Isaac Israel Hayes, who, in a moment of despair would abandon—or more truly, desert—the expedition with half its crew and all of its officers but one; William Morton, cabin boy and Kane's main confidant, who remained faithful to him (he set out in 1871 with Hall as second mate aboard the *Polaris*).

It constituted a great mine of wood, iron, and cloth. [10] Ever theatrical, Kane made a show of giving two particularly friendly Eskimos one of his highly coveted scalpels, *savik* ("iron, knife"), which had served to perform amputations on his shipmates. All the men now took their places in the two boats; they wore new clothes (finally on the Eskimo model). The expedition headed south on 19 June to attempt the dreaded traverse of Melville Bay. Open water was before them, the famous polynya so well known to whalers in the area between Cape York and Baffin Island. This year the open water extended far north of Melville Bay, to where Kane had failed in his search for a rescue ship in August 1854 and the mutineers likewise the following September.

This time Kane succeeded and did so magnificently. The two boats with their sick and infirm men crossed the vast and dangerous bay. On 6 August 1855, after unimaginable hardships and dangers, they finally reached the first Danish outpost at Upernavik. An American ship carried them soon after to the United States, where they were welcomed as heroes on 11 October 1855. It was then that Kane learned that Franklin had died aboard his ship on 11 June 1847 and that the remains of several of his crew had finally been found . . . south of King William Island, along what would become the route of the Northwest Passage. Kane, off in the north of Greenland, had in truth not had the slightest chance of finding him.

Kane and his stereotypes

Only just back, Kane worked night and day, investing himself even more than on the trail, to write his simple and sincere account of the expedition, *Arctic Explorations.* [11] This detailed and romantic book, marvelously illustrated with the author's sketches, would be the most successful travel account in the United States in 1856. But conflicts, rivalries, and betrayals were edited out, as always in expedition accounts. Twenty thousand copies were sold before publication, and 65,000 copies of its first edition. Yet though Kane avoided openly criticizing the members of his expedition who deserted, the public was perfectly able to read between the lines. Isaac Hayes was never forgiven for his "cowardice" toward Kane and would suffer from it all his life. The same disapproval was extended to the Dane Petersen and to William Godfrey. When the two wrote books critical of Kane after his death, public opinion remained with Kane. The cold condescension toward these men that can be read in the pages of Kane's private journal, now at Stanford University, is the best posthumous reply. [12] With time judgment falls on actions. And even in the frozen wastes of the Arctic, actions are not without their consequences.

Kane's book would forever fix in the minds of readers an image of the Eskimo as a savage who was uncouth, impervious to progress, and threatened with extinction. The

Kane's journal: sketch of the first meeting of the Etah Eskimos with white men. The Eskimo brandishes a spear in front of Kane, who is also armed (a fact he would omit from his account).

9) See the following chapter on Hayes.

10) Unfortunately, the Eskimos were not able to benefit from it for long. After being ransacked, the ship apparently drifted off. No mention of it survives in legends and stories. Thus are important events submerged in popular memory.

11) Two volumes, totaling 900 pages, with 300 engravings after his own drawings, and 18 scientific appendices of some 170 pages. "This book has been my coffin," wrote Kane, exhausted. This first book about American Arctic exploration, published in Philadelphia in 1857, would awaken this great nation to its responsibilities in the Arctic.

12) These men perhaps had cause to be afraid of what would be discovered in Kane's logbook. The pages concerning this tragic period of the voyage have been ripped out, as I ascertained from the copy in the New York Public Library. And when Kane learned that his sailing master, John Wilson, was planning to publish a book, Kane bought the manuscript for $350: the account was never seen again. The two men hated each other, but Kane preferred for it to be in silence.

irony is that it was the Americans whose behavior, in that environment, was the more primitive: hauling sleds by hand, succumbing to the cold, experiencing delirium at -40° F in the month of March, and being incapable of survival in that country despite having guns. [13] While the Eskimos had for centuries been happily living their culture, though they had neither bows nor kayaks, and were thus able to save the explorers from certain death.

It never occurred to Kane or his readers that the Eskimos might have a religion, a social organization, to constitute a unified people, to have a sense of poetry and a vast imaginative world, to love, to suffer, and that the "conservatism" with which they were reproached was in fact a defensive reaction. Only one tenth of the book is concerned with the Polar Eskimos! Given their narrow focus, it is not surprising that the expedition members never wondered what the Eskimos thought of them!

Beyond the lack of communication that existed between the Westerners and the Eskimos, there was a lack of communication between the classes on board the *Advance*. Kane's writings and those of his two shipmates show a rigid hierarchy: "Deference toward the officers," snickered the mutineer William Godfrey. "Absolute subordination to the officers in command," read Kane's regulations, in emulation of Navy discipline, but the effect was only to aggravate conflicts. Adding to the usual tensions of men confined within close quarters for months on end like rats in a trap was the violence of the two seamen from Brooklyn: Blake and Godfrey.

The ***Faith***, one of the two rescue boats built by Kane to bring the explorers back to the United States.

The stevedore-corsair

Believing himself to have been dishonored in Kane's published account, Godfrey responded with an account of his own, which is both interesting and little-known. He doesn't deny his insolence, but he reveals the personality of a corsair, incapable of adjusting to a silly routine, of submitting to military regimentation. Certain pages of his book are surprising. They showed him to have astonishing physical reserves and also a rare capacity for adapting to native ways—qualities that were not put to use. A more flexible and more open discipline should have been adopted, one that encouraged the individual spirit of adventure. Godfrey's case should have been pondered. At the height of the winter, in March 1854, feeling that he did not fit in, Godfrey set off to live with the Eskimos of Etah and Northumberland Island. He traveled the thirty dangerous miles between Aannartoq (where the *Advance* was anchored) and Etah on foot in thirty hours with the temperature at -40° F. Having managed to be accepted by the Eskimos—the Eskimo women in particular, who fed him meat "from mouth to mouth"—he went from one camp to another. More a seaman-stevedore-corsair than an explorer, brutal but seductive, he was the first white to be accepted into the intimacy of the Inughuit. Unschooled in literary expression, he would not relate in his book the one hundredth part of what he knew of this people. Like Hans Hendrik later, no one thought to question him . . . Anthropologists! Here are our first, mute witnesses.

Thus despite his intelligence Kane remained a prisoner of his class prejudices. He could not imagine an expedition that brought men together on an equal footing to engage in a common task. If he had delegated his authority to some extent—but was this an option with the expedition on the brink of mutiny?—if he had made an arrangement with the Eskimos to hunt for the *Advance* under the direction of a man of Godfrey's stamp, some of the expedition's more tragic episodes could certainly have been averted. Wilson, Kane's sailing master, quickly took exception to Kane, finding him a gentleman amateur, as one learns from reading his private journal, a document I found profoundly moving and saddening. After a few months of Arctic winter, these poor men started acting as though they were prisoners on the ship: they thought of nothing but eating and sleeping. Blind in their suffering and certain of their ethnic superiority, these whites had the greatest difficulty see-

13) Having traveled over the same region as Kane during April-June 1951 as part of a small expedition (four Inuit accompanied me) with equipment substantially similar to Kane's, I can testify to the ease, the joy even, with which I conducted my cartographic and geomorphological work. I can see myself at the foot of capes Grinnell and Ingersoll with their parallel sandstone striations of red, yellow, and ocher. I see, as though it were yesterday, the broad sweep of "Spring Bay" (Rensselaer). Kutsikitsoq, my companion, encouraged me, on a sunny morning when we were tearing into a seal's half-raw ribs and telling each other stories about our very different lives, to spend a year in this very place, far from the Inuit. As I watched, hares lolloped on the snowy slopes, drinking in the sunlight . . . A year of brotherhood with Kutsikitsoq and Natuk . . . I have to confess that this warm and impulsive movement on the part of my old friend made me vacillate. Sakaeunnguaq, sixteen years later, proposed the same thing to me: to stay with him at Anoritooq, not far from there, at Cape Inglefield. Apparently there is a tendency among these nomads to isolate themselves for several months with the friend who is dearest to them.

14) Margaret Fox tried to obtain recognition as his widow. Judge Kane intervened, using his influence. Margaret suffered a nervous breakdown, then lapsed into alcoholism.

ing the grandeur and beauty of the ice expanses, the rich fauna of the desert surrounding them, and their unbelievable luck to be taking part in the expedition, which would be the challenge of their lives. But just who were these whites? Conquerors who were all the haughtier for being ignorant and racist, furiously hunting down the last "savages with feathers" on the Great Plains; and they could only demonstrate once again in the country of the "savages with furs" how sterile intelligence becomes when it is elitist and racist.

Kane mastered his body, overcame the cold, the ice, the disparagement of his crew, mutiny, and the occasional hostility of the Eskimos. But men have their secrets. This Arctic hero proved unable to decide on his own life once back in New York. A few weeks before his departure to Greenland, this affection-starved man had fallen in love with the nineteen-year-old spiritualist medium Margaret Fox, whose table-rapping and spirit-calling was the talk of New York City. Victor Hugo was holding conversations on Guernsey Island with Julius Caesar and Jesus Christ at this same time. In a flight of romanticism before his departure Kane had led Fox to the family crypt, where he had eloquently expressed his passion for her. Playing the part of Pygmalion, he paid for the education of this impoverished young woman, whose parents were alcoholics; and he encouraged her to give up spiritualism. Deeply in love, he had her portrait painted by an Italian artist a few weeks before his departure and hung it on the wall of his cabin.

Kane, the romantic

Immediately on his return, Kane proposed to Margaret Fox. It was the talk of the town, and fodder for the tabloids. The two were that year's star personalities. But Judge Kane was vigilant. He refused to consent to this marriage with a commoner. Dutifully, Elisha acceded to his father. Victorian morality was spared. The bold explorer even begged Margaret to sign a document establishing that he had always "respected" her. Humiliated and contemptuous, she signed the document, in tears at the affront. Poor Kane, a prisoner to the ice inside . . .

But his heart was good. Tormented, he returned to see Margaret numerous times whenever he came to New York. Behind his father's back, he contracted a commonlaw marriage with Margaret Fox before witnesses, by mutual and public declaration.

Tireless, Kane put his private life in order, then, a national hero, hastily prepared a new expedition, a third Arctic voyage. But Fate had decided otherwise. On 16 June 1857, in Cuba where he had gone to convalesce on his return from meeting the admirable and obstinate Lady Franklin in London, Kane suddenly died. [14]

The consequences of Elisha Kent Kane's work were considerable. This first American expedition made a sensation and opened the eyes of the New World to the Arctic. Kane's book was widely read and revealed new horizons to the general public. Peary and Amundsen were no doubt greatly influenced and inspired by Kane. His deeds would probably have echoed more widely had the Civil War not eclipsed his message. It would be another sixteen years before the American government grasped the geopolitical importance of the Far North and, with Charles Francis Hall in 1871, organized the first official U.S. expedition to the North Pole. ■

Overleaf,
the crew of the *Terror*, under the command of G. Back, remove stores and lower the boats from the ship, which is in dire straits in Hudson Bay off Southampton Island, 15 March 1837. The ship was ultimately saved and returned to England after many adventures.

The *Advance*, trapped by ice, was abandoned on 20 May 1855.

Kane's view of the Inuit

The Polar Eskimos discover the fragility of the whites

Dr. Kane's medical kit. He operated without anesthesia, as when he amputated the frozen toes of Dr. Hayes in December 1854, on Hayes's return with the other deserters. Kane performed this task in a professional manner, though inwardly contemptuous of the deserter.

We were watching in the morning at Baker's death-bed, when one of our deck-watch, who had been cutting ice for the melter, came hurrying down into the cabin with the report, "People hollaing ashore!" I went up, followed by as many as could mount the gangway; and there they were, on all sides of our rocky harbor, dotting the snow-shores and emerging from the blackness of the cliffs,—wild and uncouth, but evidently human beings.[16]

As we gathered on the deck, they rose upon the more elevated fragments of the land-ice, standing singly and conspicuously like the figures in a tableau of the opera, and distributing themselves around almost in a half-circle. They were vociferating as if to attract our attention, or perhaps only to give vent to their surprise; but I could make nothing out of their cries, except "Hoah, ha, ha!" and "Ka, kaah! ka, kaah!" repeated over and over again.

There was light enough for me to see that they brandished no weapons, and were only tossing their heads and arms about in violent gesticulations. A more unexcited inspection showed us, too, that their numbers were not as great nor their size as Patagonian as some of us had been disposed to fancy at first. In a word, I was satisfied that they were natives of the country; and, calling Petersen from his bunk to be my interpreter, I proceeded, unarmed and waving my open hands, toward a stout figure who made himself conspicuous and seemed to have a greater number near him than the rest. He evidently understood the movement, for he at once, like a brave fellow, leaped down upon the floe and advanced to meet me fully half-way.

He was nearly a head taller than myself, extremely powerful and well-built, with swarthy complexion and piercing black eyes.[17] His dress was a hooded *capôte,* or jumper of mixed white and blue fox-pelts, arranged and booted trousers of white bear-skin, which at the end of the foot were made to terminate with the claws of the animal.

I soon came to an understanding with this gallant diplomat. As soon as we began talking, his companions, probably receiving signals from him, flocked in and surrounded us; but we had no difficulty in making them know positively that they must remain where they were, while Metek went with me on board the ship. This gave me the advantage of negotiating, with an important hostage.

Although this was the first time he had ever seen a white man, he went with me fearlessly his companions staying behind on the ice. Hickey gave them our greatest delicacies—slices of good wheat bread, and corned pork, with exorbitant lumps of white sugar—but they refused to touch them.[18] They evidently had no apprehension of open violence from us. I found afterward that several among them were singly a match for the white bear and the walrus, and they thought us a very pale-faced crew.

Being satisfied with my interview in the cabin, I sent out word that the rest might be admitted to the ship; and, although they, of course, could not know how their chief had been dealt with, some nine or ten of them followed readily. Others, in the meantime, as if disposed to give us their company, brought up from behind the land-ice as many as fifty-six fine dogs, with their sledges, and secured them within two hundred feet of the brig, driving their lances into the ice, and picketing the dogs to them by the seal-skin traces. The animals understood the operation perfectly, and lay down as it commenced. The sledges were made up of small fragments of porous bone, admirably knit together by thongs of hide; the runners, which glis-

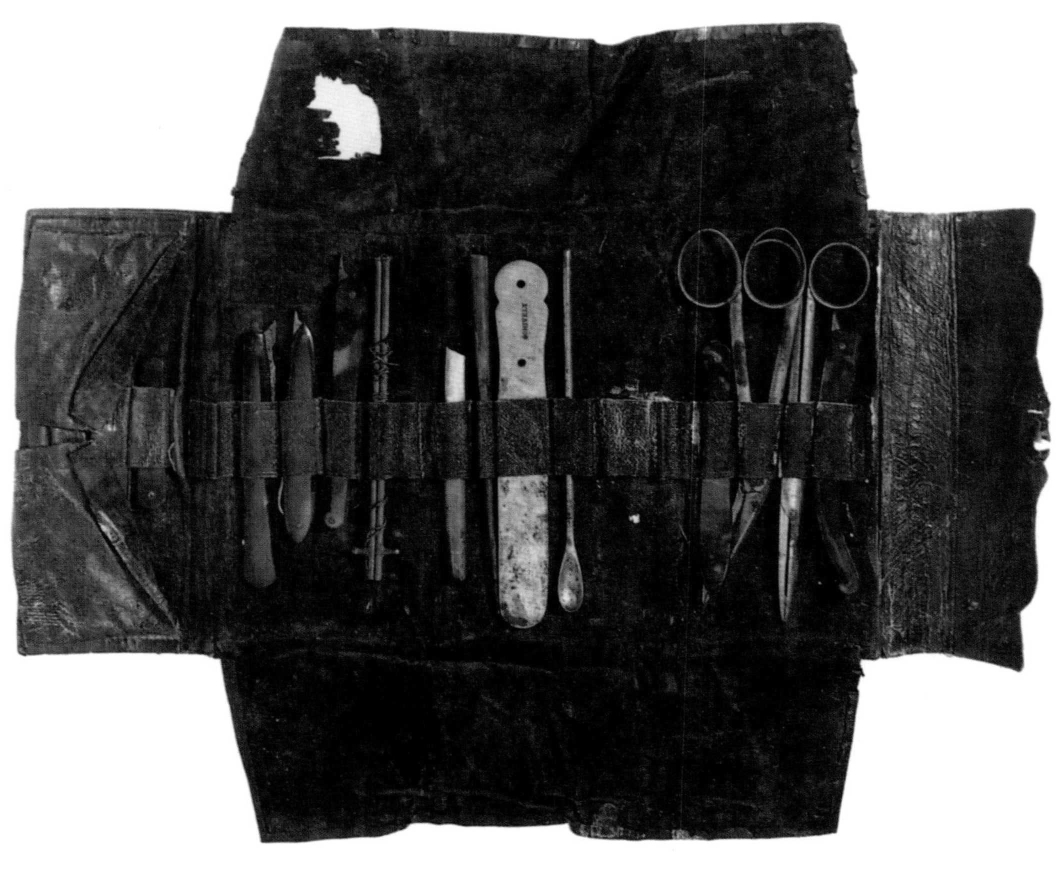

16) Aannartoq, or Rensselaer Bay, north of Etah. Kane's first encounter with the Polar Eskimos. It seems very likely that these hunters had already seen white men. The whalers put in every spring at Cape York, some even in the Carey Islands. In 1849-1850, a whaler, the North Star, is known to have wintered at Uummannaq with eight men on board after a dangerous drift in the Melville Bay ice pack—and Uummannaq therefore received the name North Star Bay. This was the first time that white men had wintered in Polar Eskimo territory. The sights witnessed by the few Eskimos who came on board (ten or so) was broadcast, in their communitarian way, throughout the group, which consisted of some forty families between Cape York and Etah. This would explain why the Etah Eskimos showed no fear of Kane.

17) Kane measured 5'3". The Eskimo in question was abnormally tall. The height of male Eskimos in 1909 ranged from 5' and 5'4", and female Eskimos were between 4'8" and 4'11". This man may have been of mixed race, as a result of passing encounters with whalers at Cape York from 1819 on; the genes might have spread through the population of forty families in a generation thanks to the practice of wife exchange.

18) It was only very gradually—some fifty years later, when the survivors from Hall's expedition were in Qallunaalik (north of Etah) in 1872-1873—that the Eskimos grew used to and then adopted, often with a passion: sugar, tea, and coffee (in that order). Tobacco

Cookpot and blubber lamp made of soapstone. Placed above the fringe of flames along the lamp's outer lip, the pot is used to prepare the *qajoq* (blood soup with chunks of more or less raw seal or walrus meat). Height of the pot: approximately 16 inches. Height of the lamp: approximately 8.5 inches. It is impossible to be absolutely certain that these objects were brought back by Kane.

Sled runner made entirely of bone segments lashed together with sealskin thongs. The runner's shoe is made of seven pieces of walrus ivory attached to the sled by a runnel bored into the ivory so that the lashing is nowhere exposed on the outside. Same technique and materials as used in 1818. (Smithsonian Institution)

tened like burnished steel, were of highly polished ivory, obtained from the tusks of the walrus.

Table manners and politics

They borrowed from us an iron pot and some melted water, and parboiled a couple of pieces of walrus-meat; but the real *pièce de résistance*, some five pounds a head, they preferred to eat raw. Yet there was something of the *gourmet* in their way of taking mouthfuls of beef and blubber. Slices of each, or rather strips, were eaten together or in strict alternation. [19]

They did not eat all at once, but each man when and as often as the impulse prompted. Each slept after eating, his raw chunk lying beside him on the buffalo-skin; and, as he woke, the first act was to eat, and the next to sleep again. They did not lie down, but slumbered away in a sitting posture, with the head declined upon the breast, some of them snoring famously.

April 26, Wednesday.—McGary went yesterday with the leading sledge; and, as Brooks is still laid up from the amputation, I leave Ohlsen in charge of the brig. He has my instructions in full, largely about the treatment of the natives.

These Esquimaux must be watched carefully, at the same time that they are to be dealt with kindly, though with a strict enforcement of our police-regulations and some caution as to the freedom with which they may come on board. No punishments must be permitted, either of them or in their presence, and no resort to fire arms unless to repel a serious attack. I have given orders, however, that if the contingency does occur there shall be no firing overhead. The power of the gun with a savage is in his notion of its infallibility. You may spare bloodshed by killing a dog or even wounding him; but in no event should you throw away your ball. It is neither politic nor humane. [20]

Life in an Eskimo igloo

The hut or igloë at Anoatok was a single rude elliptical apartment, built not unskillfully of stone, the outside lined with sods. At its farther end a rude platform, also of stone, was lifted about a foot above the entering floor. The roof formed something of a curve: it was composed of flat stones, remarkably large and heavy, arranged so as to overlap each other, but apparently without any intelligent application of the principle of the arch. The height of this cave-like abode barely permitted one to sit upright. Its length was eight feet, its breadth seven feet, and an expansion of the tunneled entrance made an appendage of perhaps two feet more. [21]

The true winter entrance is called the *tossut*. It is a walled tunnel, ten feet long, and so narrow that a man can hardly crawl along it. It opens outside below the level of the igloë, into which it leads by a gradual ascent.

Time had done its work on the igloë of Anoatok, as among the palatial structures of more southern deserts. The entire front of the dome had fallen in, closing up the tossut, and forcing us to enter at the solitary window above it. The breach was large enough to admit a sledge-team; but our Arctic comrades showed no anxiety to close it up. Their clothes saturated with the freezing water of the floes, these iron men gathered themselves round the blubber-fire and steamed away in apparent comfort. The only departure from their practiced routine, which the bleak night and open roof seemed to suggest to them, was that they did not strip themselves naked before coming into the hut, and

was immediately appreciated by them.

19) Ethnographic detail of the description. An anthropology of the gesture is already being prefigured. The quantified nutritional data are valuable: 5 pounds of meat and blubber per man per day during the winter. Elsewhere Kane states that the Eskimos ate 8 to 10 pounds of meat per day and a half gallon of a blood and broth soup. In 1950-1951, I noted that the Eskimos ate four to six pounds of meat per day in the winter, of which one half was fat (the figures varied with the circumstances), and drank 2 to 3 liters of tea, coffee, water, and broth per day.

20) The Polar Eskimos only started to be allowed to use firearms sporadically with Bessels in 1872-1873 (Hall's expedition) and extensively with Peary—some seventy-five years after their discovery. The early explorers were concerned to maintain their authority by keeping the use of firearms for themselves. Some conservative Inuit (the shaman Saqqaaq for one, the grandfather of my companion Qaaqutsiaq) refused to use guns, which they believed threatened the group's ecological balance. After 1910-1920, guns were in common use. Ammunition was very scarce during the First War of 1914-1918 at Knud Rasmussen's trading counter, opened in 1910.

21) In 1950-1951, the stones of the igloo were interspersed with chunks of sod. The technology was therefore different than the one described by Kane in 1853. The structure and dimensions of the last

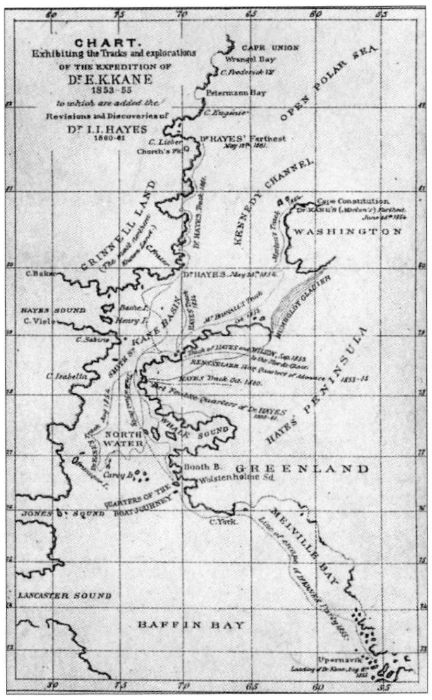

Area explored by Dr. Kane's expedition in 1853-1855. The map also shows the discoveries of Dr. Isaac Hayes (1860-1861).

Kalutunah, wearing his *kapatak* (*qulittaq*).

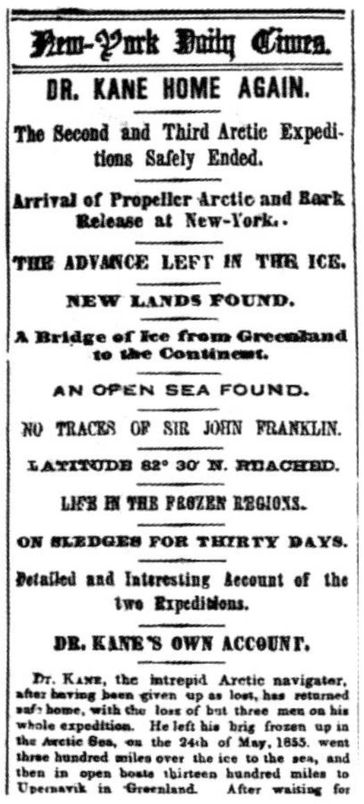

New-York Daily Times.

DR. KANE HOME AGAIN.

The Second and Third Arctic Expeditions Safely Ended.

Arrival of Propeller Arctic and Bark Release at New-York.

THE ADVANCE LEFT IN THE ICE.

NEW LANDS FOUND.

A Bridge of Ice from Greenland to the Continent.

AN OPEN SEA FOUND.

NO TRACES OF SIR JOHN FRANKLIN.

LATITUDE 82° 30' N. REACHED.

LIFE IN THE FROZEN REGIONS.

ON SLEDGES FOR THIRTY DAYS.

Detailed and Interesting Account of the two Expeditions.

DR. KANE'S OWN ACCOUNT.

Dr. Kane, the intrepid Arctic navigator, after having been given up as lost, has returned safe home, with the loss of but three men on his whole expedition. He left his brig frozen up in the Arctic Sea, on the 24th of May, 1855, went three hundred miles over the ice to the sea, and then in open boats thirteen hundred miles to Upernavik in Greenland. After waiting for

The *New York Daily Times* announced the return of Dr. Kane on 12 October 1855. Above the heading "No Traces of Sir John Franklin" is an announcement of the discovery of the open polar sea. The myth refused to die.

OPPOSITE, **saxifrage and Arctic willow,** *Salix arctophylla*. This willow is found on sunny slopes. Its roots grow horizontally at a shallow depth, the ground beneath being permanently frozen to 1500 feet.

hang up their vestments in the air to dry, like a votive offering to the god of the sea.

Their kitchen-implements were even more simple than our own. A rude saucer-shaped cup of seal-skin, to gather and hold water in, was the solitary utensil that could be dignified as table-furniture. A flat stone, a fixture of the hut, supported by other stones just above the shoulder-blade of a walrus—the stone slightly inclined, the cavity of the bone large enough to hold a moss-wick and some blubber—a square block of snow was placed on the stone, and, as the hot smoke circled round it, the seal-skin saucer caught the water that dripped from the edge. They had no vessel for boiling; what they did not eat raw they baked upon a hot stone. A solitary coil of walrus-line, fastened to a movable lance-head (noon-ghak) with the well-worn and well-soaked clothes on their backs, complete the inventory of their effects.

When all the family, with Morton and Hans, were gathered together, the two lamps in full blaze and the narrow hole of entrance covered by a flat stone, the heat became insupportable. Outside, the thermometer stood at 30° below zero; within, 90° above: a difference of one hundred and twenty degrees.

The vermin were not as troublesome as in the Anoatok dormitory, the natives hanging their clothing over the lamp-frames, and lying down to sleep perfectly naked, with the exception of a sort of T bandage, as surgeons call it, of seal-skin, three inches wide, worn by the women as a badge of their sex, and supported by a mere strip around the hips.[22]

A walrus hunt in 1854

Moving gently on, they soon heard the characteristic bellow of a bull awuk . . .

The party now formed in a single file, following in each other's steps; and, guided by an admirable knowledge of ice- topography, wound behind hummocks and ridges in a serpentine approach toward a group of pond-like discolorations, recently frozen ice-spots, but surrounded by firmer and older ice . . .

Now for the marvel of the craft. When the walrus is above water, the hunter is flat and motionless; as he begins to sink, alert and ready for a spring. The animal's head is hardly below the water-line before every man is in a rapid run; and again, as if by instinct, before the beast returns, all are motionless behind protecting knolls of ice. They seem to know beforehand not only the time he will be absent, but the very spot at which he will reappear. In this way, hiding and advancing by turns, Myouk, with Morton at his heels, has reached a plate of thin ice, hardly strong enough to bear them, at the very brink of the water-pool the walrus are curvetting in . . .

Myouk throws his harpoon. Though the awuk is down in a moment, Myouk is running at desperate speed from the scene of his victory, paying off his coil freely, but clutching the end by its loop. He seizes as he runs a small stick of bone, rudely pointed with iron, and by a sudden movement drives it into the ice: to this he secures his line, pressing it down close to the ice-surface with his feet.

Now comes the struggle. The hole is dashed in mad commotion with the struggles of the wounded beast; the line is drawn tight at one moment, the next relaxed: the hunter has not left his station. There is a crash of the ice; and rearing up through it are two walruses, not many yards from where he stands. One of them, the male, is excited and seemingly terrified: the other, the female, collected and vengeful. Down they go again, after one grim survey of the field; and on the instant Myouk has changed his position, carrying his coil with him and fixing it anew.

He has hardly fixed it before the pair have again risen, breaking up an area of ten feet diameter about the very spot he left. As they sink once more he again changes his place. And so the conflict goes on between address and force, till the victim, half exhausted, receives a second wound, and is played like a trout by the angler's reel.[23]

From Etah to Melville Bay: 8 villages, 140 persons

I can already count eight settlements, including about one hundred and forty souls.[24] There are more, perhaps, but certainly not many. Out of these I can number five deaths since our arrival; and I am aware of hardships and disasters encountered by the survivors, which, repeated as they must be in the future, cannot fail to involve a larger mortality. Crime combines with disease and exposure to thin this number: I know of three murders within the past two years; and one infanticide occurred only a few months ago. These facts, which are open to my limited sources of information, cannot, of course, indicate the number of deaths correctly. They confirm, however, a fearful conclusion which these poor wretches have themselves communicated to us,—that they are dying out; not lingeringly, like the American tribes, but so rapidly as to be able to mark within a generation their progress toward extinction . . .

The narrow belt subject to their nomadic range cannot be less than six hundred miles long; and throughout this extent of country every man knows every man. There is not a marriage or a birth or a death that is not talked over and mental-

archaic igloos seen by me in 1950-1951 were the same as for those seen by Kane, though the entrance tunnel to regulate the temperature was longer in 1853: 10.5 feet long (5 to 8 feet in 1950).

22) The Eskimos retained the custom of stripping naked inside the igloo until the beginning of the twentieth century (1910-1920), when many were converted to Christianity. The skin clothes, made damp by perspiration, are hung to dry from the igloo's warm ceiling and above the lamp during the hours of sleep. This is to ensure that one's clothes are always dry, which is vital to the hunter. In archaic times, the Eskimo rarely had any spare clothes (sealskin pants and attili). In 1950 men were sometimes half-naked, keeping on their bearskin pants and their boots; women kept on their foxskin drawers and a cloth shirt, as well as their mid-thigh boots—bare legs would have been immodest. Boots were only removed at night and slid under one's head (the same went for men).

23) A hunting technique that remained unchanged until the advent of the rifle. In 1950-1951, the walrus was still harpooned before being shot, so as not to lose the fatally wounded animal.

24) First census: a population of 140, divided between eight villages. These observations are certainly insufficient on the subject of infanticide. Female infanticide was the rule during periods of famine. Furthermore, any infant was killed whose mother died or who was considered to have an infirmity. This practice was still in vigor for the infirm in 1950. The Eskimos are thought to be primitive in their technology, but their means of demographic regulation is not understood. Their control over their population is not grasped.

ly registered by all. I have a census, exactly confirmed by three separate informants, which enables me to count by name about one hundred and forty souls, scattered along from Kosoak, the Great River at the base of a glacier near Cape Melville, to the wind-loved hut of Anoatok.

Kane placates the Eskimos robbed and humiliated by the whites

They were introduced into the oriental recess of our dormitory—hitherto an unsolved mystery. There, seated on a red blanket, with four pork-fat lamps, throwing an illumination over old worsted damask curtains, hunting knives, rifles, beer-barrels, galley-stove and chronometers, I dealt out to each man five needles, a file, and a stick of wood. To Kalutunah and Shunghu I gave knives and other extras;. and in conclusion spread out our one remaining buffalo close to the stove, built a roaring fire, cooked a hearty supper, and by noonday they were sleeping away in a state of thorough content. I explained to them further that my people did not steal; that the fox-jumpers and boots and sledges were only taken to save their lives; and I thereupon returned them.[25]

Leaving Etah: Kane abandons the Advance

July 18 [1855], Monday The Esquimaux are camped by our side,—the whole settlement of Etah congregated around the "big caldron" of Cape Alexander, to bid us good-bye. There are Metek, and Nualik his wife, our old acquaintance Mrs. Eider-duck, and their five children, commencing with Myouk, my body-guard, and ending with the ventricose little Accomodah. There is Nessark and Anak his wife; and Tellerk the "Right Arm," and Amaulanik his wife; and Sip-su, and Marsumah and Aningnah—and who not? I can name them every one, and they know us as well. We have found brothers in a strange land.

Each one has a knife, or a file, or a saw, or some such treasured keepsake; and the children have a lump of soap, the greatest of all medicines. The merry little urchins break in upon me even now as I am writing—Kuyanake, Kuyanake, Nalegak-soak!" "Thank you, thank you, big chief!" while Myouk is crowding fresh presents of raw birds on me as if I could eat forever, and poor Aningnah is crying beside the tent-curtain, wiping her eyes on a bird-skin!

My heart warms to these poor, dirty, miserable, yet happy beings, so long our neighbors, and of late so stanchly our friends. Theirs is no affectation of regret. There are twenty-two of them around me, all busy in good offices to the doctor Kayens.

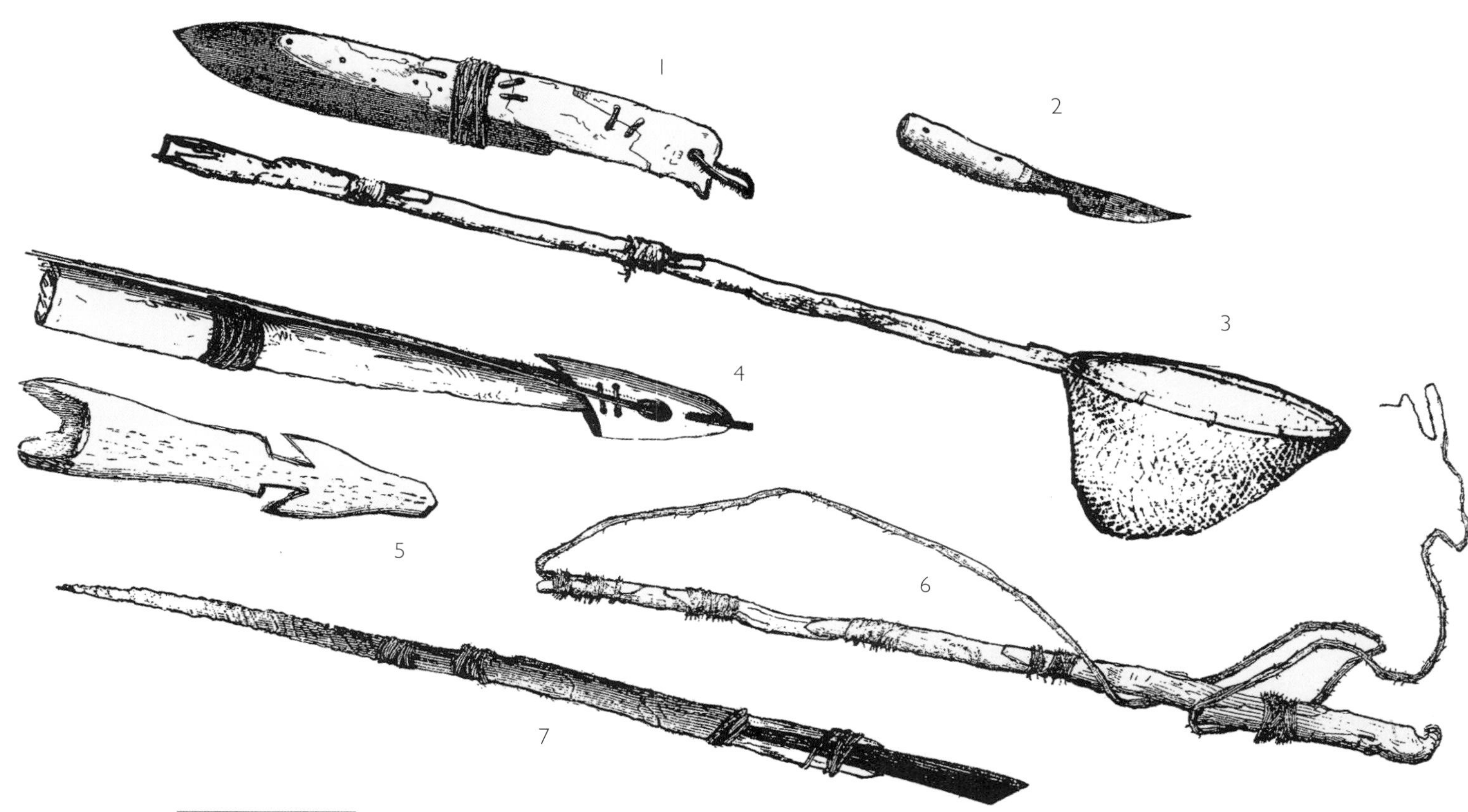

FIRST EXCHANGES

1. and 2.) Composite knives, their blades made from iron barrel hoops brought north by whalers and washed up on shore (1853-1855). 3.) Ipo *(net) used to catch cliff-dwelling auks in flight. The handle is skillfully assembled from bone fragments of marine mammals and the tusk of a male narwhal. The hoop consists of two or three seal ribs or segments of whale baleen. The net itself is a web of sealskin thongs, chewed by the women until soft. 4.) Harpoon for hunting walrus. 5.) Ivory harpoon head. 6.) Dog-sled driver's whip, consisting of five pieces of driftwood and bone lashed together. 7.) Lance made from a narwhal tusk, into which an iron blade has been embedded. The largest tusk found by Kane among the Polar Eskimos measured 8'11"; others collected later have been preserved in the Arktisk Institute of Copenhagen and at the Folketing (Parliament). Kane reported that the Polar Eskimos of the Etah region also received iron from the Inughuit of Cape York, who bartered goods with the whalers and traded with their northern cousins. Drawings by Elisha Kent Kane.*

JOURNAL OF J. WALL WILSON

111 June.
all busily employed as on any other day. – as for the prayers in the evening, not a man will attend – the officers only come out of respect & that very reluctantly. Mr Kane cannot go forward without hearing his name used in the most insolent manner by the men in the Forecastle. At our meals we are generally eddified by a spat between Mr K– & Mr Goodfellow as he can't get up a row with any one else.

A page from the diary of John Wall Wilson, evoking the tensions aboard the Advance: "June. All busily employed as on any other day. As for the prayers in the evening, not a man will attend—the officers only come out of respect and that very reluctantly. Mr. Kane cannot go forward without hearing his name used in the most insolent manner by the men in the forecastle."

The First peace treaty with the Inuit

When the three visitors came to us near the end of August, I established them in a tent below deck, with a copper lamp, a cooking basin, and a liberal supply of slush for fuel. I left them under guard when I went to bed at two in the morning, contentedly eating and cooking and eating again without the promise of an intermission. An American or a European would have slept after such a debauch till the recognized hour for hock and seltzer-water. But our guests managed to elude the officer of the deck and escape unsearched. They repaid my liberality by stealing not only the lamp, boiler, and cooking-pot they had used for the feast but Nannook, my best dog. If the rest of my team had not been worn down by travel, no doubt they would have taken them all. Besides this, we discovered the next morning that they had found the buffalo-robes and India-rubber cloth which McGary had left a few days before on the ice-foot near Six-mile Ravine, and had added the whole to the spoils of their visit.

[Morton and Riley overtook the thieves at Anoatok.]

They found young Myouk making himself quite comfortable in the hut, in company with Sievu, the wife of Metek, and Aningnah, the wife of Marsinga, and my buffalo-robes already tailored into kapetahs on their backs.

A continued search of the premises recovered the cooking utensils, and a number of other things of greater or less value that we had not missed from the brig. With prompt ceremony, the women were stripped and tied; and then, laden with their stolen goods and as much walrus-beef from their own stores as would pay for their board, they were marched back to the brig.

The thirty miles was a hard walk for them; but they did not complain, nor did their constabulary guardians, who had marched thirty miles already to apprehend them. It was hardly twenty-four hours since they left the brig with their booty before they were prisoners in the hold, with a dreadful white man for keeper, who never addressed to them a word that had not all the terrors of an unintelligible reproof, and whose scowl, I flatter myself, exhibited a well-arranged variety of menacing and demoniacal expressions.

They had not even the companionship of Myouk. I had dispatched him to Metek, "headman of Etah, and others," with the message of a melo-dramatic tyrant, to negotiate for their ransom. For five long days the women had to sigh and sing and cry in solitary converse—their appetite continuing excellent, it should be remarked, though mourning the while a rightfully impending doom. At last the great Metek arrived. He brought with him Ootuniah, another man of elevated social position, and quite a sledge-load of knives, tin cups, and other stolen goods, refuse of wood and scraps of iron, the sinful prizes of many covetings.

[After this gesture of goodwill, Kane negotiated a treaty of reciprocal engagements with the Inuit.]

On the part of the *Inuit*, the Esquimaux, they were after this fashion—

We promise that we will not steal. We promise we will bring you fresh meat. We promise we will sell or lend you dogs. We will keep you company whenever you want us, and show you where to find the game."

On the part of the *Kablunah*, the white men, the stipulation was of this ample equivalent—

"We promise that we will not visit you with death or sorcery, nor do you any hurt or mischief whatsoever. We will shoot for you on our hunts. You shall be made welcome aboard ship. We will give you presents of needles, pins, two kinds of knife, a hoop, three bits of hard wood, some fat, an awl, and some sewing-thread; and we will trade with you of these and every thing else you want for walrus and seal-meat of the first quality."

This treaty—which . . . was really an affair of much interest to us—was ratified, with Hans and Morton as my accredited representatives, by a full assembly of the people at Etah. All our future intercourse was conducted under it . . . As long as we remained prisoners of the ice, we were indebted to them for invaluable council in relation to our hunting expeditions; and in the joint hunt we shared alike, according to their own laws.

Metek, a young Polar Eskimo whom Kane encountered. *Qulittaq* of caribou hide, made the same way in 1950. The fringe of the hood, *puhihaq,* has been made of fox fur since the 1920s.

The cult of the dead and the transmigration of vital energy that project this people into the future with a shamanistic understanding of the world order were not recognized by Kane.

25) Sense of theater and protocol: Kane has grasped that, through his communal life, the Eskimo has learned above all to be an actor. He is equally taken with justice and honoring one's word. Svidlou, "two-faced, traitor, liar," is the worst insult.

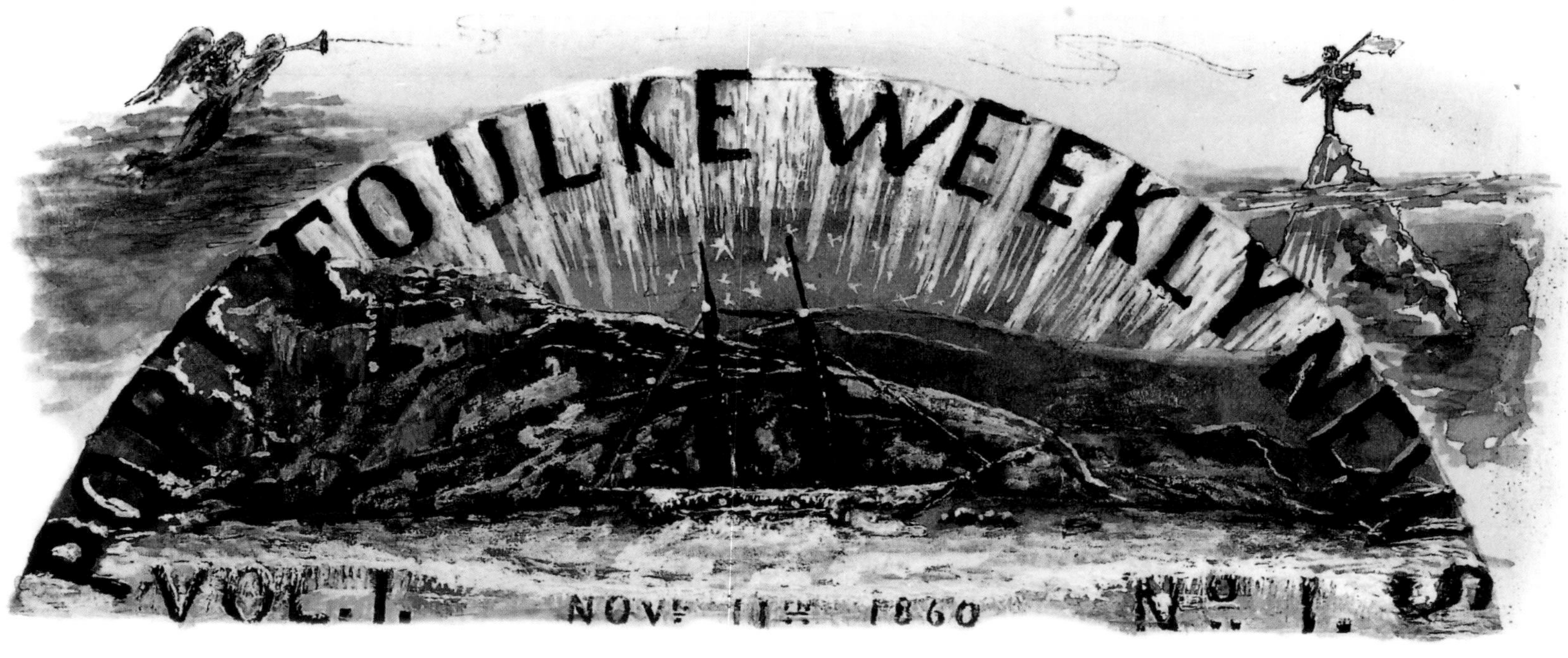

PROSPECTUS.

To the Public.

In offering this, the first number of "The Weekly News" for the consideration, and patronage we hope of the dwellers in these regions; we, after the usual custom of Editors in such cases, apologise in advance for all mistakes and errors, promising to do better next time, if we can.

We, however, take the liberty of advising borrowers and non-subscribers not to criticise, or make remarks concerning typographical appearances, as to please them we hurried our paper through the press, without using our new font of type, and as it came through so well, we shall probably reserve the type to make rifle balls of, for the purpose of sending dispatches to, and dispatching any troublesome neighbors.

Long standing newspaper hacks will readily understand the difficulty of our position, when we say, that we have not had time to thoroughly digest, and properly arrange all of the matter presented to us, in a fit, and proper manner for the private family circle, as we intend to do in future; and

Isaac Israel Hayes 1832-1881

AN INSPIRED AND DISLOYAL PHYSICIAN

He deserted his expedition leader, was aggressive toward the Eskimos, and schemed underhandedly against Hall . . . Isaac Hayes, who had a clear vision of the modern logistics of the Polar expedition, was the evil genius of American exploration in the high latitudes.

Opposite: **The first issue** of the *Port Foulke Weekly News*, dated 11 November 1860. This handwritten publication was composed and distributed on board ship during the Arctic winter. Most polar expeditions had such newspapers to keep up the crew's morale. On important holidays, plays were performed.

Dr. Isaac Israel Hayes is a little-known figure in American Arctic exploration. Courageous and inspired, he was for a long time the American explorer who came closest to the North Pole. He was the first—and with what energy!—to reach Ellesmere Island.[1] The plateau above Etah bears his name. Are only honest men worthy of statuary? If such were the criterion, our public squares would be bare. That said, posterity has reproached Hayes for three highly regrettable actions.

Hayes, a young doctor of twenty-one, shipped aboard the *Advance* in May 1853 in New York City. He was recruited as ship's surgeon by Dr. Kane despite his minimal experience—he had only finished medical school a few weeks earlier. Hayes agreed to manage the expedition's geographic and geological programs, notwithstanding his lack of formal training in these fields other than a genuine interest in natural history and especially ornithology. Kane did not know him personally, and there was no bond between them as medical colleagues. So why did he choose him? Was it the pressure of time? Inattention? Fatalism? Pride in his ability to handle any contingency? The record is silent on this point.

Two physicians—one too many?

From the first, Hayes proved to be jealous of Kane's popularity—a popularity buttressed by the establishment as well as by the Masons, to whom Hayes, it seems, did not belong. Silent, surly, and ambitious, he gradually became an opponent of Kane's. Finding the rigid authority and haughty attitude of his expedition leader irritating, he joined with the Danes and the officers who were worried about Kane's visionary daring. They tried without success to make him overwinter near Etah, near the open stretch of "North Water" so well known to the Scottish whalers who patrolled the Carey Islands' area. Kane refused, as we know, condemning his men to two winters in the Arctic, the second of which was particularly hard, for want of food.

On 13 August 1854, Hayes had reached his limit and wrote Kane that he would no longer work under his orders. Henceforth, he wrote, he would be available only at the

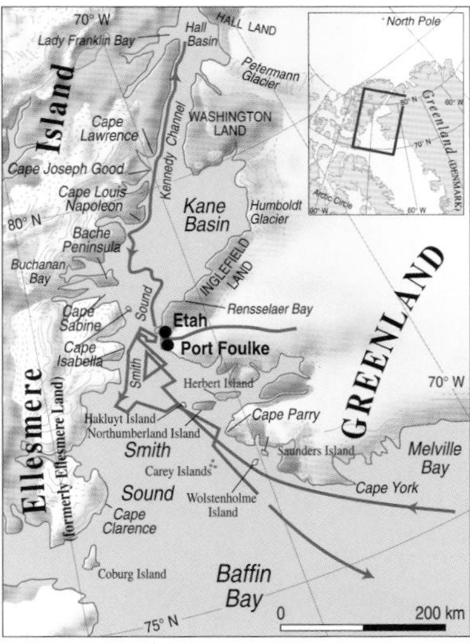

Route of Hayes's ship, the *United States*, from Melville Bay to Foulke Fjord, Etah (1860-1861), and the spring expedition along the coast of Ellesmere Island.

1) During the winter of 1853-1854, the dogs died of piblokto, or *pillortoq*, a fatal form of distemper. The men were weakened by scurvy. During a spring sledding expedition (March 1854), two men died of cold, and two others were seriously disabled. On 20 May 1854 Hayes managed to cross the strait by dog sled accompanied by William Godfrey and explore Ellesmere Island for the first time as far as Cape John Frazer (latitude 79° 43' north). On his return, he was quasi-blind for six weeks.

Sunset at Port Foulkes, 15 October 1860. It was not by chance that Hayes chose this unparalleled site for overwintering, at the entrance to the fjord, near a polynya of open water, 40 miles south of Rensselaer Harbor, where Kane had overwintered and lost his ship after being caught for two winters in the ice.

times of his own choosing. Kane skillfully sidestepped this show of ill-humor but never forgot the episode. From that moment on, Hayes had lost Kane's support and perhaps also his esteem.

Dr. Hayes's desertion

August 1854: nineteen men gathered in the central cabin of the ship. The situation on board was calamitous: rats, little or no food, cold, and, more than anything, a tension so thick that the men could only communicate through insults, at every turn attacking the man they held responsible for their distress: the rigid and distant Dr. Kane. The very prospect of a second winter in the ice struck them as unbearable. After a show of hands, all the expedition's scientists and officers (eight men, Hayes among them) informed Kane that they were abandoning the ship and going south in hopes of finding a Scottish whaler sailing in upper Melville Bay.

The stores and equipment were with difficulty divided up, and on 28 August the mutineers left the *Advance*, which had been trapped by ice in Rensselaer Harbor (Aannartoq) since the autumn of 1853. Never to return, or so they thought. They reached Northumberland Island easily, then Natsilivik, at Cape Parry. At this point matters took a turn for the worse. Despite the two boats they were hauling laden with provisions and weapons, and despite the help they received on occasion from the Eskimo villages they passed through, they did not manage in three months to reach their goal of Cape York—a journey that the Eskimos regularly accomplish in two weeks by dog sled, and which I made in February 1951, from Siorapaluk (southeast of Etah) to Savissivik (Cape York), under the same conditions, also in two weeks.

The eight deserters built themselves a stone shelter a short distance south of Natsilivik where they lived an anxious life. Food gave out. The Eskimos of Natsilivik clearly understood that the *qaallunaat* (whites) had abandoned their ship and their captain to go south. And the Inughuit—who always make a show of unity and solidarity in the face of danger—not understanding the motivations or behavior of these men, became somewhat threatening. There was no doubt that if some mishap befell these exhausted whites, the Inuit would show no hesitation in taking their equipment. Knives, needles, boats—were these not universally coveted? And especially the guns that were used to threaten them when they visited Aannartoq, near the *Advance*.

The betrayal

November 1854. Three months went by. Starving, frozen, the mutineers in their den in southern Booth Bay were living out what they imagined to be their last moments: one of them, the Dane Carl Petersen, gathered on a visit to the Eskimos that a plot was being hatched against them. They were going to be murdered! They then formed a horrible plan. They lured two hunters to their shelter and smilingly offered them bowls of soup heavily laced with laudanum. The powerful sleeping potion was administered by Hayes, the expedition's doctor. As soon as the two poor men were asleep, they stripped them of all their clothes (it was -25°F outside) and stole their sleds and dog teams. But the whites were poor dog-sled drivers, and the dogs traveled slowly, unwilling to leave their owners behind. The two Eskimos soon woke up and discovered the low trick that had been played on them. Practically naked, their feet bound in multicolored rags, they hurtled out into the night and bitter cold in pursuit of the traitors. So great was their anger that they were able to catch up with the whites—by now broken, desperate men, who begged the Eskimos to lead them "home" to the *Advance*.

Dr. I. I. Hayes.

Probably because of their solemn "treaty of cooperation" with Kane, the Eskimos—now joined by four more, with forty-two dogs—had the good grace to return the sorry crew to the ship. Perhaps they believed, Eskimo-fashion, that all of the whites, being ill-adapted to the environment and further weakened by strife, would eventually fall into their hands. Their shamanist outlook kept them from committing violence. Did not the white men have "fire-spitters" of extraordinary power? Did the Inuit expect a reward? At any rate, when the party reached the *Advance* in December, thanks to the generous hospitality of the Inuit in the villages and camps along the way, Kane gave to each of the natives, after lengthy talks and a special negotiation with Kalutunah, five needles, a file, and a piece of wood. This by way of reparation for the insult they had received. He also gave knives to two of them, Kalutunah and Shunghu, who struck him as having greater authority. The agreement was sealed with a meal in which all participated. As they left, the six men "prigged a few knives and forks—but that refers itself to a national trait," Kane wrote. On the day following the return of the mutineers, Kane amputated three of Hayes's frozen toes.

A master of logistics

After the expedition's return on 12 October 1855, Hayes lived in New York. His desertion had drawn no official censure, and Kane died in 1857. In his account of the expedition, Kane had diplomatically minimized the dissent on board and presented the desertion as an attempt to get rescue, sanctioned by him. [2]

How is a man to be judged? According to rumors? According to his actions, more or less well interpreted? "Man is a mass of little secrets," André Malraux used to say. What is important is the work. Dr. Isaac Israel Hayes deserves to be counted among the great Arctic explorers of America. His courage during Kane's expedition is undeniable.

In 1860-1861, he led a remarkable private expedition to the Far North, his commitment to that area having grown after the return of Kane's expedition, and his venture would long be seen as a model of organization. He wisely chose a small ship, the *United States* (130 tons), with a crew of fourteen men [3], and, unlike Kane, he anchored his ship at the edge of the open "North Water" near Etah, to ensure his freedom of movement. [4]

Considering that trade with the Eskimos was too chancy, he arranged for their closer cooperation by putting them on "salary." [5] The hunters, or those he had personally chosen, would drive the dog sleds on a yearly basis and hunt. In return, Hayes would supply the equipment they needed as well as the wood and iron so highly prized by the Eskimos. Hayes would thus have fresh meat all winter and for the first time in the history of Arctic exploration avoid scurvy entirely. This is what Peary egotistically called "the Peary system." But not all went as planned. One of the crew, the Greenlander Peter, committed suicide by wandering off into the mountains. Did he mean to become a *qiviqtuq*, an immortal spirit who lives in the mountains and comes out at night to haunt those who wronged him? The dogs, so crucial to the expeditions ahead, died of an epidemic. And the death of the German mathematician and geographer August Sonntag in December 1860 would particularly trouble Hayes. Some claimed that he was murdered, while on a trip with Hans Hendrik (grandfather of my companion Sakaeunnguaq) near Pitorarfik, northwest of Siorapaluk, where they had gone in search of dogs and fresh meat. [6] The rumors are probably well founded. Tensions on the trail can lead to extreme acts. We know, for instance, that Ross Marvin was murdered in 1909 by two Eskimos (one of whom I knew).] Hayes undertook a difficult mission on the east coast of Ellesmere Island without help from the local Eskimos. After quite a dangerous forced march, which he led with exceptional authority and energy, Hayes got to Kennedy Channel, on 19 May reaching a northern latitude never before achieved: lat. 81° 35' north, long. 70° 30' west. This was Cape Lieber.

What met his gaze was not ice but open water. Like Kane, Hayes was convinced that he had reached the "open polar sea": "This water was still without a limit, moved by

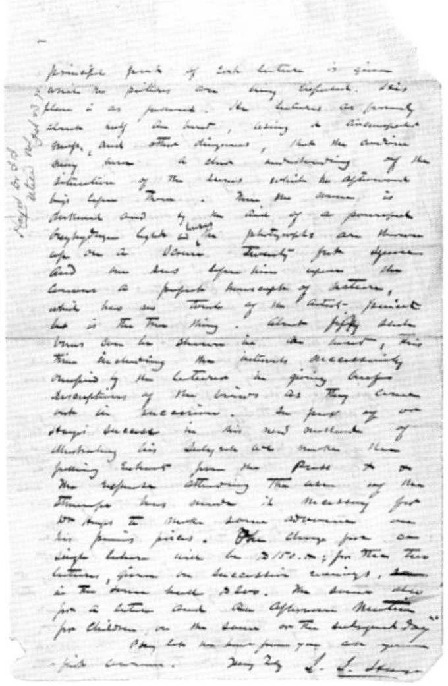

An unpublished manuscript letter by Dr. Hayes (23 February 1872).

October 1854. The eight deserters in Hayes's party traveled toward Melville Bay in two boats, hoping to be rescued by a whaler. They built a hut just south of Booth Bay (below Cape Parry). I visited the site and found the country full of game.

2) Today we know, thanks to the diaries of Kane and Wilson, what violent animosities existed between the members of the expedition.

3) Compare the practice in Franklin's day of outfitting two ships of 340 and 370 tons, with a crew of 134 men.

4) Hayes had the good sense to winter at Etah (Foulke Fjord) on the admirable site that would become the crossroads of the Peary, McMillan, and Shackleton expeditions.

5) The memory that Hayes left in their community was a hateful one, but the Eskimos are pragmatic. As whites were unpredictable, the important thing was to get the most possible out of them.

6) On 10 April 1951, while staying at Etah and trying to right the difficult problems of my own expedition, I went alone by dog sled to visit the grave of Sonntag, lost in the rocky landscape. I reset his headstone upright (it had probably been knocked down by an animal), rearranged the small scattered stones, and left, made pensive by remembering the circumstances of his death.

The grave of August Sonntag, in Etah, south of Port Foulke. The expedition's geographer, Sonntag died on the ice while traveling with Hans Hendrik, a dozen miles from Cape Alexander in December 1860. He was twenty-nine years old. Official cause of death: pulmonary congestion following a fall into a glacier.

a heavy swell, free of ice, and dashing in surf against a rock-bound shore." Surprisingly, he failed to see the high headlands of Washington Land that bounded the channel to the east some twenty miles away.[7] And why did he not listen to Hans Hendrik. We remember Hendrik's skepticism about his white companion's having seen an "open polar sea" where he saw "*sikou suak,*" or "much ice." Hayes saw what he wanted to see, and the book he published on his return was called *The Open Polar Sea.*

When he returned, the United States was caught up in the Civil War. Hayes turned over the *United States* to the Union navy and volunteered as a surgeon. He ended the war with the rank of colonel.

The racism of a young America

In his writings, Hayes discusses the Polar Eskimos in terms that are as insulting as they are incorrect. A few examples: "The Esquimaux are indeed a very strange people, and are an interesting study, even more so than my dogs, although they are not so useful; and then the dog can be controlled with a long whip and resolution, while the human animal cannot be controlled with any thing. They might very properly be called a negative people, in everything except their unreliability, which is entirely positive. . . . I cannot imagine any living thing so callous as they. . . . Merkut [Meqru, Hans Hendrik's wife] is a little chubby specimen of womankind, and, for an Esquimau, not ill-looking. . . . So much for my Esquimau subjects. October 21st—I have had another lively race to the glacier . . ."[8] In his defense, we could say that Dr. Hayes only held the common prejudices of his time. Despite the success of Kane's account and the public fascination with polar travel, Hayes, like his predecessors, took only geographers and naturalists with him but no ethnographers. His one concern was mapping the geology and glaciers. The goals of the expedition were essentially political and economic.[9]

Arctic prophet

Hayes led a summer cruise to Greenland in 1868, then in 1870 prepared a third expedition to conquer the North Pole. The plan he submitted to the American Geographical Society was perfectly thought out and very precise. It consisted of three points:

1. Two ships were needed: a sailing ship, which would stay at Etah, and a steamship, which would force its way through the ice barrier to the "open polar sea."

2. Scurvy, the plague of Arctic missions, could be avoided (as he had ascertained) by settling near an Eskimo village; the men would receive fresh meat, and the Eskimos would be in the expedition's pay to provide it.

3. An American trading post would be established in the territory of the Polar Eskimos to trade for furs and ivory; the profits would be applied to subsequent Arctic expeditions.

This was a vision of the future that Peary, then Rasmussen, would actually carry out, without crediting its originator. Was it that the name of Isaac Hayes had lost all honor? But it was Charles Francis Hall who, after a vicious struggle, would lead the first official United States expedition.

The second victim

At the headquarters of the American Geographical Society, whose founder and president was Henry Grinnell, two speeches were to be given: one by Hayes, the other by Charles Francis Hall, whose expeditions to the central Arc-

A dog can pull 90 pounds. Ten dogs will eat one ringed seal (*Phoca hispida*) every other day during the winter. Dogs always sleep outside the igloo.

7) I went to the area myself, to lat. 80° 03' north (Cape Jackson), in May 1951, and from the Greenland side could see the coast of Ellesmere Island perfectly across Kennedy Channel. There is some doubt about Hayes's exploit, which is generally accepted with reservations. His geomorphological observations on raised beaches, however, are sound, testifying to the elevation following the last warming 8000 years ago.

8) The reader will find additional examples of Hayes's racism toward the Polar Eskimos in the excerpts from his writings at the end of this chapter: whether discussing the pillage of Inuit graves or the faulty character of Hans Hendrik, the Eskimo is for him the representative of an "inferior" race. To the Americans of his day, the Eskimo meant no more than the Indian who was being exterminated, or the Black being held under slavery. In this light, Hayes's pronouncements on the Inuit seem, if anything, amiable. And remember that Hayes, Kane, and the elite of America constantly turned to the Bible . . . in support of their supremacy.

9) Arctic expeditions were conducted by officers of the navy or the cavalry when they were official, and by doctors, printers, or journalists when they were private. Only with Knud Rasmussen in 1902-1907 and Lauge Koch in 1922 would expeditions be led, respectively, by an ethnologist and a geologist.

10) To his misfortune, this excellent organizer, the first explorer of Ellesmere Island, had the true temperament of a leader. He saw and felt more quickly than others, more quickly than Kane. To have his feeling of superiority constantly thwarted by circumstance perhaps explains his base acts, his betrayals. What makes a reputation? Brilliant actions. Who destroys a reputation? The common man, public opinion. Hayes's life incorporated a number of low acts, and despite the pioneering character of his explorations, his name has gradually been erased by history, that silent court and memory. What men has history judged harshly in the past century and a half? Captain Sabine, Dr. Hayes, Dr. Bessels, Lieutenant Greely, Lauge Koch. Whereas the stature of Sir John Ross, Dr. Kane, Captain Tyson, C. R. Markham, Lockwood and Dr. Pavy, Erik Holtved, Hans Hendrik, and Knud Rasmussen have grown over time. The stature of Peary and Cook as well, naturally. Defamatory texts dishonor their authors. The history of the sciences is not only a history of ideas, but a history of careers and of dishonorable acts . . .

tic in search of Franklin had caught the public imagination. Hall paced back and forth, waiting to be called to the dais. He was preparing to give details of his upcoming expedition to the North Pole, which he had submitted to the president of the United States himself. Suddenly he saw Hayes talking with the owner of a whaling ship, an exceptional seaman, whom Hall had asked several weeks earlier to be the captain of his own ship. And Hayes was now hiring the whaling skipper. A low blow, this threatened the success of Hall's plans. Hall fulminated. "I'm ashamed of Hayes. I'm ashamed of his cowardice and weakness! I'm despise his trickery, his deviltry," he wrote in his private journal. This is but a glimpse of what the shameless Hayes might do to accomplish his ends.

Since the end of the Civil War, Hall had worked tirelessly to make the United States assume a presence in the Arctic commensurate with its power as a great nation. He met with countless senators in Washington and even with President Ulysses S. Grant. With the help of his friend Grinnell, he put pressure on one and another of them. He gave speech after speech, accompanied by an Eskimo couple, Joe Ebierbing and Hannah Tookoolito, who had followed him since his first expedition to Baffin Island. Hall stubbornly hoped that Congress would finally agree to make the next polar expedition a government one: it would be the first official U.S. mission to the Arctic. He counted on the assurances he had received . . . and on his "aura." A few more weeks and he would achieve his goal.

It was at this point that Hayes, a good political maneuverer, had the gall to propose his candidacy to lead Hall's expedition. His main argument was: "Am I not a doctor? Whereas Charles Francis Hall is not a scientist." The Foreign Affairs Committee, which was studying the matter, was thrown into upheaval. If the principle of an official U.S. expedition was accepted, thanks to Hall's efforts, the question remained: which of the two, Hall or Dr. Hayes, was the more competent to lead? Hall argued his case vigorously. An observer remarked: "Hall's energy set the train on the rails, and Hall's daring will drive it forward." Upset, worried that he would be replaced by a personality both controversial and famous, Hall abruptly left the room and wandered in a daze through the streets of New York for several hours. The following day, his courage restored, he wrote letter after letter to his friends and supporters in defense of his cause.

History is not always unfair: On 12 July 1870, Congress approved an official U.S. government expedition to the Arctic; with Hall named to lead it. The years would roll by. Hayes would publish the results of his scientific studies through the Smithsonian Institution. Elected to the New York City Council in 1875, he would die at the age of 49, on 17 September 1881, unmarried and forgotten. [10] ■

Dr. Hayes drifting on an ice floe "in search of the North Pole." The caricature, drawn by his shipmates, appeared in the *Port Foulke Weekly News.*

Hayes, on arriving at the "ice-free sea" on 18 May 1861, raised the American flag and two masonic pennants (those of Kane's lodge in New York and the Columbia Lodge of Boston). His position was lat. 81° 35' north and long. 70° 30' west, at Cape Lieber (Kennedy Channel, east coast of Ellesmere Island). This exploit would be doubted, however, because of his description of the site—"no land visible except the coast upon which I stood"—which does not correspond to reality. At that precise spot, at an altitude of 2600 feet, Washington Land on the coast of Greenland is visible only 22 miles away. I verified this from Cape Jackson (southern Washington Land) on 21 May 1951 during my dog sled expedition.

Eskimo hunters and their wives visiting the hut of the eight deserters near Natsilivik (Cape Parry), 11 November 1854. The feast was made possible by the 100 pounds of blubber and meat traded for wood and iron. Drawing by the book's illustrator (who clearly never saw an Eskimo). It is worth distinguishing between books illustrated under the author's supervision and those illustrated under the editor's.

Dr. Hayes's perspective on Inuit society

A walrus's breathing hole.

Odobenus rosmarus (*aèveq*, in Inuktitut). The walrus is 11 or 12 feet long, 10 feet in girth, and weighs one ton. The tusks are 20 inches long. In 1950, 200 walruses were killed among 70 hunters.

Looking for Hans Hendrik, July 1860

Standing close in under Cape York, I kept a careful lookout for natives. The readers of the narrative of Dr. Kane may remember that that navigator took with him from one of the southern settlements of Greenland a native hunter, who, after adhering to the fortunes of the expedition through nearly two years, abandoned it (as reported) for a native bride, to live with the wild Esquimaux who inhabit the shores of the headwaters of Baffin Bay. This boy was named Hans. Anticipating that, growing tired of his self-imposed banishment, he would take up his residence at Cape York, with the hope of being picked up by some friendly ship, I ran in to seek him. Passing along the coast at rifle-shot I soon discovered a group of human beings making signs to attract attention. Heaving the vessel to, I went ashore in a boat, and there, sure enough, was the object of my search. He quickly recognized Sonntag and myself, and called us by name. [11]

Six years' experience among the wild men of this barren coast had brought him to their level of filthy ugliness . . . [H]ad I known him as well then as, with good reason, I knew him afterward, I would not have gone out of my way to disturb his barbarous existence.

With Kane, he fed well: he grew plump and round on the *Advance* and played many nasty tricks on his master, before fleeing to the savages of this region. He behaved even worse toward me than he had toward Dr. Kane.

Looting the graves, September 1860

Jensen, whose long residence among the Esquimaux of Southern Greenland has brought him to look upon that people as little better than the dogs which drag their sledges, [12] discovered a couple of graves and brought away the two skin-robed mummies which they enclosed, thinking they would make fine museum specimens; but, unfortunately for the museum, Mrs. Hans was prowling about when Jensen arrived on board, and, recognizing one of them by some article of clothing as a relative, she made a terrible ado, and could not be quieted even by Jensen's assurance that I was a magician, and would restore them to life when in my own country; so, when I learned the circumstances, I thought it right, in respect to humanity if not to science, to restore them to their stony graves, and had it done accordingly. [13]

The same sledge as the one discovered by John Ross in August 1818

Leaving the dogs, we went to the sledges to get them ready for starting. While the preparations were being made, I examined one of them minutely. It was, almost without exception, the most ingeniously contrived specimen of the mechanic art that I have ever seen. It was made wholly of bone and leather. The runners, which were square behind and rounded upward in front, and about five feet long, seven inches high, and three fourths of an inch thick, were slabs of bone; not solid, but composed of a number of pieces, of various shapes and sizes, cunningly fitted and tightly lashed together. Some of these were not larger than one's two fingers; some were three or four inches square; others were triangular, the size of one's hand; while others, again, were several inches long and two or three broad. These pieces were all fitted together as neatly as the blocks of a Chinese puzzle. Near their margins were rows of little holes, through which were

11) Later, Hayes would express the opinion that Hans was a bad choice. He held him responsible for the unexplained death of Sonntag, the expedition's geographer and astronomer.

12) The opinions of this Danish assistant reflect the spirit of the Danish administrators at their most heinous: "The worst Dane is worth more than the best Greenlander." This racist point of view softened as mixed marriages started to occur. Hayes described Merkut, Hans's wife, as "the most stubborn of women" because she refused to sew sealskin linings into cotton and woolen clothes.

13) The Inuit are considered "human animals." In the name of science they are subjected to cultural dispossession and an underlying contempt.

run strings of seal-skins, by which the blocks were fastened together, making a slab almost as firm as a board.

These bones are flattened and cut into the required shapes with stones. The grinding needed to make a single runner must be a work of months; but the construction of an entire new sledge, I was afterward informed, was unheard of in the present generation. Repairs are made as any part becomes broken or decayed; but a vehicle of this kind is a family heirloom, and is handed down from generation to generation. The origin of some of the Esquimau sledges dates back beyond tradition.

Upon turning over the specimen before me, I found that the runners were shod with ivory from the tusk of the walrus. This also had been ground flat and its corners squared with stones; and it was fastened to the runner by a string which was looped through two counter-sunk holes. This sole was composed of a number of pieces, but the surface was uniform and as smooth as glass.[14]

The runners stood about fourteen inches apart, and were fastened together by bones, tightly lashed to them.[15] These cross pieces were the femur of the bear, the antlers of the reindeer, and the ribs of the narwhal. Two walrus ribs were lashed, one to the after-end of each runner, for upstanders, and were braced by a piece of reindeer antler, secured across the top . . .

During his absence, [the Esquimau] would not cook any food; but he would want water. He therefore carried a small stone dish that was his "kotluk," or lamp, a lump of "mannek" or dried moss, to be used for wick, and some willow blossoms (na-owinak) for tinder. These last were carefully wrapped up in bird-skin to keep them dry. He had also a piece of iron-stone (ujarak-saviminilik) and a small sharp fragment of flint. These were his means for striking a spark . . .

All being ready, the dogs, seven in number, were next brought up, led by their traces. The harness on them was no less simple than the cargo they had to draw. It consisted of two doubled strips of bearskin, one of which was placed on either side of the body of the animal, the two being fastened together on the top of the neck and at the breast, thus forming a collar.[16] Thence they passed inside of the dog's forelegs, and up along the sides to the rump, where the four ends meeting together were fastened to a trace eighteen feet in length. This was connected with the sledge by a line four feet long, the ends of which were attached one to each runner. To the middle of this line was tied a strong string which was run through bone rings at the ends of the traces, and secured by a slipknot, easily untied. This arrangement was to insure safety in bear-hunting.

The Inuit, eaters of raw flesh

We were surprised about noon by the appearance of an Esquimau. He came up the beach, and was as much astonished as ourselves. We recognized him as one of those who were at the ship last winter. His name was Amalatok. After exchanging salutations, he seated himself upon a rock with a cool dignity quite characteristic of his people, and began to talk in a rapid and animated manner. He was dressed in a coat made of bird-skins, feathers turned inward; bear-skin pantaloons, hair outward; tanned seal-skin boots, and dog-skin stockings.[17] He told us that he lives on the eastern side of the island, that he had a wife, but no children; that his brother, who had a wife and children, lived with him; and that they had been visited by whitemen (kablunet) not long since. They were evidently the same people whom Dr. Kane had met on his southern journey in August. Judging from our visitor's description, his house was distant from our camp about three miles. It could be reached, he said, only by climbing over the mountain, which was a difficult undertaking; or by walking along the beach at low tide. He carried in his hand two little auks, a bladder filled with oil, a coil of seal-thong, and two or three pieces of half-putrid walrus flesh.[18] He was on an excursion round the island to set fox-traps; and the flesh was intended for bait. While talking with us, he took up one of his auks, twisted off the head, and, inserting the index finger of his right hand under the integuments of the neck, drew it down the back—and in an instant the bird was skinned. He then ran his long thumb-nail along the breastbone, and as quickly produced two fine fat lumps of flesh, which he generously offered to anyone who would take them. He evidently intended a great courtesy; but the raw meat coming from such hands and treated in this manner was not to our liking. Petersen explained to him that we had just breakfasted, and begged, most politely, that he would not deprive himself. It did not please him that we declined his hospitality; which was evidently kindly meant, and was bestowed in a manner which showed plainly that he felt the importance of proprietorship. He did not wait for further invitation, and took his lunch with a gusto quite refreshing to see, washing it down

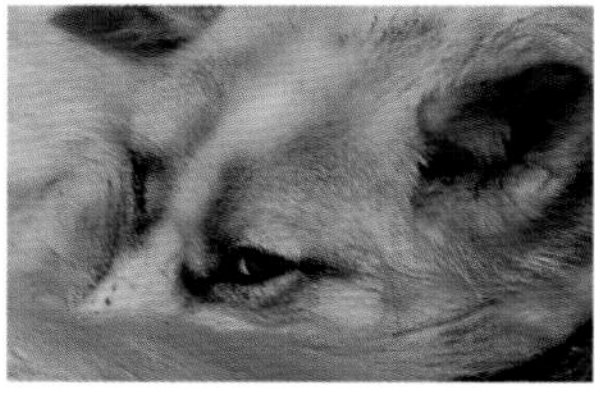

Eskimo hunting auks with a net (*kaglu*) on the cliffs near Etah. The drawing is technically accurate on the whole, except for two details: the handle of the net would probably not have been made of wood—a rare material at that time—and the cliffs are never snow-covered when the auks nest there (in July).

14) Technological conservatism: the sled brought back by John Ross (1818), though small (length: 1.42 m; width: .49 m; height: .15 m; the rear uprights: .70 m), was preserved with its structure unchanged until 1950-1951. With the more effective hunting brought on by technical progress, which accelerated after 1863 (iron knives, firearms, kayaks, etc.), sleds grew longer and wider. Just before Peary (1886), sleds measured, according to Moltke, 2.40 m in length, .56 m in width, and .15 m in height. The rear upright was .83 m high. In 1950-1951, the largest sleds were 4 meters long, .90 m wide, and .23 m high, with a rear upright of .85 m. Mine was 3.5 m long and the other dimensions proportional. Each Eskimo builds his own sled, as well as his own hunting implements—a tradition maintained until 1950-1951, and beyond, to 1970.

15) On the sled brought back by Sir John Ross and that is now in the British Museum (a different one than is presented here), the shoe of the right runner comprised 14 pieces of ivory, and of the left runner 10 pieces, not including the front right curve (3 pieces) and the left front curve (4 pieces). Left runner: 15 pieces of bone; right runner, 11 pieces.

16) The word "collar" is misleading. Clearly, he is describing a harness, the same harness that I used in 1950: a chest harness through which the head and the front legs were passed, with a cinch on the back. It took several centuries for Western man to discover this harness for the draft horse, in the eleventh century, a technical revolution that considerably increased the animal's drawing power. The Inuit, who domesticated the dog at the beginning of the Christian era, had the same harness in their primitive condition in 1852 (which is to say in 1818, if we consider the technical non-evolution of this isolated group).

17) The Eskimos' clothing remained unchanged from 1818 to 1950, with the exception of the birdskin coat (attili), which was gradually abandoned after 1910, and definitively after 1920.

18) Auks, preserved in a kiviaq, a seal that has been gutted but not removed of its blubber, was the staple food of the Polar Eskimos during the Little Ice Age, for two and a half centuries, and particularly during the cold period from 1840-1860. The adult daily ration is estimated at four to six auks. One family in 1850 needed ten kiviaqs to ensure its survival for four or five months. In 1950-1951, this form of nourishment was still employed. The kiviaq allowed me to resist the cold.

The shameful flight of Dr. Hayes, August to November 1854.

Hunter watching at a seal's breathing hole in the ice (*aqluq*).

Map of Port Foulke and the surrounding area, drawn by Hayes. In 1860, the edge of Brother John's Glacier was one half mile from Alida Lake, whereas my survey of 1950 shows it ending only 15 feet from the lake. The glacier's advance is an instance of climatic memory, a result of the cold brought by the Little Ice Age (1600-1800).

with a drink of oil which, in turn, he offered to us; but again we were compelled to commit the discourtesy of declining the proffered attention.

. . . They were clothed entirely in animal skins; their hunting weapons were carved out of bone; they had neither wood nor iron.[19]

The Eskimos refuse the white man's food

Our savage friends were kind and generous. They anticipated our every wish. One of the young women, true to the instincts of her sex, ran off to the valley, with a dozen boys and girls at her heels, and filled our bottles with water. Kalutunah's koona (wife) brought us a steak of seal, and a dainty piece of liver. All smiled at the slowly-burning canvas wick of our lamp, and at the sputtering salt fat; and the chief sent his daughter for some dried moss and blubber. We gave them a share of our meal, offered them a taste of coffee, and passed around some pieces of ship-biscuit. The biscuit proved too hard for their teeth, and, until they saw us eat, they could not divine its use. They laughed and nibbled at it alternately, and then stuck it into their boots—their general temporary receptacle for all curiosities. They made wry faces over the coffee, and a general laugh arose against the Angekok, who persisted in taking a drink of the hot liquid. We had, altogether, an amusing time with them. The evening being warm, we sat upon the rocks for several hours; and after supper, our men lighted their pipes. This capped the climax of our strange customs. The Esquimaux seemed amazed, and looked first at us, then at each other, then at us again. They evidently thought it a religious ceremony, seeing how solemn were our

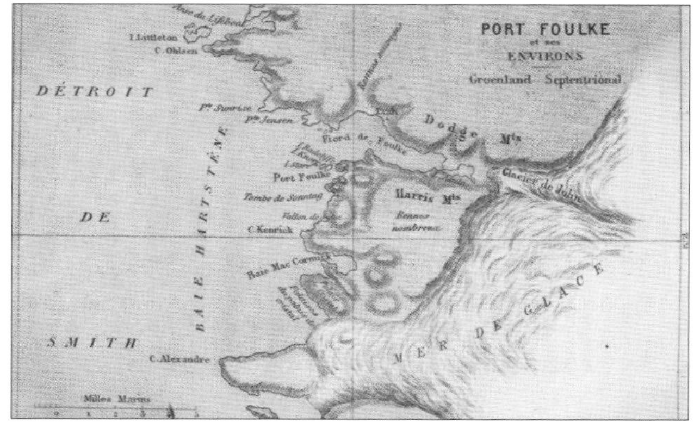

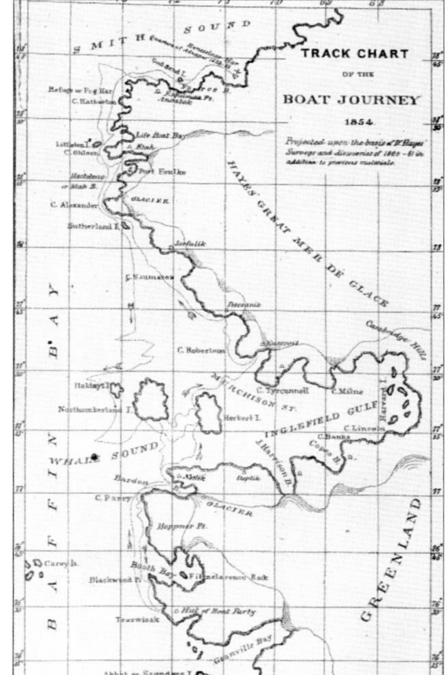

faces. At length I could not abstain from a smile; the signal thus given was followed by shouting, clapping of hands, and general confusion among the troop. They ran about, puffing out their cheeks, and imitating, as nearly as they could, the motions of the smokers. Kalutunah, who was determined to try everything, begged to be allowed to smoke a pipe. One being handed to him, he was directed to take a long and deep inhalation; this accomplished, he desired no more, and his rueful face brought the mirth of the party again upon him.[20]

Barter

Having thus established the most kindly relations, we presented a needle to each of the women, which greatly delighted them; and having nothing else to offer us in return, they started off in a body and brought us a few pieces of blubber. This was what we most wanted, and they were asked to barter more of it for a knife. The question must have been misunderstood; for, an old woman who was called Eglavfit (meaning intestines), and who seemed to be one in authority, told a long story representing how poor they were, how unsuccessful they had been in the hunt, how they would soon have no fire and nothing to eat, and how the winter would soon be upon them; in short, if we could believe her, they were just on the eve of dying. I had heard such stories before, nearer the equator, when substantial favors were likely to be required; and I began to suspect that we had commenced at the wrong end with our negotiations . . .[21] They were in fact badly provided. The hunt had latterly been unproductive, and they had not, in the whole settlement, food for three days. They were to hunt on the morrow, and, if successful, they would give us the required supplies, in case we would wait. This was all very fine, but the game was still in the sea.

The desire to learn, winter 1854

Kalutunah, the very man whom we wished most to see, came next day, accompanied by a young hunter of Netlik, and by a woman with a child, which she carried in a hood upon her back. The little creature was not six months old; and yet, wrapped up in fox-skins, and lying close to its mother's back, its fur-covered head peeping above her left shoulder, it did not seem to suffer from the long exposure.

I was never more struck with the hardiness and indifference to cold, manifested by these people than on this occasion. This woman had subjected herself to a temperature of thirty-five degrees below zero, with the chance of being caught in a gale; had traveled forty miles over a track the roughness of which frequently compelled her to dismount from the sledge and walk; she had carried her child all the way; her sole motive being her curiosity to see the white men, their igloe (hut), and their strange treasures.[22] We must at least concede that she manifested extraordinary courage and endurance in the gratifying of her desire . . .

[Kalutunah] laughed outright when it was proposed that he should sell us dogs for the journey.[23] He would not sell dogs for any purpose, or at any price; and for the best of reasons, namely, that they had none they could spare . . .

So great a courtesy [the widow] did not expect would be declined under any pretense, and she seemed quite mortified; but nothing daunted, she passed the lump [of chewed birdflesh] over to me; but no, I could not oblige her. With quite a desponding face she crossed the floor and tried Whipple. Not

9) A confirmation that until 1863, therefore until the technological revolution, Inuit society remained conservative.

20) The Eskimos started to adapt to our food in 1890-1900, and immediately—and passionately—to tobacco as well. No one is as blind and deaf as the person who does not want to see and hear. To the nineteenth-century American, the Eskimo was a primitive. Hayes and his companions could not, given their education, see the hidden complexity of this society. The Eskimo group, for its part, was too certain of its technical and moral superiority, too set within a rigid sociocultural context, to view its structures with any perspective and free itself from its rules without harming itself. As any threatened group would, it reacted by turning to conservatism. It was indifference, coupled with caution, that made the Inuit show so much patience toward the explorers when the whites were exhausted and at their mercy, and so parsimonious with their presents: needles and tools of inestimable value to the hunters.

21) In order, trade goods (at Cape York) consisted of: iron, knives, needles, wood, tobacco (starting in 1860), coffee, tea, biscuits. Only in 1890 would these trade goods be known and valued across the entire range from south to north as far as Etah. In 1900, firearms and ammunition, steel traps, tools were added.

meeting with success in that quarter she came back to Mr. Bonsall, who was already quite a philosopher in making his tastes subservient to his physical wants. "Now for it, Bonsall!" cried Petersen. These words of encouragement had the effect to call forth a hearty laugh on all sides; which, being misunderstood by the widow, she hastily withdrew her offer of friendship, bolted it herself, and in offended silence went on with her work of skinning birds and swallowing them. We all felt that henceforth we should have an enemy in the widow.

Taboos about death, 1854

This widow greatly interested me. She ate birds for conscience' sake. Her husband's soul had passed into the body of a walrus as a temporary habitation, and the Angekok had prescribed, that, for a certain period, she should not eat the flesh of this animal; and since at this time of year bear and seal were scarce, she was compelled to fall back upon a small stock of birds that had been collected during the previous summer.

This penance was of a kind which every Esquimau undergoes upon the death of a near relation. The Angekok announces to the mourners into what animal the soul of the departed has passed; and henceforth, until the spirit has shifted its quarters, they are not to partake of the flesh of that animal.[24] This may be a bear, a seal, a walrus, a lumme, a burgomaster-gull, or any other embraced within their limited bill of fare.

The widow had one practice which, notwithstanding that it related to the same serious subject, caused us not a little amusement. Her late husband, for whose sake she refrained from eating walrus,[25] met with his death last Upernak (summer) by being carried out to sea on a loose cake of ice to which he had imprudently gone to watch for seal. The tide having changed, the floating raft was disengaged from the land; and, in full view of his family and friends, the poor hunter drifted out into the middle of Baffin Bay, never to be heard of more. It happened that, during the evening, the name of this hunter was mentioned several times, always in terms of warm praise, and each time his widow shed a copious flood of tears. Petersen told us that all strangers were expected to join in this ceremony. Our first attempt, I fear, made a poor show of sorrow; but the second was perfect of its kind.

A burial, 1860

Poor old Kablunet . . . died at five o'clock in the evening; at six she was sewed up in a seal-skin winding sheet, and before it was yet cold the body was carried on Hans's sledge to a neighboring gorge and there buried among the rocks and covered with heavy stones.[26] The only evidence of sorrow or regret was manifested by her daughter, Merkut, the wife of Hans, and these appeared to be dictated rather from custom than affection. Merkut remained by the grave after the others had departed, and for about an hour she walked around and around it, muttering in a low voice some praises of the deceased. At the head of the grave she then placed the knife, needles, and sinew that her mother had recently been using, and the last sad rites to the departed savage were performed.

"A dying people," 1861

Kalutunah grew more sad than I had ever before seen him, when I spoke to him of the fortunes of his own people. "Alas!" said he, "we will soon be all gone."[27] I told him that I would come back, and that white men would live for many years near Etah. "Come back soon," said he, "or there will be none here to welcome you!"

To contemplate the destiny of this little tribe is indeed painful . . . From the information which I obtained through Hans and Kalutunah, I estimated the tribe to number about one hundred souls—a very considerable diminution since Dr. Kane left them in 1855. Hans made for me a rude map of the coast from Cape York to Smith Sound, and set down upon it all of the villages, if by such name the inhabited places may be called. These places are always close by the margin of the sea. They rarely consist of more than one hut, and the largest village but of three.[28]

The lichens on the rocks develop in concentric, colored circles. On the ground, the *Xanthoria elegans* grows by 1 millimeter per year.

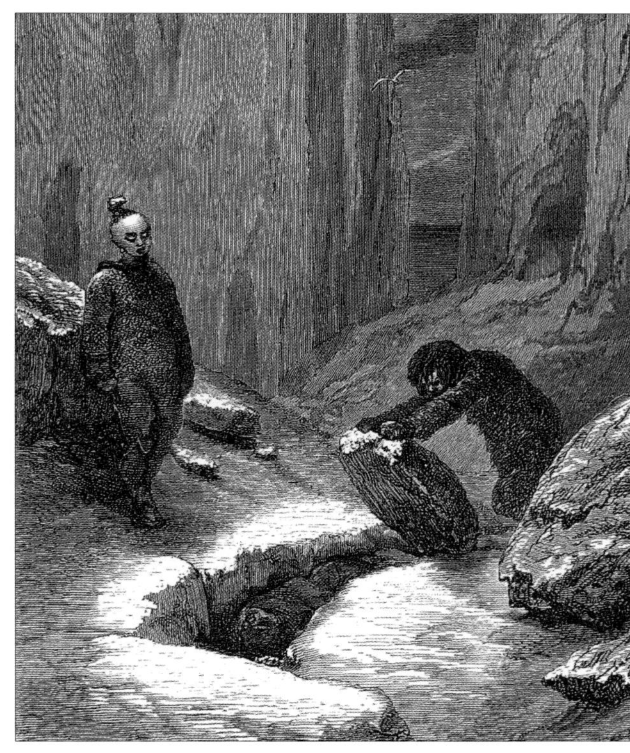

Hans Hendrik at the burial of his mother-in-law. On the left is his wife, Meqru, the grandmother of my companion Sakaeunnguaq in Siorapaluk in 1950-1951.

22) An essential trait of the Inuit: they are curious about everything, and seek to understand the why and the how; once their examination is concluded, they decide "Good or bad for the Inuit." The expression was the same in 1818 (see Ross and Sabine's accounts of the Eskimos' trial of the white man's food), in 1861 with Hayes, and in 1950-1951 with me: "The Americans at Thule," they pointed to the airbase, "bad for the Inuit." Oil polluting the sea was "bad for the Inuit." Gonorrhea, and nuak (an infectious flu brought by visiting ships), were "bad for the Inuit. "Tobacco," they told Harry Whitney, sucking on the feathers used by the American hunter to clean his pipe, were "good for the Inuit."

23) The problem—still unstudied—of the dog population among this isolated people is crucial. Without dogs, the Eskimos would be reduced to a primitive level they surpassed only at the beginning of the Christian era when they first domesticated dogs. The Eskimos' life is governed by the climate, which changes constantly. The warming trend since 1818—after the Little Ice Age of 1600-1800—has not progressed linearly. There have been periods of great cold. From 1850 to 1860, the cold was very severe. The floe grew thicker, the seals could not keep their agluq or breathing holes open with their claws and migrated south, along with the bears who fed on them. Lacking these two game animals essential to nourishment and clothing, the Eskimos killed their dogs. Subtle population control measures have always allowed the Polar Eskimos—who were completely isolated for two and a half centuries—to keep a minimum number of women and enough dogs even in the worst famines to ensure the reproduction of the one and the other. There were approximately 120 to 150 dogs in 1818 (?); 200 dogs in 1860-1861; 810 dogs in 1940-1941; 850 dogs in 1950; 1,300 dogs in 1989. Let us remember that the dog is so important to the Eskimo that the animal is accounted the progenitor of the Inuit people. The Inuit refused to sell a single one to Captain Ross in 1818.

24) The Eskimo believes that life is only a passage and continues in the beyond. His world view is vertical: the Eskimo paradise is in the sky. The world below is cruel to the hunter who has not respected the rules.

25) Taboo, or allerpoq: a body of doctrine aimed at maintaining the group in proportional relation to its ecological resources. It takes the form of sexual and alimentary prohibitions and rules for life (costume, behavior, silence).

26) Notice that Hans, a Moravian Christian from Fiskenaesset (South Greenland), did not observe the rites taught him by the priests. For good or ill, who is to say?

27) Miscommunication. Hayes misunderstands what the Eskimo is telling him. Kalutunah, like many natives, says what he believes his hearer is thinking so as to flatter him and obtain the most from him.

28) It is regrettable that this sketch map was never published. If the reference was to summer camps, these coastal hunters were always dispersed in small groups. In 1903, according to the first village-by-village census ever undertaken (thanks to Knud Rasmussen), there were eight villages (presumably winter villages) from south to north: Innaanganeq (Cape York), Apparsuit (Hakluyt Island), Natsilivik, Neqi, Kangerlussuaq, Uummannaq, Kiataq, and Qaanaaq, with one to four families in each village. In the winter of 1950-1951, there were ten villages from south to north: Savigsivik (pop. 41), Qeqertaq (pop. 13), Thule-Uummannaq (pop. 137, including 10 Danes), Nunatarsuaq (pop. 3), Qeqertat (pop. 17), Quinnisut (pop. 14), Kangerlussuaq (pop. 12), Siorapaluk (pop. 34, including 1 Frenchman, me), Neqi (pop. 10), Etah (pop. 21). (Jean Malaurie census)

The Last Migration of the Inuit

From the land of the Great Ancestors to the unknown people of Etah (1863)

Knud Rasmussen tells the story:

Among the Smith Sound Eskimos I met with some members of a foreign Eskimo tribe who had emigrated to the Cape York district, probably from the country round Baffin Island, a good fifty years before. They had become quite merged into the Cape York tribe, through wife-changing and inter-marriage. They were generally taller than the Greenlanders, and of markedly Indian type.[1]

Three or four of the actual immigrants are still living. One of these, old Merqusâq [Meqorsuaq], gave me the following details of the journey. This is probably the only example we have come in contact with among the Eskimos, of any of them, without any external influence from civilization having been brought to bear, and with only their own primitive means to assist them, having undertaken an actual tribal migration, a journey lasting several years, from one Polar region to another.

Merqusâq's tale

After Qitdlarssuaq had once heard that there were Inuit over on the other side of the sea, he could never settle down to anything again. He conjured spirits in the presence of all the people of the village.[2] He made his soul take long journeys through the air, with his helping spirits, to look for the country of the strange Inuit. At last one day he informed his fellow-villagers that he had found the new country![3] And he told them that he was going to journey to the strange people, and he exhorted them all to follow him.

"Do you know the desire for new countries? Do you know the desire to see new people?" he said to them.

And nine sledges joined him at once, and ten sledges together they set out northward to find the new country that Qitdlarssuaq said he had seen on his soul-flight. There were men, women, and children, thirty-eight in all, who started . . .

We started on our journey in the winter, after the light came, and set up our permanent camp in the spring, when the ice broke. There were plenty of animals for food on the way, seals, white whales, walruses, and bears. Long stretches of the coast along which we had to drive were not covered with ice, and so we were often obliged to make our way over huge glaciers.[4] On our way we also came to bird rocks, where auks built, and to some eider-duck islands.

As we carried all our belongings with us, clothes, tents, hunting and fishing implements, kayaks, we used very long narrow sledges. [He gave me the measure of the sledges, which were twenty feet long and four feet wide.] We had to have our

An ***angakkuq* Eskimo** preparing to butcher a narwhal.

sledges so long because the kayaks were carried on them . . .

Late in the spring we came to a place where the sea narrowed to a small channel. (Before this we had crossed two very broad inlets or fjords.) [5] Here Qitdlarssuaq pitched camp and conjured spirits. His soul took an air-flight over the sea, while his body lay lifeless behind. When the incantation was over, he announced that it was here that we were to cross the sea. On the other side we should meet with people. And all obeyed him, for they knew that he understood the hidden things.

So we crossed the sea, which was frozen over, and camped on the opposite coast. There we found houses, human habitations, but no people. [6] They had left the place. But we understood then that we had very little farther to go before meeting with people, and a great joy filled us all; our veneration for the man who for years had led us toward the distant goal knew no bounds.

It was decided that we should not seek further for the time being, but should first try to get in supplies, as the catch had for a long time been poor. The animals had been made invisible to us. And Qitdlarssuaq held an incantation to find out the reason of the failure of the fishery. After the incantation he announced that his daughter-in-law, Ivaloq, had had a miscarriage, but had kept the matter secret, to escape penance. That was why the animals had been invisible. And so he ordered his son to shut up his wife in a snow-hut as a punishment, after having first taken her furs from her. In the snow-hut she would either freeze to death or die of hunger. Before this came to pass, the animals would not allow themselves to become the prey of men.

And they built a snow-hut at once and shut Ivaloq up in it. This Qitdlarssuaq did with his son's wife, whom he loved greatly; and he did it, that the innocent should not suffer for her fault.

Immediately after the punishment had been carried into effect, we came upon a large herd of reindeer, inland, and had meat in abundance. This was at Etâ. [7]

While we were there, there was a cry one day of "Sledges! sledges!" And we saw two sledges approaching, sledges from a strange people. And they saw us and drove up to us.

They were people of the tribe, and we had been looking for them for a long time. The one man was called Arrutsak, the other Agina, and their home was at a place called Pitoravik, not far from where we were encamped. We shouted aloud with joy; for now we had found new country, and new people. And our great magician had proved himself greater than all who had doubted him.

Bow case (*atasuk*) made of seal skin, with quiver. Composite bow (*pisissi*), 34 inches long. Three pieces of antler have been bent and joined to form the bow. Bows were reintroduced to the group around 1860. They were used very little between 1600 and 1800, as hunters preferred lances and traps. The bow's range is short: 4 or 5 yards. Starting in 1900, firearms came into general use. But shot and powder were unobtainable after Peary's *final* departure (1909). A trading post was essential. Knud Rasmussen understood this in 1910.

Qaaqqutsiaq (14 years old) drawing a bow at Etah (1914).

1) This was particularly true for Uutaaq, one of my principal informants in 1950-1951 in Thule. The height and cast of features (cheekbones, shape of the eyes) of his son Kutsikitsoq contrasted with those of the natives, who were more compact, with more "Chinese" features. He was proud of this, and wore fringes along the bottom of his qulitsaq (caribou vest) in the Canadian style. The Inuit from the West are considered to be the Great Ancestors.

2) Fourteen Inuit from Baffin Island (Igloolik) immigrated to North Greenland under the leadership of Qitdlarssuaq (Qillarsuaq), who lived near Igloolik, north of Hudson Bay. He learned—probably from whalers at Pond Inlet or in Lancaster Sound—that there was a people living north of Igloolik. During the prehistoric and protohistoric eras, news moved from group to group from west to east (and vice versa). Thus, at the end of the eighteenth century, Paul Egede established that the South Greenlanders were aware of a people living in the north who had neither wood nor iron and used narwhal tusks for lance- and harpoon-shafts.

3) We shouldn't forget that the Inuit retained the memory of a people who preceded them: the Tornit, or Tunit, who were bigger, stronger, and without dogs, kayaks, or bows. Their houses were made of giant stones. They hunted caribou. It is possible that the idea of a new country was associated with the idea of a country teeming with game, an Eden, similar to the Greco-Roman idea of paradise, associated with the land of the Hyperboreans.

4) The fringe of ice, or ice-foot, along the coast is not unbroken. It is the path normally followed in the summer after the ice has melted from the fjords. The glaciers are tongues of ice issuing from the ice cap.

5) Qitdlarssuaq describes one after the other Lancaster and Jones sounds. The conjuration presumably took place near Cape Sabine, facing Smith Sound. The journey is thought to have lasted six years.

6) Presumably Anoritooq, east of Cape Sabine.

7) More accurately, according to the information I gathered at Etah in 1967, the meeting took place at Taserartalik, on the Archean rock of the north coast of the fjord, a mile or so west of Etah.

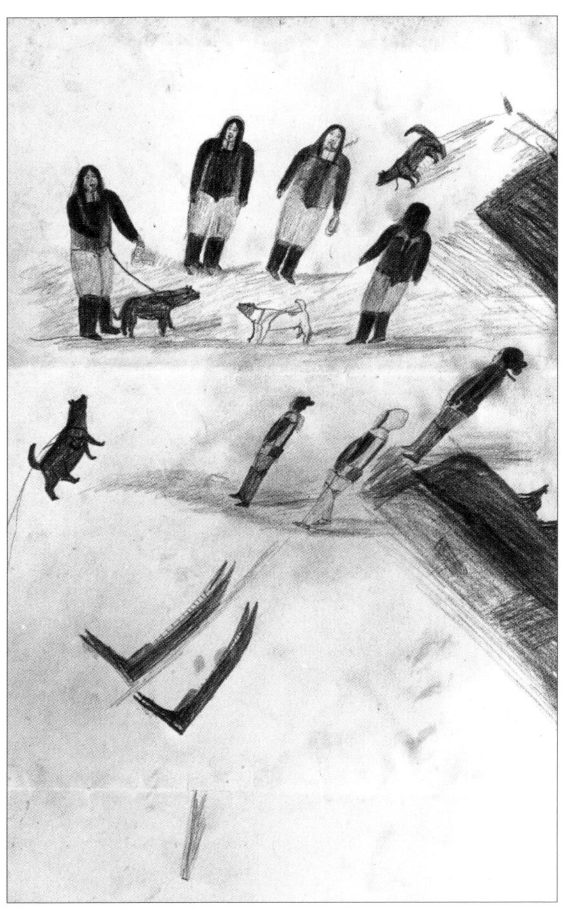

Training dogs by example: the young dog is trained by the old dog, then by the pack.

Winter scene: a malevolent spirit in the form of a monstrous dog with a hanging tail wants to enter the outer tunnel of an igloo (*tossut*) and torment the Inuits.

Arrutsak was a man with a wooden leg. Once upon a time he had fallen from a bird rock, as we learned later, and had had his one leg broken. His mother had cut off the injured part of the leg and made him a wooden leg that could be bound fast to the stump. He could run and drive just as well as if he had never lost a limb. But when we saw him come running up the first time with his wooden leg, many of us supposed that it was usual, and that the new people always had one leg made of wood.

We sat down at once to eat with the new arrivals, and they told us many things about the people we were going to see. During the meal a thing happened that amused us all.

It was customary in our tribe that, when eating together in a friendly way, all should eat from the same bone. When a piece of meat was handed to one, he just took a bite from it, and passed on the remainder to those with whom he was taking his meal. We call that Amerqatut. But every time that we handed the new arrivals a piece of meat, of which they were only intended to eat a mouthful, they ate the whole piece; and so it was a long time before we others could get anything to eat, as they were very hungry.

That was a custom the new people were not acquainted with, but now they have all adopted it . . .

We taught these people many things. We showed them how to build snow-huts with long tunnel passages and an entrance from below. When you build snow-huts that way, there comes no draught into the room where you sit. The people here did build snow-huts before we came, but knew nothing of an entrance from below.

We taught them to shoot with bow and arrows. Before our arrival they did not hunt the many reindeer that are in their country. If by any chance they got an animal, they did not even dare to eat it, being afraid that they might die, but they fed their dogs with it.

We taught them to spear salmon in the streams. There were a great many salmon in the country, but they did not know the implement that you spear them with.

And we taught them to build kayaks, and to hunt and catch from kayaks. Before that they had only hunted on the ice, and had been obliged during the spring to catch as many seals, walruses, and narwhals as they would want for the summer, when the ice had gone.[8] They generally went for the summer to the islands where the eider duck hatched, or near razorbill rocks, as here at Agpat, or inland, or to a country where the Little Auks bred. They told us that their forefathers had known the use of the kayak, but that an evil disease had once ravaged their land, and carried off the old people. The young ones did not know how to build new kayaks, and the old people's kayaks they had buried with their owners. This was how it had come about that kayak hunting had been forgotten.

But we adopted their type of sledge, for it was better than ours, and had uprights on it.

All the people took us in as kinsmen, and we stayed here many years without thinking of returning home. But it came to pass that old Qitdlarssuaq was again taken with the desire for a long journey. He was very old then, with children and children's children. But he said that he wished to see his own country again before he died. And he announced that he was going to start back. He had been among the new people then for six years. All those who had followed him here were unwilling to desert him, and made ready to start back with him. Only his son, Itsukusuk, decided to remain, because he had a little child who was ill.[9]

[Rasmussen, Knud, *The People of the Polar North*, comp. and ed. by G. Herring (London: Kegan Paul, Trench, Trübner & Co. Ltd., 1908).

8) In August 1818, Sir John Ross reported that the Polar Inuit had no knowledge of kayaks. The expression is incorrect. The error is due to John Sacheuse's relative ignorance of the language of the North Greenlanders. Meqorsuaq's statement, made in 1902, plausibly establishes that the Inuit preserved the memory of the kayak but had lost the art of building it when the "old people" died, and that they refused, for unconscious reasons of population control, to develop an economy oriented toward the sea during a time of dearth. It took forty-five years for these Inuit to believe in the warming trend that began in 1818, for them to accept the technology of the kayak, and only because it was taught to them by the Great Ancestors, the Inuit from the West, who by their own vitality attested to its value. The recommendations of Hans Hendrik (Ashé), who was very familiar with kayaks—his skill with the kayak was one of the reasons Kane had recruited him in 1853—were not followed by the Inuit during his long stay among them in 1855-1860. Nor did he teach them the use of the bow, which he practiced shooting in the hold of the Advance, killing the rats that Kane ate. He came from the south and collaborated with the whites, who had little credibility in the field of technology—their overwinterings generally ended in tragedy.

9) Ittukusuk, the "Little Anus."

Arrutsak, the man with the wooden leg. He took to wearing the prosthesis after falling from a rock as a child while hunting auks with a net. His mother had to cut off his broken leg.

POLARIS.

Charles Francis Hall 1821-1871

THE MISFORTUNE OF NOT BEING A SCIENTIST

Charles Francis Hall was the first to understand that the Pole could not be conquered without the active help of the Inuit. He would be murdered by one of his companions. After this tragic expedition, white men lost whatever prestige they had in the eyes of the Eskimos, never to recover it.

"They're trying to kill me, this cup of coffee is poisoned!" shouted Captain Charles Francis Hall, the leader of the first American expedition to the North Pole commissioned by the president of the United States. It was early autumn of 1871.

On 30 August of that same year the *Polaris* (380 tons) reached a new farthest north at latitude 82° 11' north and longitude 61° west, thanks to an unusually warm summer. Hall was on the northwest coast of Greenland two hundred miles farther north than reached by Kane's ship the *Advance* in 1853-1855, not far from the Arctic Ocean.

This desolate land of rock and ice received daylight for only a few hours each day at that season. The polar night with its continual darkness would descend in six weeks (13 October), bringing with it a train of anxieties . . .

In the captain's cabin, Hall felt extraordinarily ill. He anxiously considered what might have brought on his weakness and pain. After several days of delirium, he rose and wandered around the *Polaris* looking for the enemy who was trying to kill him. He instructed his faithful Eskimo companions to watch over all the food and drink that was brought to him. Seaman Joseph Mauch had orders to taste every dish and beverage . . .

The expedition had been commissioned by President Ulysses S. Grant, who was won over by the great explorer's simplicity and communicative power. Hall's reputation was international. Lady Jane Franklin, now 77 years old, had traveled to New York to convince Hall to search for her husband's expedition, using his own methods, which were similar to those of the Eskimos. Hall replied that it would be a great honor, but only after his return from the Pole.

A fervent patriot, Hall was distressed that the British were still the only ones to explore and map the north coast of America from Labrador to the Bering Strait. In his address to Congress, Hall said: "It is high time for Washington to stake a claim to the Arctic. Planting the star-spangled banner at the Pole, the earth's axis, would be a first step." And his voice would be heard, echoing as it did the deep feelings of a young America. "The Pole must be American; the earth's sum of knowledge can only be increased by settling this enigma; and vast new whaling grounds may be found in the ice-free Polar Sea."

Charles Francis Hall (seated in the center), who led the first official polar expedition of the United States government, did not succeed in planting the stars and stripes at the North Pole. Born in Rochester, N.Y., in 1821, he died on 8 November 1871 aboard the *Polaris*, trapped by ice in Robeson Channel at latitude 81° 37 north and longitude 62° west. He was buried nearby on land that bears his name. From left to right around Hall: J. Lupton, J. H. Stanton, P. Clarke (Washington, D.C., 1870).

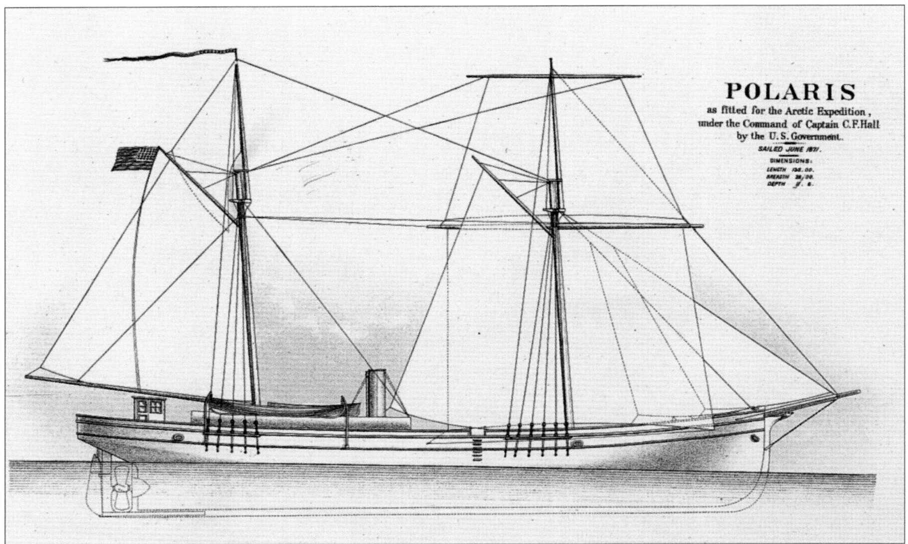

The *Polaris* was a former tugboat, refitted for Arctic service. Its interior layout (below) was adapted for wintering in the ice.

A few politicians objected that Hall was not a scientist, and that Dr. Isaac Israel Hayes (who was maneuvering to take his place, as we have seen) would be a more competent choice of leader. He answered haughtily: "No, I am not a scientist, but the quest for the Pole has never been conducted by men of science. Neither Sir John Franklin, nor Sir Edward Parry, nor Frobisher, nor Davis, nor Baffin, nor Bylot, Hudson, Foxe, Back, or M'Clintock, nor Osborne, Dean, or Simpson, nor Rae nor Ross were scientists. Yet they loved science and did much to enrich it." Hall ended with a famous quote from Goethe: "The more I live, the more I am certain that the difference between men is based on energy and unconquerable determination."

Hall of the Far North

Who exactly was Charles Francis Hall? He was first a blacksmith, then a printer, and finally a reporter on a newspaper that he had started in Cincinnati. An unconditional admirer of Kane and deeply religious, Hall became convinced at the age of thirty-eight that he had been called to the Far North. He left his wife and four children and decided to search for Franklin and his 129 shipmates in the frozen regions. Having read everything there was in the public library about the Arctic and made extensive notes, he went to New York to complete his research. He concluded that the massive British rescue expeditions were bound to fail because they were too rigid and military. Nearly a million pounds sterling had been spent with no decisive results. To slip into the Arctic expanses Eskimo-fashion was, according to him, the key to success. And he was the first from the United States to say so. [1]

For eight years he explored Baffin Island, Foxe Peninsula, and the Keewatin district, learning from the Eskimos and living in intimacy with them. In the course of two expeditions—the first a two-year expedition (1860-1862) alone with the Eskimos of Frobisher Bay, [2] the second a five-year expedition (1864-1869) to the central and eastern Arctic—he would not only prove an excellent self-taught geographer and cartographer but collect an enormous amount of ethnographic material, much of it ignored even today. To organize and publish this material would bring much glory to an American scientific institution.

Hall also contributed to our knowledge of the true fate of the British explorers aboard the *Erebus* and the *Terror*. The Inuit told him that they had seen the bodies of the expedition's members (led by Crozier after the death of Franklin—whose death has still not been explained and whose grave has never been found), several of which had been mutilated. Hall was horrified to learn that there was evidence of cannibalism. Only thirty-six of these seamen, with two Eskimos, managed to reach the mouth of the Back River after a forced march, and to reach Montreal Island. [3]

Hall's first and only book, written on his return from his first expedition, is dense but exceptionally full of information and shot through with mystical and poetic insights. It has not had the success it deserves. It was published while Hall was starting off on his extraordinary second expedi-

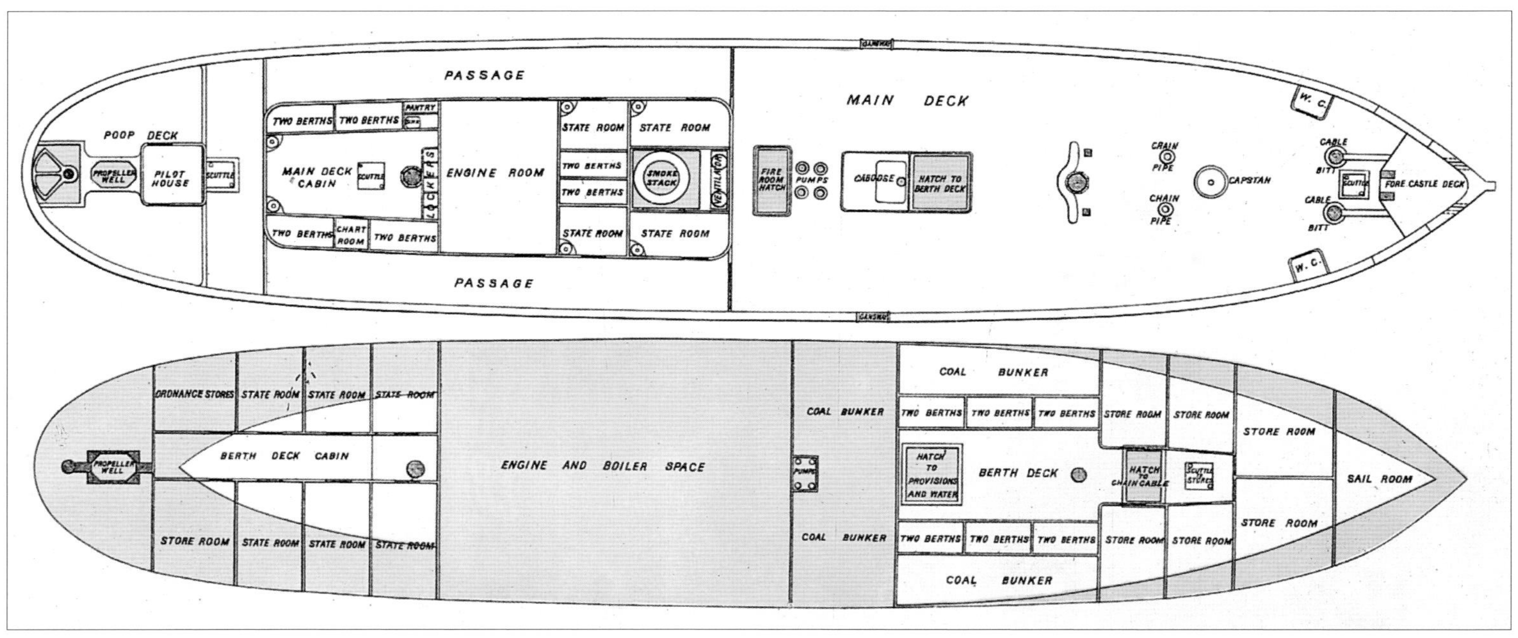

tion (1864-1869), which would take him as far as King William Island. The book notably disproves the conventional wisdom that to overwinter is to sign one's death warrant, and it is the first to give a voice to the Eskimo people.

Envy and jealousy, the plague of Polar expeditions

Willful, ambitious, and of uncommon energy, a giant of a man at 220 lbs., bearded, and with a permanently ironic expression, Hall found himself for the first time the only master on board ship—or at least so he thought. The *Polaris* was a steam-driven former tug-boat refitted for Arctic duty, carrying twenty-seven men beside himself (eight officers and quartermasters, three scientists, fourteen seamen, and two Eskimos). After lengthy hesitation on the part of the government bureaus concerned, Hall had been named to lead the expedition, but his appointment had been a difficult one. And though Hall intended to be the heart and soul of the expedition, he could not, lacking university ties, assume the role of chief scientific officer. With no sailing experience, he could not command the ship, either. A captain was needed, a master sailor with Arctic experience: the whaler Sidney Budington was chosen. The fate of the *Polaris* would thus be in the hands of a triumvirate. Hall should have asserted himself early on, but given his character, his extreme sensitivity, his habit of settling problems Eskimo-fashion, by letting conflicts ripen, and given also the various players involved, an unbearable tension soon overwhelmed the expedition. It would have been infinitely better to have this antagonistic and multinational group under the authority of a single man. The chief antagonist and enemy of Charles Francis Hall was the rich and arrogant Dr. Emil Bessels, a twenty-four-year-old geographer and doctor. This young graduate of Heidelberg University, who had taken part in the German Arctic expedition of 1869 (aboard the *Hansa*), had been asked, along with Dr. Meyer, to take part in collecting scientific information.[4]

The two youngsters, proud of the German victory over France in 1871 after the Franco-Prussian War (in which they took part), tried to assert their authority over the crew, especially as the expedition was jointly sponsored by the German Academy of Sciences and the Smithsonian Institution and they had been selected personally by Augustus Petermann, the famous German geographer and the author of the theory of the Open Polar Sea.

By their constant sarcasm, and with the support of the nine Germans on the crew, they attempted to undermine Hall's authority and dignity. Yet the expedition had been remarkably organized. The *Polaris*, reinforced to withstand the ice, was sailing under one of the best whaling skippers, Sidney Budington, a friend of Hall's and a veteran of eleven previous Arctic outings. But Hall was unaware that Budington drank. Then too there was the presence of Captain Tyson, the original choice for sailing master, who joined the expedition late as Budington's second in command, a situation that inevitably created conflict. On the other hand, there were excellent and loyal subordinates: the Eskimo couple from Frobisher Bay, Joe and Hannah, who shipped aboard in New York, and the veteran Hans Hendrik, with his wife Meqru and his children, who joined the expedition in Upernavik.[5]

After leaving New London on 3 July 1871, Hall met with nothing but tension and difficulty. At Godhavn (Disko Island), the insolence of the German scientists was so marked that the two American officers of the transport ship resupplying the *Polaris* with coal felt obliged to call them to order officially; Dr. Meyer was even impelled to sign his employment contract a second time. But the law could not overcome the general antagonism and reverse the disintegration of the crew. Budington, wearied by these quarrels, sought refuge in drink. His only concern was to save the boat and bring it back safely to port. Of course he wanted the *Polaris* to continue northward, but not beyond Etah and the stretch of open water near Pond Inlet and the Scots whaling fleet operating out of Melville Bay. He believed that Hall should use dog sleds to reach the Pole while he himself maintained the ship as a rear base. Everyone argued, but Hall made the decision. The *Polaris* must push as far north as possible immediately. Fortune smiled on him. Kane Basin and the sea beyond as far as the Arctic Ocean were remarkably free of ice. In honor of George Robeson, U.S. secretary of the navy, Hall named the last channel to the ocean Robeson Channel.

Provoking jealousy and envy is the fate of strong personalities. The arenas of politics and science see this on

First official U.S. expedition to the Pole, led by C. F. Hall aboard the *Polaris*. Course of the ice floe bearing the drift party toward Labrador (1871-1873).

Augtuq. The hunter crawls over the ice toward the basking seal (May-June).

Instruments from the *Polaris*: sounding-line and compass.

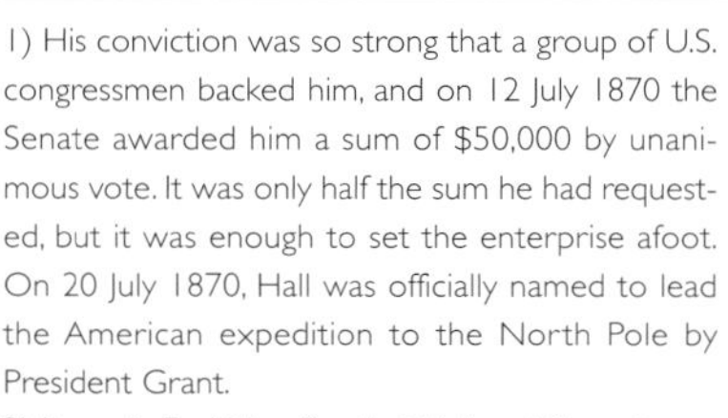

1) His conviction was so strong that a group of U.S. congressmen backed him, and on 12 July 1870 the Senate awarded him a sum of $50,000 by unanimous vote. It was only half the sum he had requested, but it was enough to set the enterprise afoot. On 20 July 1870, Hall was officially named to lead the American expedition to the North Pole by President Grant.

2) It was in Frobisher Bay that Hall met the extraordinary Inuit couple Joe and Hannah, originally from Repulse Bay, who would accompany him for the rest of his life, even to New York (they called him "Father Hall"). On his second expedition to the Canadian Central Arctic, they served as his interpreters and guides. They had first been picked out by whalers in 1855 and taken to London where they spent two years. They were even presented to Queen Victoria. Hannah spoke English quite fluently. This extraordinary couple deserves a book of their own.

3) A note discovered under a cairn at Cape Felix established that the expedition was proceeding south under the greatest peril. No other trace was ever found in the sector between western King William Island and the Back River. I made inquiries about this tragedy on the site itself, in April 1963, from the Eskimos and the sergeant of the Canadian Mounties who accompanied me while investigating the causes of a famine among the Utkuhikhalingmiut. See Jean Malaurie, *Hummocks I*.

4) Dr. Bessels received a salary of $100 per month, exclusive of board.

5) Hendrik was simply following tradition. A woman accompanied her husband on the hunt, and if she was a mother, the children necessarily rode along on the sled.

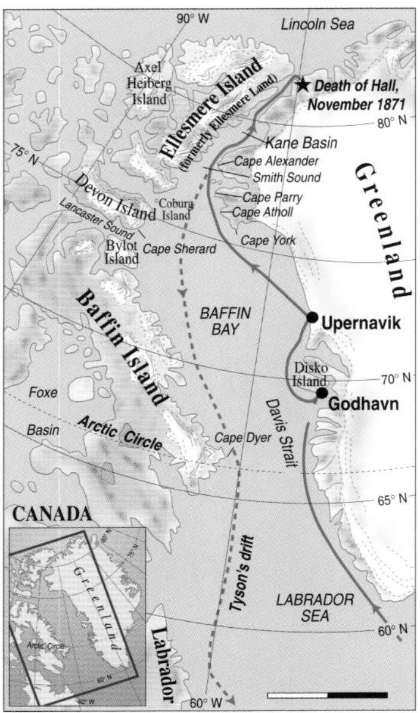

Route of the *Polaris*'s exploration (1871-1873). On the return, in November 1872, the *Polaris* was shipwrecked north of Etah. One group returned in two launches. Another group (Tyson's) drifted on the ice to Labrador.

Lifeboat Cove, or Qallunnaalik, site of the winter quarters of the fourteen Germans and Americans shipwrecked with the *Polaris* north of Etah at the foot of Cape Hatherton. The cabin was built by the expedition. The two igloos belong to the Inuit of Etah, who gave the explorers occasional help. The first launch has been built. On the left, the stranded *Polaris*, a trove of wood and iron for the Inuit after the departure of the whites.

a daily basis. One might think that the Arctic regions, which require unusual physical and moral attributes, would work against this tendency. The opposite is true. It appears that fear, isolation, cold, and group living in the prison-like setting of a ship exacerbate it. Jealousy and envy have plagued Arctic expeditions large and small up to the present day. There was Captain John Ross, maligned by Edward Sabine; and Hayes, who criticized his colleague Kane behind his back. Hall, the mystic of the North, whose almost mythical voyages among the Eskimos of Baffin Island were already legendary, would not escape the plague. The list is long, and this malignant disease remains an active threat. Alas!

The *Polaris* meanwhile was able to reach the Lincoln Sea and the extremely high latitude of 82° 11' north. A victory, this represents the farthest north ever attained by a traditional ship. But Hall wanted to press on even farther. The ship should be maneuvered into open leads and driven forward. Ever northward! Budington refused. He stormed out of a meeting called to decide the matter. Tyson and Chester supported Hall, but Hall was reluctant to override his sailing master and decided, after some hesitation, to winter farther south in a suitable cove. The road ahead would be explored by sledge. The *Polaris* drifted south in the dangerous ice for four days then was brought into a harbor on the extreme north coast of Greenland in the shelter of an enormous iceberg (lat. 81° 37' N, 62° W), some distance back from its extraordinary advance into the Arctic Ocean. Hall disembarked, draped in the American flag, and claimed formal possession of the land for the United States government. The land would eventually bear his name. Hardly had the expedition settled in than Hall, true to his nature, decided to explore the area, taking a dog sled north to scout the route that he would follow toward the Pole in the spring—one that would perhaps lead him past the barrier of ice hummocks to the mythical Polar Sea and to the North Pole itself, which he said he was certain to reach. His chances were exceptionally good. Morton, the very man who saw the southern shores of the Open Polar Sea from Washington Land in 1854, was on board the ship and daily urging him on. So Hall set off with Chester and his two Eskimo companions, Joe and Hans, driving two sledges pulled by 14 dogs (or 12, the accounts differ), from 10 to 24 October, on a first reconnaissance of the coast to 82° north (Cape Brevoort). He discovered land stretching to the west of Robeson Channel. From a high point, he was able to determine that it extended to 83° 05' north. The former printer from Cincinnati, embarked on his last exploration, had seen accurately. Later expeditions would confirm it.

The murder of Charles Francis Hall

There followed one of the greatest dramas in the history of the Arctic. On his return from this brilliant reconnaissance mission, Hall was greeted by Morton and lingered on deck, in perfect health, only a little tired. He asked for a cup of coffee, then went down to his cabin, where he complained of the oppressive heat. Having drunk his coffee, whose taste he found sweet (it was served to him by the steward John Herron), he immediately felt nauseous. He took to his bed and became delirious. He was feverish and partially paralyzed, with a stomach ache and an irregular pulse, and he had difficulty speaking. The fragments of speech he was able to utter were unambiguous: in his moments of lucidity he accused Dr. Bessels of having poisoned him. He categorically refused Bessels's care or his medications. Dr. Bessels, the chief scientific officer, was the ship's doctor.

Bessels, the "little German," the "little dancing master," as Hall nicknamed him—intense dark eyes, high forehead, and a forked mephistophelean beard—never left Hall's side. Was it not his duty as a doctor to attend to Hall? Although he could not object to Hall's food being tasted, it was still he and he alone who administered the patient's quinine shots, over Hall's vehement objections. But, one might ask, was it really quinine?

Hall, whose health was legendary, seemed to recover very quickly once all his food was being checked. The official report states clearly: "The refusal of all medica-

tion seems to be benefiting him." He rose from bed, spoke on deck with several of the seamen, whose company he visibly preferred to the officers', and lingered particularly with the Eskimos, with whom he felt more than sympathy—a veritable symbiosis. He chatted often with Morton, who held him in tremendous respect. He continued to want his meals cooked solely by the Eskimo Hannah. On 4 or 5 November he ate a large dish of boiled seal meat. But on 6 November he relapsed abruptly. Seated on his bunk, his eyes glazed, Hall tried to talk and articulate syllable by syllable the word "murder." Dr. Bessels rubbed his body as a last resort with mustard. The end was near. He fell into a coma and died in the early hours (3:25 am) of 8 November 1871, at the age of fifty. All the seamen as well as Tyson, the assistant navigator, accused Bessels of having betrayed his duties as a doctor. [6] The four Eskimos were in despair. They left the ship to live some distance away in an igloo.

But why would the young German doctor have murdered Hall in this way? Out of hatred, or spite, or in the hope of taking command of the expedition? Who can say? Everything is so quickly exacerbated in these desolate spaces, where the effects of a man's conflicts and phantasms are unpredictable. The conditions on these ships inflames the vilest impulses.

The matter is hushed up

On the expedition's return, the congressional board of inquiry, anxious to hush up the murder of the leader of the first official U.S. expedition to the Pole, would lose itself in a tangle of conjectures. The private journal in which Hall recorded every incident up to the eve of his death curiously disappeared; Budington, to whom the journal had been entrusted, could not find it. In his last two days when he was feeling slightly better, Hall apparently burned some papers that might have proved compromising to his "old friend," who had lapsed into alcoholism. One fact has always been clear, which is that Hall did not commit suicide. A further fact is that not only Bessels but Budington (despite his closeness to Hall) loudly expressed their satisfaction at Hall's death. To them, his death could only prove "beneficial for the accomplishment of the aims of the expedition and for the survival of all." According to the seaman Noah Hayes, Dr. Bessels even said that "Hall's death was the best thing that could have happened to the expedition." Hayes added: "He even laughed when he said it!" [7] Naturally the private journals of the expedition members were read and analyzed, but by whom? With what purpose? What instructions? The board of inquiry, to all appearances, preferred to cover up for the witnesses, who for their part had all the time to prepare their testimony in the two years of overwintering that followed the murder of their leader and moving force.

Hall's two Eskimo friends were briefly heard from—very briefly. Hans Hendrik's interrogation was handled in such a way that he actually said nothing; his wife Meqru was not even questioned. Thus the possibility that a man with a great mission to accomplish had been stopped in mid-career by a criminal act could be erased from public consciousness. It is worth noting that the board of inquiry did not think it worthwhile to have Hall's body examined! An analysis was made only in 1968, when a private expedition led by the American Chauncey Loomis dug up Hall's body in northern Greenland—where his remains still lie, in the frozen land that bears his name. The results from the laboratory in Toronto were unequivocal: the arsenic levels found in Hall's hair and nails were fatal and had been absorbed by Hall in the last two weeks of his life.

Yet the answers given by the steward John Herron at his interrogation were clear enough: "I did not prepare the coffee. . . . He never took medicine during his illness. . . . I understood that the doctor (Dr. Bessels) gave him quinine injections; what he said was quinine . . ." To the question: "Did Hall accuse anyone in particular?" he answered: "Yes, sir." Question: "Who?" "Answer: "Doctor Bessels."

The only funeral oration that would have pleased him was the declaration by his faithful Eskimo friend Joe

6) See page 123 for Tyson's horrific account.

7) Quoted in Pierre Berton, *Arctic Grail*, p. 392.

The burial of Charles Francis Hall, on 10 November 1871, occurred at 11:00 a.m. during the polar night. Seamen pulled the coffin on a sled draped in the American flag (which would be discovered almost intact in 1968) and followed by Hall's four Eskimo companions. The grave was shallow (about two feet deep) because of the hard-frozen ground, and Hall, wearing his blue uniform, was interred in a simple pine coffin, his head to the east and his feet toward the icy waters of the strait.

The chaplain, Brian, read a few prayers.

A British expedition led by Captain George Nares was the only one to erect a stone over the grave to honor this American hero. The United States would bring honor on itself by doing homage to Captain Hall, either by holding a ceremony or building a monument to him on the land that bears his name, or, better yet, by burying this Arctic celebrity and pioneer with all honors at Arlington National Cemetery.

The wreck of the *Polaris,* November 1872, south of Cape Hatherton in what would become Qallunnaalik. Drawing by a seaman.

Ebierbing: "Captain Hall? A man with heart. I was very unhappy when he died. I'll never go to the North again without him. I don't know anything else."

An indication of the secretary of the navy's desire to squelch the whole affair can be seen in the following few lines: "The daily life of the expedition was as harmonious as could be expected. Discipline was maintained and good order was generally respected on board." The navy wished Hall to be seen as having died of apoplexy, and his public accusations of murder to be taken as the ravings of a paranoiac. [8]

As to Bessels, he was exonerated by the board of inquiry. The Smithsonian Institution designated him to translate and prepare the scientific reports. But his Prussian arrogance exasperated all his colleagues. An interview in the *New York Herald Tribune* of 16 February 1880 gives some idea of the "little dancing master"'s style. Asked about an Arctic expedition organized by Captain Howgate of the Signal Corps, he answered: "The plan proposed by Howgate has no merit. It demonstrates that the man is without even the most elementary experience of the Arctic. . . . He is nothing more than an agitator, an officer with no more competence in science or navigation than a cabin boy." Bessels went on: "Let me tell you that we know from experience that the white man cannot live at high latitudes, due to the polar night: the longer his stay, the lower his resistance."

Polar history is rife with commentators whose exaggeration and spirit of disparagement are a reflection of their own mediocrity. *Ultima Thule* is the expression, chapter by chapter, of this poverty of the human condition: vanity and jealousy, the levers of history.

Yet the very Captain Howgate that Bessels dismissed so contemptuously would prove an innovative spirit: his plan for the creation of new bases—permanent Arctic stations from which exploring parties could be organized along military lines under a single operational command—was to have considerable importance for the geostrategic future of the Arctic nations. The history of the stations in Alaska, Canada, Greenland, and Siberia have proven Howgate's foresight and the wrongheadedness of Dr. Bessels.

At the Smithsonian, Bessels's competence as a geographer was generally recognized, as was his talent for collating the diverse observations made on the *Polaris* expedition and compiling a record, but his vanity was growing more and more unendurable. Bessels's contract, renewed annually for nine years with increasing reticence, was finally denied a further renewal. This accounts for the fact that the second volume of the scientific report of the Hall expedition was never published. [9] The U.S. Navy prepared a *Narrative of the North Polar Expedition* under the direction of Admiral C. H. Davis. Highly official and uncritical, the report compiles official documents, private journals (obviously chosen for political reasons), and various experimental results.

For Bessels, nothing would ever go right again, even to the most minor details: his ethnological mission to the Pacific Northwest ended in shipwreck; his suitcase full of the documents and notes he had managed to bring back from the Arctic was stolen from him on a train in London; in 1885 a fire burned his house, his manuscripts, and his collection. The gods of the North have a long memory. Back in Berlin, he would die suddenly, on 30 March 1888, of an actual apoplexy.

George Tyson's party, adrift on a floe

With the death of Charles Francis Hall, the *Polaris* expedition witnessed another drama. After 8 November 1871, the *Polaris* was literally and figuratively adrift. "Nothing but chiefs on board," said the four Inuit, Joe, Hendrik, and their wives. Three groups took shape: the Americans, the Germans, and the Eskimos. Bessels meticulously maintained the schedule of geographic and meteorological observations. The winter and spring passed with the various factions at each others' throats. Petermann Fjord was explored at the end of the winter, as well as the east coast of Robeson Channel as far as Cape Bryant. But the energy level of the first month diminished with the passing weeks. Alcohol was now consumed on a daily basis. In August 1872, Budington was looking for the quickest way south, his ship's hull severely dented by the pressure of the ice against its sides. Meqru gave birth to a son, who was named Charles Polaris in Hall's memory. The ship steamed south without major difficulties as far as Smith Sound. On 15 October 1872, north of Etah Fjord (Littleton Island), the ship was caught in a storm and, unable to maneuver among the ice floes, was wedged against a gigantic iceberg to the point of almost sinking. Drunk, Budington gave contradictory orders. The storm raged with increasing violence. The crew was called to bring the ship's cargo on deck—cases of stores, ammunition, etc. The stern seemed to have been stove in. In the general panic, nineteen men, women, and children—nine white men, eight of them German, a black cook, four Eskimos with their five children (including Meqru and Hans's newborn)—reacting to confused orders, disembarked from the ship onto the ice floe with the dogs, a portion of the equipment (including two boats, kayaks, guns and ammunition) and provisions for a few months—along with the boxes containing all the scientific observations, letters, and private journals. Suddenly, the ship righted itself and set off crazily toward the south with the remainder of the crew and its drunken captain. Some ran along the ice trying to catch up with the ship, which was steaming rapidly away, but in vain. The expedition had been cut in two! The nineteen men and women found themselves stuck on an island of ice five miles in circumference, which, as it drifted south, occasionally spun on its axis in the currents. Tyson, the assistant navigator, who had disembarked onto the ice on Budington's orders, tried in the dark to organize this disparate crew, which would drift on the floe for six months across the North Atlantic and, after surviving the long polar night, reach Labrador in April 1873.

Their inventory: fourteen cans of pemmican, eleven and a half sacks of flour, one sack of dried apples, fourteen hams, ten dozen cases of meat, ten pounds of chocolate, and some ammunition—such were their reserves. On the first two days, the stranded crew saw the *Polaris* in the distance sailing and even steaming! Their frantic calls, dispersing into the frozen air amid the crashing of the ice and the howling of the wind, drew no response.

They were alone on the ice, with the added injury of believing they had been callously abandoned. The stranded party survived the winter thanks to the igloos built by the two devoted Eskimos, Joe and Hans, and especially thanks to their hunting. It was they who kept the blubber lamps attended by Hannah and Meqru supplied with oil. Tyson, who had been Assistant Navigator aboard the *Polaris*, had difficulty imposing his authority; stealing was widespread; the Germans, who spoke almost no English, terrorized the group as a whole. They were armed and, when food was scarce, openly declared that there were too many Eskimo children. Did they want to eat them? When famine struck (in the month of March and from 13 to 17 April), the Eskimo families stayed huddled together, watching day and night to ward off any attack from the Germans. The hardest times, in point of fact, were when spring returned, and the ice floe started to break up in early April. Each day, the group had to move to a new floe. Off the coast of Labrador, the ice rafts were no more than small cakes washed by the waves. Some sought shelter under the ship's boat, others tried to reach a more substantial iceberg. Every hour was a struggle.

On 1 April the party crammed together into the boat and steered a course between the jagged and dripping icebergs, which were melting in the spring weather. From time to time the party would stop and rest on one of the masses of ice. After having been adrift for one hundred ninety-six days, their torture—unparalleled in Arctic history—came to an end. On 30 April 1873, two days before a terrible storm that would certainly have drowned them—they were picked up by a sealer, the *Tigress*, off Newfoundland. Hans Hendrik, wanting to make sure that the ship did not miss them in the fog, courageously set off in his kayak to intercept it.

The ice-drift party on their fragment of ice floe, 6 April 1873. They were saved only thanks to the three ship's boats, which they quickly launched. Engraving after the description in Tyson's journal.

And the party aboard the *Polaris*?

Captain Tyson, whose character seems more and more admirable as the narrative progresses, had barely landed in St. John, Newfoundland, before organizing a rescue mission to bring back the fourteen men left aboard the *Polaris*, which was thought still to be near Etah. Tyson certainly didn't hold a grudge. Although he continued to doubt Sidney Budington's good faith—he despised his behavior toward the dying Hall—he nonetheless decided to rescue him. And so he arranged for the American government to outfit the *Tigress* immediately for this mission. [10]

What had in fact happened to the *Polaris* since the dramatic separation? Had it sunk? No, in this surreal setting, it had first drifted south, then north, wafting back and forth along the coast of Inglefield Land before it was finally run aground in a cove four miles north of Etah.

There the fourteen men on board settled in. They made themselves a cabin with boards from the superstructure of the *Polaris*, and left the steamer to take on water from the incoming tides. All hands made ready for a

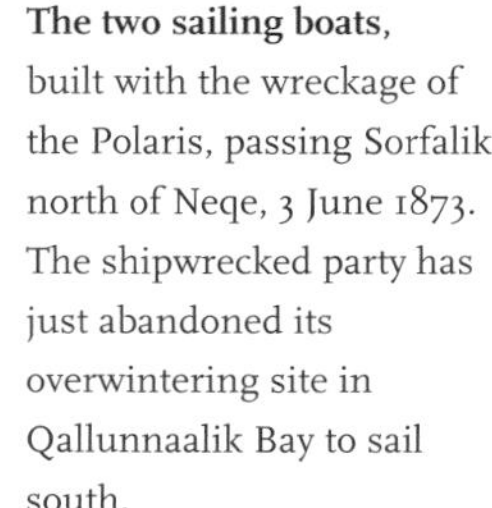

The two sailing boats, built with the wreckage of the Polaris, passing Sorfalik, north of Neqe, 3 June 1873. The shipwrecked party has just abandoned its overwintering site in Qallunnaalik Bay to sail south.

8) There was some surprise that, in light of Chauncey Loomis's discoveries in the summer of 1968, which established a strong presumption of poisoning, the case was not immediately reopened by the American authorities. The memory of the first leader of a U.S. Arctic expedition deserves greater respect. The British Admiralty mobilized all its resources to save Franklin, and a memorial to him was erected at Westminster Abbey. The publication of an official reconsideration would do the U.S. Navy honor.

9) It is certainly regrettable that Bessels's study of the Inuit at Qallunaalik and Etah, to which he devoted considerable time and energy, could not be published. His thoroughness and attention to detail would have provided us a useful ethnological report on this people just after the last immigration from the Canadian Arctic (1860-1861). Where is the manuscript? Was it stolen from a train in London or did it burn up with his house?

10) The *Tigress* was officially requisitioned for this rescue mission, and Captain Greer was named to command it.

The two boats in Melville Bay, 23 June 1873, sighting the Scots whaler *Ravenscraig.*

long winter. Yet it was not to be a solitary one, as two Polar Eskimos, "having smelt the smell of the White man," arrived from Etah on 19 October to join them. They wore dog-skin blouses and trousers of polar bear fur. They drove a sledge made from small segments of bone, with ivory shoes on the runners, and pulled by a team of nine dogs. Their names were A-wah'took and Mi'ouk. They recognized Morton, who had traveled with Kane. They helped to unload the ship and were surprised to find a cat and five lemmings on board. The bay would henceforth be called Qallunaalik, "where the white men are."

Other Inuit would follow on 21 October. They built an igloo near the *Polaris* and then a second. But these Eskimos, who put their dog teams to work helping the whites perform various heavy jobs, eventually stayed in the white men's cabin, sleeping on the floor. There were nine men, three women, and eight children—the whole population of Etah. Though it is hard to fathom, they developed close ties with the desperadoes of the *Polaris*, who gave American nicknames to the Inuit: Jimmy, Joe, Sharky, etc. All winter there was constant traffic: Eskimos from the villages south of Etah came to visit the shipwrecked crew. The women sewed clothes for them out of skins. By 24 March, seventy-seven Eskimos had come to visit. The Inuit used a gun for the first time in their history (Hayes, in 1861-1862, had not allowed them to fire the guns themselves); they discovered starches, alcohol, and violence. Bessels, in particular, grossly threatened some Eskimos, who fled. "One cannot give the Eskimos orders," said Bessels. "They have their customs . . ." And what they saw of the white man did not encourage them to give up their customs. A woman named Akrutak was particularly rebellious toward Bessels's orders. And an Eskimo family that worked for the shipwrecked men saw them at close range and judged them harshly. Despite his great ships, the white man seemed incapable of solving even the simplest problems. For example, the white man's sledge slid poorly and broke, while the Inuit's, which was made of bone, was light and quick.

The white man loses face

On 3 June 1873, the fourteen men of the shipwreck party finished building two large boats for their escape. One would be commanded by Budington, the other by Chester. Hall's Arctic library was placed in a box and set under a cairn. The men embarked in total disorder: provisions, equipment, ship's logs, books, etc,. were abandoned on shore, and no offer was made to the Inuit, comparable to Kane's offer in July 1855, to help themselves to whatever they might find useful: wood, iron, tools. Kane had even had the courtesy to present his ship, the *Advance*, to the Inuit. The disorder left by the shipwreck party would be described by the British mission aboard the *Pandora*, Sir Allen Young commanding, which examined the *Polaris*'s last winter site. Eventually the two gerry-built boats (one of which carried the expedition mascot, a cat, which disappeared during a brief layover south of Natsilivik) encountered a Scots whaler, the *Ravenscraig*, off Cape York, on 23 June 1873,

A stop on the west coast of Northumberland Island, 9 June 1873. After fourteen days of sailing and sledding through the pack ice, which was mostly broken up, the party was rescued on 23 June by the Scots whaler *Ravenscraig* in Melville Bay, 25 miles south of Cape York, at lat. 75° 38' N and long. 65° 35' W.

which carried the men back to Dundee. The party returned to the United States in two groups, some in a steamer from Liverpool, the others in a Glasgow vessel.

Thus this first official expedition of the United States government, which set out for the Pole in May 1871, succeeded by an extraordinary sequence of events in joining its separated halves. All except Charles Francis Hall, who was murdered.

The Inuit would never forget what they had witnessed: brutality, incompetence, and laxity. The white man's society was decidedly not for them. With Captain John Ross, with Elisha Kent Kane, with Isaac Israel Hayes, they had remained silent and reserved. But the Inuit would henceforth be not only "impertinent" but aggressive. The white man had at length lost whatever prestige he still had with the Polar Eskimos, a prestige he would never regain. "Jim and his family were loath to part with the "*Kodlunahs*" [whites], but the other Esquimaux did not display any feeling," wrote Budington in July 1873.

Qallunaalik and Qeqertaraq, April 1951

I was twenty-nine years old and the leader of an expedition. I had set out north of Etah in Inglefield Land alone. My spring-season geomorphological mission faced grave difficulties. We had to travel 1000 miles with our three dog sleds in order to make a geomorphological map of Inglefield Land, southern Washington Land, and Ellesmere Island (Alexandra Fjord, Bache Peninsula). The hunters of Etah/Taseq, a settlement of four igloos, had gone hungry during the past winter. Nasaapaluk could not set aside the walrus and seal quarters I had been counting on: in their distress they had eaten even their dogs. . . . We were five in Qaaqqutsiaq's igloo, a space of a dozen square yards, and tension was rising: my companions Kutsikitsoq and Qaaqqutsiaq and their wives were speculating in muttering tones about the future of my solitary venture. To give ourselves something to do we were busily checking over our equipment, each silently aware of the terrible dangers we might face if we ran low on food in the implacable deserts of Inglefield and Washington lands, and on Ellesmere Island, which lay 200 miles from the nearest settlement. I was deeply concerned that they would not agree to follow me on this expedition, which was turning into a desperate adventure.

On a sledge journey in February of that year, Kutsikitsoq had given me a detailed account of Knud Rasmussen's tragic expedition of September 1917. Lauge Koch, sledging 80 miles from where we were, and thirty-four years earlier, had been forced to abandon his white traveling companion, Dr. Thorild Wulff, who was dying of starvation. On Ellesmere Island forty miles to the east, near Cape Sabine, he described to me a small rise where nineteen Americans from Greely's expedition had died of hunger sixty-seven years before, some after eating their own dead. In Inglefield Land I would truly be in the middle of it, with these two tragic sites only a few days' travel from my sector of operations.

Having set out across the ice on 2 April, I was alone ten miles to the north on the snow-covered beach of Qallunnaalik. It was very cold (-30°C). The day before, a blizzard had blown, heralding a storm. I was alone, intentionally alone, in front of my igloo. In tragic Inglefield Land I had wanted to advance, setting the example, to establish a physical distance between me and the Eskimos so that my companions would have the time to make up their minds. And I wanted to show them that, though in a place where polar bears prowled, I was afraid of nothing. I had proclaimed my absolute confidence in my Inuit friends by leaving my sledge with them and asking them to return for me on a given date, after they had caught enough seal and walrus to feed our dog teams for two or three weeks.

I walked back and forth in front of my little snow igloo, thinking of Hall's expedition. I had in fact just stumbled on a piece of debris from the *Polaris*—part of its machinery, a section of the propeller's drive shaft. I was exactly on the ill-fated campsite of an expedition that had been in full retreat. Among the fourteen Americans and Germans who in 1873 formed the rearguard of the first large American expedition ever commissioned by a U.S. president was the man known by all to be a murderer. A cursed place: on the land that I was treading, a few hundred yards from my igloo, Sidney Budington had ignobly decided to abandon his companions, adrift on an ice floe.

I came and went in front of this section of frozen sea, mapping the raised beaches, the cliffs with their rockfall: I examined my memory. How does an expedition arrive at such an extreme? The fault must be ascribed in the first place to the expedition leader, however great his merits. In fact, Hall had committed at least two errors: an error of judg-

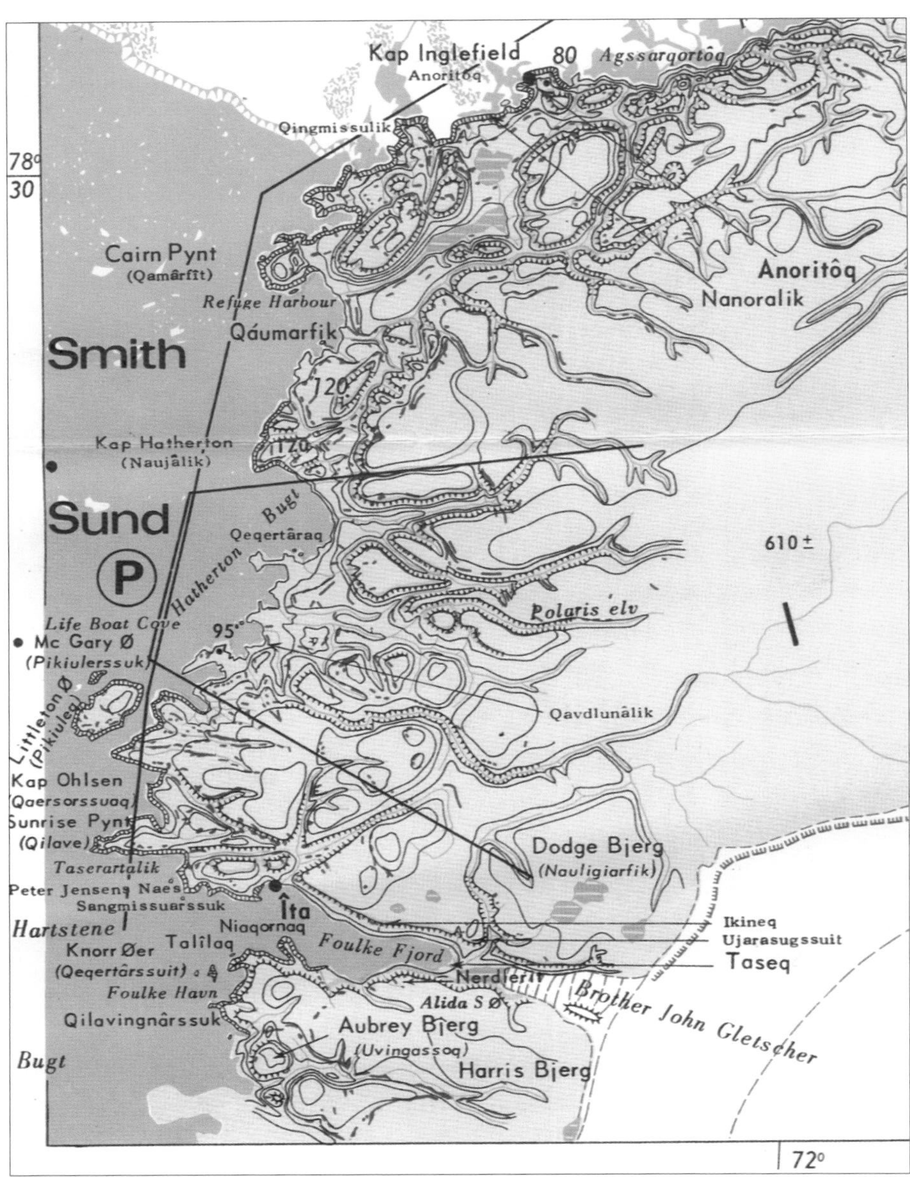

Excerpt of the map of Inglefield Land, Humboldt Glacier, and southern Washington Land, plotted by me in April-May 1951 on a scale of 1:100,000 and published at 1:200,000 by the Imprimerie Nationale.

Opposite:
Polar night, pastel, by Jean Malaurie.

ment and intuition in choosing his companions; and an organizational error in bringing together so heterogeneous a group—different in background, nationality, and language. Hall should have foreseen the rivalry between Budington and Tyson. He should have sensed the deterioration in human relations. In order to maintain the highly fragile unity of his crew, an expedition leader must be able to detect the signs of a powerful storm—even when the sea is apparently calm . . . It takes a deep knowledge of human nature, much subtlety, and also the talent—which may be based on authority, on charm, or on humor—to mend gracefully any tears in the group fabric while they are yet barely perceptible. If you wait it is too late.

I pondered these problems all the more as I would have to deal with a difficult rivalry between my two Eskimo companions, both of whom had very strong personalities: there was Kutsikitsoq, with his cheekiness; and Qaaqqutsiaq, with his unpredictable violence. Qaaqqutsiaq later told me on a journey we made together over the plateau that he sometimes experienced such violent impulses that, when he felt them come on, he would ask those around him to put all the knives and axes out of his reach . . . My relations with these two hunters, who were among the most hot-blooded in the group, would be further complicated by the fact that I had wanted their wives to accompany them. [11] They had come to know me, a young white man, over the eight months of the past summer and winter, and I understood that they had decided to risk everything with me—their dog teams, even their lives. The expedition would be difficult: the ice of the past winter was thicker than normal, the lack of pemmican for the dogs was worrisome, and the pay was modest. But what did it matter? In some measure they had chosen to go on adventure with a young scientist, and that is what kept them going. We had only two days' worth of meat for the forty-three dogs and we would have to hunt every day until mid-June for us to have enough to eat.

For my part I believe in the virtue of differences. Everything seemingly set us apart—our origins, our ways of life—even though I had not used a fork or a plate for months but eaten frozen meat standing up, stamping my feet, and drunk their broth of blood and seal blubber; even though I spoke only their language, slept cheek by jowl with them in their igloos of rock and sod, snow huts, and tents. For these very reasons it was essential that I put some distance between us and that I be more vigilant. Then too, the respect we feel toward civilizations other than our own obliges us to show ourselves in the best light.

In 1948 and 1949 I signed on as a geographer in the glaciological expeditions led by Paul-Emile Victor. I'll never forget all I owe this great explorer, the founder of French polar research after World War II. He first put my foot in the stirrup. And I am convinced that the hardest thing is to lead an expedition such as Hall's (or Victor's) that comprises only "civilized" men and no "savages." [12]

Was it this experience that led me, after 1950, to pursue solitary missions? I truly believe so—even if it is rarely a comfortable solution to count solely on oneself in these countries with intensely hostile climates. But at least, when all is said and done, one is not harassed by the problems of people's relations, which otherwise occupy a portion of your thoughts and threaten to handicap the progress of your own work severely, even the quality of your inspiration. ■

11) This hyperborean community is governed by the women.

12) I was able to verify the acuteness of these problems during the shooting of my films, *The Last Kings of Thule* and *Inuit*, for which I led four successive crews of six to eight people in Alaska, Canada, Greenland, and Siberia. I encountered difficulties on multiple levels: first, due to the cold (we sometimes shot at -50°C); due to the relations between the Inuk and the white man; due to the divide between me and the French television technicians, who saw that I spoke their film-makers' language (*pan, tilt, dailies*, etc.) only imperfectly; and finally due to political problems, in Siberia particularly, where two "Soviet assistants" accompanied me constantly, while I directed a Soviet crew from wildly different backgrounds (Georgian, Jewish, Russian, Yakut) in intensely cold weather and with three hours of light per day—repeatedly encountering prohibitions against filming, and patiently having to renegotiate.

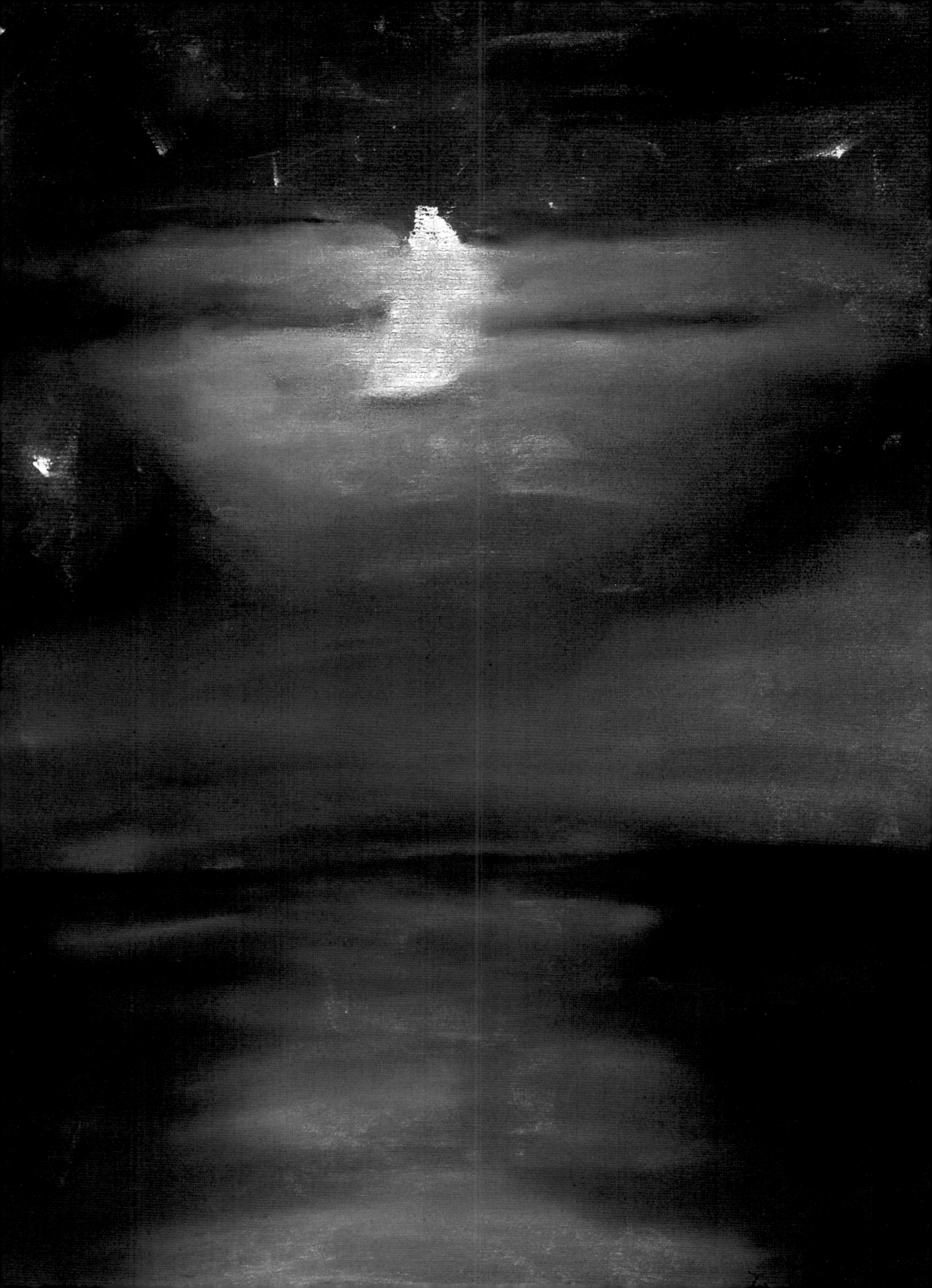

Robinson Crusoes of the Ice

1

THE POLARIS WAS RUN AGROUND NORTH OF ETAH FJORD ON 15 OCTOBER 1872.

Food, scientific equipment, and specimen collections were unloaded onto the pack ice. 1.) The ice broke up, stranding nineteen men on the fragmented floe, while the Polaris was swept off, carrying fourteen men and a drunk captain. 2.) The Polaris stranded in Lifeboat Cove after the tragic night when the expedition was separated. 3.) The shipwrecked party prepare to leave their winter cabin made of wood salvaged from the dismasted ship. A small meteorological station allowed them to collect hourly data. They would embark on 3 June 1873 in two launches (each of the fourteen men was allowed only eight pounds of luggage). The crates of specimens were left behind. The scientific equipment and the logbooks (except Hall's) were put in a box and set under a pile of stones, eventually to be picked up by the British expedition commanded by Sir Allen Young in the Pandora.

2

3

Inquest into the death of Charles Francis Hall

Horrifying testimony. Washington, 5-7 June 1873 (report signed 16 June)

Hannah, whose Eskimo name was Tookoolito, the wife of Joe Ebierbing and one of Hall's most loyal companions, meditates over Hall's grave. Drawing by Dr. Emil Bessels, Hall's likely murderer.

Notes from the private journal of Captain Tyson

[His state] grew rapidly worse. He seemed out of his mind and died on the eighth of November. Was buried on the eleventh. Captain Budington and several others could not conceal their joy at his death. Budington wished the officers to join him in a game of cards that evening Capt. Hall died in the morning. The body of Capt. Hall was not cold. When he Budington call[ed] me out in the post alley way he there told me he believed the Dr. had poisoned Capt. Hall. I was surprised at this for I had not a thought of foul play going on. I told him I did not believe any such thing. He said he did. But [. . .] he since then has tried to make most if not all the ship's company believe that Dr. Bessel poisoned Capt. Hall and he has said to me if this damn German organ grinder says anything about me at home or tries to take any honor from me I will accuse him of killing the old man. I make this statement not knowing whether I shall get through this affair with life. I have told Joe and Hannah should anything happen to me to save these books and carry them home. Their is some bad spelling as it is writen in the dark hut and with very cold fingers. This man Budington endeavored in every possible way to prevent the vessel going up [?] Smith Sound . . .

Torn-out pages The viewpoint of Captain Greer of the Pandora, *a British rescue vessel*

Captain Greer reported that exactly "one month and four hours after having left New York, [he] had found the spot occupied by the crew of the *Polaris* the preceding winter. It was then in the possession of Esquimaux, who had also appropriated two canvas tents belonging to the *Polaris*.

"The camp was situated at latitude 78° 23' north and longitude 73° 46' west. The sight that met our eyes was one of willful disorder and destruction: furniture, instruments, books, stove, medical stores and a quantity of provisions were scattered in every direction. It was difficult to tell how much was the work of the crew that had retreated hastily or of the Esquimaux who now occupied the site. No effort had been made to conceal or to protect from the weather the manuscripts, books, or scientific instruments. Despite an extensive search, no written trace was found to indicate the time of departure nor the route they planned to follow.

One eloquent discovery was made: a log-book from which all mention of the death of Captain Hall had been ripped out."

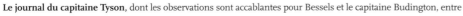

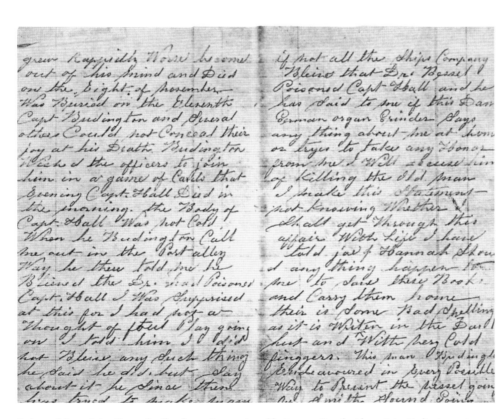

Le journal du capitaine Tyson, dont les observations sont accablantes pour Bessels et le capitaine Budington, entre

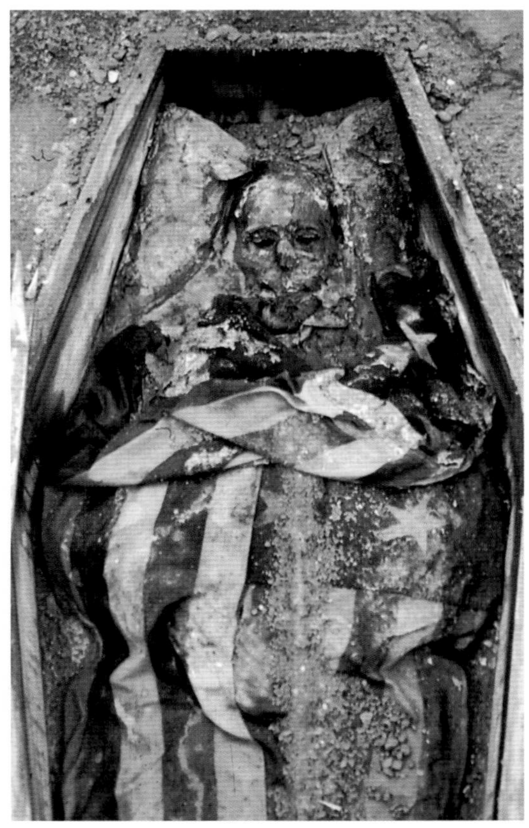

Hall's body, preserved intact under the ice, as it appeared when exhumed by Chauncey Loomis in August 1968. Loomis discovered abnormally high levels of arsenic in samples from Hall's fingernails. Was the poisoning a criminal act, or due to an overdose of medicine? We will never know.

Testimony of two of the Eskimos on the expedition

Questioning of Hans Christian [Hendrik] and Hannah Tookoolito: biased interrogations

Q: Do you speak English?

A: Very little. [The witness spoke largely through Joe and Hannah, who interpreted.] Was in the boat when Captain Hall died; was with him when he went into the north; with Mister Chester and Captain Hall.

Q: Was Captain Hall in good health?

A: Yes, very good. Came on ship in afternoon; very soon he fell sick; not know what he had.

Q: Were you with him when he was sick?

A: I was next to him after he was sick.

Q: Was he crazy?

A: I don't know. (Urged by Joe.) Yes, all the time. I remember the night when we lost the boat.

Q: How did you save yourself?

A: I took my wife and my children and put them on the ice. I thought the boat was gone. The ice soon let go. The cable broke and the boat went away in the dark. Not much good on the ice. We floated on the ice for six months. Killed two bears and may seals and then picked up by the *Tigress*.

Charles Francis Hall in 1870.

Hannah was instructed to ask Hans if he had anything further to say.

Hannah: He has nothing more he wants to say. Too hot here; children sick, he wants to return home right away. (Hans was very happy about a promise to return to Greenland.)

Hannah (the wife of Joe) was questioned in Joe's presence.

Q: You are Joe's wife?

A: Yes.

Q: And you sailed on the *Polaris* with Captain Hall?

A: Yes.

Q: Did anything unusual happen before you reached Disko?

A: Nothing. We went to the north, stopping at Upernavik and Tessiusak, then we continued until the ice stopped us. Once the ice stopped us, the ship had to come back and take its winter quarters. I remember Captain Hall's departure for the North and his return. I went onto the ice to see him. He was happy with his voyage. Went well. He said he would finish the next spring.

Q: When did you see Captain Hall on board after that?

A: About an hour after going on board, Captain Hall sent the girl to get me. I found Mr. Morton undressing him and washing his feet. Captain Hall was sick. He said he was sick and that he had vomited. He said he had vomited three times since coming back on board. I asked him if he had caught cold. He answered that in the morning he had felt quite well.

Q: Did he have no feeling on one side?

A: He did not mention it.

Q: What else did he say?

A: Nothing else that time. He wanted me to prepare things for the journey with Chester and Tyson. He thought he would get better right away and wanted me to be ready the day after next.

Q: Did he say anything about the coffee?

A: Not that time.

Q: When did he say something about it?

A: The next day. Very sick at that time. Worse than the day before. I looked at him closely. He was very tired. He felt bad. He wanted to stay still. Did not say much.

Q: Did he say anything about the coffee being bad?

A: After being bad in the head, he started to be better. Then he talked about the coffee. He said the coffee had made his stomach upset. Too sweet for him. "He made my stomach upset and made me vomit."

Q: He said it was too sweet?

A: Yes, that's all. I prepared coffee and tea for him. He said he had never known anything like the coffee he had when he came back on board.

Q: Did he say anything to you about someone poisoning him?

A: When his head was not well and he was making loud cries and wandering, he said that someone had poisoned him, but only when he was crazy.

Q: Did you believe that someone had poisoned him?

A: No, I did not believe it.

Q: Had Captain Hall argued with anyone?

A: No arguments that I know.

Q: You were with him every day during his illness?

A: Yes, sir.

Q: You never heard him accuse anyone of poisoning him except when he was delirious?

A: No.

Q: After his first discomfort, did Captain Hall talk to you about how he felt?

A: Captain Hall told me after his first discomfort that his stomach was better and that he thought he would get well.

Q: Did he say anything to you on the subject of his papers?

A: Oh, yes. He said to take care of his papers and to give them to the secretary. If anything happened to the secretary to give them to someone else. After his death I talked to Captain Budington several times about this responsibility. He told me he would give them to me soon.

Q: And were you near him when he died?

A: Yes, sir.

Q: How was he when he died?

A: Very bad. He was shouting. He wanted Captain Budington to come up. Joe stood up. All the others stood up. Did not recognize us then. He thought he was dreaming. I asked him what he was doing. He didn't know what he was saying. He looked at me and asked where was Hannah. He didn't recognize me. Then, until the ship went south, Joe went to hunt and I stayed on board.

DR. EMIL BESSELS TESTIFIES

Report of the Secretary of the Navy to the President of the United States

As I have already said, I returned to the observatory after seeing Captain Hall. After about an hour and a half, Mr. Meyer called for me to say that the captain was sick.

I went to the captain, finding him in bed. It was rather hot in his cabin, and the first thing I did even before speaking to him was to open the door. He told me that he had vomited, that he had a stomach ache, and that his legs felt weak. While I was speaking to him, he suddenly fainted. I tried to rouse him, but this had practically no effect. His pulse was irregular, at 60 to 80 beats per second, and alternately weak and forceful. . . .

Dr. Emil Bessels, "the little dancing master."

While he was unconscious, I applied a mustard plaster to his legs and chest, cold water to his head, and cupping glasses to his neck. After twenty-five minutes, the captain came to. I noticed a hemiplegia. His left arm and all his left side including his face and tongue were paralyzed; his left cheek swelled every time he breathed out.

The muscles of the tongue were affected (due to the paralysis of the hypoglossal nerve) in such a way that when I asked the patient to stick out his tongue, the tip deviated to the left. I made him take purgatives. . . . This caused his bowels to move three times, but without much production. He had hardly eaten during the entire time of the sledge journey. During these outings, it is necessary to be sparing with provisions. That night he slept for several hours. Mr. Morton stayed by his bedside.

On the morning of the 25th, he took some tapioca for breakfast, though he had trouble swallowing. He complained of difficulty moving his tongue. He was sometimes almost entirely incapable of articulating clearly. I gave him another dose of castor oil and croton oil, upon which he recovered from his paralysis.

On the morning of the 26th, after a sleepless night, he had no appetite. He asked for tapioca but could not eat any of it. He had some canned food, peaches if I remember, and perhaps also some pineapple, but I am not certain. He complained of being very cold, and his temperature was in fact oscillating rapidly, as one observes in cases of intermittent fever . . .

***Question:** Mentally, what was his state?*

***Answer:** Mentally, he was himself, and his mind perfectly clear. He never presented delirium, either before or after this episode. And even during it, it was not what I would call delirium. After his temporary coma, he fully recovered his mental faculties.*

Given his condition and the sudden fluctuations in his temperature, I gave him an injection . . . of quinine to see what effect it would have. I observed a clear remission . . .

Let us concentrate on the facts: Hall was liked and respected by all the members of the expedition with the exception of Captain Budington and two of the German scientists: Bessels and Meyer. "Hall's death was the best thing that could have happened to the expedition . . ." Bessels said to Noah Hayes, Hall's companion. "And the next day he was laughing about it." All of Hall's papers, journals, and notes have disappeared. "Some were burned," Tyson admitted. The arsenic that poisoned Captain Hall was administered to him "during the last two weeks of his life," according to the experts consulted by Chauncey Loomis: the arrogant and ambitious Dr. Bessels is the number one suspect. The claustrophobic conditions aboard a vessel in the Arctic can turn a man of complex psychology into a monster.

GEORGE STRONG NARES 1831-1915

THE LAST BRITISH EXPEDITION TO THE NORTH POLE IN THE NINETEENTH CENTURY

The 1875-1876 expedition of the *Alert* and *Discovery*, because of its inappropriate military methods, was the last British attempt in the nineteenth century to conquer the Pole.

Captain George Strong Nares, who had taken part in the famous voyage of the *Challenger* (December 1872 to May 1876), had a great deal of experience with scientific expeditions. He also took part in a rescue mission by sledge in the Canadian Central Arctic, brilliantly led by Captain Francis M'Clintock (1853). The son of a high-ranking officer, solidly built and with clear eyes, Captain Nares was forty-four years old when he led his expedition; a conscientious, disciplined officer who had been in the Royal Navy since the age of fourteen, he yet lacked the passion and mysticism that have carried so many explorers beyond their own capacities. Placid and pragmatic, devoid of any lyricism, he prepared his expedition with military attention to detail. At the Admiralty, he was assisted by an Arctic committee.

Great Britain gives up on the North Pole

This expedition—whose objective was the Pole—overwintered in the Arctic uneventfully but ended in defeat. Returning from the Arctic Ocean, Strong sent a famous telegram to the Admiralty: "Pole unattainable." By exploding the theory of an ice-free polar sea, he discouraged any further British attempts to reach the geographic Pole. History would judge Nares harshly for not having overwintered a second year, though he was equipped to do so. [1]

On 29 May 1875, the *Alert* (a seventeen-cannon sloop refitted for arctic service) and the whaler/sealer *Discovery*, carrying 120 officers, scientists, junior officers, and seamen, left the dock at Portsmouth. The expedition had been overseen at the highest level and approved by Prime Minister Benjamin Disraeli himself. Many of the expedition members were volunteers—polar journeys were at the height of their prestige, and arctic service offered a rapid path to promotion.

On 15 July, after crossing the Atlantic, the expedition left Godhavn (Disko Island) on the west coast of Greenland carrying 24 newly purchased Eskimo dogs. On 19 July, the ships anchored in Pröven, near Upernavik, just south of Melville Bay, and the well-known Greenlander Hans Hendrik embarked. From 22 to 28 July, the *Alert* and the *Discovery* had an easy crossing of Melville Bay and visited the Eskimo settlements between Cape York and Etah. Few ethnographic observations were made, only that the Inuit were in good health and retained the use of their traditional equipment. On 28 July, near the entrance to Smith Sound,

Captain George Strong Nares.

OPPOSITE: **The *Alert* being towed by its seamen** through the fractured pack ice of Kennedy Channel. A scout walks ahead of the seamen who pull the ship.

1) The first Briton to conquer the North Pole was Sir Wally Herbert, on 6 April 1969, during a historic surface crossing of the Arctic Ocean by sledge with 34 dogs. Herbert left Barrow, Alaska, and arrived fourteen months later in Svalbard. He received several airdrops of food and equipment and had continual radio direction guidance.

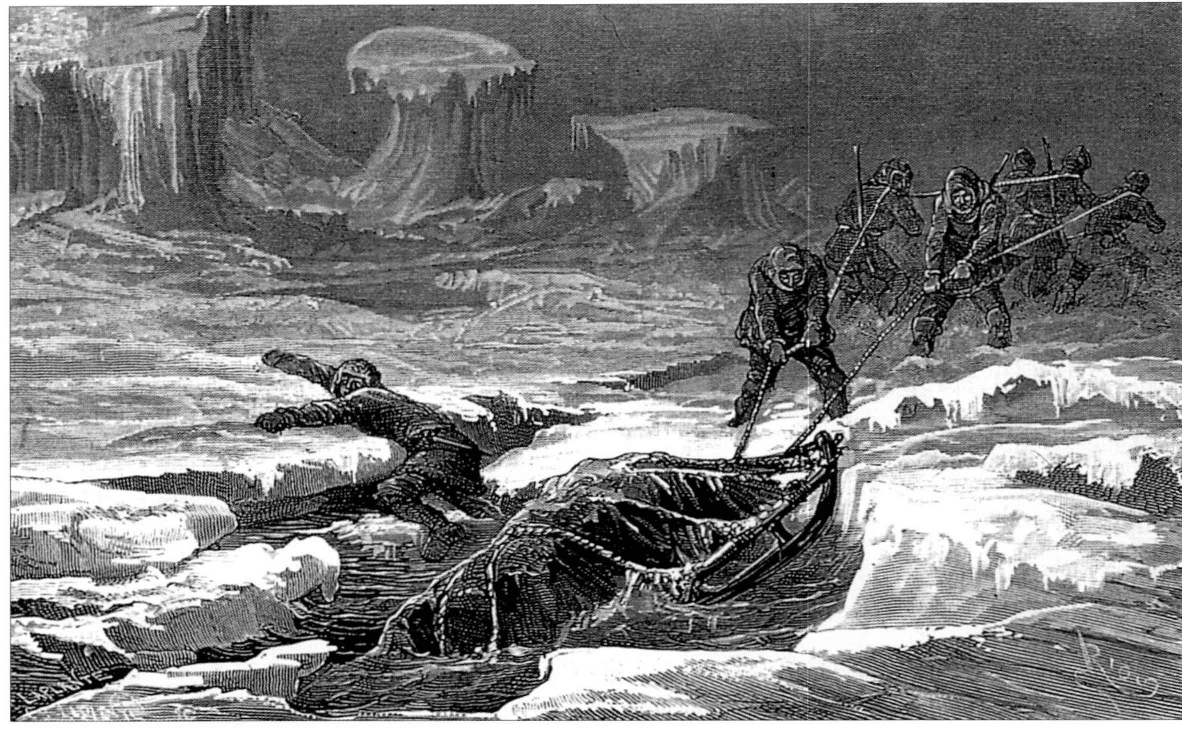

The foot journey to the Pole (Markham party) and the exploration of the north coast of Ellesmere Island (Aldrich party.)

the two ships anchored at Etah, north of Port Foulke (where Hayes had wintered in 1860-1861). Two parties reconnoitered Etah and Qallunaalik, where fourteen members of Hall's expedition, including Captain Budington, overwintered in 1872-1873 after the stranding of the *Polaris* in Inglefield Land. On his way north, Nares had stored 3600 rations on the southeast coast of the Carey Islands in case of an emergency retreat, 3600 rations at Cape Hawks (Ellesmere Island), and 1000 more at Cape Lincoln.

After the difficult crossing of Kane Basin and the passage up Kennedy Channel, the *Discovery*, under the command of Captain Henry Stephenson, dropped anchor on 25 August in Discovery Bay. Captain Nares decided that the *Discovery* would overwinter in this bay to serve as a rescue ship in case the lead ship, the *Alert*, was unable to break loose from the ice of the Arctic Ocean during the following summer. The *Alert* then proceeded boldly northward, threading leads through the moving pack ice, and came to anchor at Floeberg Beach in the shelter of grounded icebergs, in lat. 82° 25' N and long. 63° 50' W, the highest latitude reached by a ship to date. Were they on the edge of an ocean or was it a large bay bordered on the north by more land? Cautious, the British avoided jumping to conclusions. Only further exploration could establish whether the Pole was in an ice-free sea, or on an island, or on a peninsula extending from Greenland to 90° N and beyond.

The British Admiralty's last expedition (1875-1876). Captain George Nares commanded the *Alert* and the *Discovery*. He rode the *Alert*, which sailed in the lead, while the *Discovery* stayed in reserve, wintering north of Lady Franklin Bay in what became Discovery Bay. Exploratory expeditions on foot and by sled are indicated.

Inappropriate military methods

The expedition focused primarily on geography and geology. It provided valuable geomagnetic data and coastal maps, established the tidal variations in the Arctic Ocean at its winter site (1.5 to 3 feet), and identified pine logs that had drifted from Siberia, an observation that would lead the Norwegian Fridtjof Nansen to mount the famous *Fram* expedition (1895-1896). Curiously, no ethnological or technological lessons were learned from the misfortunes of Hayes and Kane, or the disastrous Franklin expedition. Had Eskimo hunters been incorporated into the plans, this expedition might have had extraordinary impetus. But the army and the navy both have great powers of inertia. The British Admiralty's inability to revamp its polar logistics and undertake a critical examination of the lessons of the past proved significant to this expedition, the last to capture the attention of all Britain, even Queen Victoria. Despite the lessons suggested by Hall's travels in Hudson Bay and by the extraordinary exploration of the Canadian Central Arctic by the American lieutenant Frederick Schwatka, the expedition continued to ignore the Eskimos and despise their technology. [2] Thus Captain Nares and his officers would hear nothing of building igloos but, being good military men, used standard-issue military tents instead. They inevitably recruited Hans Hendrik to serve them as a "native guide," but without drawing any advantage from his broad experience. [3] The expedition used heavy oak sledges (145 lbs. apiece), whose runners sank in the snow unlike the lighter sledges used by the Inuit, and the British sledges were still pulled by men. Nares dismissed Eskimo dogs outright, calling them "picturesque." The expedition would stick by the good old British practice of man-hauling the sleds, which taught discipline and inured men to suffering, just as their celebrated forebears had done. Their clothes were woolen. They had no wool inner boots, and no fur sleeping bags, instead using woolen blankets that quickly became damp. Their food was once again totally ill-adapted. On their overland excursions, the men became unbearably thirsty. After a few months, the expedition inevitably

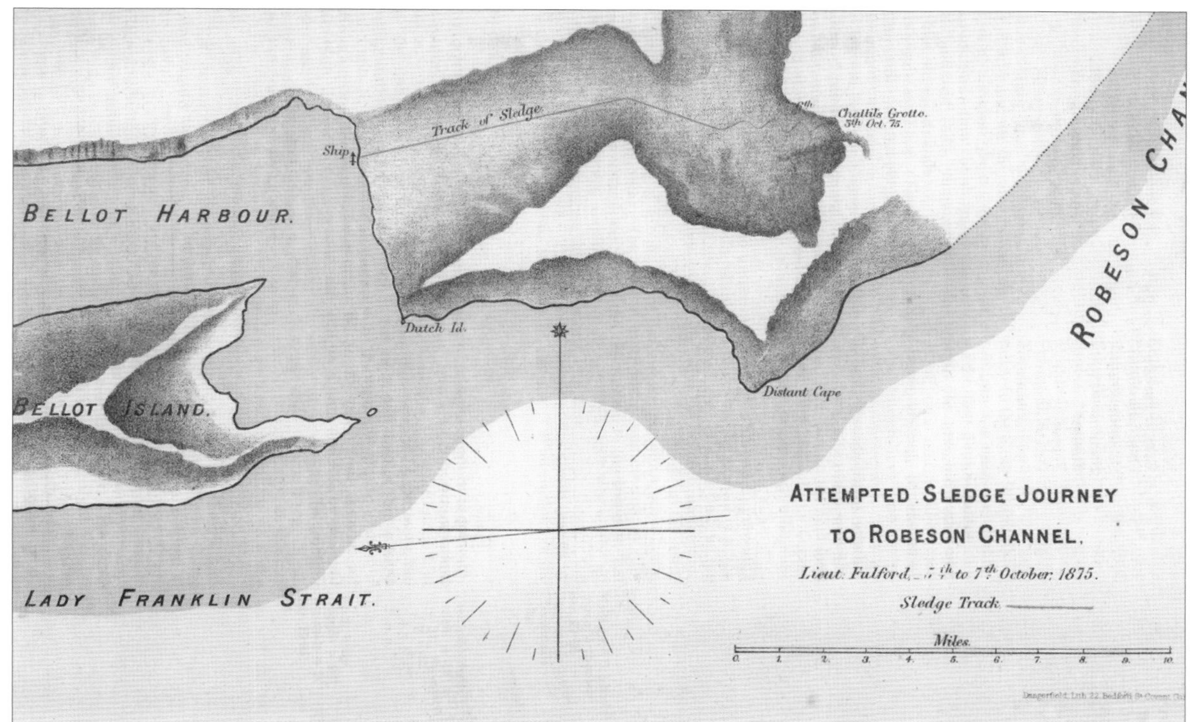

The party from the *Discovery* under Lieutenant Archer mapped the area around Robeson Channel (Bellot Island).

showed signs of scurvy. [4] The Admiralty deliberately ignored the recommendation of John Ross (reiterated up to the time of his death) to use fresh locally caught meat rather than the traditional salt meat. The ship's living quarters were deplorably damp, as the hatches closed improperly and had no drying mechanism. In March the temperature sank to -58.7°C on the deck of the *Alert*, and -57.2°C on the deck of the *Discovery*. Not wearing slitted snow goggles as the Inuit did but glasses with tinted lenses that offered poor protection from the ultraviolet rays on the ice, the explorers also suffered from painful eye inflammations. Yet the program of scientific research and exploration was nonetheless maintained with magnificent courage and obstinacy. The ultimate goal was the North Pole.

During the autumn, after a preliminary excursion to set up depots for the main expedition across the Arctic Ocean in the spring, eight men were frostbitten and some required amputation. The polar night would last for one hundred and forty-two days. In the spring, after considerable effort, Albert Hastings Markham and his lead party (seventeen men, two sledges) reached the furthest north yet attained in an attempt on the Pole: on 12 May 1876 they stood at latitude 83° 20' north, longitude 64° west. The return to the ship was fraught with hardship. The explorers grew exhausted (eleven of the seventeen were sick, and five had to be pulled on the sleds). The tents, covered in rime, were twice their normal weight, and the overheavy sleds were further burdened by the second boat (eventually abandoned to make room for the sick), the ransom paid to the persistent myth of the "open polar sea."

On board ship, the situation was no better. In June 1876, Nares had only nine seamen who were still healthy, out of a crew of fifty-three men. Despite having enough stores for a second winter, the fateful decision was taken to head south. The expedition—for all its might—was no match for the Arctic.

On 31 July, using explosive torpedoes to open a channel, the *Alert* skillfully freed itself from the ice and headed toward the *Discovery*. On 9 September, the two ships turned toward England, reaching Portsmouth on 2 November 1876.

Their reception was at first warm. The commission of inquiry acknowledged the remarkable quality of the vast scientific work performed (the mapping of northern Ellesmere Island and northern Greenland, the data on tides and weather, and the heroism of Markham's extraordinary excursion), but it judged Nares harshly. [5] The captain was blamed for not having forced the issue and for having let his crew ruin its health by not following the prescribed rules for warding off scurvy, notably by substituting sweet lime

2) Lieutenant Frederick Schwatka is a neglected explorer. After wintering near Chesterfield on the west coast of Hudson Bay (1878-1879) with four white men, including his friend Gilder, fourteen Eskimos, and enough food for a month, he proceeded in April 1879 to explore the last stages of the Franklin expedition in an area reputed to be gameless (King William Island). He was away from his base for twelve months and covered 2819 miles overland. He discovered numerous remains of the unfortunate crew of the Franklin expedition in scattered locations.

3) Assigned to the *Discovery*, he saved Lieutenant Beaumont, going out to rescue him by dog sledge on his return from an audacious excursion along the north coast of Greenland on 22 June 1876 and, against British rules, feeding him seal meat.

4) Scurvy, as we know today, results from a deficiency of vitamin C. It develops after twenty-five or thirty weeks of a strongly unbalanced and salty diet. The officers, who had private stores of food (butter, milk, eggs, rice), suffered from scurvy less than the men.

5) "The expedition set off like a rocket and came back like a log," the press wrote, all the angrier for the tremendous expectations the expedition had raised. The newspapers even clamored for Nares to be court-martialed. After this last attempt on the North Pole, London turned its attention to the Antarctic.

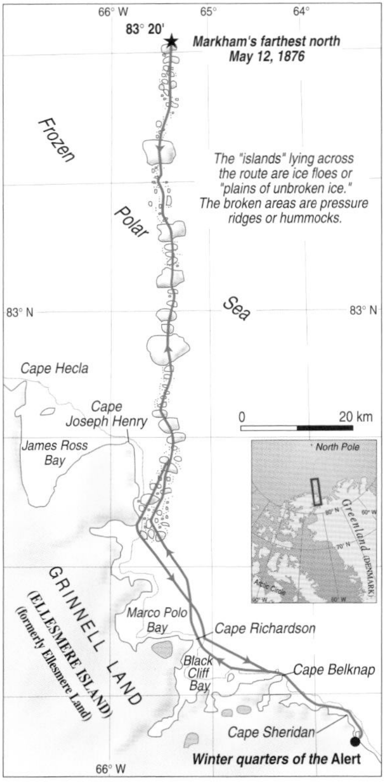

Markham's historic dash to the Pole using man-drawn sleds. The party set out on 10 April 1876 with two sleds, seventeen men, and two ship's boats. On 12 May 1876 they reached lat. 83°20' N, long. 64° W.

for the recommended lemon juice. What the British regretted was that despite the courage of the Markham party, they had not managed to plant the Union Jack at the North Pole.

Having made only a short stop at the Eskimo settlements on the outward journey—Cape York, the Carey Islands, Port Foulke, Etah—the expedition had virtually no impact on the Eskimo population. But its passage nonetheless had psychological import: it confirmed to the Eskimos that they were not an isolated people. "We are alone in the world," they had told Ross in August 1818. Now their territory was being visited at intervals of five to ten years by large expeditions and by overwintering whaling ships: 1849-1850, the *North Star* (Captain Saunders); August 1852, Inglefield; 1853-1855, Kane on the *Advance*; 1860-1861, Hayes aboard the *United States*; 1871-1873, Hall on the *Polaris*. Since 1818, there had been contact between Eskimos and whalers every year at Cape York. Barter had gradually allowed all the natives as far as Etah along a 200-mile strip of coast to have a sufficient quantity of wood and iron knives, whose use seems to have become widespread by 1872—a fact confirmed by the scientific notes of the *Polaris* expedition. The use of the bow and arrow spread after 1862 (date of the Inuit migration from the Canadian Arctic), and food became more abundant and more varied. The population, which had remained in equilibrium at 100 or 150 souls, grew rapidly. In 1895, the population of the Polar Inuit stood at 253.

But the consequences were most profound in the long term. There is no doubt that interbreeding occurred through short-lived sexual pairings, and that the bloodlines of this small, isolated group of thirty to fifty families, where inbreeding was a fact despite taboos against the marriage of close kin, were thereby enriched. But the effects were more than anything cultural. The three American expeditions of Kane, Hayes, and Hall convinced this people with its archaic technology that the white man was incapable of putting his powerful resources into play at these high latitudes. The hunters became increasingly aware of their own cultural, sociological, and ethnic power, and of their technological superiority in this harsh environment. "They become impertinent," John Ross had observed in August 1818. And they grew more impertinent with time. The realized that they were the masters of a space that the white man was trying to appropriate little by little. Because of their weakness in numbers, the Eskimos "collaborated" with the whites, but without ever forgetting what was owed them. Though armed with a static perception of history, they prepared themselves mentally to live with and accept the changes brought by major shifts in technology: guns, steel traps, and, in 1910-1920, money and Christian missions.

Great Britain declares its sovereignty over Ellesmere Island

The work of Lieutenant Pelham Aldrich, Lieutenant Archer, Lieutenant Beaumont, and Dr. Richard Coppinger to the east and west of the *Alert* and the *Discovery* resulted in the discovery of enormous lands, surveyed from their coast lines.

The Nares expedition thus spared Canada (a British possession) the loss of its northernmost territory. Ellesmere Island and the entire Arctic archipelago would be declared a part of Canada in 1895 and in 1909 (Bernier expedition). Britain's was a theoretical possession—since Canada did not occupy the territory—which would be implicitly called into question by other nations: Norway, by virtue of the arctic expeditions led by Sverdrup in 1903; Denmark, because of its rule over Greenland and the Polar Eskimos (whose administrator starting in 1909 was Knud Rasmussen and whose vital hunting ground and historical origin lay on Ellesmere Island); the United States, through Peary's repeated expeditions to Ellesmere Island (Cape Sabine, 1898-1902; Cape Columbia, 1905-1906, 1908-1909).

A station of the Royal Canadian Mounted Police would be established on Bache Peninsula, in Alexandra Fjord, and maintained from 1926-1932 by two sergeants who made reconnaissance trips around the island to assert Canada's dominion over it.[6] Ottawa hadn't forgotten the misfortunes of Kane and of the *Polaris* expedition, the tragedy of the Greely expedition, and the enormous difficulty of reaching as far as Cape Sabine, north of Cape Isabella, on the west coast of Smith Sound.

Getting the supply ship to the station on a yearly basis would prove problematic. In 1928, 1929, and 1930 the supplies and equipment could only be deposited on the ice at some distance. As the permanent station could not be securely provided for, the Canadians turned to the Inuit for help in supplying provisions. And who among the Inuit could explore and hunt for the Mounties if not the Etah Eskimos? The policy was made possible only because the

Mounties recruited two Inuit families from Etah: Nukappianguaq, that incomparable Polar Eskimo, his son Sakaeunnguaq (my companion in 1950-1951), and their wives. Supplying food for the dog teams, but also providing fur clothing for the men, with all the labor of sewing it, was the responsibility of these two families. Thus the Polar Eskimos played an important role in the claim of Canadian sovereignty over Ellesmere Island.

Was there indifference or latent racism? The Etah Inuit always told me that they felt very poorly rewarded for their work, outside the modest salary they received of three to five dollars per month, paid in kind. [7] For about one thousand dollars, therefore, Canada was able to lay claim to an island—the historic birthplace and vital territory of the Greenland Inuit—whose strategic importance would be enormous, with the construction of the base at Alert.

The least Canada could do to express its gratitude would be to erect a tall marker in Alexandra Fjord on Ellesmere island with the inscription: "To Nukappianguaq and to Sakaeunnguaq, Inuit hunters of North Greenland (Etah, Siorapaluk), and to their wives, Inalunnguaq and Birthe, from the grateful Canadian nation." ■

6) This station, by then uninhabited, was the base of my study area during my expedition of June 1951.

7) This issue was raised at the request of my old friend Sakaeunnguaq in my *Last Kings of Thule*, fifth edition, 1989, p. 459 and pp. 721-725. I entered a plea on their behalf to the general of the Canadian Royal Mounted Police. Ottawa responded that the plea was denied after consideration because the payment in kind was judged to be sufficient. At my renewed request, the governor of Greenland, Nils Otto Christiansen, modestly increased the pension of the only survivor, Sakaeunnguaq, who never felt he had received his due.

Nares testifies. Inadequate equipment.

In this unpredictable country, military rigidity can lead to absurd situations, even disaster.

The clothing worn when on board the ship was a thick under flannel and a pair of drawers and socks; a thick woollen shirt with a turn-down collar and a naval black silk headkerchief, a knitted waistcoat with sleeves, a pair of seal-skin trousers and box-cloth shoes; the ship's company wore knitted jerseys instead of the waistcoats.

When going on deck or on the ice, a duck jumper, or a seal-skin jacket, was worn in addition, with a naval blue comforter around the neck, a thick pair of fisherman's stockings, duffle knee-boots with thick soles, and a leather cap with ear-laps lined with lamb's skin, with mitts as necessary.

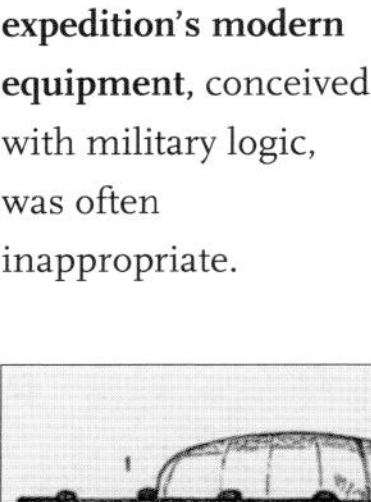

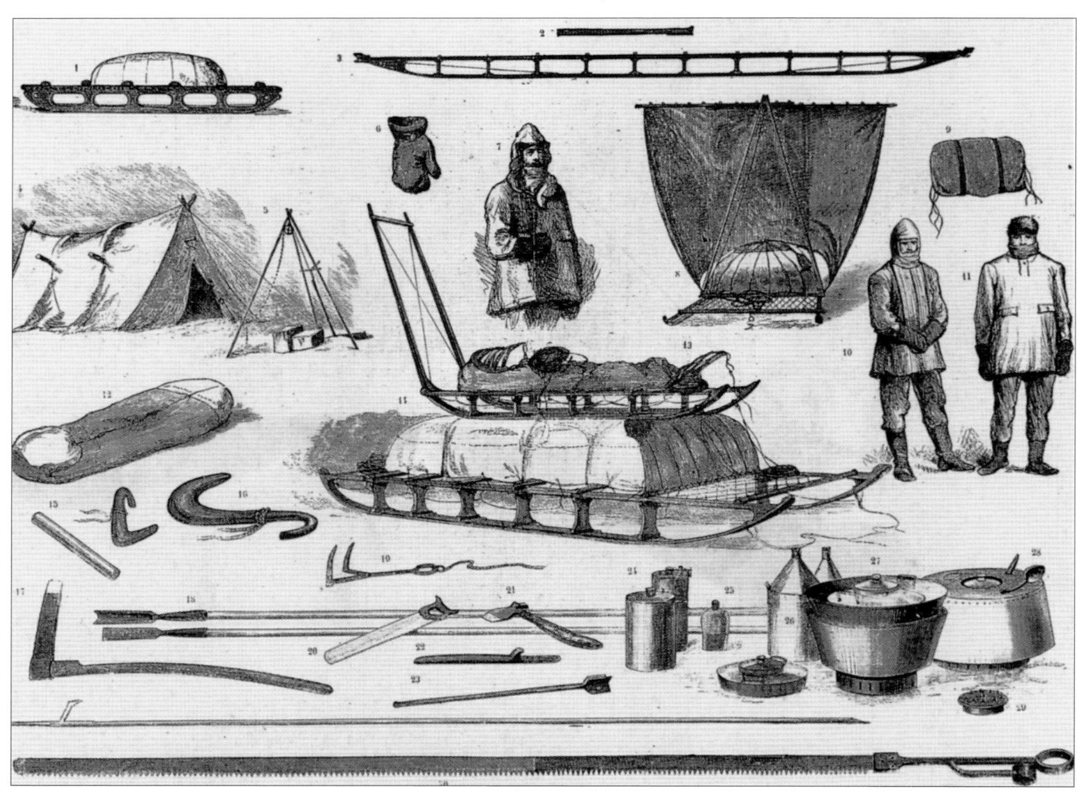

The Admiralty expedition's modern equipment, conceived with military logic, was often inappropriate.

The rough duffle cloth leggings on the boots were found to catch the snow badly. Except during very cold weather the snow turned into ice from the heat of the leg, and by clinging to the hairy cloth gave much trouble in removing it.[8]

Death of the dogs

About this time the dogs on board the "Discovery" showed the first signs of disease, owing probably to close confinement, wet decks, and want of natural exercise. Fits were frequent, and a few deaths occurred after symptoms of madness. Dr. Colan and Dr. Ninnis took great trouble to discover the nature of the disease and to arrest it. It was evident that this alarming and very often fatal malady could not be true rabies or hydrophobia, for in several instances the affected dogs recovered.[9]

The day's routine

As is usual in Arctic ships, all expected that during the winter there would be ample time for reading and writing; now the general complaint is how little can be done in that way.

The men breakfast at 7:30 a.m., then clear up the lower-deck. After an hour's work on the ice we muster at divisions, and read daily prayers at a quarter past 10 a.m. The officers breakfast at 8:30, after which there is too little time to settle down to any particular occupation before the general muster on deck about 10 a.m. After prayers, all hands leave the ship, the men for work, and the officers either for exercise or to visit the "Kew" or "Greenwich" observatories. The crew dine at 1 p.m., then out on the ice again until 4 p.m., when their official work is over for the day.

The officers generally remain on the ice until about 1 p.m.; between which time and dinner at 2:30 p.m. the time slips away in a surprising manner. After dinner and a smoke the ship is very quiet, so probably many take a siesta; but there is plenty of noise at tea-time at seven. Then comes school on the lower-deck until 9 p.m.,[10] after which one sits down for the first time in the day perfectly ready for study, and with a certainty of not being disturbed. We need not wonder then, when the regular lamps are put out in the ward-room at 11 p.m. most of the cabins and the ward-room itself remain lit by private candles for some time longer . . .

On Sundays, after church on the lower-deck, the general muster is held outside the ship, then all hands scatter over the ice and land; the distance of their wanderings being dependent on the temperature and the amount of moonlight. On sacrament Sundays, by mustering before church, the service is not interfered with.[11]

Sledding calculations

After calculating the weights most carefully, I finally decided to follow the plan of Sir Edward Parry, namely, for the travelers to advance the requisite weights each day by stages; first dragging forward the boat, then to return and transport a second sledge laden with provisions. From my former experience I well knew, as is stated in the fifteenth paragraph of my orders, that *"in the absence of continuous land, sledge traveling has never yet been found practicable over any considerable extent of unenclosed frozen sea."*[12]

An inexorable illness: scurvy

As the Expedition subsequently experienced a severe attack of scurvy, which has been attributed in some quarters to errors in the sledge dietaries, I may here conveniently refer to the subject, [and give my reasons for adopting the scale of diet used by the travellers from the "Alert" and "Discovery"]. In doing this, I fear that I shall leave the actual cause of the outbreak of scurvy in as undefined a state as others who have endeavoured to explain it.

On the return of the Expedition to England a committee, consisting of three admirals and two medical men, was appointed to inquire into the causes of the outbreak of scurvy. On the 7th of May, 1877, they reported, 'We attribute the

A reading from the Bible on the deck of the *Alert*. The revelations of the Apocalypse, of John, the Second Coming, Gog and Magog, the Last Judgment were present in the minds of all the seamen, for whom Anglicanism was the state religion.

early outbreak of scurvy in the spring sledging parties of the Expedition to the absence of lime-juice from the sledge dietaries.' The italics are my own.

Soon after the publication of this report Admirals Sir George H. Richards and Sir Leopold M'Clintock, the two surviving members of the Arctic Committee of 1875, and whose experiences in the Arctic sledge-travelling are certainly greater than those of any other living men, thus expressed their views in the public press. Sir George Richards wrote under date of 20th of May, 1877:—

'This can be no more than an opinion, as it is positively unsusceptible of proof; but it is entirely opposed to all former experience on similar service. It appears in the evidence taken before the Committee that Sir Leopold M'Clintock in all his varied Arctic journeys, extending over some thousands of miles, never carried lime-juice or considered it necessary. Certainly the evidence of Dr. Rae in regard to his own remarkable journeys and his long experience as an officer of the Hudson's Bay Company in Arctic America does not justify the conclusions arrived at by the Committee.

'For myself I must say that, during some seven months passed on the ice at different times, and with, perhaps, larger parties than any one person ever had the charge of, my crews never used lime-juice. The same may be said of the early and extended sledging parties of all previous expeditions. Lime-juice was undoubtedly used by some of the parties which made short excursions in moderate temperatures; but there remains the fact that many previous parties exposed to the same temperatures and pretty much the same hardships as those experienced by the late Expedition, and for considerably longer periods, did not use lime-juice, and were practically exempt from scurvy, or the cases which did occur were so few in number, and of so mild a character, that opinion actually differs at the present time among medical

The *Alert* overwintered on the north coast of Ellesmere Island. An unusually warm summer allowed the ship to reach latitude 82° 25' north, longitude 62° 20' west, at noon on 1 September 1875—the farthest north reached by a ship to that date. The site where the *Alert* wintered, in Lincoln Bay, was named Floeberg Beach. It was protected from the ice pack by great masses of grounded ice and proved ideally suited for spending the winter. The *Discovery* wintered much farther south, in Lady Franklin Bay, which it reached on 25 August 1875.

8) The equipment points to a total disregard for Eskimo techniques, based on the principle of cushions of air between loose layers of fur clothing. The clothes were worn with the fur outward.

9) April 1988: a rabies epidemic on a scale not seen for more than a century afflicted five villages in Polar Inuit territory. Of 1000 dogs, only 300 were saved, after being vaccinated. A nationwide collection in Greenland helped the Polar Inuit to rebuild their teams.

10) School was of course obligatory for the entire crew, which included three men who were completely illiterate. Education was not widespread among the British populace at this time. The navy sought by schools such as this to raise—though only slightly—the social level of its sailors.

11) Nares instituted military discipline. Prayers and services were led by the chaplain H. W. Pullen. The officers ate in a separate mess. The Eskimos, who are individualists, would never have tolerated military discipline. In 1906, after clashing with the authoritarian Peary, eight Eskimo families resumed their free life. They left the expedition. It took them eight months to cover the hundreds of miles between Cape Columbia and their base in Etah. Among them were several pregnant women. They accomplished what Greely, with all the means at his disposal, had been unable to do in 1883. The Inuk, as I know, is a man of heart and very sensitive, who gives only if he is treated as an equal and if "your" adventure is also his own.

12) The history of the Eskimos shows just the opposite. Peary (1893-1909), Cook (1907-1908), Rasmussen (1903-1904), and afterwards Lauge Koch (1922-1925) would establish by their expeditions, as I would later in my own (1950-1951), the inanity of this military arrogance and the danger of holding an unfamiliar traditional society in contempt. How much suffering the members of Nares's expedition could have been spared if the Admiralty had only adopted a few simple techniques (drafting with dogs, fur clothing, Inuit diet) from these "primitive" men, to whom Sir John Ross in 1818 gave the proud name "Arctic Highlanders"!

Departure toward the Pole of the seven sledges from the *Alert* on Monday, 3 April 1876: the Marco Polo, the lead sled, and the Challenger, both equipped with ship's boats, followed by the Victoria, the Poppy, the Bulldog, the Alexander, and the Blood Hound. Fifty-three men took the place of dog teams on this spring expedition to the Pole, in -30° C to -40° C weather. Each man had to pull a load of 145 pounds. Before the departure, the chaplain conducted a prayer service, ending with the hymn "Praise God from whom all blessings flow."

men as to whether they were cases of scurvy or not.

The fact is that it has always been regarded as unnecessary and impossible to administer frozen lime-juice to sledge crews, and in the Arctic regions it is always frozen during the month of April and the greater part of May; at any rate the expedient has never been tried.

I state, moreover, without fear of contradiction, that there is not one experienced Arctic officer living who would not have followed precisely the course Captain Nares did in regard to his sledge diet.'

Sir Leopold M'Clintock wrote:—

'I think it due to Sir George Nares and his officers that former Arctic experience should not be lost sight of. If Sir George Nares erred in not having supplied his sledge-parties with lime-juice, then we Arctic travellers have all likewise erred.

'I have myself made several sledging journeys, varying in length from 20 to 105 days each, without either lime-juice or scurvy in any of my parties; and the experience of my brother officers in the Franklin search agreed with my own. Briefly, we lived upon pemmican, and enjoyed sound health. Therefore, acting as I have always done upon experience when obtainable in preference to any number of suggestions, however valuable they may appear, had I been in Sir George Nares' place I also would have left the lime-juice behind.'

As two of the members of the Committee appointed to inquire into the outbreak of scurvy had personal experience in Arctic travelling, it is to be regretted that in their report they did not draw conclusions from the knowledge gained during the numerous sledge journeys that have been successfully undertaken in the Arctic regions, on practically similar dietaries and without any lime-juice whatever; such as those of Baron von Wrangel, Parry, Franklin, Richardson, Back, Richards, M'Clintock, Sherard Osborn, M'-Clure, Collinson, Kellett, Rae, Hamilton, Mecham, Clements Markham, Hayes, and many others.

On the other hand, parties commanded by Sir James Ross, Allen Young, Mr. Kennedy, and Mons. Bellot suffered from scurvy.

Sir James Ross, starting from Port Leopold in 1849 on the 15th of May, when the weather was warm, was able to issue a daily ration of one ounce of lime-juice to his sledge crews; but nevertheless, at the end of thirty-seven days, his men returned to their ships as completely prostrated by what is said to have been debility as the sledge crews of the 'Alert' and 'Discovery' were from scurvy. [13]

Departure toward the Pole

The temperature being settled and favourable, ranging between minus twenty-five and minus thirty degrees below zero, typical for early April, I gave the order for departure. The party consisted of fifty-three officers and men, all apparently in robust health; those remaining on board the 'Alert' numbered six officers and six men. All hands assembled for prayers on

13) The Eskimos who live on these shores have never suffered from scurvy. This committee of three admirals and two doctors could have used an Inuit hunter, and appended a brief study of the Eskimo diet. This polemic about lemon, worthy of Molière, would thus have been avoided. In the course of my missions I have never used lemon and never contracted scurvy, living like the Eskimos on the fresh or frozen meat of seal, walrus, and gamey auk (kiviaq).

14) For all the majesty of the departure, the expedition was an inhuman one: because of the loads they brought the heroic explorers often had to cover the day's distance up to three times.

15) The tinted glasses used by the expedition gave little protection against the glare and reflected light of the Arctic in the blue, violet, and ultra-violet range. They would have done better to adopt Eskimo goggles, of which a version is used today by skiers in competition. The wooden goggles in the material brought back by the expedition were collected by Captain Felden and destined for exhibitions on primitive societies at the British Museum and the pleasure of schoolchildren.

Equipment of the expedition members: parka, boots, flask, and lamp.

the ice alongside of the laden sledges, which were drawn up in line, their silk banners lightly fluttering in the breeze. Every man of our company was present, the ship being tenanted only by poor Petersen, who was bearing his sufferings and trials most patiently. Mr. Pullen ended the usual daily prayers with the doxology, in which everyone joined. It was a most impressive scene; each heart being inspired with enthusiasm, and with a feeling of confidence that the labours, privations, and hardships that the travellers were about to undergo would be manfully battled with.

They started at 11 a.m., each man in the northern division dragging 230 lbs., and those of the western division 242 lbs. The programme was as follows: Lieutenant Aldrich, assisted by a sledge crew under the command of Lieutenant Gifford, was to explore the shore of Grant Land towards the north and west, along the coast-line he had discovered the previous autumn. Commander Markham, seconded by Lieutenant Parr, with two boats, and equipped for an absence of seventy days, was to force his way to the northward over the ice, starting off from the land near Cape Joseph Henry: three sledge crews under the commands of Dr. Moss and Mr. George White, accompanying them as far as their provisions would allow. [14]

Warding off snowblindness

The white painted boats being objectionable for snow-blind travellers to gaze on, Dr. Moss has been painting those belonging to Markham's party with diversified colours, but the paint does not appear inclined to dry. The backs of the travellers' white-duck jumpers have also been marked with appropriate designs, in order that when pulling at the sledge-ropes the men may have a dark colour to rest their eyes on. As every individual has been left free to choose his own crest, the variety and originality displayed is somewhat quaint. [15]

Three healthy men on the return

Legs *very* stiff, but the idea of soon getting on board the ship acted as a good restorative. Observed the dog-sledge coming over Mushroom Point. Hoisted colours. Sent Winstone, Lawrence, and Harley to the ship on May's sledge. Arrived on Mushroom Point at 8:30. Deposited, in tent pitched there, all provisions. Resumed the march, arriving alongside the ship at half-past one on the morning of Wednesday the 14th of June.

Out of my original party of fifteen men, three only—namely, Radmore, Joliffe, and Maskell—were capable of dragging the sledge; the remaining eleven having been carried alongside on the relief sledges.

The utter impracticability of reaching the North Pole over the floe in this locality

After his return Commander Markham reported: 'I feel it impossible for my pen to depict with accuracy, and yet be not accused of exaggeration, the numerous drawbacks that impeded our progress.

Dramatic scenes during the polar journey: the return of Markham's sledges. The energetic and admirable Albert Markham led the lead expedition, which left from the north of Ellesmere Island (lat. 82°24' N) with seventeen men and two sledges carrying heavy ship's boats, in the event that an "open polar sea" surrounded the Pole, which they could cross to reach Asia. At their farthest north, they were only 73 miles in a direct line from the *Alert*, though they had actually traveled 300 miles because of detours around hummocks and pressure ridges.

Lieutenant A. A. C. Parr, thanks to a twenty-three-hour solitary forced march, brought a message back to the ship, and a rescue party was sent for Markham and his men.

Crossing the hummocks. This dangerous environment was not friendly to dogs, whom Nares characterized as "picturesque" elements of polar expeditions. Their own dogs were killed by rabies during the winter.

The expedition's return. From our vantage point it is hard to understand the adventures these brave men underwent. Everyone knew that many who set off on these ships into the unknown would not return. No communication was possible, either by radio or other means, between the Admiralty, the seamen, and their families. One can appreciate the strong emotions of the women on finding their brothers, husbands, and lovers alive, truly alive!

One point, however, in my opinion is most definitely settled, and that is, the utter impracticability of reaching the North Pole over the floe in this locality; and in this opinion my able colleague, Lieutenant Parr, entirely concurs. I am convinced that with the very lightest equipped sledges, carrying no boats, and with all the resources of the ship concentrated in the one direction, and also supposing that perfect health might be maintained, the latitude attained by the party I had the honour and pleasure of commanding would not be exceeded by many miles, certainly not by a degree.'

In this I most fully concur. Markham's journey, coupled with the experience gained by Sir Edward Parry in the summer of 1827, and more recently the memorable retreat of Lieutenant Weyprecht and his companions after having abandoned the 'Tegetthof' off the coast of Francis Joseph Land, proves that a lengthened journey over the Polar pack-ice with a sledge party equipped with a boat fit for navigable purposes is impracticable at any season of the year. The much-to-be-deplored outbreak of scurvy in no way affects the conclusions to be derived from the journey.[16]

16) The danger of snap judgments: on 21-23 April 1908 and 6 April 1909, F. A. Cook and R. E. Peary respectively claimed to have reached the North Pole by dog sled, guided by Polar Eskimos. The exploit would be repeated on 19 April 1968 by the American Ralph Plaisted by snowmobile and with aerial assistance, and on 19 March 1971 by the Italian Guido Monzino, with the help of air drops and aerial reconnaissance. In March-April 1969, the Japanese Naomi Uemura covered the distance alone by dog sled with only air drops of food to assist him. On 6 April 1968, the Englishman Wally Herbert was at the Pole. On 11 May 1986, a Frenchman, Dr. Jean-Louis Etienne, reached the Pole alone on skis with the help of five air drops, as did Will Steger, with seven men and one woman, on 2 May 1986, with techniques identical to Peary's and without air drops, although some of the expeditions returned from the Pole by air: the American Ralph Plaisted, the Guido Monzino expedition (from T3), Dr. Jean-Louis Etienne, and the crew of Will Steger.

Live as the Eskimos or die

Meeting of 25 July 1875. Socializing between whites and Inuit. "Cape York. Seventeen natives, fifteen men and two women, with three dog-sledges, visited the ship. They appeared poorly clad in hooded seal-skin jumpers, and bear-skin trousers cut off at the knees; wearing nothing underneath, they showed a broad margin of body between the two garments. On being given some of the narwhal they ate it in great quantities, tearing the raw flesh asunder with their teeth. Their hair was long and matted, but their splendid row of even white teeth showed to advantage out of the setting formed by the flat mahogany-coloured visage. They were given a supply of lucifer matches, biscuits, knives, &c., which appeared to please them greatly." Nares offered no other observations on the Inughuit in his report. This document is one of the few known photographs of the Nares expedition with Inughuits. Photograph taken by Thomas Mitchell or George White.

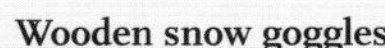

Wooden snow goggles (contemporary with the Nares expedition); their wide lower section protects the eyes from the sun's reflection on the ice. These "sunglasses" were collected at Etah by the expedition's naturalist, Captain Henry W. Feilden.

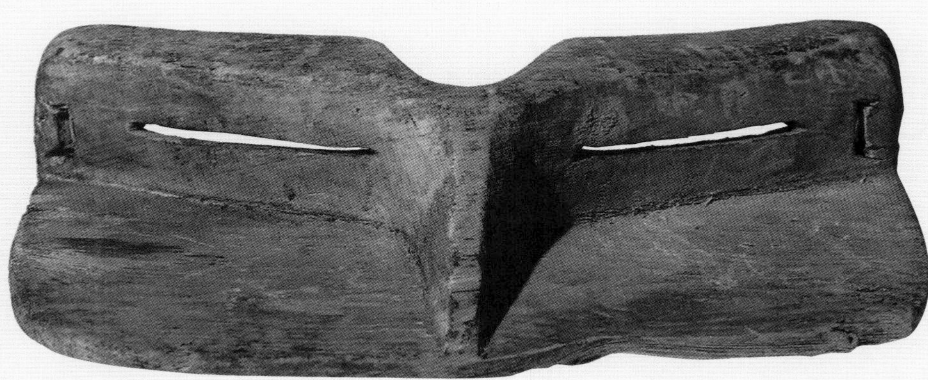

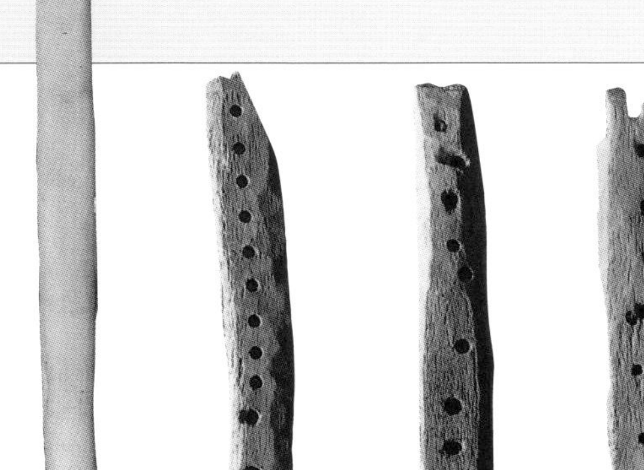

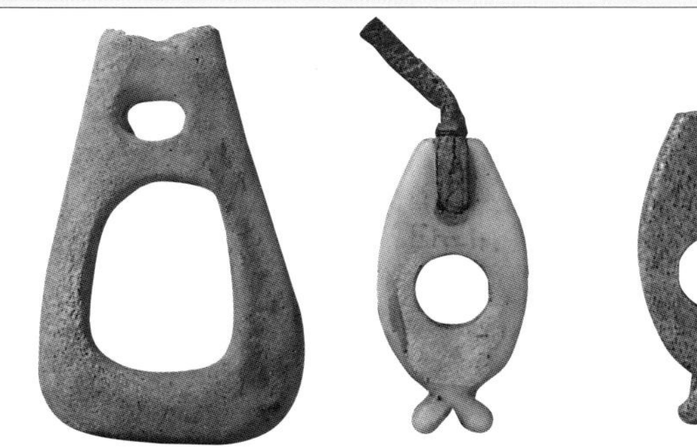

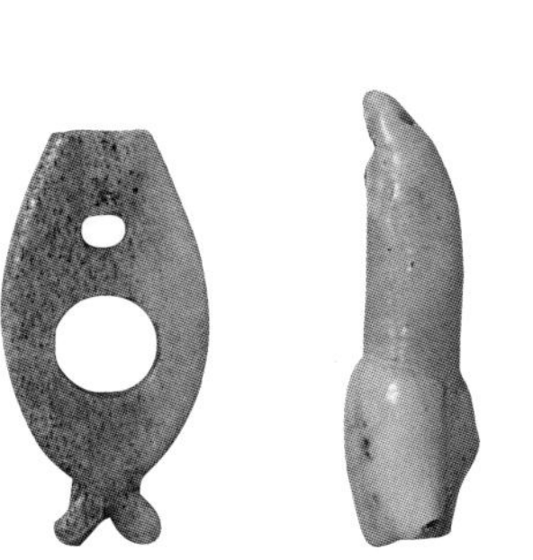

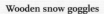

Inuit objects, some contemporary and others from excavations, brought back by Nares's expedition. Left, artifacts excavated on Ellesmere Island: harpoon point of polished narwhal ivory, and bone sled runners with holes for lashings made either of sealskin or baleen. Right, objects collected from the Inuit by Nares: three buckles for dog harnesses (the two smaller were carved in the shape of a seal, whose tail fins can be seen) and a tooth pierced at the root.

Knife with caribou antler handle, fitted with a riveted iron blade of European make (obtained by barter).

Hans Hendrick

HANS HENDRIK 1834-1889

THE FIRST GREENLANDIC EXPLORER

A veteran of five expeditions—those of Kane, Hayes, Hall, Nares, and Nordenskjöld (aboard the *Sofia*)—and of eight winters spent among the Polar Eskimos, Hans Hendrik was a legendary Inuk, who led an extraordinary life . . .

On the morning of 1 July 1853, the *Advance* dropped anchor in the small South Greenland port of Fiskenaesset (lat. 63° N., long. 50° 40' W.), the domain of Moravian missionaries. The local population had gathered on the rocks to welcome the visitors. Elisha Kent Kane, navy surgeon and captain of the ship, was worried about the prospects of his expedition. Worn out from seasickness and heart trouble, Kane had faced dissension and near-mutiny among his crew (from two men in particular) ever since leaving New York on 30 May (see page 77).

During the long Atlantic crossing, Kane had meditated on possible solutions. He would have to find a Greenlander who was capable, loyal, well viewed by all, and who could provide a useful link to the Inuit. At this his first port of call he applied to the Moravian authorities, who unhesitatingly sent him a stocky Inuk of nineteen with a grave and attentive air: Hans Hendrik. The young man's gentle aspect immediately struck Kane. After testing his dexterity with the harpoon and his skill at handling a kayak, Kane signed him on for the trip.

Hans Hendrik raised no objections. In his heart, he wanted to leave Fiskenaesset anyway, a stilted environment, extremely religious, where the Moravian pastors in their Van Dyke-style doublets ruled as tyrants. He hated the confinement imposed by the pastors on his people: no boats were allowed in the port, for fear that the "heathens" might use them to travel the twenty miles to Godthaab, run by Danish Lutheran "heretics." And Hendrik had to help his mother, a widow with five children.

Intrepid, Hans Hendrik was also endowed with extraordinary curiosity: he was not afraid of meeting his distant ancestors in the north though legend held them to be fierce, even cannibalistic. This young Moravian Greenlander was not afraid of white men either. He had heard so often in his childhood that "The worst Dane is superior to the best Greenlander" that by dint of repetition it had become his philosophy. And no matter how much he heard of atrocities committed by the whalers, his respect for the white man—and for Danes in particular—remained unwavering. It was an inherent part of his education.

In search of his Great Ancestors

Hendrik wanted only to embark on this large ship, which was sailing to North Greenland to find a certain *tuluk*, Franklin. It would take him among the Inuit, the

1) *Tuluk* means "Englishman." It is derived from the English words "do you."

Hans Hendrik, with Meqru, his wife since 1855, and two of their children, Charles Polaris and Tobias. Tobias was born among the Polar Eskimos around 1855 (a year after Hendrik's desertion). Hendrik is wearing a whaler's cap and smock, while Meqru is dressed in the South Greenland summer style: red seal boots, caribou skin pants, cloth anorak with a fur collar, and a knotted scarf around her head.
This photograph was taken in Upernavik in the summer of 1869 by a crew member of the *Panther*, an exploring ship led by Isaac Israel Hayes and carrying the artist William Bradford.

Hans Hendrik in 1853, at age nineteen. He was hired by Kane at Fiskenaesset. "He was fat, good humored, and except at the most thrilling moments of the hunt as phlegmatic and self-possessed as a North American Indian."

Avanersuarmiut, who call themselves the Inughuit, to discover his Great Ancestors[1] And to that end this young man, who wanted to live another life and see everything with his own eyes, was ready for anything. In fact he would see more than his share . . .

First he would experience the pitiless discipline of the *Advance*, the rigid hierarchy instituted by Kane. He discovered a quasi-military society aboard the American ship—ten of the officers and crew belonged to the Navy—where men announced their rank by visible signs: uniforms, staterooms, specific activities, etc. Seamen were expected to show their deference by always saying "Yes, sir" and "No, sir." The food served to the seamen was far inferior to what the officers received, a jarring custom from the Greenlander's egalitarian perspective. Hendrik's Moravian and Christian upbringing had taught him—particularly in Fiskenaesset—to despise money and material goods. It would not be long before the natives of the north would despise the white man, as a result of rubbing shoulders with him on a daily basis.

Corporal punishment astonished Hendrik: this was behavior the Greenlanders sanctioned only toward dogs! And so the white man, whom he had been taught to respect, did not respect other white men. A man could be locked in the brig for the least infraction with his hands and feet bound. Blows from the cat o' nine tails on a man's bare buttocks—an old British custom—were meted out in cases of gross indiscipline or drunkenness.

Before long tensions had risen to a high level from prow to stern, pitting white man against white man in steadfast, sordid opposition under the eyes of Hans Hendrik, the only Greenlander. The Danes questioned Kane's authority. And Kane, in order to acquire proper respect as captain of the ship and leader of the expedition, carried a pistol at all times. One day he threatened to shoot down a mutineer, and an Eskimo suspected of having put a hole in a ship's boat. But the crew started to experience scurvy and starvation, with all the suffering this entailed. Hatred had to be put away, men had to get along. Everyone's life was at stake.

Kane, at first fatherly, became more distant and condescending to Hans Hendrik as the months went by. Wasn't Hendrik no more than a hunter and a guide? As Kane himself admitted, he paid him "very modest wages." A trifling salary, plus two barrels of biscuit and fifty-two pounds of pork for his mother, in addition to a gun and a kayak, the minimum for a two-year voyage. Yet Kane always had a special affection for Hendrik. Had not this Greenlander immediately volunteered to follow him?

Lost illusions

His "superiors" were disunited, cowardly, thieving, treacherous, and mutinous. No matter. With his Asiatic eyes and imperturbable smile Hans was already the perfect example of the Greenlander of the future, seemingly complying with the oddness of the white man and expressing no judgment. Obedient to the code of the U.S. Navy, he would remain loyal to his leader, whom he called "Tarti-Kene," when almost the entire crew and all the scientific men of the *Advance* fled the ship a year later.

Hans's life recapitulates the Inuit's relations with polar explorers: strengthened by his experience the young Greenlander would secretly change after six Arctic winters with white men, and the white man would no longer be a model, but simply a means. Certainly in the beginning Hans was an adventurer like many others; but his destiny gradually became clear to him, and with it his personality. Negotiating with the Inuit of North Greenland for fresh meat to supply the starving explorers, whose ship was frozen in the ice north of Etah, he rediscovered the calm and the courage of Eskimo society, whose only law is sharing. He was not long in choosing between the two peoples. Just as he had broken with the

Moravians when the time came, so he would break with the white man.

Without the slightest hesitation, he joined the Inuit in April 1855—those same men whom the sailors called "savages" and "primitives." What did he care if he was risking his life (Kane shot unhesitatingly at deserters)? What did he care if he was judged to be a deserter in Fiskenaesset? His mother was in charge of the lamps in the church, and his brother worked for the pastors; both might fear reprisals from the Moravian church. But his decision was irrevocable.

In April 1855, after spending twenty months with Kane, Hans used the pretext of going on an errand for boots to desert. He joined the Etah Eskimos, who helped him hide and even spirited him away to one of the Inuit camps in the central islands of Northumberland and Herbert. Hans was in love with Meqru, and Kane was a bit jealous.

Stone and bone

Who were the Inuit among whom Hans had chosen to live? In Uummannaq, Natsilivik, Qaanaaq, Qeqertat, and Neqi—camps and settlements north of Cape York, scattered along the coast from Savissivik to Etah—the hunters still lived without bows or kayaks, and even without wood or iron. Thirty-six years after their historic discovery by Captain John Ross in Melville Bay, they still opted not to change their technology or their culture, based since the dawn of time on stone and bone. It was their culture that had saved them during the Little Ice Age from 1600 to 1800.

These men had survived by observing very strict rules of mutual help and dietary taboo. They were forbidden, for instance, to eat caribou or salmon even under the direst circumstances. "As strange as it might seem," wrote Knud Rasmussen in 1910, "the caribou (*tuttu*) was then considered by the Polar Eskimos as an unclean and inedible animal, just as the ptarmigan was." The group attempted to maintain a balance between its population (thirty-five to forty families) and the game supported by the environment and provided by its hunting technology. Pressed by the white man, the group clung to the hard core of tradition, its rules and taboos. To change was to go into the unknown. A group that is in danger is always conservative; it keeps what it has.

"Are you an Inuk?" a Polar Eskimo asked Hans Hendrik when Kane's expedition arrived in Rensselaer Harbor (Inglefield Land) in November 1852. This was the first Polar Eskimo that Hans had met.

"Yes, I am an Inuk," he answered, though he understood the other's language only imperfectly.

"Have you caught any hares?"

"Yes, with my gun," he said, holding out his weapon.

"'Gun'?"

The word meant nothing to the native hunter. He looked at the weapon in silence.

"It goes very far," Hans explained, "killing any animal: hare, seal, ptarmigan, fox . . ."

As Hans Hendrik tells it: "On hearing this, the Inuk said nothing more to me. He went away shaking."

Hans observed the laws of the group, just as he observed the harsh laws of nature. He would have to face the polar night. Still deeply influenced by the Bible, darkness was for him a symbol of the end of the world and of Hell. But as he had turned away from Kane, he would break with these "white" notions, these *qaallunaat* ideas, that had been fed to him over the years. Christianized and "Moravianized," he would recover his deep per-

Places where Hendrik overwintered, as the companion of five explorers.

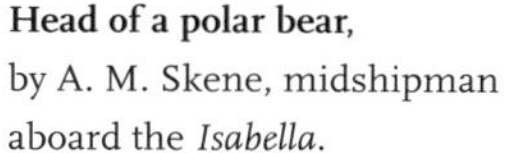

Head of a polar bear, by A. M. Skene, midshipman aboard the *Isabella*.

The ice at Inglefield Fjord, south of Qaanaaq (abandoned camp of Kangerdlugssuaq). This fjord was used as a shelter by the Inuit in times of famine and was also a breeding ground for narwhals. Precambrian sandstone and limestone cliffs, capped by a glacier that rises to more than 3200 feet.

sonality on contact with his Great Ancestors. And he would slowly slip and meld into the group—humbly, modestly, and without trying in any way to change the precarious equilibrium that held it together. Nor did "Ashé" (as the Polar Eskimos called him) give in to habit or comfort and introduce the technologies of South Greenland, particularly the kayak, though he was a skillful paddler. He kept what he knew to himself. His knowledge was not synonymous with power.

"Ashé," explained the famous Eskimo shaman Meqorsuaq [2] in 1910, "quickly learned the techniques for hunting. He let his hair grow, because the short hair he had when he arrived displeased us. He was never a good bear hunter and only had a dog team in his last year with us. Like us, he had no kayak."

Hans accepted the Polar Eskimos' shamanistic rules, even to their most constraining restrictions: no eating of salmon or caribou, and no kayaks. Unlike his white companions on the *Advance* (Petersen and Godfrey in particular), he never mocked the Inuit belief that the celestial vault is populated with wandering souls and animals: Orion, a seal hunter who lost his way in ancient times; the Big Dipper, a troop of caribou; the Pleiades, a pack of dogs harassing a bear . . . He believed in the *qiviqtuq*. [3] When Meqru ("Needle"), Shunghu's daughter, whom he married in 1855, was granted sight of the invisible and heard what is hidden from others during her trances (*piblokto*), he did not doubt her for an instant. Much later, after he had returned to the whites, he reported the least words spoken by Meqru, with whom he remained until the end of his life. [4] His choice of wife was all the more courageous for a man raised by the Moravians in that she was a heathen. As far as we know Hans would not try to have her baptized before 1865, in Upernavik, during their first prolonged stay in this Danish colony. At any rate he never spoke of it, and if his conscience troubled him it went unmentioned in his memoirs.

Mr. Hendrik or Ashé?

The Christian Hans did not disappear entirely. Though he had assumed the character of Ashé, he sometimes spoke to the Polar Eskimos about the "other" society in which he lived. Despite the resistance and inertia of the Inuit toward anything foreign, they listened at night to the Greenland legends he related to them. For Ashé did not deny his past. He was the first to speak at those high latitudes of a God of charity, a Son—God crucified and resurrected—the concepts of humility, sin, and redemption—ideas that till then were totally foreign to Inuit thought. What is remarkable is that in the two hundred tales and myths collected in 1933-1936 by Erik Holtved and earlier (in 1903-1920) by Knud Rasmussen, no trace of this layer of Christianity is to be found. The evangelical message was blanked out by the Inuit.

Woodcut, after a photograph. Hans Hendrik, already an old man though only 49 years old.

Without panegyrizing Hans Hendrik, it is appropriate to take stock of his role and remember his personality. It was certainly not money that motivated his repeated engagements: it was not for money that he joined the *Advance* from 1853 to 1856; nor the *United States* in 1860-1861. After living in the Upernavik region he was personally recruited in Pröven on 20 August 1871 by Charles Francis Hall for $300 a year. He took part in both the happy and tragic times aboard the *Polaris*, and drifted on the ice floe to Labrador in the autumn and winter of 1872-1873. At the personal request of George Strong Nares, [5] he took part in the British *Discovery* expedition of 1875-1876, saving Lieutenant Lewis Beaumont from certain death. In August 1883 he took part in the Swedish expedition to Cape York led by Nordenskjöld on the *Sofia*. Was it only to assuage his thirst for adventure, or was it also to conduct his own "exploration" of his Great Ancestors? At all events, he was undeniably the first Greenlandic explorer. And on those grounds he deserves international fame, having paid the price of many tragic and exceptional adventures.

Hendrik intervened on numerous occasions to help his white companions out of desperate straits. [6] Out of friendship? or because he was a faithful servant? After Hall was murdered in 1871 while leading the American *Polaris* expedition, Hans fell into deep distress. Was it because Hall, a man of modest origins, had understood him? No one will ever know. His friendship for the patrician "Tarti-Kene" cannot be denied either.

A true Inuk, Hans Hendrik was able to adapt to the diverse personalities he encountered. Again as a true representative of the Inuit, he never offered the least public criticism of the members of the polar expeditions he took part in. He passed no judgment on Kane or Budington. He never criticized Hayes, though from all the evidence their relations were bad—not even during the official interrogation he underwent in Washington in 1873 after Hall's death, nor in the book he wrote in Eskimo with the encouragement of his Danish friend Dr. Rudolph, and more or less at the request of the Danish inspector for Northern Greenland, Karup Smith. (Despite his celebrity, Hendrik never realized the slightest profit from this book.) These are truly Eskimo character traits: adaptability, disinterestedness, and a perfect loyalty toward the white explorers whose hardships he had shared. Another Eskimo trait: modesty. He never talked of the dangers he had faced, or of his own courage. He showed the same intelligence and humanity toward the Polar Eskimos. A Greenlander and a Christian, he wintered among them for eight years without trying to alter to their culture. His manner was to slip into a foreign society, not to appropriate it.

Though like other natives he was extremely sensitive to marks of disrespect and injustice, he voluntarily kept silent in his book on the disagreements and other humiliations that he and his people experienced. We know only that he was disgusted by Hayes's racism, particularly over the business of the skeletons (see page 186). But one has to put oneself in the context of the period. Hendrik belonged to a generation of aboriginals who

2) See photograph p. 280.
3) See page 148.
4) Meqru was the grandmother of my dear companion Sakaeunnguaq, the first to welcome me in Siorapaluk in July 1950. He spoke of her to me.
5) "My primary purpose in stopping at Pröven was to secure the services of the Greenlander Hans Hendrik . . . Upon being asked, Hans agreed immediately." This points to the extreme availability of these men, who are nomads at heart.
6) "He rendered invaluable services to his companions," said Captain Nares, speaking of Hendrik's part in Kane's expedition.

July 1860. The *United States*, commanded by Hayes, put in near Cape York to look for Hans Hendrik, who deserted from the Kane expedition in 1854. He was "making signs to attract attention . . . Six years' experience among the wild men of this barren coast [with his wife Meqru, a young Polar Eskimo woman for whom he deserted the *Polaris*] had brought him to their level of filthy ugliness." He embarked immediately.

were frightened—when not terrorized—by the Americans, Danish, and British, who gave orders at pistol point that it was inconceivable to resist. For this reason, and despite their having an anarcho-communist society, the Eskimos of this period had a clear preference for military discipline in their relations with whites. Already reduced by their "masters" to the lowest rung of the social ladder and paid accordingly, they hated nothing more than fluid and ill-defined work relations. The Eskimo, a man par excellence, likes his work to be well executed and hates any shoddiness. He performs to the utmost of his competence, or he leaves. Discipline—even the iron discipline of a Captain Hayes—struck them as preferable to any other way of proceeding: it was the lesser evil.

Yet the Eskimos understood perfectly well that in times of danger, responsibility would rest solely on them—their experiences with Kane, Hayes, and Hall proved this clearly. In 1891, Peary would face the first challenges arising from the Inuit's realization of this. Though he hid it, the great explorer had terrible difficulty with Uutaaq, the leading dissenter, who argued bitterly over wages and other arrangements. Knud Rasmussen would be the first, starting in 1917, to treat the Polar Eskimos as equals, thus securing a truce of sorts with this often-scorned people just as their acrimony toward whites was growing. Despite the proclamation of autonomy in 1953, this acrimony did not disappear but became more strident as growing numbers of ever more critical native voices joined in.

Today, the Inuk is conscious of his power and of the justice of his struggle. Whites, all whites, reap only the anger of a people conscious of the despoliation it has suffered for generations.

Hendrik kept his secrets and his truth to the end of his life, when, still a nomad, he worked up and down Greenland's west coast from Upernavik to Disko Bay as a laborer and boatswain. He seems never to have had much money. He never returned to the land of his Great Ancestors. He died and was buried with his secrets in Godhavn, on Disko Island, on 11 August 1889, at the age of fifty-five. I went to pay my respects in September 1949, bringing a bouquet of tundra flowers, while camping alone in the vicinity of the scientific station there.

It would be well for the children of Greenland to honor this legendary Inuk as he so richly deserves . . . ■

The Memoirs of Hans Hendrik.

Hans Hendrik (at age 41) with his daughter and youngest son on 3 July 1875 aboard the *Discovery*, captained by George Strong Nares. Hendrik has opted for adventure, that is, freedom. In Fiskenaesset in South Greenland, where he lived in a Moravian community, men and women were kept separate by the missionaries and assigned to fraternities or *herrnhut*. Mates were chosen by community decision or by lottery.

I, Hans Hendrik, who first lived at Kekertarsuatsiak [Fiskenaesset], belonging to the Germans [Moravians], have now moved north, to Kangersuatsiak, belonging to Upernivik.

I was born in the German [missionary station of] Kekertarsuatsiak, which had three priests, and my father served the priests. He used to go to the other stations to lead divine service there on the great holidays. His name was Benjamin. My mother was in charge of the church lamps. Her name was Ernestine. She had come from the south, from Agdluitsok, from the end of the country [Cape Farewell]. . . . My father's children by his first wife were seven altogether, three sons and four daughters; but by my mother he had five children, four sons and a female child, scarcely to be mentioned, because she died as an infant.

The horror of a polar night, 1853-1854

Then it really grew winter and dreadfully cold, and the sky speedily darkened. Never had I seen the dark season like this, to be sure, it was awful. I thought we should have no daylight any more. I was seized with fright,[7] and fell a weeping, I never in my life saw such darkness at noon time. As the darkness continued for three months, I really believed we should have no more daylight. However it finally it dawned and, brightness having set in, I used to go shooting hares.

The men of the polar regions— murderers? 1853

When I first saw these people, whom I knew nothing about, and nobody had examined, I feared they might perhaps be murderers, as they lived apart from any Kavdlunak; but, on the contrary, they were harmless men. In the evening they went to sleep on board the vessel. The Tuluks[8] offered them something to eat, bread and beef, and such like, with

HANS HENDRIK'S MEMOIRS

These memoirs—the first to have been written by a Greenlander—were published in 1878, thanks to the Danish inspector Hans J. Rink, a thoughtful and feeling man.[9] Rink, also the publisher, added: "My doubts about Hans Hendrik's ability to make the text as readable as possible for the reader were relieved by my friend Professor G. Stephens, who assumed the responsibility for editing it."

These are "failed" memoirs, "masked" memoirs. One reads them with a feeling of regret for all that this first explorer from Greenland might have told about his white companions. Only forty-eight pages are devoted to his time with Kane and the five years he spent with the Avangnamiut [Avanersuarmiut], the Polar Eskimos he had the privilege of witnessing from 1855 to 1860 during a decisive period in their history. How many crucial thoughts and observations, accumulated over these eight years, have been lost! At fault was Hans Rink, who should have encouraged Hendrik to speak more about the Polar Eskimos. A hunter, used to expressing himself orally, will naturally feel inhibited by the pen and the effort of composition. An attentive man could have helped him by asking pertinent questions so as to bring this Eskimo society to life, transmitting to paper this extraordinary civilization— until little over one hundred years ago, was among the most primitive on earth— at a crucial juncture in its history, just before the great technological shift of 1863.

Hans unfortunately lived at a time when there was little or no communication between peoples, and no one took an interest in his extraordinary knowledge.[10] The loss is irreparable. Whole fields of knowledge concerning this people will always elude us. White men risked their lives for glory, carrying to the far ends of the planet their haughty and majestic indifference to all lives but their own.

7) The same fear existed among the whalers.
8) Tulut, "those who speak English."
9) Memoirs of Hans Hendrik (London: 1878).
10) The manuscript notes of Hans Hendrik have not all been published.

Pressure ridges: looking for a safe passage for the dog team and the sledge.

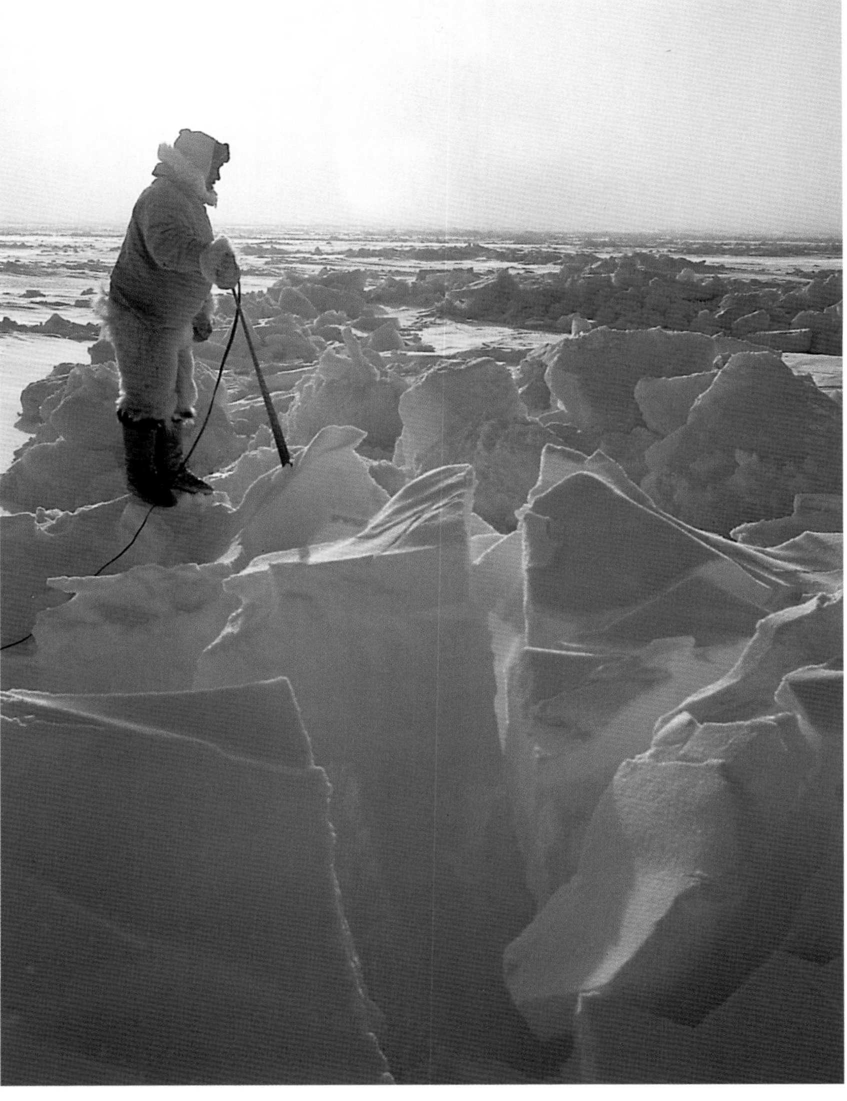

tea, but they did not relish them, they only tried some little bits. They said: "We cannot eat it;" and added, that they should like to have some hare-meat. But our Commander was careful of our hares. The next day, when they left us, our Master gave them wood, needles, iron, and matches, and they went off very thankful and cheerful.

Kane addresses the Eskimos threateningly, 1854

After their departure the [frozen up] boat was found broken asunder ... and the sails in patches—only think! a native found it, and being unable to make out what this thing was amidst the ice, he had broken it into pieces. Our Commander, Kane, grew angry, as he knew not who had done it. Later on, a native arrived on foot named Majok. When I returned from hare-hunting I saw him shut up in the ship. [11] The Master ordered me to examine him as to who had spoiled the boat. He said: "I don't know, I have not done it." The Master said he would shoot him if he did not confess. On hearing this I took fright; at once pitying him, and afraid to look at him, I uttered: "He says he will shoot you if you do not tell." He replied: "I have not done it, I don't know it."

Finally, unable to overcome him, they grew silent. Our Commander said to me that he intended to shoot him. I answered: "What a pity!" We went to sleep, while he was kept prisoner. In the beginning of the night I heard a noise. I went out and saw him running off speedily. I wonder how he managed to get out, the hatch-way being very high. [12] After his departure no more natives made their appearance, I think they were frightened.

The memory of three centuries of history [13]

In the days of yore their ancestors used to visit Upernivik [Hendrik's spelling], for which reason they still speak of "Southlanders." Those northern people had for their merchandise walrus-teeth, for which they got wood, whereas the Southlanders had wood to barter with. Their ancestors also possessed Kayaks. One man, named Kassuk, when undertaking a journey, was told not to visit the Southlanders, because they used to kill their guests when they were going to depart. [14]

How you become a qiviqtuq, *1861*

In the beginning of winter one of these natives turned a Kivigtok [fled from human society, to live alone up country]. [15] We were unable to make out what might have induced him to do so. The only thing we remembered he had uttered was—"What does J___ say when he whispers in passing by me?" When he asked me this, I answered—"I don't know at all." Also of the others he inquired in the same way, but we were quite ignorant of what he meant. Once, when the sea was frozen, he went outside towards tea-time, as we supposed, without any particular purpose. But fancy! all of a sudden he had run away. After tea, on going out, I said to my wife—"Hast thou not seen Umarsuak?" She

OPPOSITE:
Hans Hendrik would live out his life in Upernavik with his four children. It was in this small port and during this same period that the ships commanded by Schley dropped anchor, carrying the survivors of the Greely expedition. In the United States, Hendrik was famous, having participated in five major expeditions. The *Polaris* saga was well known to the general public. Photograph taken in 1884.

---

11) Sir John Ross wanted to subjugate the Polar Eskimos to the British Crown. They preferred to disappear rather than obey Ross's injunctions and lead him to the "chief" of their group and show him where the meteorites lay. Ross claimed the territory in the name of the prince regent. Kane, who was more intently observed by the Polar Eskimos than he observed them, made himself respected by firearms. He put Majak "in prison" aboard the Advance.

12) The Eskimo becomes panicky at being shut up in a dark place.

13) When no date is indicated, the event emerges from one or another of Hendrik's expeditions.

14) Ross reports that the Polar Eskimos told Sacheuse, his Greenlandic interpreter, that they were alone in the world. Did he understand correctly? Sacheuse did not know the Polar Eskimos' dialect and spoke English poorly, as Sabine reminds us. Furthermore, Ross interprets the incident according to the ideas of his period. To him, the Polar Eskimos are "primitives" on the brink of extinction, judging from their technology; hence they are isolated. Hans Hendrik—whom ethnographers paid little heed to during the 1920s and 1930s, taking isolation as a given—left no doubt on the point: the Polar Eskimos retained the memory of trips to the south, where they traded ivory for wood. If they did not build any Kayaks and umiaqs, as their cousins to the south did, it was due to a cultural choice and not an inability.

15) The idea of the qiviqtuq is related to the visceral fear felt by the Eskimos toward all transformations. Man, as he slowly becomes human, remains in danger of turning back into an animal. When this happens, he speaks a language that only the animals understand ("We were quite ignorant of what he meant"). A qiviqtuq is a man who, having suffered at the hands of the Inuit, leaves the sea and goes toward the mountains or the glacier and lives alone. Through his suffering he becomes immortal. He is dangerous to humans, trying to get revenge on them by taking their souls and tormenting them if they stray into his territory.

Hans Hendrik is sitting in the boat on the right, his left hand on the gunwale and a child beside him. Meqru is to the child's left. Standing at far right is Fred Meyers, one of the formidable Germans in the company. On the far left stands Captain Tyson, leader of the nineteen members of the *Polaris* expedition who drifted on an ice floe five miles in circumference all the way from Etah in Greenland to Labrador, from 15 October 1872 to 26 April 1873. Hendrik and Joe Ebierbing—a Canadian Eskimo, who lies on the left side of the boat beside his wife, Hannah—showed that the ingenuity and experience of Inuit hunters could rescue whites from the most desperate straits. It was Hans who set out by kayak toward the sealer *Tigress* and saluted it with his Russian-style cap. Photograph taken on 13 May 1873 in Saint John, Newfoundland, a few days after the sealer rescued them.

answered—"He went out after having handled his bag. I thought he was going to take his tea, but he said, 'That is the only awkward thing, to understand neither Danish nor English.'" As soon as he was missed, some of the crew lighted torches and set off in search of him. At last I found his foot prints going to the hills. I followed them and shouted to him, but got no answer. When I had reached the top of the hills, also there he had still run farther. But, as I grew exhausted, and his track disappeared in the darkness, I gave him up wholly and returned to the ship, where the rest had now arrived. Although we still kept up a faint hope of his return, he was quite lost, and his memory left a deep impression upon me, he being the only friend whom I loved like my brother.

Eskimos and Christianity, 1853-1860

It is a great pity that people there in the north have no idea of a Creator.[16] Only by me were they informed about the Maker of heaven and earth and everything else, of all animals, and even of ourselves. Also, about His only begotten Son, who came in the flesh for the sake of sinful men, for the purpose of saving them, teaching them faith, and performing wonderful deeds amongst them, and afterwards was killed on a wooden cross, and arose from the dead on the third day, and will come down again to judge the living and the dead. On hearing this the Northlanders were rather frightened as to the destruction of the world in their life as well as in their death.[17]

Hans describes the Inuit's method of hunting

They pursue white whales along the edge of the ice,[18] using five hunting bladders in connection with one line, but on the big ice only one bladder. They get the seals, which lie near their breathing holes upon the ice, by creeping up to them and harpooning them. They pursue the walrus with two hunting lines, both ends of which are furnished with a harpoon, and their spears are headed with a Tok [chisel]. As soon as the line becomes tightened [pulled by the stricken animal], they thrust this into the ice to hold.[19]

They also catch seals by having many breathing holes at once occupied by men. One man then generally catches a great number, while the others only get a few, as the seals, when at the point of choking, have recourse to a few holes without leaving them.

Bears they kill by spearing them, after having brought them to bay by the dogs. They capture foxes in traps of four different descriptions. For hares they use nets made of sealskin thongs. For birds they also use an implement like a catcher.

Hunting seals at the breathing holes, during day, they call Marpok; during the night, Nirpapok.

A few words of the original Eskimo language

I also remember the following words of their language: sirlla pirnerkariarnarkark irnurk pirniarkark irgijarnarkark pirnirkark arllirnarkark narparpurk karparpurk pirniarllune arllarpurk sarnivarpurk irmirnirk narnurnijarpuk kirmursirgarpuk tirmirsarnut karllurpurk. Some of their word I have forgotten, as I left them after a few years' stay.[20]

A year's pay

The next day we landed, to our great delight, and were lodged in the house of Julius. The Captain came too and proposed to convey me to Fiskernaes, but I answered that I wanted to remain at Upernivik, and he consented. Our Master now appeared to be quite changed, full of love towards me, and liking me as he did in former years. He gave me a gun, which I took, but another rifle, which likewise he offered, I refused, as it did not shoot straight. He also added tea and other provisions and pork, and a wage-sum of 72 dollars [Danish].[21]

---

16) First dialogue between the Polar Inuit and a Christian: 1853-1855. Yet the Inuit appeared to ignore Christianity altogether, according to subsequent expeditions, until 1910.

17) The Inuit believe that man represents only a moment in the history of nature and that the earth and sea are supernatural forces which might come from a supreme power. The Inuit world concept is vertical: the afterlife is simply the invisible pursuit of earthly life "up there" in good circumstances—if one has respected all the Inuit taboos. If not, the hunter lives "down there" in misfortune. The Christian vision of man's redemption through a Man-God might to some extent be comprehensible to the Inuk. What is incomprehensible to them, though, is that the Earth should not be part of a Divine Whole but instead be subject to destruction. It is remarkable that the Inuit obliterated Hendrik's stay among them from collective memory, along with the revelation of a crucified Man-God.

18) Having no kayaks, the hunters used the floe as a pontoon.

19) This technique was practically unchanged in 1950.

20) Only sample of the protohistoric Polar Eskimo language.

21) The Eskimos, expert guides on American as well as British Arctic expeditions, were always exploited—until Knud Rasmussen. John Sacheuse received the same salary as the least skilled seaman of John Ross's crew in 1818: £ 3 per month. Peary paid his black manservant Matt Henson $ 40 per month—half what a white man received. A seaman on a whaler received a monthly wage of £ 2.72. In 1861, Hayes paid $ 72 for a year's work—and its attendant dangers—plus two firearms . . . one of which was unsuitable for hunting.

Hans Hendrik as described by whites.

Elisha Kent Kane *1855* [22]

Hans, the devoted son and ardent young lover of Fiskenaesset, my loyal friend, has been absent for almost two months.... In our work during the following month, we missed Hans terribly.... Hans was sought after by all and especially by the best—and considered an excellent prospect, one of the greatest men in the country. I must summon my former feeling of affection for him in order to suspend my judgment.... I have spared no effort to get to the very bottom of it; at every occasion I have asked questions about the business.... But the story is always the same: Hans, loyal Hans (though I'm afraid he does not hold to his word), was last seen on an Eskimo sledge travelling toward Peteravik [Pitorarfik], to Uwarrow Suk-suk, at the very head of Murchison Fjord, with a young woman at his side.... Alas for Hans, a married man!

Isaac Israel Hayes *1869, the* Panther *expedition*

The doctor entered his room one day and said in his hearty voice: "You know this man! you know this scoundrel, hey?" From behind his jacket he drew forth a sinister-looking individual that I had certainly not forgotten: Master Hans Hendrich [Hendrik]. This Hans had enjoyed a certain celebrity. In 1853, Doctor Kane had taken him from Fiskenaesset, in South Greenland, to serve as his interpreter on his famous voyage into Smith Sound. At that time the Eskimo was twenty years old. He ate well on the *Advance*, grew round and fat, and played many tricks on his master before running off to the savages of this region and marrying a young savagess, Merkut [Meqru]. I found him again in 1860 and took him on board with his wife and their child, Pingasuik. It was folly on my part; he behaved even worse toward me than he had toward Doctor Kane. I have no doubt that he caused the death of two of my men, but it was never possible to gather enough evidence to pass judgment on him. Where to find a witness in a desolation where there is no eye to see or ear to hear? I therefore returned him to the hands of the Danish authorities, from whom Dr. Kane had taken him eight years previously. Since then he has never ceased to practice his art of meanness: his wife sulks continually because she is no longer able to live entirely like a savage; his children (they now have two) are being raised by public charity. I gave Merkut a little money to buy them clothes; in less than an hour she had exchanged it at the trade counter for some dried figs and sugar candy.

The savage in the "state of nature" is not a likable creature, though one puts him in the best possible light. He has very primitive notions of mine and thine, and "the truth inhabiteth him not." It seems that "truth," along with manners, are properly to be ranked among the fine arts; a man may be endowed with them only by culture. But Hans was no longer a savage: the missionaries had taught him to read the New Testament and Thomas à Kempis; he could write his own name. The story of his progress is told at length in a Sunday school book that I came across a year or two ago; it goes on blithely about the Christian charity that he showed in accompanying us to the far north—as though these fine appearances had not served to cloak his true character, like Uriah Heap playing his part before Creakle and the visiting committee.

22) From *Arctic Explorations* (Philadelphia: 1856).

November. The clouds darken threateningly: it is the month of storms. The polar night (*kapirlaq*) gains on the horizon.
Pastel by Jean Malaurie.

Near Cape York. Sketch by E. K. Kane, drawn during his expedition of 1852-1854. Engraved by J. Hamilton.

William Bradford painter, and friend of I. I. Hayes, voyage of summer 1889 aboard the Panther

In 1860, Dr. Hayes found Hans Hendrik in a state of great misery at Cape York. Believing his knowledge of the country could prove useful to the expedition, he took him on board ship and brought him back to the Smith Sound area. Hans revealed himself to be an excellent hunter, but he was morose of temperament, sulky and ungrateful, and displayed the worst traits of the Eskimo character, though he had been converted and partly educated by the missionaries. He was strongly suspected of having plotted the death of two members of the expedition. . . . He was brought back to Upernavik, where he has lived since; he is a lazy, shiftless man, or so I judged him to be. His wife is only a little better. The Danes would happily pay to have the family deported, if they would consent to go. Hans cannot be considered a good specimen of the Greenlandic convert, nor held up as an example of the missionary work in this country.

Captain Tyson's journal adrift on the floe

22 January 1873.—Hans sometimes acts like a madman. This is the same Hans who abandoned Dr. Kane and who caused Dr. Hayes to lose two good partners in his expedition. He played the "good Moravian" with Kane, who was tender-hearted, and Hayes was unable to pin a criminal conviction on Hans in the United States; but I could never read the account of Sonntag's death [Hayes's astronomer] and the material benefit that Hans drew from it for his whole family without feeling slightly uneasy about him. But he has worked well for us and is now somewhat older and responsible for a wife and four children, which increases one's sense of trust for him.

23 January.— . . . He is a thoughtless or egotistic Esquimau. He is not a skillful hunter like Joe, or he lacks his intuition. He does not know how to build a hut for himself. In any case he does not do it. Joe built it for him. He does not take care of himself in this place with so little game. I am not surprised that Sonntag froze to death or suffered some other mishap. Any White man left in the hands of so vile a creature as Hans is in danger. This afternoon he threatened us with "no more hunt." We'll leave him and see. He will get hungry because I won't allow him to draw on our supplies if he continues in this vein. He was recruited for the purpose of hunting for the expedition (and will be paid for it, if we manage to return to the United States). Hunting is not a favor on his part, but a duty.

George Strong Nares 1875-1876[23]

Hans proved himself to be an admirable hunter and an excellent dog-driver. Hans when a lad of nineteen joined Dr. Kane's expedition in 1853. After rendering invaluable services to his companions during their two winters' stay at Rensselaer Harbour, Smith Sound, he married Merkut, the daughter of Shanghu, one of the "Arctic Highlanders," who tended him when lying sick at Hartstene Bay; he remained behind with his wife when Dr. Kane abandoned his vessel and travelled south to Upernivik in boats. In 1860, after he had passed five years with the "Arctic Highlanders," Dr. Hayes finding Hans at Cape York, took him and his wife and child on board his vessel the "United States"; on the homeward voyage in 1861 he was landed with his belongings at Upernivik. In 1871 he joined Captain Hall in the "Polaris," taking his wife and three children with him. He was one of the party who were separated from the "Polaris" in a gale of wind, and drifted during the long winter of 1872-73 from Smith Sound to the southward of Hudson's Straits; during that time he and Joe, another Eskimo, preserved the lives of their companions by their indefatigable and noble exertions in hunting and procuring seals.

A. E. Nordenskjöld, leader of a Swedish expedition along the west coast of Greenland, June 1883, en route to Smith Sound

Hans is now old, and his appearance no longer reminds one of the young conqueror of native belles. . . . The sense of his own worth has given Hans a certain dignity. I welcomed him warmly and gave him the best treatment. Nonetheless, the conversation languished. Hans found great difficulty expressing himself in a European language. The coffee and the wine finally loosened his tongue, and our interview became more animated. The memories of his youth at Cape York were still vivid, and his eyes lit up just at the thought of revisiting the site again. But he prudently added that he would return there only in the summer.

---

23) From Narrative of a Voyage to the Polar Sea.

Baron Nils Adolf Erik Nordenskjöld

This multifarious and feverishly active scientist attempted to conquer the Pole from Spitsbergen using reindeer, and set off across Greenland on skis . . . That same summer, an exploration into northern Melville Bay by the expedition's ship determined that the Polar Eskimos, discovered 60 years before by Sir John Ross, still refused to emerge from their prehistory.

The son of a geologist and the director of the Ministry of Mines in Finland, the future commander of the Vega was born in Helsinki. At age twenty-five, he was named lecturer in physics and mathematics at the University of Helsingfors. This appointment confirmed the young Nordenskjöld in his vocation for science. In 1857 he was expelled from the duchy of Finland, at that time under the tsar's rule, because of his independence of mind. He had presented an address that went counter to the censorship laws: "The Memories and Hopes of Finland." He took refuge in Sweden, where he was named to the Academy of Sciences. A few years later he took part in an expedition to Spitsbergen, where he performed remarkable work in paleontology. In 1864, collaborating with Dunér, he produced a remarkably accurate map of Spitsbergen based on eighty geodesic points, far more detailed than any maps of arctic lands then in existence.

Nordenskjöld would lead the first two Swedish expeditions to the Pole. On 19 September 1868, accompanied by Captain von Otter, he reached the furthest north yet attained in a ship (lat. 81° 42' N, long. 17° 30' W).[1] On his second expedition (1872), which set off north from Spitsbergen, he would attempt to journey to the Pole over the chaotic hummocks and pressure ridges of the pack ice using a sled pulled by reindeer! This expedition, with its novel source of locomotion, quickly came to grief. The route from Spitsbergen to the Pole, though the shortest, turns out to be the least practicable because of the opposing currents (northeast to southwest).

In 1878-1880 Nordenskjöld headed the scientific, geographic, and oceanographic mission of the 300-ton Vega in a courageous transit of the Northeast Passage under Swedish navy captain L. Palander. The Vega left Tromsø on 21 July 1878 with nine officers and twenty-one seamen and succeeded in making the first crossing from Europe to the Far East via the northern Siberian route. After passing Cape Chelyuskin on 19 August and wintering north of Chukotski Peninsula (northeastern Siberia),[2] at Pitlekaï (lat. 67° 07' N, long. 173° W), 120 miles west of Dezhneva Cape, the Vega rounded East Cape (northeastern Siberia) in July 1879, then visited Saint Lawrence Island and, after a further stopover in Yokohama on 2 September 1879, reached Stockholm on 24 April 1880. The voyage received international acclaim. April 24 was made the official day of the Swedish Anthropological and Geographical Society, to which Nordenskjöld belonged. In February 1883, Nordenskjöld acquired a steamship from the Swedish postal service, the Sofia, though it was not well adapted to ice. But Nordenskjöld had exploration in his blood. With twenty-three men, he attempted an expedition to the south and northwest of Greenland to explore the ice cap and to study (and bring back to Sweden) one of the famous meteorites reported in August 1818 by Ross's expedition.

According to native reports, collected in 1788 by

Portrait by Jungstedt

Paul Egede, northern Greenland was free of ice north of the more or less mythic strait separating Greenland in two, marked on the west by Jakobshavn. The gravelly soil was covered with shrubs. Game was plentiful. The natives, who were few in number, spoke a language close to the language of South Greenland. For lack of wood or iron, these Eskimos—whose night lasted several months—used the tooth of the narwhal.

These rumors affirmed that Greenland was an island, a fact only scientifically proven by the Lauge Koch expedition of 1920-1922. They affirmed that Peary Land (reached by Peary in 1892) was free of ice and teeming with game (musk oxen). Perhaps this information dates from the migration of Canadian Inuits via Peary Land in the fourteenth century. It supports the idea that communication existed between different population groups in Greenland, despite the enormous distances and the rivalries dividing them.

The Sofia put in at Upernavik on 22 July 1883, and Hans Hendrik was hired as the expedition's indispensable guide. The ship crossed Melville Bay without any major difficulties, noting that the water changed from a "dark color" to a "greenish" one, and arrived on 26 July fifteen miles south of Cape York. Because of the fog, the Sofia was unable to land but hugged the coast as whalers had always done, following a narrow channel through the ice. The ship entered Ivssugissoq Bay, where I traveled by dog sled in March 1967 with Qaaqqutsiaq and Sakaeunnguaq to collect peat for an archaeological study of pollen and climate over the past thousand years.

The party met a few Eskimos, whom they perceived as being in a state of great misery and who were unable to provide any detailed information on the blocks of meteoric iron. Sir John Ross's report had justly placed them much farther south, near Savissivik. But the expedition could not linger, as the ice was closing in and threatened to overtake the ship at any moment. The captain nonetheless learned that to the north "the captain of an American ship had been murdered by his crew." This must refer to Hall (1871). The whites traded for a narwhal tusk, a complete suit of clothes, "vases of serpentine," and walrus tusk animal figures. In return they offered knives, saws, and axes.

On 29 July at 8:00 a.m. the ship freed itself from the moving pack ice and headed south at full speed. West of Cape York, the pack suddenly became impenetrable. As the Sofia's hull was of unreinforced steel sheets, the ship was in extreme danger. And there was only enough coal to last two days! This excursion by the Sofia, made at Nordenskjöld's behest, showed reckless courage, given the ship's unreadiness. Thanks to providential openings in the pack and the adroit maneuvering of the pilot, the Sofia arrived in Upernavik on 1 August, and at Egedesminde on 16 August, where Nordenskjöld rejoined the ship. He had traveled on foot with two Laplanders to longitude 50° 30' W. Though the crew returned safely, the "Meteorite Excursion" had been a failure; yet in science, discoveries are sometimes made in marginal and seemingly ancillary areas of investigation. Nordenskjöld had the audacity and luck that characterizes great explorers, as his danger sortie onto the ice cap and the Sofia's exploits prove. And he possessed an open mind: ethnography seemed no less important to him than mineralogy—a rare attitude among specialists.

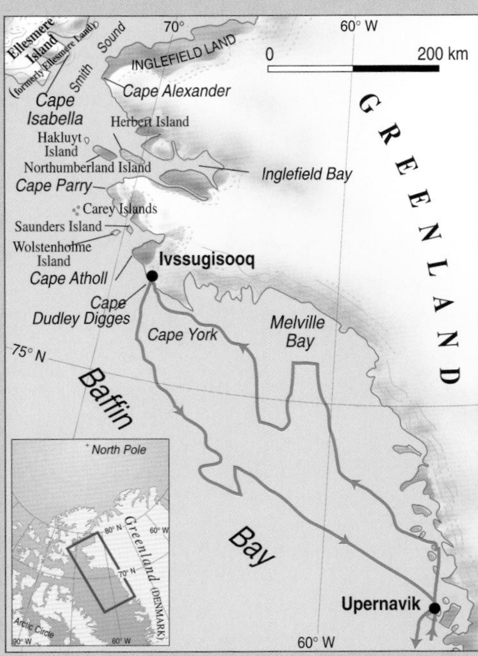

1) His mark would be surpassed two years later by the American Charles Francis Hall on the Polaris; in 1875 by the Englishman George Strong Nares commanding the Alert and Discovery; then in 1881 by the American Adolphus Washington Greely aboard the Proteus and in 1908 by Robert Edwin Peary aboard the Roosevelt.

2) During the winter, Nordenskjöld gathered a unique collection of Chukchi ethnographic material, preserved today in the Stockholm Museum.

LIEUTENANT ADOLPHUS WASHINGTON GREELY 1844-1935

NINETEEN DEAD, SIXTEEN FROM STARVATION

A new chapter in arctic history, revealing a new facet of human relations in cramped quarters and an extreme climate. After the era of privately funded expeditions, marred by quarrels, qualms, and dramas, the era of official arctic stations began. The U.S. Army decided to spearhead American participation in the First International Polar Year, establishing that effort's northernmost station. The tragic outcome of the Greely expedition showed that the military can conduct scientific research properly—the station was perfectly equipped and the observations regularly taken—but cannot deal with the unexpected, as individual initiative is discouraged. In these regions the unexpected is the order of the day.

"Tall, straight-backed, humorless, and a stickler for military discipline": thus was Lieutenant Adolphus Greely, head of the first American arctic station of the International Polar Year, described by the most loyal of his companions, Sergeant David Brainard. "Tall, straight-backed," also myopic, puritanical, and lacking in the spirit of initiative and adaptability so necessary at high latitudes. And he lacked the humor indispensable for group leadership. Yet his courage was beyond doubt. He proved it during the Civil War. His beard hid a sword cut he received in the Indian wars. A dutiful man—for him, discipline was a troop's primary strength—he was concerned that the expedition should fulfill its scientific mission in its entirety. Respectful of the hierarchy and its rules. he acted so as to bring the expedition back as a body, without losing a single man. Such were the vows taken by cavalry lieutenant Adolphus Greely before his hour of destiny struck.

A revolutionary plan for the Arctic

The International Polar Year was a joint research program instigated by scientists from Germany. Gathered in conference in Hamburg on 1 October 1879 with Prince von Bismarck presiding, scientists from eleven nations led by the Austrian climatologist Karl Weyprecht agreed to cooperate for a year in the arctic region.

Thanks to the energetic and imaginative Captain H. W. Howgate, the United States was one of the first nations to go "into the field." Captain Howgate of the U.S. Signal Corps understood that the fragility of arctic expeditions—all of them more or less private despite official patronage—was due to there being no fixed base with a military infrastruc-

Greely aboard the *Thetis*. The photo was taken in late June 1884, that is, a week after his dramatic rescue from Camp Clay (Cape Sabine).

ture offering a framework of rules and support. The plan—at that time revolutionary—was to establish a station as far north as possible with a complement of fifty men, stores for three years, and a prefabricated cabin. This station would be the base for repeated dashes toward the Pole. Collecting meteorological and geographic data, it would tie in to an international network of stations. Thus data from the Arctic could be integrated with meteorological data from all over the world and readily interpreted to provide a global picture.

Howgate was an important precursor of the modern era. He grasped that the meteorology of the future would progress only by adopting a synoptic perspective. [1] But Howgate was a troubling, nettlesome presence. He was basely attacked by Emil Bessels, who felt jealous of his growing authority on arctic matters. [2] After a difficult preliminary expedition on the *Florence* in 1877 to Cumberland Bay and another unfortunate expedition in the *Gulnar* in 1880 toward Lady Franklin Bay, the indefatigable Howgate found himself barred from any further expeditions by Congress, which was dismayed at such ambitious projects. Deeply hurt, Howgate engaged in acts of virtual suicidal—for such is the only explanation for his swindling $200,000 from the U.S. War Treasury. He escaped after his arrest and disappeared forever.

It was in this climate of uproar and scandal that Lieutenant Greely was named by Congress to continue for Howgate and organize a second U.S. arctic expedition to coincide with the International Polar Year. Lacking arctic experience, Greely nonetheless pulled together in a few weeks an expedition with international responsibilities. He came immediately into conflict with the War Department, which was financing the operation. The Secretary of War, in particular, was hostile to the project. Orders and countermands were issued in succession, and delays accumulated. [3] The proposed vessel was also problematic. It was the *Proteus*, a 467-ton sealer with two 100-horsepower engines, unfit for navigation through thick and abundant ice which had accumulated over years. Yet this was the ship the U.S. Navy had chosen. Greely was forced to sacrifice precious equipment and seek private funding from New York patrons to have the ship's bow reinforced with metal and its bottom with teak. Why so many difficulties? After the Kane and Hall expeditions, American bureaucrats and politicians were unwilling to risk their careers on such uncontrollable enterprises. Any incident could hurt their careers—rescue missions, additional appropriations . . .

The northernmost station in the Arctic

Fort Conger, at latitude 81° 44' N. and longitude 64° 45' W., whose somewhat martial name harks back to the Indian wars, was a prefabricated cabin 60' long and 17' wide. [4] The expedition consisted of three officers and twenty-one men, all of them members of the military, many with the makings if not the rank of officers, excepting (as in the expeditions of Kane and Hayes) a civilian meteorologist and an astronomer, two South Greenlanders, and a French doctor, Dr. Octave Pavy, who was belatedly recruited in west-central Greenland, and who kindly doubled as the expedition's naturalist. Trained as a biologist, he became the expedition's Chief Scientific Officer. This doctor from the Charente in western France had taken part in Howgate's first expedition. Having arrived on 20 July from Ritenbeck (West Greenland), he was stopping over in Godhavn when Greely arrived on the *Proteus*. He had been a friend of Charles Francis Hall. That same day he was sworn in as Surgeon 2nd Grade on the American expedition for the First International Polar Year.

This North American expedition, like the three that preceded it, focused solely on the meteorology, magnet-

The twenty-two members of the expedition before their departure from New York in spring 1881. Seated in the first row from left to right: Connell, Brainard, Lieutenant Kislingbury, Lieutenant Greely, Lieutenant Lockwood, Israel, Jewell, Rice. Standing, from left to right: Whisler, Ellis, Bender, Cross, Frederick, Lynn, Biederbick, Henry, Long, Ralston, Salor, Dr. Pavy, Gardiner, Ellison. The engraving was made after a photograph, on which Pavy did not appear, since he was recruited only on Disko Island in west central Greenland. The engraver thus added him subsequently to the group gathered for the departure.

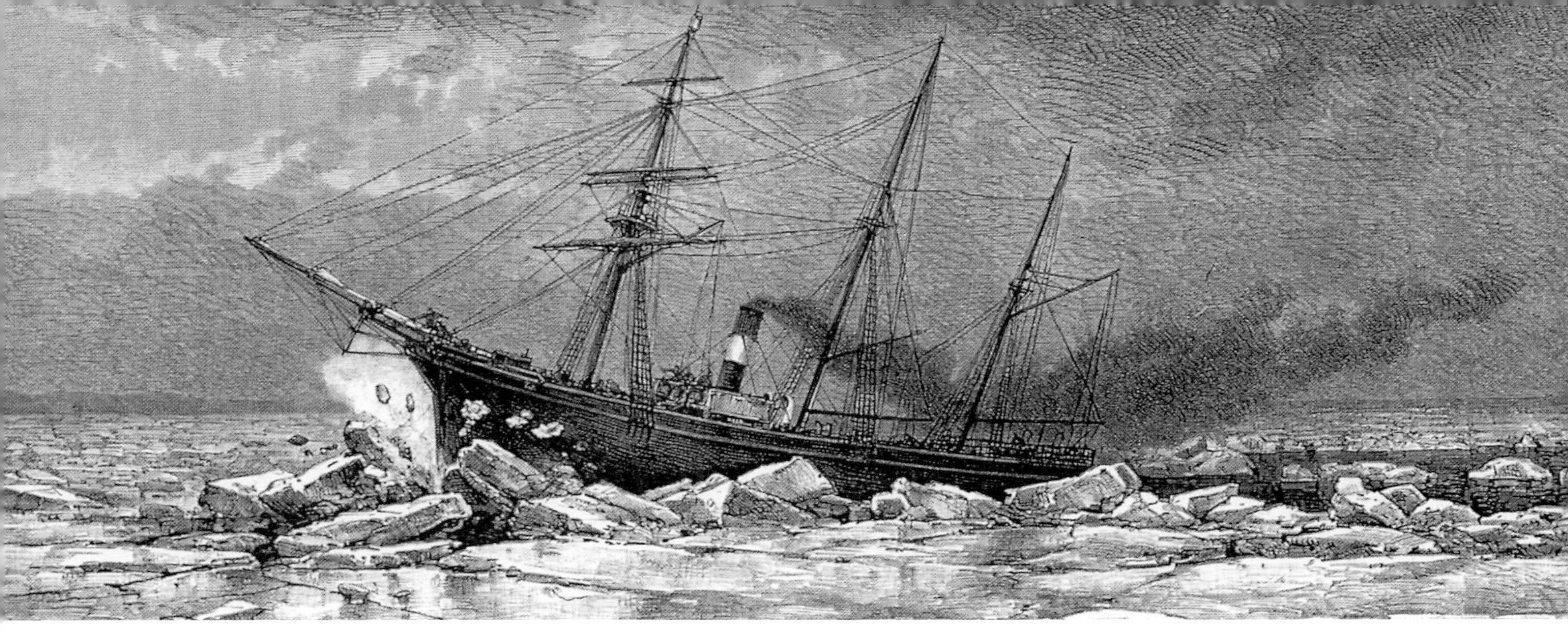

The former sealer **Proteus** (460 tons, oak-lined, with metal sheathing) advanced with difficulty into the pack ice of Hall Basin. It set a record of thirty-six hours in crossing Melville Strait and on August 11 reached Lady Franklin Bay, the winter quarters of the *Discovery*. There it stayed for eight days to unload men and equipment before returning home.

ism, geology, and geography of the arctic territory, which is to say on appropriating it politically and economically. It brought no archaeologists or ethnologists: the native was considered of no importance. Not only was there no plan to study the Polar Eskimos, but their participation in the expedition was not sought. "The power of resistance of the Eskimos has been much exaggerated," said Greely. "I dispute the truth of this . . . These people, who are absolutely incapable of appreciating the purpose of such a voyage, can they do otherwise than pine away and lose all moral strength?" This was the first American arctic expedition not to employ the services of the celebrated Hans Hendrik, though he had been highly valued by the British captain George Nares in 1875-1876, after his service to Kane (1853-1855), Hayes (1860-1861), and Hall (1871-1873). There was no question of stopping over at an Inuit camp near Etah (40 miles from Cape Sabine, in a barren spot designated as a meeting place in case of dire emergency) in order to establish neighborly relations that might eventually prove valuable. Greely's way of thinking, which betrays his belief that he knew the arctic region better than its own inhabitants, was partly responsible for the expedition's final catastrophe.

Returning to the chronology: on 7 July 1881 the *Proteus* sailed from Saint John, Newfoundland. The crossing of Melville Bay was accomplished in 36 hours. On 11 August, Greely had successfully passed through Smith Strait and Kennedy Channel to reach Discovery Bay (lat. 81° 44' N., long. 64° 58' W.). The sea was exceptionally clear of winter ice. The coastal slopes were green and flowering. The omens were favorable.

The American expedition would overwinter in Discovery Bay, where one of the ships of the last British arctic expedition, led by Nares, had passed the winter of 1875-1876. A dozen miles away lay Thank God Harbor (lat. 81° 37' N., long. 62° W.), where Hall's *Polaris* had spent its first winter. This choice of a winter site was fortunate from a scientific point of view: the meteorological, oceanographic, and magnetic data they collected could be compared to regionwide data over an extended period.

Eight days after offloading the expedition and its equipment, the *Proteus* prepared to return south. An incident then occurred that would affect the expedition at its highest levels. It is not set forth with clarity in any text—only a full-blown psychodrama could paint the daily life of polar explorers on the way to their destination. On 26 August, Kislingbury, the expedition's second-in-command, announced his immediate resignation. A friend and admirer of Greely's (he had known him during the civil war, when he helped build a telegraph line to the West), Kislingbury had apparently made some ironic comments in response to Greely's solemn announcement of the regulations governing daily life: general wake-up call at 7:00 a.m., no lying on one's bed during the day, no frivolous talk on Sundays, etc. Having thought long and hard, Kislingbury asked to be sent back to the United States immediately aboard the *Proteus*, which was preparing to depart.

By the time he had written his letter of resignation and received Greely's formal acknowledgment—on which Greely insisted—Kislingbury had missed the *Proteus*'s departure. Not that he didn't run after the *Proteus* along the shore! But he was too late, the ship had slipped out through a sudden opening in the pack ice. Out of breath, Kislingbury signaled with his arms. In vain. And there was no radio. His fate was sealed. His race along the shore, as it turned out, was a race against death.

So Kislingbury stayed ashore with Greely, though he was no longer under his command. Having resigned his post, he became a civilian supernumerary, a guest with-

Lieutenant Kislingbury. After fifteen years in the military, he was the first to volunteer for this expedition. He joined to "get a fresh view of the world" (he had been widowed twice in three years) but was quickly pushed to the limit by Greely's authoritarianism and resigned on landing in the Arctic. Yet he missed the ship's departure to the south by minutes and was condemned to suffer the general fate of the expedition, dying three years later of starvation among the ice fields he had sought to leave, perhaps guided by a premonition. Having resigned, he remained a bystander during the whole expedition.

1) No man is a prophet in his own country. The first permanent arctic stations in high latitudes were only established by the Americans and the Russians in the 1920s and 1930s. Germany and the Soviet Union were pioneers in this respect. The Ardennes offensive (December 1944) was possible only because of the secret German meteorological stations in Greenland and Svalbard that allowed weather conditions to be predicted a week in advance.

2) See the chapter on Hall, p. 116.

3) Decisions about food stores and clothing were put off until the last moment: seventy-two hours, in fact, before the expedition's departure.

4) The name also honored a senator who had sponsored the project and urged U.S. participation in the International Polar Year.

Fort Conger, the base of the U.S. expedition. Built in 1881, it was the northermost meteorological station of the International Polar Year. Its design, in keeping with the ideas of Lieutenant Howgate of the Signal Corps, provided every possible comfort. Its floor plan (60' x 17'), below, was established by Greely himself.
1 to 6. Double bunk beds, in pairs. 1. Biederbick, Connell, Henry, Whisler. 2. Ellison, Schneider, Cross, Lynn. 3. Salor, Long, Bender, Ellis. 4. Brainard, Frederick, Ralston, Gardiner. 5. Jewell, Israel, Rice. 6. Christiansen, Jens. 7. Dr. Pavy. 8. Lt. Kislingbury. 9. Lt. Lockwood. 10. Lt. Greely.
A. Base for pendulum.
B. Bathtub. C. Chimneys.
D. Greely's desk.
E. Ladder to loft.
F. Recorder for chronometer and anemometer.
G. Chronometers.
L. Canvas porches.
P. Coal storage. R. Kitchen equipment. S. Stove.
T. Tables. W. Reservoirs.
Exterior wall lined with ice and snow.

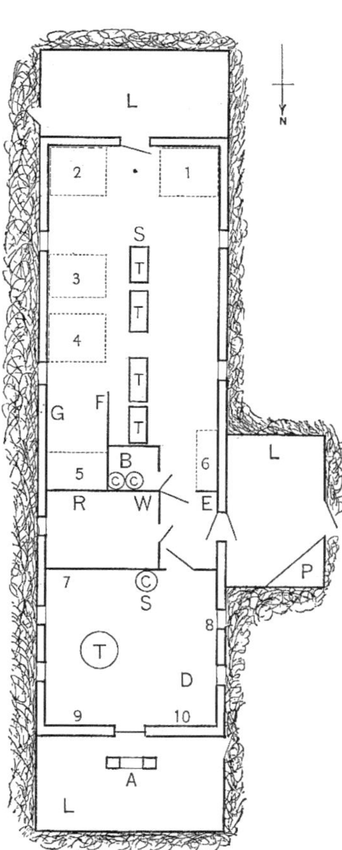

out functions, a tourist condemned to encounter his former friend, the expedition's leader, on a daily basis. Greely wrote that they were reconciled at the time of Kislingbury's death, but who is to know? If there was conflict with the second-in-command, there was also conflict with the chief scientist (and science was the expedition's chief object). Dr. Pavy—himself irritated by the military regulations, which he considered inappropriate to a polar research expedition—would take opposition to Greely with all a Frenchman's irony. This admirer of Charles Francis Hall, an ingenious and courageous man, the only doctor and biologist in the group, wanted to make his mark on polar history. And why not? It had been his ambition in 1869, as it was Greely's, to plant his country's flag at the Pole with his compatriot Gustave Lambert. Greely was jealous and described him as a "bohemian." Why should a "Frenchie" go to the Pole? The animosity and distrust of the Anglo-Saxons for the unpredictable French, their francophobia, has ancient and complex roots. Against regulations, Pavy refused to share his private journal with Greely, whom he disliked thoroughly and even considered a menace to the general safety. Greely wanted to check on the criticisms leveled at him. Pavy refused. Greely would allow no discussion and ordered Sergeant Brainard to put the doctor under arrest. He stripped him of his title of Chief Scientist. He even forbade him to go more than a mile from the "fort" (a thousand miles from any court, they were surrounded by the Arctic waste, and the fort, as we've seen, was no more than a winter hut). Forced to comply, Pavy handed his journal to Greely, who told him it was about time, that he would have had him shot except that as a doctor he was considered indispensable to the other members of the expedition, and that, in any case, he would be court-martialed on their return. How could Greely expect to create sympathy and unity with his delayed-action threats?

So Pavy now found himself relieved of his duties, as Kislingbury had been. He responded by announcing that he would only provide medical assistance to the company on a private and voluntary basis. A remarkable explorer, a French hero of the Arctic whom American accounts have neglected and distorted, he showed exceptional energy in his exploratory mapping expeditions. Pavy held the current French record for farthest north, and he displayed extreme devotion, helping his comrades in distress until his last moments and dying of hunger in June 1884, days before the expedition's rescue. [5]

Thus the final tragedy took shape. So great were the tensions during the next two years that Kislingbury and Dr. Pavy tried to brand Greely as mentally ill and have him discharged of his functions. According to one of the officers, Lieutenant Lockwood, they were extremely pessimistic about the outcome of the expedition given the character of their leader. But though part of the company was secretly in favor of removing Greely from authority (which might have saved the expedition), it was Lockwood who managed to block the action, citing Article 185 of the Navy Code concerning discipline and the preservation of unity in a detachment engaged in an operation.

The largest high-latitude scientific research project

Such was the atmosphere. But being a military expedition, its disciplinarian structure allowed it to resist the internal challenge, where a looser authority would have had to resolve it. And the expedition's intense level of activity, spurred by Greely's energy and obstinacy, masked the conflicts during the first two winters. The expedition undertook the vastest and most remarkable program of scientific research ever seen at these high latitudes. Systematic records of the magnetism, climate, and tides were made daily. At the end of a year, in July 1882, an enormous cartographic, geologic, glaciologic, botanical, and zoological program was undertaken. Lieutenant Lockwood conducted a preliminary cartographic

5) In his account of the expedition, Greely failed to pay tribute to him—or to Lockwood. Instead he leveled charges and criticism at them both—unverifiable charges, as the men could no longer respond and their journals have never been published.

survey of the north coast of Greenland. He even surpassed Markham's farthest north on the Nares Expedition and reached latitude 83° 24' N, to America's great pride. On the north coast of Ellesmere Island he conducted a party to the farthest west, the farthest north, and the farthest east. America could well be proud. The time for the expedition's return was drawing near. Did not the plans call for a ship to relieve the expedition in August 1882? The southern horizon was scanned daily with feverish impatience by every man, each of whom hated all the others. How could there be any doubt of their being relieved? Was this not an official expedition? And everyone remembered how easily the *Proteus* had reached Discovery Bay in July 1881. But what had been true in 1881 was no longer so in 1882. The Arctic is like that: the seasons are highly variable and the ice always shifting. Pack ice—not insuperable to a good whaling skipper—in fact obstructed the sea lanes between Discovery Bay and Smith Sound.

Orders are orders

September 1882. There was consternation at Fort Conger, and morale was low. The relief ship *Neptune* had in fact reached Etah (lat. 78° 18' N, long. 73° W) but the captain cautiously refused to venture any farther. The ice in Kane Basin struck him as dangerous. Moored near Etah in Pandora Fjord (lat. 78° 14' N), 280 miles from Greely, he failed to notice that the pack ice of Smith Sound and Kane Basin had broken up for several days after a storm, perhaps as far north as Fort Conger. The arctic whalers would not have hesitated to slip into these open leads, but the expedition leader aboard the *Neptune*, Sergeant William Beebe, was a functionary with little appetite for risk. He was the private secretary of the head of the Signal Corps, the expedition's sponsoring organization, and history would reveal that he was a notorious drunk.

He went as far as to leave a cache of provisions on Littleton Island, but did not try to reach Fort Conger using dog sleds borrowed from the Eskimos, a stratagem that would have allowed him to communicate with Greely and even bring back the expedition members. Cooperation with Eskimo "primitives" was seen by this official organization as so outlandish that the idea was never even explored.

The rescue expedition therefore returned to Newfoundland carrying seven tons of canned meat, fruit, and other foodstuffs. They didn't even think of distributing this mass of stores along the coast in depots—except for the 250 rations left at Littleton Island and the 250 more left near Cape Sabine on Ellesmere Island. Beebe was covered: his orders were to bring back the supplies if the ship was unable to meet with Greely!

And Greely? Concerned at not seeing the relief ship arrive, he made preparations for evacuating his good and solid base after the second winter, following instructions in the (foreseen) event that the relief ship might not appear before then. During the spring of 1882-1883 he prudently sent out dog sled expeditions to establish food caches along the return route.

Summer 1883. A second year had passed and tensions now reached a high point. Greely still saw no sign of the relief ship. On 23 July 1883, the *Proteus*—the second ship sent from Washington—had in fact been shipwrecked in Smith Sound, not far from Cape Sabine, the meeting place designated in Greely's written instructions in case of severe difficulties. In the panic and chaos of evacuating the ship, two thirds of the *Proteus*'s supplies were lost. The crew was rescued by whalers cruising the Melville Bay grounds. Cavalry lieutenant Garlington, who led the *Proteus* rescue mission, also did not consider sending out a dog sled party toward Greely to meet him en route. Greely therefore knew nothing of the decisions taken, the attempts made, or the failure and chaos of the rescue party 280 miles away.

Trapped by ice

For a variety of reasons, a replacement vessel for the *Proteus* was not immediately named by the authorities in Washington, who were terrified at how treacherous—and costly—the ice fields were proving. The Treasury did not want not to expend any more public funds. But Congress showed some conscience—harassed as it was by the explorers' families, in particular Henrietta Greely, the wife of the expedition leader, and General Lockwood, father of Greely's aide—by delegating its responsibilities to others . . . and abdicating from its own. Twenty-five thousand dollars were promised to any person not belonging to the U.S. Army or Navy who contributed to the evacuation of Fort Conger, which had been out of contact for twenty-four months. What needed to be done? And who should be called on? Neither the whalers, those veterans of the icy seas who had been navigating Melville Bay for three generations,

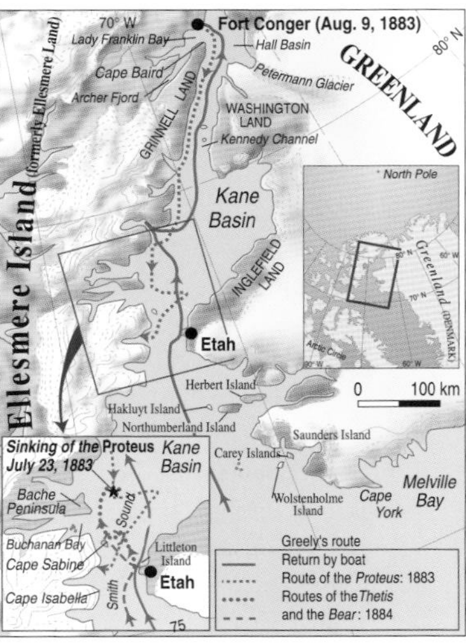

American expedition led by Greely.
Outward journey to Fort Conger and return in three ship's boats. Route of the rescue expeditions (summer 1883) and of Commander Schley (1884).

The expedition leader's quarters at Fort Conger (1881-1882).

On 21 August 1883, the heavy boats that were able to navigate for a few days through open leads in the pack ice were unpacked and loaded onto sleds. The expedition continued on over the perilous ice. To the left is the small steam-driven whaleboat.

nor the Eskimos were induced to participate in the rescue effort by the offer of an appropriate reward. Wasn't it obvious? Hadn't the Eskimos saved Kane's expedition from certain death, as his *Arctic Explorations* eloquently attested? The very first step should have been to bring news to Greely, trapped by the ice with his twenty-three men, and to update him on the evacuation plans. The Eskimos—had they been asked specifically—could have carried messages and brought help to the explorers. Though Hall had shown the way in 1867-1868, it would not be until 1891 with Peary that the Eskimos would be massively involved in polar expeditions, and in 1905 with Knud Rasmussen that the Inuit would be treated as equals. The racism at the headquarters of the young American army, engaged as it was in the Indian wars, would have its price: to the army, the Inuit did not exist.

The retreat to Cape Sabine

In the month of July 1883, the Greely expedition still had another year to survive in the Arctic. The alternatives were straightforward: to stay where they were (in an area with much game and with considerable reserves of food, as well as a good local source of coal) or to leave (toward the unknown, and an area where the conditions for supporting life had never been tested). After long and difficult consultations between Greely and his men, the decision was taken to leave. It is possible that the poisonous psychological climate at Fort Conger was responsible for this adventurous decision. For twenty-four men to leave a safe base stocked with supplies to last three years is more than a little risky. But it was clear that Washington couldn't simply overlook its official base for the First International Polar Year. Rescue missions comparable in scale to those organized for the Franklin mission would have to be organized. To my mind, it would have been wiser to wait. This was also Dr. Pavy's opinion: he suggested that, if no ship came to pick them up in summer of 1883, a return expedition be mounted using dog sleds in the spring of 1884.

On the day of departure—was it to stiffen a wavering discipline?—Greely put on his dress uniform with his sword and epaulettes. Fort Conger was evacuated on August 9 1883, the day following the first breakup, in a steam launch, a whaleboat, and a longboat. Greely brought rations for sixty days, four shotguns, two rifles, and one thousand rounds of ammunition. The convoy headed for Cape Sabine (Smith Sound), 280 miles away, hoping to intersect the relief ship's course before 15 September 1883.

To save food, the expedition's plucky dogs, who had been so faithful during the winters and spring sledge trips on the pack ice of the Arctic Ocean, were abandoned on the beach. The steam-driven Lady Greely led the way, towing three other vessels: the *Narwhal* (a whaleboat), the *Valorous* (a dinghy), and the *Lieutenant Beaumont* (a longboat). One of the dogs, the most faithful of them all, dashed into the water to reach the boats; he swam until he was exhausted, then, after looking intensely at the men with his beautiful brown eyes, sank like a stone. The anguished look of this dog, abandoned by his masters, was watched by all with horror. It would prove premonitory.

In accordance with the written instructions "to be followed in case of emergency" Greely navigated along the west shore of Kennedy Channel and Kane Basin, down the east coast of Ellesmere Island, which was uninhabited and heavily iced over. This was a crucial error, one that is difficult to understand after the experiences of the Americans Kane, Hayes, and the crew of the *Polaris*, who were greatly assisted (if not actually saved) by their knowledge of the Greenland coast and by the help given them by the Polar Eskimos of North Greenland during their expeditions of 1853-1855, 1860-1861, and 1872-1873 respectively. These explorers always traveled along the Greenland coast, which is freer of ice—I experienced the phenomenon myself in April-June 1951. Being too thick, the ice along the coast of Ellesmere Island is barren of game, and Greely's strange itinerary thus offered no chance of making contact with the Etah Eskimos or of getting help from them. I have already mentioned how frenziedly the expedition was organized in Washington. Greely would have found it hard to argue with his written instructions in January 1881, and he therefore countersigned them. But he could have objected to one or another of its arbitrary provisions, such as this one.

On 21 August, the three boats were halted by drifting ice. They were hauled out onto an ice floe, then launched again as soon as possible. The men were exhausted by these maneuvers, which were foreign to them (they were not seamen). They navigated from open lead to open lead. The general southward drift grew more sporadic, until in the area of

7) In any case, Article 186 of the U.S. Navy regulations, concerning extraordinary circumstances, is explicit: "Bold initiative, based on sound reasoning, is a primordial quality of the naval officer, and it is important not to discourage its use in cases of this nature."

Smith Sound the currents became variable in direction.

From 6 to 10 September, a vain attempt was made to reach the deserted Canadian coast at Cape Albert, a distance of three or four miles. A stroke of bad luck swept Greely and his boats back into the middle of Kane Basin in September.

Greely now had a chance to take the initiative. Where should he go? Toward Cape Sabine on the Canadian coast, which was uninhabited, or toward Etah in Greenland, with its Eskimo village? The group decided to vote. And the majority voted to follow the original orders and proceed to Cape Sabine.

When Greely finally arrived near Cape Sabine, after fifty-one days at sea, he discovered from the top of a small hillock the cases of food hurriedly left by the *Proteus* after its shipwreck on 23 July 1883: only five hundred rations of bread, tea, and preserved food, dumped in obvious haste. Thus did Greely learn that the long-awaited *Proteus* had foundered south of Cape Sabine, at this very spot, only nine weeks before, that it had spent four hours at Cape Sabine and did not seize the opportunity to leave its awaited tons of food: eager to push farther north, it had taken advantage of an opening in the pack, where it had sunk. In fact Cavalry Lieutenant Garlington, devoid of any experience in ice navigation, had ordered the unwilling captain of the *Proteus* to proceed north immediately through the open leads. The captain asserted that it was essential to wait, in order to negotiate the perilous leads one by one. In a message Greely found among the cases, the young and peremptory Garlington, leader of the *Proteus*'s rescue expedition, rashly affirmed that the U.S. government did not despair of saving the expedition: "Greely and his companions should not lose heart," he said in substance. He came from the Great Plains where he, too, had fought the Indians and did not know that the high latitudes are ruled by unpredictability.

Greely, confident in the instructions and promises given to him—as a good soldier should be—put off until a later date any further retreat by boat toward the south. Might he not expect relief at any moment?

After several days of reflection (29 September to 11 October) during which a lightly equipped party could have made the boat journey to Etah thirty miles away carrying the news of their whereabouts, the expedition settled on a site for its winter camp: the north beach of Pim Island, fully exposed to the wind, at so-called Camp Clay, west of Cape Sabine. Greely decided to build a shelter against the cold. A large cairn was erected on Stalknecht Island (south of Brevoort Island, east of Cape Sabine) giving directions to their camp for any ship that might be searching for them. The twenty-four men then made their camp on the other side of the cape: a speck in the vast expanse of unknown islands and fjords. The cairn would prove their salvation . . . a year from then.

It was a fatal error, I repeat, not to take one of the boats to the Eskimo village of Anoritooq or Etah, a few dozen miles away. That summer's rescue mission (on the *Thetis*) would in fact meet Eskimos at Saunders Island who had spent the previous winter (1883-1884) in Etah. The error was all the more inexcusable as the draconian written instructions did give the expedition leader some freedom of initiative, a freedom Greely did not avail himself of: "Full liberty is given to the leader of the expedition to alter the details according to the circumstances, but the expedition leader should consider to be of major importance the main outlines of the instructions cited above . . ." [7] Concerned about his career, Greely took no risks. He knew that he had a rendez-vous at Cape Sabine, and he stayed there.

The starvelings of Cape Sabine

Camp Clay: 78° 54' N, 71° 03' W. The winter of 1883-1884, the expedition's third in the Arctic, started with provisions for forty days, under a hut using the overturned whaleboat for a roof. This boat had been abandoned after the camp was established, then carried back to them miraculously by the currents several days later: it was an omen Greely should have read as a sign, or as a gift from the fates. In these dire circumstances, he should have ripped up his absurd and threatening instructions, which he probably reread every day. It was urgent to head east toward Etah—or at least send a scout there. The providential return of the whaleboat was one more reminder.

But what did Greely do? Having missed his chance for a summer crossing of Smith Sound in the boat that now served them as a roof and that his frozen men would dismantle piece by piece to keep themselves warm, did he send a message to Etah, the village from which they could get

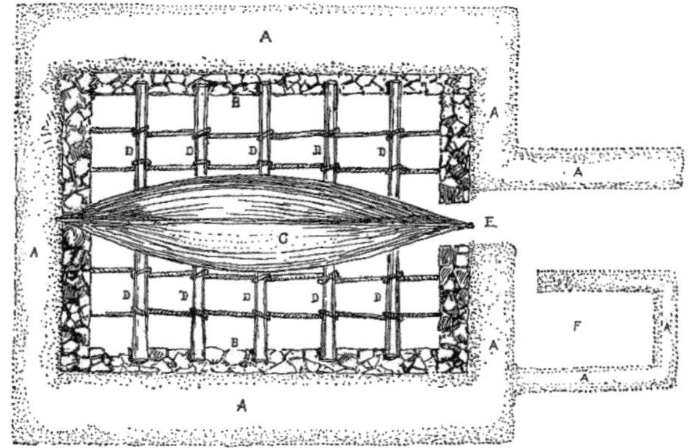

The expedition's winter quarters. Note the longboat, which could have saved their lives, being used as a roof. Spring was near, but rations were short, and the men living in this shelter would almost all die one after the other, while the Eskimo camp at Etah was only forty miles to the southeast. But orders were orders, and Greely's orders were to wait. Military discipline also saved this expedition, which Washington neglected, and the rescue efforts were chaotic.

George Rice, the brave expedition photographer, died of exhaustion in the arms of Frederick, one of his companions, on 9 April 1884. He devoted himself to the general good, always with a smile on his lips, and had just been promoted to sergeant.

help? No. He organized several sorties on foot, by famished men, toward the uninhabited west of Ellesmere Island, that is, in the opposite direction. [8] Orders, orders: stay at Cape Sabine.

The wait, performed according to instructions, would continue for two hundred and fifty days. To kill time, Greely held sessions on the geography of each state in the union. There were readings from the Bible. The men grew to hate each other quietly as they starved. The rescue ship would only arrive for them on 22 June 1884. That year the ice was particularly extensive. The many whalers sent to their rescue (appropriate rewards finally having been offered) could not get to them any sooner.

Dying of hunger at Cape Sabine? Alexandra Fjord is full of seal, walrus, rabbit, fox, and, in the north, musk ox. I know this from having hunted there on 3 to 5 June 1951 and having decided to go there after discussions with the Inuit with three sleds, five men and women, without my cases of food, taking only my ammunition, at the risk of being cut off from my base by the drifting pack ice at the beginning of the breakup (June). In a few hours we secured large supplies of food for ourselves (*uutoq* seals).

But Greely and his men, who now hated each other, were desperate. They had exhausted all their resources. The hunting was unproductive, despite their two skilled South

The seven survivors, west of Cape Sabine. Some of them were within hours of death when Captain Schley discovered them under their tent. Nineteen Americans died of starvation here and at Camp Clay, a short distance away.

Greenlanders. Only the Polar Eskimos, whom Greely should have recruited, had any experience of this area, the cradle of their history, which they had been visiting for many generations. Only they knew how to find seal breathing holes in this thick ice, a difficult task without dogs. But Greely, unlike his predecessors, visited none of the Polar Eskimo settlements. The two South Greenlanders, unaccustomed to the high latitudes, died accidental deaths in the spring, one of them from drowning while in his kayak.

Do I exaggerate in saying that this region teems with game? Are there indications of earlier settlements there? Yes, archaeology has shown that Vikings lived on the Ellesmere coast in the fourteenth century. The recent exca-

vations by Peter Schledermann on Skraelling Island confirm this. Furthermore, Dr. F. A. Cook established in 1906-1907 that Ellesmere Island is a noted hunting preserve for the Polar Eskimos, who go there to secure complementary supplies of bear, caribou, and musk ox, which are particularly numerous.

The American explorers, defeated by misfortune, were reduced to eating lichen, and their clothes were in rags. In the beginning, they caught a few shrimp on the edge of the floe. They even trapped a few foxes and ate them. But things quickly disintegrated: the fishermen would use rotting human flesh for bait.

The tragedy

In fact, nineteen of these young explorers in succession would die of cold and starvation, after inconceivable sufferings. Only one man died during the polar night (on 18 February); six died in April, four in May, seven in June, and the last in Godhavn on 8 July, after the rescue. Among the dead were the admirable Lockwood, who explored the northern tip of Greenland in 1881-1882; the charming and clever Israel; Kislingbury, the original second-in-command, with whom Greely was reconciled only on his death bed; and Octave Pavy, the French doctor-explorer, who was liked by all and who, feeling doomed, committed suicide by throwing himself into the water after swallowing the remains of the medicine chest, notably the flask of ergotamine. His relations with Greely were bad until the very end. Was he afraid of being eaten by the survivors? It is not impossible that the dead—at least seven of them—became a last resource for the starving party, and it is generally thought that Dr. Pavy put his scalpel to work carving the flesh of the dead, notably the thighs, the arms, the legs, and the ribs, thus allowing some of the remaining men to live. But who can declare it with any certainty? As a last mark of respect, the face, hands, and feet of the dead were not touched. After Pavy's death, four new corpses were cut up by the starving crew and dismembered to such an extent that it proved impossible to gather the scattered remains. Officially these four were considered to have been lost at sea, as was Pavy. In the coffins the rescuers from the *Thetis* placed rocks to complement

8) Alexandra Fjord, whose boulder-strewn fields and slopes I myself studied during my excursion in June 1951 from Inglefield Land.

9) The bodies of Kislingbury, Jewell, Ralston, Henry, Whisler, and Ellis were mutilated.

the skeletons. [9] Henry would be shot for theft four days before the rescue—discipline could only be maintained by making an example of him, Greely believed. But let us listen to Greely's horrific account, taken from his detailed, pitiless journal:

February 25th. Lieutenant Lockwood's condition. . . . alarmed me very much, and on April 6th I commenced issuing him extra food—four ounces daily of raw dovekie, all and really more than we could spare. On the 8th he fainted, and his mind wandered much during the evening. . . . May 20th. In order to give Israel the last chance, and on Dr. Pavy's recommendation, four ounces of the raven was given him today, that being our only meat. . . . May 23rd. Ralston died about 1 a.m. Israel left the [sleeping] bag before his death, but I remained until driven out about 5 a.m., chilled through by contact with the dead. May 26th. How we live I do not know, unless it is because we are determined to. We all passed an exceedingly wretched night. Summer opened wretchedly, with a howling gale and driving snow. . . . We were yet fourteen in number, but it was evident that all must soon pass away. . . . June 4th. We had not strength enough to bury Salor, so he was put out of sight in the ice-foot. . . . Our condition grows more horrible every day. June 5th. A clear, calm, and fine warm day. I crawled on the rocks today, and got a canful of tripe de Roche [lichen]—half a pint. June 6th. [C. B. Henry] admitted he had taken from [our old winter-quarters], contrary to positive orders, seal-skin thongs; and, further, that he had in a bundle, concealed somewhere, seal-skin. He was bold in his admissions, and showed neither fear nor contrition. I ordered him shot, giving the order in writing:

Near Cape Sabine, June 1884.

Sergeants Brainard, Long, and Frederick: Notwithstanding promises given by Private C. B. Henry yesterday, he has since, as acknowledged to me, tampered with seal-thongs, if not other food at the old camp. This pertinacity and audacity is the destruction of this party, if not at once ended. Private Henry will be shot to-day, all care being taken to prevent him injuring any one, as his physical strength is greater than that of any two men. Decide the manner of death by two ball and one blank cartridge. This order is imperative, *and* absolutely necessary *for* any *chance of life.*

A. W. Greely

First Lieutenant Fifth Cavalry, U.S.A., and Assistant, Commanding L.F.B. Expedition

About two o'clock shots were heard. . . . . Everyone, without exception, acknowledged that Henry's fate was merited. June 8th. Clear and calm all day. . . . Managed to pick about two quarts of tripe de Roche . . .Obliged to eat the last seal-skin thongs in stew this afternoon, with which we mixed the tripe de Roche and reindeer-moss. June 9th. Schneider shows signs of scurvy in his swollen, stiff knees. . . . Schneider this evening appeared to wander a little. Had nothing but tripe de Roche, tea, and seal-skin gloves for dinner. Without fresh bait, we can do little in shrimping. . . . Ellison expressed a desire that his arms and legs should go to the Army Medical Museum in the interests of science. His case is most singular. . . . Biederbick is engaged in writing up the medical case. . . . June 20th. Six years ago to-day I was married and three years ago I left my wife for this Expedition. . . . When will this life in death end! Today I crawled out a few yards behind the tent to pick lichens. June 21st. 11 a.m. South gale. . . . June 22nd. Through the energy and devotion of Frederick or Brainard, I do not remember which, we obtained, about noon, some water. . . . Near midnight of the 22nd I heard the sound of the whistle of the Thetis. . . . I feebly asked Brainard and Long if they had the strength to get out, to which they answered, as always, that they would do their best. Brainard came back reporting that Long had gone over to set up the distress flag, which had blown down. A fruitless discussion sprang up as to the noise. . . . We had resigned ourselves to despair, when suddenly strange voices were heard calling me. . . ."

On 22 June, the day after the summer solstice, a few seamen disembarked hurriedly from an American ship, the *Thetis*, which had been boldly and adroitly navigated

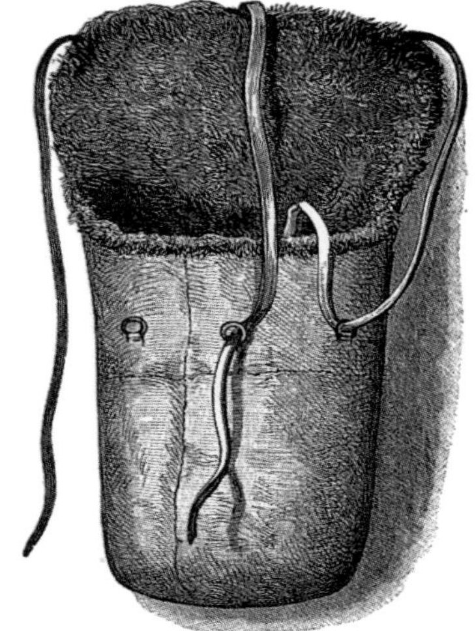

One-man sleeping bag. At Camp Clay, the men doubled up in them.

Skraelling Island, Alexandra Fjord, west of Cape Sabine and Pim Island, 19 August 1995. The area was explored by an exhausted party of Greely's men (Long and Christiansen, a Greenlander) in autumn 1883.

The big cairn on Stalknecht Island (October 1883). "The clock in its case, mounted on the top, served as a signal. The most important papers were in the sextant case." This precaution was taken because Camp Clay was very isolated and likely not to be noticed by rescue crews coming from the south or east.

through the pack ice by Captain, later Admiral, Winfield Scott Schley. The seamen were horrified to see two men dragging themselves along the beach. Then on a little knoll they spotted a wind-battered tent, from which moaning escaped. One of the seamen burst into tears. When the door to the shelter could not be readily found, the canvas was slit open with a knife.

"It was a sight of horror. On one side, close to the opening, with his head towards the outside, lay what was apparently a dead man. His jaws had dropped, his eyes were open but fixed and glassy, his limbs were motionless. On the opposite side was a poor fellow, alive to be sure, but without hands or feet, and with a spoon tied to the stump of his right arm. Two others, seated on the ground, in the middle, had just got down a rubber bottle that hung on the tent pole, and were pouring from it into a tin can. Directly opposite, on his hands and knees, was a dark man with a long matted beard, in a dirty and tattered dressing-gown with a little red skull cap on his head, and brilliant, staring eyes. As [Lieutenant Colwell of the *Thetis*] appeared, he raised himself a little, and put on a pair of eyeglasses.

"Who are you?" asked Colwell . . .

One of the men spoke up: "That's the Major—Major Greely."

Colwell crawled in and took him by the hand, saying to him, "Greely, is this you?"

According to the doctor on the *Thetis*, the seven survivors were in desperate condition. With the exception of Ellison, they would all have been dead within forty-eight hours had they not been rescued. Tea and warm milk, spiked with rum and beef extract, were served to the group every ten minutes in tiny quantities for the next ten hours. Then the survivors were carried onto the ship despite the terrible weather. Only Julius Frederick, supported by two seamen, was able to walk as far as the boat.

Harsh judgment of the Eskimos

The Eskimos once more became aware of the inability of the whites to master even the simplest techniques. They saw search expeditions arrive in July 1883 and July 1884, expeditions that had been planned in great haste and with little organization, and no fewer than nine whaling ships attracted by the reward, but without any overall strategy. The personnel on the official ships had been poorly selected. The rescue expedition of the *Proteus* was led, as we've seen, by a cavalryman, Garlington, back from fighting the Indians in the Dakotas. He had never been to sea before. Only two men, the soldiers in the launch that landed on Cape Sabine, knew how to handle a boat. The Eskimos saw the shipwreck not only of the *Proteus* but of the white man's reputation. The spectacle of these sailors desperately trying to leave this "northern hell" was a pitiful one. With their own eyes the Eskimos saw the wastefulness of these expeditions, which dumped off vast quantities of food before rushing back to the safety of the south. The idea of using these stores to help the Inuit (if only to make allies) never crossed their minds. They saw the whites unable to cross Smith Sound in the summer with large sail and motor boats, while they themselves had crossed it twenty years earlier in modest skin-covered kayaks and umiaks. And the treacherous ice floes? The Greenland Inuit make them their allies, pontoons, and cross them briskly each spring to hunt bear, as I did myself in a single day by dog sled on 5 to 6 June 1951, from Ellesmere Island to Greenland. One might object that Greely and his men were in a weakened state. Yet Frederick Albert Cook and his two starving Eskimo companions, when returning on foot if not from the North Pole at least from the Arctic Ocean via Cape Sparbo (Jones Strait) in March 1909, managed to cross the strait between Cape Sabine and Cape Inglefield. What was feasible for the starving Cook must surely have been feasible for the soldiers of the Greely expedition!

The white man, in all truth, had little aptitude for the Arctic. The army, massive and disciplined, certainly accomplished magnificent forays from Fort Conger in 1881-1883, when it was regularly supplied, and discovered vast areas of unknown land to the north, west, and east. But the first reversal of fortune, the first unexpected turn, provoked a disaster. Eskimos would have held on until the end, but they never would have accepted such discipline. From my experience as an expedition leader, I can testify that any participation of the Polar Eskimos in the Greely expedition with its rigid discipline and prevailing racism would have ended in their desertion. Greely would have had to invent—sixty years before its time—the spirit of the commando mission. Sitting in silent judgment, the Eskimo community actually grew stronger in its conviction of its own cultural and technological superiority.

Before dying at 91 on 20 October 1935, Greely (promoted to brigadier general in 1887) became the head of the Signal Corps, serving it as a loyal and disciplined officer despite the horrible way it had let him down. He helped found the American Geographical Society, publishing many papers on the Pole. He became a prominent figure in organizing the rescue and relief effort for the San Francisco earthquake. David Brainard, his loyal sergeant, also survived and became a general. Honor belongs to all these heroes and, it seems to me as a Frenchman, to Dr. Octave Pavy in particular. Yet these tragic events reflect poorly on the U.S. Army. Peary would look back and declare that the Greely expedition represented "a black mark on American polar exploration." Greely would never forgive this Parthian shot and obtained his revenge when Peary encountered adversity in his turn and was abandoned by many of his peers. ■

Opposite, **unknown Smith Sound Eskimo.** Greely and his companions paid dearly for their contempt of Inuit technology, which alone could have saved them.

Precarious survival inside the winter hut at Camp Clay (18' x 25'). The inner walls were of stone, the outer of snow; the whaleboat has been overturned to form the roof; the oars, their blades sawn off, have been held together by cables.

Lieutenant A.W. Greely's report

Government unwillingness and improvisation

The organization and equipment of the Lady Franklin Bay Expedition were accomplished under very great disadvantages, arising not only from inadequate means but from the avowed hostility to the work of the Cabinet Chief, under whose charge it necessarily was.... The preparation in this case devolved entirely on the commanding officer of the expeditions. [11]

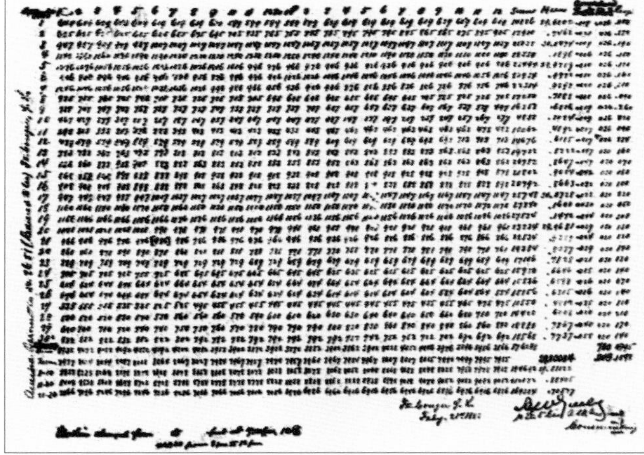

Handwritten record of aneroid barometer readings (21 February 1883). On Lieutenant Greely's orders, all the documents were recopied and put in a safe place (30 July 1883) before the dangerous voyage to the south was undertaken (9 August) to meet a nonexistent rescue ship. The scientific results of the Greely expedition: two fundamental volumes comprising more than 1300 pages and covering several disciplines (meteorology, astronomy, geography, oceanography, biology, and archaeology), which revitalized knowledge of the Arctic.

Arrival at Fort Conger, general regulations

The Proteus landed one hundred and thirty tons of coal and was discharged. The ship made an attempt to leave the harbor on the morning of the 19th, but was only able to reach Dutch Island, where the heavy crowded ice in Lady Franklin Bay, driven in by the easterly storm of the 18th, prevented her departure. She returned to the point adjacent, which was named Proteus Point, where the rest of her stay was occupied in taking on ballast...

On the 25th Lieutenant Kislingbury spent the day on the Proteus and the next day, dissatisfied with the expeditionary regulations, requested that he be relieved from duty with the expedition. He was relieved and ordered to report to the Chief Signal Officer. [12] Unfortunately the Proteus got under way just as Lieutenant Kislingbury was leaving the station, and he was obliged to return to Conger. He remained consequently at Conger, doing no duty, and with no further requirements than that he should conform to the police regulations of the station. He at no time requested to return to duty as an officer of the expedition. An excellent shot and an assiduous hunter, he contributed by his skill at various times to our stock of game and thus to our health and comfort. He accompanied several short sledge parties, as will be noted hereafter.

These unfortunate episodes emphasize the necessity of selecting for Arctic service only men and officers of thorough military qualities, among which subordination is by no means of secondary importance. If in all military commands that element is of great importance, it is of predominating weight in Arctic work, where isolation and self-dependence impose peculiar and rigid conditions...

On August 28th all unnecessary work was discontinued. At ten o'clock the entire party were assembled, and the programme for future Sundays outlined.

In dealing with the religious affairs of a party of that kind, which included in it members of many varying sects, I felt that any regulations which might be formulated should rest on the broadest and most liberal basis. [13] I said to them that, although separated from all the rest of the world, it was most proper and right that the Sabbath should be observed. In consequence, I announced that games of all kinds should be abstained from on that day. On each Sunday morning there would be read by me a selection from the Psalms, and it was expected that every member of the expedition should be present, unless he had conscientious scruples against listening to the reading of the Bible. After services on each Sunday, any parties desiring to hunt or leave the station should have free and full permission, and such exercise was deemed by me especially suited to our surroundings, as serving to break in on the monotony of our life, and thus be conducive both to mental and physical health. The selection of Psalms for the 28th day of the month was then read . . . I felt obliged that morning to especially invite the attention of the party to that verse which recites how delightful a thing it is for brethren to dwell together in unity. A few words were added upon the depressing effect which an isolated and monotonous life produced upon men experiencing the trials and hardships of a long Arctic winter.

Scientific program

The expedition took every care, it goes without saying, to put into practice the program of the Hamburg conference, our expedition's primary goal. The observations were begun in Newfoundland on July 1st 1881 and were carried on uninterruptedly until June 21st 1884, forty hours before the survivors' rescue.

Our observations were calculated according to the mean time in Washington, to which we added 49 minutes to get the mean time at Fort Conger.

A few of our most costly spirit thermometers showed so much variation that I was never able to use them. If I had given them to our sledging parties, they would have had no difficulty recording temperatures from minus 62° to minus 67° C. Whenever the recorder is not absolutely sure of his instrument, I tend to look with skepticism at the extreme colds reported at polar or other stations. Researchers who are honest but unaware of one fact or another may easily mislead the public, having first been misled themselves.[14]

Medical problems

About the 10th of December was the critical period of our life at Conger, as a number of the men gave indications of being mentally affected by the continual darkness. Their appetites for a time failed, and many signs of gloom, irritation, and depression were displayed. The Eskimo, however, were more seriously affected than any of the men. These symptoms of restlessness and uneasiness were noted by me as early as the 8th, and every effort was made by personal intercourse to restore these Greenlanders to a cheerful mental condition.

On the 13th Jens Edward disappeared, leaving the station in early morning, without eating his breakfast, or even taking his seal-skin mittens. The morning was a dark, gloomy one, with threatening aspect, which soon manifested itself in a fall of snow. To ensure striking the right trail, Sergeant Brainard was sent directly north of the station for nearly half a mile, and Sergeant Rice to the south, both parties being provided with lanterns, which would enable them to describe a half-mile circle around the station to determine positively the direction taken by the Eskimo. His tracks were found with some difficulty southward toward Dutch Island and Robeson Channel. Sergeants Brainard and Rice, with Private Whisler, pursued him, followed later by Dr. Pavy and a sledge. He was overtaken near Cape Murchison travelling rapidly northward, but returned to the station without objection, and in time recovered his spirits. No cause for his action in this respect could be ascertained other than his intense desire to return to his home, or place himself in some situation in which, according to the superstitions of Greenland, he could have supernatural knowledge of it.[15]

Sledging rations and base camp rations

The question of sledging rations was one of vital importance . . . Sir Edward Parry, in 1827, adopted nineteen ounces' solid food as his sledging ration, an amount which he found to be entirely insufficient for his men. Dr. Rae in one journey adopted twenty-nine ounces, which was not enough, and later took thirty-four ounces, which was supplemented somewhat by game. Other parties have found thirty-two ounces, when *all* pemmican, enough

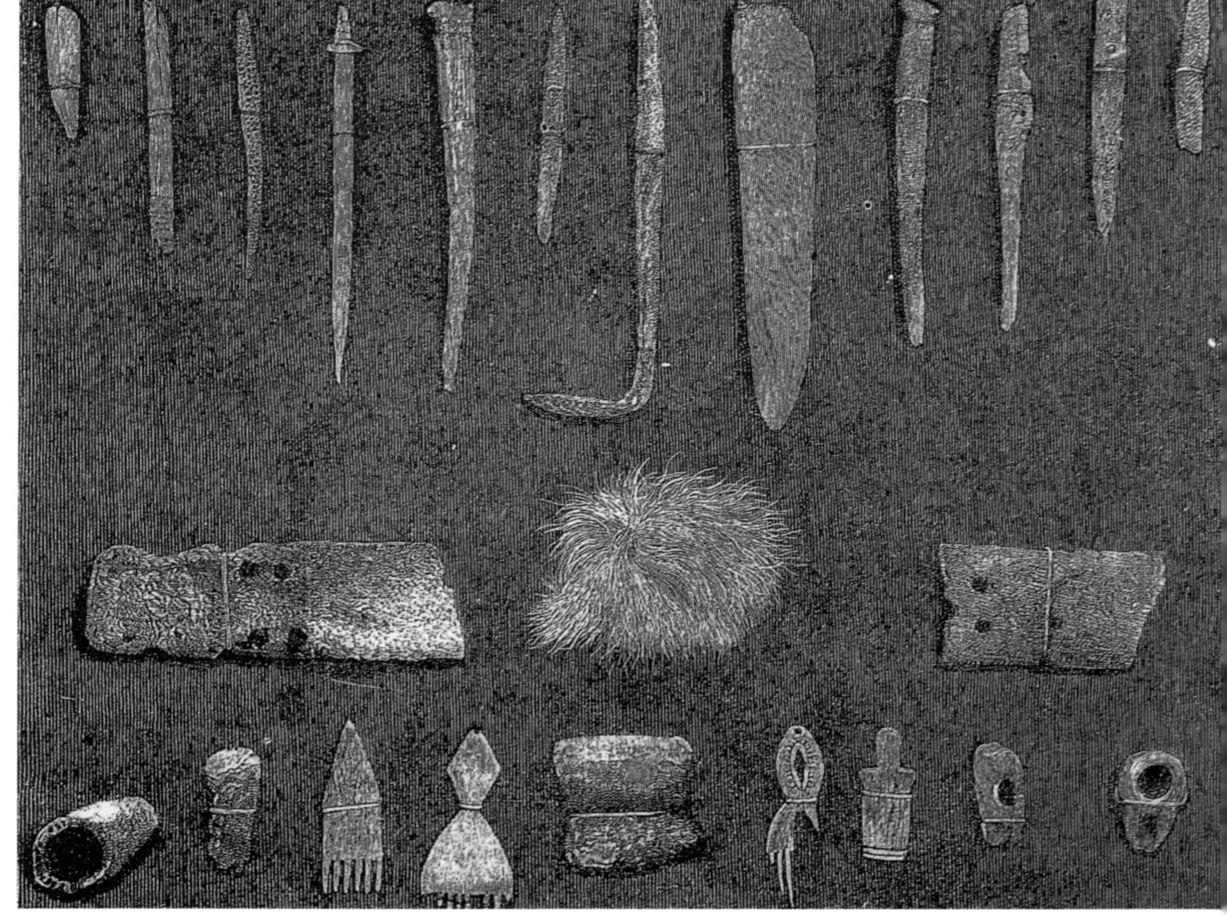

Objects collected by Greely at latitude 81° north. From top to bottom: various handles and awls, knives, fragments of sled runners, combs, scrapers, sled rings made of bone, shafts and heads of harpoons made of walrus bone and ivory.

11) The U.S. government's second official expedition was as badly organized as the first ten years before under Charles Francis Hall. Preparations were completed in only two months. The expedition leader had to dip into personal funds to have the hull of the ship strengthened. The secretary of war was tired of taking unknowable risks for operations that the businessmen who ran his government considered of limited importance.

12) Note Greely's condescension toward his subordinate, as he writes in the quiet of his home in the United States in 1885-1886. Greely seems to forget that, by his myopic leadership, he caused the horrible death of this man and eighteen of his companions.

13) A Puritan, Greely imposed his strict observance on a group whose origins and beliefs were diverse (Christian, Jewish, agnostic, and atheist). Lacking even the most limited insight into social psychology, Greely confronts his group with a choice between violence and insubordination. The Puritan ministers acted in the same way toward their Inuit parishes: hunting, dancing, singing, and games were forbidden on Sundays. I witnessed this myself in the Anglican group in Igloolik (Q'apuivik, Jens Munk Island) in 1960. And this was not an isolated case.

14) Note that the scientific expedition sent by American government to represent the United States in the first International Polar Year included only two scientists among its twenty-five men: an astronomer and a meteorologist, under the leadership of a French physician, Dr. Octave Pavy. The military personnel could only follow orders. Scientists would have been better able to reconceive and adapt their scientific program in this extraordinary place and these unusual circumstances, finding dead ends and new trails as they proceeded with their experiments. The idea of using military men (the Signal Corps) for a polar research expedition derives from a fairly common misconception: that you have facts and the analysis of facts. Facts are inert. Thought takes shape from the study of these facts. The history of modern science tells us that it is while experimenting or collecting information that the scientist thinks as it were kinetically, and that it is during the research into facts—which are always relative to a given set of data, and therefore variable—that ideas emerge.

15) Perhaps it would have been useful to interview Jens himself?

Tragic death of Jens Edward (recruited in Upernavik), a Greenlander, on 29 April 1884, while chasing a large seal (*Phoca barbata*) in his kayak.

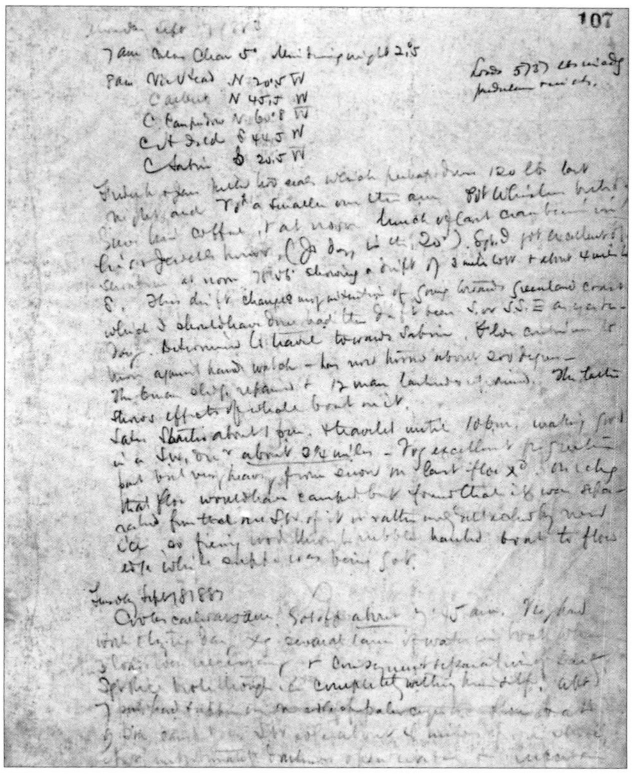

Page of a journal by one of Greely's companions, at the time of the retreat from Fort Conger to Cape Sabine. On Monday 17 September 1883 at 8:00 a.m. he notes (second line) the results of his sightings: "Cape Victoria, north 20° 5' west. Cape Albert, north 45° 5' west. Cape Camperdown, north 60° 8' west. [Illegible] south 44° 5' west. Cape Sabine, south 20° 5' west." On the eighth line, the party's goal is reconfirmed: "Determined to travel towards Sabine."

solids. Convicts at hard labor in England receive fifty ounces solid food—mostly bread and vegetables...

I concluded to increase the solids to thirty-nine ounces, and to add an ounce of lime-juice and a half ounce of fuel, by substituting food, etc., for rum.[16] The sledge ration of 1882 was viewed as a tentative one, and, while the parties remained in perfect health and did remarkable work, yet, owing to the general representations, I deemed it necessary, in 1883, to increase it and to modify the character of the food by replacing bread with butter and meat. The ration I finally decided on for the latter year was twenty-two ounces of meat, two of butter, four of vegetables, ten of bread, two of sugar, one-half ounce of milk, one ounce of tea and chocolate, salt one-fourth, and pepper one-twentieth of an ounce. The alcohol allowance of 1882, four and a half ounces after April 30th, (five ounces *before*), was increased the following year to six, as being the smallest amount on which a party of three or four could properly cook their food. The ration of 1883 consisted, besides beverages, of forty and a half ounces of food...

As a result of my experiences, I would now recommend the same quantity of solid food,[17] but would place the vegetable ration at three ounces preserved potatoes, replacing the other ounce by a half ounce each of milk and of extract of beef. Of the twenty-two ounces of meat, I do not think that more than eleven ounces should be pemmican, the balance to be divided between bacon and fresh meat; the latter to be sliced fine and frozen.* In case fresh meat cannot be obtained, it would seem to me well to make the remaining eleven ounces of meat consist of four ounces of bacon and the balance of sausage and canned fresh meat, the latter to be cooked as little as is possible consistent with its preparation...

The use of butter and condensed milk in the field cannot be too highly commended. Tea, the true Arctic drink, should be used for three-fourths of the meals in the field; the balance should consist of coffee in preference to chocolate, which seemed to induce thirst during the day if used before the march. The use of extract of tea and extract of coffee would probably reduce the weight of beverages to one-half ounce, and in place might be substituted curry-paste or some other powerful condiment. . . . No rum was ever sent as a sledge ration, but a liberal amount was always furnished as medicine, with authority for it to be used on extraordinary occasions at the discretion of the officer in charge. . . . As to tobacco, each man was expected to carry on his person such as he desired to use. One or two of our men regularly abandoned the habit while serving in the field.

The resistance of the Arctic wolves

Much surprise and excitement was caused, September 13th, by the appearance of a large band of wolves upon the harbor-floe near the house. Their gaunt, slight forms showed up in a remarkable manner as the light fog, which at that time covered the country to the westward, magnified greatly their size, and some of them appeared to be as large as calves.

Thirteen to eighteen were counted in the pack. While they showed no signs of timidity, yet they were very careful to keep a proper and discreet distance, and none of our hunters were able to get within gun-shot. This caution, while in keeping with the general habits of the Arctic wolf, which has been rarely killed by hunters, seems surprising, when we reflect that these animals could never have been hunted, and doubtless had never seen anything but a bear which could injure them.

The tenacity with which Arctic animals hold to life was frequently instanced in our experiences, and it occurred to me whether it did not arise from the survival of the strongest and hardiest in a clime where nature ever seems at strife with nature's life.

September 26th, a wolf came within a hundred yards of the house, and in the early twilight was for a time mistaken for one of the dogs. He was eventually pursued by Lieutenant Kislingbury and several men, and was shot through the body by that officer. The wolf, knocked down by the ball, lost at least a cupful of blood, and afterward continued to lose it steadily. He was chased again for some time without any one getting again within gun-shot. He was let alone for a time in the hope that would die, and pursued by the hunters later, travelled on, leaving drops of blood on the snow, until he fell down dead, with his body substantially bloodless.

Retreat: preparations and objections, August 1883

I decided to establish the necessary depot of provisions at Cape Baird, which was twelve miles distant, on the south side of Archer Fiord, and in immediate view of the station. That point well supplied we would be able to cross the fiord under any circumstances, and leave there fully rationed and equipped at such time as might seem most favorable to us.

Dr. Pavy was an excellent physician, but his previous Bohemian life made any restraint irksome and subordination to military authority particularly obnoxious. A man of active mind and quick parts, his lack of any order or system proved most injurious to the natural history interests, which were in his charge.[18]

On May 1st the naturalist of the expedition was directed to furnish by May 31st as complete a report concerning the natural history

DR. PAVY'S REFUSAL

Was the expedition's doctor obliged to provide the expedition leader with his private journal? No, said the doctor. Yes, said Lieutenant Greely. When Dr. Pavy refused, Greely put him under arrest for insubordination. Dr. Octave Pavy's journal has, to my knowledge, never been published. Did he leave it to Lieutenant Greely before dying of hunger at Cape Sabine on 6 June 1884, or did he keep it with him when he jumped into the water to commit suicide?

of the expedition as was possible. A description of all specimens on hand was to be given, and such notes made as would facilitate the speedy rendering of a report on the return of the expedition.

Lieutenant Lockwood classified and arranged the entire collection of natural history specimens, which, labeled and systematically put up for transportation, were securely packed in boxes and barrels. These collections could have been loaded on the expected steamer in a couple of hours, but were necessarily abandoned, except the botanical specimens ...

The surgeon, who had declined to renew his contract that expired on July 20th, refused, on the 19th, to turn over to Lieutenant Lockwood his diary, sealed and addressed, for transmission to the Chief Signal Officer ...

By July 29th all arrangements had been made for the retreat, and an order was issued announcing that the station would be abandoned on August 8th if no vessel should arrive. A party was detailed to proceed to Cape Baird with the launch at the earliest possible moment. The launch and boats had been overhauled, and were pronounced by the engineer to be in excellent condition. Five thousand pounds of carefully selected coal was screened, bagged, and carried to Dutch Island, where the launch lay ...

For the greater part of the year, with my clerk, I had been engaged in reducing, arranging, and copying the scientific observations, which, by August 3rd, were completed to July 31st. These records, weighing about fifty pounds, were packed in three tin boxes, which were soldered and thus made water-tight. Two boxes were to be in my charge. These contained original reports, field journals, my own diaries, original sheets of magnetical and meteorological observations, and other official papers. Lieutenant Lockwood was to take charge of the third box, which contained letter-press copies of all scientific observations, star sheets, and the official collection of plants. The work of duplicating these records was great, but I hoped thus to save one set in case of any disaster during our retreat ...

[We brought] four rifles, with about a thousand rounds of cartridges, and two shot-guns, with ample ammunition, were also selected.

The greater part of the men turned in their private diaries, sealed and addressed, which, with forty-eight photographic negatives, were carefully packed in a stout water-tight box. Medical stores designated by Dr. Pavy were handily arranged by Hospital Steward Biederbick, on whom that duty fell. The medical liquors were also taken in as great a quantity as I felt was possible.

In addition to my own baggage, I also carried needles, bodkins, gimlets, thread, yarn, etc., not only for trade with the Etah Eskimos, if we should reach them, but for our own use.

The last survivors of the Greely expedition, who on 22 May moved 200 yards southwest of their hut to settle in a large tent, where they faced the strait and caught more sunlight. Sketch made from life at Camp Clay by one of the rescuers (23 June 1884).

Within sight of Cape Sabine: Greely's private journal, September 1883

September 3rd. Israel got an excellent meridian observation to-day: our position is 79°15.6' N., 74° W. None of the men have been very despondent during our besetment, yet is noticeable now that they are very much encouraged by our latitude [confirming a slow southward drift]. September 9th. At this time occurred to me the idea of attempting to reach Cape Sabine over the moving pack in order to communicate with the relieving steamer, whose presence we expected, which was soon to leave Smith Sound, September 15th being the date mentioned. Such an attempt, while involving possible death for those venturing, might also save the party from great future suffering and perhaps death.

Why not a crossing toward Littleton Island?

It may seem strange to uninformed readers, that

The order to evacuate Fort Conger (Order No. 5): "In case of the non-arrival of a vessel by August 7 1883, this station will be abandoned, and a retreat southward by boat to Littleton Island will be attempted. Sixteen pounds of personal baggage will be allowed to each officer and eight pounds to each man."

16) The official daily rations prescribed by Great Britain and the United States for polar expeditions are from 19 to 39 ounces. The concept of weight is absurd. Everything depends on the caloric value of each food, especially the meat.

17) And what of the seal, walrus, and musk ox, whose meat and fat was the staple food at high latitudes for Knud Rasmussen (1910-1916), Lauge Koch (1921-1922), and myself (1950-1951)? The diet of all three of us was about 80% native. And it was one of the main reasons for our success: we traveled light and ate highly caloric food.

* GREELY'S FOOTNOTE: During Franklin's second voyage, his men had managed with great stealth and patience to stalk close to a herd of reindeer and were just congratulating themselves when, to their great dismay, the prey took flight, its noisy honking establishing its identity beyond any doubt: the noble animals were nothing more than a flock of wild geese.]

18) This obituary notice is particularly distasteful as it concerns a man who devoted himself body and soul to the survival of his companions. Dr. Pavy did not agree with the retreat to the south and the evacuation of the base at Fort Conger, and he favored close cooperation with the Inuit. The only foreigner on the expedition, and possessed of a strong character that intimidated Greely, Dr. Pavy deserved at the very least the honors due to an arctic hero who died on expedition. And the secretary of war's board of inquiry should have published the journals of those who were opposed to Greely's actions: Kislingbury and Pavy. These were not just any two men: one was the expedition's second-in-command, the other its chief scientific officer. Both have been condemned to everlasting silence.

my diary in those days makes no mention as to the non-feasibility of crossing Smith Sound to Littleton Island, and the expected relief party or the Etah Eskimos. The impossibility of such a passage was so patent to every one, that not even the most querulous and impractical of the party ever suggested it. The conditions were as follows: Smith Sound in shape resembles a partly opened fan, the open part to the southward, and has a southerly running current of four to eight miles per day. Our experience of eighteen days had proved that, even when working for our lives, we could not average more than two miles daily across a moving pack. The chances of crossing a channel twenty-five miles wide at the narrowest part, by travelling two miles to the east and drifting four miles to the south, where the channel soon becomes fifty miles wide, are obvious.

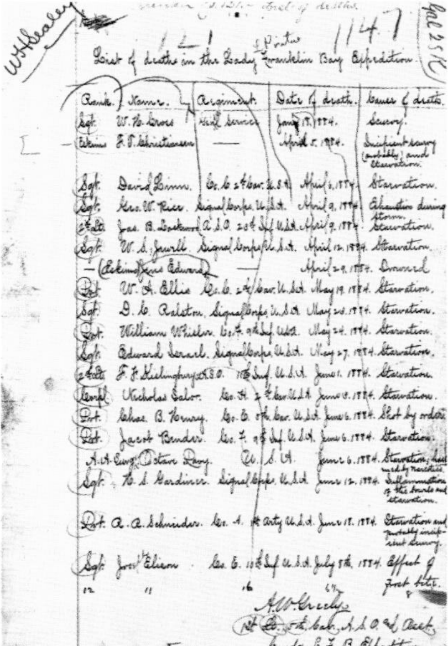

List of deaths in the Lady Franklin Bay Expedition.

Rank.	Name.	Regiment.	Date of death.	Cause of death.
Sgt.	W. H. Cross	Gen'l Service	Jany 18. 1884.	Scurvy.
Eskimo	F. T. Christiansen	—	April 5. 1884.	Incipient scurvy (probably) and starvation.
Sgt.	David Linn.	Co. C. 2d Cav. U.S.A.	April 6. 1884.	Starvation.
Sgt.	Geo. W. Rice.	Signal Corps. U.S.A.	April 9. 1884.	Exhaustion during storm.
2d Lt.	Jas. B. Lockwood	A.S.O. 23d Inf U.S.A.	April 9. 1884.	Starvation.
Sgt.	W. S. Jewell.	Signal Corps U.S.A.	April 12. 1884.	Starvation.
—	(Eskimo) Jens Edward	—	April 29. 1884.	Drowned
Pvt.	W. A. Ellis	Co. C. 2d Cav. U.S.A.	May 19. 1884.	Starvation.
Sgt.	D. C. Ralston.	Signal Corps, U.S.A.	May 23. 1884.	Starvation.
Pvt.	William Whisler.	Co. F. 9th Inf U.S.A.	May 24. 1884.	Starvation.
Sgt.	Edward Israel.	Signal Corps U.S.A.	May 27. 1884.	Starvation.
2d Lt.	F. F. Kislingbury A.S.O.	11th Inf. U.S.A.	June 1. 1884.	Starvation.
Corpl.	Nicholas Salor.	Co. H. 2d Cav U.S.A.	June 3. 1884.	Starvation.
Pvt.	Chas. B. Henry.	Co. E. 5th Cav. U.S.A.	June 6. 1884.	Shot by order.
Pvt.	Jacob Bender.	Co. F. 9th Inf. U.S.A.	June 6. 1884.	Starvation.
A.A. Surg.	Octave Pavy.	U.S.A.	June 6. 1884.	Starvation, hastened by narcotics.
Sgt.	H. S. Gardiner.	Signal Corps. U.S.A.	June 12. 1884.	Inflammation of the bowels and starvation.
Pvt.	A. A. Schneider.	Co. A. 1st Arty U.S.A.	June 18. 1884.	Starvation and partially incipient scurvy.
Sgt.	Jos. Elison	Co. E. 10th Inf U.S.A.	July 8th. 1884.	Effect of frost bite.

A. W. Greely
1st Lt. 5th Cav. A.S.O. & Acct.
Comdg. L. F. B. Expedition.

Handwritten list of the expedition's nineteen dead, written on 8 July 1884. The document was written by Greely and countersigned by representatives of the rescue expedition. Note that most of the deaths came in June. Within a few more days, all would have been dead.

Near Cape Sabine
June 6th. 1884.

Sergts Brainard, Long and Fredericks:

Notwithstanding promises given by Pvt C. B. Henry yesterday he has since acknowledged to me having tampered with seal thongs, if not other food at the old camp. This pertinacity and audacity is the destruction of this party if not at once ended. Pvt Henry will be shot today, all care being taken to prevent his injuring any one as his physical strength is greater than that of any two men. Decide the manner of death by two ball and one blank cartridge. This order is imperative and absolutely necessary for any chance of life.

(Signed) A. W. Greely
1st Lieut. 5th Cav. A.S.O. & Acct.
Comdg. L. F. B. Exp'd

A true copy of the order for the execution of Private C. B. Henry
D. L. Brainard

Greely's order, dated 6 June 1884, for the execution of Private C. B. Henry. He would be shot by sergeants Brainard, Long, and Frederick firing "two balls and one blank cartridge. This order is *imperative* and *absolutely necessary* for *any chance* of life."

Greely's journal and Lockwood's pessimistic commentary

October 3rd.—I selected a general site for building; and, as there was a variety of plans proposed for constructing the houses, I permitted each squad to build its own house in accordance with its own ideas ... The boat, with two oars, rudder, and boat-hook, was disposed of by lot, and fell to Sergeant Brainard's party. I ordered that it should be so used, in constructing the houses, that its future serviceability should not be impaired. Everybody worked very hard and cheerfully during the day. My own party will first put up an ice house, and then construct a stone one inside. The others have decided to build stone houses first, and then surround them with ice. Our house will be eight feet by eighteen in the clear. We nearly half-finished our house to-day. Many Eskimo caches and a number of relics have been found in and around these permanent houses. Among other articles was a toggle of walrus ivory for tog-traces, a narwhal horn, and large bones of whale ...

October 4th.—Our ice wall is substantially done, and the stone wall commenced. Stopped work at 2 p.m., and hauled a load from our old camp. The temperature to-day has been down

to 6°, and at 4 p.m. was only 8°. In accordance with the doctor's advice, I increased the ration, commencing this evening, to four ounces of pemmican, eight ounces of bread, and one and a half ounces of potatoes, which is to last until we are through with the present hard work. The hunters are not working upon the houses, but are out for game. Long saw many walruses in the straits, all in the open water ...

Lieutenant Lockwood says: "We have now three chances for our lives: First, finding American cache sufficient at Sabine or at Isabella; second, of crossing the straits when our present rations are gone; third, of shooting sufficient seal and walrus near by here to last during the winter." [19]

Thoughts on the tragedy at Cape Sabine

Later.—An eventful day. Sergeant Rice, whom Lieutenant Kislingbury had gone over the glac-

RESIGNATION OF THE MEDICAL OFFICER, DR. PAVY

Fort Conger, Grinnell Land
18 July 1883

To the Commanding Officer
Sir:
As my second contract expires on the 20th of this month, I respectfully submit to you my wish that it not be renewed.
As I do not intend to remain in the service and as (according to your own assessment) our work will be virtually concluded within a month or two by the arrival of a ship in Discovery Bay, or by our meeting with this ship in Kennedy Channel, any activity on my part is therefore of secondary importance.
Naturally, I offer my services to the expedition, on a voluntary basis, to perform the same duties as in the past, bending all my efforts to the health of all and the success of our endeavours.
I understand perfectly that the Department owes me no remuneration whatsoever, and that any costs deriving from my presence here are to be borne by me.
I remain, dear Sir, your most devoted servant,

Octave Pavy
Acting Assistant Surgeon
U.S. Army

ier to meet, was reported returning, from the front of the glacier. As he said, he brought both good and bad news. The Proteus sank July 24th, this year . . . The record brought back by Rice comprised a notice of the proceedings of the Beebe expedition of 1882, and the following notice from Lieutenant Garlington, as to the loss of the Proteus and his intended movements:

United States Relief Expedition
Cape Sabine, July 24, 1883

The steamer Proteus was nipped midway between this point and Cape Albert, on the afternoon of the 23rd instant, while attempting to reach Lady Franklin Bay. She stood the enormous pressure nobly for a time, but had to finally succumb to this measureless force. The time from her being "beset" to going down was so short that few provisions were saved. A depot was landed from the floe at a point about three miles from the point of Cape Sabine as you turn into Buchanan Strait. There were five hundred rations of bread, sleeping-bags, tea, and a lot of canned goods; no time to classify. This cache is about thirty feet from the water-line, and twelve feet above it, on the west side of a little cove under a steep cliff. Rapidly closing ice prevented its being marked by a flag-staff or otherwise; have not been able to land there since . . .

It is not within my power to express one tithe of my sorrow and regret at this fatal blow to my efforts to reach Lieutenant Greely.

I will leave for the eastern shore just as soon as possible, and endeavor to open communication.

E. A. Garlington,
First Lieutenant, Seventh Cavalry, A.S.O., Commanding.[20]

This record speaks in varying ways; but to the party and to me it meant we trust that "every-

Whale Sound, Qeqertarsuaq (Herbert) Island, in the heart of the country from which the Inuit could have brought immediate help to Greely and his men, if they had been asked.

19) Lockwood, an admirable explorer who accomplished remarkable journeys in north Greenland in 1882 and 1883, has analyzed the situation perfectly. His first and third options having been tried, only the second was left. Lockwood was a friend of Greely's and the sole remaining officer after the resignations of Kislingbury and Dr. Pavy. Why was he not listened to?

20) Garlington was a careless officer. After his brave words: "I will leave for the eastern shore [of Ellesmere Island] just as soon as possible, and endeavor to open communication," he in fact headed south ("the flight of Commander Wildes," as Greely justly notes) with a crew "wracked by dissension and indiscipline."

21) Greely, a disciplined and blinkered officer, clung to his visibly outdated orders. His arguments were unconvincing: he had four boats and two kayaks, and should have sent out a party to carry their news to Etah (a one- to three-day trip) or to the south (a week's trip at most) to talk a whaler into sailing further north. The main party would have waited, as instructed, at Cape Sabine. This is what Kane did successfully in July-August 1854, traveling to Beechy Island. Remember Kane's retreat in improvised boats (1855) and Budington's (Polaris expedition, 1873).

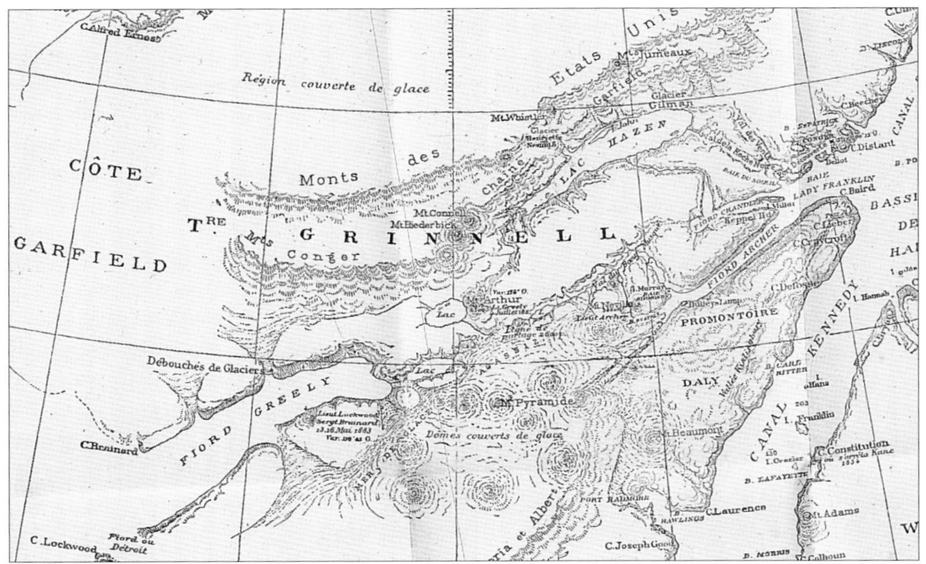

Map of Grinnell Land drawn on the basis of surveys by Greely and Lockwood in 1882 and 1883. It also shows the furthest points reached by Kane and Hall.

List of provisions furnished each of the three ships of the Greely Relief Expedition.

Articles.	Quantity.	Articles.	Quantity.
Bread .... pounds	31,201	Cibil's extract beef .... pounds	288
Oat-meal .... do	1,160	Vegetable soup .... do	288
Corn starch .... do	144	Assorted soup .... do	1,104
Flour .... do	8,200	Olives .... kegs	8
Corn-meal .... do	1,176	Pickles .... do	40
Tapioca .... do	144	Vinegar .... gallons	576
Farina .... do	144	Onions .... pounds	1,210
Arrow-root .... do	70	Lime juice (concentrated) .... do	240
Macaroni .... do	300	Lime juice (for ship's use) .... do	3,904
Vermicelli .... do	300	Sauces .... dozens	16
Royal baking powder .... do	294	Garlic .... pounds	49
Dry-cooked sugar cakes .... do	1,155	Cabbage (pickled) .... do	285
Hominy .... do	550	Sauer-kraut .... do	1,197
Samp .... do	600	Tomatoes .... do	2,352
Barley .... do	300	Prepared pumpkins .... do	168
Rice .... do	2,320	Plum pudding .... do	576
Buckwheat .... do	1,125	Mince meat .... do	1,152
Beans (marrow) .... gallons	587½	Evaporated apples .... do	300
Dried Lima beans .... do	299	Apple butter .... do	588
Dried green peas .... do	300	Peach butter .... do	588
Dried Shaker corn .... do	300	Candied lemon peel .... do	30
Split peas .... do	300	Tamarinds .... do	140
Carrots (canned) .... pounds	1,116	Figs .... do	575
Potatoes (fried) .... do	4,680	Citron .... do	150
Pemmican (for crew) .... do	9,752	Dried fruit (assorted) .... do	1,676
Pemmican (for dogs) .... do	7,332	Raisins .... boxes	4
Pork, salt .... do	11,700	Preserved cranberries .... pounds	576
Breakfast bacon .... do	7,050	Jams (assorted) .... do	288
Pig's jowl and feet, scrapple .... do	1,175	Nuts (assorted) .... do	1,121
Beef, salt .... do	9,400	Butter (assorted) .... do	3,520
Dried and smoked beef .... do	300	Sugar .... do	10,284
Beef tongues (smoked) .... do	1,175	Coffee .... do	1,020
Hams (boiled) .... do	1,655	Tea .... do	3,048
(raw) .... do	3,000	Chocolate .... do	576
Roast chicken .... do	1,364¼	Cheese .... do	1,736¼
Roast turkey .... do	564	Dessicated eggs .... do	96
Roast beef .... do	4,704	Sirup .... gallons	288
Roast mutton .... do	2,352	Pepper, black .... pounds	74
Cove oysters .... do	966	red .... do	36
Spiced mackerel .... do	600	Lard .... do	2,040
Spiced salmon .... do	575	Condensed milk .... dozen	146
Head cheese .... do	288	Eggs, boiled and scalded with lard, dozen	648
Sausages .... do	288	Celery-seed .... pounds	36
Sausage meat .... do	288	Mustard .... do	72
Cooked corn-beef .... do	288	Currie powder .... do	72
Bologna sausage .... do	150	Hops .... do	20
Spiced beef .... do	288	Spices .... do	25
Sardines .... boxes	288	Citric acid in crystal .... do	39
Philadelphia pepper pot .... pounds	576	Olive oil .... dozen	17
Turtle soup .... do	288	Dried herbs .... pounds	144
Mock-turtle soup .... do	2 8	Salt .... do	430
Ox-tail soup .... do	288	Flavoring extracts .... bottles	36
Mutton broth .... do	288	Turnips (canned) .... pounds	828
Beets (canned) .... do	468		

List of the provisions loaded onto each of the three ships of the expedition sent to rescue Greely. They had orders to discharge none of their cargo in the Arctic, so as not to have to return for it later.

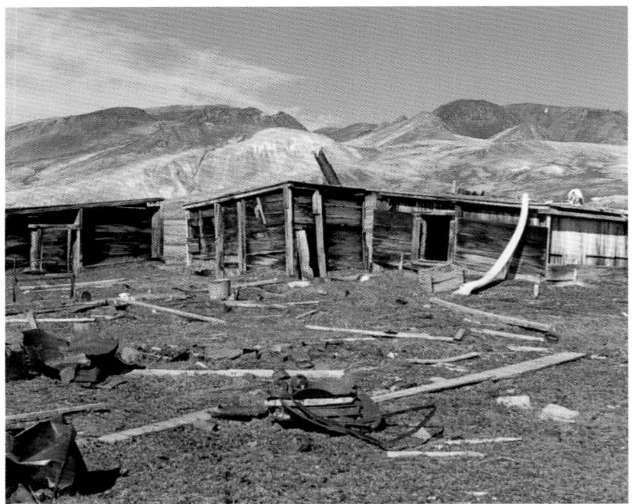

ABOVE: **Fort Conger** as it looked in the 1980s. It was rebuilt and occupied by Peary.

RIGHT: **The remains of Camp Clay,** identified by the archaeologist Peter Schledermann during a trip to Grinnell Land in 1977.

thing within the power of man" would be done to rescue us, and on the strength of that promise I at once decided to proceed to Cape Sabine and await the promised help.[21]

We now had four boats, and, although the sun was about leaving us for the winter, we could yet travel southward, there being open water visible at Cape Isabella. Had I been plainly told that we must now depend upon ourselves, that trouble and lack of discipline prevailed among the Proteus crew, that the Yantic was a fair-weather ship, and that its Commander and Lieutenant Garlington were acting independently of each other, I should certainly have turned my back to Cape Sabine and starvation, to face a possible death on the perilous voyage along shore to the southward …

It is perhaps best here to break that silence maintained by me for the many months since my return, through the long and bitter discussions regarding the responsibility for our great disaster, but I intend to weary no one with a lengthy and uninteresting argument.

There exists no doubt that in 1881 I should have done more than arrange for a retreat to Cape Sabine if we should not be reached at Conger. Although not under orders to do so, I should have provided against shipwreck and all other mischances. There is no doubt either, that General Hazen regrets that Memorandum No. 4 of his orders was not allowed to stand, as being in the direction of greater safety for all.

The neglect of these points would have been uncriticised, had the Proteus disaster not occurred. As to the responsibility for that disaster, others are better qualified than I to speak.

Similarly, the neglect of Lieutenant Garlington to replenish the stores he knew to be damaged, although he was under orders to do so, would have been unnoticed. I am already on record as pointing out the disastrous effect of such disobedience.

His action in taking every ounce of food he could carry when turning southward cannot be justified …

The Proteus disaster, and the subsequent failure of Commander Wildes to extend relief, did not alone determine the fate of the party. I have already concurred in the views of Chief Engineer Melville, and the opinions of the sealers of Newfoundland, that our relief was practicable during the autumn of 1883. I can understand the unwillingness of the Secretaries of War and of the Navy to send again northward the officers who had just failed us in Smith Sound, but not even this reason seems sufficiently urgent to justify the final adverse decision. … Had a stout sealer—and there were many available—left St. John, under a competent officer, within ten days after the return of the Yantic, the entire Lady Franklin Bay Expedition, in my opinion, would have safely returned.

WHITE MAN'S BUSINESS

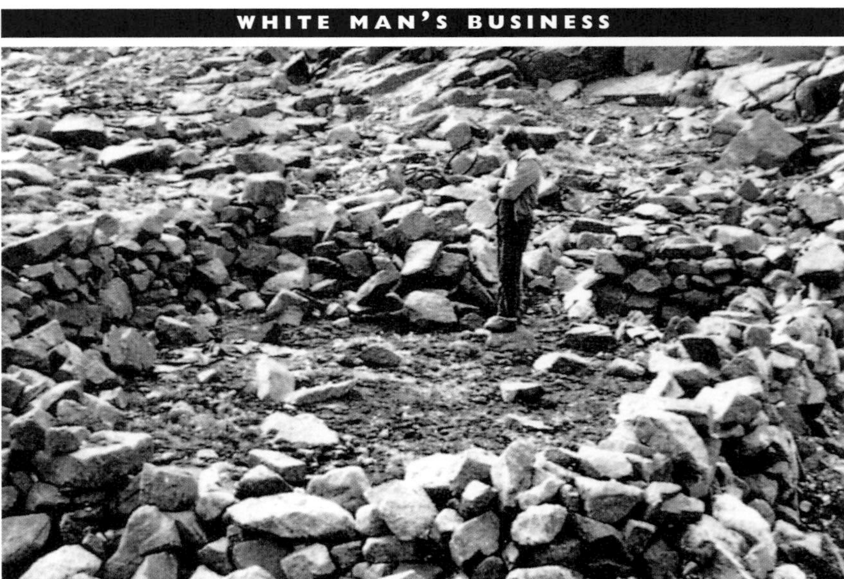

On 5 June 1951, on my return from Alexandra Fjord, I discovered the tragic site of the Greely expedition's winter hut. It still surprises me that I felt nothing in this place of despair and suffering but distance, as though all emotion froze before such majesty. The reaction of the Eskimo accompanying me: "Qaallunaat's (white man's) business!" I observed a minute of silence and fired a long salvo with my rifle in their honor.

"Greely, is this you?"

Cape Sabine. Elevation of the coast drawn by an officer of the *Thetis*. Camp Clay is west of Cape Sabine, the site designated as a meeting place by Greely's military superiors. Greely duly erected a big cairn on Stalknecht Island. Captain Schley spotted it, found the message inside the cairn, and immediately began searching on the north side of Pim Island, the most unlikely place imaginable for a winter camp.

On board the *Thetis*, early July 1884, at Upernavik: 1) Commander Schley, who led the rescue expedition (he was later promoted to admiral and became one of Dr. Cook's most ardent defenders); 7) Lieutenant Colwell, who discovered the first survivors of Camp Clay; 22) Lieutenant Greely; 23) Frederick; 24) Brainard; 25) Biederbick; 26) Connell; and 27) Long.

The Arctic waters in June-July, in the area of Smith Sound.

ADMIRAL ROBERT EDWIN PEARY 1855-1920

THE CONQUEST OF A DOUBLE MYTH

Willful as a corsair, inarguably charismatic, and ruthless in his methods, Robert Edwin Peary took extraordinary risks of every kind during his eight arctic expeditions. The only thing that counted for him was the goal he had set himself: to reach the Pole first and plant the American flag on that sacred spot.

Inveniam viam; aut faciam.[1] Peary scratched this motto (a quotation from Seneca) into a beam while bedridden in one of the three run-down cabins at Fort Conger during the desperate weeks of January 1898 after the amputation of seven toes. It is also found on the inside cover of his journal.

Walking with great difficulty, Peary advanced inexorably toward the conquest of the myth that haunted him. He squinted his steely blue eyes, the better to scan the great white desolation where his life's goal was hidden: the North Pole, axis of the earth. A second and more secret myth also motivated him: to share ever more intimately the life of the Inuit, far from the vanities of Boston and the sophistications of Washington.

"I must have fame"

Over twenty-three years, he made eight expeditions. Obstinacy, physical courage, and an indomitable will in the service of a well-defined project—the cardinal virtues of the greatest conquistadors in fact belonged to this man of iron. His determination that he, Peary, should reach the North Pole first is evident in the many expeditions he made crisscrossing the southeastern Arctic Ocean, North Greenland, and Ellesmere Island. "I fight not for fortune, but for the pure glory of it." By no choice but his own, his life would indeed be a series of sacrifices on the personal, familial, and social levels. Peary had a great deal of charm; a public man, he was admired by the Washington establishment; from the scientific perspective, his mathematically accurate reports were particularly valued by geographers. He could have been an ethnographer. The prime witness of a decisive change among this Eskimo people—a change he was all the more capable of appreciating in that he was the cause of it—he showed in his technical notes an ability to observe this people's material culture accurately and fairly. He had a pragmatic understanding of their psychology, to the point that he became something of a legend among the Inuit. Although Peary had a classical college education, he showed little literary aptitude. His writings—books and journals—are engineering reports, stripped of all emotion, written in a laconic, military style. His later books, as history would reveal, were not even written by himself but by ghostwriters.

Tall (5'11") and red-haired, Peary (whose name is an anglicization of "Pierre"—he was of partly French descent) had a strong constitution. His big handlebar mustache gave him

1) "I shall find a way or make one."

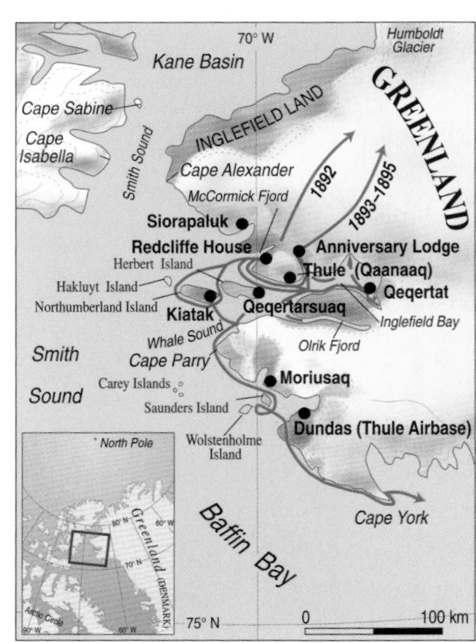

Peary's first expeditions over the Greenland ice cap (1892 and 1893-1895).

OPPOSITE:
Robert Edwin Peary, the legendary image of a Polar explorer.

Right, **Robert and Josephine Peary** (standing at far right) on a visit to the boatyard in Buckport, Maine during the construction of the *Roosevelt*, 24 October 1904. The ship was 200 feet long overall (180 feet at the waterline) and 27.5 feet wide. Its hull was entirely made of wood, which gave it strength and elasticity.

Above, **the cross section** of the oval hull, on which the pinching of the ice could gain no purchase. Pressure from the side would make the ship rise without breaking it.

a gruff dignity. Somewhat distant and taciturn, he was generally of even temperament. A slight stutter betrayed his secret sensitiveness.

Generous with his companions—according to the whaling skipper Robert Bartlett—he could prove extremely harsh toward anyone who was disloyal to him. During the expedition of 1891-1892, one of his young companions, John Verhoeff, a geologist who had contributed $2000 to take part in the expedition, was pushed to the limit by the cynicism and authoritarianism of the Pearys as a couple and committed suicide, or in any case vanished, on the eve of the expedition's return. [2] During the expedition of 1898-1902, at Cape Sabine, he broke off Dr. Tom Dedrick's contract during the winter of 1901, and sent him away without any provisions, forcing him to throw himself on the mercy of the Etah Eskimos, who took him in. It is harrowing to read Dr. Dedrick's journal, because we learn that the Eskimos were facing an epidemic and we feel the doctor's consternation in trying to help them, given Peary's indifference. But Peary had eliminated him from his mind (though Dedrick personally amputated seven of Peary's toes in 1898). His divorce from Peary was also unbearable to him. We should further note Peary's poor relations with Dr. Goodsell in 1908-1909. Yet the attachment that most of his companions and all of the Inuit felt for him through thick and thin is striking. This iron man, so often reviled, was complex and masked. If he provoked real hatred, he also elicited extraordinary affection, admiration, and respect. [3]

It is remarkable that he gained the respect and admiration of such a diverse set of people. President Theodore Roosevelt was his most unshakable friend. Visiting Peary on board his ship on the eve of his departure, Roosevelt said: "I believe in you, Peary, and I believe in your success." Another friend was the president of the American Museum of Natural History, Morris K. Jesup, who would support him and provide financial help on a large scale. Bankers and captains of industry staked their good names on his success by joining the Peary Arctic Club. And he was well-liked by his black

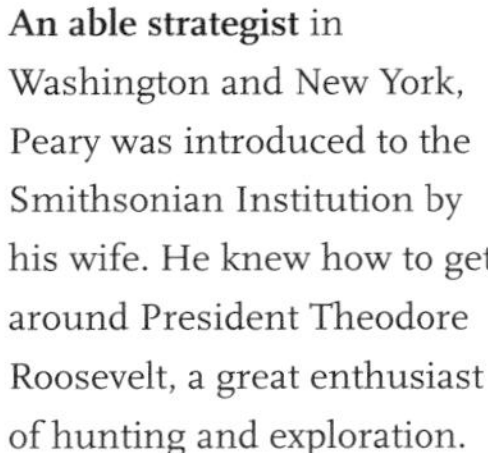

An able strategist in Washington and New York, Peary was introduced to the Smithsonian Institution by his wife. He knew how to get around President Theodore Roosevelt, a great enthusiast of hunting and exploration.

2) It might seem somewhat cynical of Peary, as the leader of the expedition, to set out as a newlywed while all his companions were single and lived under one roof with him. Considering the importance of sexual urges in a group living in a confined environment, this could be seen as a provocation to the rest of the crew, an incitement to debauchery with the Eskimo women in the neighborhood. Verhoeff's last words: "I hate them, her and him both!"

3) Bob Bartlett, the dour whaling skipper from St. John's, Newfoundland who, as captain of the *Roosevelt*, accompanied Peary in 1905-1906, and again in 1908-1909, never doubted the fact of his having reached the North Pole on 6 April 1909, six days after they separated on the pack ice. The Scottish geographer Lyall (Bartlett's companion on the *Karluk* and the tragic overwintering on Wrangel Island in 1903-1905) personally reminded me of this during our only interview, recorded in Glasgow in 1970: "Oh, Bartlett had absolute faith in Peary. The Pole? To him Peary had unquestionably been there."

4) This was told and repeated to me by the Eskimos during my first expedition in 1950-1951, and on each successive one, in 1967, 1969, 1979, and 1982.

5) The Navy wrote him pointedly to remind him that his use of the title was unauthorized and contrary to regulations.

6) In 1907, Peary was deeply in debt. The *New York Times*, to whom Peary sold the exclusive rights to his story, insisted that he repay the $4000 advanced to him if he did not reach the Pole.

7) Yet Josephine, a remarkable character, was not simply a muse. Highly feminine, she found it painful to be so often separated from her husband and experienced periods of depression: "The Pole will never thank me for the anxiety and suffering I have endured," she wrote in a note dated 25 September 1906.

8) This famous research organization, headquartered in Washington D.C., was founded in 1846.

9) At one of our meetings, Anaakkarsuaq asked me to transmit to his father, who was then living very modestly in New York and who seemed to have forgotten him, an invitation to his house. I can still see Anaakkarsuaq saying to me: "Write it down in your notebook: white men always forget ..." Unfortunately my means were very limited when I returned from Thule in 1951, and I was only able to go to New York in 1956, by which time Matt Henson had died. I saw Anaakkarsuaq again in 1982: "You didn't see him. I would have liked him to hear my invitation. And he never wrote me. Many thanks to you for having come back to see me. And I'll write it out for you, here and now, so that everyone will know how I was abandoned."

servant Matthew (Matt) Henson. Finally, the Polar Eskimos—his second family, literally—remember him in respectful and fearful terms. [4] Though somewhat distant in temperament, Peary loved them in his own shy way.

"Remember Mother, I *must* have fame," he wrote to his mother, his closest confidante. And only the Pole, ever at the center of his thoughts and actions, could give him that fame. His relations with others were entirely a function of the accomplishment of this goal.

Peary was an independent operator, contrary to what rumors might suggest. All his expeditions were privately mounted, with the help of more and more powerful organizations. Peary was not well liked by the U.S. Navy, though a product of their training, and he was actively disliked by many of his Navy colleagues. One reason was that he adopted navy titles somewhat inexactly, calling himself "Commander" when he was in fact a Civil Engineer. [5] Also, his "unpaid leave" was repeatedly extended on the orders of President Roosevelt, himself an explorer and big-game hunter. And finally, Peary's unorthodox personality, breathlessly reported by the press, infuriated the Navy, both at the top and the bottom. Jealousy—that powerful motor in the affairs of men and most especially in arctic history—is too often neglected in historical analyses, yet its effects were appreciable. In 1902, the U.S. Navy curtly refused to send a ship to Peary's rescue at a time when he faced grave difficulties in the Arctic.

His expeditions were expensive—the eighth and last cost $500,000. Yet Peary was not a wealthy man. After 1908 he even faced serious financial difficulties. Consequently it took an important commitment on his part to organize his expeditions, which were heavily manned and equipped. Before the 1893 expedition, Peary gave 168 lectures in ninety-six days, in order to raise $13,000! Such sums were insufficient in his eyes for the realization of his projects. In 1898 the Peary Arctic Club was formed, whose goal was the conquest of the North Pole, with twenty-five millionaires each promising to contribute one thousand dollars per year for four years. [6] But where did this man come from, who, like a hero from Plutarch, wanted to raise himself to the height of the greatest names in history?

He was the only son of a poor family, encouraged from childhood by his mother, who played a decisive role in his life and helped him financially until her death. Peary was so attached to her that she accompanied him even on his honeymoon! But Josephine Diebitsch, his wife, of German ancestry, soon became equally important to Peary. [7] Endowed with rare energy, this young woman, whose father worked at the Smithsonian Institution, [8] would support and perhaps inspire the arctic destiny of the great explorer. She fearlessly accompanied her husband during his first arctic winter, and gave birth to their first child in 1893 during the second winter among the Inuit, thirteen degrees from the Pole. Josephine also accompanied Peary on the 1897 voyage and overwintered for a third time at Cape Sabine in 1900. And she joined Peary for the first weeks of the 1902 and 1903 crossings.

When she stayed home, it was at their house near Portland, Maine—not a fashionable watering hole at the time. Their large wooden house, designed by Peary, was not far from Bowdoin College, where he had managed by dint of hard work to be enrolled as a scholarship student. It was at Eagle Island that all the plans for Peary's expeditions to the Pole were drawn up, and there that his wife, daughter, and son waited so anxiously for the news that he had finally conquered it.

Drawing by Kiutikaq Dunek, born in 1932. Qaanaaq, 1991.

A Bostonian and "his" Eskimos

To Josephine it was intimately clear that her husband had a more complex nature than was readily apparent. In fact, he would very soon lead a true double life. Among the Polar Eskimos he found a second country. It was not so much to Eagle Island that he went to repair his strength and collect himself, but among the "primitives," whose language he spoke poorly and whose social conduct he was never interested in enough to study seriously. His quite extraordinary wife transcended her love for him and, in the spirit of the Arctic, accepted his having an Eskimo family. From 1898 to 1902, Peary lived for three whole years in the region of Etah and Cape Sabine. His health was then poor, and had to have seven toes amputated during the winter of 1898-1899, without anesthetics. He knew that he would have to wear prostheses, which were in fact fitted to him when he returned to New York in 1903. But on no account did he want to return to the United States without having achieved his goal.

Ehré, born in 1880, son of the shaman Sorqaaq, photographed at age 30. Of phlegmatic temperament, he was derisively called the "Strongman."

At that time, he lived with Aleqasina, by whom he had two sons: Kaalipaluk, born in 1906 (who would become one of my close friends in Thule) and Anaakkaq, born in 1900. Like master, like servant: Peary's black manservant Matt Henson mirrored his master's deep tendencies in this area. Mattipaluk (as the Eskimos called Henson) was also very popular among the Polar Inuit, and he also had a son, with an Eskimo woman named Akratanmguak. This son, born in 1906, was Anaakkarsuaq, whom I often met in Savissivik, and whom I queried about his father's silence. [9] Peary, of Puritan stock, was modern and emancipated in his morals, but he was also cynical. After his successful Polar expedition, he abandoned his Eskimo wife and their two children without ever sending them the slightest compensation. "The presence of women," Peary wrote, "is an absolute necessity to keep men happy." In his book, he published a naked photograph of Aleqasina (nostalgia?) without raising any eyebrows in prudish America.

Ittukusuk, at the age of about 24 (in 1892). Undoubtedly one of the greatest Inuit shamans.

From 1898 to 1902, Peary dallied among the Eskimos without the least hope of reaching the Pole (he had no prostheses). It is impossible to understand so long a stay among

Captain Robert Bartlett, extremely capable, had sailed extensively on Newfoundland whalers and was able to maneuver the *Roosevelt* through the pack ice and the dangerous leads of Kane Basin and Kennedy Channel to the Arctic Ocean and back again in 1906. It was he who, in March-April 1909, led the penultimate party breaking trail toward the Pole, until Peary ordered him to turn back so that he could go on alone. Ironically, a cousin of Bartlett's (with the same family name) was captain of the *John R. Bradley*, Cook's ship, in July 1907.

them without imagining a "second Peary," who found happiness in intimacy with the Eskimos. It is true that no account exists of this happy life, but Peary was, in his deepest heart, Rousseauvian and Thoreauvian. [10] Although he never dared publicly admit to his second life, he had the audacity to live the utopian existence of these "anarchistic philosophers of the Far North."

No doubt he sensed that Eskimo society had from the outset conferred on him, by a deep and irreversible conviction, the rank of leader, and he therefore sought out that society in the midst of the difficulties (and doubts) that assailed him, preferring it to the hermetic and moralizing society of Boston or Washington. Peary knew all too well that America and the U.S. Navy in particular would never grasp the deep meaning of this double life. They would see his greatness only on one condition, that he conquer the Pole with irrefutable evidence, showing only one of his faces, that of the stern and noble Anglo-Saxon explorer.

A geopolitical vision that interested no one

Peary fought on singlehandedly for his country, trying to convince Washington that his cartographic explorations, his uncontested authority over the Polar Eskimos, and their inhabited territory (not claimed, even by Copenhagen) were important assets and that the United States could claim territorial rights and rule over an arctic area that might prove of great strategic importance in the modern world.

In 1909-1910, back from his eighth and last expedition, Peary tried to draw the attention of the Secretary of State to the disadvantages to the U.S. in the short, medium, and long terms if the Danes built a station in North Star Bay (Thule)—but in vain. Peary made no more impression on Washington in 1909 than Sir John Ross had on London in 1818. The halls of government have neither the pioneering spirit nor a sense of the politics of the future. In 1917, Washington and Copenhagen would exchange mutual concessions: by ceding its interests in the Virgin Islands to the United States, Denmark gained full sovereignty over the entire island of Greenland. Peary's political views, which would have given Washington a first-class opening onto the Arctic, from North Greenland to Ellesmere Island, were not taken into consideration.

Peary on the deck of the *Roosevelt*. He left Aleqasina and their two sons on board: Annakak, born in May 1900, and Kaalipaluk, born in May 1906. It was common knowledge that the Commander had become attached to Aleqasina ever since first seeing her in 1892: she was then ten years old. While taking ethnographic photographs, he had been struck by her personality. He published photographs of her as a naked adolescent in his 1898 book, noting her name, Alakasingwah, and her American nickname, Ally. Though an adventurer, Peary was concerned to maintain his own good name and avoid shocking puritan Bostonians. He thus maintained a sort of double life, which he took care not to make public.

But who could have foreseen, in point of fact, that this Navy officer and civil engineer, whose research started in Nicaragua, would suddenly become interested in the Arctic? Tasked with re-examining the route of the Panama Canal, Peary had spent four difficult years exploring the terrain with Indian crews and had proposed a shorter and better route for the U.S. canal. Matt Henson was already working at his side.

In 1886, Peary suddenly decided to undertake an exploration of the Greenland ice cap. The urge did not arise from nowhere but was the outcome of a secret inner progress, spurred by his childhood delight in the fabulous tales of arctic journeys such as the bold exploration of the Greenland ice cap in summer 1883 by Nordenskjöld and the expeditions of Elisha Kent Kane (1853-1855), two heroes who were much admired by American youths . . .

Eight bold expeditions

At the earliest possible moment, Peary asked the Navy for a short leave of absence, borrowed $500 from his mother, and shipped for Disko Bay. Although he spoke no Danish, within a few days he had convinced a young civil servant in Godhavn (Disko), Christian Maigaard, whom he had not known previously, to accompany him to Pakitsoq Fjord on the ice cap for a reconnaissance mission. His goal was to reach the interior of Greenland and examine the conditions with a view to further exploration. Of the eight Greenlanders who accompanied him, six deserted and only two continued on past the moraine. Advancing on skis and with an ice ax from 5 to 19 July 1886 through the worst of the melt season, past glacial rills [11] and crevasses, followed by two sixteen-foot sleds loaded with biscuit, pemmican, condensed milk, dried meat, and beans, Peary succeeded in walking "farther across the inland ice than any other white man." [12] With only six days' food left, at an altitude of 7500 feet, and 100 miles in from the west edge of the ice cap, he was forced to turn back. Using a sail and setting the two sleds abreast of each other, he quickly regained the coast.

During his second expedition in 1891-1892, in the country of the Polar Eskimos, Peary crossed the unexplored North Greenland ice cap with a fourteen-dog sled team. He was accompanied only by an American of Norwegian descent, Eivin Astrup, and took no native guide. This daring expedition allowed Peary, traveling without the Inuit, to map the northernmost land in the world—to which he gave his name— and to demonstrate for the first time that Greenland was truly an island. [13]

The six expeditions that followed (1893-1895, 1896, 1897, 1898-1902, 1905-1906, 1908-1909) all shared a single goal: the conquest of the North Pole. Methodically planned, they grew increasingly massive in men and materials, and a large part of the native population was mobilized to assist them. In this, Peary was unlike his predecessors, able through his innate authority and charisma to bring the Inuit to his cause.

Matt Henson, originally from Virginia, quickly became an excellent dog sled driver. Through all adversity, he maintained absolute discretion and loyalty toward his boss. Peary never discussed his relations with this man, who was his most intimate confidante, his interpreter (Henson spoke Eskimo perfectly, unlike Peary), and who continued to address him as "Sir" while blizzards howled around them! Matt Henson never discussed their relations either, or only in the most laconic terms.

His other companions were for the most part white Americans, chosen more for their physical and psychological qualities than for being scientists. Bound by draconian contracts that prevented them from publishing or even saying anything without their expedition leader's express consent, they too remained—even in times of hardship—totally loyal to Peary. The exception was Dr. Frederick Albert Cook, who was the only man among them to have, like Peary, the stature of a conqueror.

A worthy competitor: Dr. F.A. Cook

In contrast to the increasingly massive expeditions of the aging Peary, Cook adopted in 1907 the stripped-down style the "young" Peary had used at the time of his bold and solitary crossing of north Greenland in May-August 1892.

Cook began to feel that Peary's expeditions were too massive to be successful, and that the overall strategy needed to be reconsidered. Furthermore, he had noticed that the increasing energy Peary showed sverged on paranoia. Unable to make progress toward the Pole, Peary had started to believe that he was being threatened on all sides, notably by the Norwegian Otto Sverdrup, who had come along to map and study Ellesmere Island. He had even forbidden any of his Eskimo hunters to cooperate with other explorers.

The reader should know that the obstacles presented by the Arctic Ocean are truly formidable, inhuman. George Nares's term for it, as we remember, was "impassable." In contrast to his predecessors Kane and Hayes, Peary set him-

Peary and Cook arguing over the discovery of the North Pole.

self with frank obsession to overcome them one by one. The navigation logs of his expeditions, with the exception of the last two, are detailed: latitude, longitude, and magnetic variation were scrupulously noted at every stage. Peary left nothing to chance: he examined his failures and those of his predecessors to draw every possible lesson from them. [14]

The Pole, Peary believed, could only be conquered from a base established on the shores of the Arctic Ocean. Only a ship such as the *Roosevelt*, built to his specifications in 1904 with an egg-shaped hull, thanks to a gift of $100,000, could bring him there. As long as he did not have access to an extremely maneuverable ship, built to his specifications, with a 1000-horsepower main engine that would enable a new technique of navigation through the arctic pack with direct steam injection, Peary was sure he would be condemned to aborted expeditions—because the base from which he had to start, like the one at Cape Sabine (78°43' north, 74°07' west), was so far from the Pole.

In 1908 all the elements were in place: it would be his last expedition. Peary was aboard "his" ship, the *Roosevelt*, with enough food to last for two years. "My last chance," he said, "the last arrow in my quiver." Just before leaving he confided to a journalist from Portland that he had every intention of reaching the Pole . . . or not returning.

His finances were in critical straits. His main supporter, the banker Morris K. Jesup, had just died. Peary was fifty-three years old, and he needed a resounding success to jus-

Peary's great rival, Frederick Cook, photographed in Copenhagen, August 1909, before his claim to the Pole was disputed. He was indifferent to money and honors, and naive in his dealings with the media. Cook impressed his contemporaries with his simplicity and dignity.

10) Henry Thoreau (1817–1862), author of *Walden, or Life in the Woods* (1854), advocated a return to nature.

11) pockets of melting ice within a glacier.

12) Despite his claims, this excursion was shorter than that of Nordenskjöld and his Lapp companions (though the Lapps are of course not whites!).

13) This was an exceptional expedition, as much for its means of navigation as for the courage it demonstrated. It should be noted, however, that it engendered a serious cartographic error. Peary Land is not separated from Greenland by a channel. This error would lead to the death of Mylius-Erichsen and his Greenlandic companion during an expedition in November 1907.

14) On his next to last expedition (1905-1906), he was cut off by a lead six miles wide. Nonetheless, he managed to reach 87°6' north after getting across the open water channels in the polar pack with great daring, despite his lack of provisions. Uutaaq, his Eskimo companion, told me in February 1951 emotionally and in detail about the terrible hardships of the last stages of the polar journey in 1905, and of Peary's strict fairness in sharing the food in silence under their tent: grave and smiling, he served himself last. "For the first time I saw Piulersuaq (Peary) truly human and attentive toward each of us."

The June-July breakup.

tify his past pronouncements. The sarcasm of his detractors was getting increasingly boisterous: enough of the Farthest North . . .

On 6 July 1908 he sailed on the *Roosevelt* out of New York harbor. Seven Americans accompanied him, including the excellent ice navigator Captain Bob Bartlett, of St. John, Newfoundland, who had skippered the ship in 1905-1906. Their destination was Etah. Between Cape York and Etah, eighteen Eskimo men, along with their families (forty-nine souls in all, a fourth of the total population of the Polar Eskimos), and one hundred twenty-three dogs were taken aboard the *Roosevelt*, along with seventy tons of whale meat, and the blubber of fifty walruses. Everything was progressing according to a rigid plan. Peary felt confident.

R. E. Peary aboard the *Roosevelt* in 1908. "I fight not for fortune, but for the pure glory of it." And, one might add, for the honor of the United States of America.

Haunted by the vision of Cook marching to the Pole

But in Etah, Peary was struck as though by lightning: he learned that Cook had left America a year earlier (July 1907), also to conquer the Pole. Accompanied by a young German, Rudolph Franke, he had apparently mounted a lightweight expedition, and tried a new itinerary, farther to the west, from Cape Svartevoeg on northern Axel Heiberg Island, which was very well adapted to his goal. Had Cook already reached the Pole? And if so, why had he not returned? Peary made detailed inquiries about Cook's expedition and grew worried. The Eskimos said that he had left Anoritooq on 9 February 1908 under the guidance of Pualuna, Uutaaq's brother, with nine Eskimos, eleven sledges, one hundred and five dogs, and a load of three tons. [15] He struck off across the Arctic Ocean for the Pole on 18 March with four Eskimos, then with only two. There had been no news since.

Peary knew the determination of his old companion better than anyone. He judged him to be "an honorable man and an excellent traveling partner." [16] Cook was very much admired, as Peary knew, by his friend Roald Amundsen, the future conqueror of the South Pole. Cook had played an important role in rescuing the first expedition to overwinter in the Antarctic: the *Belgica* expedition (1897-1899). By his daring actions, he had saved the ship, but always modestly underplayed his part in favor of his comrades and his leader. Peary, who was subject to depressions, felt wounded to the quick. Cook personified his own intrepid youth. To see the doctor from his first expedition use his methods and draw on the collaboration of "his" Eskimos plunged him into a deep rage. He didn't hesitate to write the president of the United States from Etah to denounce Cook as a trouble-maker. "This man puts my enterprise in danger," he said, in substance, in a peculiar letter sent back via the *Erik*, the supply ship they had met with in Etah. But what was Cook doing? This disturbing question haunted Peary day after day and night after night. Peary was literally taken over by this "other self," who threatened to forestall him at the finish line. It was thus a wounded Peary who left Etah for Cape Columbia. The same thing happened to Scott in his rivalry with Amundsen, when the latter reached the South Pole before him (14 December 1911, to Scott's 17 January 1912).

But where was Cook? At that very moment, the younger explorer was several hundred miles to the northwest, somewhere in the Arctic Ocean, surviving with difficulty on the drifting ice and struggling dramatically to save his life and that of his two young Inuit companions. As his journal indicates, he would soon have neither dogs nor firearms. A piece of wood from his sled served as a tool handle and harpoon shaft for the throwing weapons he manufactured. In desperate straits, he tried, on 15 April 1909, to return to his base at Anoritooq (Cape Inglefield) north of Etah. He would arrive back after traveling for eight months. This exploit by itself was one of the most phenomenal in all Arctic history.

---

15) Pualuna was one of my principal informants in the winter of 1951 during my study of the genealogy of the Polar Eskimos. He was the central individual in a genealogy I drew up with the help of many elders of four generations (1400 individuals).

16) Peary knew Cook intimately and was aware that he was an extraordinary arctic explorer, of a caliber similar to his own. Cook was the only adversary that Peary feared. He also knew—because he was aware of his own regrettable tendencies—that Cook was as capable as himself of "taking a few liberties with the truth" in cases of extreme necessity. Let us not forget that the supposed channel mapped by Peary (when in fact Peary Land is a peninsula) could only be distantly glimpsed. Crocker Land, north of Ellesmere Island, was imaginary. The name, whether spelled with a "c" in the middle or not, brought bad luck— it was the Croker Mountains that John Ross saw barring the end of Lancaster Sound, an imaginary sighting that all but ruined his career.

17) The Peary Arctic Club was also a commercial enterprise. Its accounts have never been made public.

18) The *Roosevelt* fared better in this year than it had in 1905-1906. On that trip, the ship was holed below the waterline with an opening large enough for a child to crawl through. It was only by working the pumps night and day that they were able to limp back from the Arctic Ocean and arrive, one year later, at Etah.

19) Each sledge carried a load of 550 pounds, with food for fifty days.

20) Not counting the detours around fractures and hummocks, which increase the distance by 25%. Uutaaq, Peary's companion from 87° N to the Pole and back informed me in February 1951 that Peary's sledges broke down often, thus slowing progress. The distances seem particularly long as Peary, now exhausted, was most often riding on his sledge. This was confirmed to me by Uutaaq. By way of comparison, Nansen traveled 23 miles per day (28 maximum); Cagni, 6.23 miles; Cook, 29 miles; Ralph Plaisted, 11 miles (by snowmobile); Will Steger, 8.5 miles; Wally Herbert, 26.4 miles (this maximum was achieved for only one day in sixteen months of ice travel—the ice was smooth, the dogs fresh, and the loads light).

July 1908: Peary, for his part, was making slow progress, and after entering Smith Sound he suddenly ordered the *Roosevelt* to stop at Anoritooq. He disembarked, standing on the very site of Cook's winter camp. On Cook's abandoned cabin, containing spare food and equipment, Peary had the temerity to post a sign saying: "Dr. Cook is long ago dead and it is no use to search for him." This miserable sign does no honor to the third president of the Explorers' Club, who had been decorated by that club's second president, none other than Dr. Cook.

After installing two of his seamen in Cook's cabin (in reality, two crooks) with instructions to trade with the Eskimos for ivory and furs during the winter, Peary ordered Captain Bartlett to hurry their passage through the ice of Kane Basin and Kennedy and Robeson channels. [17] But navigation was extremely difficult, the pack ice proving much denser than in 1905-1906. Bartlett maneuvered the ship daringly. [18] A few miles beyond the overwintering site of the *Alert* (where Nares's ship spent the winter of 1875-1876) at Cape Sheridan, the *Roosevelt* finally dropped anchor. It was the farthest north a ship had ever wintered up to that date. On the very shores of the Arctic Ocean, Peary was within reach of his goal.

The dash to the Pole: February-April 1909

During the months of the polar night (November to March), the polar expedition was meticulously planned aboard the *Roosevelt*: clothes were sewn by the hunters' wives, and sleds, dogs, traces, and harnesses were seen to. The expedition was organized according to the system developed in previous years: Peary's "traveling machine," in which successive parties relayed each other in breaking trail so as to leave the last party (Peary's) fresh and strong for the final push. Nothing was left to chance.

After four months of winter, Peary ordered the departure toward the Pole. He set off on 1 March 1909 from Cape Columbia (latitude 83° 9' north), slightly east of Cape Sheridan. He decided to follow the Cape Columbia meridian closely. The polar night had not yet lifted. The group comprised twenty-four men (including seven Americans), nineteen sledges, and one hundred thirty-three dogs, with different teams alternating in the lead. [19] The level of enthusiasm was very high. Each man, whether American or Eskimo, knew that the effort had to succeed. It was a last-chance expedition.

But was success so certain? Peary's mind seems to have been elsewhere. He had changed. Some of his abrupt decisions in those early days of March—such as leaving on shore part of the equipment for taking ocean depth soundings—make one wonder, as the soundings could have provided an additional chain of proof. Peary seemed abnormally distant. He was, in fact, increasingly obsessed with Cook.

Cook at that precise moment was living in a stone hut he had built on a deserted island north of Devon Island at Cape Sparbo, a 600-foot cliff (lat. 75° 49' N, long. 83° 48' W). With no firearms, no bow and arrows, no dogs, he had to protect himself from the bears that threatened him daily. He was living a stone-age life with two young Eskimos. The collapsible boat that, unlike Peary, he had sensibly brought along would save the lives of all three men. Cook was preparing to start walking the 500 miles toward his base at Anoritooq, Cape Inglefield, in northern Greenland.

On 1 March 1909, Peary's traveling machine went into motion. A route was hacked with an ax across the hummocks. But conditions were unfavorable from the start: a strong east wind (ultimately fatal to his plans) made him drift far from the meridian he needed to follow so as not to miss the Pole. The drift of the ice along the coast opened large leads that the sleds, oddly unequipped with boats, had somehow to cross. In fact, the expedition had to wait for new ice to form on the leads before they could go on. Peary was falling behind.

The mystery of the last stages

On 1 April, in bitter cold, Peary reached 87° 47' N. This northing—independently confirmed—was in itself a record. (But is it so sure? Bartlett confirmed the astronomical sighting as to latitude but not longitude. If Peary was truly on the meridian of Cape Columbia, he was 133 miles from the Pole.) It seems certain that Peary could reach the Pole from there in eight days, if the ice remained solid and covered with frozen snow. But for a feat of this kind it was crucial to have an independent witness. As the pack ice drifts with the currents, Peary could leave no permanent mark at the Pole. Bartlett could and should have been that witness. He had always wanted to belong to Peary's final assault party, and Peary never tried to dissuade him from it. Yet on 1 April, more authoritarian than ever, Peary suddenly ordered him to turn back. Bartlett was so bitterly disappointed that he almost decided during the night to continue anyway, alone and on foot. But the next day, mastering himself, he bowed to orders and left Peary to face his destiny alone. Did Peary want to proceed without witnesses? It is not impossible that the great explorer was rattled by the possibility of Cook's suc-

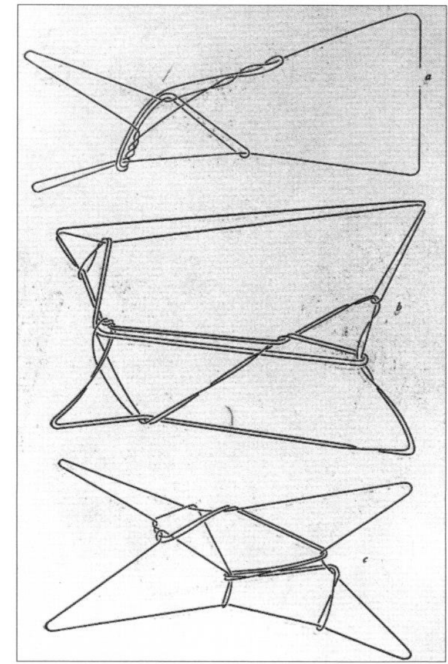

Ajaraarutit: according to custom, cat's cradle is played only in the winter, during the polar night. In the summer, the kayaker could become entangled with his harpoon line and drown.

BELOW, LEFT: **Christmas menu,** from the base at Redcliffe House, where Peary overwintered in 1891-1892. Drawing by Eivin Astrup.

BELOW, RIGHT: **Weekly menu** of the expedition of 1893-1894, as it appeared in Davidson's journal. The food is typically American, except for the reindeer roast. Seal and walrus meat were reserved for Eskimos and dogs, with the dogs fed only every other day.

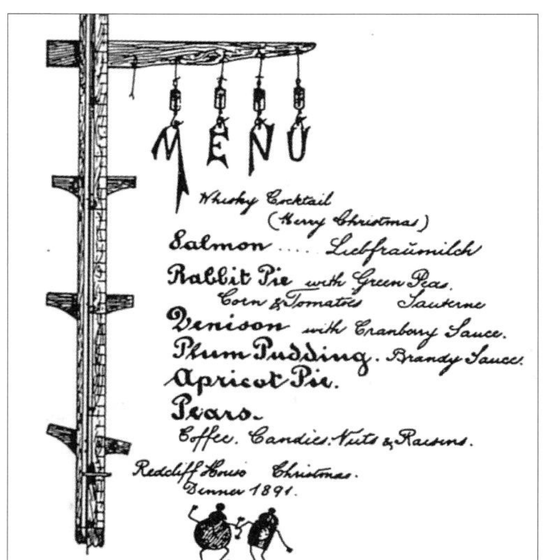

MENU

Whisky Cocktail
(Merry Christmas)
Salmon .... Liebfraumilch
Rabbit Pie with Green Peas.
Corn & Tomatoes Sauterne
Venison with Cranberry Sauce.
Plum Pudding. Brandy Sauce.
Apricot Pie.
Pears.
Coffee. Candies. Nuts & Raisins.

Redcliff House Christmas.
Dinner 1891.

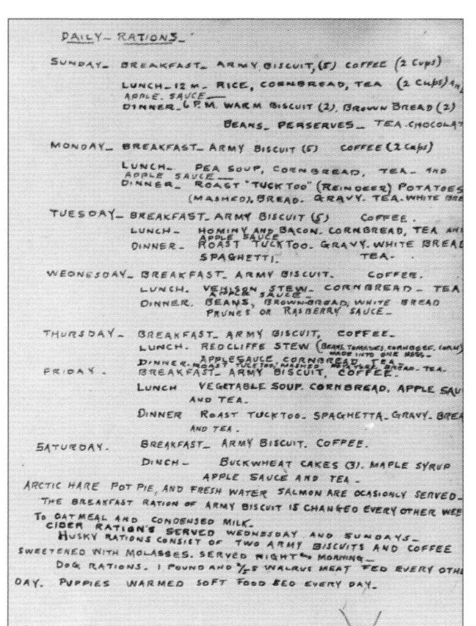

DAILY – RATIONS –

SUNDAY – BREAKFAST – ARMY BISCUIT, (5) COFFEE (2 Cups)
LUNCH – 12 M. – RICE, CORNBREAD, TEA (2 Cups) ...
APPLE. SAUCE –
DINNER – 6 P.M. WARM BISCUIT (2), BROWN BREAD (2)
BEANS – PERSERVES – TEA. CHOCOLAT...

MONDAY – BREAKFAST – ARMY BISCUIT (5) COFFEE (2 Cups)
LUNCH – PEA SOUP, CORNBREAD, TEA – AND
APPLE SAUCE –
DINNER – ROAST "TUCK TOO" (REINDEER) POTATOES
(MASHED), BREAD. GRAVY. TEA. WHITE BRE...

TUESDAY – BREAKFAST – ARMY BISCUIT (5) COFFEE.
LUNCH – HOMINY AND BACON. CORNBREAD, TEA AN...
APPLE SAUCE
DINNER – ROAST TUCK TOO. GRAVY. WHITE BREA...
SPAGHETTI. TEA.

WEDNESDAY – BREAKFAST – ARMY BISCUIT. COFFEE.
LUNCH. VENISON STEW – CORNBREAD – TEA
APPLE SAUCE –
DINNER. BEANS, BROWNBREAD, WHITE BREAD
PRUNES OR RASBERRY SAUCE –

THURSDAY – BREAKFAST – ARMY BISCUIT, COFFEE –
LUNCH. REDCLIFFE STEW (...)
APPLESAUCE, CORNBREAD, TEA.
DINNER. ROAST TUCK TOO, MASHED POTATOES, BREAD – TEA.

FRIDAY. BREAKFAST – ARMY BISCUIT, COFFEE.
LUNCH VEGETABLE SOUP. CORNBREAD, APPLE SAU...
AND TEA.
DINNER ROAST TUCKTOO – SPAGHETTA – GRAVY – BRE...
AND TEA.

SATURDAY. BREAKFAST – ARMY BISCUIT. COFFEE.
DINCH – BUCKWHEAT CAKES (3). MAPLE SYRUP
APPLE SAUCE AND TEA –

ARCTIC HARE POT PIE, AND FRESH WATER SALMON ARE OCASIONLY SERVED –
THE BREAKFAST RATION OF ARMY BISCUIT IS CHANGED EVERY OTHER WEE...
TO OATMEAL AND CONDENSED MILK.
CIDER RATIONS SERVED WEDNESDAY AND SUNDAYS –
HUSKY RATIONS CONSIST OF TWO ARMY BISCUITS AND COFFEE
SWEETENED WITH MOLASSES. SERVED NIGHT AND MORNING –
DOG RATIONS. 1 POUND AND 1/2 WALRUS MEAT FED EVERY OTH...
DAY. PUPPIES WARMED SOFT FOOD FED EVERY DAY –

Matthew Henson in Eskimo clothes. A veteran of seven arctic expeditions, he reached the Pole on the last. Black historians have argued that there were two conquerors of the North Pole: Peary and Henson. With President Reagan's support in 1980, Henson was re-interred in Arlington National Cemetery in a twin tomb to Peary's. He always stayed out of the Peary-Cook controversy.

cess. And it was at this stage that events began to gather speed. Peary had been in the habit of traveling 12 miles per day, from 83° N to 87° N, but on the subsequent stages he traveled 43 and 49 miles![20] According to his journal, which was only partially made public, Peary at no time between 87° and 90° N made a noon sighting. Was he still on his original meridian? Who knows? He sensed that he was drifting as he had in 1905-1906. He guessed his route, especially as the ice was drifting in the opposite direction . . . From 87° N to the Pole, despite his custom, Peary did not have his sightings countersigned by Matt Henson, who knew how to take a sighting but not how to translate it into positional data. On 6 April 1909, Peary's journal announces that the goal had been achieved. Not in the notebook itself, where the approach to the Pole is mentioned neither on the journey out nor back, but on loose sheets, which cover the crucial days of 7 and 8 April.[21]

On the continental glacier at the South Pole, Amundsen had had several members of his expedition take astronomical sightings to eliminate any possibility of error. But as Peary was alone, what categorical proofs could he give of having actually been at the Pole? His journal? It would be kept from public examination (and continues to be so). Wally Herbert, the only researcher to have been allowed by the family and the National Geographic Society (in 1989) to examine the journal, remained skeptical as to Peary's attainment of the Pole (see Note 21). At 90°, a latitude shot was made, but the magnetic variation was not recorded.[22] Yet Peary, who was an excellent navigator, had always made scrupulous note of it on all his expeditions. On this occasion, however, he had no wristwatch with which to check the astronomical time. As to the photographs (a hundred or so) taken at his insistence by Matt Henson, they were never returned to their author or published, although an examination of the shadows could have provided evidence in the debate as to whether Peary reached the Pole.[23] Another regrettable fact was that the sounding gear, an essential piece of equipment for establishing the expedition's presence at the Pole, was partly unusable. Peary had, as mentioned, left part of it on shore at the start of his dash to the Pole, and was only able to confirm Nansen's hypothesis that the ocean above 85° N was more than 600 m deep.[24]

On the final stages, Peary had with him only four Eskimos and Matt Henson. The Eskimos—as I was informed in January 1951 by Uutaaq, their leader—were very concerned about the return trip, since the 1905-1906 expedition had almost met with disaster on its return. Everyone felt great tension. As the sea ice drifts, the pack can break off from shore, leaving a fracture zone that is uncrossable by sled. Peary had not brought a collapsible boat. And the sledges, according to Uutaaq, had to be constantly repaired, causing serious delays. Finally, it appears that Peary and Matt Henson had a heated argument at the Pole—or what passed for the Pole—but we will never know its subject. The group was in danger, and its members were in disagreement.

Had Henson, who was ten years younger than Peary (by then severely handicapped by the loss of his toes), offended his master and elder by arriving at the "Pole" first? Whatever the cause of the argument, Henson remained loyal to Peary until his death and only mentioned that Peary barely spoke to him four times from the Pole until they were back aboard the ship.

Peary's return to Cape Columbia was particularly strange because of its speed. Yet his party could not simply retrace their outward path on the return, since the drift of the sea ice had disrupted some of their passages through the pressure ridges. A comparison of Bartlett's times with Peary's is surprising. Peary was exhausted (he was fifty-four years old), yet he traveled, inexplicably, at a speed never equaled in the history of arctic journeys. Bartlett left 87° 47′ N on 1 April and reached the ship in 24 days (24 April). Peary left 90° N on 8 April and reached the ship in eighteen days (26 April), only two days after Bartlett.

As laconic as Peary could be in daily life, his behavior on arriving back at the ship was nonetheless surprising. His

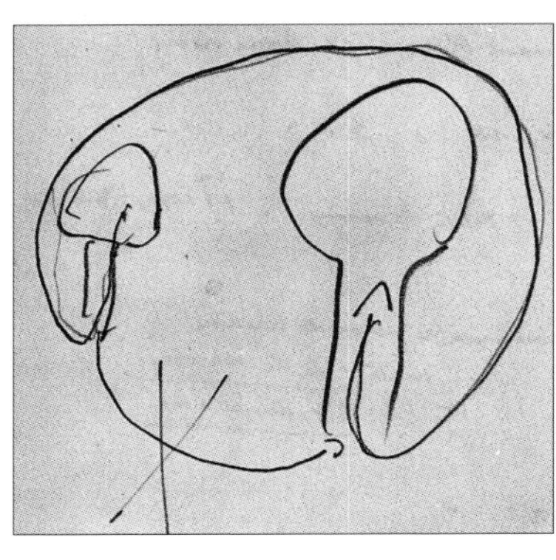

The route that must be taken by a woman who is under taboo (miscarriage) to visit a neighboring family in another igloo. (Siorapaluk, 1967: Imina.) These taboos among people traumatized by the Church have been insufficiently explored by ethnologists. They reveal a pantheistic understanding of the universe and space. Left, right (male, female; north, south); the four cardinal points; the continent (at the igloo's back) versus the sea (facing the igloo's entrance). Feng-shui, the yin and yang of the Eskimos of Asia, is the inspiration for this spatial pantheism, distant and obscure as it is.

MATTHEW HENSON

Matt Henson (1865-1955) was born in Virginia. Peary's junior by ten years, he always remained loyal to him, only saying, in substance: "Peary could sometimes be cold, but over the years we got used to each other. We had a little argument at the Pole, but that's all I'll ever say." His complex, Melvillian personality has never been adequately studied.

companions watched with emotion, a single question racing through their minds: success or failure? To Bartlett's question, he answered coldly and cryptically: "The northern trip was entirely satisfactory."

Was Peary sure that he had reached the Pole? He was in fact haunted by the idea that Cook had been successful. Psychologically, he was a broken man, and his anxieties would become nightmares. The *Roosevelt* steamed south from the Arctic Ocean and put in at Etah on the way. The Eskimos in Etah informed Peary that Cook was very much alive. They had seen him. Furthermore, after a year's expedition over the Arctic Ocean and on Ellesmere Island, he was traveling toward Denmark. At Cape York a few days later, a whaling captain confirmed that Cook had been seen and claimed furthermore to have reached the Pole. The effect on Peary was electric. [25] Until then he had repressed his fears and lingered in the beloved land of the Inuit (to which he would never return), but he now announced clearly to his companions that he had reached the Pole and abruptly decided to sail at full speed for the nearest North American telegraph station in Labrador. On arriving in Labrador, he cabled the news of his victory with characteristic terseness: "Stars and Stripes nailed to the Pole."

He would wait before describing his trip to the press. Wait for what? Perhaps until he had seen the article Cook wrote for the *Herald Tribune* (a 250-word telegram on 8 April, and a 2500-word one on 9 April) describing his route and the geography of the Pole. As Hugh Eames remarked: "Dr. Cook's account is his own. . . . Peary was only the second to report on his arctic voyages out and back." And Eames has claimed that Peary read a copy of Cook's account before sending out his own telegram. This point is hard to confirm.

It is at any rate noticeable that in all his writings on the region near the Pole, Peary is laconic and sticks close to Cook's observations: variable cold from latitude 88° or 89° N to the Pole, ice conditions improving after 88° N, no land, ice unbroken by open water.

The confrontation

On his return to New York, Peary not only expressed his contempt for Cook in violent terms, he now publicly raised the question of Cook's veracity. At the same time he experienced a long and serious bout of depression—a fact that has only recently come to light. What did it mean? And why was it hidden? Public opinion favored Dr. Cook, who had traveled more or less alone and reached the Pole first. Americans like pioneers. His elegance and high-mindedness were admired. Peary, on the other hand, seemed to deal poorly with the press and scientific organizations. He hid behind institutions and grew ever more distant. The information he gave was sometimes contradictory. He agreed to be judged only by the National Geographic Society, a private organization that was undividedly on his side, since it had sponsored his expedition. He asked to be believed on the strength of his word. The Société de géographes in Paris wisely proposed the formation of an international committee of arbitration, with no American experts, a suggestion that Peary and his group regarded as insulting. [27]

But Peary would soon find insults and defamatory accusations leveled at him. Cook wrote the president of the United States a letter accusing his competitor of being "a degenerate, a debauchee, a pornographer, a seducer, and an assassin." A campaign led by a small group of senators and

Drawing by Igguanguaq-Uutaaq, born in 1919. Qaanaaq, 1982.

Tupilak of walrus ivory, which I received as an *aarnguaq* (amulet). A good spirit, *pilluarnaqtuq*, sculpted by Pualuna (brother of Uutaaq) and slipped into my pocket by him to protect me during my expedition. Siorapaluk, 22 December 1950.

Detail of the theodolite used by Peary in 1898.

21) "In search of Peary's entry for the sixth of April—that date so fateful, so memorable, I came upon one headed 'Thursday, April 8,' then had to turn back past four blank pages before finding one headed 'Wednesday, April 7'—his second day at the Pole. This also was blank. The pages before it, his entry for April 6, made no mention of the Pole. Instead, a loose leaf had been inserted: 'The Pole at last!!! The prize of three centuries, my dream & ambition for 23 years. *Mine* at last. I cannot bring myself to realize it. It all seems so simple & commonplace . . .' "When did Peary write that note, and why is it on a separate piece of paper? If, as Peary says in his book *The North Pole*, he wrote it 'after awaking' the afternoon of April 6, then one would expect it to appear right on the diary page for that date. But it does not. Dismayed that his diary offered absolutely no record of Peary's activities during the 30 hours he and his companions spent in the vicinity of the North Pole, I then stumbled upon another mystery. On the cover, in his own hand, there is a surprisingly incomplete inscription: 'No. 1, Roosevelt to ____ & Return, Feb. 22 to Apr. 27, 1909, R. E. Peary, U.S.N.' He gives the date of his return to land, crosses it out, and puts his return to the ship. Why did he not insert 'North Pole,' those two words that spelled out his very reason for living?" (Wally Herbert, "Did Peary Reach the Pole?" *National Geographic Magazine*, September 1988, p. 389) This is by the same Wally Herbert who, for his part, unquestionably did reach the Pole by dog sled on 6 April 1969 and wrote these superb words: "It had been an elusive spot to find and fix—the North Pole, where two separate sets of meridians meet and all directions are south. Trying to set foot upon it had been like trying to step on the shadow of a bird that was hovering overhead, for the surface across which we were moving was itself a moving surface on a planet that was spinning about an axis beneath our feet."

22) The first magnetic measurements at the Pole would be made on 26 May 1926 by General Umberto Nobile, who flew there with Amundsen and was therefore the first scientifically verifiable discoverer of the Pole.

23) The analysis of these rare photographs by Peary and Cook has allowed experts to make certain deductions on the basis of the shadows cast and thus to give the latitude on a stated day.

24) Mapping of the ocean floor has subsequently shown that in reaching the Pole, Peary would have followed the west slope of the Lomonosov Ridge, whose maximum depth is 1000 meters. The Pole itself is east of the Lomonosov Ridge in Fram Basin, which has a depth of 4150 m (± 10 m). Had Peary taken depth readings, his itinerary could have been fixed with more certainty.

25) A wealthy hunter named Harry Whitney, who boarded the *Roosevelt* at Etah and rode it to North Star Bay (which would be renamed "Thule" in autumn 1909), has testified that Peary and his eight companions did not state clearly that they had reached the Pole.

26) "Stars and stripes, nailed to the Pole."

27) The Royal Geographical Society of Britain awarded Peary its gold medal, but only with the greatest reluctance. The results of the determining vote were: eight for and seven against, with two abstentions.

Column raised in 1930 by the Peary family in the explorer's honor. It stands on top of Cape York, surveying Melville Bay, where the Polar Inuit were discovered by Sir John Ross on 10 August 1818.

Trail-marking cairn of flat stones, of a kind traditionally built on high spots at major points along a route. Knud Rasmussen, 1917. South of Washington Land.

orchestrated by Senator Henry Hegelsen (North Dakota) tried to have Peary stripped of his title of admiral. He was publicly called a "fur trader," and a "deliberate liar." Senator Robert Macon denounced him as a crook, the author of "a lie pure and simple." In Cook's book, *My Attainment of the Pole* (New York: 1913), there appears a photograph of Aleqasina, the mother of Kaalipaluk, whom the Eskimos knew to be Peary's son. In the Danish census he now bears his father's name. Cook captioned the photograph: "Polar tragedy: a deserted child of the Sultan of the North and its mother." [28]

But let us leave these miasmas for the more solid ground of astronomical proof. The course that Peary followed to the North Pole is so unclear that the Naval Affairs Subcommittee, charged with investigating the matter in 1911, concluded its long hearing, during which Peary was vague, evasive, and unable to recall, with these words from its chairman, Senator Butler: "We have your word for it, and we have these observations to show that you were at the North Pole. That is the plain way of putting it, your word and your proofs. To me, as a member of this committee, I accept your word; but your proofs I know nothing about."

In 1911 the Naval Affairs Subcommittee passed the Peary Bill, recognizing that the admiral had reached (but not discovered, the words were debated) the North Pole. The vote, after heated discussion, was four to three. One senator on the committee, dissenting, said: "The more I investigated and studied the story, more thoroughly convinced I have become that it is fake pure and simple." We should note that Peary refused to show his astronomical data to the committee for obscure reasons of copyright. As Professor Gustave Galle, an astronomer from Berlin, said after studying Peary's documents: "None of Peary's methods are certain. Even had he reached the Pole, he would not have known it!"

"When Peary returned," wrote General Greely, head of the American expedition during the First International Polar Year (1882-1884), "I thought he had reached the Pole and, like every American, I was delighted. Yet after reading his various, rather contradictory, accounts, I came to the sad conclusion that he had not reached his goal." From 7 to 10 November 1983, during the 1st International Scientific Congress on the Pole, over which I had the honor to preside at the CNRS in Paris, a commission directed by Michael Richey, president of the (British) International Association of Navigation Institutes, examined the documents communicated to our congress by the geographical societies that awarded medals to the conquerors of the Pole and concluded that the matter lay beyond all scientific debate, for lack of appropriate documentation. Such was the verdict of a commission reporting to an international congress of polar experts that counted four explorers who had reached the Pole. [29] This assessment was delivered dispassionately seventy-four years later. The investigations conducted by the geographical societies at the time concerning the polar navigation of Peary and Cook were practically nil. "A determined fraud," remarked Michael Richey, "would, after all, have had no difficulty falsifying his observations. It is unfortunate that so little first-hand evidence is available to the serious researcher."

Peary's last years: silence and isolation

Let us return to 1910: Peary refused to take part in any debate with the press or the public, or in any scientific discussion. He wrapped himself in his role as a public figure—the conqueror of the Pole—and lived in seclusion at his house on Eagle Island with his mystery. He died of pernicious anemia on 20 February 1920 at the age of sixty-five and was buried at Arlington National Cemetery with full honors.

As to Matt Henson, that other conqueror of the Pole, who was ignored because of his race, he wound up with a small post at the federal customs house in New York. There is no evidence that Peary ever made provisions for his well-being, any more than for his faithful friends the Polar Eskimos. No trust or foundation was ever established by Peary to benefit them, although he knew at first hand their poverty and deprivation.

Though he received invitations from the Explorers' Club of New York, Matt Henson often declined because he was unable to pay for his meal there. [30] His death on 8 March 1955 went unnoticed. Yet he too was a Polar conqueror. The same goes for the four Inuit, Peary's companions in 1909, who would die neglected by American government and media.

---

28) In the text Cook says only: "In the white, frozen North a tragedy was enacted which would bring tears to the hearts of all who possess human tenderness and kindness. This has never been written. To write it would still further reveal the ruthlessness, the selfishness, the cruelty of the man who tried to ruin me. Yet here I prefer the charity of silence, where, indeed, charity is not at all merited."

29) Present were (with the date of their attainment of the Pole in parentheses): Wally Herbert (6 April 1969); Captain MacLaren (8 August 1978); Waldo Lyon (17 March 1959); Guido Monzino (19 May 1971). On hand as well were the widow of General Umberto Nobile (26 May 1926), Iggiannguaq Uutaaq, the son of Uutaaq, Peary's companion in 1908-1909 (6 April 1909).

30) In Thule in July 1951, Uutaaq, a member of the Explorers' Club, showed me the gilded invitations he received in the mail from them.

31) "My name is Iggiannguaq Uutaaq, I am sixty-three years old, I am a hunter, and I come from Qaanaaq (Thule). I thank the scientists who invited me, and especially Malaurie, and who have made it possible for me to be here today. My father was Uutaaq. Uutaaq was the leader of the Eskimos who were Piulersuaq's (Peary's) partners during his expeditions to the Pole. Uutaaq was the leader of the Eskimos for very many years. He went to the North Pole in the spring with Peary and four other people. Uutaaq, my father, said that he planted the flag at the North Pole and that Peary was the leader of that expedition; and all the Inuit said the same thing. Uutaaq, my father, and all the Inuit also said that Tatsekuk—which was our name for Dr. Cook—did not go to the Pole. He did not tell the truth. Dr. Cook didn't tell the truth. He was with two young men, Aapilaq and Ittukusuk, and I myself heard Aapilaq and Ittukusuk say that Tatsekuk did not tell the exact truth about the North Pole. Tatsekuk left Anoritooq in the winter to go to Canada. He stayed in Canada during the summer, the fall, and the winter. In the spring he came back to Anoritooq." Such was the statement (spoken in Greenlandic), by Iggiannguaq at the International Polar Congress, the 10th International Congress of the Center for Arctic Studies, CNRS, Paris, 7-10 November 1983. The statement was published in *Pôle Nord 1983* (Paris: 1987), pp. 203-205.

Peary's best defenders: the Inuit

Speaking to me of the conquest of the North Pole, one of the last living witnesses to it, Uutaaq, described Peary's victory to me thus: "*Piulersuaq kisiani*," or "the great Peary, he alone." Thirty-two years later, I found the same admiration for Peary in his son, Iggiannguaq Uutaaq. Invited by the CNRS Congress on the Pole, from 7 to 10 November 1983, he gave an official endorsement of Peary. [31] Most of the Polar Inuit will never doubt his victory, and I can testify to the great respect they felt toward the man they called their "great tormentor."

It was that same "great tormentor" who, in 1897, took their four meteorites away—their source of metal since time immemorial—to sell them for personal profit for $40,000.

The Inuit are more or less aware of this plunder. But they are honored nonetheless to have helped accomplish a feat that redounds to their credit, even if the Polar myth was foreign to them. By his systematic policy of giving the natives modern equipment—rifles, tools, wood, boats, household goods—in return for services, Peary radically transformed Eskimo life. Of course, Peary took good care that the Inuit would have no ammunition for their firearms after he left and would therefore be at his mercy on his return. Living in the iron age (thanks to whaling vessels, to Kane and the *Advance*, and to the *Polaris* beached north of Etah, which were vast sources of iron and wood), the fifty hunters of the Polar Eskimo obtained guns in the years 1890-1900, constituting the greatest technological and social revolution in these high latitudes since prehistory. But in addition to their respect and their gratitude, the Polar Eskimos felt a deep and somewhat tender attachment to Peary. After all, he had lived in their midst for nine and a half years, and was never far from them in thought or in deed for fully eighteen years. This the Inuit expressed to me again in 1982 when I spoke to them of the column with the initial *P* that rises proudly above Cape York.

If Peary's life was devoted to one end, which was to link his name to the conquest of the North Pole, the key to the mystery of his personality is perhaps to be found, when all is said and done, in the personality of his Eskimo son, Kaalipaluk, living in Qeqertarsuaq, North Greenland. He is the proof that Peary never left them. Robert Edwin Peary found in this place his own most secret shore. ■

R. E. Peary writing his memoirs in the study of his legendary house on Eagle Island, Maine. Full of energy but complex in nature, Peary was subject to depression. He lacked literary talent, writing like a technocrat. His *The North Pole* was ghostwritten by A. E. Thomas at the publisher's request. It contains regrettable errors.

Call to an American Zola

I would like to return to certain lesser-known traits in the personality of Robert Peary, who differed considerably from his predecessors—and not only because he was one of the first to lead well-endowed private expeditions.

Minik, an Eskimo "invited" to New York by Peary in 1897 with five relatives, discovered the skeletons of his father, brother, and cousins (who had died shortly after their arrival) on display in the Museum of Natural History. In fact, at the time Minik recognized the remains of his family, he was already an adult doing odd jobs around New York. Image from Kenn Harper, *Give Me My Father's Body: The Life of Minik, the New York Eskimo* (Steerforth Press, 2000).

The behavior of the official discoverer of the Pole has its shadowy areas, one of which particularly shocks me—namely, his relations with the Eskimos. We have to remember that Peary was one of the last explorers of the colonial age. Yet given his exceptional stature as a North American icon, may we not expect a somewhat exceptional attitude toward those who were his absolutely faithful companions? Peary's relations with the Inuit are, it must be admitted, feudal. Looking out over the empty floe, swept by glacial winds, I reflected on the complex psychology of this man of somber will: I imagined Jo (Peary's wife, Josephine), Mattipaluk (Henson). Kuluntanguaq, Sivssuk, Ooqqaak, and particularly Uutaaq, father of my companion Kutsikitsoq. . . . During the long polar night, Peary could not help but appreciate the irreplaceable help he received from his Inuit companions, who were faithfully devoted to his cause and didn't hesitate to risk their lives to further his ambitions. Kaalipaluk never in the least spoke resentfully about his father, but he told me many times that he had been profoundly saddened never to receive a sign from him, either of emotional or financial support, though he remembered perfectly well living on the *Roosevelt* with him in 1908. He confided to me that his mother had on a number of occasions recommended, out of modesty, that he not vaunt being the son of the great explorer.

In these extraordinary places, one is prepared to take the modern view and respect Peary's liberated morals, yet how can we not contrast his behavior with the admittedly post-colonial behavior of Knud Rasmussen, who married in Denmark and never took an Eskimo wife in Thule, or of Peter Freuchen, who never kept house with Navarana, sister of my old friend Inuterssuaq, until he had married her and decided to live his entire life among the Inuit.

I feel compelled to discuss another aspect of Peary's behavior, which is just as reprehensible—if not more so. Peary needed ever increasing sums to finance his expeditions, a part of which he earned through his lecture tours, which were widely publicized. In order to make his publicity more sensational, Peary dreamed up the idea of "inviting" six Eskimos to take part in the tours. Standing in their furs and brandishing their harpoons, they created a sensation, but within a few months two of them died of acute tuberculosis. Peary knew perfectly well that this people had been too long sheltered to endure such brutal contact with civilization. And he willingly accepted that the skeletons of his beloved companions be given (or sold) to the American Museum of Natural History in New York. Worse still: Minik, one of two survivors of the original six, a young hunter of twenty who became a taxi driver in New York to survive, discovered on going to the museum one day in New York the skeleton of his own father displayed behind glass in an ethnographic display. There could be no doubt about it: the Eskimo's name was there on the label. Poor Minik! It was certainly his father, the father he had been searching for in this strange land, and about whose whereabouts Peary had kept a resolute silence. Minik contacted the press, and scandal erupted—before the usual cloak of silence settled over the incident.[32] As to the other young hunter, Uisaakassak, who was probably tubercular and in any case carrying pathogenic germs, he was quite simply sent back to Thule, the land of his birth, where his mere passage could have severe epidemiological consequences. This is a long way from the strict—and fair—traditions of international Arctic research. Years have passed and yet the questions raised by this incident are still open.

One cannot but be surprised that in our own era the American government has not delegated an independent and respected scientific institution to investigate the historical truth of these reports. That Peary should be presented unreservedly as the discoverer of the North Pole in even the most scholarly encyclopedias is an unfailing source of wonder, and one notices that the voices that have been raised in criticism against him—those, among others, of Senator Hegelsen, of General Greely, of Dennis Rawlins, of Hugh Eames, of Theo Wright, of Pierre Berton, of the International Congress of the CNRS on the Pole (Paris, 1983), of Sir Wally Herbert himself in *National Geographic Magazine*—have fallen largely on deaf ears in the court of public opinion. America, which likes to imagine the star-spangled banner over the Pole, seems little inclined to award the title of discoverer of the North Pole to Umberto Nobile—is it because he is Italian?—who first flew over it with Roald Amundsen and Lincoln Elsworth in the *Norge* on 26 May 1926. What we need in the field of polar history is an American Zola, a muckraker. There is never a statute of limitations on correcting an error or discovering an impostor.

And that is the reason why I have opened this question once more.[33] J.M.

32) "You are a race of scientific criminals. I know that I will never recover the bones of my father from that American Museum of Natural History," wrote Minik, before being promptly embarked for Greenland, where he was reduced to silence (1909). Another indecency: in 1897, the skeletons of recently deceased Eskimos were carried away in five large barrels—Eskimos that Peary had known personally. These remains, removed from graves, were sold to an American museum (Wally Herbert, Noose of Laurels, p. 107 and 281).

33) On 28 July 1993, the bones of the four Eskimos were transported to the Thule airbase, and from there transferred to the cemetery in Qaanaaq, the territory's capital. The publication of Kenn Harper's Minik (1986), of Wally Herbert's Noose of Laurels (1989), and the present book, Ultima Thule (1990), finally convinced the authorities at the American Museum of Natural History to concede to the earnest request of the government of Greenland.

The Journal of Josephine Diebitsch-Peary [1]

"Queer, dirty monkeys."

Josephine Diebitsch Peary performing good works among the Inuit during her husband's first expedition, 1891-1892.

August 15/06
EAGLE ISLAND
SOUTH HARPSWELL, MAINE
My Dearest.
God grant you may read
these lines not later
than Sept. 15. 06. We are all
well + waiting. I don't
feel as though I could
wait much longer.
I am very near the
end of my line
Robert is a fine boy
considering how

Letter from Josephine Peary to her husband, 15 August 1906: "My Dearest, God grant you may read these lines not later than Sept. 15, '06. We are all well and waiting. I don't feel as though I could wait much longer. I am very near the end of my line. Robert is a fine boy considering how . . ."

These Eskimos were the queerest, dirtiest-looking individuals I had ever seen. Clad entirely in furs, they reminded me more of monkeys than of human beings.[2] Ikwa, the man, was about five feet two or three inches in height, round as a dumpling, with a large, smooth, fat face, in which two little black eyes, a flat nose, and a large expansive mouth were almost lost.

Infanticide by young widows

The little girl Tookymingwah, whom we all call "Tooky," is a neat little seamstress, but is not very rapid. A few days ago her mother, named Klayuh, but always called by us the "Widow," arrived with her two younger daughters, the youngest about five years old. I asked her if she had only the three children, and she burst into tears and left the house without answering me. Turning to M'gipsu, I asked her what it meant, and she said it was "peuk nahmee" (not well) for me to ask Klayuh about other children. When I insisted upon knowing why, she took me aside and whispered that Klayuh had just killed her youngest child, about two years of age, by strangling it.[3] She went on to explain that it was perfectly right for Klayuh to do this, as the father of the child had been killed, and she could not support the children herself, and no man would take her as a wife so long as she had a child small enough to be carried in the hood. I asked her if this was always done, and she said: "Oh, yes, the women are compelled to do it."

Ethnographic inventory of a family's belongings

They brought their dog, a sledge, a tent, a kayak (or canoe),[4] and all their housekeeping utensils and articles of furniture, which consisted of two or three deerskins, on which the family slept; a stove made of soapstone and shaped like our dust-pans, in which they burned seal fat, using dried moss as a wick; and a dish or pot made of the same material, which they hung over their stove, and in which they melted the ice for drinking purposes and also heated their seal and walrus meat (I say heated, for we would hardly call it cooked when they take it out of the water). The skin tent put up, and these articles put in place, the house was considered furnished and ready for occupancy. Wood being almost impossible to procure, the tent was put up with narwhal tusks, which are more plentiful and

answer the purpose. The tent itself is made of sealskin tanned and sewed together with narwhal sinews.

Eskimo drawings. Josephine is recognizable by her long dress, Peary by his hat. Both were very tall, towering over the Inuit.

34) The journal of Josephine Diebitsch-Peary, Robert Peary's wife, is of great interest. Freer, full of examples, of scenes witnessed, it reveals customs that her husband's journal ignores.
35) "More of monkeys than of human beings": this is the way a young American woman of good education and from a Christian family described the Inughuit, in a text that is for the most part cheerful and high-minded.
36) Female infanticide is practiced when the mother dies, or during famines, when no neighboring family can adopt the child (and only during periods of dearth).
37) Here is proof that the Eskimos of this locality used kayaks in 1892. They were introduced in 1860-1863. In 1818, when first discovered by Ross, the Polar Inuit used ice cakes broken from the floe as rafts.
38) The Roosevelt was anchored east of Cape Columbia, at

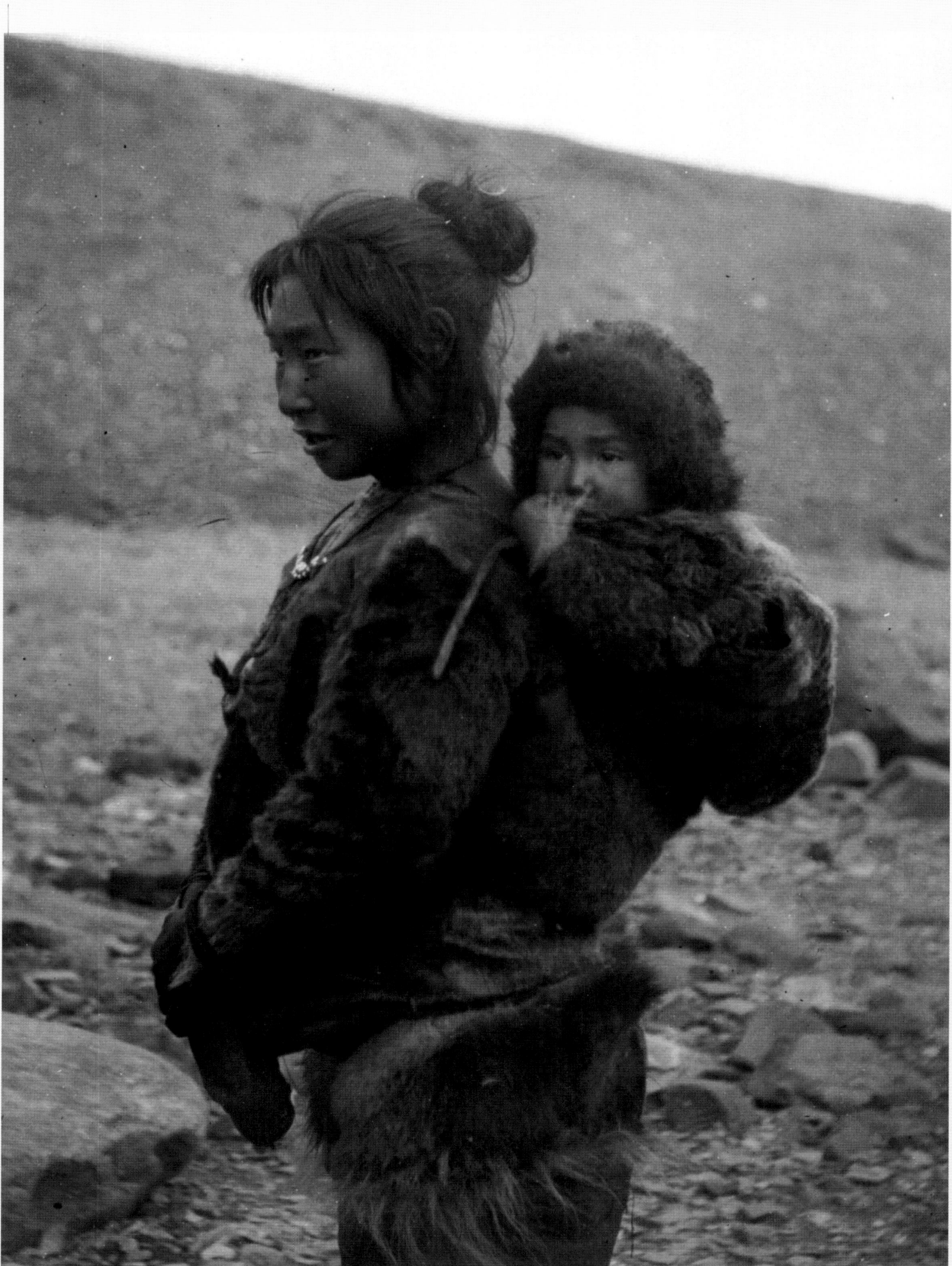

Young woman carrying her child in her *amaaq* in the traditional Inuit way, with the child "sticking" to its mother's skin. The child will suckle until the age of two or three. Inuit society is marked by a violence that is kept under control by the group. Yet there are exceptions and lapses. A hunter in his kayak killed Uisaakassek with a rifle shot to the head in 1910. Murders are often crimes of passion, there being fewer women than men in part because of female infanticide.

Two young women, Arnaruniak (21 years old) and Inadtliak (24 years old). The younger, apparently under taboo, wears the characteristic hood. Photograph taken in Thule by T. N. Krabbe, 31 June 1909.

The conquest of the Pole

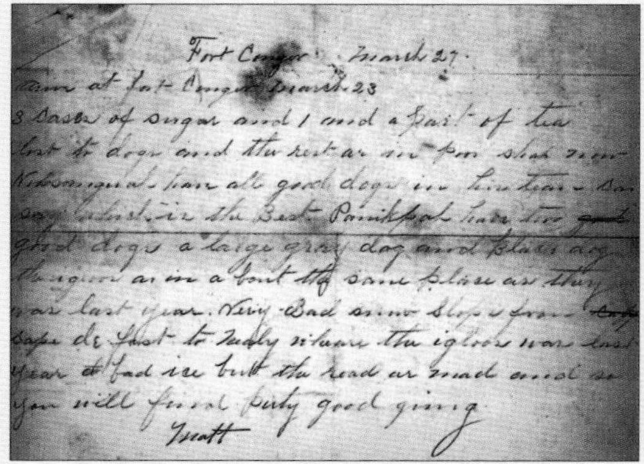

Fort Conger March 27
Arrive at Fort Conger March 23
3 casks of sugar and 1 and a part of tea
lost to dogs and the rest are in poor shape now
Nipsanguak have all good dogs in his team. Can't
say which is the Best. Panikpah have two good
good dogs a large gray dog and black dog
igloos are in about the same place as they
was last year. Very Bad snow slopes from
Cape [illegible] to nearly where the igloos was last
year bad ice but the road are made and so
you will find pretty good going.
Matt

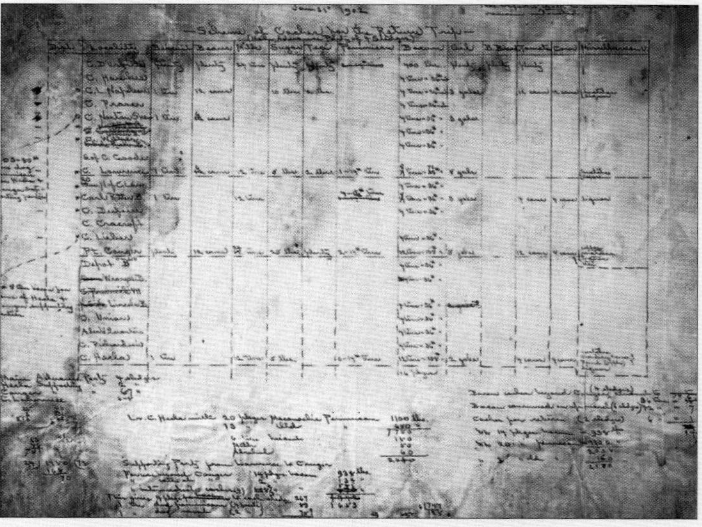

NEAR RIGHT, **letter from Matt Henson** to Peary, dated 27 March 1900: "Arrive at Fort Conger March 23. Three casks of sugar and one and a part of tea lost to dogs and the rest are in poor shape now. Nipsanguak has all good dogs in his team. Can't say which is the best. Panikpah has two good dogs, a large gray dog and a black dog. The igloos are in about the same place as they was last year. Very bad snow slopes from Cape [illegible] to nearly where the igloos was last year. Bad ice but the roads are made and so you will find pretty good going. Matt"

RIGHT, **organization chart** drawn up by Peary, 31 January 1902, detailing the food caches to be made from Cape d'Urville to Cape Hecla in anticipation of the return trip with four sledges and six men, four of them Eskimos.

CHRONOLOGY OF A FAILED EXPEDITION (1898-1902)

Equipped with weak engines, the *Windward* was unable to progress beyond Cape Sabine and enter Smith Sound at the entrance to Kane Basin. The ship therefore wintered at Cape Sabine, a few miles from the Greely expedition's Starvation Camp (1884).

The advanced base was established at Fort Conger in Lady Franklin Bay by a dog sledge expedition during the winter of 1898-1899. Peary set off impulsively in the middle of the polar night to occupy the "fort," the now-ruined cabin left by the Greely expedition. He went into a rage on learning that Otto Sverdrup was in that area on Ellesmere Island, though somewhat to the west, with a strong Norwegian expedition of cartographers and geologists. Peary feared that Sverdrup would occupy "his" territory and pre-empt "his" Eskimos. Might Sverdrup not be looking beyond his geological research toward the Pole? Who was to know? In the course of this six-week sledge journey, Peary froze both his feet and had to return to the ship to have his toes amputated.

In March 1900, Peary took up quarters at Fort Conger again and reconnoitered the north coast of Greenland as far as Cape Morris Jesup. He established that Greenland was an island. Peary spent the winter of 1900-1901 at Fort Conger. His attempts on the Pole in the spring of 1901 fell short. Peary returned to Cape Sabine for the winter of 1901-1902. In January 1902, he readied an expedition to establish a chain of caches from Cape Sabine to Cape Hecla on the Arctic Ocean in view of a dash to the Pole in March. A meticulous route was planned from cape to cape, from Cape d'Urville in the south where the ship wintered in Buchanan Bay to Cape Hecla in the north.

On 6 March 1902, Peary left Cape Sabine with new Eskimo sledges for Cape Hecla at the north end of Ellesmere Island. The polar dash over the Arctic Ocean reached latitude 84° 16' north on 21 April 1902. Peary was in despair: he had failed to reach Fridtjof Nansen's farthest point north of April 1895 (86° 13'). "The game is off. My dream of sixteen years is ended," he wrote in his journal. "I close the book and turn to others less interesting, but better suited for my years.... The goal still remains for a better man than I, or more favorable conditions, or both."

FOOD DEPOTS

A chart of the transport missions to be made in January 1902 from Cape d'Urville to Cape Hecla was drawn up in Peary's hand on 31 January 1902 to ensure caches for the return from the Pole, anticipated for the spring of 1902. The assault party of four sledges was to be manned by four Eskimos plus Matt Henson and Peary.

The chart shows Peary's cumbersome logistics and a provisioning scheme that was ill-adapted to local realities, given the partly native composition of his expedition. The food in these caches consisted, as can be seen, primarily of biscuits, beans, milk, sugar, tea, bacon, tomatoes, flour, and above all pemmican. Under "Miscellaneous" Peary lists: matches, coffee, tea, blueberry sauce, apples, and alcohol. Peary and Henson were not used to native food, which consisted primarily of dried seal, walrus, and musk ox meat. Thus a *de facto* hierarchy divided Peary and Henson from the Eskimos. Contrary to what one might think, Peary did not adapt greatly to Eskimo life. While he used Inuit labor on a massive scale, he maintained a "white" mode of existence.

Food for the Eskimos does not figure in the document. It is lumped in with the dog food: pemmican and seal, walrus, and musk ox meat. Other than the tea, the white man's food would have been largely distasteful to the Eskimos, who do not eat bacon or vegetables. The whole of this provisioning scheme is intended for two of the six men in the party. We should mention that Peary and the other whites drank alcohol in front of the Eskimos, though they avoid mentioning it.

The primary assault party consisted of four sledges; the support party at Cape Hecla of two sledges; the support party at Fort Conger of six or seven sledges; the Lawrence support party of six to eight sledges.

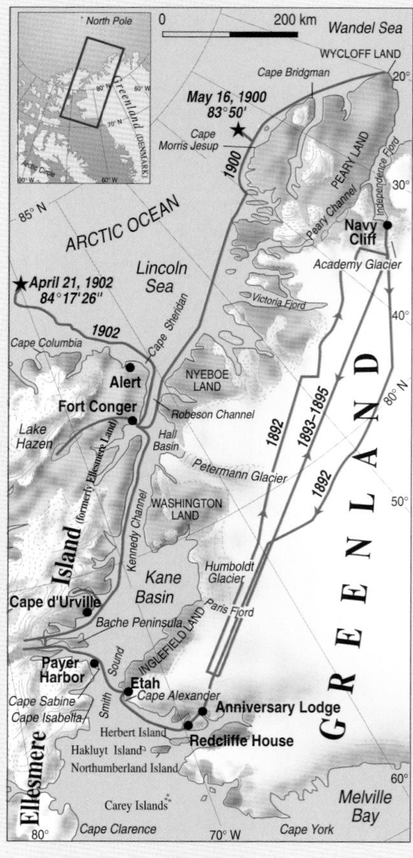

Peary's expeditions toward the Pole, across the ice cap in 1892 and 1895, and on the Arctic Ocean in 1900 and 1902.

The
American Geographical Society
No. 15 West 81st Street
New York

May 24, 1904

Dear Sir;

I send you under separate cover a map for your consideration in connection with my article.

I enclose suggestions concerning the same, the idea being that the map be reproduced as a full page.

Very truly
R. E. Peary

Mr. Wm. Taylor

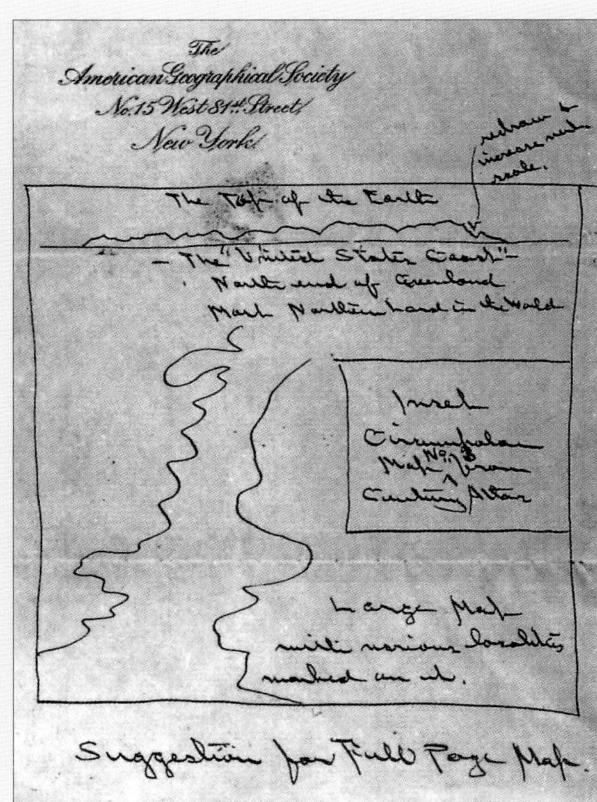

The
American Geographical Society
No. 15 West 81st Street
New York

The Top of the Earth

– The "United States Coast" –
North end of Greenland
Most Northern Land in the World

Insert
Circumpolar
Map No. 3 from
Century Atlas

Large Map
with various localities
marked on it.

Suggestion for Full Page Map.

Unpublished letter from Peary to the journal of the American Geographical Society, 24 May 1904, along with a map and suggestions for the layout. His instructions reveal his ambition, which is to give North Greenland to the United States: "The 'United States Coast,' North end of Greenland, Most Northern Land in the World." At the top of the map he had sketched an elevation of "The Top of the Earth." A prescient vision, if one considers the ambitions of the U.S. Air Force in Thule since 1951.

THE EXPEDITION OF 1905 TO 1906: a new farthest point north of 87° 6' (21 April 1906)

Route of Peary's dash toward the Pole in 1906:
a. route of the *Roosevelt* in summer 1905 from Etah to Cape Sheridan;
b. route by dog sled along the coast in winter 1906 from Cape Sheridan to Point Moss;
c. dash in winter 1906 from Point Moss to 87° 6' and return to the ship via Cape Morris Jesup;
d. summer 1906: homeward route of the *Roosevelt* along the Greenland coast.

Peary's route toward the Pole in the spring of 1906 was a daring one, and he reached 87° 6' north. His experience had been primarily on the ice cap, not on the polar pack, which is subject to drifting. The caches deposited on the sea ice were lost due to the action of the currents, which trend west from 86° to 88° and southeast from 88° to 90°. At 85° north, 50° west, Peary was carried toward the southeast. The return to Cape Morris Jesup was dangerous as food ran out and the party met large open-water channels they were unable to cross. Oddly, Peary carried no collapsible boats on his sledges. Nor would he carry any in 1909. The *Roosevelt* only managed to free itself from the ice at Cape Sheridan in late August. Note that the ship was only able to travel south by hugging the Greenland coast, a further demonstration of the faulty instructions given Greely to stay along the Canadian coast, which is always obstructed by ice from the Arctic Ocean.

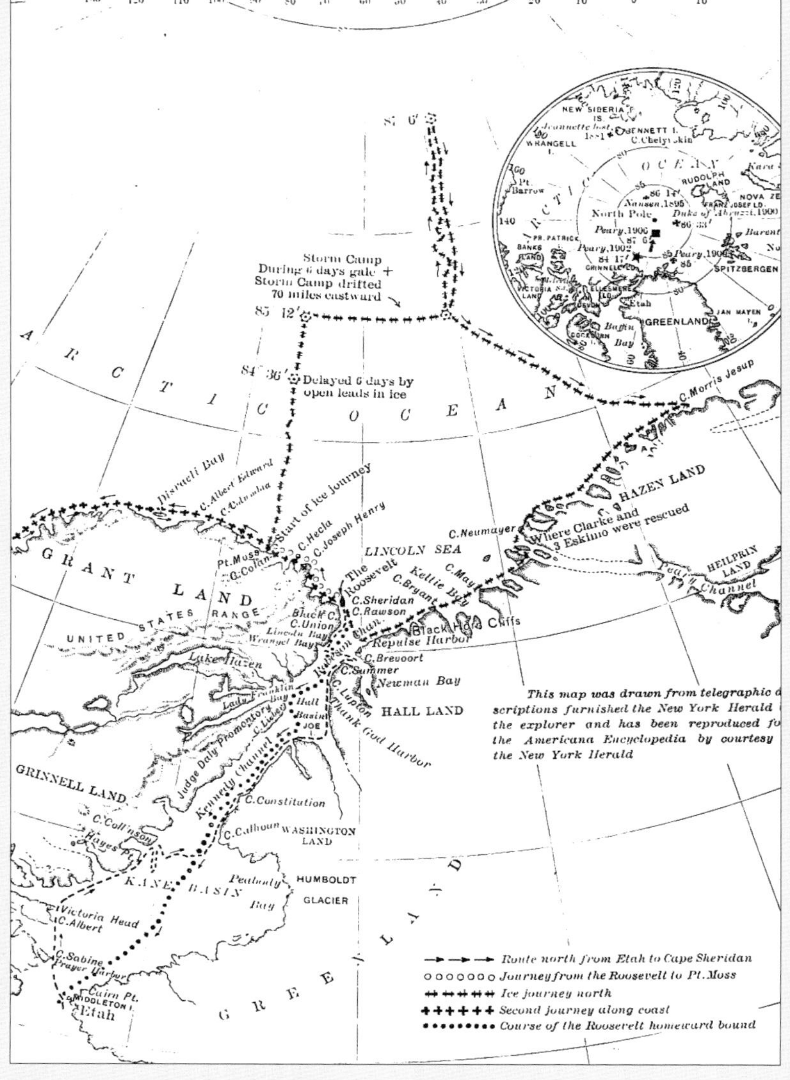

Map of the 1905-1906 expedition, drawn up by the *New York Herald* according to Peary's descriptions. Notice the long eastward drift at 85° 12' caused by a storm that lasted six days. The expedition almost ended tragically. Peary proved to have exceptional courage and sang-froid, which was confirmed to me by Uutaaq.

Message in Peary's handwriting left under a cairn on 28 June 1906 and found by McMillan on the north coast of Greenland during his expedition of 1914-1917.

The Arctic Ocean is a large undersea trench more than 3000 meters deep, traversed by three major ridges: the Lomonosov Ridge, the Nansen Ridge, and the Alpha Cordillera. The North Pole is situated above the eastern slope of the Lomonosov Ridge.

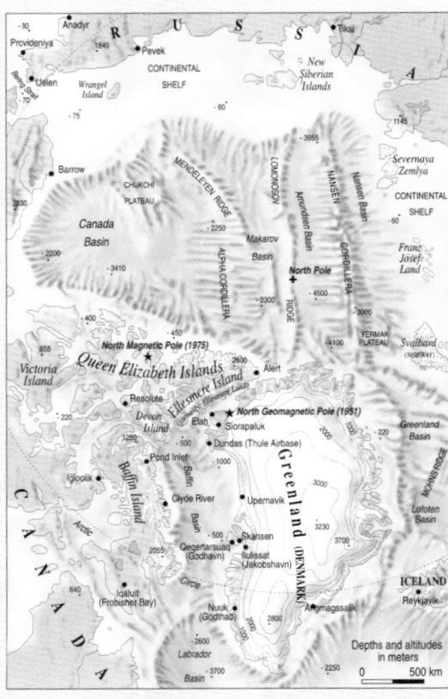

Map of the territory of the Polar Inuit drawn up in 1893-1894 by Jason W. Davidson, the expedition's cartographer. On McCormick Bay sits Redcliffe House, where Peary wintered with Cook and where his first daughter, Anighito, was born. At the head of Bowdoin Bay is Anniversary Lodge, Peary's second overwintering site in 1893-1895. In Robertson Bay, Kokan (Kughat) lies across from the site of the future village of Siorapaluk, where I wintered in 1950-1951.

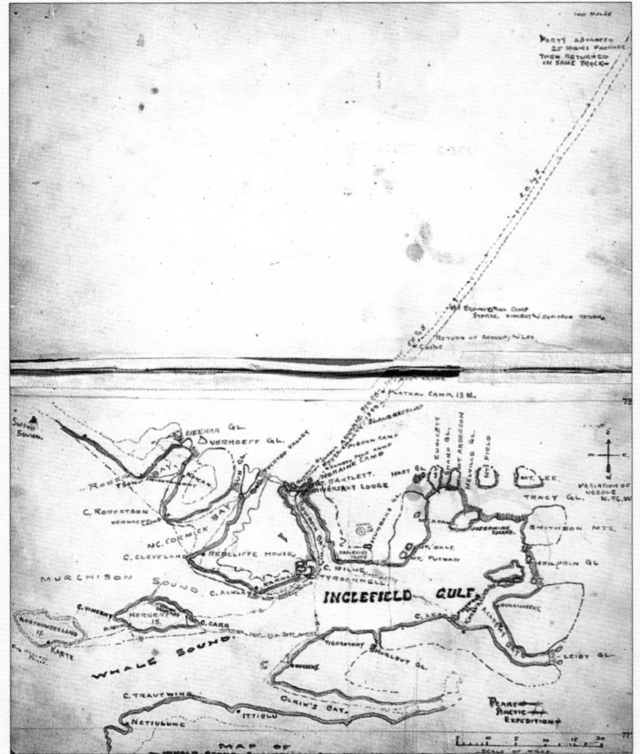

THE "PEARY SYSTEM"

His expeditions were organized along military lines with ultra-modern equipment and dog teams fed an overabundance of pemmican. He used a system of relays, with successive parties breaking trail, leaving food depots, and falling back to base, until the final polar party of five sledges carried on from 87° 47' north.

Peary and the Eskimo Uutaaq, along with Peary's black companion Henson and three other Eskimos, were forging ahead across the hummocks of the polar pack that sometimes rise to fifty feet. The Inuit played an essential role: they directed their light, flexible sledges bravely and intelligently through the least fractured sections. Peary's more massive sledges often broke in falling from the hummocks up which they had been hauled. The Inuit who remained at base camp—the *Roosevelt* off Cape Sheridan on northeastern Ellesmere Island—formed a group of some fifty individuals, who had been helping with preparations for the push to the Pole of March-April 1909 since July 1908. Women and children wintered near the ship in snow igloos. This suggests the intimacy of the Peary expedition with each of the twenty Polar Eskimo families taking part in the endeavor. The Eskimos were motivated simultaneously by their taste for adventure, their respect and admiration for Peary, and their growing need for wood, iron, rifles, tools, boats, foodstuffs, and the various goods and benefits in kind that were part of the salary Peary offered, with bonuses promised for the successful attainment of the Pole. It became apparent that the polar explorers, spurred on by a desire to set records, were often approximate or wrong in their sightings, either because their training was inadequate—they were after all doctors (Kane, Hayes, Cook), engineers (Peary), printers (Hall)—or because of the adverse conditions.

The first accurate maps were made by the geographer Bessels (1872), British navy officer Nares and his crew (1875-1876), and cavalry lieutenant Greely (1881-1884), who led a scientific expedition that included cartographers.

The errors made by Peary in his geographical surveys are legendary: the nonexistent Crocker Land of the arctic seas, and the supposed insularity of Peary Land, etc. And Cook was neither a geographer nor a navigator. But the earlier transgressions place the debate over Peary and Cook in their proper context.

It should be noted that the Peary archives have been withheld from public scrutiny and their contents only partially revealed. Peary's journal, in which he recorded his astronomical observations, was never given to the Naval Affairs Committee for examination. If we are to believe his account, the average distance per day that he covered in his last eight days of sledging—exclusive of any detours—was forty-four miles. Sir Wally Herbert, in sixteen months of the polar pack in 1968-1969, only once made good 26 miles in a day. And this performance was the result of "fifteen hours of sustained progress over an excellent ice surface, with fresh dogs and light loads."

In the United States, as in Europe until the end of the nineteenth century, science was the province of a coterie of men of honor, each believing in the others' word. It was the Peary-Cook controversy that, in the field of geographic exploration, put an end to this ancient and tacit covenant. The competing claims of the two explorers quickly gave rise to sharp and inconclusive debate.

When Geographical Societies gave Peary and Cook gold medals, thus authenticating the exploits claimed by these polar explorers, it was on the basis of rumor and reputation. A scientific review of the records was never undertaken. The statements and publications of the explorers were accepted as sufficient evidence. It is worth noting that the gold medal bestowed on Peary by the Paris Geographic Society does not explicitly refer to Peary as the North Pole's discoverer.

The sail-assisted sledge used by Peary on his trek across the ice cap in 1891-1892. Photograph by Robert Peary.

The voice of Peary

Departure toward the Pole

It was ten o'clock on the morning of February 22d—Washington's Birthday—when I finally got away from the ship and started on the journey toward the Pole. This was one day earlier than I had left the ship three years before on the same errand. I had with me two of the younger Eskimos, Arco and Kudlooktoo, two sledges and sixteen dogs. The weather was thick, the air was filled with a light snow, and the temperature was 31° below zero . . .

When I finally got away from the ship, there were in the field, for the northern work, seven members of the expedition, nineteen Eskimos, one hundred and forty dogs, and twenty-eight sledges. As already stated, the six advance divisions were to meet me at Cape Columbia on the last day of February . . .[38]

When I awoke before light on the morning of March 1st, the wind was whistling about the igloo. This phenomenon, appearing on the very day of our start, after so many days of calm, seemed the perversity of hard luck. I looked through the peep-hole of the igloos and saw that the weather was still clear, and that the stars were scintillating like diamonds. The wind was from the east—a direction from which I had never known it to blow in all my years of experience in that region. This unusual circumstance, a really remarkable thing, was of course attributed by my Eskimos to the interference of their arch enemy, Tornarsuk—in plain English, the devil—with my plans . . .[39]

One by one the divisions drew out from the main army of sledges and dog teams, took up Bartlett's trail over the ice and disappeared to the northward in the wind haze. This departure of the procession was a noiseless one, for the freezing east wind carried all sounds away. It was also invisible after the first few moments—men and dogs being swallowed up almost immediately in the wind haze and the drifting snow.

The "Big Lead"

All the next day we were still there beside the lead. Another day, and we were still there. Three, four, five days passed in intolerable inaction, and still the broad line of black water spread before us. Those were days of good traveling weather, with temperatures ranging from minus 5° to minus 32°, a period of time which might have carried us beyond the 85th parallel but for those three days of wind at the start which had been the cause of this obstruction in our course. 40

During those five days I paced back and forth, deploring the luck which, when everything else was favorable—weather, ice, dogs, men, and equipment—should thus impede our way with open water . . .

Each day the lead continued to widen before us, and each day we looked anxiously southward along the trail for Marvin and Borup to come up. But they did not come.[41]

Only one who had been in a similar position could understand the gnawing torment of those days of forced inaction, as I paced the floe in front of the igloos most of the time, climbing every little while to the top of the ice pinnacle back of the igloos to strain my eyes through the dim light to the south, sleeping through a few hours out of each twenty-four, with one ear open for the slightest noise, rising repeatedly to listen more intently for the eagerly desired sound of incoming dogs—all this punctuated, in spite of my utmost efforts at self-control, with memories of the effect of the delay at the "Big Lead" on my prospects in the previous expedition. Altogether, I think that more of mental wear and tear was crowded into those days than into all the rest of the fifteen months we were absent from civilization . . .[42]

The protracted delay, hard as it was upon all the members of the expedition, had a demoralizing psychological effect upon some of my Eskimos. Toward the end of the period of waiting I began to notice that some of them were getting nervous. I would see them talking together in twos and threes, just out of earshot. Finally two of the older men, who had been with me for years and whom I had trusted, came to me pretending to be sick. I have had sufficient experience to know a sick Eskimo when I see one, and the excuses of Pooadloonah and Panikpah did not convince me. I told them by all means to go back to the land just as quickly as they could, and to take with them a note to Marvin, urging him to hurry.[43]

A fix: 85° 48' north

Up to this time no observations had been taken. The altitude of the sun had been so low as to make observations unreliable. Moreover, we were traveling at a good clip, and the mean estimate of Bartlett, Marvin, and myself, based on our previous ice experience, was sufficient for dead reckoning. Now, a clear,

Peary's parallel watches.

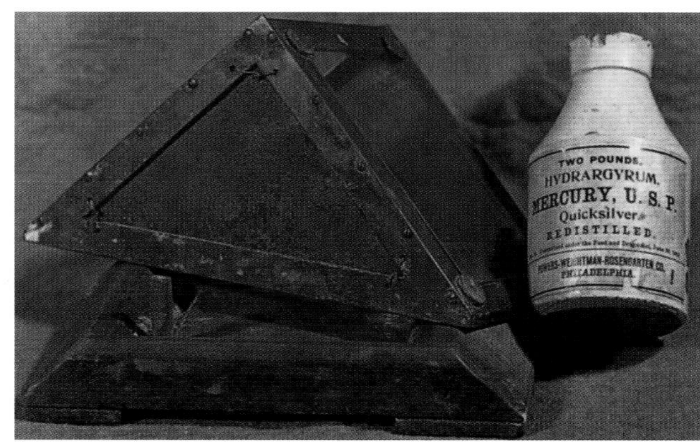

An artificial horizon and a flask of mercury that belonged to Peary.

Cape Sheridan, and it was from Cape Columbia that Peary wanted to start north over the Arctic Ocean.

39) The east wind in North Greenland is the wind coming off the inland ice-cap, the land of the qiviqtuq, supernatural beings who rob the souls of those who have tormented them.

40)It is incomprehensible that Peary had no collapsible boat or raft. Cook included in his equipment a collapsible canvas boat, which saved his life (and that of his two companions) on several occasions. Peary was a victim of the "heaviness" of his military-style operation. In 1891-1892, and 1893-1895, he had operated as a commando. Peary had aged, and knew it.

41) Marvin and Borup had been sent back to base camp for supplies of alcohol and petrol, the rations having been poorly calculated at the start.

42) Peary tactfully omits any mention of his troubles with Eskimos at this stage.

43) Only the authority of Piulersuaq (the "Great Peary") prevented the Eskimos from quitting all at once and disbanding Eskimo-style. Uutaaq, who had a difficult temperament, played a key mediating role at this crucial juncture—I heard this from his own lips in 1950. What terrified the Inuit was the possibility of being cut off from the continent by fractures, as in 1906, and losing their dogs and their lives.

44) It is inconceivable that Peary could have maintained an accurate course without any coastal landmark, in fog that veiled the sun, among ice barriers that hemmed the horizon, for hundreds of miles from the coast to 85° 48' north. The contrary drift of the pack, during the frequent stops to repair the constantly breaking sledges, and the detours around pressure ridges inevitably led to a sinuous route. Constant astronomical observations were necessary to maintain one's orientation. Later expeditions to the Pole (Wally Herbert's in 1968-1969, and Guido Monzini's in 1971) have proven this amply. Though they had air support and radio direction finders, these expeditions were initially off by seven and six miles respectively. Nansen took longitude observations daily during his traverse of the Arctic Ocean, and he was still anxious about his actual position, given the sporadic and contrary drift of the pack.

Difficult progress over ice hummocks, which form barriers fifteen to thirty feet high. Photograph apparently taken in April 1909.

The "Peary System" of relaying parties in action. The dogs of the forerunner teams, performing double duty, were killed to provide fresh meat. "It was hot, and [the Eskimos] seemed thoroughly to enjoy it."

calm day, with the temperature not lower than minus forty, made a checking of our dead reckoning seem desirable. So I had the Eskimos build a wind shelter of snow, in order that Marvin might take a meridian altitude for latitude. I intended that Marvin should take all the observations up to his farthest, and Bartlett all beyond that to his farthest. This was partly to save my eyes, but principally to have independent observations with which to check our advance.[44]

Constant mortal danger

I was just dropping off to sleep when I heard the ice creaking and groaning close by the igloo, but as the commotion was not excessive, nor of long duration, I attributed it to the pressure from the closing of the lead which was just ahead of us; and after satisfying myself that my mittens were where I could get them instantly, in an emergency, I rolled over on my bed of deerskins and settled myself to sleep. I was just drowsing again when I heard some one yelling excitedly outside.

Leaping to my feet and looking through the peephole of our igloo, I was startled to see a broad lead of black water between our two igloos and Bartlett's, the nearer edge of water being close to our entrance; and on the opposite side of the lead stood one of Bartlett's men yelling and gesticulating with all the abandon of an excited and thoroughly frightened Eskimo.[45]

Awakening my men, I kicked our snow door into fragments and was outside in a moment. The break in the ice had occurred within a foot of the fastening of one of my dog teams, the team escaping by just those few inches from being dragged into the water. Another team had just escaped being buried under a pressure ridge, the movement of the ice having providentially stopped after burying the bight which held their traces to the ice. Bartlett's igloo was moving east on the ice raft which had broken off, and beyond it, as far as the belching fog from the lead would let us see, there was nothing but black water. It looked as if the ice raft which carried Bartlett's division would impinge against our side a little farther on, and I shouted to his men to break camp and hitch up their dogs in a hurry, in readiness to rush across to us should the opportunity present itself.

Then I turned to consider our own position. Our two igloos, Henson's and mine, were on a small piece of old floe, separated by a crack and a low pressure ridge, a few yards away, from a large floe lying to the west of us. It was clear that it would take very little strain or pressure to detach us and set us afloat also like Bartlett's division.

87° 46' 49" north: Peary and Bartlett separate

On Bartlett's return the Eskimos built the usual wind shelter already described, and Bartlett took a latitude observation, getting 87° 46' 49".

Bartlett was naturally much disappointed to find that even with his five-mile northward march of the morning he was still short of the 88th parallel. Our latitude was the direct result of the northerly wind of the last two days, which had crowded the ice southward as we traveled over it northward. We had traveled fully twelve miles more than his observation showed in the last five marches, but had lost them by the crushing up of the young ice in our rear and the closing of the leads.

Bartlett took the observations here, as had Marvin five camps back partly to save my eyes and partly to have independent observations by different members of the expedition. When the calculations were completed, two copies were made, one for Bartlett and one for me, and he got ready to start south on the back trail in command of my fourth supporting party, with his two Eskimos, one sledge, and eighteen dogs.

. . . I had given him the post of honor in command of my last supporting party for three reasons: first, because of his magnificent handling of the *Roosevelt*; second, because he had cheerfully and gladly stood between me and every possible minor annoyance from the start of the expedition to that day; third, because it seemed to me right that, in view of the noble work of Great Britain in Arctic exploration, a British subject should, next to an American, be able to say that he had stood nearest the North Pole.[46]

With the departure of Bartlett, the main party now consisted of my own division and Henson's. My men were Egingwah and Seegloo; Henson's men were Ootah and Ooqueah. We had five sledges and forty dogs, the pick of one hundred and forty with which we had left the ship. With these we were ready now for the final lap of the journey.

We were now one hundred and thirty-three nautical miles from the Pole.

"Let us now praise famous men"

My four Eskimos carried the dogs, sledges, ice, and cold as their racial heritage. Henson and Ootah had been my companions at the farthest point on the expedition three years before.[47] Egingwah and Seegloo had been in Clark's division, which had such a narrow escape at that time, having been obliged for several days to subsist upon their sealskin boots, all their other food being gone.

And the fifth was young Ooqueah, who had never before served in any expedition; but who was, if possible, even more willing and eager than the others to go with me wherever I should elect. For he was always thinking of the great treasures which I had promised each of the men who should go to the farthest point with me—whale boat, rifle, shotgun, ammunition, knives, et cetera—wealth beyond the wildest dreams of Eskimos, which should win for him the daughter of old Ikwa of Cape York, on whom he had set his heart.

All these men had a blind confidence that I would somehow get them back to land. But I recognized fully that all the impetus of the party centered in me. Whatever pace I set, the others would make good; but if I played out, they would stop like a car with a punctured tire. I had no fault to find with the conditions, and I faced them with confidence.

No racial inheritance of daring and initiative

Henson, with his years of arctic experience, was almost as skillful at this work as an Eskimo. He could handle dogs and sledges. He was a part of the traveling machine. Had I taken another member of the expedition also, he would have been a passenger, necessitating the carrying of extra rations and other impedimenta. It would have amounted to an additional load on the sledges, while the taking of Henson was in the interest of economy of weight.[48]

The second reason was that while Henson was more useful to me than any other member of my expedition when it came to traveling with my last party over the polar ice, he would not have been so competent as the white members of the expedition in getting himself and his party back to the land. If Henson had been sent back with one of the supporting parties from a distance far out on the ice, and if he had encountered conditions similar to those which we had to face on the return journey in 1906, he and his party would never have reached the land. While faithful to me, and when *with me* more effective in covering distance with a sledge than any of the others, he had not, as a racial inheritance, the daring and initiative of Bartlett, or Marvin, MacMillan, or Borup. I owed it to him not to subject him to dangers and responsibilities which he was temperamentally unfit to face.

. . . As the Eskimos worked away at repairing the sledges while we rested there on the first day of April, they stopped from time to time to eat some of the boiled dog which the surplus numbers in Bartlett's returning team had enabled them to have.[49] They had killed one of the poorest dogs and boiled it, using the splinters of an extra broken sledge for fuel under their cooker. It was a change for them from the pemmican diet. It was fresh meat, it was hot, and they seemed thoroughly to enjoy it. But though I remembered many times when from sheer

Peary and the media. The Peary Arctic Club proved very effective at international publicity.

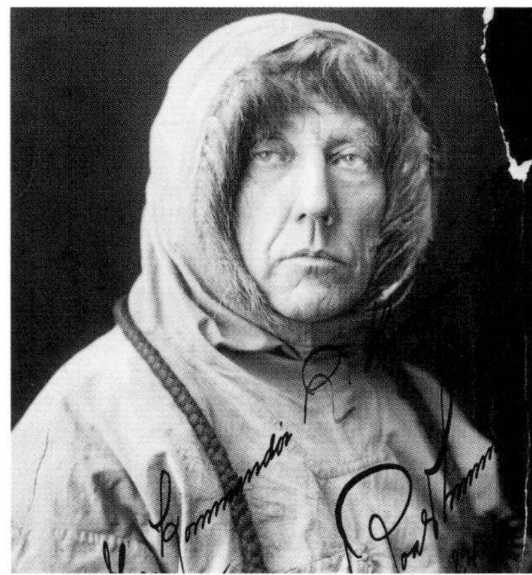

Roald Amundsen (Oslo), a great explorer, the first to transit the Northwest Passage (1905) and the first to reach the South Pole (1911), remained a staunch friend of Cook. But he had clear reservations about Peary, who was feared, fragile, and a loner.

45). Peary's laconic manner and natural reserve give little indication of the extreme physical dangers that he faced during his eight expeditions.

46) Bartlett was Canadian, and Canada was under British dominion. Loyal as he was, he rebelled against this decision for a brief moment, so near and accessible did the Pole seem. Bartlett's presence at the Pole with Peary a week later would have removed all ambiguity about whether the long-sought goal had been attained. In the racist America of 1910, Peary was reproached in the inner circles of Boston and Washington society for allowing a "Negro" to reach the Pole before himself. He would never have been forgiven for opening the door for a "Brit."

47) Uutaaq was the leader of the Eskimo group. A strong personality, he asked his son Kutsikitsoq to be my companion. The reference books make no mention of these discoverers of the Pole. For the first time in November 1983, at the First International Polar Congress, the Paris Geographical Society at my insistence honored a Polar Eskimo, Uutaaq's son, Iggiannguaq (Kutsikitsoq, who died on 10 November 1979, was his half-brother), awarding him before the entire congress the same silver medal of the Geographical Society as had been awarded to the other discoverers. In 1910, no honors were given to them by any American scientific society. On my 1:200,000 map, Uutaaq has been honored with a fjord in his name, near Cape Agassiz.

48) Matt Henson posed a problem for Peary, who was attacked by white racists in Boston, New York, and Washington for the exceptional place he gave him. Peary always remained faithful to him. Note the white man's condescension toward the black, who "lacked initiative." Henson could fix their position approximately by dead reckoning, noting the hours traveled and the speed of the sledges in his notebook. Marvin had introduced him to solar observations. He was the first to arrive at the Pole ("Commander, isn't it here?" he said), and Peary never forgave him this discourtesy, refusing to speak to him until they reached New York. He reviewed the text of Henson's book and confiscated the 100 photos Henson had taken. He never helped Henson find employment commensurate with his title of discoverer of the Pole. Henson held a lowly job at the federal customs house in New York and retired with a very modest pension.

49) Dog gave more "strength" than pemmican, according to the Eskimos.

Peary on the bridge of the *Roosevelt* in Inuit-made fur clothes such as he wore on his eight expeditions to the Pole.

starvation I had been glad to eat dog meat raw, I did not feel inclined to join in the feast of my dusky friends.

The ice smoother toward the top of the globe

It was a fine marching morning, clear and sunlit, with a temperature of minus 25°, and the wind of the past few days had subsided to a gentle breeze. The going was the best we had had since leaving the land. The floes were large and old, hard and level, with patches of sapphire blue ice (the pools of the preceding summer). While the pressure ridges surrounding them were stupendous, some of them fifty feet high, they were not especially hard to negotiate, either through some gap or up the gradual slope of a huge drift of snow. The brilliant sunlight, the good going save for the pressure ridges, the consciousness that we were now well started on the last lap of our journey, and the joy of again being in the lead affected me like wine. The years seemed to drop from me, and I felt as I had felt in those days fifteen years before, when I headed my little party across the great ice-cap of Greenland, leaving twenty and twenty-five miles behind my snowshoes day after day, and on a spurt stretching it to thirty or forty.[50]

...The moon had been our friend during the long winter, giving us light to hunt by for a week or two each month. Now it seemed no longer a friend, but a dangerous presence to be regarded with fear. Its power, which had before been beneficent, was now malevolent and incalculably potent for evil.

When we awoke early in the morning of April 3, after a few hours' sleep, we found the weather still clear and calm.

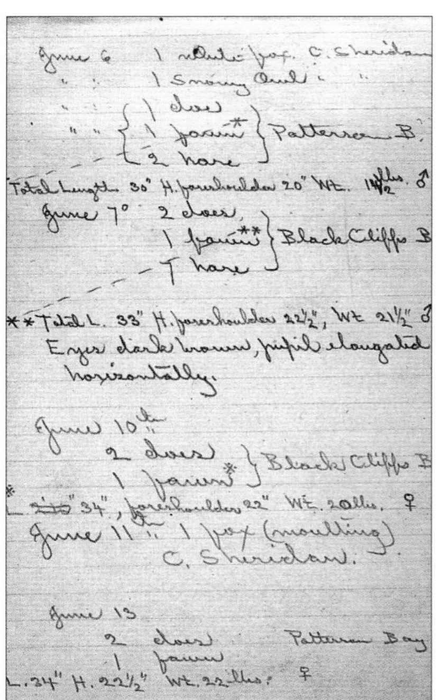

June 6 1 white fox. C. Sheridan
" " 1 Snowy Owl " "
" " { 1 doe / 1 fawn* / 2 hare } Patterson B.
Total Length 30" H. foreshoulder 20" Wt. 14½ lbs. ♂
June 7° 2 does, / 1 fawn** / 1 hare } Black Cliffs B
** Total L. 33" H. foreshoulder 22½", Wt 21½" ♂
Eyes dark brown, pupil elongated horizontally.
June 10th 2 does / 1 fawn* } Black Cliffs B
* L 34", foreshoulder 22" Wt. 20 lbs. ♀
June 11th 1 fox (moulting) C. Sheridan.
June 13 2 does / 1 fawn Patterson Bay
L. 34" H. 22½" Wt. 22 lbs. ♀

Peary's journal from 6 to 11 June 1909, that is, between his arrival back on the *Roosevelt* and the ship's departure for the south and the United States. There was nothing of a personal nature about the conditions met by the expedition on its return but, instead, details of the game caught: fox, owl, deer, hare; and a dry listing of the hunting grounds: Patterson Bay, Black Cliffs, Cape Sheridan.

50) In July 1886, on the Greenland ice-cap, at 68° north (the so-called Disko expedition.

51) The ice became harder and more unified beyond 88°. The fear that haunted Peary—and the Inuit he had in tow—was of being cut off from land (North Greenland) by channels of open water, as in 1905-1906; but he did not know that on that particular year the pack became increasingly uniform near the Pole. Cook had observed the same phenomenon the year before.

52) The Marvin affair is obscure. Having talked to Eskimos loyal to him, Peary knew immediately that it was the Eskimos who had killed Marvin—a fact we now know thanks to an official Danish investigation. We also know: 1) that Peary covered for the Eskimos; and 2) that it is against Eskimo rules to kill a white companion, the expedition leader's friend, and to throw away the victim's personal effects, particularly his private journal. From Marvin's correspondence we know that he was shocked, as Peary's secretary, at his chief's hatred for Cook—this as early as July 1908—and sensed that trouble was brewing. His posthumous letters confirm it. What could this lost journal have contained?

There were some broad heavy pressure ridges in the beginning of this march, and we had to use pickaxes quite freely. This delayed us a little, but as soon as we struck the level old floes we tried to make up for lost time. As the daylight was now continuous we could travel as long as we pleased and sleep as little as we must. We hustled along for ten hours again, as we had before, making only twenty miles, because of the early delay with the pickaxes and another brief delay at a narrow lead. We were now half-way to the 89th parallel, and I had been obliged to take up another hole in my belt.

Some gigantic rafters were seen during this march, but they were not in our path. All day long we had heard the ice grinding and groaning on all sides of us, but no motion was visible to our eyes. [51]

Peary's only astronomical observation after 87° 46' is at . . . 90°

The last march northward ended at ten o'clock on the forenoon of April 6. I had now made the five marches planned from the point at which Bartlett turned back, and my reckoning showed that we were in the immediate neighborhood of the goal of all our striving. After the usual arrangements for going into camp, at approximate local noon, of the Columbia meridian, I made the first observation at our polar camp. It indicated our position as 89° 57'.

. . . Everything was in readiness for an observation at 6 p.m., Columbia meridian time, in case the sky should be clear, but at that hour it was, unfortunately, still overcast. But as there were indications that it would clear before long, two of the Eskimos and myself made ready a light sledge carrying only the instruments, a tin of pemmican, and one or two skins; and drawn by a double team of dogs, we pushed on an estimated distance of ten miles. While we traveled, the sky cleared, and at the end of the journey, I was able to get a satisfactory series of observations at Columbia meridian midnight. These observations indicated that our position was then beyond the Pole.

Return to the Roosevelt: why was Marvin killed?

We reached Cape Hecla in one march of forty-five miles and the *Roosevelt* in another of equal length. My heart thrilled as, rounding the point of the cape, I saw the little black ship lying there in its icy berth with sturdy nose pointing straight to the Pole.

. . . As we approached the ship I saw Bartlett going over the rail. He came out along the ice-foot to meet me, and something in his face told me he had bad news even before he spoke.

"Have you heard about poor Martin?" he asked.

"No," I answered.

Then he told me that Marvin had been drowned at the "Big Lead," coming back to Cape Columbia. The news staggered me, killing all the joy I had felt at the sight of the ship and her captain. It was indeed a bitter flavor in the cup of our success. It was hard to realize at first that the man who had worked at my side through so many weary months under conditions of peril and privation, to whose efforts and example so much of the success of the expedition had been due, would never stand beside me again. The manner of his death even will never be precisely known. No human eye was upon him when he broke through the treacherous young ice that had but recently closed over a streak of open water. [52]

THE ARCTIC OCEAN IS CLAIMED BY THE UNITED STATES.

6 April, 1909. 90° Lat. N. North Pole. I have today raised the flag of the United States on this spot, which my observations inform me to be the North Pole of the earth's axis, and I have formally taken possession of the entire region and those adjacent to it for and in the name of the president of the United States of America.

I leave these documents and this flag as a sign of possession.

ROBERT PEARY
U.S. Navy.

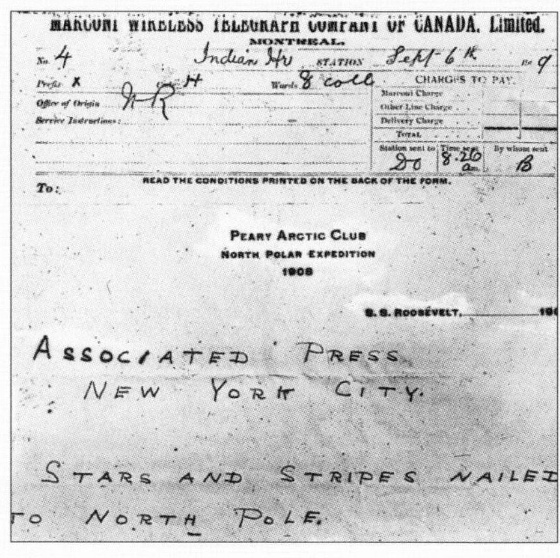

MARCONI WIRELESS TELEGRAPH COMPANY OF CANADA, Limited.
MONTREAL.
No. 4 Indian Hr STATION Sept 6th 19 9
Prefix X Code H Words 8 coll CHARGES TO PAY.
Office of Origin IHR
Service Instructions:
Station sent to Do Time sent 8.26 am By whom sent B
READ THE CONDITIONS PRINTED ON THE BACK OF THE FORM.
To:
PEARY ARCTIC CLUB
NORTH POLAR EXPEDITION
1908
S. S. ROOSEVELT, 190
ASSOCIATED PRESS
NEW YORK CITY.
STARS AND STRIPES NAILED TO NORTH POLE.

Peary's famous telegram announcing his victory: "Stars and Stripes nailed to North Pole."

"All the News That's Fit to Print."

The New York Times.

THE WEATHER.

NEW YORK, THURSDAY, SEPTEMBER 9, 1909. ONE CENT

COOK NOT NEAR POLE, SAYS PEARY; PROOFS STILL HELD BACK BY COOK

Two Eskimos Cited by Cook Told Peary He Never Went Far from Land.

SAYS "I HAVE COOK NAILED"

Cables His Wife Not to Worry About the Doctor's Claim to the Pole.

COOK TO ASK FOR AN INQUIRY

COMMANDER PEARY'S PRELIMINARY ACCOUNT OF HIS SUCCESSFUL VOYAGE TO THE NORTH POLE

He Sends to The Times by Wireless a Summary, to be Followed by His Full Report—Record of His Swift Progress to the Utmost North.

FROM CAPE COLUMBIA UP IN 37 DAYS, BACK IN 16 DAYS

Prof. Ross G. Marvin, of Cornell, Drowned on April 10, Forty-five Miles North of Cape Columbia, While Leading the Supporting Party.

BATTLE HARBOR, Labrador, Via Wireless Cape Ray, N. F., Sept. 8.—As it may be impossible to get my full story through in time for to-morrow's TIMES, partly as a prelude which may stimulate interest and partly to forestall possible leaks, I am sending you a brief summary of my voyage to the North Pole, which is to be printed exactly as written.

SUMMARY OF NORTH POLAR EXPEDITION OF THE PEARY ARCTIC CLUB.

The steamer Roosevelt left New York on July 6, 1908; left Sydney on July 17; arrived at Cape York, Greenland, August 1; left Etah, Greenland, August [illegible]; arrived Cape Sheridan, [illegible] September 1; wintered at Cape Sheridan.

The sledge expedition left the Roosevelt February 15, 1909, and started for the North. Arrived at Cape Columbia March 1; passed British record March [illegible]; delayed by open water March 2 and 3; held up by open water March 4 to 11; crossed the 84th parallel March 11; encountered open lead March 15; crossed 85th parallel March 18; crossed 86th parallel March 22; encountered open lead March 23d; passed Norwegian record March 23d; passed Italian record March 24th; encountered open lead March 26th; crossed 87th parallel March 27th; passed American record March 28; encountered open lead March 28; held up by open water March 29; crossed 88th parallel April 2; crossed 89th parallel April 4; North Pole April 6.

All returning left North Pole April 7, reached Cape Columbia April 23, arriving on board Roosevelt April 27.

The Roosevelt left Cape Sheridan July 18, passed Cape Sabine August 8; left Cape York August 26; arrived at Indian Harbor with all members of expedition returning in good health except Prof. Ross G. Marvin, unfortunately drowned April 10, when forty-five miles north of Cape Columbia, returning from 86° North Latitude in command of the supporting party.

ROBERT E. PEARY.

MAP SHOWING PEARY'S ROUTE TO THE POLE.

NORTH POLE
ARCTIC OCEAN
GREENLAND SEA
GREENLAND
BAFFIN BAY
BAFFIN LAND
DAVIS STRAIT

The *New York Times* on 9 September 1909. In the three left-hand columns, Peary's dismissal of Cook's claims: the controversy had begun. Cook would respond from Copenhagen by asking for an investigation and the convening of a jury of scientists. In the two right-hand columns, above the map, Peary's preliminary account, describing the stages of his expedition.

Did Peary reach the Pole?

The data at our disposal today do not allow us, in point of fact, to arrive at a certain scientific conclusion in the controversy between Peary and Cook. The first incontrovertible discoverer of the Pole by the overland route, in this case by snowmobile, was the American Ralph Plaisted, on 20 April 1968. The Englishman Sir Wally Herbert reached the Pole by dog sledge on 6 April 1969.

JEAN MALAURIE,
President of the First International Congress on the North Pole, CNRS, Paris 1983.
First Frenchman to the North Geomagnetic Pole (29 May 1951)

FAR RIGHT, **a photograph** taken by Peary at the "Pole." From left to right, Sigloo (Sivdlu), Uutaaq with his musk ox boots, Matt Henson, Eginwah, and Ooqueah.

NEAR RIGHT, **return from the Pole.** The Morris Jesup camp, on the way to Cape Columbia.

Sir Wally Herbert arbitrates

Departure toward the Pole

The mass of floating ice that covers the Arctic Ocean like a skin is in constant motion. Driven by the winds and currents as though it were boiling, the ice forms a chaotic expanse of broken floes and pressure ridges, whose fractures, leads, and sometimes even "seas" of open water lie across the path of those whose ambition it is to reach the Pole.

Yet Peary claimed that in the spring of 1909, in a stupendous time of 53 days, he was able to reach the Pole directly and return to his point of departure at Cape Columbia on the north coast of Ellesmere Island, crossing this fractured and moving surface, without once taking the trouble to measure his longitude, check the drift of the pack, or consult a compass to orient himself.

From my own experience, I know perfectly well that such a feat is impossible. But I also know from having studied this unusual man for twenty years that Peary had no intention of deceiving the world. It is my firm conviction that in fact he was unaware of his error when he made his first solar observations at what was to be his northernmost camp. And my conviction is corroborated by the behavior of his loyal companions, who in their innocence believed him at his word and were persuaded they had reached their goal.

To understand the nature of Peary's error, there is no need to look farther than his inextinguishable—and destructive—thirst for glory, and his tragic illusion of having been "elected" to discover the North Pole. This explains why a man of such great experience could have neglected to take into account the drift of the ice and, in consequence of this neglect, chose the *wrong* direction.

But even though he failed in his last attempt on the Pole (by one degree, I believe), there is not the shadow of a doubt that Peary showed extraordinary willpower and a truly exceptional courage.

And what is to be said about his rival, Dr. Cook, who claimed that he reached the Pole with two companions a year before Peary? I have never ceased, and will never cease, to admire the *known* exploits of this much-maligned man, in particular his 1908 journey whose route I followed step for step in 1967 along with two companions and three dog teams. But even if we can attest to the first part of his extraordinary voyage, as far as the great cliffs of Svartevoeg, when it comes to the remainder of his progress over the Arctic Ocean, the affable doctor's claims are supported neither by his Eskimo companions, nor by the photographs in his book which he claims

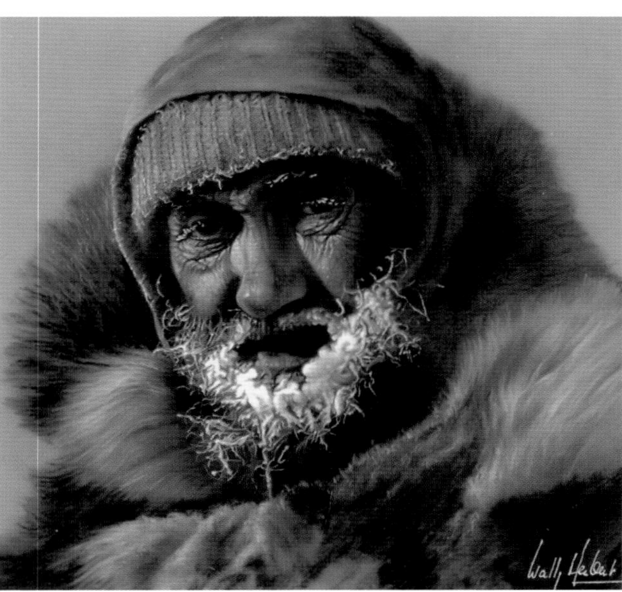

Wally Herbert, at the Pole on 6 April 1969.

Likely route of Robert Peary toward the North Pole in March-April 1909, according to Sir Wally Herbert.

(or seems to claim) to have taken during his voyage on the pack ice in the spring of 1908. Some of his partisans still claim that one of these photos—entitled "Bradley Land"—does represent an island of ice. Another snapshot is described—rather confusedly—as showing a submerged island in the Arctic Ocean (according to Cook, a floe several years old at a latitude of 88 degrees—some 120 miles from the Pole). Alas, these photographs, far from confirming Cook's claims, undermine them completely.

As an instance, the photo of his two companions entitled "First camp at the North Pole, 21 April 1908" shows one of them wearing *kamiks*, or boots, made of musk-ox hide, whereas these were not made until several months later when the three men were at Cape Sparbo. The "Bradley Land" photo is another fake, as an attentive examination makes clear: it is not an island of floating ice some 200 miles from all land, but the northwest coast of Axel-Heiberg Island.

Yet it was the fortuitous discovery in the Library of Congress of an original snapshot of the island said to be "in the Polar Sea" that finally convinced me: Cook had used a photograph of a glacier (after cropping the land that could be seen on one side) and claimed in the caption and the corresponding passage in his text that the photo had been taken on his outward voyage, only two degrees from the Pole . . .

It is the explorer's responsibility to obtain proof of his exploits. Unquestionably, neither Peary nor Cook returned with sufficient proof to support their claims. Of the two possible conclusions, this is the more generous; the other is that the two men lied . . . If one were to measure those lies in terms of distance from the Pole, Cook's would be the bigger by far.

SIR WALLY HERBERT
British discoverer of the North Pole, 6 April 1969.
(Unpublished text, 17 July 1989)

Peary's sledges were massive and rounded in front (unlike those of the Inuit, which were light and slender); they often broke in getting across the hummocks, thus slowing the pace in 1909, according to Uutaaq.

A hydrographer's opinion

More than eighty years have now passed since Robert Peary announced that he had reached the North Pole on 6 April 1909. A navy engineer, he was subsequently promoted to the rank of rear admiral, after lengthy and heated discussions in the United States Congress. Since then, debate about his exploit has continued, forming the noose of laurels that gives the title to Wally Herbert's latest book on this subject (April 1989).

Three months earlier, on 9 January 1909, Ernest Shackleton reached a point 97 miles from the South Pole, for which he was knighted by King Edward VII and acclaimed by all. How are we to explain the difference? The key was in their methods of navigation: it is up to the explorer to provide the proof of his discoveries and to make them public. On his Antarctic foray, Shackleton traveled with three members of his expedition: Adam, who recorded meteorological observations; Marshall, who registered topographic data; and Wild, who noted the geology. When Shackleton took an observation of the sun, he had each member of the crew verify it. All this was published and used by Scott and Amundsen, who followed him, and not the slightest objection was ever raised on this score.

With Peary the situation was entirely different. On his last voyages, in 1906 and 1909, Peary eliminated all white companions from his party, keeping with him only his black servant and four Eskimos who were incapable of taking observations or judging those made by Peary. Furthermore, Peary kept no meteorological records, though the wind plays a determining effect on the drift of the pack—and on the position of the explorer. Finally, he claimed to have reached the Pole after traveling 413 nautical miles as the crow flies without any observations of his longitude or magnetic declination. The U.S. Congress questioned Peary at length but asked the wrong questions and accepted his unlikely account—as did the National Geographic Society, which has defended Peary for the past eighty years. In September 1988 the society published an article by Wally Herbert which for the first time cast serious doubt on Peary's claims. In point of fact, Wally Herbert, a confirmed British explorer of the Arctic and the Antarctic, was the first to reach the North Pole by dog sled, on 6 April 1969.

In the last ten years, several explorers have retraced Peary's voyage: the Japanese Uemara in 1978, the American Steger and the Frenchman Etienne in 1986. Their daily distances are commensurate with each other, but only half of what Peary claimed to have attained after his last white companion turned back. As to the astronomic observations made by Peary on 6 and 7 April 1909, everything points to his having falsified them to make it appear as though he had been at the Pole. Peary kept his expedition journal private, but Wally Herbert was recently allowed to examine it at the National Archives in Washington: it proved to be fabricated and unprofessional. Yet nine years earlier, Peary had discovered and located the northernmost point in Greenland, Cape Morris Jesup (R. Lillistrand, *Canadian Surveyor*, 1970). Why would a man of his competence and courage fake results? Wally Herbert points out that the discovery of the Pole had become his unique obsession. We should add that he had no alternative to claiming victory—there were his backers in the Peary Arctic Club, Cook's competing claim (even if false), public opinion, and his promises to the president of the United States, Theodore Roosevelt. A year later, Scott would face similar pressures, and, because of his integrity, he and his companions met with a tragic death.

BERTRAND C. IMBERT
Chief Hydrographic Engineer (CR),
Leader of the French Antarctic Expeditions of the International Geophysical Year 1956-1959, 23 June 1989

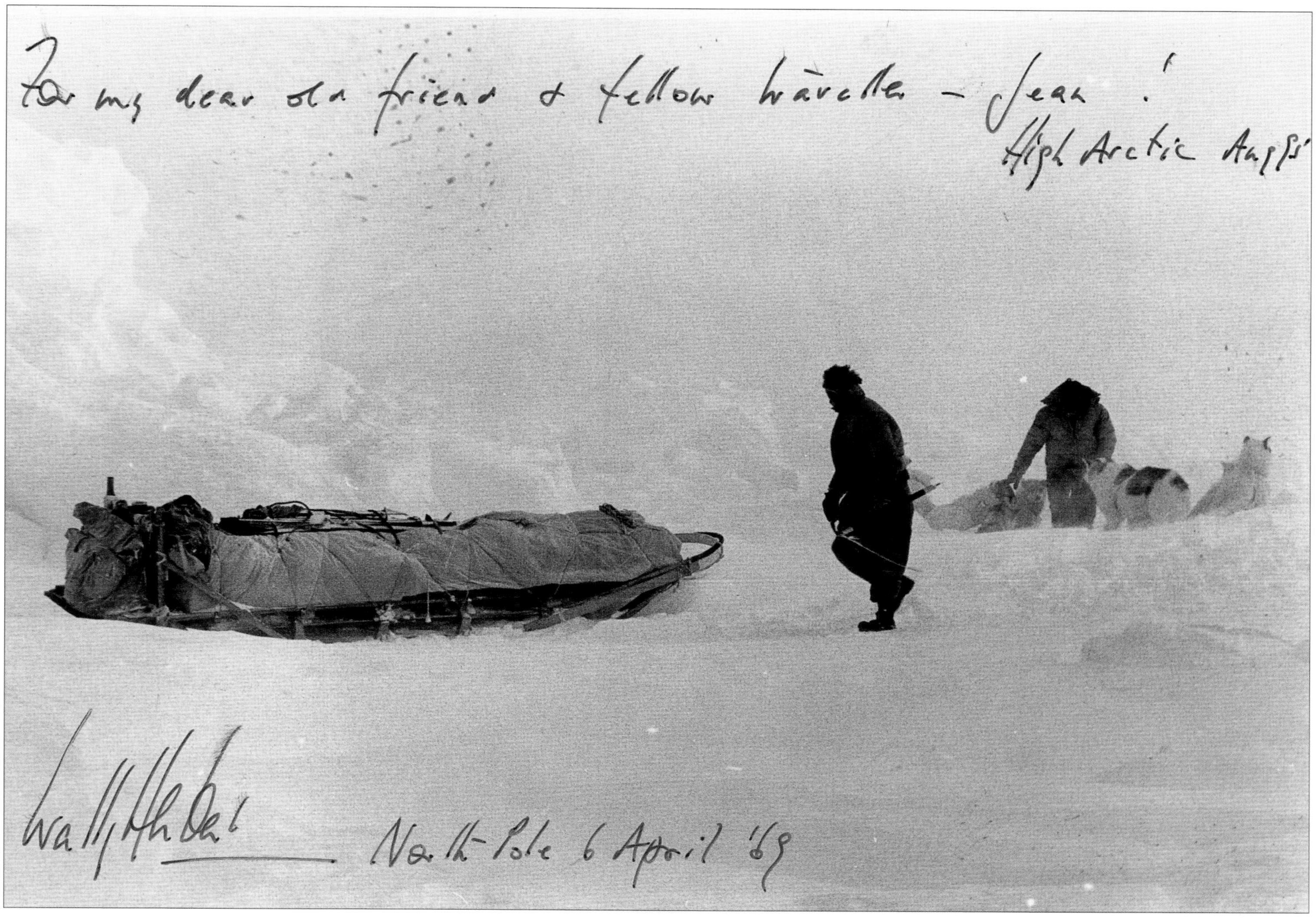

Sir Wally Herbert (knighted in April 2000) reached the North Pole on 6 April 1909 during the first recorded surface transit of the Arctic Ocean from Alaska to Spitsbergen. This photograph was inscribed to the author during a joint trip in the high Arctic in August 1995.

The Polar Eskimos: a walrus hunt, 1990.

The meteorite known as the "Tent" as it looked in 1896, half-buried in the ground at Savissivik. Peary christened it "Ahnighito," the Eskimo name of his daughter Mary, born in 1893.

THE THEFT OF THE SACRED METEORITES

News of the Cape York meteorites caught the attention of the scientific world after Sir John Ross learned of their existence on discovering the Polar Inuit in August 1818.

"We find the metal (*savik*) for our knives and harpoon points in large stones that are not far from here." The metal proved on analysis to be meteoric in origin. The Eskimos gave no further information as to the location of their "iron mountain." To all indications it lay at no great distance from where they were discovered, in Prince Regent Bay south of Cape York.

Peary was able, thanks to his intimate contacts with the Eskimos, to locate the meteorites. A more or less intensive search had been under way since 1818 but had remained inconclusive. Ross had looked for them during his few days of dialogue with the Inuit, so had the *North Star* in 1849-1850, Nares in 1875-1876, and Nordenskjöld in the summer of 1883. Peary's informant was the hunter Tellikotinah. He personally led Peary to three of the four sites spread over eight miles around the Eskimo village of Savissivik. Payment: one rifle. Value of the meteorite when sold to the American Museum of Natural History in New York: $ 40,000.

The four meteorites were named: the Tent (11 ft. long, 7 ft. high, 6 ft. wide, 36.5 tons); the Woman, which was trapezoidal (3 tons); the Dog, which was oval (0.5 tons); and a block discovered in 1913 by Knud Rasmussen weighing 7,483 lbs, which was transported to the mineralogical museum of Copenhagen in 1925. It is massive and irregular.

According to the Inuit, the three largest meteorites represented a seated woman engaged in sewing, her tent, and her dog. They were hurled to earth by the evil spirit Tornaarsuk. Meteoric iron, which proved of such great use to the Inuit, lifting them partly out of the Stone Age and into the Iron Age, was therefore identified by them with Evil. Only the Woman was used by the Inuit for tools, it being the easiest to fragment (by pounding it with a hard stone), into flakes the size of a fingernail.

These meteorites are meteoric fragments, that is, metallic substances that have come to earth from interplanetary space in the wake of an explosion and dispersal across a finite area. The largest known meteorite to date is in Hoba, South Africa, and weighs 60 tons. The surface of the earth is believed to have one meteorite per square kilometer per million years of existence.

Unlike most meteor sites, there is no visible crater here, leaving us to suppose that the four blocks fell during the Ice Age and burrowed into the overlying glacier. When warm weather returned 8000 years ago, the meteorites were slowly lowered to their present positions near the shoreline.

As the meteorites left no sub-glacial crater, the glacier into which they fell is calculated to have been at least 200 meters (650 ft.) thick. The Dog and the Woman lie on top of the ground, while the Tent is (or was) sunken into the soil and rock. Savik lies in a gravel moraine. The meteorites have not been dated, but they are thought to have fallen either during the period of glacial melting 8000 years ago or during the Little Ice Age (1600-1800).

The meteorite fragments, which should be more numerous, were deposited either in a line or a shower. Most must have disappeared into the great glacier to the east, or into the sea. Time will tell whether the meteorites that should have been buried in the glacier to the east will be carried toward the coast by the glacier's dynamic forces. Given the size of the largest block, the impact when it fell must have been considerable.

This type of meteorite is rare, accounting for only 5% of those known. The surface has oxidized, giving the meteorites a black color. They have many holes, most from 0.5 cm to 1 cm in diameter and a few millimeters deep, some larger and deeper. Small cup-like cavities were formed by burning on entry into the atmosphere.

After a first attempt to remove the Tent in 1896, a second was made in August 1897. The giant meteorite was placed on rollers laid across rails and loaded with great difficulty on the *Hope* in July 1897. A storm almost swallowed up the ship on the day after the meteorite was brought on board, leading everyone to believe that the theft would not go unpunished. The two smaller meteorites, the Woman and the Dog, were loaded onto the *Kite* in 1895.

The meteorite called the "Tent" (Ahnighito) was loaded onto the *Hope* by means of rollers on rails (July 1897). The only meteorite from which the Eskimos chipped flakes was the "Woman," which was redemptive in character, like Nirrivik, who lives at the bottom of the ocean.

ABOVE,
the Eskimos extracting iron from the meteorite the "Woman." This scene, as captured by the painter Albert Operti, was recreated *in situ* in 1896 at Peary's request. At left center, a hunter strikes the ridge of the meteorite with a large round stone to chip off flakes. His father, seated on the sledge, inserts these flakes into a split bone to make a scraper. To the left, in front of the *k'angmah* (stone shelters), a woman in a hood prepares a dish of seal over the oil lamp, while her child eats a piece of it with both hands.

LEFT,
Masonic ritual in front of the Tent meteorite. From left to right, in aprons: Figgins, Peary, Bartlett, Hunter, Operti. During the second day of the *Hope's* return journey, the ship was caught in a terrific storm. The Eskimos on board guarding the Tent were convinced that the meteorite's spirits were starting to take revenge (July 1897).

Robert Peary looks at the Inuit

An Inuit settling of accounts

One day, Kyo was asked to accompany a hunting party, little suspecting that he was to be the object of the hunt. About five miles from camp he was struck from behind, and fell, hardly realising what had taken place. Then lest his spirit should escape, he was buried and weighted with stones.

An Eskimo execution is always done in this manner. Lacking government and laws of any kind, even subsisting without a leader, the avenger is at liberty to decide the fate of the criminal. The execution is never done openly, always by stealth. Yet Eskimos are far from cowardly—as proved when attacking the polar bear and musk-ox.

Piblokto, or "polar hysteria"

There exists among these people a form of hysteria known as *piblocto* (the same name as given to the well-known madness among their dogs), with which women, more frequently than men, are afflicted. [53] During these spells, the maniac removes all clothing and prances about like a broncho. In 1898 while the *Windward* was in winter quarters off Cape D'Urville, a married woman was taken with one of these fits in the middle of the night. In a state of perfect nudity she walked the deck of the ship; then, seeking still greater freedom, jumped the rail, on to the frozen snow and ice. It was some time before we missed her, and when she was finally discovered, it was at a distance of half-a-mile, where she was still pawing, and shouting to the best of her abilities. She was captured and brought back to the ship; and then there commenced a wonderful per-

Peary's young friends, on the deck of the *Roosevelt* in 1908-1909. From left to right: Arnaluk, Ivalu, Atitak (who would marry my companion Pualuna), Tukumeq (the mother of the shaman Sorqaq), and Ivnartarssuaq. (The last two young women have not been identified.)

53) "Polar hysteria" has been studied among the Polar Eskimos only hastily and never clinically. It does not appear to be neurological in origin and occurs primarily in autumn and primarily among women. It is never seen in children or the elderly, but only in adults. The release of a psychological oppression, the "hysteria" is ritualized. The patient shouts out what is oppressing him or her, while mimicking the cries of animals and singing ancestral songs. The person may tear the upper part of his garment to breathe, walk barefoot, and not feel the effects of cold. His skin becomes darker, his body is hot, he drools, becomes violent, and shows unusual strength. He picks up solid-looking objects from the ground: wood, pebbles. He covers his face with dog feces and sometimes eats them. Settling down outside on the frozen sea if it is autumn, on an eminence (iceberg), he spews invective at the village and at all who accompany him. The crisis passes in a half hour at most. The sufferer's face is pale, his irises yellow, and his skin cold. He falls into a deep, untroubled sleep, and when he wakes up remembers nothing. No "hysteric" has ever killed anyone. The Inuit protect the piblokto victim from doing any harm. In 1950-1951, the Inuit told me they considered these crises to be liberating, expressing the difficulties of communal life: "They are good for you." With modern life less constricted and the modern diet lower in animal fat and blood, these crises have become quite rare since 1960. Piblokto in dogs is fatal. According to Kane, who observed his dogs with scientific detachment, a perlerorneq dog first barks constantly, yaps and whines, and walks in a zigzag, as though feeling some internal pain. He looks out of bloodshot, sightless eyes, drools, nods his head, and then falls down, his jaw slack. Patting calms the dog. Then he dies. Foxes may also contract piblokto, as I witnessed in April 1967.

54) That is, three years after the onset of puberty.

55) On the unbalanced sex ratio, see my genealogical study published in Population, Paris, 1953, and in Inter-Nord, no. 20 (Paris, CNRS, 1990).

56) In a century that saw the publication of works by Lévy-Bruhl, Mauss, Frazer, and Boas, this representative of Anglo-Saxon America describes the primitive Eskimo religion as "a collection of miscellaneous superstitions and beliefs in good and evil spirits." Peary is a reductionist. How could he have loved the Eskimos and not grasped that they are first of all a religious, pantheistic people?

57) These conflicts did not always end peacefully. Affairs of passion were the number one cause of murders. In 1910, an argument between Uutaaq and a rival led to a fatality.

formance of mimicry in which every conceivable cry of local bird and mammal was reproduced in the throat of Inaloo. This same woman at other times attempts to walk the ceiling of her igloo; needless to say, she has never succeeded.

A case of piblocto lasts from five minutes to half-an-hour or more. When it occurs under cover of a hut, no apparent concern is felt by other inmates, nor is any attention paid to the antics of the mad one. It is only when an attempt is made to run abroad that the cords of restraint are felt.

An unbalanced sex-ratio

Though not lacking in warmth of blood they are not a prolific people. The females arrive at the age of puberty neither very early nor very late, but according to their own statements they rarely have children, even with every possible provocation, till at least three years later, and I am inclined to think the statement is substantially correct.[54]

As the males are considerably in excess[55] there is a constant demand for wives, and girls frequently marry while still as flat-chested and as lank-hipped as a boy.

The Eskimos "have no religion"

Of religion, properly speaking, they have none. The nearest approach to it is simply a collection of miscellaneous superstitions and beliefs in good and evil spirits.[56] It may be said, in relation to this latter subject, that information in regard to it is extremely difficult to obtain, and probably, the facts will be known only when some enthusiast is willing to devote five or six years of his time to living with them and doing as they do, becoming, in fact, one of them.

Duel over a woman

The rivalry between these two waxed so intense that it was evident something serious would occur, and no one was surprised when Koko entered the igloo where Nowdingyah, seated upon the edge of the bed-platform, was trimming a whiplash, jerked the lash from his hands, and seating himself beside him, threw his arms about his waist, and attempted to force him upon his back upon the platform. Not a word was said by either or by anyone in the igloo, yet everyone knew, as the two strained and twisted with quick, loud breath, that the struggle was for the widow. For several minutes the struggle continued, till Koko, at last, with a supreme effort, crushed his antagonist prone upon his back, then, jumping quickly to his feet, left the igloo and, harnessing his dogs, drove off with the widow on a bridal tour to the lodge. He had won the prize in a bloodless Eskimo duel.[57] An interesting sequel to this was that, after spending a brief and blissful honeymoon of two or three days at the lodge, Koko returned to Karnah, when my previously staid henchman Ikwah, though already possessed of a wife and child, became enamoured of the widow, strayed from the paths of propriety, vanquished Koko in another bloodless duel,

ALEQASINA

***Summer 1894**, Anniversary Lodge base. Aleqasina, quartered in an outbuilding, was hired by the Peary expedition to do household work. The Eskimos disrobe indoors without compunction, if only to dry the clothes in which they have been perspiring.*

Aleqasina would become Peary's Eskimo wife and the mother of his two sons: Anaakkaq (1900-1926) and Kaalipaluk (born in 1906). She was the aunt of Imina, who would be my companion in Siorapaluk. Peary displayed an open and widely acknowledged affection for Aleqasina as early as 1891.

Josephine Peary's words when she came north to rescue her husband, 28 August 1900: "You will have been surprised, perhaps annoyed, when you heard that I came up on a ship . . . but believe me, had I known how things were with you here I should not have come." Quoted in Wally Herbert, The Noose of Laurels *(London: 1989), pp. 138-139.*

Bowdoin Fjord, 1894. Eskimo women photographed by the Peary expedition. Two of them wear hoods, being under taboo. Note the iron and aluminum containers received from the white man.

Armanguaq, who for a time was the wife of Minik in Ummannaq. His return to his own people (1910-1916) was ill-fated. Misunderstood and poorly adapted, he no longer spoke the Inuit language.

This woman was "very lazy," according to Peter Freuchen. Here she is carrying Meqqusaaq, the son of Peter Freuchen and Navarana.

left him to proceed alone and disconsolate to Cape York, and installed the rotund siren, with all her wealth and witchery of charms, in his own igloo.

Hyperboreans farther to the north

They have a general idea of land far to the north. They are aware that the land is inhabited by the musk-ox, and there are misty traditions of the existence, somewhere in that region, of a race much larger than themselves. [58]

Technical progress in the last twenty years: wood, iron, kayaks, and firearms

The effect of my expeditions on the children of the north has been to bring prosperity to the entire tribe. Seven years ago, many men in this community had no knife, and many women no needles. [59] Rare was the man who had a kayak or skin-covered canoe; and he who possessed a lance or harpoon shaft made from a single piece of wood was truly well equipped. Today the men and women are provided with an abundance of knives and needles; every male, from the adolescent to the adult, has his own kayak; most men have firearms, and each hunter has the best wood available for his lance, his harpoon, his seal-lance, and his sled. The effect of this improvement in their arms has had an immediate effect on the well-being of the tribe, due to the considerably improved efficiency of the hunters. The men and women are better clothed, and they may keep a greater number of dogs (their only domestic animal): by reason of their improved nutrition and their greater capacity to resist the constant severities of their life, mortality has declined and the birth rate has increased noticeably in the course of the last six years. [60]

The meteorites: a heavenly woman . . .

According to the natives, the "Saviksue" (great irons) have been where I discovered them from time immemorial; but they were originally an Innuit woman and her dog and tent hurled from the sky by Tornarsuk (the Evil Spirit). They say that at first the "woman" was in shape like a woman seated and sewing, but that the constant chipping off of fragments through successive ages has gradually removed the upper portion of her body and reduced her size one-half or one-third. [61] Years ago her head became detached and a party of Eskimos from Peterahwik or Etah (settlements north of Whale Sound) attempted to carry it away, motivated probably by the desire to have a supply of the precious metal more convenient, and save themselves the long and arduous journey to Cape York and into Melville Bay, when they needed to replenish their stock of iron. The head was lashed upon a sledge and the party started for their home, but when well out from the shore the sea ice suddenly broke up with a loud noise, and the head disappeared beneath the water, dragging down with it the sledge and dogs. The Eskimos themselves narrowly escaped with their lives, and

58) This presumably refers to the Tunit or Tornit, the giants from the North, the Hyperboreans of legend. They were nomadic Eskimos, hunters of musk oxen, whose traces were discovered on Ellesmere Island by Greely (Lady Franklin Bay). Other traces have been found in Peary Land.

59) This is misleading. Knives of meteoric iron had been in use since time immemorial. The Eskimo cannot live without knives. The same goes for needles, traditionally made of bone. Peary, who is often inaccurate on ethnological matters, is referring to European knives and needles.

60) The transition from a material culture of bone and stone to a culture of wood (40 years), iron (40 years), and firearms (80 years) manifested itself in larger dog teams, more extensive hunting grounds, and increased yields from the hunt. These technological changes coincided with a climatic warming after 1818, though the period from 1840 to 1860 saw a return of severe cold. Though this people have an oral culture and no writing, they are able to foresee changes in climate three to five years in advance: the general warming started in 1817 and the Eskimos cautiously refused to believe in it. Yet the Polar Eskimos (40 to 60 families) deliberately altered their population control measures (taboos relating to sex, diet, technology, euthanasia and voluntary death of the elderly, female infanticide) during the period from 1850-1870, right in the midst of the cold snap, in anticipation of the substantial climatic warming that they sensed ahead from their reading of natural signs—measures they had not been willing to change during the two and a half centuries of the Little Ice Age, from 1600 to 1800, and the years after, from 1818 to 1850. Contrary to Peary's belief, the population increased before his arrival in 1892-1893. The group's rapid expansion dates to 1860-1870, a generation before the census. Between 1855 and 1895, the population increased by 80.7%. The group decreased in size by 4% from epidemic between 1895 and September 1906, when the population was 207. In 1854, the population was 140. In 1920, it was 250; and in 1950-1951, it was 302. Arrivals from the outside to this genetically isolated people: 14 Canadian Eskimos, 1863-1867. Unions with whalers and explorers: 9 known between 1818 and 1950.

61) According to the Danish mineralogist Buchwald, a noted authority on meteorites, especially the meteorites of Greenland, it is strictly impossible for the Eskimos to have detached even a small flake from the meteorites with their basalt strikers (10,000 stones have been found around Anighito, the largest meteorite). They must have bent their efforts on pieces already detached and ready to be dislodged or already scattered on the ground.

62) The interplanetary meteorites always fall in clusters and radiating patterns. They fall with greater frequency in the region of the geomagnetic pole. More then 1000 lbs. of meteorites reach the earth every day. Every 150 years, a meteorite of more than 220 tons reaches the earth. The Cape York meteorites (lodestones) contain 92% iron and 5% nickel.

since that time no attempt has been made to carry away any but the smallest fragments of the heavenly woman.[62]

"Philosophic anarchists of the north"

I have often been asked: Of what use are Eskimos to the world? They are too far removed to be of value for commercial enterprises and, furthermore, they lack ambition. They have no literature nor, properly speaking, any art. They value life only as does a fox, or a bear, purely by instinct. But let us not forget that these people, trustworthy and hardy, will yet prove their value to mankind. With their help, the world shall discover the Pole . . .[63]

I know every man, woman, and child in the tribe, from Cape York to Etah. Prior to 1891 they had never been farther north than their own habitat. Eighteen years ago I went to these people, and my first work was from their country as a base.

Much nonsense has been told by travelers in remote lands about the aborigines' regarding as gods the white men who come to them, but I have never placed

Peary on the *Roosevelt*, personally "remunerating" the Eskimo women who took part in the expedition. Eighteen Eskimo hunters and guides, along with their families (49 people in all), were employed full time, from July 1908 to July 1909, 300 miles north of the northernmost village (Etah). The lead party, which took considerable risks during the three months of the Polar journey, was paid at most a boat, a tent, a gun, tools, and a telescope, worth in all some $ 2000, or $ 170 per month. Housing costs were nil, as the Eskimos lived in snow igloos near the ship all winter. Out of gratitude, Peary and his partners might well have created a North American foundation, a spin-off of the Peary Arctic Club with its U.S. millionaires, to guarantee the Polar Inuit the bare minimum to survive in the long term and make steady material progress. Peary would never have discovered the Pole—or what he designated as such—without the help of the Eskimos. The ingratitude of "Piulersuaq" and his sponsors is embarrassing. The American admiral lost all concern for this people's welfare once the Pole had been discovered.

Women sewing on Peary's ship. On the deck are the patterns used to make clothes and boots for the explorers. Sometimes they employed a more traditional way of measuring by passing a thong directly around their client's body and then setting it against the skin they planned to cut and sew (in 1950 I observed the same techniques). Peary always had a large fraction of "his" Eskimos follow him (about a fifth or a sixth of the population), including men, women, and children.

Qaassaaluk, in her animal hide tent with her two children, 30 July 1909. Suckling at her mother's breast is Natuk, born on 2 January 1909. She would become the wife of the famous shaman Kutsikitsoq, hero of *The Last Kings of Thule,* then would take part in my expedition to Inglefield Land in March-June 1951. Inuterssuaq, on the left, would be one of my principal informers from 1967 to 1982.

The Inuit hunters became Peary's oarsmen during the great summer hunts he organized for the group's benefit, in order to ensure a sufficient supply of walrus meat to feed the 500 dogs. At the end of an expedition, before heading back to Cape York, he would organize a great hunt so that the Inuits would have a supply of meat to last them through the winter when he was no longer there. Bowdoin Fjord, August 1894.

much credence in these stories. My own experience has been that the average aborigine is just as content with his own way as we are with ours, just as convinced of his own superior knowledge, and that he adjusts himself with his knowledge in regard to things in the same way that we do. The Eskimos are not brutes; they are just as human as Caucasians. They know that I am their friend, and they have abundantly proved themselves my friends . . .

They are savages, but they are not savage; they are without government, but they are not lawless; they are utterly uneducated according to our standard, yet they exhibit a remarkable degree of intelligence. In temperament like children, with all a child's delight in little things, they are nevertheless enduring as the most mature of civilized men and women, and the best of them are faithful unto death. Without religion and having no idea of God, they will share their last meal with any one who is hungry, while the aged and the helpless among them are

taken care of as a matter of course. They are healthy and pure-blooded; they have no vices, no intoxicants, and no bad habits—not even gambling. Altogether, they are a people unique upon the face of the earth. A friend of mine well calls them the philosophic anarchists of the North.

Trial marriages

The trial marriage is an ineradicable custom among the Eskimos. [64] If a young man and woman are not suited with each other, they try again, and sometimes several times; but when they find mates to whom they are adapted, the arrangement is generally permanent. If two men want to marry the same woman, they settle the question by a trial of strength, and the better man has his way. These struggles are not fights, as the disputants are amiable; they are simply tests of wrestling, or sometimes of pounding each other on the arm to see which man can stand the pounding the longer.

Their fundamental acceptance of the

63) One has to look critically at Peary the writer and his cookie-cutter views, which demonstrate a great ethnographic ignorance. It is absurd to say that the Inuit have no religion: shamanism is the basis of their thought. But there is also another Peary, the hidden man, who deeply admired and respected this unique people in his Anglo-Saxon way—as strong, disciplined, and loyal men. His writing offers quick, short, dismissive judgments. He obviously possessed a vast knowledge of this people that he did not know how to organize. On the other hand, he can be credited with not having tried to interfere with the beliefs of the Polar Inuit, steering away from schooling or proselytizing. He can also be credited with having given a man's calling to these Eskimos whom he admired: the job of expedition guides, much like sherpas. He allowed them to participate in his adventure, which was also theirs to the extent that it was the search for the mythical Great Ancestors, the Tunit or Hyperboreans, people of the Arctic Ocean. And no doubt in his introverted way he loved them. In this respect, he led a liberated, modern life in their midst, taking an Eskimo wife and having children.

64) A custom linked to other rules: there is a prohibition against the union of individuals related up to the sixth remove. A young man of 18-25 in fact has a choice between four or five girls in his age group, unless he marries the widow of a man having the same name as himself.

65) A man's name carries his spirit. At birth, an infant is given the name of a relative or a person who died within the year. An Inuk never calls another by his name: he addresses him in an oblique way. A name can be masculine or feminine.

66) Anaana: "Mommy"; Ataata: "Daddy."

67) These sometimes derive from a union between the families of the parents. Unlike the Inuit of eastern Canada (Igloolik), these pre-marital unions decided by the parents are not binding on the children. The group supports marriages made outside the will of the parents, thus preventing the formation of dynasties.

68) "Studying" is an inapposite word—"using" would have been more accurate.

69) The height of cynicism. Given Peary's substantial means, the payments he made were truly modest: 50 knives, 50 tools, 100 boards, 10 boats, 40 tents, and 40 rifles per expedition, for the work of an entire year, entailing the greatest danger, on the part of vigorous men equipped with their dogs and sleds. Let us consider the fairness of these contracts. Their "austerity" saved the Eskimos from a possibly fatal inflation. It was in Peary's interest to have the Eskimos dependent on him and attending on him during the whole of his stay. Peary says explicitly what many explorers have thought to themselves in an era of Christian dominance: that there is one truth (no salvation but through baptism) and a faith in technological progress and industrial civilization, which tramples over the global aspects of a culture (art, thought, and systematic perception of life); and that some peoples are superior while others are archaic, and that it is in our interest as conquerors to keep the latter dependent on us.

70) An engineer, Peary remained a technologist bound to the assumptions of his time: externally he showed Christian good will, while inside he was prey to a merchant's cynicism, the spirit of conquest, and the conviction of belonging to a superior race.

proposition that might is right in such matters sometimes extends to a man saying to the husband of a woman: "I am the better man." In such case the husband has either to prove his superiority in strength, or yield the woman to the other. If a man grows tired of his wife, he simply tells here there is not room for her in his igloo. She may return to her parents, if they are living; she may go to a brother or a sister; or she may send word to some man in the tribe that she is now at liberty and is willing to start life again. In these cases of primitive divorce, the husband keeps one or all of the children if he wants them; if not, the woman takes them with her.

The group: an aggregate of personalities, not families

The Eskimos do not have many children, two or three being the usual number. The woman does not take her husband's name in any case. Akatingwah, for instance, will remain Akatingwah, whether she has had one husband or several. Children do not address their parents as father and mother, but call them by their names, [65] though sometimes very small children use a diminutive which corresponds to our "mamma." [66]

...As there are more men than women among the Eskimos, the girls marry very young, often about the age of twelve. In many cases the marriages are arranged between the parents when the children are quite young; but the boy and girl are not bound, and when they are old enough they are permitted to decide for themselves. [67]

Yankee cynicism

I have been studying [68] the Eskimos for eighteen years and no more effective instruments for arctic work could be imagined than these plump, bronze-skinned, keen-eyed and black-maned children of nature. Their very limitations are their most valuable endowments for the purposes of arctic work. [69] I have a sincere interest in these people, aside from their usefulness to me; and my plan from the beginning has been to give them such aid and instruction as would fit them more effectively to cope with their own austere environment, and to refrain from teaching them anything which would tend to weaken their self-confidence or to make them discontented with their lot.

...[B]ut the cardinal graces of faith, hope, and charity they seem to have already, for without them they could never survive the six-months' night and the many rigors of their home.

Their feeling for me is a blending of gratitude and confidence. To understand what my gifts have meant to them, imagine a philanthropic millionaire descending upon an American country town and offering every man there a brownstone mansion and an unlimited bank account. But even this comparison falls short of the reality, for in the United States even the poorest boy knows that there is a possibility of his attaining for himself those things on which he sets his heart, if he will labor and endure, while to the Eskimos the things which I have given them are absolutely out of their world, as far beyond their own unaided efforts as the moon and Mars are beyond the dwellers on this planet.

...The fundamental point in all my dealings with them has been always to mean just what I say and to have things done exactly as ordered...

I have made it to their interest to do what I want done. For example, the best all-round man on a long sledge journey got more than the others. A record was always kept of the game secured by each Eskimo, and the best hunter got a special prize. Thus I kept them interested in their work. The man who killed the musk ox with the finest set of horns and the man who killed the deer with the most magnificent antlers were specially rewarded. I have made it a point to be firm with them, but to rule them by love and gratitude rather than by fear and threats. An Eskimo, like an Indian, never forgets a broken promise—nor a fulfilled one.

...I have saved whole villages from starvation, and the children are taught by their parents that if they grow up and become good hunters or good seamstresses, as the case may be, "Pearyaksoah" will reward them sometime in the not too distant future.

Fear of the dead and belief in the beyond

Strictly speaking, the Eskimos have no religion, in the sense in which we use the word. But they believe in the survival of the person after death, and they believe in spirits—especially evil spirits.... The beneficent spirits are those of their ancestors (another Oriental touch), while they have a whole legion of malevolent spirits, led by Tornarsuk, the great devil himself. [70]

They are constantly trying to propitiate Tornarsuk by incantations; and when they kill game, an offering is made to him. The devil is supposed to have a keen appreciation of these tidbits. On leaving a snow igloo the Eskimos are careful to kick the front out of it, that the evil spirits may not find shelter there, and when they throw

Payday. Redcliffe House, McCormick Fjord, 1892.

Masaitsiaq, one of the Inuit group's most visionary *angakkuqs.*

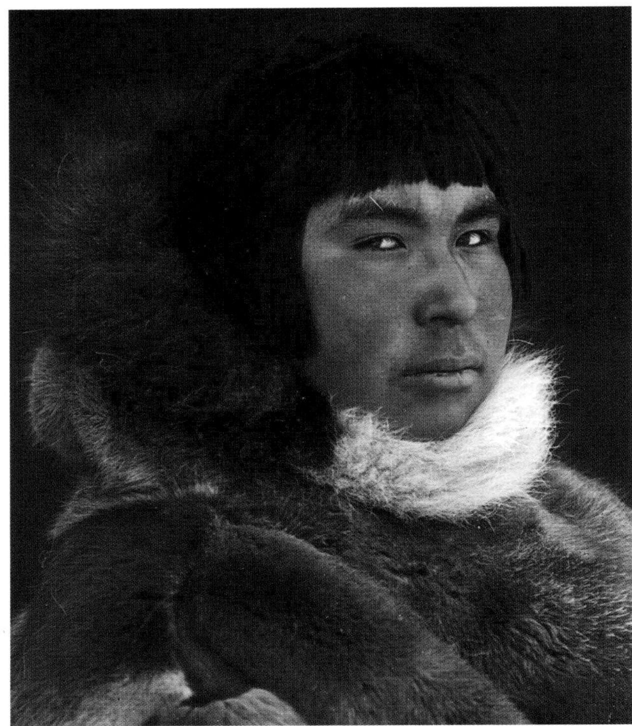

Ayakou, one of Knud Rasmussen's favorite Inuit (he was present in September 1917 when Dr. Wulff was tragically left to die along the trail). The elder brother of my companion Qaaqqutsiaq, he died of typhoid in Upernavik in 1922 on the point of leaving with Rasmussen for Canada on the Fifth Thule Expedition.

Talitsining, or arm-wrestling competition. The Inuits customarily settle disputes with public competitions or endurance tests. Photographed by Peary in 1896.

away a worn-out garment it is never left intact, but is torn in such a way that the devil may not use it to warm himself. . . . Any sudden and unexplained barking or howling among the dogs indicates the invisible presence of Tornasuk, and the men will run out and crack their whips or fire their rifles to scare away the invader. When, on board the *Roosevelt* in winter quarters, I was suddenly aroused from sleep by the crack of rifles, I did not think there was a mutiny aboard—only that Tornasuk had ridden by upon the wind.

When the ice presses hard against the ship, an Eskimo will call on his dead father to push it away; when the wind blows with special violence, ancestors are again appealed to. Passing along a cliff, on a sledge journey, a man will sometimes stop and listen and then say: "Did you hear what the devil said just then?" I have asked the Eskimo to repeat to me the words of Tornasuk, up there on the cliff, and I would not dream of laughing at my faithful friends at such a time; the messages of Tornasuk I receive with a respectful gravity.

There are no chiefs among these people, no men in authority;[71] but there are medicine men who have some influence. The angakok is generally not loved. [His] business is mainly singing incantations and going into trances, for he has no medicines. If a person is sick, he may prescribe abstinence from certain foods . . . and the incantations take the place of the white man's drugs . . .

Their burial customs are rather interesting. When an Eskimo dies, there is no delay about removing the body. Just as soon as possible it is wrapped, fully clothed, in the skins which formed the bed . . . Then a strong line is tied round the body, and it is removed, always head first, from the tent or igloo. The Eskimos do not like to touch a dead body, and it is therefore dragged as a sledge would be. Arrived at the place selected for the grave, they cover the corpse with loose stones, to protect it from dogs, foxes, and ravens, and the burial is complete.

According to Eskimo ideas, the afterworld is a distinctly material place. If the deceased is a hunter, his sledge and kayak, with his weapons and implements, are placed close by, and his favorite dogs, harnessed and attached to the sledge, are strangled so that they may accompany him on his journey into the unseen.

. . . The relatives of the dead observe certain formalities in regard to food and clothing, and the name of the lost one is never mentioned. If any other members of the tribe have the same name, they must take another until an infant is born to which the proscribed name can be given. This appears to remove the ban.

The Eskimos' remuneration

One of the first things done after reaching the ship and bringing our sleep up to date was to reward the Eskimos who had served us so faithfully. They were all fitted out with rifles, shotguns, cartridges, shells, reloading tools, hatchets, knives, and so on, and they behaved like so many children who had just received a boundless supply of toys. Among the things I have given them at various times, none are more important than the telescopes, which enable them to distinguish game in the distance. The four who stood with me at the Pole were to receive whale-boats, tents, and other treasures when I dropped them at their home settlements along the Greenland coast on the southward journey of the *Roosevelt.*

ANTHROPOMETRY OF THE INUIT

The Polar Inuits were studied at the beginning of the twentieth century (1909) according to the anthropometric methods then in fashion. Setting aside their racist underpinnings, let us consider the raw data they produced, which provide a quantified picture of this people in the course of their millennial evolution.

Average male height was 5'2", while average female height was 4'9". The Inuit's physical characteristics were close to those of the American Indians. Their lung capacity was large, their heart rate generally slow, their blood pressure high. Captain Sabine noted in 1818: "The Eskimos are prone to violent nosebleeds." Their essentially all-meat diet, of low energy efficiency, was completed by glycogen, a direct muscle nutrient, derived from the liver of sea animals.

More than half of the women had a child only every 32 months; 18% gave birth every 2 years; nearly 10% every 4 years; nearly 5% every 5 years. Young women had their first child between the ages of 19 and 23 (while girls reached puberty between the ages of 12 and 14). Women reached menopause between 45 and 50 years of age. Winter amenorrhea was recorded in 1891. Male sexual excitement and female fecundity were at their height when the sun returned, in May, June, and July. The sex ratio was tipped toward men. One cause was female infanticide during periods of famine or when a parent died.

71) Their society can be defined as anarcho-communist, egalitarian, and of revolving authority. All acquired goods are shared according to hierarchical rules. There is no appropriation of territory. Every five to seven years houses are exchanged from sector to sector. The people do not like to stay in one place: "We would grow bored." They also fear that groups of allied families might appropriate key sectors (flint mines, meteorite sites, hunting grounds for bear or walrus). Fearing that families might consolidate around the potentially solid core of the parents, one child out of every three or four is given for adoption to an unrelated family.

Ittukusuk (Little Anus) and his sister Qaassaaluk, photographed on 30 July 1909 in front of their tent, two miles northeast of North Star Bay. Ittukusuk wears sealskin boots and bearskin trousers that come up to his hips and are gathered just below the knee. Qaassaaluk wears foxskin shorts.

The third evolutionary leap (1891-1892). Technological capital.

The artifacts gathered by the first Peary expedition (366 numbered objects) were accessioned by the World Columbia Museum on 31 October 1893.*

The main portion of the material was collected by Dr. Cook at Nettik (Natsilivik) and Kiatak (Northumberland Island); another portion was collected at Cape York by members of the Philadelphia Academy who were passengers aboard the *Kite*, which had just carried Peary's party to McCormick Fjord in July 1891 and would return for them in July 1892. This second collection, the portion from Cape York, appears to have been lost. Parts of the collection went by sale or exchange to the Dahlem Museum in Berlin and the British Museum in London.

The sum offered to Peary by a Mr. Putnam for the purchase of the ethnographic collection was $2000. There is no doubt that this collection of artifacts exactly represents the technological state of this isolated society of boreal hunters, the northernmost in the world, before Peary's influence on it was felt. In that respect, it is unique. Neither Ross (1818) or Kane (1852-1855) or Hayes (1860-1861) made so systematic a collection, a mirror of the people.

Until 1891, the date of Peary's first expedition, the Polar Eskimos were practically virgin (to use Rasmussen's term) of any external contact. There had been barter on a yearly basis with the whalers who put in at Cape York from 1818 on. Yet in July 1852, thirty-

Wooden snow goggles, or *ixxaun*, 5.9 inches in length.

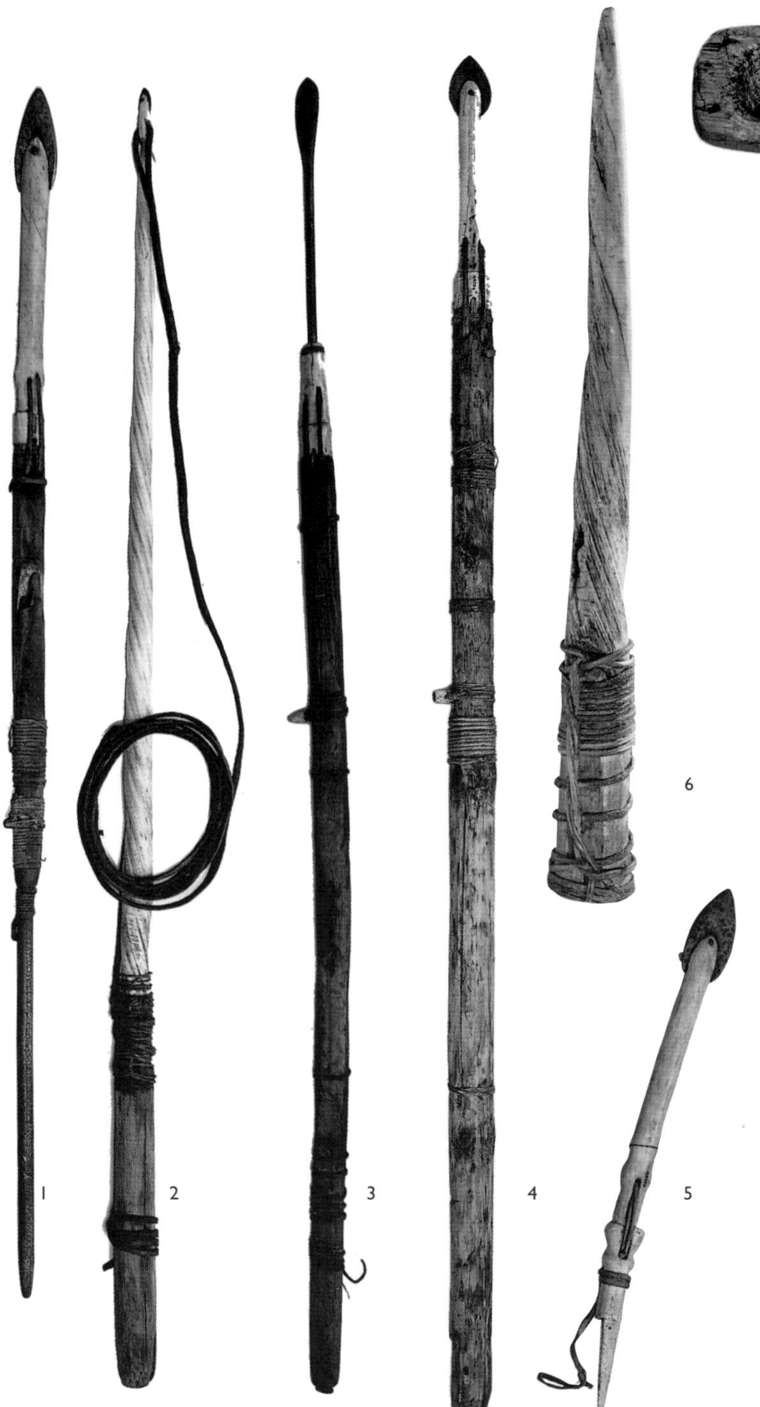

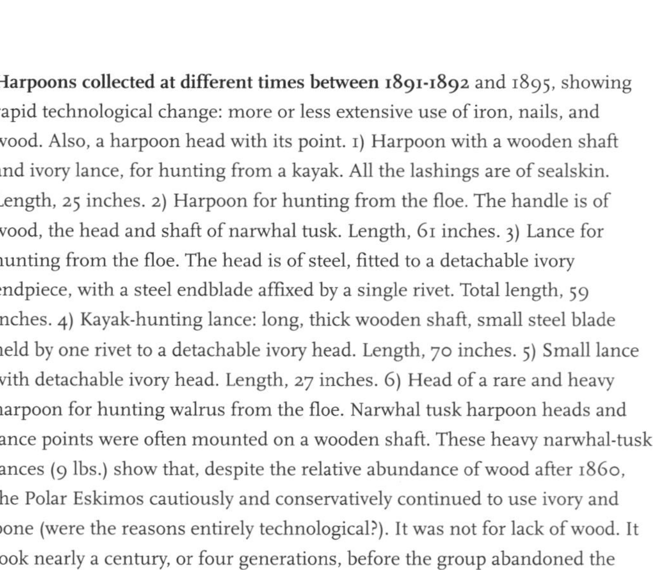

Leister, or three-pronged fish spear (*kakivak*), reintroduced to northern Greenland by the fourteen Canadian Eskimo immigrants: wooden shaft, and a fork with two teeth. The flexible tines are of antler. The central point, on which the fish is impaled, is missing. In 1950-1951, the *kakivak* used was identical to this one.

Harpoons collected at different times between 1891-1892 and 1895, showing rapid technological change: more or less extensive use of iron, nails, and wood. Also, a harpoon head with its point. 1) Harpoon with a wooden shaft and ivory lance, for hunting from a kayak. All the lashings are of sealskin. Length, 25 inches. 2) Harpoon for hunting from the floe. The handle is of wood, the head and shaft of narwhal tusk. Length, 61 inches. 3) Lance for hunting from the floe. The head is of steel, fitted to a detachable ivory endpiece, with a steel endblade affixed by a single rivet. Total length, 59 inches. 4) Kayak-hunting lance: long, thick wooden shaft, small steel blade held by one rivet to a detachable ivory head. Length, 70 inches. 5) Small lance with detachable ivory head. Length, 27 inches. 6) Head of a rare and heavy harpoon for hunting walrus from the floe. Narwhal tusk harpoon heads and lance points were often mounted on a wooden shaft. These heavy narwhal-tusk lances (9 lbs.) show that, despite the relative abundance of wood after 1860, the Polar Eskimos cautiously and conservatively continued to use ivory and bone (were the reasons entirely technological?). It was not for lack of wood. It took nearly a century, or four generations, before the group abandoned the "unicorn horn" as a material for harpoons.

Measurements and ethnographic descriptions after J. W. van Stone, "The First Peary Collection of Polar Eskimo Culture," *Fieldiana Anthropology*, vol. 63, no. 2, Chicago 1972. Ethnographic vocabulary, Erik Holtved: *Contributions to Polar Ethnography*, MOG, Copenhagen, 1962.

four years after their discovery, Inglefield traveled from village to village looking for Franklin and found only one knife (made in Britain), a length of cord, and a few iron blades inserted into bone handles. In 1852-1855, Kane found the Inuit extremely poor in wood and iron. His ship, the *Advance*, abandoned north of Etah in 1855, was never stripped or exploited as the prodigious source of wood and iron it was, capable of propelling this group of forty to fifty families out of their material culture of bone and stone into one of wood and iron. Apparently the Eskimos burned the ship, which sank that same year, before the residents could raid it. Supporting this is the testimony of Hayes, who wintered near Etah in 1860-1861. He noted that the hunters had no firearms but that, thanks to him, they had iron, knives, needles, and pieces of wood, received in exchange for dogs and clothing. If wood and iron had been abundant Hayes would have said so, and the Eskimos would not have exhibited an urgent need for these raw materials.

The Polar Eskimos had lost the art of hunting caribou, and the use of the bow, the kayak, and the three-pronged salmon spear, or leister. Only when a small group of Eskimos migrated to Smith Sound from Baffin Island in the Canadian Arctic did they reacquire these technologies, along with the art of building snow igloos with long entrance tunnels to keep out the cold.

The second technological and mental revolution occurred fully forty years after their discovery, as the reports of Kane (1853-1855) and Hayes (1861-1862) attest. The Inuit did not change their cautious population control practices (which had been followed resolutely since 1600, probably, and at all events since 1818, despite the inducements of Kane, Hayes, and the whalers) until the arrival from Canada of the fourteen Inuit, their cousins and ancestors.

The kayak was gradually reintroduced during this period. The two kayaks in the Peary collection were unfortunately preserved poorly by the museum, deteriorating so badly they were removed from the collection. What we know from Peary's photographs is that they were of primitive construction and related to the caribou-skin kayaks of the Canadian Central Arctic.

But the Eskimos' third technological revolution did not really take shape until Peary's five expeditions, the first in 1891-1892 and the last in 1908-1909. The first revolution (1818-1850) was primarily a revolution in thought ("we are no longer alone in the world") and took place in the south of the Polar Eskimo territory, at Cape York, through modest annual exchange with the whalers. This allowed this materially poor group, who were still living in the age of stone, bone, and meteoric iron, to acquire wood and iron. Iron quickly became an essential material. Wood, whose origin was then unknown, did not have the ritual value of ivory and bone, being of vegetable and not animal origin.

* *In Chicago (Peary Fieldiana Anthropology).*

Bow drill. An indispensable tool for making harpoon heads, sled joints, etc., its technology was rediscovered in 1860-1863 following the migration of fourteen Canadian Eskimos to northern Greenland. It is hard to imagine the Eskimo hunter without his bow drill, so useful is this tool to him on a daily basis. The bow is made from a walrus rib. The strap is 17 inches long. The drill (12.5 inches long) is of iron at the top end, over which the drill bearing fits. It is with the bow drill that holes are pierced in ivory, bone, and antler. It is used to make harpoon heads, and harness rings for sled dogs. The bow drill, identically made and of the same materials, was still being used in 1950-1951. (Purchased in London in 1899, and probably collected by Peary's second expedition of 1893-1895.)

Women's knives (*ulu*) with metal blades. After 1850, women used less and less stone and meteoric iron. The handles of these knives are of ivory. The Polar Eskimos adopted European iron quite quickly, if only for knives and harpoon points. Wood, by contrast, remained of secondary importance for a long time (70 years) in the making of harpoons and lances. Wood was used for the handle of the *ulu* only toward 1920-1930: a coarser material than ivory, it was less highly prized. The crescent shape of the woman's knife no doubt had practical advantages, but it is well to note that in Inuit cosmology the Sun and Moon are respectively female and male.

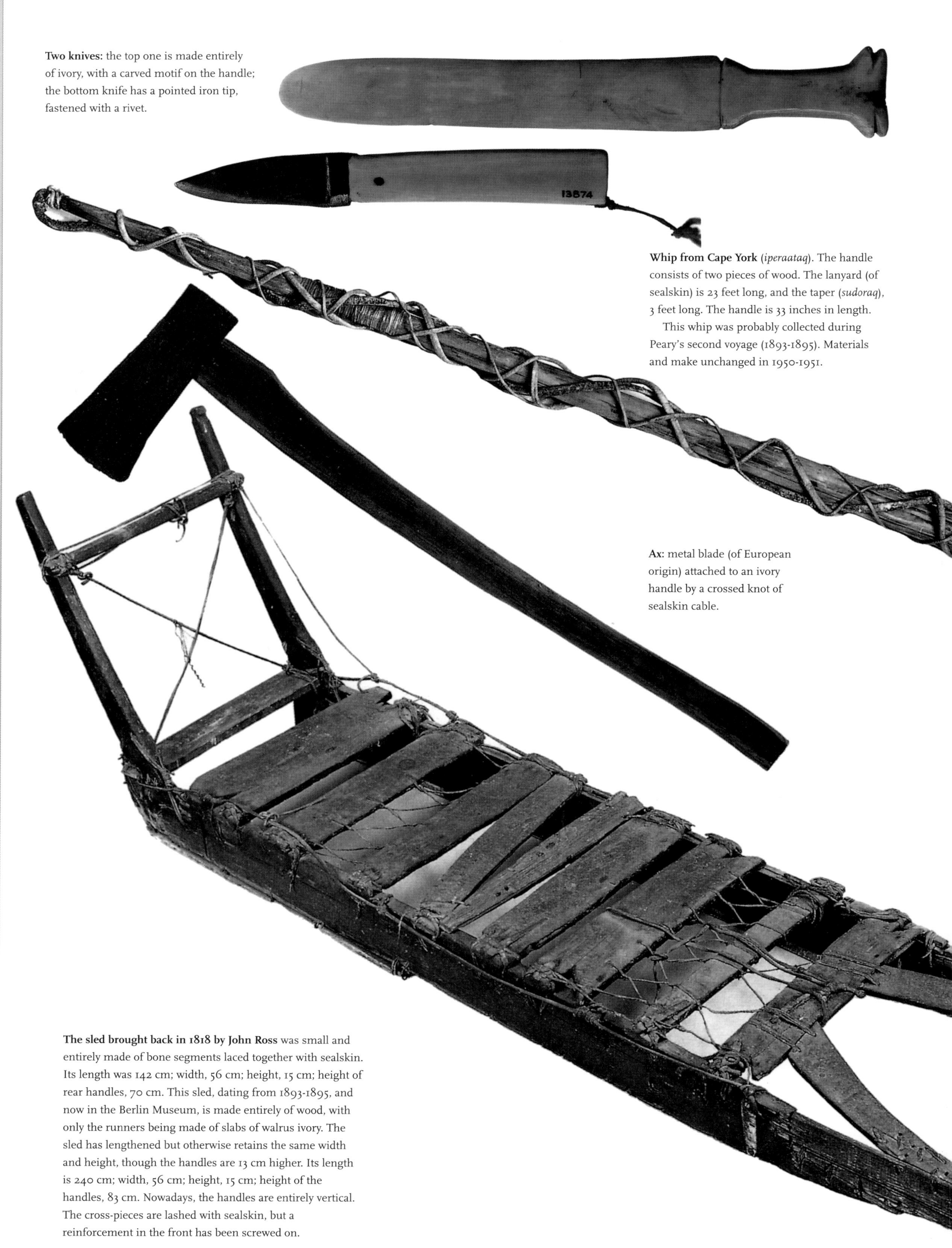

Two knives: the top one is made entirely of ivory, with a carved motif on the handle; the bottom knife has a pointed iron tip, fastened with a rivet.

Whip from Cape York (*iperaataq*). The handle consists of two pieces of wood. The lanyard (of sealskin) is 23 feet long, and the taper (*sudoraq*), 3 feet long. The handle is 33 inches in length.

This whip was probably collected during Peary's second voyage (1893-1895). Materials and make unchanged in 1950-1951.

Ax: metal blade (of European origin) attached to an ivory handle by a crossed knot of sealskin cable.

The sled brought back in 1818 by John Ross was small and entirely made of bone segments laced together with sealskin. Its length was 142 cm; width, 56 cm; height, 15 cm; height of rear handles, 70 cm. This sled, dating from 1893-1895, and now in the Berlin Museum, is made entirely of wood, with only the runners being made of slabs of walrus ivory. The sled has lengthened but otherwise retains the same width and height, though the handles are 13 cm higher. Its length is 240 cm; width, 56 cm; height, 15 cm; height of the handles, 83 cm. Nowadays, the handles are entirely vertical. The cross-pieces are lashed with sealskin, but a reinforcement in the front has been screwed on.

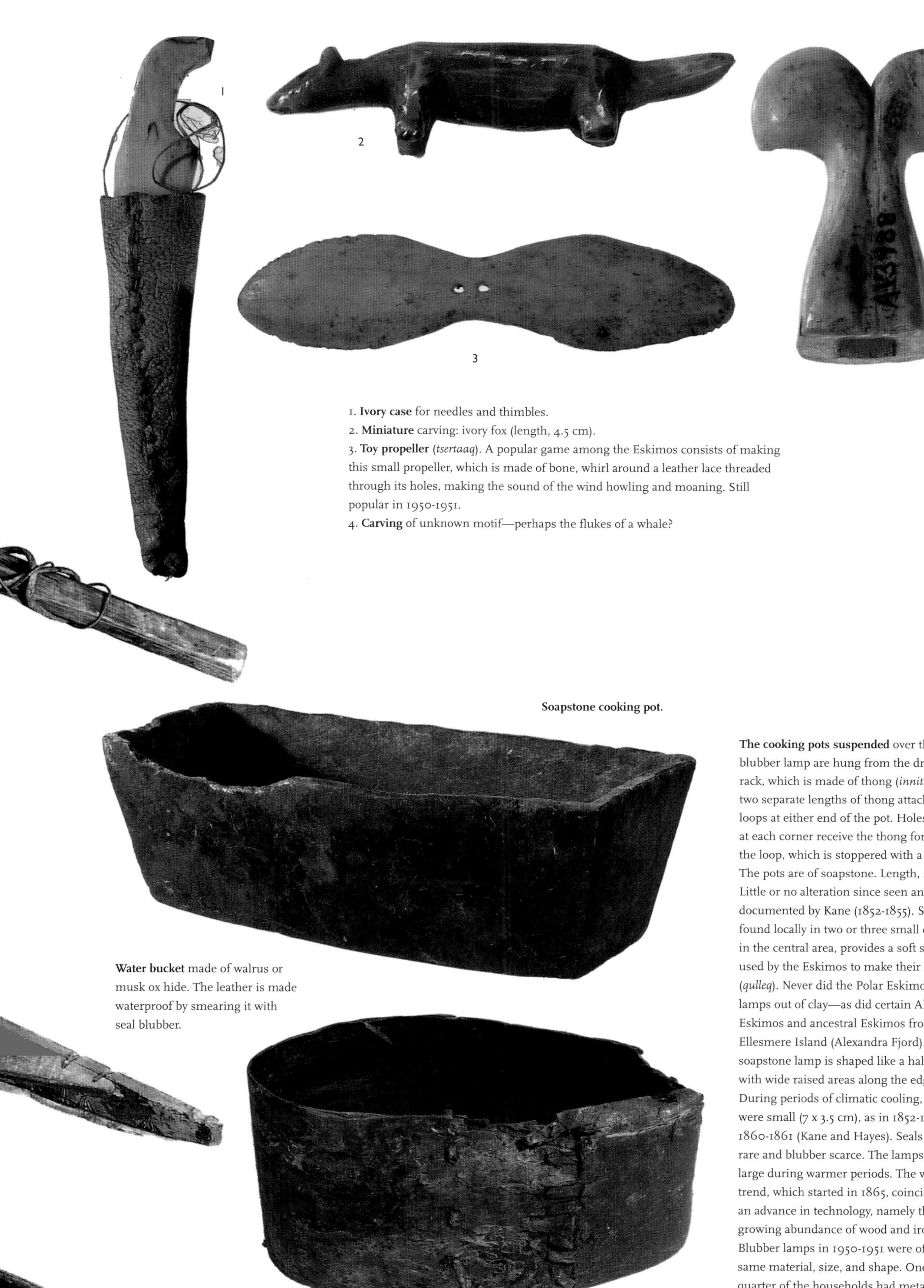

1. **Ivory case** for needles and thimbles.
2. **Miniature** carving: ivory fox (length, 4.5 cm).
3. **Toy propeller** (*tsertaaq*). A popular game among the Eskimos consists of making this small propeller, which is made of bone, whirl around a leather lace threaded through its holes, making the sound of the wind howling and moaning. Still popular in 1950-1951.
4. **Carving** of unknown motif—perhaps the flukes of a whale?

Soapstone cooking pot.

The cooking pots suspended over the blubber lamp are hung from the drying rack, which is made of thong (*innitsat*), by two separate lengths of thong attached to loops at either end of the pot. Holes bored at each corner receive the thong forming the loop, which is stoppered with a knot. The pots are of soapstone. Length, 28 cm. Little or no alteration since seen and documented by Kane (1852-1855). Steatite, found locally in two or three small quarries in the central area, provides a soft stone used by the Eskimos to make their lamps (*qulleq*). Never did the Polar Eskimos sculpt lamps out of clay—as did certain Alaskan Eskimos and ancestral Eskimos from Ellesmere Island (Alexandra Fjord). The soapstone lamp is shaped like a half moon, with wide raised areas along the edges. During periods of climatic cooling, lamps were small (7 x 3.5 cm), as in 1852-1855 and 1860-1861 (Kane and Hayes). Seals were rare and blubber scarce. The lamps were large during warmer periods. The warming trend, which started in 1865, coincided with an advance in technology, namely the growing abundance of wood and iron. Blubber lamps in 1950-1951 were of the same material, size, and shape. One quarter of the households had metal (steel) lamps.

Water bucket made of walrus or musk ox hide. The leather is made waterproof by smearing it with seal blubber.

Full woman's outfit (the model is Aleqasina, mother of Peary's two Eskimo sons), photographed in 1893. From left to right: *natseq*, or sealskin coat with hood, front and side view, and *aaqqatit*, or furred sealskin mittens with polar bear fur trimming; inner coat of bird skin, with hood (worn under the *natseq*), and outer boots, or *kamik*, of sealskin; the same coat worn with inner boots, or *alersit*; in the last picture, the young woman is almost naked, with the exception of the *nano*, made of fox fur, and stitched of twenty-three black and white pieces: note the dark-colored rectangular section at the height of the pubes. This outfit was unchanged in 1950-1951, except for the bird skin coat, which was no longer in use.

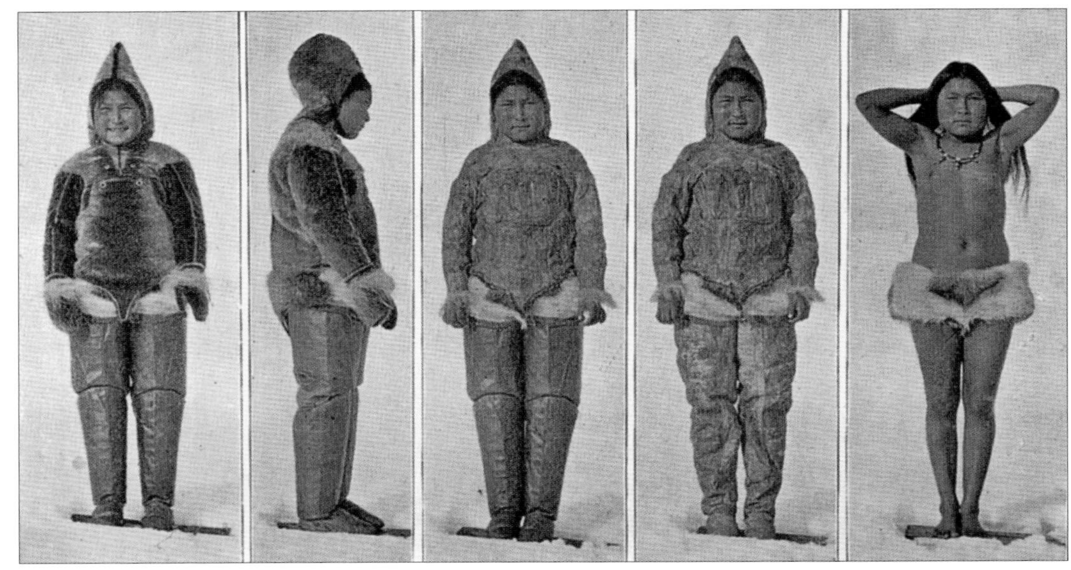

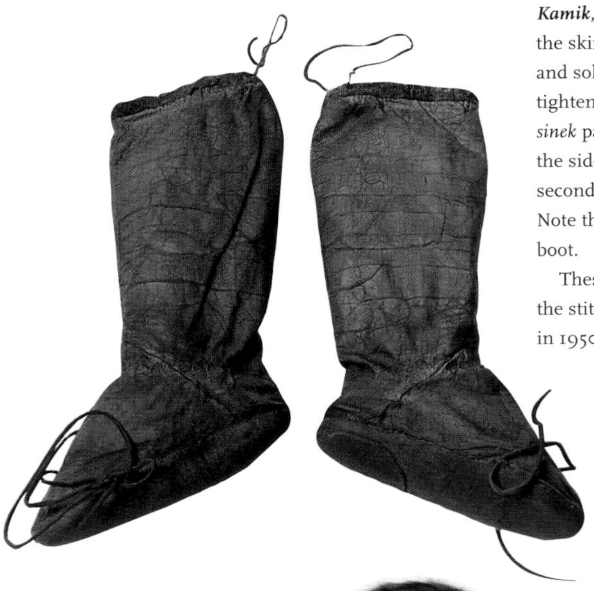

Kamik, or outer boots, with uppers of the skin of the ringed seal, dehaired, and soles of bearded seal. They are tightened at the bottom by a lace or *sinek* passing through a double loop on the sides and knotted at the instep; a second lace tightens them at the calf. Note the patch on the sole of the right boot.

These boots are only waterproof if the stitching is very tight. Unchanged in 1950-1951.

Young boy wearing a man's *natseq*. Three skins: Kardah, Etah, 1916. Unchanged in 1950-1951.

Natseq or woman's summer sealskin coat with an *amaat* or hood for carrying an infant. It is made of two sealskins. Notice the two tabs at the lower edge of the coat: the *akoq* behind, large and triangular; and the smaller, rounded *kineq* in front. Unchanged in 1950-1951.

Sealskin necklace (*ujamik*): three pendants of glass beads obtained from whalers. One still sees necklaces in photographs from 1909, although this decoration (luxury) gradually disappeared along with the amulet (witchcraft) as Christianity became established (1910). Necklaces had disappeared by 1920. They were totally absent in 1950-1951.

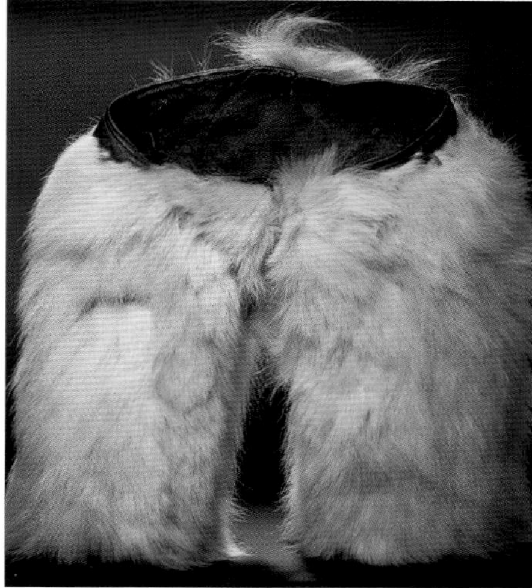

Nannuk or man's trousers. In winter as in summer, the *nannuk* is worn directly against the skin. The fur sheds snow. The legs are cut off just below the knee and above the hips. It rises higher behind than in front. Its cut would only change in 1920, when it rose higher on the hip by 1 cm. A belt 5 cm wide, sewn to the top of the trousers, girdled a man's waist in 1950-1951.

Kapatak or woman's fox-skin coat, still worn in 1950. Seven foxes are needed to make one. The inserts—the white band on the breast and the tabs in the front (*kineq*) and back (*akoq*)—are traditional and were preserved until 1950.

Bag of dehaired sealskin. Still used in 1950-1951.

Bird-skin coat (*atisaq*), worn against the skin. The man's and woman's garment were identical. Two hundred and fifty auks were needed to make this warm, fragile garment, worn from time immemorial by the Inuit. Vermin, notably fleas, infested the *atisaq*. It was abandoned toward 1920. Feathers facing outside and in. This *atisaq* is worn here by Qaaqqutsiaq, age 14. (Photographed by McMillan, Etah, July 1916.)

Frederick A. Cook

DR. FREDERICK ALBERT COOK 1865-1940

THE MOST REVILED MAN IN THE HISTORY OF THE ARCTIC

Dr. Frederick A. Cook, one of the greatest travelers in Arctic history, claimed that he reached the North Pole first, on 21 April 1908. The surprisingly vivid account that he left of his exploration is modest in tone and appears on first examination to be entirely true in its main points ...

Cook's story is a sad one. An explorer of extraordinary courage, he was already well known before his dash to the pole, [1] and was the founder and second president of the Explorers' Club of New York. [2] He was attacked for two months without let-up and his reputation destroyed by a campaign organized against him in the newspapers by Peary, who had close ties with men in power and the media.

Yet the first meeting between Peary and Cook in 1891 was cordial and the two men got along well from the outset.

Recruited as an unsalaried doctor and ethnologist, Cook was on hand to treat Peary when the expedition leader broke his leg on his first expedition in 1891-1892. "Thanks to my doctor's professional skill," Peary declared, "I soon recovered completely." But Cook also accomplished his second task with energy and discernment, gathering ethnographic records on the populations of several villages. His notes, or at least what Peary allowed of them to be published, were of high quality. Cook described the natives' material culture and noted the women's amenorrhea during the winter months.

On this score also Peary commended him, but Cook refused to take part in Peary's second expedition. On their return Peary had barred Cook from publishing his ethnographic findings in a medical journal, and Cook was surprised and angered by this autocratic ruling on publication. When Peary again invited him to join a later expedition, Cook again refused, but he did give a medical examination to the men Peary planned to bring on that expedition (1898-1902). The two men still held each other, therefore, in mutual esteem.

In 1897-1898, Cook played a brilliant part in de Gerlache's voyage to Antarctica aboard the *Belgica*, which saw the first overwintering of a ship in Antarctic seas. Then, in July 1901, he sailed for Etah on the relief ship *Erik* at the request of the Peary Arctic Club, still without salary. Peary had just had most of his toes amputated in primitive conditions, and the club wanted to have him examined by a friendly doctor. Cook gave him a thorough examination. Peary's energy was undiminished, but Cook was concerned about his general state and detected signs of the pernicious anemia that was eventually to kill Peary in 1920.

1) The king of Belgium had bestowed on him a medal for his part in the *Belgica's* expedition to Antarctica (see note 5 below).
2) The first was Greely.

OPPOSITE:
Doctor F. A. Cook, eminent physician and first-rate explorer, was utterly selfless and by his own testimony had only $40 when he disembarked in Copenhagen in August 1909.

It was a strange meeting. Eight years later, the two men would square off against each other on the American stage with a violence never before seen in polar history.

If one is to credit the American press, Cook was not only an impostor but the greatest crook in the history of exploration. Every day's journey and every camp on his fourteen-month expedition (19 February 1908-15 April 1909) with two Eskimo companions past Ellesmere Island, onto the drifting polar pack, progressing tortuously over and around hundreds of pressure ridges, was the pure product of his imagination. Who is to say definitively? His companions were two young Inuit, Aapilaq and Ittukusuk. Only his journal could offer the necessary credibility, along with his navigational data and the confused testimony of his native companions. The one thing that is certain, given that his navigational data is missing and the testimony of the Inuit contradictory, is that his reported itineraries from August 1907 to April 1908 and his crossing of Ellesmere Island are absolutely accurate. Uusaaqqaak, the son of Aapilaq, one of his

The first meeting of Cook (second from right) and Astrup (Norwegian-born geographer and explorer who would commit suicide after an argument of undisclosed nature with Peary). The two are at Kiatak on the south coast of Northumberland Island in the company of Polar Eskimos. The photograph was taken between 12 and 19 August 1891, during Peary's first expedition, on which Cook was the expedition doctor.

companions, confirmed this to me directly in 1951; and the great British explorer Wally Herbert, who would later reach the North Pole by dog sled on 6 April 1969, traveled Cook's route step by step all the way to his camp on Cape Sparbo. But Cook's journey on the Arctic Ocean and the moving polar pack is conjectural at best.

Frederick Cook was the eldest of five children. His father (whose name was Koch, the spelling was anglicized during the Civil War) was a German immigrant and a doctor. Cook lost his father at an early age (as did Peary), and his childhood was one of deprivation and unhappiness. He managed to support his medical studies at Columbia by starting a milk delivery route. He was of medium height but powerfully built, with blond hair, light blue eyes, a large nose, and a neatly trimmed mustache. Again like Peary, he spoke with a slight stutter, slowly and in a low voice. Always calm and in control of himself, he impressed those who met him with his naturalness and amiability. Women seem to have played only a minor role in the life of this solitary man. [3]

Daring and selflessness

Cook felt a romantic passion toward nature and held the Polar Eskimos, who lived close to nature, in profound respect. His anthropological and medical records of this society—unfortunately still not published in their entirety—are of vivid interest. His extreme probity in moral matters is striking. Cook, a patient psychologist, proved the key figure in the first Belgian Antarctic expedition, which might well have ended tragically without his decisive intervention to curb scurvy. This comes out in the accounts of his shipmates, as his own account of that journey, *Through the First Antarctic Night,* tells his part in it with great modesty. [4] His key role in the successful overwintering of the *Belgica* would have remained unknown if his comrades—Roald Amundsen in particular—had not reavealed it. [5]

Throughout his life, Dr. Cook—who was possessed of true nobility—showed little aptitude for business. Governments and universities never sponsored his expeditions. A private individual, he was probably the only man among the great arctic explorers not to harbor any scientific or political ambitions. Yet parts of his life remain obscure. Close scrutiny only opens more questions.

Cook's one interest was in adventure for its own sake. In the various exploits that he attempted, he never took any precautions to ward off his possible detractors. His first ascent of Alaska's Mount McKinley (20,320 ft.), in 1906, after an earlier failed attempt in 1903, seems to have been a turning point in his life. It would have devastating consequences. The metal container he left on the summit in proof of his exploit was never found. [6] Furthermore, the summit photograph proved to have

3) Cook had hardly married before he took off for the Arctic and the Antarctic. When his first two wives—who were sisters—died, he married a third, a young French-born widow, with whom he had his only child, a daughter.

4) Frederick A. Cook, *Through the First Antarctic Night* (New York: 1900).

5) The great Norwegian explorer Roald Amundsen, who would later discover the Northwest Passage (1903-1906) and the South Pole (14 December 1911), was a member of this expedition. He called Cook "the finest traveler I ever saw." He added: "Cook is the most honest and reliable man I have ever known. Of all men, he is the one I trust most." In January 1926, when the explorer was beset with adversity, Roald Amundsen went to visit him in Leavenworth Penitentiary and once again declared his admiration and called him "a genius and an intrepid explorer." This is all the more significant as Amundsen rarely gave compliments.

6) Was Cook pursued by bad luck? A terrible earthquake shook Mount McKinley in July 1912, perhaps providing a natural cause why his summit capsule disappeared.

7) This seems to be in the Arctic tradition. Though Hayes is known to have explored Ellesmere Island, his claimed farthest north is open to debate.

8) Frederick A. Cook, *To the Top of the Continent* (New York: 1908).

been taken on a smaller peak nearby. The greatest authorities all doubted Cook's claim to a first ascent. From then on, fate was against Cook. Sir Wally Herbert has reported that, among the photographs Cook brought back from the Pole, one at least is an obvious fraud, readily detectable from available documents. Cook has therefore been suspected of manically falsifying his claims.[7] And Cook never showed his navigational data to any institutional body.

Cook left for Greenland without having reread the proofs of the book he wrote on his ascent of Mt. McKinley.[8] He was severely reproached afterward for the errors that found their way into the text. But the same happened to Peary on occasion, when his quantitative data proved contradictory. Some mountain climbers supported Cook, while others denounced him. The guide who accompanied him, a certain Barrill, seems to have been an unreliable witness, first confirming Cook's claims for several years, then all of a sudden accepting a considerable sum ($1,500) and contradicting himself to expose Cook as a fake. These blots on Cook's record—in a country ruled by money and the iron claw, to use Jack London's phrase—would later be used maliciously against Cook by a faction bent on destroying him, particularly Peary's coterie of millionaires who had staked their reputations on Peary's success and invested heavily in his enterprise.

In point of fact, Peary refused to enter into the controversy when the Mt. McKinley affair first surfaced, citing his admiration for Cook. But the discovery of the Pole would bring these two men into opposition and arouse, at least on Peary's side, an implacable and permanent hatred. Cook left Anoritooq (Cape Inglefield, north of Etah) on 19 February 1908 in the direction of Cape Sabine and northwest Ellesmere Island (Cape Svartevoeg). He reached the Arctic Ocean on 15 March 1908—three weeks behind Peary's schedule of the following year. His plan was based on an remarkably acute study of Arctic currents by Otto Sverdrup, which described an eastward drift. At Cape Svartevoeg, Cook was 500 miles from the Pole. His supplies, both of dried meat and ammunition, were considerable. After sending back his large group of Eskimo followers, he set off north across the Arctic Ocean on 18 March 1908. His equipment was light and carefully chosen (flexible sledges, unsinkable rubber boat). His push to the Pole was envisioned as a commando raid with the two young Eskimos Aapilaq and Ittukusuk, two sledges, and twenty-six dogs. For the first three days, Cook was accompanied onto the polar pack by two other Eskimos, Qulutannguaq and Inukitsoq,

Cook censored by Peary

The invaluable collection gathered by Cook, a doctor and excellent observer, and his rare written report on native ethnology have unfortunately disappeared, confiscated by Peary. This is extremely regrettable in ethnographic terms, as the "primitive" Polar Eskimos had not yet been studied rigorously. Cook was one of the rare doctors to have reported on winter amenorrhea. Where is that report? His study was made just prior to a period of rapid demographic expansion (1855: pop. 140; 31 August 1895, pop. 253, with 140 men and 113 women) and the establishment of a dual economy, part traditional and part modern, with salaries and the use of firearms and steel traps.

Cook (first row, second from left) on the deck of the Danish ship *Hans Egede*, which carried him back from Greenland in August 1909. They are heading for Lerwick, Scotland, where Cook would send out his first message by telephone. In Upernavik he met Knud Rasmussen, who wrote to him admiringly. A senior Danish civil servant, Jens Dangaard-Jensen, cabled ahead to Copenhagen to have a reception prepared for the explorer commensurate with his great exploit—an exploit he did not in the least doubt.

Uutuuq. In May the seal sleeps on the ice. The hunter is behind a screen of white cloth mounted on a sled. Kiutitak Dunek (born 1932), 1967.

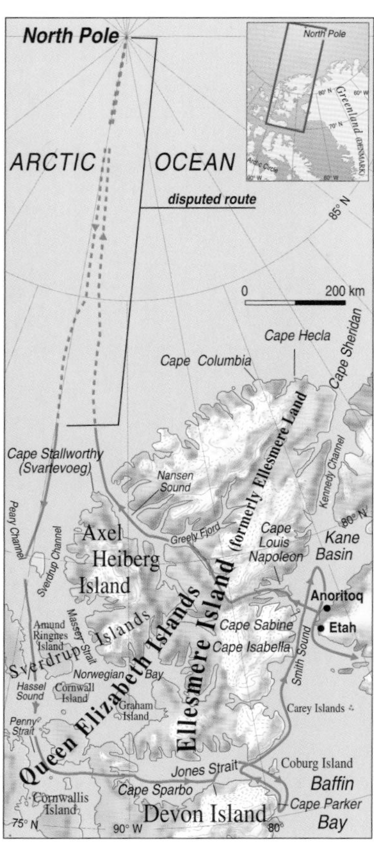

Cook's route to the "Pole," February 1908 to April 1909.

who turned back on 21 March. Thirty-four days later, after numerous adventures, the expedition supposedly reached the Pole.

Shadows

Cook stayed at the Pole the 21st, 22nd, and 23rd of April 1908. His return was eventful, due to the westward drift of the polar pack, which carried the two sledges far from the caches of food they had made on the coast. Between 400 and 300 miles from the Pole, Cook experienced a terrible storm. While northeast of Meighen Island, a point of land unknown until Cook discovered it, the party battled through thick fog for twenty days (24 May-13 June). They ate their dogs one by one and wintered at Cape Sparbo in Jones Sound, which they reached in September. Cook did not have food, rifles, or dogs. On 18 February 1909, having built a small sledge, Cook tried to get back to his starting point north of Etah (Cape Inglefield), where he arrived on foot after inconceivable dangers and hardships on 15 April 1909. [9]

Cook then made another foolish mistake. Having decided to return south by a bold and rapid dog sled journey across Melville Bay, he left his navigational instruments and his original documents at Etah in the hands of the wealthy sportsman Harry Whitney, an honorable but somewhat thoughtless man and not one to court trouble. Cook wanted to spread the risk of losing his effects. A month later (July 1909), Whitney was still at Etah when Peary came through aboard the *Roosevelt* on his return to New York from the Arctic Ocean. Afraid of spending a second winter in the north, Whitney asked for passage home. Not only did he omit to bring back the key documents Cook had left with him, but he helped Captain Bob Bartlett to cache them somewhere along the rocky cliff foot at Etah. [10] The papers and journals would most likely be there still if they hadn't been destroyed or scattered (who knows?) on a subsequent voyage to Etah in August 1910 by Bartlett, Whitney, and a photographer who wrote about the excursion in an article published in 1911. What sorry heroes! "What use," Bartlett declared, "can Dr. Cook have in going back to Etah for 'Proofs' when there are none? The only articles belonging to Dr. Cook at Etah are some clothing and such like and possibly a sextant. But as for records, you can stake your life that there are none." Certainly, but on 25 July 1910 Bartlett was rummaging in the rocks of Etah with Whitney. And if he could say that there were no notes, it was because he had opened the trunk . . .

Oh, America! Bad weather took care of the rest. Peter Freuchen, the Danish explorer and friend of Rasmussen who, in 1910, managed the trading post at Thule, has written that Cook's sextant (of French make) was seen at that time in the Eskimos' igloos. It belonged to Ittukusuk. Freuchen took it to use as a base for an alarm clock. Cook's trunk had also contained a barometer and a thermometer . . .

I am probably the first to have tried—without much conviction—to uncover the truth and find the trunk during my geomorphological expedition to Inglefield and Washington lands, while spending a few days in Etah (March-April 1951). All I had were hazy indications from the Eskimos ("under a little stone igloo . . ."). But their information on the subject came from the vaguest rumors. "Ittukusuk . . . yes, but we don't know anymore . . ." And their behavior was definitely cautious. While making my survey, I walked back and forth over certain sections of the rocky ground, following contradictory information. Nothing came of it. The rock-fall is vast and had already been visited by concerned parties. I quickly gave it up on 15 April 1951, the day before my second and final departure for Inglefield Land.

Companions of Dr. Cook, portrayed by Harald Moltke. They include Pualuna (brother of Uutaaq), and Piuaitsoq, who accompanied Peary and was killed by an American explorer on McMillan's 1914 expedition (according to Minik, and reported by Kenn Harper).

A RE-EXAMINATION OF DR. COOK'S LIFE

If Cook was a fraud—no possibility should be discarded, particularly as Cook had the unfortunate habit of falsifying photographs—consider the extraordinary risk he took in "imagining" what the Pole was like. The Pole could have been a volcano, an island, a mountain, a chaotic field of ice hummocks . . . But what Cook described—and he was the first ever to do so—was an accurate picture of the Pole: an ice surface that grew smoother beyond 88° N. He declared that the atmosphere had a reddish tint, that it was colder between 88° and 89° than at the Pole itself. He also reported a current at 84° N trending south and west, one that had

9) From 1 March to 1 April, Cook's journal was not maintained regularly. He dated his arrival at Cape Inglefield to 15 April, but it was in fact 18 April, Cook having lost three days during his fourteen months alone with his two Inuit companions.

10) Whitney, who had been at Anoritooq when Cook arrived, had promised not to mention to Peary or anyone else that Cook had reached the North Pole on 21 April 1908. Cook, who had no transport south, wanted to reach Upernavik by dog sled and from there catch a Danish ship to Europe so that he could announce his news before Peary reappeared.

11) Michael Richey was President of the International Society of Navigation in London (1983).

never before been described and nearly proved fatal to his expedition, and an ice island between 87° and 88°, again unreported but subsequently confirmed. Why would Cook have risked his life far from his food caches if he had simply wanted to make a short trek over the polar pack? Finally, the shadow cast by a sledge's upstander in one of his photographs is at the correct angle for the Pole.

Proofs and the sum of evidence

Cook's daily record of his journey is detailed and colorful. At first glance, it has all the appearance of truth. Temperature, barometric pressure, wind speed, animal life, and new westward currents are all indicated, but the navigational data are entirely insufficient given that he had no accurate knowledge of the time for two months, and did not make corrections on his return twelve months later. Cook was therefore unable to establish his correct longitude. His fragile instruments, furthermore, suffered from hard treatment on the pack. Daily variations in the compass were not recorded. Cook declared that the compass pointed south at the Pole . . . but with a tolerance of 30°. At least two of the photographs claimed to have been taken near the Pole were falsified—this has been clearly established by Sir Wally Herbert (see page 199). Did Cook reach the Pole? Did he believe he had reached it? Or did he make up the fact that he had gone there? The second and third of these possiblities appear closest to the truth.

Cook had the advantage of publishing his report and his data first (on 2 September 1909), without any knowledge of Peary's findings. Peary, who had Cook's text transmitted to him, confirmed his general description in an interview with a journalist from the *Sydney Times* published on 28 September. And Peary on his return from his historic expedition of March-April 1909 had no more navigational data to support him for the region beyond 87° than Cook had. The only proof possible would be the concurrence of an international committee of experts from geographical societies, a navigational institute, or an academy of science, after investigating and re-investigating. But neither one nor the other received such proof. The medals Peary and Cook received from various rival geographical societies prove nothing at all.

The First International Congress on the Pole, held at the CNRS in Paris from 16 to 19 November 1983 and attended by five men who had traveled to the Pole, established how skimpy was the evidence presented to the geographical societies—this came out in the session on the history of the discovery of the North Pole and the report by that session's chairman, Michael Richey. [11] And the Explorers' Club of New York, represented at this historic congress by its archivist, added to the confusion by pointing to the fact that the club had honored both Peary and Cook (the latter having been its second president).

Cook in explorer's costume. This studio photograph was taken in Alaska during Cook's questionable 1906 ascent of Mount McKinley, North America's highest summit.

1909: the scientific organizations bow out

In 1909 this debate took on a polemical and scandalous character. Yet no international body of geographers shouldered the responsibility of examining and re-examining the evidence so as to produce a neutral judgment. The Swedish scholar Nordenskjöld, discoverer of the Northeast Passage, called for such an investigation but in vain. The caution exhibited by the world of polar travelers is both surprising and disappointing . . . The Smithsonian Institution, the United States Academy of Science, and the American Geographical Society remained strangely silent, although the secretary general of the International Polar Committee (Brussels), Professor Georges Lecointe, came out in favor of Cook.

It is symptomatic that, when this great historical debate on the discovery of the Pole raged in 1910—a debate that concerned everyone—no independent scientific organization felt called upon to act. These organizations all kept silent, which left the way open for any amount of blather and mudslinging in the international press.

The great problem is that even if Cook and Peary had reached the Pole, they could not have known it with any certainty. Sightings of latitude and longitude have to be taken frequently, which is not always possible given the weather at the Pole in April. At most, both explorers truly believed that they had reached the Pole—or its general vicinity, according to one of Cook's later remarks.

Let us continue with the investigation. Concentrating on Cook, what are we to think of his expedition on a tech-

687 Bushwick Ave
Brooklyn N.Y. Sept 16 1901

My Dear Mrs Peary—

By this time I presume you have gotten a goodly supply of worldly pleasures and are again breathing a normal life. Let the good work go on—

I have sent Marie a little birthday token by this mail which I hope you will accept for her with my sincerest and best wishes for her future happiness.

Yours faithfully
Frederick A Cook

Unpublished letter, dated 16 September 1901, from Dr. F. A. Cook to Josephine Peary. It shows the excellent relations between Cook and the Pearys during these years. Peary never forgave Cook for betraying him by mounting a polar expedition in 1907-1908, at the very time that Peary was, after twenty years, organizing a final push to the Pole.

Peary and Cook with their Uncle Sam, who proposes to judge between them by flipping a coin.

nical level? His sledges were light (55 lbs.) and made of white hickory; [13] his food was appropriate (pemmican, dried meat); he carried a folding canvas boat, whose frame doubled as part of a sledge. His equipment was well designed, and of a quality rarely seen in polar expeditions. Cook also had considerable native help: nine Eskimos, eleven sledges, and 102 dogs accompanied him to the north end of Axel Heiberg Island. "I was able to verify that it would be difficult to conceive a more intelligently equipped expedition," said Rasmussen, who saw Cook at Etah in February 1907 before his departure for the Pole. Pualuna, Cook's companion in February-March 1908, confirmed to me over the course of many interviews in November 1950 while I wintered in Siorapaluk that the expedition cached great stores of food and game in northern Ellesmere Island. He never spoke a critical word about Daagitkoorsuaq. [14] He answered my questions with a weary and dismissive "White man's business!"

The primitive existence that Cook led for a year (1908-1909) without guns, dogs, or a kayak, and his survival using the most archaic tools (slings, lances, and bows fashioned from sledge parts), are the basis of one of the most extraordinary tales ever told. This part of his account, concerning his prehistoric living conditions for eight months on Cape Sparbo, is known to be true. The extracts from his account, published below, speak for themselves.

The first photographs of the "Pole," taken by Cook: the film is enclosed in two brass tubes and packed in a cigar box, just as it was sent from Copenhagen to the offices of the *New York Herald* in Paris to be developed.

Cook's technical evidence

And what of Cook as an explorer and navigator? Many of his compatriots, including Lieutenant, then Brigadier General, Greely, Captain Baldwin (meteorologist on Peary's 1893-1894 expedition), and Admiral W. S. Schley (an eminent figure in Arctic history, who rescued the Greely expedition from Cape Sabine in June 1884), and many foreigners, including the Norwegian captain Otto Sverdrup and Roald Amundsen, continued to believe in Cook through thick and thin.

Admiral Schley, in a letter dated 7 January 1911, wrote to him: "I have never subscribed to the belief that Civil Engineer Peary was alone to reach the Pole. Having read each day—and in a critical frame of mind—the accounts written by you both, I am led to the conclusion that their similarities are such as to make each of you the ocular witness of the other's victory. I have always tried to put my finger fairly on the proof inducing me to believe that there is room enough at the Pole for two discoverers, and I have never had so narrow a mind as to believe that only one man reached it." Greely, who led the American expedition of the First International Polar Year (1882-1884), declared: "Dr. Cook is the discoverer of the North Pole." And Dagmar Rasmussen, Knud's wife, was quoted in *Le Matin* on 5 September 1909 as saying: "My husband has not the slightest doubt about the truth of Dr. Cook's assertions."

Let us append a statement by Otto Sverdrup, the Norwegian explorer of Ellesmere Island: "I believe that Cook reached the Pole because he did not cling to the same route that had always been followed—the one Peary was still attempting. The fast currents along that route carry the ice away and make it impossible to reach the Pole." The final word goes to Erik Nordenskjöld: "The polar controversy must be decided by an international commission."

13) The weight of Peary's sledges, according to Cook, was 90 lbs.

14) One of Cook's Inuit names, the other being "Tatsekuk."

15) As late as 1983, the controversy could have poisoned the First International Congress on the Pole at the CNRS if the executive committee had not prevented it. An advertisement aired in New York in December 1983 promoting a film favorable to Cook claimed that Congress had made certain statements when in fact it had said the opposite.

16) He had said that Cook exploited his two companions, having not paid them. Recently, however, Inuterssuaq, an old friend, recalled that he had ("I have no doubt that they received guns, knives, etc. and perhaps a bit of wood") and that they hold no grudge against Daagit Koorsuaq. "I know that the Eskimos have nothing bad to say with respect to Daagitkoorsuag, or regarding his stay in 1891–1892." Inuterssuaq, in his report published by the Society of Greenland and, in English, by Slr Wally Herbert (1988), testified in detail that the two Eskimo companions didn't think they were headed to the Pole, a point of view contrary to that expressed to Knud Rasmussen by "members of the tribe you can trust," and published in September 1909.

The controversy (again)

"Reached the North Pole, April 21st 1908. Discovered land far North," signed F. A. Cook, 5 September 1909. "Stars and stripes nailed to the Pole." This was signed R. E. Peary, 10 September 1909. The two telegrams broke on the world five days apart.

Cook welcomed Peary's achievement graciously. Peary was furious and, after looking into it, contested Cook's claim. So began the imbroglio that was to stir American public opinion until the United States entered into the war in 1917.[15]

Within two months, Cook, the national hero who had received the keys to New York City, was being vilified. Two further errors would be used to discredit him. In preparing his final report, Cook hired assistants to help him organize his material and work out his mathematical calculations—a customary practice. But he chose poorly and the men stole his papers and said he had asked them to make up a route to the Pole. They went to the newspapers with this story, and the press trumpeted the accusations irresponsibly. Then Cook gave an interview to *Hampton Magazine*, and the published account had Cook saying the opposite of what he thought. The reporter admitted to having twisted Cook's words in his pseudo interview—a particularly sorry instance of journalism. The slightest detail of Cook's story was attacked on the basis of ridiculous and derogatory fabrications. For instance, he had said that the Eskimos loved the gum drops he gave them, and a certain newspaper sniggered that the explorer bribed his two companions to slog on toward an imaginary Pole "with gumdrops."

"Few men in all history, I am inclined to believe, have ever been made the subject of such vicious attacks, of such malevolent assailing of character, of such a series of perjured and forged charges, as I," said Cook later. Even when he responded with dignity, he was ridiculed and dragged in the mud. And when Peary made Cook's Eskimo companions "confess" the opposite of what they had just told Knud Rasmussen,[16] Rasmussen (regrettably!) made no protest.

At no time did the American authorities decide to have the two Eskimos in question brought to New York so that they might be questioned in depth by an independent jury. Cook expressly requested this of the Danish authorities in Copenhagen in September 1910. They did not act on Cook's request, saying that Rasmussen's inquiries had been favorable to him. And at no time did they consider sending a fact-finding commission to Etah, despite Cook's repeated pleas. Meanwhile, Cook was trying to get back the documents that had been hidden by Whitney on orders from Peary in the rock-fall at Etah.

Despite the virulent attacks, Cook always took the high road in his responses. His attitude throughout these weeks of scandal deserves to be noted—it had

The "North Pole,"
21 April 1908. Photograph by Dr. Cook.

Shamanistic séance: the giant female soothsayer (Eskimo legend from South Greenland).

nothing in common with the classic image of a crook. Cook showed rare dignity, a real indifference to power, and unmistakable naivete.

London, 1910: in the midst of the crowd, unrecognized, Cook stands leaning against a column while Peary speaks about his discovery of the Pole. It would be interesting to know what thoughts are passing through the mind of this wounded and solitary adventurer while listening to Peary's speech and the applause that followed it.

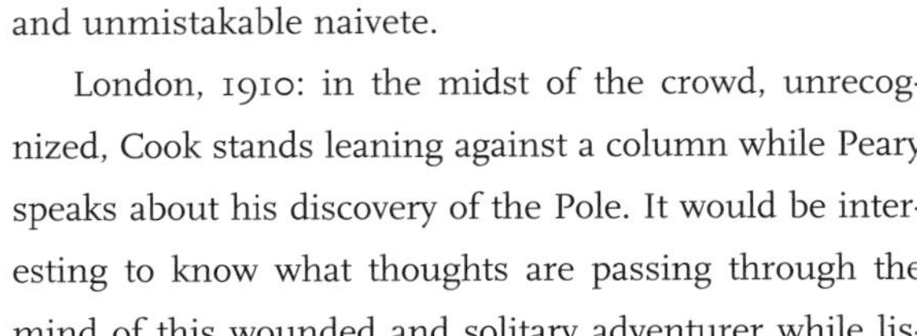

Cook's published account, *My Attainment of the Pole,* appeared before Peary's and was accompanied by a solemn appeal to the president of the United States for justice, asking that his feat be acknowledged and that an international committee of experts examine the data brought back by the two explorers. Alas, this elementary justice was denied him, due to the indirect but nonetheless decisive pressure of Robert Peary, who refused to lend himself to the mediating process called for by the Geographical Society of Paris, the dean of all geographical societies.

Anonymous Eskimo drawing of a white man next to a *tupilak.* Cook was victim of jealousy and lies, as though one of these evil spirits had attached itself to him.

In December 1910, events started to come to a head. The University of Copenhagen, pressured by the publicity and nettled by the difficult position it faced because of the Cook affair (the Danish government and even the royal family were also under attack from Cook's detractors) decided to hurry the process along. They also decided to hurry the verdict, on the basis of a proposal by Cook to return personally to Etah in summer 1910: without the original records, which had been left among the rocks, he could provide no proof for his navigational data. On 20 December 1910, the University of Copenhagen announced its verdict: "Not proven." Yet only a year earlier, in 1909, after the explorer had met with the most notable mathematicians and astronomers at the university, their leader Professor Torp had declared: "I am bold to say that there is not the slightest reason for anyone to cast the shadow of a doubt on Dr. Cook's assertion that he reached the Pole, nor on the means he claims to have used to get there." So it goes. *Verba volant,* even in the highest research institutions. This last blow left Cook exhausted and in despair. Canceling his scheduled speeches, which would have allowed him to earn $200,000 in five years, he left for Nepal with the intention of climbing Everest, only to flee to Borneo under an assumed name.

In the United States meanwhile, a nationwide campaign was building in support of Cook's claim to be the rightful discoverer of the Pole. Cook's friends in Congress had stayed fanatically loyal to him and now began questioning Peary—the too successful Peary—on his own proofs. The sea ebbed, and a new wave rolled in. Under the leadership of Helgesen, a U.S. representative from North Dakota who tracked Peary accurately and implacably, a national campaign was mounted against Peary in Congress, which went so far as to accuse him of being "immoral and a liar." The formidable Helgesen wanted to get to the bottom of Peary's statements, which he judged as unsatisfactory as Cook's. He even asked that Peary be stripped of his title of rear admiral for fraudulence. But Helgesen died suddenly on 10 April 1917—the gods seem to have been protecting Peary.

At that point the United States entered the First World War. Congress had other matters to attend to. Peary retired to Eagle Island. Cook, flamboyant as ever, was almost arrested by the British secret service in India as a German spy.

F. A. Cook, president of a petroleum company

Cook did not reappear in the public eye until 1923. By then he had become an oilman in Texas, at the head of a small but powerful company, buying weak companies and promoting his stock through mail campaigns. He fell a victim to the obscure but determined war fought by large companies against small: in November 1925 he was condemned to fourteen years and nine months in prison for false advertising.

The presiding judge had ties to the plaintiff oil companies (he was a member of the famous "Ohio gang"), and the court made only a cursory examination of Cook's holdings—a very cursory one, because one of the wells did start to produce oil while Cook was in prison! This well would be one of the largest producers in Texas. Following the trial it was sold to a financial group for whom it earned 110 million dollars. In the five years that Cook (prison number 23218) actually served of his sentence, he became one of the most popular inmates in the U.S. penitentiary system, editing a newspaper by and for prisoners.

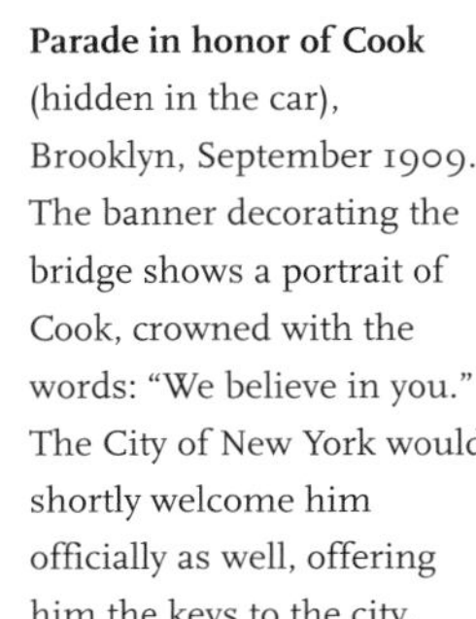
Parade in honor of Cook (hidden in the car), Brooklyn, September 1909. The banner decorating the bridge shows a portrait of Cook, crowned with the words: "We believe in you." The City of New York would shortly welcome him officially as well, offering him the keys to the city.

Honor to the fallen great

When Cook was released from prison on parole in May 1930, he was sixty-five years old. He had $50 in his bank account. He would live another ten years, heading a Chicago organization for the rehabilitation of social misfits and writing his last book, *Return from the Pole.*

"Read what I have written," said Cook, "compare the reports. I trust your decision." And before his death, he would fight on: "I want my name, which is an honorable one, entirely cleared." Alas, he would die at the age of seventy-five before his name was "entirely cleared." On his death bed, he was granted a presidential pardon by Franklin Roosevelt, who restored him to full citizenship.

"You can't sling mud without splashing your own face and hands," Cook liked to say. And he was not wrong. Since the 1970s, the balance has started to shift in his direction—as a man and a victim, if not as the discoverer of the Pole. He has been the subject of a returning interest, and the focus of many societies and books. "Justice to Peary, mercy to Cook," said Stefansson, a severe critic of Cook. But today the situation is reversed: mercy to Peary, justice to Cook. With neither of the explorers able to furnish valid evidence, Cook has regained a certain advantage.

Cook's dignity in misfortune and his eminently generous spirit lift this extraordinary traveler out of the mists of oblivion. In 1958, a U.S. representative, J. R. Pillion, again proposed that the discovery of the Pole, whether one accepted or rejected Peary, be attributed to Cook. ■

Cook in an arctic decor, recreated in a studio (probably in New York) in September 1909. The explorer holds his notebooks in his left hand, his theodolite in his right. The two Eskimos are clearly stand-ins, and the dog is not from North Greenland.

Dogs are trained to attack bears. They pursue the bear in silence, pulling the sled at great speed. Released from the sled by the hunter, they encircle the bear and try to bite his paws. The bear (ten feet tall, and 650 to 1400 lbs.) tries to get away into the open water if the pack is broken up, or by backing up against an iceberg. Facing the dog pack, he grabs a dog by the harness and throws him like a bullet at his adversaries. Powerful and cunning, the bear attacks with its left paw. Melville Bay.

Cook speaks

Cook tells his story: "... One of them seemed much older because of his quiet courage and also the maturity and calm of his way of thinking and acting. His name was Etukishook (Ittukusuk) ..."

Arrival at the Pole, 21 April 1908

Our course when arriving at the Pole, as near as it was possible to determine, was on the ninety-seventh meridian. The day was April 21, 1908. It was local noon. The sun was 11.550 above the magnetic northern horizon. My shadow, a dark purple-blue streak with ill-defined edges, measured twenty-six feet in length. The tent pole, marked as a measuring stick, was pushed into the snow, leaving six feet above the surface. This gave a shadow twenty-eight feet long. [17]

Several sextant observations gave a latitude of a few seconds below 90°, which, because of unknown refraction and uncertain accuracy of time, was placed at 90°. (Other observations on the next day gave similar results, although we shifted camp four miles toward magnetic south.) A broken hand-axe was tied to the end of a lifeline; this was lowered through a fresh break in the ice, and the angle it made with the surface indicated a drift toward Greenland. The temperature, gauged by a spirit thermometer, was 37.7° F. The mercury thermometer indicated -36°. The atmospheric pressure by the aneroid barometer was at 29.83. It was falling, and indicated a coming change in the weather. The wind was very light, and had veered from northeast to south, according to the compass card.

The sky was almost clear, of a dark purple blue, with a pearly ice-blink or silver reflection extending east, and a smoky water-sky west, in darkened, ill-defined streaks, indicating continuous ice or land toward Bering Sea, and an active pack, with some open water, toward Spitzbergen. To the north and south were wine-colored gold-shot clouds, flung in long banners, with ragged-pointed ends along the horizon. The ice was nearly the same as it had been continuously since leaving the eighty-eighth parallel. It was slightly more active, and, showed, by new cracks and oversliding, young-ice signs of recent disturbance.

The field upon which we camped was about three miles long and two miles wide. Measured at a new crevasse, the ice was sixteen feet thick. The tallest hummock measured twenty-eight feet above water. The snow lay in fine feathery crystals, with no surface crust. About three inches below the soft snow was a subsurface crust strong enough to carry the bodily weight. Below this were other successive crusts, and a porous snow in coarse crystals, with a total depth of about fifteen inches. [18]

John Murphy and Billy Pritchard, the two American sailors—one of them a brute—left by Peary to trade with the Eskimos at Anoritooq (Cape Inglefield) and Etah during the winter of 1908-1909 to bolster his expedition's finances. Peary installed them in Cook's cabin, where Cook had stored emergency supplies in case of dire need. Cook bitterly complained of this later, as he arrived back starving and exhausted to find that his supplies had been stolen by the two sailors.

Return from the Pole, May-June 1908

Thus had a mutual confidence long since grown up between us. They called me "Doto." [19] Though the men were twenty years old, one of them seemed much older because of his quiet courage and the maturity and calm of his manner of thinking and acting. His name was Etukishook [Ittukusuk]; I called him Etuq. The other was quick, theatrical, young in spirit, hasty and light in his actions. His name was Ahwelah [Aapilaq]; I called him Wela.

Both had a great deal of experience with hunting, as must any savage who relies on meat for nourishment. The art of hunting was a profession to them, an art of life that required a well-trained mind and a harmoniously developed body. If we see the Eskimo as a primitive artist, his calling provides us a study of the progress of humanity through the work of all subsequent generations. My Eskimo companions were ill at ease, though they were on the whole more satisfied and less worried than I. They alternated between periods of extreme agitation and periods of emotional repression and frozen desires. Other than ourselves and our dogs, we had not seen a living soul for almost two months. For me, this absence of life on the vast expanses we were crossing was profoundly depressing; but for them, everything that surrounded us was alive. Even the storms and the ice that broke and parted represented a living energy. When the spirits of the air or the gods of the sea were at war, humankind had to suffer.

They showed a stoic resignation toward the setbacks occasioned by the forces of nature and a willingness to wait and watch for a greater harmony. Physically, at this time, they lived in a world full of promises. Almost every day they saw signs of the presence of seals, birds, bears, and land.

They scented the odor and the taste of the land breezes, and they heard the sounds of a mysterious activity, where for me there was only the frozen wasteland of an infinite expanse of lifeless ocean.

Return to land: Ringnes Island, April 1908

At about six o'clock we were awakened by a strange sound. Our surprised eyes turned from side to side. Not a word was uttered. Another sound came—a series of soft, silvery notes—the song of a creature that might have come from heaven. I listened with rapture. I believed I was dreaming. The enchanting song continued—I lay entranced. I could not believe this divine thing was of our real world until the pole of our tent gently quivered. Then, above us, I heard the flutter of wings. It was a bird—a snow bunting trilling its ethereal song—the first sound of life heard for many months.

We were back to life! Tears of joy rolled down our emaciated faces. If I could tell you of the resurrection of the soul which came with that first bird note, and of the renewed interest in life which it gave us, I should feel myself capable of something superhuman in powers of expression.

With the song of that marvelous bird a choking sense of homesickness came to all of us. We spoke no word. The longing for home gripped our hearts.

We were hungry, [20] but no thought of killing this little feathered creature came to us. It seemed as divine as the bird that came of old to Noah in the ark. Taking a few of our last bread crumbs, we went out to give it food. The little chirping thing danced joyously on the crisp snows, evidently as glad to see us as we were to behold it. I watched it with fascination.

Fighting the bears, Devon Island, Cape Sparbo, winter 1907-1908

Bears headed us off at every turn. [21] We were not permitted to proceed beyond an enclosed hundred feet from the hole of our den. Not an inch of ground or a morsel of food was permitted us without a contest. It was a fight of nature against nature. We either actually saw the little sooty nostrils with jets of vicious breath rising, and the huge outline of a wild beast ready to spring on us, or imagined we saw it. With no adequate means of defense, we were driven to imprisonment within the walls of our own den.

Cook's discovery of the Pole. Cover illustration of the German magazine *Simplicissimus*. The figure on the left is Peary.

From within, our position was even more tantalizing. The bear thieves dug under the snows over our heads and snatched blocks of blubber fuel from under our very eyes at the port without a consciousness of wrongdoing. Occasionally we ventured out to deliver a lance, but each time the bear would make a leap for the door and would have entered had the opening been large enough. In other cases we shot arrows through the peep-hole. A bear head again would burst through the silk covered window near the roof, where knives, at close range and in good light, could be driven with sweet vengeance.

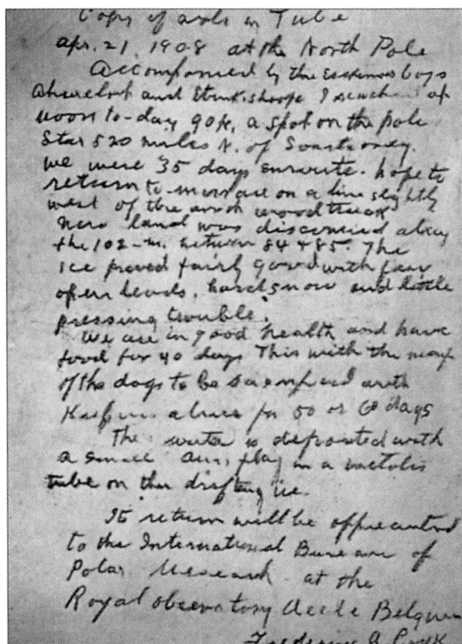

Copy of note in Tube
Apr. 21, 1908 at the North Pole
Accompanied by the Eskimo boys Ahwelah and Etukishook I reached at noon to-day 90°, a spot on the pole star 520 miles N. of Svartevoeg.
We were 35 days enroute. hope to return to [illegible] on a line slightly west of the [illegible] route.
New land was discovered along the 102 m. between 84 & 85. The ice proved fairly good with few open leads, hard snow and little pressing trouble.
We are in good health and have food for 40 days. This with the meat of the dogs to be sacrificed [illegible] [illegible] for 50 or 60 days.
This note is deposited with a small [illegible] flag in a metallic tube on the drifting ice.
Its return will be appreciated to the International Bureau of Polar Research at the Royal Observatory Uccle Belgium
Frederick A. Cook

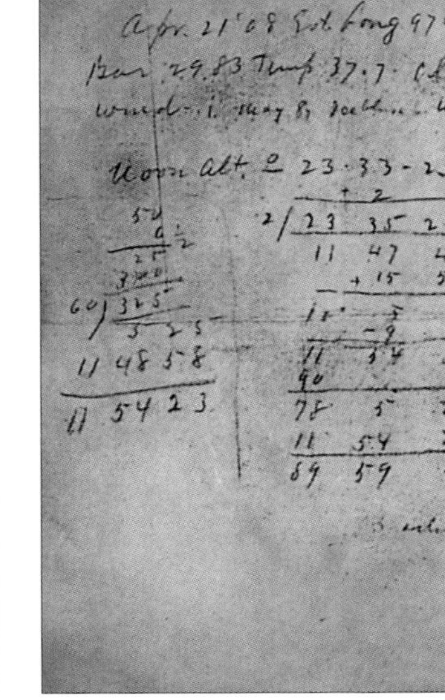

Apr. 21 '08 [illegible] Long 97 W.
Bar. 29.83 Temp. 37.7 [illegible]
[illegible]
Noon alt. [illegible] 23.33.25

Left, **the journal of Dr. Goodsell**, Peary's doctor aboard the *Roosevelt*, dated 25 August 1909. "The Roosevelt arrived at Cape York this morning. The balance of the Inuits leave us here: Koodlooktah and Aletah. We heard that Dr. Cook claims to have reached the North Pole April 22, 1908."
Middle and right, Dr. Cook's notes at the "Pole" on 21 April 1908.

17) This first geographical description of an entirely unknown spot was published in the newspapers on 2 September 1909, that is, before any appearance of Peary's account. The full account appeared on 15 September and 17 October 1909.

18) Cook knew the work of Sverdrup, the Norwegian oceanographer and companion of Nansen, who concluded from his explorations of Ellesmere Island that the ocean currents ran east. Hence Cook set off from east of Axel Heiberg Island (95° longitude) so as to allow the currents to carry him toward 90° of longitude.

19) In 1950-1951, the memory of Cook as retained by the Inuit, and notably Inuterssuaq, could be summarized in two words: charm and daring. There were no recriminations. Uusaaqqak, the son of Aapilaq, never voiced the slightest criticism of Cook to me.

20) 13 June 1908: as a result of the polar pack drifting south and west, a fact unknown to geographers and first revealed by Cook, the party missed finding its cache of food on the Canadian shore near Cape Stallworthy (Svartevoeg). Cook had only ten dogs left and a little pemmican, perhaps twenty days' food for three men. They were hungry and anxious. They survived three hundred days. This text was written in 1930-1935, when Cook was seventy years old, but we shouldn't be startled by the clarity of his recollection. Such events become sharper with time.

21) In the Arctic, if a man is without dogs, he must constantly fight to survive his immediate enemy, the bear. The stone igloo with its long narrow entrance corridor, the Polar Eskimos' main dwelling, was primarily a shelter against bears. Cook's text brings us back to the time when men still contended with bears for their very survival.

The *Erik*, Peary's supply ship on several expeditions, at Etah. It was at this site and on this ship in July 1908 that Rudolph Franke, Cook's faithful companion, badly wounded in the leg, obtained Peary's permission to embark for the United States on condition that he turn over his stock of furs and ivory.

Ovibos moschatus, part mountain goat and part ox, with its sharp and powerful horns. It weighs from 450 to 650 lbs.

As a last resort we made a hole through the top of the den. When a bear was heard near, a long torch was pushed through. The snow for acres around was then suddenly flashed with a ghostly whiteness that almost frightened us. But the bear calmly took advantage of the light to pick a larger piece of the blubber, upon which our lives depended, and then with an air of superiority he would move into the brightest light, usually within a few feet of our peep-hole, where we could almost touch his hateful skin. Without ammunition we were helpless.[22]

A further enemy, the musk ox

Two lances were crushed to small fragments before they could be withdrawn by the light line attached. They inflicted wounds, but not severe ones.

Noting the immense strength of the animals, we at first thought it imprudent to risk the harpoon with its precious line, for if we lost it we could not replace it. But the destruction of the two lines left us no alternative.

Ah-we-lah threw the harpoon. It hit a rib, glanced to a rock, and was also destroyed. Fortunately we had a duplicate point, which was quickly fastened. Then we moved to encourage another onslaught.

Two came at once, an old bull and a young one. E-tuk-i-shook threw the harpoon at the young one, and it entered. The line had previously been fastened, to a rock, and the animal ran back to its associates, apparently not severely hurt, leaving the line slack. One of the others immediately attacked the line with horns, hoofs, and teeth, but did not succeed in breaking it.

Our problem now was to get rid of the other three while we dealt with the one at the end of the line. Our only resource was a sudden fusillade of stones. This proved effective. The three scattered and ascended the boulder-strewn foreland of a cliff, where the oldest bull remained to watch our movements. The young bull made violent efforts to escape but the line of sealskin was strong and elastic. A lucky throw of a lance at close range ended the strife. Then we advanced on the old bull, who was alone in a good position for us.

We gathered stones and advanced, throwing them at the creature's body. This, we found, did not enrage him, but it prevented his making an attack. As we gained ground he gradually backed up to the edge of the cliff, snorting viciously but making no effort whatever either to escape along a lateral bench or to attack. His big brown eyes were upon us; his sharp horns were pointed at us. He evidently was planning a desperate lunge and was backing to gain time and room, but each of us kept within a few yards of a good-sized rock.

Suddenly we made a combined rush into the open, hurling stones, and keeping a long rock in a line for retreat. Our storming of stones had the desired effect. The bull, annoyed and losing its presence of mind, stepped impatiently one step too far backward and fell suddenly over the cliff, landing on a rocky ledge below. Looking over we saw he had broken a foreleg. The cliff was not more than fifteen feet high. From it the lance was used to put the poor creature out of suffering. We were rich now and could afford to fill our stomachs, contracted by long spells of famine. The bull dressed about three hundred pounds of meat and one hundred pounds of tallow.

The musk ox now supplied many wants in our Robinson Crusoe life.[23] From the bone we made harpoon points, arrow pieces, handles, fox traps, and sledge repairs. The skin, with its remarkable fur, made our bed and roofed our igloo. Of it we made all kinds of garments, but its greatest use was for coats with hoods, stockings, and mittens. From the skin, with the fur removed, we made boots, patched punctures in our boat, and cut lashings. The hair and wool that were removed from the skins made pads for our palms in the mittens, and cushions for the soles of our feet in lieu of the grass formerly used.[24]

The meat became our staple food for seven months without change. It was a delicious product. It has a slightly sweet flavor, like that of horseflesh, but still distinctly pleasing. It possesses an odor unlike musk but, equally, unlike anything that I know of. The live creatures exhale the scent of domestic cattle. Just why this odd creature is called "musk" ox is a mystery, for it is not an ox and does not smell of musk. The Eskimo name, ah-ming-ma, fits it much bet-

Telegram from Dr. F. A. Cook to the *Daily Mail* of London. Cook was convinced that the scientific community, once it had seen his records, would recognize his achievement.

Statstelegrafen. Ktr. J. Nr.

Gebyr: Kr. Ø. — Tilsammen: Kr. Ø. — Modt. af:

Telegram til fra Kjøbenhavn.

Befordret App. til St. den / . T. M. af:

Nr. , Ord, (Ø, Gr.) / 190 , T. M. — Tj. Bm.

Telegrammets Adresse og Tekst:

Copenhagen

September 5th, 1909.

To the Editor of the Daily Mail

London

When the scientists of England and the rest of the world have had an opportunity of examining my astronomical observations, I cherish the utmost confidence they will unreserevedly recognise my claim to the discovery of the North Pole. I believe our data to be indisputable. It is the result of comprehensive, detailed compilation with the aid of the most modern apparatus, and I am entirely prepared to accept full responsibility for its accuracy.

Frederick A. Cook.

ter. The bones were used as fuel for outside fires, and the fat as both fuel and food.

Dramatic return from Cape Sparbo (Canada) to Anoritooq (Greenland)

At the end of thirty-five days of almost ceaseless toil we managed to reach Cape Faraday.[25] Our food was gone. We were face to face with the most desperate problem that had fallen to our long run of hard luck. Famine confronted us. We were far from the haunts of game; we had seen no living thing for a month. Every fiber of our bodies quivered with cold and hunger. In desperation we ate bits of skin and chewed tough walrus lines. A half candle and three cups of hot water served for several meals. Some tough walrus hide was boiled and eaten with relish. While trying to masticate this I broke some of my teeth. It was hard on the teeth, but easy on the stomach, and it had the great advantage of dispelling for prolonged periods the pangs of hunger. But only a few strips of walrus line were left after this was used.

Traveling as we must in a circuitous route, there was still a distance of one hundred miles between us and Cape Sabine, and the distance to Greenland might, by open water, be two hundred miles. This troublesome expanse could not be crossed in less than a month. Where, I asked in desperation, were we to obtain subsistence for that last thirty days?

To the east, a line of black vapors indicated open water about twenty-five miles off shore. There were no seals on the ice. There were no encouraging signs of life; only old imprints of bears and foxes 5were left on the surface of the cheerless snows at each camp. For a number of days we had placed our last meat as bait to attract the bears, but none had ventured to pay us a visit.

In sight of Anoritooq, Inglefield Land

So weak that we had to climb on hands and knees, we reached the top of an iceberg, and from there saw Annoatok [Anoritooq].[26] Natives, who had thought us long dead, rushed out to greet us. There I met Mr. Harry Whitney. As I held his hand, the cheer of a long-forgotten world came over me. With him I went to my house, only to find that during my absence it had been confiscated. A sudden bitterness rose within which it was difficult to hide. A warm meal dispelled this for a time.

In due time I told Whitney: "I have reached the Pole."

Uttering this for the first time in English, it came upon me that I was saying a remarkable thing. Yet Mr. Whitney showed no great surprise, and his quiet congratulation confirmed what was in my mind—that I had accomplished no extraordinary or unbelievable thing; for to me the Polar experience was not in the least remarkable, considered with our later adventures.[27]

Cook, speaking in September 1909 to the Danish Royal Geographic Society in Copenhagen, points out his route to the Pole before a gathering of 1,500 guests that included the king of Denmark and the leading scientific minds of the nation. The University of Copenhagen had just conferred an honorary doctorate on him after he was questioned by Professor Torp, rector of the University, and Professor Stamgreen, the great Danish astronomer. "There was never a detail or a question that he failed to answer in the most satisfactory manner," Professor Torp concluded.

22) It was in the middle of the winter, by the light of the tallow lamp (using musk ox fat) that Cook copied down each day with care in a tiny hand his journal and notes. Intutek, the brother of Aapilaq, and Ivalu, the sister of Itukusuk, told me the story of this winter with the following detail: "He wrote, he wrote all the time, in tiny little characters on tiny, tiny pieces of paper, by the light of the musk ox tallow lamp.

23) One of Cook's great deeds was to have revealed new hunting grounds to the Polar Eskimos, namely the musk ox range of Ellesmere Island. In the history of the Polar Eskimos, it amounted to a revolution in their economy, increasing the resources of the group considerably.

24) Cook's account of his prehistoric life at Cape Sparbo (on the north of Devon Island, four miles west-southwest of Cape Hardy) is fundamental if one is to grasp how prehistoric man survived. Unfortunately, Cook's book is unknown to specialists. Sir Wally Herbert was the second explorer to visit Cook's shelter (1968). Cook's stone house is on a small inlet, on the site of a prehistoric settlement. It was earlier visited, in August 1910, by the photographer Paul J. Rainey, who claims to have photographed the hut. I was there briefly in August 1995.

25) February 1909, Ellesmere Island, Cape Faraday, south of Cape Isabella (discovered by Captain John Ross): Cook is en route toward Cape Sabine, Anoritooq, and Etah. The text shows what Greely and his men should have attempted in February-March 1884 to reach the Etah Eskimos—a feat that Cook and his companions accomplished, despite their exhaustion.

26) 18 April 1909. At the end of April ("the third week of April"), the indefatigable Cook undertook an extremely bold journey across the vast expanse of Melville Bay, accompanied by Inuit hostile to Peary, from Anoritooq to Upernavik, in part over the ice-cap. He first reached Tasiussaq in mid-May, then Upernavik (in a skin boat) on 20 May 1909. His crossing of Melville Bay was accomplished in the record time of three weeks.

27) Cook's survival experience with his two Eskimo companions on the north of Devon Island was unquestionably unusual. Did he, driven by the same demon that made him claim his dubious ascent of Mount McKinley in 1906, invent a scenario of a savagery to rival the solitary expanses through which he traveled? His falsification of photographs has been devastating to his reputation.

The Polar Eskimos, whom Cook for the first time examined from an ethnographic perspective.

Cook looks at the Inuit

On board the yacht were busy days of barter. Furs and ivory were gathered in heaps in exchange for guns, knives, and needles. Every seaman, from cabin boy to captain, suddenly got rich in the gamble of trade for prized blue-fox skins and narwhal tusks.

The Eskimos were elated with their part of the bargain. For a beautiful fox skin, of less use to a native than a dog pelt, he could secure a pocket knife that would serve him half a lifetime.

A woman exchanged her fur pants, worth a hundred dollars, for a red pocket handkerchief with which she would decorate her head or her igloo for years to come.

Another gave her bearskin mitts for a few needles, and she conveyed the idea that she had the long end of the trade! A fat youth with a fatuous smile displayed with glee two bright tin cups, one for himself and one for his prospective bride. He was positively happy in having obtained nine cents' worth of tin for only an ivory tusk worth ninety dollars! [28]

Speaking quietly to the shadows (1907-1908)

A strange and eerie sight confronted me. Along the seashore, bending over the lapping black water, or standing here and there by inky, open leads in the severed ice, many Eskimo women were gathered. Some stood in groups of two or three. Bowed and disconsolate, her arms about them. I saw a weeping mother and her children. Standing rigid and stark, motionless graven images of despair, or frantically writhing to and fro, others stood far apart in desolate places, alone.

The dull, opaque air was tinged with a strange phosphorescent green, suggestive of a place of dead things; and now, like the flutterings of huge death-lamps, along the horizon, where the sun had sunk, gashes

28) First official admission of the injustice to which the ill-informed Eskimos had been subjected since 1819, most likely, and since 1892 when Peary first visited them. Cook raised the veil . . . and was the first to discuss trading in specific terms. The two hundred Polar Eskimos were targeted first by Peary, then by Cook in 1907-1908, for active organized trading. In a note to the Peary Arctic Club in January 1903, Peary had written: "My Eskimos and my dogs cost practically nothing" (quoted in Wally Herbert, The Noose of Laurels, p. 192). The keys to Peary's trading could be analyzed from the (privately held) archives of the Peary Arctic Club. The way had certainly been shown by the whalers, who made enormous profits: a tightly packed stack of blue fox skins would be traded against a knife of the same height. The little said by Peary and Cook tells volumes: they gave a needle, a knife, a piece of wood, some tobacco, tea, glass beads, ammunition, or rifles for fox skins that were worth fifty to one hundred dollars apiece on the American market. It was thus possible to make a considerable profit. For the Inuit, who had nothing at all, the trade was a bargain. The whites, under no supervisory authority, could easily realize profits on the order of 1000%, and collect it in the name of civilization. We can now see why Peary always tried to keep any competitors away from the area—his whole system of payment with the Eskimos could have collapsed. The furs collected by Cook at Anoritooq through trading in 1907-1908 were estimated by him to be worth some $10,000, the profit of a few months' work. And Cook accused Peary of having turned a profit of one million dollars (1909 dollars!) in his eight expeditions between 1892 and 1909, through trading furs and ivory.

29) Need one emphasize that the Polar Eskimos are the only people in the world to live from November to February in the polar night? The sky is lit by the stars (when the heavens are clear), by the milky light of the moon (when it is

of crimson here and there fitfully glowed blood-red in the pall-like sky.[29]

A friendly look at a hunting society

A little farther along was Al-leek-ah, a middle-aged woman, with two young children by her side. She was hysterical in her grief, now laughing with a weird giggle, now crying and groaning as if in great pain, and dancing madly. I learned her story from a chatter that ran through all her anguish. Towanah, her first husband, had been drawn under the ice, by the harpoon line, twenty years ago. And though she had been married three times since, she was trying to keep alive the memory of her first love. I went on, marveling at a primitive fidelity so long enduring.

Still farther along toward the steep slopes of the main coast, I saw Ahwynet, all alone in the gloomy shadow of great cliffs. Her story was told in chants and moans. Her husband and all her children had been swept by an avalanche into the stormy seas. There was a kind of wild poetry in the song of her bereavement . . .

These women were communicating with the souls of their dead.[30] To those who had perished in the sea they were telling, ere the gates of ice closed above them, all the news of the past year—things of interest and personal, and even of years before, as far back as they could remember.

Inuit cuisine (1907-1908)

The making of native ice cream is quite a task. I watched the process of making it Christmas Day with amused interest. The native women must have a mixture of oils from the seal, walrus, and narwhal. Walrus and seal blubber is frozen, cut into strips, and pounded with great force so as to break the fat cells. This mass is now placed in a stone pot and heated to the temperature of the igloo, when the oil slowly separates from the fibrous pork-like mass. Now tallow from the suet of the reindeer or musk ox is secured, cut into blocks, and given by the good housewife to her daughters, who sit in the igloo industriously chewing it until the fat cells are crushed. This masticated mass is placed in a long stone pot over the oil flame, and the tallow reduced from it is run into the fishy oil of the walrus or seal previously prepared.

This forms the body of native ice cream. For flavoring, the housewife has now a variety from which to select. This usually consists of bits of cooked meat, moss flowers and grass. Anticipating the absence of moss and grass in the winter, the natives, during the hunting season, take from the stomachs of reindeer and musk oxen which are shot, masses of partly digested grass—which is preserved for winter use. This, which has been frozen, is now chipped in fragments, thawed, and, with bits of cooked meats, is added to the mixed fats. It all forms a pistachio-green paste, with occasional spots like crushed fruit.

The mixture is lowered to the floor of the igloo, which, in winter, is always below the freezing point, and into it is stirred snow water. The churned composite gradually brightens and freezes as it is beaten. When completed, it looks very much like ice cream, but it has the flavor of cod liver oil, with a similar odor. Nevertheless, it has nutritive qualities vastly superior to our ice cream, and stomach pains rarely follow an engorgement.

With much glee, the natives finished their Christmas repast with this so-called delicacy.[31]

Anivunga: "I am born"

There is a little cry. But there is no doctor, no nurse, no one, not a kindly hand to help. A piece of glass is used as a surgical knife. Then all is over. There is no soap, no water. The methods of a mother cat are this mother's. Then, in the, cold, cheerless chamber of ice, she fondly examines the

Koolatinguak and Inugito (Qulutannguaq and Inukitsoq) accompanied Cook on the first three days of his polar dash over the Arctic Ocean, 18-20 March 1908. Torn between Peary, whom they admired deeply, and Cook, whom they respected for his medical help, the Inuit found themselves very ill at ease with the tension between the whites and sought to protect their own interests first. In the photograph are two faithful companions of Cook, a man and a woman.

present), and, at the start and end of the polar night, by the crepuscular light of the distant sun below the southern horizon.

30) The dead live invisibly in the midst of the living. The Inuit place near a grave small-scale models of what the dead will need in the next life. For a man: harpoon, knife, sledge, favorite dogs (strangled, and harnessed to the sledge). For a woman: needles, an ulu, or rounded knife, a blubber lamp. They tell the dead the events in the village, lacing their tales with endearments. The grave is a mound of stones piled over the body, and one moves round it in the direction of the sun's rotation: five times around for a man, three times for a woman. These visits to the dead occur only for a few years after their death. Where have the dead gone? Who knows? They have gone to a place farther from the living: the Inuit "paradise." In 1896 and 1897, these beliefs in the supernatural life and the presence of the dead in and near the grave were very strong. All the more reason to find Peary's attitude shocking: "The ship's men brought off the cask containing Qujaukitsoq and his wife and the little girl together with the accessories of his grave." (Peary's diary, quoted in Herbert, Noose of Laurels, p. 107.)

31) Eskimo food is much more varied than might appear: meat is eaten raw, frozen, boiled, deep-frozen in a more or less gamy state, and with eggs, vegetation (roots, berries), algae, shellfish, auks gone gamy and left to steep in grease in the gutted carcass of a seal (kiviaq). Recipes like uruner (consisting of liquid partridge droppings collected frozen from the snow and mixed with seal blubber, which is then beaten and eaten hot) are numerous and have practically escaped study. The study of the traditional diet might be all the more important if, as Dr. Sinclair of Oxford has reported, the Eskimos were entirely free of cancer until their diet was Americanized and Europeanized. They are believed to consume a daily average of 4000 to 5000 calories.

Myak and Kessuk in a family group in front of their summer tent. Western opinion about native peoples in the nineteenth century and beyond was seriously flawed: "I am white and therefore better. He is savage and therefore inferior. I am Christian and he is pagan, an idolater."

little one. Its eyes are blue, but they turn brown at once when opened. Its hair is coal black, its skin is golden. It is turned over and over in the search for marks or blemishes. The mother's eyes run down along the tiny spine. At its end there is a blue shield-shaped blot like a tattoo mark. This is the Eskimo guarantee of a well-bred child. If it is there, the mother is happy, if not, there are doubts of the child's future, and of the purity of the parents. Now the father and the grandmother come. All rejoice. [32]

The fierceness of the hunt is what has formed the Inuk. In their souls, the Inuit are still hunters in the year 2000. Saunders Island.

Seasonal sexuality

During all of the long arctic night, secretions are diminished and the passions obliterated, which causes a great muscular debility. Our own group suffered in a like manner. This singular state is due to the prolonged absence of the sun, and I would draw the conclusion that the sun is as essential to animal life as it is to vegetable life. The passions of this people are periodical, and their season of love generally comes after the return of the sun. In fact, at that time they practically tremble, so intense is their love frenzy, and for several weeks almost all their time is taken up with its satisfaction. It is thus not surprising that children are born at the start of the arctic night, nine months after this period. [33]

During the arctic night, menstruation is generally suppressed; not more than one woman in ten continues to have regular menstrual periods. Menstruation resumes before the start of the arctic day, on a cycle of twenty-eight or thirty days. [34]

32) Women give birth in the kneeling posture. Delivery is induced by compressing the mother's belly with a belt and massaging it forcefully. Sometimes the husband sits behind the woman with his legs apart, squeezing her and helping her push with his loins. The blue stain on the baby's lower back is the very expression of Inuit ethnic identity. Deformed and sickly infants are allowed to die. By the "artificial" selection of the strongest, the group only allows those individuals to survive who have the physical characteristics it needs.

33) This is an instance of the group's organic intelligence, which sometimes allowed it to tell up to three years in advance when a change in climate was due and adapt to it using population control measures such as sexual, dietary, and technological taboos, infanticide, and euthanasia. Births were seasonal, the periods of fertility and sexual activity being linked to the return of the sun. Furthermore, in a note of great medical interest, Cook notes that in the case of sterility in a couple, the husband might lend his wife to another man to impregnate. The child belonged to the mother. Cook did not believe that masturbation was common, though he ruled cautiously on this for lack of specific information. Women reached puberty late: at 18 to 20 years of age. Cook's journals and notes from 1891-1892 have unfortunately not been found in the National Archives in Washington. Perhaps they are in Peary's private archives.

34) One of the first medical mentions of winter amenorrhea. In 1950-1951, in the rare cases where I was able to gather any information, menstrual flow was very light during the winter months.

Pressure ridges
on the pack ice.
Looking for bear . . .
Melville Bay.

Cook the ethnographer: 1891-1892

Note from Dr. Cook to R. E. Peary, expedition leader

REDCLIFFE HOUSE, NORTH GREENLAND, 30 DECEMBER 1891

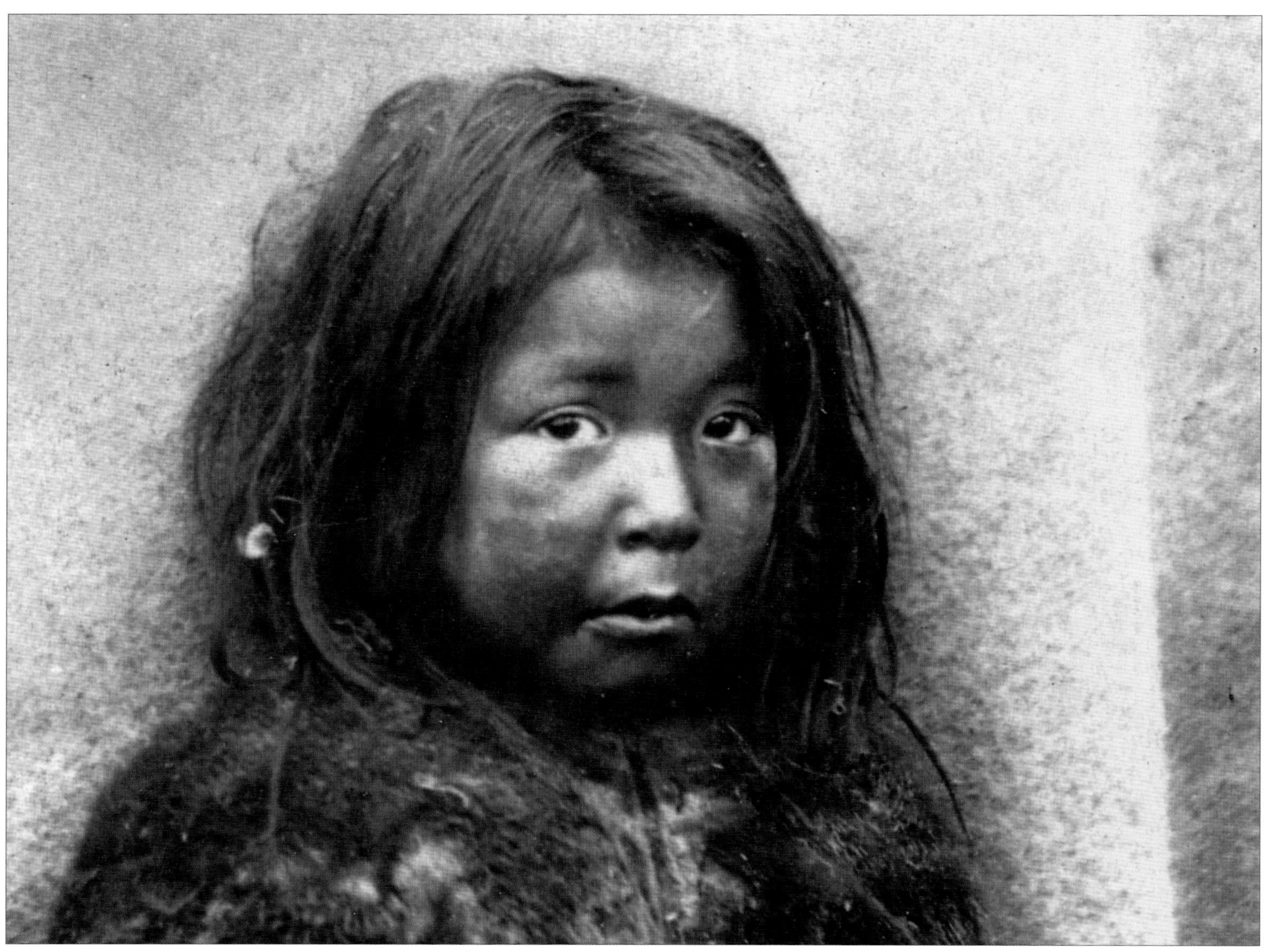

"The women nurse their children for a period of three to six years."
F. A. Cook

Sir, in accordance with your instructions of 12 August 1891, I submit the following report, concerning the tasks you assigned to me during the cruise around Hakluyt and Northumberland islands from 12 to 19 August.

When they were here (spring, June, July), the men, women, and children must have eaten nothing but birds and hares. I found no large bones, for example of seal or of walrus, such as I invariably found at their winter settlements. Feathers and bird bones were scattered in every direction.

The first trace of Eskimo habitation that I discovered on Northumberland Island was in a bay and west of a large glacier. Between the village and the glacier was quite a large stream. The name of this village was Ooya-huk-sua-sue. Its people moved to Inmomioma, according to Annooka, some ten years ago.

The abandoned village consisted of two stone igloos, six huts for dogs, and eight caches for birds and blubber. All the entrances to the igloos as well as to the dog huts faced directly south. The roofs of the igloos and the *toshue* [entrance tunnels] had been removed or had collapsed. The general method of construction was in no way different from those we studied elsewhere, excepting that large-sized bones, such as the bones of whale, walrus, and narwhal—their skulls, shoulder blades, and vertebrae—formed the major part of the walls, with leather lanyards threaded through the holes, natural or artificial, in these bones.

When we perceived these igloos from a distance for the first time, we saw no sign of life, but as we drew closer and were about to land, we saw a man climbing down some nearby hummocks. His behavior resembled that of a wild beast more than of a human being. He showed no sign of fear and gave us a hand with the boat; he smiled and talked at length several times. Of course, we could understand nothing of what he said, with the exception of Chimo. A woman and two children also appeared. We took our lunch and offered to share our food with them. Our generosity seemed to gratify them; they tasted our food, but none was apparently to their taste except the coffee and biscuits; the same proved true at the next settlement as well.[35]

Here is the list of my trades [36]

I pair of *kamiks* [boots] . . . . I hunting knife
leather bucket and knife . . . . file
2 small women's knives
and a needle case . . . . 5 needles
2 reindeer skins . . . . I saw-knife
2 packets of sinew . . . . I woman's knife
I casket of ivory toys . . . . . . I hunting knife
I bow and
some arrows . . . . 3 needles (iron)
I harpoon and I line . . . . ditto
3 rolls of line . . . . ditto
I lamp . . . . ditto
I needle case and
I needle . . . . 2 needles (iron)
2 slingshots . . . . ditto
I sealskin seat . . . . ditto

Inuit isolation and interbreeding

This people is absolutely pure from a racial standpoint, [37] with the possible exception of a number of individuals who came from the American coast and chose to settle here. [38] I was incapable of discovering any form of government in this people whatsoever or any social organization. The *angakkuk* are apparently the only ones to have any authority. Any man of greater than average intelligence who knows how to sing is accounted an *angakkuk* of greater or lesser power.

They are subject to very few illnesses, as long as they hold to the native diet, but as soon as they begin to eat civilized food, they all complain of discomfort. Respiratory ailments are common. They often contract the flu year after year in a very mild form. Pulmonary disease—pneumonia and pleurisy—seems to be the major cause of death.

The women often die in childbirth as well. The oldest women that we met would have been around seventy years old.

The mothers always nurse their children, and for a period of three to six years. If the mother or the father dies before a child reaches the age of two, the child is also put to death. This operation is performed by attaching a cord around the child's neck and strangling it. Male children are preferred to female.

What do they eat?

Their food consists only of meat and a small quantity of fat. They drink a great deal of blood, which they draw from half-boiled meat.

Most of the food they eat is raw food; in my opinion reports greatly exaggerate the quantities that they supposedly ingest. If one could weigh these substances, if one could somehow weigh the amount of food that they have eaten in a given week, it would provide information of the highest interest.

They drink abundant quantities of water, especially women when they are nursing. I have seen some of them drink three pints of water in one draft.

In misfortune, it is "every man for himself," 1891-1892

Monee told me that her sister had been eaten by the Great Spirit. The circumstances struck me as bizarre and I submitted Monee to a close questioning on the details. She answered me that she had never seen the Great Spirit eat the young girl, nor had any other member of her family, excepting her father. She told me that it had happened during the long arctic night. The weather was cold and lugubrious. They had not eaten any food for two weeks when, all of a sudden, the Great Spirit made his appearance. The young girl and her father walked around the point and disappeared, and the father came back with fresh meat. My own opinion is that the fresh meat was the body of the young girl, and I believe the family ate the young girl and made use of the Great Spirit to explain her disappearance. Monee told me that the meat only lasted them a week, and they were again without food for several weeks, until the return of the sun. I do not doubt that by gaining the confidence of this people more, one might hear other stories of this kind. I also think that it shows their belief in the Great Spirit to be highly convenient to explain all natural phenomena and all the things they can't explain. [39]

Manigssok, twenty-four years old. A shaman? Yes, if he can reach that status after long fasting and acquire a knowledge of the invisible. If he makes a mistake, he will be killed.

---

35) By 1892, the Eskimos had formed a taste for coffee and biscuits, whereas in 1853-1855 (Kane) they could not stand them and spat them out.

36) Precious information on the rates of exchange. This people, whose technology was based on stone, bone, and ivory, was not lacking for wood or iron (nails, barrel hoops), which it conserved with great care. Note that the Inuit did not ask for these raw materials from Cook. What they needed at this point were sophisticated tools: knives, needles, saws, files, axes. They had known of the existence of guns since Kane (1852-1854), and how to use them since the Polaris (Qallunalik, north of Etah, 1872), but they did not use them for lack of ammunition.

37) Debatable statement. Every summer from 1819 on, sexual encounters took place with the crews of whalers at Cape York. In this population counting some forty isolated families, the women at the small Cape York encampment could only have numbered between ten to fifteen. The young women (most often five or six of them) were pregnant or nursing infants and therefore infertile during the season when the whalers were passing through (July-August). But it would only take a few mixed-blood children per generation for the whole group to be genetically modified. The photographs taken by Peary in 1892-1893 and in 1895 are significant.

38) The immigrants from America were the fourteen Canadian Eskimos who came in 1860-1863. Peary identified six of them in his census of 31 August 1895: Ak-ki-gi-ah'-soo (m), Ah-say'-oo (f), E-too-shak'su-ah (m), Ko-man-ah'-pik (f), Merk-to-shar (m), Ok-pud-i-ah-pe (m). Merkusaq's stories to Knud Rasmussen allow us to identify others: Qumangapik, Minik, and, naturally, Qidtlarssuaq, the shaman who instigated the migration.

39) Cannibalism, incest, and neglect of the ancestral rules are proscribed. These rules offer working mental and behavioral guidelines when the society is strong and in a position to share. In times of dearth and famine, it is "every man for himself." This communitarian and ecologico-shamanistic society is not static: it becomes degraded during periods of greater cold. All efforts are aimed at recovering the group's balance, trying to rebuild parental, socio-economic, and mental structures. History has shown that a society is not simply a structure for survival, but a culture aimed at appeasing tensions through establishing complementary structures.

Ludvig Mylius-Erichsen 1872-1907

THE FIRST ETHNOLOGICAL EXPEDITION AMONG THE POLAR ESKIMOS, THE INUGHUIT (1902-1904)

This expedition, consisting of a journalist, a painter, a doctor, a South Greenlander, and a young Greenland-born Dane, was innovative in that its sole object was to study the Eskimos.

The goals of this first multidisciplinary expedition,[1] conceived by the journalist Mylius-Erichsen, were: to explore and study the native populations of Greenland's west coast from Cape Farewell to Cape York, gathering data on the natives' physical anthropology; to make oral recordings of their folklore; to poll the Greenlanders on their personal opinions about their future; and to document them photographically. The expedition's members wished to share closely in the life of the South Greenlanders and the Inughuit in the north and to gather their opinions and beliefs first-hand. To do so, they would proceed the first summer (1902) up the southwest coast by umiak (large skin boat) from Cape Farewell to Jakobshavn and spend the winter of 1902-1903 in Jakobshavn, a large village in Disko Bay where the best dogs in Greenland are to be found. From there they would proceed to Cape York by dog sled, thus establishing Danish Greenland's first official link between South Greenland and the Polar Eskimo territory in the north, which had practically been under Peary's administration since 1892.[2]

The expedition was undertaken independently of any academic or official organization. Harald Moltke, Prussian in origin, and descended from one of the oldest and most illustrious Danish families, joined the expedition out of friendship for the young Knud Rasmussen, though he had no previous experience in the Arctic.[3] The journalist Mylius-Erichsen, the expedition's leader, had no arctic experience either. He was said to be an ambitious young man and hard to pin down because of his many projects, but Moltke's name opened many doors for him in Copenhagen. In particular, it was Moltke who introduced him to Knud Rasmussen, then nineteen years old.

Knud Rasmussen, who was born in Jakobshavn, Greenland, spoke the native language fluently and was eager to take part in an expedition to Greenland so as to be initiated into the life of research and study. He had no

Opposite, **the five members** of the expedition. From left to right: the South Greenlander Jørgen Brønlund from Ilulissat (Jakobshavn); Doctor Bertelsen (who would not go beyond Upernavik); Ludvig Mylius-Erichsen, the expedition leader; the young Knud Rasmussen; and Count Harald Moltke. Two Greenlanders are missing from this photograph: Gaba (Gabriel) Olsen of Kuuk (Upernavik district); and Elias of Nutaarmiut (Upernavik district).

1) Det Danske Literaere Grönlands Ekspedition, or Danish Literary Expedition to Greenland.
2) Peary, as we've noted, claimed North Greenland for the United States. Copenhagen had not yet confirmed its authority over the island as a whole.
3) Moltke said as much to me in 1953. He had met Rasmussen at a party in Copenhagen in 1898 and immediately fallen under his spell.

At work on the north coast of Greenland, the cartographer Mylius-Erichsen and the painter Moltke (May 1903).

university training. Rasmussen's father, a noted linguist in Greenlandic studies, encouraged his son and took a leading role in the preparations. He recommended that the men take with them a South Greenlander, Jørgen Brønlund, whose useful and loyal service would prove of great help to them in the face of dangers great and small. The first expedition, in which Rasmussen took part, was a turning point in his life and in the lives of the Polar Eskimos, whose fate would be linked for three decades with the trading post he established in 1910 and with the administrative system he conceived for this small population of 250 hunters scattered over ten villages and encampments.

Moltke under the care of shamans

The expedition reached Godthaab, or Nuuk, the island's administrative center, in the summer of 1902 and set out according to plan from Jakobshavn by dog sled in February-March 1903. On arriving at Cape York after a difficult crossing of Melville Bay, the four men faced a serious predicament: Harald Moltke, the expedition's guiding light and resident diplomat, was gravely ill. He had contracted typhoid fever, and at that latitude there was evidently no doctor to take care of him. [4] There was the further danger that the illness could spread and ravage the virgin native population.

The Eskimo group whose life the expedition intended to share was living in a state of utter deprivation—despite Peary's claim to have left them "millionaires." There had recently been a famine and a severe flu epidemic, communicated by Scottish whalers. In two years, the population declined by 15 percent. And it was these very Eskimos, traumatized by misfortune, who undertook to look after Moltke. Some incurred a serious risk of contamination by providing meat for the explorers' party, which had quarantined itself in an isolated stone igloo on Saunders Island.

Tensions

Communal life in the igloo proved difficult. Mylius-Erichsen, rough by nature, feuded with his comrades—Rasmussen in particular, whose vibrant and extroverted personality visibly made him jealous. In fact, Mylius-Erichsen hated him, as his recently published journal reveals. Moltke, lying on his sick-bed, played the part of conciliator. For better or worse, the winter passed in this way. Was it during this winter that Mylius-Erichsen realized he could never compete with Rasmussen in knowledge of the Polar Eskimos? At any rate, his subsequent explorations took him to the northeast coast of Greenland, where his cartographic work earned him the fame he coveted as a great polar explorer. Moltke drew and painted as his health improved. He was the first painter to document the Polar Eskimos. Mylius-Erichsen recorded everything that went on around them, which he later consigned to the fine book Moltke and he produced together: *Groenland.* [5] He had only four years left to live.

The first ethnological expedition among the Polar Eskimos

On Saunders Island, Rasmussen was also collecting tales and legends. The notes gathered by expedition members filled eighteen expedition notebooks—not counting two sketchbooks of Moltke's and a further notebook of Rasmussen's—the harvest of this rugged winter. A number of the documents remain unpublished.

The young Rasmussen published nothing on his return in 1904, concerned that he had only impressions to relate.

Realizing how complex and original the Inughuit were, he preferred to return among them first to verify and extend his observations. It is interesting to see how Rasmussen, who had no formal training in anthropology, approached his work on this expedition. In a letter to the editor of *Verdens Spalet* dated 20 November 1904, he gives a clear picture of the method and spirit of his work:

"You have asked me to describe my own work within the expedition and the results of those two and a half years of travel. Well, as I have said, for the moment I have returned to Denmark with material that still needs to be worked up. Nothing is finished, and therefore there are no results.

"My method was to fling off all civilization and to become like one of the Eskimos whose way of life I was to study. . . . If you travel in Greenland with the slightest official character, you run the risk of finding only what you want to see. We shucked off our overcoats immediately, replacing them with the Greenlandic anorak, and the Eskimos' door, in a spiritual sense, opened to us at once. What set us off from other expeditions is that we lived, in the most literal sense, with the subjects of our study. We shared the good and the bad with them, and we gained their trust."

The Danish Literary Expedition was the first in North Greenland whose main object was the study of man among the Polar Eskimos. It also pioneered in being multidisciplinary, as noted above, and in incorporating physical and medical anthropology, ethnography and folklore, painting and art, journalistic reporting, and photography. These data are of the greatest interest because in 1903 the Polar Eskimos were at a pivotal moment in their evolution—at the third turn in their history. In 1863-1866, the group had seen its second technological revolution since 1818, when it learned or relearned to use the bow, the bow-drill, the kayak, and the salmon spear from Inuit immigrants from the Canadian Arctic. With Peary's arrival in 1891-1892, the group entered on its third technological revolution: the gun, the steel trap, and a secondary barter economy.

On the spiritual plane, the Inuit's lives still took inspiration from shamanism, which established man's umbilical relation with his natural environment. The old unquestionably continued to believe. "What we believe," the wife of an elderly *angakkuq* said to Mylius-Erichsen, "was taught to us by our ancestors, and we will teach it to our children because it is good." Yet Peary's expeditions and the American explorers' intimacy with the native hunters had begun to undermine the Eskimos' ancestral beliefs and philosophy—despite Peary's precautions to respect and protect the cultural independence of this people.

"The young," the old *angakkuq's* wife continued, "neglect our teaching, unfortunately. They defy our customs and make fun of them. Only when they grow old do they become reasonable and once again obey the ancient rules."

A young mother carrying her baby in her hood emerges from her tent to go meet her returning husband (Eskimo drawing). Peary collection.

A heroic fate

In September 1904, the entire expedition returned to Copenhagen. Mylius-Erichsen's bubbling mind was already elsewhere. Sensing that the land of the Polar Eskimos would always be "Knud's land" and that he could never compete with this young Danish Greenlander who spoke the language so well and was exceptionally empathetic, Mylius-Erichsen turned toward the

Ludvig Mylius-Erichsen, 19 April 1902. Drawing by Harald Moltke.

4) The expedition lost its doctor in Upernivik, when Dr. Bertelsen chose not to adventure north of Melville Bay.

5) Ludvig Mylius-Erichsen and Harald Moltke, *Groenland* (Copenhagen: 1906).

The Danish Literary Expedition among the Polar Eskimos. Left, a South Greenlander who has bartered his fur vest for a woolen pullover. The two women wearing hoods (rear right) are perhaps under taboo.

northeast coast of Greenland. In a frenzy of activity he made preparations for a new expedition to the unexplored coast between Germania Land and Peary Land, leaving Harald Moltke to ready the notes of the Danish Literary Expedition for publication. [6]

Mylius-Erichsen obtained financial backing from the Danish government and kept the budget for his expedition astonishingly low: 15,000 pounds sterling. He bought a fifty-one-year-old ship in Peterhead, Scotland, rechristened it the *Dannmark*, and left on 24 June with food supplies for three years. Among the expedition's twenty-eight members were eminent cartographers: J.–P. Hoch, H. Hagen, and a meteorologist who became famous as the first to describe continental drift, Alfred Wegener.

Mylius-Erichsen acted on what he had learned from the Polar Eskimos and made his dog sled journeys during the winter. On 28 March 1907 he started north with six sledges, three Greenlanders, and two companions: Hagen and Koch. Their goal was to reach the headlands in Peary Land identified by Peary himself. The expedition would end in tragedy. It was planned on the basis of Peary's data (1891-1892), but Peary's map was incorrect, throwing off all Mylius-Erichsen's calculations of distances and food supplies.

One of Mylius-Erichsen's last messages (8 April 1907), discovered several years later in a metal tube, eloquently describes their plight: "We reached the point of Peary's glacier and discovered that there was no Peary Channel, Navy Cliff being joined to the continent by Hielprin Land."

On returning to Copenhagen in August 1908 minus its leader, the expedition described the tragedy in a laconic telegram: "Goal achieved, coast explored, entire outline of Greenland surveyed, important scientific results obtained, Commander Mylius-Erichsen, Lieutenant Hoëg Hagen, and the Eskimo Brønlund dead after a heroic struggle against the elements." Hagen died on 15 November 1907, Mylius-Erichsen two days later, and Brønlund at the end of November.

The bodies, journals, and notebooks of these two heroes were never found, but Brønlund, the last to die, managed to save the map compiled by the expedition. So that it might be found, he had dragged himself to the cache, the point of rendezvous. The map established that Greenland was in fact an island. That headland now bears the name of Mylius-Erichsen, and the fjord the name of Brønlund. ■

6) This book is one of the richest sources on the Polar Eskimos, though little known by English-, French-, or German-speaking specialists, having remained in Danish.

A Wise Society

Excerpts from L. Mylius-Erichsen and Harald Moltke Groenland, (Copenhagen, 1906.)

Discovery of a North Greenlandic language

When Elias and Gabas had recovered a bit from their surprise at finding a "pagan savage," they started to ask Massannguaq many questions in their Upernavik dialect about the encampment on Agpat [Saunders] Island: the number of houses and inhabitants, and what animals the people up there hunted and fished to stay alive. Massannguaq understood only half of what they were asking him, then, trying to imitate the Upernavik dialect, he laughed a good deal at their use of the vowel "i" instead of "u" (for example *marllik*, which means "two" instead of *marlluk*). [7]

The world maintained in equilibrium by taboos

[Taateraaq] has not always been crippled as he is today. . . . He tells the story of how he became an invalid: "I was no bigger than this one [Inukitsoq, a boy of thirteen] when I got my first kayak, at the same time as my brother Majak, who was several years older than me . . .

"One day I was kayaking beyond Uummannaq [North Star Bay] . . . when we saw a seal and chased it . . . but when I cut it up I discovered that it was a *dubilaliark* (an animal made from a man to bring misfortune on another man); it looked just like a seal, but its bones were those of a fur-bearing seal and a walrus, and its meat was like kidney. We didn't eat it but gave it to the dogs instead. And here is what happened: the next winter I fell ill, my legs hurt and became paralyzed, and I never moved again." [8]

Sorqaq's medical practices and prescriptions

25 April. I was finally obliged last night to authorize Sorqaq and Kaali to organize a [witchcraft] séance for Moltke. We are not running any risk. And we have to follow the local customs or leave. The evil spirits entered the encampment with Moltke's ill body, and they must therefore be summoned and chased away. . . . It was a strange séance. . . . Sorqaq stood in front of Moltke's cot and struck the stretched gut of his drum with fanatic force, uttering almost incomprehensible phrases. He would rise up then fall to his knees, bending his body to left and right to the rhythm of the drum. [9] His long hair fell in strands before his face and swung this way and that; from time to time we could see his half-closed eyes and his face clenched in a frightening grimace. Sometimes his song seemed to address a question to the world of spirits, which was followed by a pause during which Sorqaq listened intently for an answer . . .

Sorqaq ended his treatment by giving us a solemn list of prescriptions that were to be scrupulously followed if Moltke were to recover . . . I describe them here:

1. The invalid must eat quantities of seal and walrus meat, but only from male animals.
2. He must not cut the meat with a knife but tear it from the bones with his teeth.
3. Women who visit must not sit on the main bed [bench] but only on the side bench.
4. He may eat reindeer meat in addition to the meats already mentioned.
5. He must not breathe in any smoke, so the lamps must be carefully trimmed.
6. He must never prepare his own food.

The hunter Inagssanguaq in a *kapatak* (or *kapetah*) made from eight fox skins. He is holding the coiled traces of his dog team, made of seal skin. This was the first Polar Eskimo encountered by the Danish Literary Expedition (1903).

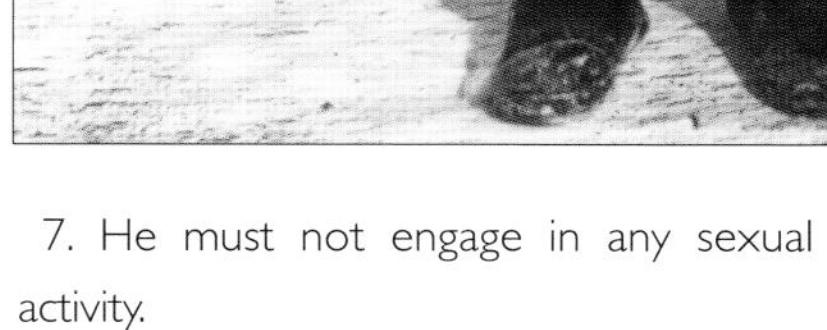

7. He must not engage in any sexual activity.
8. He must then show his gratitude toward the *anggakkuq* in every way possible.
9. He must give him a large dog and
10. A good rifle.

He would then certainly recover, but slowly, little by little. [10]

On Peary's spelling of Eskimo words

The spelling used by Peary for the names of people and places strikes me as unsatisfactory. When you read the word aloud to an

7) Language, dialect, and accent: the Inuit language is one language, from Eastern Siberia (the Chukotka coast) to the east coast of Greenland. It is divided, however, into two major groups: Yupik (Siberia, Southeast Alaska) and Inupiat (Northern Alaska, Canada, and Greenland). The fragmentation of Inuit society over a vast area has given rise to forty dialects just among the Inupiat and fifteen dialects among the Yupik. The language spoken in Thule, harsh and raucous, is a Greenlandic language, set off (to the point of not being readily comprehensible to the South Greenlander) by its phonetics, its vocabulary, and especially its rapid, syncopated rhythm. Certain words are different: in Thule, "yes" is lèh, but it is Hap! south of Melville Bay. The sound of the vowel "u" replaces that of the vowel "i," which is much used in South Greenland. A radical of two or three syllables gives the general sense, to which the speaker adds affixes to give his exact shade of meaning. The letters "k," "q," "t," "d," "g," "dl," and "r" have a different sound than in French. Finally, the rhythm is fundamentally different among the Polar Eskimos: the last syllables are swallowed down the back of the throat; the guttural accent applies to the three final syllables. But as Erik Holtved has noted, the Polar Eskimos—who are strong-minded and highly individualistic—vary their expression according to mood and circumstance. The three final syllables are not always swallowed: some Eskimos express themselves in so elliptic a fashion that, speaking from the throat, they seem to communicate more by looks and gestures. They "speak" in this way when they are displeased and want to avoid being understood by a foreigner.

8) The spirits must not be offended. The Polar Eskimo lives in a magical world, and everything is a sign to him. Only the many rules handed down by tradition, which vary according to sex, age, and historical circumstance, preserve the balance between the Inuit, the sky, the sea, the animals, and the plants. To neglect them is to risk being instantly turned into a dog or a monster. Uutaaq, the father of my companion Kutsikitsoq, said to Knud Rasmussen: "We follow our old customs so as to keep the world in balance, for the spirit powers must not be offended." The Inuk's vision of the world is vertical: there is an above (the sky) and a below (a dark world below ground), and whoever does not observe the taboos will be punished after death. The taboos (agligtuq) are therefore not only social rules but sacred ones.

9) The drum is a sacred instrument. Only its sound can, according to the rhythm, establish communication with the invisible.

10) These prescriptions may be seen as intended to provide the invalid with an abundance of fresh local meat, while isolating him from common objects (knives), keeping him from any sexual (or even tactile) contact with women, and having him breathe uncontaminated air.

The shaman Sorqaq, who was missing his left eye (1903). He is sitting on a *nikorfautaq*, or traditional seat made of bone and seal skin whose three feet are padded with bear fur so as to make no noise on the surface of the ice that might alert a seal. He was against all change, which he thought harmful, and was the grandfather of my companion Qaaqutsiaq (1951).

Eskimo, he generally does not understand what you mean. All of a sudden, someone grasps the word's meaning. There is a general roar of laughter, and they pronounce the proper word, which has only the most tenuous relation to Peary's transcription. Of course, one has to stick to a firm principle in order to transcribe sounds. Jørgen Brønlund [a South Greenlander on the expedition] will always pronounce Polar Eskimo words according to the written language of the western Eskimos, but it is absolutely necessary, next to this justified transcription, to restore phonetically as accurately as possible the pronunciation of the Polar Eskimos. That is what Peary wanted to do, but he had no knowledge of the written language of the Eskimos, and his interpretation of their sounds was therefore wavering and uncertain. He writes the same sound in several different ways. For example, the name Ihré or Ehré is given by Peary as Ihlie. And Angutivluardsuk (which is almost pronounced "Angutidluahw" in Peary's rendition) becomes Ahngodoblahho.[11]

On Peary and the Eskimos

This American has an iron will. The Eskimos speak of him with fear and respect. They don't really understand why he wants to make journeys "far from men," but they respect his will and they bend to it. There is no doubt of it: he orders them as he pleases—their labor is the precondition for all his sledging expeditions, and they say he pays them satisfactorily in arms and tools, but in my opinion this course of action is indefensible, as he never gives them enough ammunition. He carries off their bows and many other primitive implements as museum curiosities, but these are not replaced by firearms with sufficient ammunition. Until Peary's repeated visits overturned their lives, these Eskimos lived a well-regulated existence. As I've said, the Eskimos speak of Peary favorably and respectfully, but they are also afraid of him and do not dare do anything against his will. He commands and they obey. He has revolutionized their tribe in ten years or so, he has torn them from a more or less Stone Age existence and given them a foretaste of our modern culture and technology—perhaps more of it than they can assimilate.[12]

Samik asks us if Peary is not returning soon to the land of the Eskimos. All of them received the impression when he left the last time that he would return soon and try once more to reach the "Center of the Earth" (Silakrekra), which is to say the North Pole. As to the "Big White," which is to say the *Fram*, the Norwegian Arctic ship, Samik saw it a few years ago near Etah but he did not go on board "because Peary did not want the Eskimos to go on board." "Why not?" I asked.

Majaq's family, in front of his spring tent, made of seal skin (1903).

Samik laughed and answered: "Yes, Peary and the master of the "Great White" (Sverdrup) were enemies. So we stayed with Peary and the "Great White" went away, and only a few of us visited Peary's ship the following winter when it lay on the other side of the sea. When the ice melted, he sailed south and we never saw him again."

Twenty years before Greely, Eskimos survived by eating each other

Meqorsuaq answered me: "We attach small pieces of narwhal or walrus tooth on a seal skin thong and drop them into the water, drawing them in and throwing them back out several times to attract the salmon, which we then spear with a two-tined fork. But as the sun had disappeared and we had almost no food, some people died of hunger. One of them was my father. I can remember six people who died of hunger. Others were killed by the survivors, who were so hungry that they wanted to eat the corpses of the dead. Minik and Mattak (two men) were the ones who wanted most to kill the others and eat them. At first, we didn't know that they were killing to satisfy their hunger; but my mother was killed and taken by them, because these men lived at another place, and then we understood what had happened." [13]

Avoidance of inbreeding, an Inuit concern

Among the local families, I especially noticed the Inapaluk, relatives of the beautiful Pualuna. The woman is named Idoshwarsuaet, which is spelled Igtuggarssuak in South Greenlandic. The man is quiet and reserved. The woman is beautiful and imposing, truly majestic in carriage. She is the sister of Panigpark and Asayuk. Together they have five children, all of exceptional beauty. A girl of fifteen, who lives with her parents, is said to have been married to a cousin, Kresunguaq, but was taken back from her husband because an *angakkuq* saw their close kinship as a danger to the family line. In general, they try to avoid marriage between close kin, and the same goes for extramarital relations. But it would be extraordinary if the marriage of kin could be entirely avoided in a tribe of 200 persons. Clearly it would not hurt such a tribe to receive new blood from Eskimos who came from elsewhere. The tribe's members have benefited physically and mentally, as we know, from the immigration of Eskimos from the other side of Smith Sound, which we learned about through Meqorsuaq. From what we can tell, this immigration brought them new knowledge of the kayak. [14]

Arctic tales

And Sorqaq told an extraordinary story about Peary: "Peary told us that once, when he was a young boy he came here on a whaling ship, and that while he was sledging with another white boy they started to argue because the boy would not obey him—that is how Peary was, he always wanted to give orders and be the boss!—so Peary killed his companion and buried him right there. I saw

Training dogs for hunting bear. They must learn to stay absolutely silent during the stalk, then attack the animal on the right side (near the shoulder blade where it is most vulnerable) and on the legs. In an actual hunt, the traces are cut as short as possible so that the bear cannot seize them with the claws of its left forepaw and whirl the dog like a toy over the heads of the pack, knocking them senseless.

1909. Kruli (the poorest widow in Uummannaq, according to Steensby), aged sixty-five. Note her cane, which is made of two joined pieces.

11) Peary never thought of himself as an ethnographer. An engineer by training, Peary was only mildly interested in the traditional life of the Inuit, whose lives he shared during six expeditions spread over twenty years (1891-1909). It is remarkable, in fact, that he spoke Eskimo poorly and butchered the names of places and people in his writings.
12) Respect and admiration based on fear: the Polar Eskimos respected and feared Peary more than they held him in affection. They were proud to have taken part in such major expeditions and to have undergone, thanks to Peary, a veritable technological revolution, using the most modern equipment and firearms. "My Eskimos!" Peary was accustomed to say. More an expedition leader and a businessman than a politician, he wisely chose to respect Eskimo customs and avoided proselytizing to them, a practice that did not begin until his final departure in 1909. Unlike the British, he never brought a chaplain on his expeditions. He claimed all of northern Greenland for the United States. Washington rejected the idea in 1912, determining that North Greenland belonged geographically under Danish rule. In a diplomatic agreement concluded in 1914, Denmark relinquished all claims to the Danish Antilles. Peary frightened the Inuit. Perhaps they saw him as a great white shaman, gifted with unknown powers. Uisaakassak told Moltke in 1907-1908 that whenever he slept in the same igloo as Peary, he never took off his amulets for invulnerability, so as to ward off Peary's "aggressions"! And much later, in September 1967, an old hunter from Siorapaluk told me that as a child he had seen Peary land and that, frightened by his authority and his love of giving orders, he had nicknamed him the "Great Tormentor"! Before telling me this, he checked twice outside the door and spoke to me in a low, fearful voice, as though frightened that Peary's ghost might hear us.
13) Cannibalism is the last resort. This was from an account of the last migration from Canada to Greenland (1860-1863). The fourteen Eskimos from Baffin Island (Igloolik area) taught the Polar Eskimos once again the use of the kayak, the bow, the bow drill, reindeer hunting, salmon fishing, the eating of reindeer meat, and the construction of snow igloos. After five or six years of communal living and intermarriage, the Canadian Eskimos decided to return to their native land under their leader, the shaman Qillaarsuaq. A number died along the way. Those who reached Ellesmere Island murdered each other south of Cape Sabine, near Cape Isabelle, and there were instances of cannibalism. Patdloq, the wife of my companion Qaaqqutsiaq in 1951, was the daughter of Tornit, one of the few survivors. In 1950, 14% of the Polar Eskimos were related to the Canadian immigrants.
14) Parental choice: my genealogical study of 1200 Eskimos across four generations (1950-1860), studied in Paris by J. Sutter, L. Tabah, and myself (Population, Paris, 1956, 507-530) established that parents guided their offsprings' choice of marriage partner. Everything points to a prohibition against the union of cousins (to the sixth degree). The parental rules governing marriage were exceptionally strict in this small group of fifty families (1902). Note that Moltke describes nonmarital relations between close relatives as being avoided. And wife exchanges were organized so as to respect parental taboos.

Aleqasina, 1903. Known as "Ally" by the Americans, she bore Peary's two Eskimo sons. She was married to Piuaittuq Ulloriaq, with whom Peary shared her during his stays, and became the mother-in-law of Inuterssuaq, who had a son, Talilenguaq. Aleqasina had a strong personality and a very open mind for the period. The daughter of Asivaq, she died in Qaanaaq in 1921. Peary first noticed her in Bowdoin Fjord in 1892 when she was twelve. At a time when Peary was held up at Fort Conger, she happened to meet Josephine Peary near Cape Sabine (1900). Peary's wife had come from New York to seek news of her husband, who was thought lost. After a stormy reunion with Peary, she seems to have accepted the situation.

Two *ulut*: women's knives from Cape York. The first, from 1905, measures 2.5 inches in length. The second, from 1924, is 3.7 inches long.

the grave near Cape York with my own eyes," said Sorqaq.

On the subject of wife exchange, Jørgen had the following conversation with Puivatsork's wife, Aleqasina (Peary's former servant), one of the most appealing women in the area, almost of refined character. Jørgen asked her: "How can you agree to change men like that?" To which Aleqasina answered resignedly: "Yes, it is something we must do. We wives have no say when the decision is made. A stranger is sent to us to share the bed in which we are sleeping with our children and we must, as it were, become his wife." . . . Infidelity in marriage is judged very harshly when it is the woman who is guilty. Only the man has the right to lend out his spouse, whereas the woman must not do it on her own initiative. Uissakassek is known as someone who tends to borrow the wives of others too much, that is, without the husband's consent. [15]

Funerary rites, a contribution to Verdens Spilit *by Knud Rasmussen, 1904*

We give in what follows a summary of the fifteen points traditionally observed during the time of the Danish Literary Expedition: burial of the dead as soon as possible. The body is laid under stones, the head toward the rising sun, completely clothed and with all the person's hunting weapons. The soul continues to live and might have need of its harpoon. The body is bound in a skin and dragged to the spot where the stones are to be mounded over it. For five days no one must cross the tracks made by the dragged body. For five days, those who have touched the corpse must stay indoors, they must not dress, and they must not prepare their food themselves. If anyone has to sew, they must first blacken their eyebrows with soot. Every day for five days they must walk in procession to the grave, following the course of the sun. After five days they must wash their hands and their bodies.

Those who are present when a person dies must block their left nostril with straw: this is necessary for a long life. The nostril must stay blocked until the burial is over. The Polar Eskimos believe only in their *angakkuqs*, their spirit callers, and they say that they are obliged to believe in them, otherwise the animals they killed would become inedible and they themselves would fall sick and die. [16]

15) The Arctic, like every land of exploration, is rife with more or less imaginary stories, passed on by whalers, missionaries, traders, colonial administrators, passing travelers . . . Spiteful rumors are common and of little interest. I have heard my share of them about one man or another: the policeman, the anthropologist, the manager at the trading post, not to mention the missionary, who may be ill-liked and have led a less than blameless life. Saints certainly exist, but they are few. Bastard children are attributed to this one or that one, even to the missionary, who finally confesses. The story told above is clearly invented, as Peary never traveled on a whaling ship. The only companions of Peary who died were Verhoeff (1891-1892) and Marvin (1909). Peary gave Verhoeff's name to the strait where he disappeared near Siorapaluk. Verhoeff had left Peary in July 1892 to explore a glacier on his own, one week before he was due to return to the United States; the relief ship had been sighted. Some say he committed suicide, unable to stand the criticism and sarcasm he received from the Pearys.

16) The dead are the shadows of the living. For a year and sometimes more, close kin make visits to the deceased, speaking to their relative in low tones and walking around the grave in the direction of the rotation of the sun. It is forbidden to speak the name of the dead person until he has been reincarnated into the body of a newborn, to whom his name is given. The survivors do not so much feel grief at the loss of a loved one as fear that the spirit of the dead might wreak revenge on them—a revenge their relative was not able to mete out in life. Any social and religious wrongs committed by the living—failure to observe a taboo—would leave them defenseless before the "breath" of the dead, who are great enforcers of justice.

OVERLEAF:
Inglefield Fjord. Hunting for narwhal east of Qeqertaq, along the edge of the glacier.

LEFT:
In Upernavik, on the way to the Polar Eskimo territory. In the first row, from left to right, are Harald Moltke (with the arm of a South Greenlandic woman around his neck), Ludvig Mylius-Erichsen, and Knud Rasmussen. With them are several Polar Eskimos, some South Greenlanders, and two unidentified Danes (1903).

BELOW:
a hunter from Saunders Island in 1903. After Peary's departure, stories and rumors circulated. Marvin, Peary's secretary, was said to have been killed on the polar pack. Rasmussen investigated. The Eskimo Kuluttu apparently preferred to kill Marvin than to abandon his Eskimo brother in danger.

Portrait of Arnaruniak, by Harald Moltke (Appat, 21 June 1903).

FAR LEFT: **a white man** photographing the Eskimos. A woman cuts up a seal, while another woman eats, seated, using her *ulu*, and a man raises his whip (1911). Drawing by In-ah-waho (from Borup, *A Tenderfoot with Peary*).

Hunting auks on the bird cliffs, which might be at Cape York. In the foreground are four loaded sledges by a tent. Whaling boats tow a whale toward shore, followed by kayaks. Drawing by In-ah-waho (from Borup, *A Tenderfoot with Peary*).

Knud Rasmussen 1879-1933

ETHNOLOGY TO THE FORE

By giving the little village of Ummannaq in North Star Bay the legendary name of Thule, which he did in 1910, Rasmussen would endow the Polar Eskimos with a mythical fate, which obliged them to surpass themselves and become the figurehead for all the Inuit peoples from Siberia's Chukotka Peninsula, their land of origin, to the east coast of Greenland.

Only nineteen years old and with no college education, Knud—as he quickly became known among the Inuit—set himself the task with his friend Peter Freuchen of bringing North Greenland under Danish rule. At the time, the Danish government was entirely indifferent to foreign undertakings at high latitudes, whereas the United States had every title to claim that territory for itself. [1] Norway, for its part, had designs on the area for commercial reasons. A new expedition to be led by Nansen's companion Otto Sverdrup (whose earlier presence on Ellesmere Island in 1898-1902 had so confounded Peary that he forbade "his" Eskimos to fraternize with the Norwegians) had been announced for 1910. A Norwegian sealing station was even planned for Saunders Island, across from Thule, with all the imaginable consequences for the local population.

Knud Rasmussen brought together the Eskimo's imagination, sense of grandeur, and pragmatic and dramatic sides with the realism, decisiveness, and enterprise of the Dane.

He was rightly concerned about the Inuit's economic situation. The annual arrival of the Scots whalers at Cape York and the Carey islands (1819-1910) and the American expeditions of Kane (1853-1855), Hayes (1861-1862), Hall (1872-1874), and especially Peary (eight expeditions, starting in 1891) and Cook (1907-1909) created an irreversible situation in North Greenland. Peary's Americans came and went from village to village. They hired Eskimo hunters for wages. Temporary unions developed—which of them did not have "his" Eskimo wife? Hybridization, both physical and cultural, increased. The native hunters became habituated to the modern equipment they had been using for the past twenty years. Now they needed ammunition for their firearms, preferred wood to bone, and tools such as axes, saws, and files. Tobacco was virtually a necessity. As to the use of imported iron, it had become widespread. [2] A dependent material culture and a barter economy had gradually developed since 1892.

Yet no trading post, American or Danish, had been established in the Thule region to date. Hayes, Peary, Cook, and Sverdrup had certainly thought of it because of the great wealth of fox fur in the country—a thousand white

1) At least if one believed the political and geographical appropriations Peary announced to the State Department.

2) According to Peary, metallic slivers from the four meteorites in Savissivik had not been used since 1860. An iron barrel hoop, which could supply the needs of the group for a year and more, was of infinitely greater use.

The many faces of Knud Rasmussen: at once a Dane and a Greenlander, an expedition leader and a poet, a "savage" and a charmer, an administrator and an ethnologist.

Maisanguak, by Harald Moltke, 17 June 1903, Agpat.

Drawing by Iggiantuak-Uutaaq (born 1903). Qaanaaq, 1982.

The central problem for a primitive people is to survive without betraying itself as it enters into relations with the modern world.
There is an ethics of science, just as there is an ethics of discovery expeditions. Peary and Cook owed it to themselves, after virtually forcing the Inuit to make their indispensable contributions to the discovery of the Pole, to bring help to this threatened people in the form of a foundation. The revolutionary technologies the American explorers had brought the Inuit were brutally yanked away when they left. The Inuit children they had fathered were abandoned unacknowledged. In both cases this was a dereliction of duties.
It is to Knud Rasmussen's honor that he created the nomadic native university known as the "Thule Expeditions." The translation of the work of the Thule Expeditions into Greenlandic should be one of the high priorities of Greenland's Ministry of Culture.

and blue foxes were caught annually. [3] Rasmussen boldly started a private company, Kap York Stationen, to fill the void, though Danish banks refused to stand guarantor because of the lack of government backing. If Copenhagen cautiously refused to open a trading post north of Upernavik and Melville Bay—the provisioning of posts in the north from Disko to Upernavik was already headache enough—then Rasmussen would do it himself.

He considered the problem at great length during his dramatic overwintering with Moltke and Mylius-Erichsen in 1902-1904 and again when he returned alone in 1906-1907. The profits earned by the sale of skins had to support the costs of a post where the Eskimos could buy wood, tools, ammunition, and food items such as tea, coffee, sugar, etc.

And the financing? The initial investment in the company would be raised through lectures on Greenland that he and Freuchen would give in Denmark, calling on the better nature of businessmen and bankers. "During these negotiations," Freuchen later wrote, "I saw human nature in its worst light. My respect for it diminished greatly."

Yet the sponsorship of one Danish businessman, Adam Bjerring (who never met Rasmussen; he lived in the Caucasus) and the gifts of a Danish engineer, Nyeboe, provided the startup funds for the Thule trading post. Places in the region around the post still bear the names of these founding sponsors—thus did Rasmussen show his thanks.

The Eskimos sponsor the study of their own history

The small ship chartered by Rasmussen in 1910 put in at Godhavn (Disko) and Upernavik after crossing the Atlantic. In a replay of history, it carried the daughter of Hans Hendrik and Meqru, Vivi. Widowed at a young age after the death of her Polar Eskimo husband and feeling herself to be poor among the poor of Godhavn, she had decided to return to the birthplace of her husband. And so the great shadow of Hans Hendrik—the companion of Kane, Hayes, Hall, and Nares—would accompany the founder of Thule to the country of the "Arctic Highlanders." Vivi was to be the grandmother of my companion Sakaeunnguaq and of Olepaluk in Siorapaluk.

A violent storm brought Knud Rasmussen's ship into North Star Bay. "We had not planned to make this site our base, but we had no choice. And as it turned out, it was the best-suited spot in the entire district." Chance is the handmaiden of fortune: this was the only bay that could be used for a large-scale port project. Uummannaq ("Seal Heart") was the name of the age-old Inuit village. It lay at the center of the territory.

Rasmussen's most innovative decision—I might almost call it revolutionary in terms of policy toward natives—was to link the trading post he established to a series of expeditions devoted exclusively to the history and ethnology of the Eskimos: studies based on the past of the inhabitants of this land.

On this economic and scientific foundation, the administration of the territory only gradually developed. The modest trading post of 1910 did not allow all the various branches of a regular administration to be established. The budget for missions, education, and health were more or less tied during those early years to the profits made by the post. The first missionaries arrived in 1910. The population as a whole became Christian by 1920. [4] The church was built in 1930. In 1928 all of the adults were taught to read and write by catechists from South Greenland. A hospital with a doctor and a nurse was established in 1925.

When you consider that Peary and all those who preceded him—Britons, Americans, and Norwegians—had launched expeditions exclusively to allow the West to conquer the Pole, acquire new territory, and find new routes to China, with the Eskimos taking part only as hired hands, then the novelty of the period ushered in by Rasmussen can be understood. By integrating the Inughuit into the Western world, through trade and medical assistance, through science and Christianity, he guaranteed their protection and bolstered their strength. By bringing them into his expeditions as equal partners with the whites he reinforced their Greenlandic and circumpolar destiny. By making them ethnologists of their own history, he laid the foundations of a future arctic university. Through a kind of pedagogy, of teaching through action—in his so-called Thule expeditions—Rasmussen actually devised a new form of development for traditional societies: first strengthening them through a knowledge of their historic greatness, then encouraging them to choose their own mode of development.

Springtime: the floe begins to fracture. A seal is harpooned across a lead. (After 1910.)

An autodidact schooled by the Eskimos

What roots could such a man have had? What family heritage compelled the young Knud to devote himself to the study of the Eskimos? Knud's father, Christian Rasmussen, a Danish pastor and teacher, lived in Greenland for eighteen years before retiring to Denmark to give well-regarded courses in Eskimo linguistics at the University. He was the author of a Greenlandic grammar and a Greenlandic dictionary. His wife, Knud's mother, was the daughter of Karl Fleischer, a remarkable man, who married a Greenlandic orphan found half dead of starvation in Christianshaab. This was Knud's maternal grandmother, and it was she who taught him the Eskimo language. The Fleischers were a well-known family of colonial administrators in Greenland, and they had many relatives. From the start this provided Rasmussen with solid allies on the island of Greenland, where clan affiliation is an important feature.

Knud Rasmussen was born in June 1879 in Jakobshavn (Ilulissat) in a large house that is now a museum devoted to the explorer.[5] He spent his first years with the children of Disko Bay, speaking their language, sharing their games and taking part in their dog sled and kayak races. The missionary assistants in Thule were childhood friends of his, in particular Inuk Christiansen, whom I knew in 1950-1951 in Siorapaluk; he was my neighbor. I spent many evenings listening to tales of his early years as a missionary among the "pagans."

At a young age Knud heard the old myths with their giants, cannibals, *qiviqtuq*, *tupilaat*, and bears. Listening to these fantastic stories of the past no doubt affected the course of his life and endowed him with his extraordinary permeability to Inuit thought. His education in Denmark did not go far, despite his father's ambitions for him. As his friend Peter Freuchen remarked: "He studied without pleasure and with no great success." Knud hesitated between several possible careers. Should he be an actor? an opera singer? He discovered a talent for language and after reporting from Lapland was tempted to try a career as a writer. But in the end, Knud's extraordinary personality was to manifest itself in another way.

"His glance was kind and piercing. . . . His laughter preceded him," noted Peter Freuchen. And whites generally found him extremely handsome. The Eskimos for their part admired Rasmussen largely for his mental qualities. Here is how one of them expressed it to him, with typically double-edged Eskimo humor: "It's obvious that everything has a reason: your ugliness forces other people to pay attention only to your intelligence and your worth, which are qualities one notices less when a man is handsome." Whether handsome or ugly, it is certain that he had a great deal of charm and exercised a very real power over those who came in contact with him. He was also generous, and he set great store by friendship—a trait that is all too rare, as we have seen, in the Arctic.

A camp of native hunters in the warmth of a Greenland spring. May-June 1910.

The painter Harald Moltke, his close friend, wrote me on my return from Thule to Paris in 1951 that though Knud was only nineteen years old at their first meeting in 1898, he had vividly experienced Rasmussen's rare talent for enlarging his interlocutor and enhancing his faith in himself.

The academic establishment in Copenhagen looked askance at Rasmussen in the beginning—he hated mathematics, mapmaking, and geodesy, and he had a reputation for being unmethodical and working too impulsively. Yet he managed to come to terms gradually with his enemies by involving them one by one in his projects. He was an able diplomat, as his good friend Countess Moltke used to remind me during our annual dinners, and he had the valuable ability to get public opinion on his side in the many interviews he gave. And public opinion carried great weight with the very traditional university, which was proud of its past and its rules, and dubious toward this "half-breed" with no university degree. Some scholars were already critical, jealous of the aura surrounding him. The field of Eskimo studies was then dominated by William Thalbitzer, but it is unclear whether this ethnolinguist, who specialized in Greenland's east coat, ever worked with the young explorer and administrator of Thule.

When Rasmussen's plan took shape, the government of Greenland was skeptical that an isolated trading post in North Greenland could prove viable, but it eventually decided that this enterprise—undertaken without regard for distance, for isolation, or for the vagaries of commerce—was sound. Financially independent, able to use the press (which he never neglected) to keep the Danish people on his side, and always aiming at the highest level of knowledge, Rasmussen, an excellent diplomat, quickly became an undoubted hero. What a great distance he had come, this man of mixed race, a schoolteacher's son, taking his place among the most honored members of the Danish government and Danish academe!

27 October 1927: Knud Rasmussen receiving an honorary doctorate from St. Andrews University in Scotland. He was forty-eight years old, and it was time to collect honors. He had only six years left to live.

3) Fox skin was extremely valuable. Before the First World War, fox pelts fetched 50 to 100 dollars apiece (in 1910 dollars).

4) The last adult to be baptized was the querulous Nukappianguaq, from Etah, father of my friend Sakaeunnguaq, in 1934.

5) I know it well. In 1949 it was the residence of the vice-bishop of Greenland, Mathias Storch, the first Greenlandic novelist. He honored me with his friendship, as did his son Johan; many times have I played chess with Mathias Storch. From time to time he would speak of the past for my benefit and of Rasmussen.

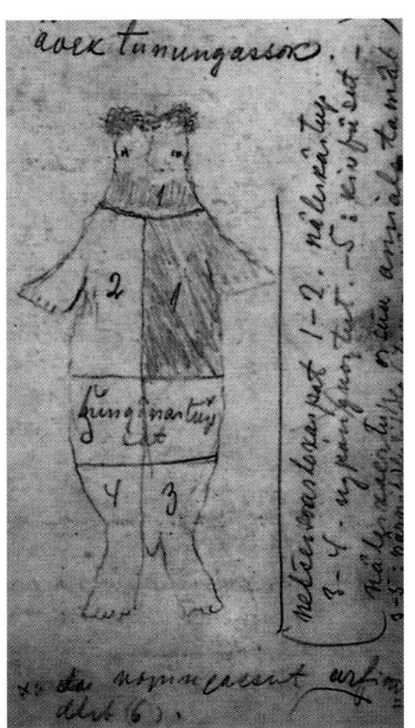

A page from an ethnographic notebook kept in Greenlandic by Knud Rasmussen. It sets out the rules for dividing a walrus after the hunt.

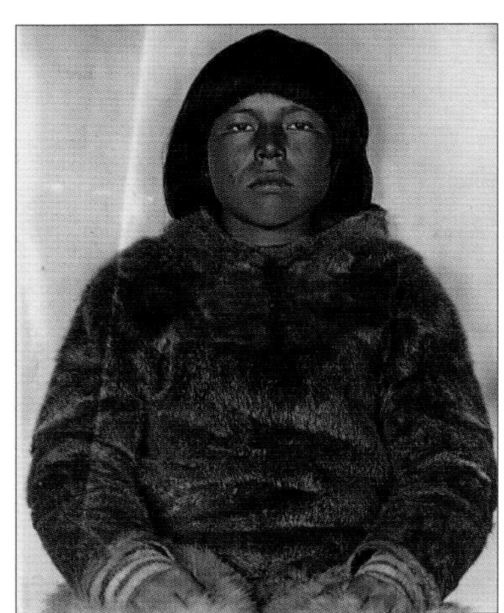

Ki-We-Ark-Shah (Qaavigarsuaq), a young Etah Eskimo, photographed in 1914-1917. Nicknamed Miteq ("the Duck"), he became one of the members of the Fifth Thule Expedition in the Canadian Central Arctic and Alaska (1922-1925). "He [Knud] often questioned me about my reactions when we were among the Netsilingmiut, comparing his own interpretations with mine and those of Arnarulunaguak," Qaavigarsuaq told me in December 1950.

And it was partly out of jealousy that Lauge Koch, a former companion of Rasmussen's, wrote a perverse biography of him after his death, in which he introduced two or three long and venomous thorns among the flowers. The Danish people—to its credit—met the book's publication with disdainful silence. When a great man dies, one who has given you a leg up, you don't write: "To receive an honorary doctorate was the great dream of his life; and one may well ask whether he should have been awarded such an honor? . . . I am not alone in harboring some doubt as to the value of Knud Rasmussen's collections of myths. Knud wrote what he thought was science, and what has become the subject of novels." What hateful villainy on the part of Lauge Koch! He has told me that he never understood my contempt for this form of denigration by a colleague in print—pillorying a friend who has died.

Understanding the world of Inuit religion

Let us leave these miasmas behind, the expression of an old and twisted jealousy, to return to Rasmussen. Religious by nature, he wanted to understand the basis of the Inuit's world view, that is, their religious vision of the world. When he met the journalist Mylius-Erichsen in 1902, Knud Rasmussen's fate as an Arctic ethnographer was sealed. The university might not be interested in North Greenland, but Mylius-Erichsen wanted to mount an expedition to the area. This was to become the Danish Literary Expedition to Greenland's west coast, intended to collect as much about the past of Arctic societies as possible—before it was too late—from the south to the extreme north. The expedition left Disko Bay by dog sled, had a difficult crossing of Melville Bay, then reached Saunders Island. Being poorly equipped, it faced serious problems, among them the terrible illness of Harald Moltke. The Eskimos welcomed the four members of the expedition with extraordinary generosity, particularly Knud, the youngest, who charmed them by his intelligence, his open mind, and his understanding.

As Moltke put it: "Rasmussen drank in the nature of Greenland through all his senses." He proved an excellent ethnolinguist. He soon grasped how fragile were the society and culture of the isolated Polar Eskimos, after their enrollment in the American expeditions whose emphasis was on sporting and media matters, rather than scientific ones. And he diagnosed the dangers of social and economic collapse that were beginning to threaten the Polar Eskimos.

Rasmussen and the first missionaries; Rasmussen as trader

But how could Rasmussen protect the Inuit's traditions and their rules? Having heard their conversation, he knew that the Inughuit were worried and felt their terrible isolation. Peary reached what he called the Pole on 6 April 1909 and never afterward returned. Now that the whalers were growing scarcer and scarcer, who would bring the Inuit the iron, wood, ammunition, firearms, tools, and tobacco that they had acquired an urgent need for? They had not abandoned their ancient hunting techniques (bow, stone traps), but the poverty and inefficiency of these means were now clear to them.

Furthermore, the Eskimos now understood that the white man had a different god and that the ancient shamanistic religion was perhaps open to question. This utterance (from 1900), reported by Peter Freuchen, is significant: "We are only poor, silly people. We have few ways of protecting ourselves for the sake of our children, so we only do as our forefathers have taught us to do. If you need not do the same thing, it is convenient for you, but you should not laugh at us merely because you are the stronger. We think that if we do this we shall not die at least until the sun returns next year. Even if it does no good, we enjoy life so much that we do anything to keep it."

At the same time, the Polar Eskimos had taken profound stock of their moral superiority over the whites—ever since the first days of their meeting with Captain John Ross. Let us not forget the astonishment of the egalitarian Inuit in August 1818 at seeing officers seated on sledges and being pulled by men playing the part of dogs. Kane was the first to winter among them (1853-1855). They witnessed the dramas, rivalries, mutinies, assassinations, suicides, and betrayals that occurred during the thirteen expeditions that followed. Hayes's desertion and his treachery toward the Inuit (1853) remained in their memory. The wintering of the *Polaris* north of Etah (1872), the business of the rescue of the Greely expedition from Cape Sabine (1884) with all its local consequences (food caches, the sexual fraternization of the crews of the rescue ships with the Eskimos), the suicides, the crises during the Peary expedition—all made a profound mark on the minds of these simple people. Peary's Minik affair left a lasting impression: the Inuit are pained to know that the skeletons of five of their relatives lie far from their ancestral capes and mountains. The skeleton of Minik's father was sold or given to the American Museum of Natural History.

Thus when Rasmussen arrived, the Polar Eskimos were being swept by conflicting currents of thought. It is noteworthy that in the tales and legends he presented, Rasmussen totally ignored the troubled history of the Eskimos in their contacts with the white man, from their discovery to the present day. This people hung between two radically divergent worlds, which Rasmussen, by virtue of his mixed Danish and Greenlandic heritage, had the capacity to bridge.

After the first, so-called literary expedition, led by the journalist Mylius-Erichsen, Rasmussen returned to Denmark and in the fall of 1908 married Dagmar Andersen,

Knud Rasmussen (left) at the age of twenty-four with his friend Harald Moltke at the time of the Danish Literary Expedition to the southwest coast of Greenland (1903). He wears a quietly ironic expression that one often finds among the Inuit.

the wealthy daughter of one of Denmark's largest builders and a state deputy and councilor. She helped him—this she told me during one of our meetings in Copenhagen—-to write his first book, the best of them, which was the literary and scientific sensation of 1905: *Nye Mennesker,* "New Men—the Polar Eskimos," which he himself translated into Greenlandic.

But Rasmussen was a nomad. Nothing and no one could keep him from setting off again. On 4 August 1909 he was back in Greenland as the co-founder of a Christian mission in Kangerluarsuk, Inglefield Fjord, south of Siorapaluk, intended to convert the group gradually to Christianity. A pastor's son, Rasmussen at the same time respected Eskimo tradition and believed in missionary work. Among the missionaries was Gustav Olsen, [9] who lived very simply by hunting in order to be with the Inuit. Rasmussen, as we've seen, had brought several of his childhood friends to help the pastors. Enok Christiansen was one of them. Rasmussen, though convinced because of his upbringing of the need to propagate Christ's word throughout the world, was always respectful of the Inuit's traditions, a contradiction that lay at the heart of Danish Greenland as founded in 1721 by Bishop Hans Egede. The thought was to bring the Christian message while respecting Eskimo language, songs, dances, and beliefs. It might thereby be possible to establish a respect for the law and abolish such accepted forms of aggression as rape, crime, and infanticide, but through consensus and without resorting to authoritarianism. This was a far cry from the spirit animating the Order of Mary Immaculate, the one Catholic missionary order that practiced in the Canadian East Arctic, and from the spirit that animated the Anglican missionaries of the early days with their Puritan ethic and their "sins of the flesh." I visited a village where the pastor had outlawed hunting on Sundays, the Lord's day, presumably on the same principle by which embroidery was permitted on Sundays, while knitting, which would have been an offense to the Lord, was proscribed.

A dual society

Despite the external change in the new converts—their long hair, a sign of nature's power and of the Eskimos' close ties to it, had now to be cut short and the bowl haircut became obligatory—their deepest thoughts rebelled. [10] The *ayaya,* traditional songs and dances, continued to be performed, though less publicly. Rasmussen certainly intervened with the missionaries on the Eskimos' behalf in this matter. The conversion was a gentle one.

The rituals of shamanism—dietary taboos, sharing of sexual favors, burial rites, spouse exchange—continued to be tolerated and were practiced until 1930; the various taboos and archetypes were current until 1950-1951 and beyond. The church's tolerance allowed a form of dualism to become gradually established: the ancient beliefs were buried in the minds of individuals to greatly differing degrees; the shamans (*angakkuq*) no longer practiced in front of all, but shamanist thought persisted, emerging from time to time and particularly in moments of crisis, as I witnessed often enough.

It was in 1909, the year he co-founded this missionary station, that Rasmussen had a serious accident (a fact too often ignored): his spine was seriously injured and two of his ribs were broken, so that he was never again able to bend down, or to push or haul a sled. Furthermore, he ran the risk of becoming paralyzed at any moment. This terrible handicap, which he gracefully hid, did not keep him from leading seven expeditions and traveling thousands of miles over the ice and tundra.

The Danish Greenlander Knud Rasmussen in a park in Copenhagen.

6) "Already during my childhood I had heard a great deal about the Polar Eskimos . . . stories of wild cannibals, terrible hunters who lived in the north wind at the edge of the world where it is permanently night and where the sea stays frozen in summer . . ."

Rasmussen could also be wild. Countess Moltke told me the story in 1982 of a formal dinner given in his honor in Stockholm (1920). Knud was nowhere to be found. It was she who discovered him, entirely by chance, hiding in a wardrobe, hunched up like a troll, his evening clothes in disarray, his eyes crazy, shouting "Go away! Go away!"

7) Mylius-Erichsen died of starvation in 1907 on a second expedition to Peary Land. Peary's erroneous mapping of the area contributed to the disastrous fate of Mylius-Erichsen's exploration, in which both he and his Greenlander companion, Jørgen Brønlund lost their lives.

8) Peter Freuchen, Arctic Adventure: My Life in the Frozen North (New York: Farrar & Rhinehart, 1935), p. 319.

9) He too was the father of another friend, Ammalortoq Olsen, Greenlandic delegate to the First Pan-Inuit Conference in Rouen in 1969, which I had the honor of co-chairing with René Cassin, Nobel Peace laureate in 1968.

10) Who decided to humiliate the Inuit in this way? It was the Lutheran missionaries from South Greenland, in a spirit of Christian modesty.

Inuit hunters walking along the fragile floe edge to hunt walrus where a storm has created open water (February-March). Drawing by Asiajuk, collected by Knud Rasmussen (1910-1920).

Uqaluktuaqtuk, telling a legend (1990). The elders are held in particular respect. They are the keepers of the tribe's memory.

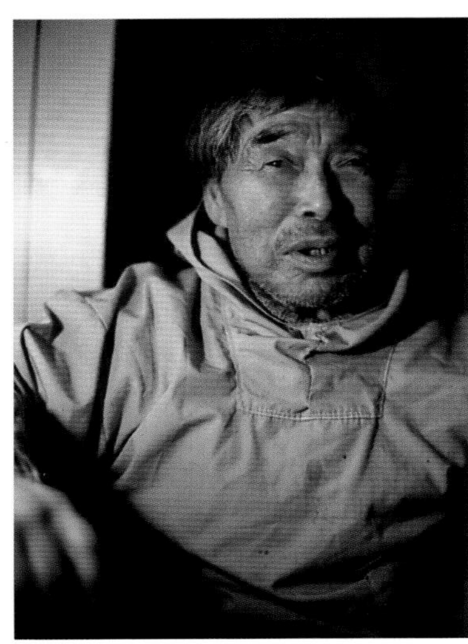

The coming of the trading post and the end of the barter economy

With his friend Peter Freuchen, Rasmussen created the Thule station on 19 August 1910, whose main function was to provide a trading post for North Greenland. To start this establishment running Rasmussen had only 200 fox skins, or 12,000 kroner—but the very modesty of the funds was to prove beneficial to the Eskimos, as it kept the post from being modernized too rapidly. Rasmussen had received his training for this venture in 1905 when, under contract to the Ministry of Greenland, he traveled along Greenland's west coast from trading post to trading post. An excellent observer, he learned all the administrative techniques necessary for the functioning of his trading company.

A trading post where the prices were fixed in advance provoked an upheaval in the minds of the Arctic hunters. In July 1910, the Eskimos had not the least notion of a "fixed trading price." As Freuchen observed: "Many would have accorded a higher value to their goods if they had cost them more." This only shows how rapacious were Rasmussen's predecessors in setting the terms of trade.

Modern methods of trapping foxes had arrived with Peary and Cook, and the practice was now systematically encouraged so as to provide the Eskimos with a cash commodity. [11] Trapping foxes had been a woman's task until 1910, but it now became a man's job. The Eskimos settled immediately into a dependant economy. Steel traps were sold at low prices. From being intermittently available in Peary's time, the trading post now offered them continuously. As the trading post was a private one (and there was only one in all the district administered by Rasmussen at North Star Bay), it sold a minimum of different goods: knives, tools such as axes and saws, cloth, wood, rifles and ammunition, steel traps, matches, coffee, tea, sugar. A local currency was introduced.

The trading post met some competition when McMillan's expedition settled in Etah in 1914-1917. The Americans followed Peary's old practices, though not as systematically as had been done in the days of the Peary Arctic Club. The American guns and knives were of better quality, yet Rasmussen inspired confidence in the Eskimos and he kept his "clients." The trading post's future was safe. It nonetheless faced harsh economic conditions. Exchange rates dipped and fresh goods were unavailable during the four years of the First World War (1914-1918), which led to rationing. Freuchen has written that in 1914 a family could receive only two boxes of matches and a hunter only 30 cartridges per year. The Inuit were under no illusion. The trading post offered only a wispy echo of Western technology. Daily life provided a constant reminder of old times, which were still recent. And the vicissitudes of history (the war between the whites, for instance) could force them to revert to their old technologies, such as building igloos of snow or sod without wood or canvas, or using bows, lances, and harpoons (for want of ammunition), or once again having to use stone traps (for want of steel traps), or being obliged to light fires with the bow drill (for want of matches), or of having to repair clothing or the dog traces on the trail during an all-male hunting expedition. And when an Inuit hunts, he may be swept away on a drifting floe where his survival will depend entirely on his adaptive capabilities. Hence the necessity for a dual society; or more accurately, the Inuit have a dual mentality so as to adapt to their two lives.

The dispersion of the villages and hamlets (twelve in 1923, ten in 1950-1951, six in 1989), dictated by hunting, was maintained and discreetly encouraged: Eskimo society had to preserve its ability to be self-sufficient. The use of imported wood, for example, only gradually became widespread. Its first use was for the sleeping platforms of dwellings, then (in 1950-1960) for walls, ceilings, and

11) The first steel traps were brought by Peary in 1893-1895; until then, foxes had been trapped in stone traps, with the stone door tripped by sealskin thongs. A few of these traps still existed in 1969, and I filmed them in action.

12) The Thule trading post only came under official Danish administration seventeen years before my arrival (1933 being the year Rasmussen died), or actually fourteen years before (1936). Rasmussen proved on the whole conservative toward "his" Eskimos and rather shy of the white man's influence (doctors and schools, for instance, were only established quite late). In trading posts other than Thule, the only education was from the catechist, a Polar Eskimo who could more or less read and also tended the store. Only Siorapaluk and Savissivik had a catechist from South Greenland who was both a teacher and the manager of the post. Education covered only reading, writing, and arithmetic until 1960.

13) The Greenlandic edition, which I translated into French (winter 1950) to perfect my knowledge of the language, differs considerably from the original Danish edition.

14) The film was produced, directed, etc. in Germany (1932-1933).

15) It is odd that Rasmussen did not think to shoot this film on the northwest coast of Greenland, where he could at once have been an inside witness, actor, and interpreter of the Eskimos' life. The first film shot in Thule was by Jette Bang in 1936, a short ethnographic documentary; the next by Jorgen Roos (*Ultima Thule*, 1968, 28', 16mm and 35mm, black and white)—both are Danish film-makers. Finally there is my own *Last Kings of Thule* (1969, 120', color): 1. "The Polar Eskimo as Hunter"; 2. "The Eskimo, Unemployed and Unpredictable" (INA, Paris, 1970).

At the end of spring, Qaaqqutsiaq and Ah-now-kah travel along the ice foot between the rocky shore and the open sea. The Inuit use this "sidewalk," which allows them to travel by dog sled from fjord to fjord, until about mid-June. The ice foot can collapse suddenly, tumbling the hunter and his team to the bottom of the cliff.

floors. It was not universally used in dwellings in 1950. Several were still of sod and piled stones, with stone floors. The best rifles, fox traps, and tools were sold to the Eskimos. By assuring them a steady supply of everything that they naturally lacked through the Thule trading post, Rasmussen was obviously putting more power into the hands of the Danish authority. [12] Nonetheless, by so regulating matters that the Christian mission was not a direct part of the trading company, Knud created a real separation of church and state, which is to say that he "secularized" Danish Greenland.

The Eskimos subsidize Eskimo studies

His independence from the church probably allowed "our Knud" (*Kununnguaq*, as the Eskimos called him) to seem a real ally, an alliance that would be sealed when Thule became an expedition base (profits from the post being used to sponsor research) and the birthplace of Eskimo studies. Thanks to his extraordinary vision, Rasmussen laid the groundwork for the longtime future of the Inuit by interesting them in every possible way in the knowledge of their past and their thousand-year civilization.

Ethnology was to save the Eskimos from the more or less brutal trauma they had suffered since 1892 in their close encounter with Peary and the Western world. Rasmussen, fascinated by Arctic myths and legends, listened attentively and transcribed faithfully, thus showing the greatest respect for a tradition that until then had been despised and unknown. Shaken in its deepest matrix, this people found its character reinforced by Rasmussen's respect for its intellectual culture. Rasmussen's prescription was to encourage the knowledge of culture at the very moment when traditional society was forced to change, and in 1908 he became one of the founders of the Greenland Literary Society. He both wrote and translated its first book, *Avangarnisalerssarutit*, or *Nye Mennesker* (1909). [13] Thus, no sooner did they become literate than the people of Thule were able to read their own history. It was unique in the history of primitive peoples that a small people should subsidize the scientific expeditions that researched the history of such great nations as Canada and the United States.

In 1925 Rasmussen received an honorary doctorate from the University of Copenhagen and, in 1927, from St. Andrews in Scotland. He felt the honor deeply. The scientific community recognized the considerable work he had accomplished in Greenland as well as in Canada and Alaska. The rich ethnological collections assembled by Rasmussen gave the Danish National Museum one of the foremost Arctic holdings in the world. His new dream was to internationalize the study of the peoples of the Arctic and examine the great questions concerning the northern and prehistoric European peoples.

In the last years of his life Rasmussen saw the importance of film for understanding a people. *Palo's Wedding*, for which he was an advisor, was a masterwork. [14] Thanks to his influence over the Eskimos, he was able to enthuse the hunters in one hamlet after another and get their cooperation to reconstruct many extraordinarily vivid scenes. The main aspects of daily life in summer were recorded. The winter scenes, however, were never filmed. [15] It was after the shooting of one of the great summer sequences in *Palo's Wedding*, under technically demanding conditions that—Rasmussen poisoned by spoiled meat and weakened by pneumonia—was transported urgently back to Copenhagen, where he died after four months of illness, at dawn on 21 December 1933. He was fifty-seven years old. [16]

Knud Rasmussen:

Avángarnisalerssârutit.

Oĸalualât

kuisimángitsut Uperniviup avangnâne
Ivnângarngup erĸâne pivdlugit.
ássiliartagdlit.

Københavnime,
A. Rosenberg-ip naĸiteriviane.

Cover of the Greenlandic edition of *Nye Menneker* (1909). This book, Rasmussen's first, was published in Danish in 1905, bringing him lasting fame at home.

Alerted by a dog, the musk oxen have taken up a defensive formation, facing outward. Three Eskimos level their rifles at them at short range (1914-1917, Ellesmere Island).

The narwhal (Monodon monoceros) is hunted collectively at the head of Inglefield Fjord in August-September, near the glacier that calves into the sea. The male has two teeth, a short one in the upper jaw and a long one growing out of its skull which can measure ten feet in length. It is used by the narwhal during his mating display. Narwhal's teeth have great symbolic value to the Inuit (symbolizing an elderly woman's sacrifice) and to Westerners (allegorical creature symbolizing the incarnation and death of Christ). "My horn shalt thou exalt," (Psalms: 92, 10). In 1950-1951, the hunters in the Thule district caught 130 narwhals. The male narwhal was chosen by the Inughuit as the tutelary animal for the crest of Qaanaaq-Thule.

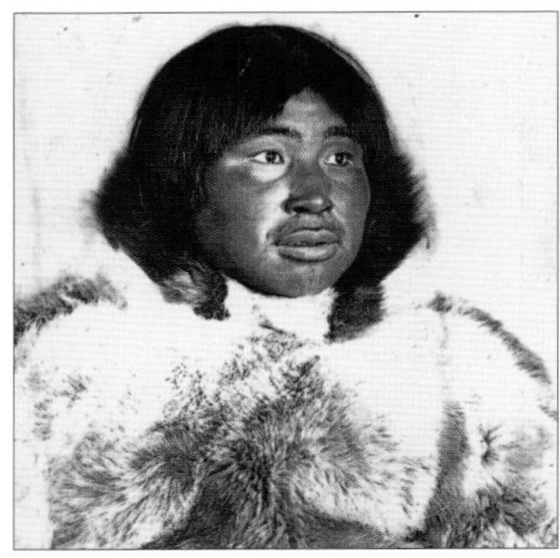

Ittukusuk, one of Cook's Inuit companions (1914-1917).

My great personal debt

Whatever trail you take in Thule, Knud Rasmussen's shadow envelops you. For me, he was an example and a model, about whom I learned from the Inuit, which is to say *after* my first expedition to Thule. A geomorphologist, I confess to having known little about him beforehand. "The man whose laughter preceded him," said his closest friend, Peter Freuchen. I might have put it: "The man whose charm preceded him," taking the word in its shamanistic sense of "under a charm." The dictionary defines "charm" as "the supposed effect of a magical operation that consists mostly of words." I owe to Rasmussen my enthrallment with Inuit cosmogony, first during the long evenings of November 1950. One night at the end of October, feeling I had solved the problems besetting me—establishing my cabin base, learning to understand the language, what the Inughuit left unspoken, their manners (I found them *very* touchy), learning to drive my dogs, to travel at night, to adapt to the Inuit diet, which I adopted 90 percent— I went alone to "find myself" on a small deserted beach just north of the nine igloos of Siorapaluk. The moon that night lit an empty bay, harmonious in its arc; the chalky light revealed my pallid skin. The sea, thickened with grease ice, the crystals starting to coalesce, moved heavily. In the inlets, a fine film of ice crackled with the cold. Vast icebergs, come from a mythic elsewhere, loomed in the distance, craggy and seemingly alive in their slow progress. Under careful scrutiny, the black sky revealed a few remaining spots of madder and mauve. Leaning against the cliff (silent since the departure in early October of its millions of auklets), facing the floe, I allowed myself to be drawn into this phantasmagoric world, so strange to a young European.

The Danish Literary Expedition taking coffee with some South Greenlanders.

Summer camp on Neqi Bay, near Siorapaluk (1914-1917). In the foreground, the traditional sealskin tent, this one belonging to Ahl-nay-doo. Behind, to the left, in the frozen inlet, a wooden boat, probably received from Peary.

And Inuit legends sprang to my lips spontaneously. I had in fact been improving my grasp of the Polar Eskimo language in the past month by translating the Inuit myths that Rasmussen had written down in Inuktitut: *Avangarnisalerssarutit Oqalualat.* [17]

The Inuit, assisted by the South Greenlandic catechist, helped me with my translation, making me understand unknown words and obscure passages by paraphrasing them, or by drawings and gestures. Nerrivik, the goddess of the sea, Kivioq, the humiliated but victorious orphan, the child-eating ogre—each of these heroes seemed to spring from their hands and from the narrators themselves as they stood up to act out the story. The wife of Sakaeunnguaq, who was friendly toward me, visibly took pleasure from coming to my cabin in the evening and telling me all over again the legend of Igimarassugsuq, the unpredictably voracious ogre, (she made me a surrealist drawing of the most violent part).

That night, at my feet, the lips of the crevasses in the land-fast ice creaked as they rubbed against each other with the movement of the rising tide. Kutsikitsoq had been right when he had whispered to me: "Yes, yes, that's what the Inuit say. They are the terrible cries of our children, abandoned at Atikerluk by a horrible shaman long, long ago, and they are still moaning. The poor children moan, they are freezing. The spirits of those who died that year continue to roam around the igloos, in the Inuit tradition. They come and go, and the wind blowing is the sound of their voices. You must listen to the wind when it hisses, when it roars, when it hoots: they are speaking to us." I looked at the milky slopes rising in the gloom, searching for a *qiviqtuq* that might be coming toward me. All of a sudden the man-shaped rocks along the cliff base seemed to move; there was a ghostly silhouette. A stone suddenly rocketed down the slope. Might it not be one of these beings in flight from the Inuit? Now immortal, they come down at night, with their clawed hands, their castrators' mouths with sharp white canines, to catch souls and torment them. Sakaeunnguaq, who was a bit of a shaman, saw them often in his nightmarish dreams. He showed me the print of one of their enormous feet in the snow. I felt a breath. There was no doubt, "he" was behind me, "he" was going to touch me. The Inuit, as I was told every day, are never wrong. It was true, there was a *qiviqtuq* near my house and he was harassing me.

The night wind rose, the air was dry, the silence tomblike. *Taaq*, "it's dark," everything was dark. I shivered. Was a *qiviqtuq* going to carry off the young *qaallunaat* into his mountain fastnesses? It was the first time that I had felt so intensely the geopoetic power of the primeval forces. Then I gathered myself. My rational education seemed to close me off from these powers, which explains how I was able so quickly to dominate this fear, before it became an existential panic and paralyzed me there on the beach, or later on the trail, when I was alone with my dogs. But I confess to having taken pleasure in courting these feelings of fear. Rasmussen, because of his mixed blood and of having grown up in Greenland, was also eminently susceptible to these voices from elsewhere when he listened to the old tales. These texts, which I was translating word for word each night, no doubt had the maieutic power of changing me little by little and bringing to the surface the primitive man in me, imperfectly contained by schooling and Christianity. The mantle of education that had secularized me gradually slipped off, and, thanks to Knud Rasmussen, the university graduate became a new man sensitive to the messages from the archipelago of the dead, in an omnipresent shamanistic experience. When I slept next to Ullulik and heard him breathe heavily and groan, I was no longer surprised to see him virtually paralyzed in the morning by his confrontation with the dreaded *tupilak*.

This sensitivity, which came to me through the movement of the air, the sounds and the language of the night, its colors and smells, never again left me. When, later that winter, I went dressed in Eskimo clothes with my dog sled from igloo to igloo, laughing, suffering, loving, I became reflective for long periods, inspired by these tales of the hyperborean genesis, folded into a vaster myth, the myth of Thule "the mist-enshrouded," which sprang up again on these shores thanks to the great poet of the Arctic, Knud Rasmussen.

The seven so-called Thule expeditions

The multidisciplinary expeditions known as the "Thule" expeditions, undertaken between 1912 and 1933, were no doubt the sharpest expression of Rasmussen's scientific persona. These expeditions led to fundamental studies in ethnography, archaeology, linguistics, geography, and cinematography. The work they encompass is at the basis of all study of the northern societies of Northern Alaska, Canada, and Greenland. The different disciplines had until then competed amongst themselves but now became complementary, thanks to the authority and conciliating spirit of the non-specialist Rasmussen. His exceptional knowledge of the Inuit language, his great psychological intensity, and, as we mentioned, his mixed blood allowed him to grasp the complexity of the tortured and imaginative Inuit psychology from the inside. His books are the indispensable base from which any attempt at understanding the religious and shamanistic thought of the arctic peoples must start. His expeditions always had a substantial component of Polar Eskimo members.

The first expedition (1912-1913) counted four men at the start (Rasmussen, Freuchen, and two Eskimos), with thirty-four sleds and three hundred and fifty-three dogs. The expedition mapped the northwest coast of Greenland

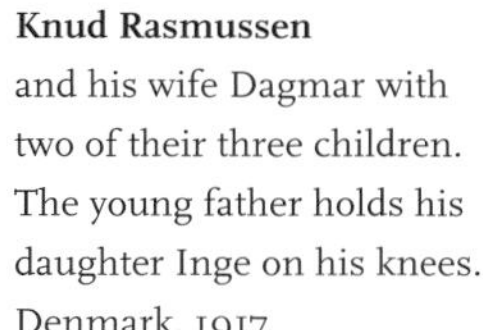

Knud Rasmussen and his wife Dagmar with two of their three children. The young father holds his daughter Inge on his knees. Denmark, 1917.

and confirmed that, contrary to Peary's assertions, the land known as Peary Land was not an island. The two-thousand-mile crossing of the inland ice cap (counting the voyage out and back) was extraordinarily bold and dangerous. From it Rasmussen and Freuchen gained a reputation among the Inuit equal to that of *Piulersuaq*, the "Great Peary."

Rasmussen earned his title among the Inuit. He was no longer *Kunupaluk*, "Little Knud," beloved of everyone, but *Kununnguaq*, "Our Knud."

With the Thule Inuit

The Second Thule Expedition (1916-1917), primarily a mapping and exploratory mission, counted seven men, three of them whites, with six sleds and seventy-two dogs. The expedition members planned to spend five months in the north but were there for seven. The expedition was conducted "Eskimo-style," which is to say that it was improvised in its details from day to day and obtained food entirely from hunting (musk ox, caribou, and seal), with all the attendant risk. The expedition was under collective leadership, the Eskimos taking part in every decision. For the first time in the history of the Arctic, the equal rights of white and Eskimo partners were written out. Lauge Koch always charged that this expedition was anarchic, in the Eskimo way, and carried the seeds of catastrophe. He said as much to me in 1951. In fact, it would end with the tragic deaths of two of its members, one of them the Swedish botanist Thorild Wulff (see page 269), who, exhausted, asked to be left behind on 29 August 1917 at Qaaqqaitsut in Inglefield Land.

The Fifth Thule Expedition (1921-1924) was the largest of them all. It was financed from the proceeds of the trading post, of course—fox skins having gone up enormously in price after the war—but also by public and private contributions from Denmark. It lasted three years and took Rasmussen and two Polar Eskimos (one of them Qaavigarsuaq[18]) as far as Alaska. During the first two years, Ras-

Knud Rasmussen in the prime of life: the visionary hunter was also a scientist and a skilled diplomat.

16) Last point: Rasmussen was not a civil servant. The Thule trading post provided a sound financial base for him and his family: the Kap York Station post was a private company run by him and Peter Freuchen. It was bought from the family by the Danish government in 1933 at its founder's death, and the beneficiaries received financial compensation.

17) "The Men of the North Speak to You."

Appat, summer 1929. Rasmussen resting with the Danish writer Axel Ahlam on the sleeping platform of an abandoned igloo.

mussen, along with the geographer and ethnologist Birket-Smith, the archaeologist Mathiassen, and the geographer Freuchen, studied the land and the peoples of Hudson Bay. Ten crucial volumes on the arctic peoples of North America resulted, in the fields of geography, botany, linguistics, archaeology, and ethnology. Twenty thousand ethnographic specimens were collected, which have made the National Museum in Copenhagen the foremost in the world.

The sixth and seventh expeditions (1931 and 1932-1933), directed toward the southeast of Greenland, were supported by modern logistics (motor boats, airplanes). Massive and complex, counting thirty native hunters and incorporating cartography, geology, geography, archaeology, ethnography, and film, they were precursors of modern-style expeditions. Participation from Greenlanders was minimal, though it remained at the forefront of the expedition leader's concerns.

The first Eskimo reading primer in Thule was used throughout Greenland from 1910 to 1955. The letter "c" does not exist and is replaced by "k." The wide diffusion of this reader had the effect of "south greenlandizing" the language of the Polar Eskimos, who have resisted this pressure.

The council of the Thule Inuit

At thirty-five, Rasmussen was already an advisor to the Danish authorities for Greenland as a whole. He designed the basic structure of a self-managed Inuit government in Thule, such as was later established. It incorporated respect for the past and flexibility toward the future, assigning the land to the Inuit in egalitarian and anarcho-communist terms.

Sixteen years later, on 7 June 1930, the old customs that could be adapted to modern circumstances were codified and an administrative law was established. The Eskimo formulators of this law, who were still living in 1950-1951 and whom I questioned privately (Borseman, Inukitsupaluk, Imiina, etc.), told me that the law was adopted after numerous and sometimes heated discussions in which the entire population (women as well as men) were able to make their views known. It was abolished only on 1 January 1963, when the Thule district was integrated into Greenland's territorial system—a development that was highly prejudicial to the local people, whose specific interests were buried under more general municipal interests, and one in which the concerns of the ever more numerous Danes and South Greenlanders (10 percent of the population in 1989) played an increasingly prominent part.

Ambivalence toward a Danish Greenland

In 1925, in a famous speech, Rasmussen declared himself in favor of a Danish Greenland and of the Kongelige Grønlandske Handel (Royal Greenland Trading Company), a monopoly for buying and selling, though on condition that the monopoly should gradually loosen. Rasmussen also voiced his belief that bilingualism was useful, since it allowed the Inuit to open outward to the wider world. But he looked favorably on cooperation with the white man only if it was regulated and positive for the Eskimo. And he countenanced the immigration of whites to Thule only to the extent that they offered a positive stimulus, and only if provincial and paternalist tendencies could be avoided.

From 1929 on, Rasmussen was considered the representative of the Danish government in Thule. The Danish administration was anxious to redress a situation that it considered abnormal in administrative law: a private trading post (Kap York Stationen) in the context of Danish Greenland—yet from 1910 to 1933 (the date of Rasmussen's death), the company remained private. Thus North Greenland, while under Danish rule, was privately administered. The situation was unusual enough to merit note.

If it was, of course, as the defender of the inalienable rights of Denmark over Greenland's east coast—which Norway was contesting—that Rasmussen took the stand at the International Court in The Hague on 7 January 1933, it was also (and perhaps primarily) to protect the Eskimo community. This is certainly how that community read it. This decisive intervention of Rasmussen's on the international stage not only earned him Greenland's undying loyalty but also extraordinary popularity. He was the greatest Danish hero, and Greenland was profoundly honored that one of its sons should stand at center stage in Greenland, its tutelary power. And it was Knud Rasmussen's personality, the breadth of his scientific programs, that decided the Danish government to defer administering Thule directly. Although Danish administration was declared in 1933 after Rasmussen's death, it did not become effective until 1936.[19]

The mirror of others

Courage, will, diplomacy, breadth of intellect, high-mindedness—these are the characteristics that emerge from the life of this extraordinary man, as one examines its different stages and the work it produced. Rasmussen was above all a man who paid personally all his life by taking considerable physical risks. With neither the university nor the government to support him, Rasmussen struggled as a private individual against ever more difficult material conditions. The fifth, sixth, and seventh expeditions were particularly massive and costly.

Many questions might be asked on this score: shouldn't the university and the government have subsidized Rasmussen's expeditions on a large scale? Only the fifth (though only very partially) and the seventh expeditions (the second part) were subsidized at all. It is remarkable that Rasmussen never challenged this state of affairs, and that a number of his unpublished works did not see the light of day for fifty years. If they were published, it is thanks to the patient work of Regitze Margrethe Søby, a Danish Eskimologist of the first order.[20]

Rasmussen was a Dane and a Greenlander not only in fact but in mentality—which is no doubt what allowed him to look at Eskimo society both from the outside and the inside. But one shouldn't forget his very real attachment to Danish life: his primary residence, his home port, was at Hundested, Seeland. I went there at the invitation of Mrs. Knud Rasmussen. It is a house with a thatched roof by the seashore. I saw the desk where Rasmussen wrote a number of his admirable and fundamental works on the thought, psychology, and shamanistic religion of the Inuit. While he lived at Hundested with a small secretarial staff, his family lived in Copenhagen. Rasmussen chose to be a Dane. None of his three children received an Eskimo first name, and none pursued their father's work in the field of Eskimology. Unlike Peary and Freuchen, Rasmussen had no Eskimo descendants.

Was Rasmussen afraid of giving more rein to his Eskimo side? Was he held back from a hypothetical "double life" by his Lutheran education? He could not forget that his actions in fact had a dual nature (cultural and commercial) and a dual purpose: to further the joint interests of Denmark and the Inuit, as well as his own career. From a certain perspective, one can also see his actions as fostering a policy of regionalization and protection of the Danish interests.

Finally, though I have refused to lend an ear to it, I have heard young intellectuals from Greenland criticizing the liberties Rasmussen took in interpreting Inuit legends, "rasmussenizing" them—though the critics seemed to regret their words even as they spoke. You have to choose, for Rasmussen was not a classical philologist. He was a great writer and possessed of a Greenlandic sensibility. Regitze Søby confirmed to me the great quality of the translations of Greenlandic myths and legends. Two or three malicious tongues in Thule, belonging to the Inuit, tried to tell me their misgivings about the financial practices at the trading post. I have always avoided this sort of arctic gossip, which some of the locals adore: "Fox skins were not bought at a fair price, we waited many years for a doctor, the post was too primitive, didn't have enough goods . . . we were poor." The general population has always considered these criticisms irrelevant and in poor taste. Ferreting in the trash bins of history is a good way to get one's hands dirty.

Looking again at his work, we can say that Rasmussen was above all an observer who looked and listened well and who understood the crucial importance of gathering and collecting materials for posterity. He fanatically gathered everything that came his way before it was too late: the rules regulating taboos, the lives of the shamans, the language and practices of the sacred, the tales of legends, the things that are spoken of or left unsaid—avoiding any comparative analysis, which he thought premature. But it is certain that his natural modesty (he never criticized anybody) and his lack of a university degree were at the root of unfortunate complexes. He was truly deferential toward "science" as it is understood in university circles—and he had important predecessors in Eskimology: Franz Boas, Diamond Jenness, Vladimir Bogoraz, William Thalbitzer—though his own tendencies intuitively led him to a more immediate and even literary understanding of arctic man. He instinctually understood the ambivalence of the Eskimo mind, which was still deeply linked to nature and trying to universalize its duality. It is likely that Rasmussen's respect for the university had both a positive and a negative influence on his work: positive because it obliged him to surround himself with truly able specialists (such as Mathiassen and Birket-Smith) and with strong scientific personalities (such as Lauge Koch, whom he never feared as a competitor, though others did), seeking a multidisciplinary approach in all his expeditions and a multiplicity of points of view; negative because it hampered him in his personal approach, which was sensitive, poetic, literary, and exceptional. Birket-Smith has put his finger on it: "Others have approached the Eskimos with the goal of understanding them. In the best cases, the results have been honorable and flat. A deep inner resonance was missing. But Knud Rasmussen indisputably had that." In a sense, he was a pioneer of narrative anthropology.

One shouldn't forget that this incomparable ethnographer, collector of legends and tales, and analyst of Eskimo religious thought might well have become—with more con-

Lauge Koch at Etah in March 1917. Departure of the Second Thule Expedition toward Peary Land. It was on the return from this trip, in Inglefield Land, that Lauge Koch and his two Eskimo companions were forced to abandon the Swedish botanist Thorild Wulff, who was at the end of his strength and determined to stay behind and die. He categorically refused to follow the others, who were themselves in great danger.

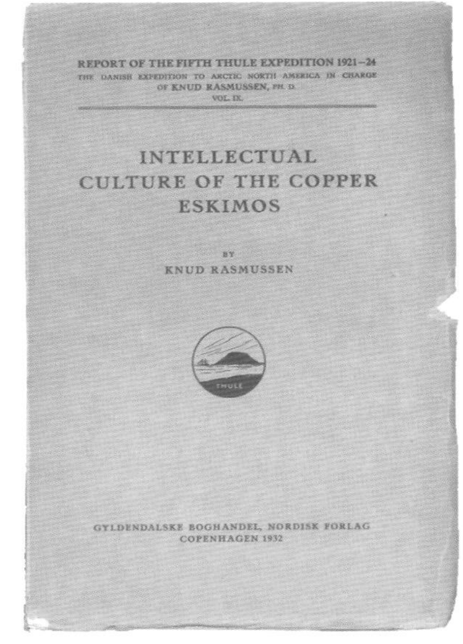

REPORT OF THE FIFTH THULE EXPEDITION 1921–24
THE DANISH EXPEDITION TO ARCTIC NORTH AMERICA IN CHARGE OF KNUD RASMUSSEN, PH. D.
VOL. IX.

INTELLECTUAL CULTURE OF THE COPPER ESKIMOS

BY
KNUD RASMUSSEN

THULE

GYLDENDALSKE BOGHANDEL, NORDISK FORLAG
COPENHAGEN 1932

18) In Thule in 1950, I found him still perfectly loyal to Rasmussen. He declared his joy at encountering his Great Ancestors from Canada and Alaska. He admitted to having at times found himself in danger from these distant Inuit tribes, whose distrust of strangers is strong. Along with Amarulunguak, he traveled by dog sled with Knud Rasmussen to Alaska.

19) I had the opportunity to know Hans Nielsen well, who became Peter Freuchen's successor as manager of the Thule post. In 1948-1949 he was the Danish administrator at Godhavn while I was part of an expedition to Skansen, south Disko. He helped me understand the pro-Greenland politics of the South in legal and commercial matters. Absolutely loyal, he administered the "post-Rasmussen" era in Thule.

20) Regitze Margrethe Søby, *Knud Rasmussen: Tales Told by the Inuit; Greenlandic Myths and Legends* (Copenhagen: Bogan, 1981), 2 volumes (in Danish).

Ivalu Quumanngapik, visiting the base of McMillan's American expedition at Etah. This unusuallly beautiful young woman was probably of mixed blood (1914-1917).

The Etah Eskimos discover the white man's music (1914-1917), thanks to the McMilllan expedition's gramophone. In 1950-1951 and afterward, the Inuit struck me as largely insensitive to Western classical music. But I have seen them moved and sometimes even anguished by the plaintive notes of the Andean pipe.

fidence in his vocation—a writer of the class of Jack London. As such, his literary work (still unknown outside Denmark) is of great value. Unlike Thalbitzer, Rasmussen only made literal translations of 128 myths and legends, which he collected in Canada, Alaska, and the east coast of Greenland; the original documents are now in the Danish national archives. The other tales and legends he adapted for the general public. He never described the men or animals he saw in a literal fashion; instead, he tried to translate the "truth of the impression," in Jean Cocteau's term, often with astonishing success. And this truth was one he was likely to feel more deeply than a stranger since not only was he "also" Eskimo but he had spoken the language fluently since early childhood.

Peter Freuchen said of him: "He never shows any trace of superiority. He is never in the least impatient. He assimilates with the Eskimos and manages through various customs and ways of being to bring out things of real value!" Rasmussen led his expeditions in the Eskimo manner, suggesting a course without ever imposing his authority, and giving others every chance to have their say. This modesty was paired—just as it is among the Eskimos—with a keen fear of ridicule, which showed itself in a concern with appearances. Unlike most white men in the Arctic, Rasmussen always wore impeccable clothes, and Peter Freuchen even mentions—not without a certain irony—that at the worst moments of an expedition he would take out a little mirror and a pair of scissors to trim his beard!

This aspect of Rasmussen's "double personality" was also apparent on the Danish side, where he was known always to be ready to play the starring role, which he did with great skill, to the irritation of his colleagues. Yet at least two great men in his field always stayed on his side: Steensby, an anthropologist and geographer who died at an early age in 1914, and Thomas Thomsen, the curator at the National Museum in Copenhagen.

In the vast trove of work that he left to posterity—both books and films—Rasmussen set himself high standards of scientific rigor, often at the cost of considerable trouble. In his film on the Fifth Thule Expedition, the director wanted to create a lively reportorial tone to express the living realities, whereas Rasmussen insisted on static shots of faces and as classically ethnographic a tone as possible. The director protested, saying that this sort of shot went against the camera, but Rasmussen held firm. He wanted a film that was "ethnographically flawless." In his books, which earned him fame in Copenhagen, he exercised the same care, sometimes bringing a Polar Eskimo to Copenhagen to question him and confirm his notes. If he seems an innovator in mixing Eskimo poems and legends into his accounts of his life and thought, he always fought against the "perceptible excesses" of his literary temperament.

Mixed blood, but an Inuit nature

Given how strong Rasmussen's personality was, it is certain that he only fell in with those influences that corresponded to his own deep tendencies. We know that in 1910, at the height of his popular acclaim after the publication of *Nye Mennesker*, he behaved not only as an ethnographer but as a specialist, refusing—despite the considerable funds offered him—to make a movie on the discovery of the Pole, saying that his only interest was in studying the Eskimos. [21] And when a Danish sponsor offered him 40,000 kroner in tribute to his work, he refused the money and asked that it be given to a scientist. [22]

At his death, Rasmussen was certainly the Dane of his era who held the most official honors and decorations. His unusual charm, his inexhaustible energy, his high-mindedness (he never criticized a colleague), his great skill in dealing with others, his stubbornness in carrying out a long-term program against wind and tide—all of these combined to give this "mixed-breed" an extraordinary victory: he was accounted a great man by the general public and the elite of two widely divergent civilizations.

In the history of the Arctic, but also in the history of the third world, his personality was truly unique. ■

21) The only film on Rasmussen is by Jorgen Roos (McGraw Hill Company, 1965, 16mm, black and white, 30 minutes). An homage by ten Danish specialists has been published: *Bogen om Knud* (Westermann: Copenhagen, 1943), 310 pages.

22) It was thanks to this gift that the Danish Arctic Station in Greenland was established at Godhavn (Disko).

Knud speaks

The Inuit's status

I wish beforehand to emphasize that during the Expedition there must be no difference in standing between the Eskimos and ourselves, the Eskimos being members of the Expedition with rights and duties equal to the scientists', and no man but the leader must have command over them. [23]

Maage makes a prophecy

A memory still remains among the tribe of a woman named Maage (Gull), who prophesied that a big boat with tall poles would come into view from the ocean. And sure enough, one summer's day, just as the winter ice broke and steep Cape York lay separated from the sea merely by a narrow strip of ice, the ship arrived and lay to by the edge of the ice. [24] It was a marvel of ingenuity—a whole island of wood which moved along on the sea on wings, and in its depths had many houses and rooms full of noisy people. Little boats hung along the rail, and these, filled with men, were lowered on the water, and as they surrounded the ship it looked as if the monster gave birth to living young.

This visit at first caused great anxiety and fear among the Eskimos, but later much joy. They did not believe that the white men were real human beings, but looked upon them as spirits of the air, who had come down to the Inuits.

The sense of sharing

One has tried to counter-balance even the fickleness of fortune by dividing all the larger animals into pieces which are distributed to everybody who, during the hunt, has not had the luck to be the first to harpoon, say, a narwhal. By this distributive arrangement every hunter is entitled to meat if only he will keep in the vicinity of the one who kills the quarry. This seems to be the result of humane sentiments developed during the fight for existence against niggard Nature.

There is yet another point. Men are not all born equally strong and supple, and it is generally only a select few who are able to avail themselves of the chance to throw the first harpoon into an unwounded animal. But if once the animal has got the huge bladder with its heavy trailer dragging behind it through the water, even the mediocre hunter can take part in the kill. It is for this work that he receives his just and generous part of the booty. For the maintaining of one's position as a breadwinner in this community one thing only is required—this is industriousness. The lazy man who will not take up his share of the work must go his own way.

Inuit religion

The Polar Eskimos do not believe in a God to whom one must pray, but they have as a foundation for their religious ideas a series of epic myths and traditional conventions, which are considered an inheritance from the very oldest time. In these their ancestors laid down all their wealth of experience, so that those who came after might not make the same mistakes and harbour the same erroneous notions as did they themselves. [25]

Rasmussen beside his sled during a hunting expedition in Thule (1910).

14 April 1912, the first so-called Thule Expedition north of Neqi. The cartographic survey carried out by Rasmussen and Freuchen, who traveled alone with the Inuit, would show that Peary Land was not an island and was therefore an integral part of Greenland. At the start there were 34 sleds, with 353 dogs. Decisions were made collectively, as the Inuit informed me: "Knud and the Inuit, we made decisions together."

23) It is the first time in the history of the exploration of North Greenland that the Eskimo companions on an expedition were regarded as partners with equal rights. The Americans Kane, Hayes, Bessels, Peary, and Cook in their different ways considered the Eskimos less as partners than as dog sled drivers, very inferior in rank to themselves.

24) Ross's expedition aboard the Isabella and the Alexander in August 1818 was prefigured by an annunciatory legend.

25) A body of ancestral beliefs and epic tales is the foundation of the Inuit religion, which is expressed in the perception of the sacred in the environment, a great respect for numerous complex and shifting taboos, the will to maintain in its main aspects the social equilibrium, and finally a belief in supernatural beings and the punishment of wrongs. It is remarkable that Inuit legends and tales never concern the white man, though there has been more or less permanent contact with whites since 1818. This portion of their history has been suppressed.

Shamanistic scene inside an igloo. A seated *angakkuq* (shaman) looks at the body of a patient stretched out on the sleeping platform. A relative looks on, while a white man—probably Peter Freuchen—reads his newspaper. Drawing by a young Eskimo woman, collected by Knud Rasmussen in 1910-1920. "All that is best, strongest, most important, and profoundest in the creative realm—whether in science, art, philosophy, or religion—has its source in the thought of death and the terror it inspires," wrote Leo Tolstoy. The seer is instilled with a living energy, thanks to which he has the power shamans call "penetrating vision."

The myths, which are handed down from generation to generation by the oldest to the youngest within the community, are to be looked upon as the saga of the Inuit people. These myths are partly simple narratives, partly a warning against those who will not submit to the demands of tradition, and for the rest they are tales of heroes who in every possible danger acquitted themselves in such a way that they are held up as glorious examples for coming generations.

Osarsaq, a wise and intelligent man, once defined to me their own conception in the following words: "Our tales are narratives of human experience, and therefore they do not always tell of beautiful things. But one cannot both embellish a tale to please the hearer and at the same time keep to the truth. The tongue should be the echo of that which must be told, and it cannot be adapted according to the moods and the tastes of man. The word of the new-born is not to be trusted, but the experiences of the ancients contain truth. Therefore, when we tell our myths, we do not speak for ourselves; it is the wisdom of the fathers which speaks through us."

A religious society

Those who have been engaged in burying the dead must keep quiet within their houses and tents for five days. During this period they must not prepare their own food or divide up the cooked meat. They must not take off their clothes during the night or push back from their heads their fur hoods. When the five days have elapsed they must carefully wash hands and body to rid themselves from the uncleanness which they have contracted from the dead. The Eskimos themselves give the following explanation of the reason for observing this rule:

"We are afraid of the big evil power which strikes down men with disease and other misfortunes. Men must do penitence because in the dead the sap is strong, and their power is without limit. We believe that, if we paid no attention to that over which we ourselves are not masters, huge avalanches of stones would come down and crush us, that enormous snowstorms would spring up to destroy us, and that the ocean would rise in huge waves while we were in our kayaks far out at sea." [26]

But one may also acquire additional strength through one's life and increased powers to resist danger, with good fortune in all matters of chance, by using amulets and magic formulas.

The amulet is a protector against danger, and imparts to its owner certain qualities; under certain conditions it may even change him from man into the animal from which the substance of his amulet is derived. An amulet of a bear which was not slain by human hands renders the owner immune from wounds; a part of a falcon gives certainty in the kill; the raven makes one content with little; the fox imparts cunning. Often the Eskimos wear a Poroq of a stone from a fireplace, because this has been stronger than the fire; or they smear an old man's spittle round a child's mouth, or put some of his lice into a child's head, thus transferring the vital force of the old one to the young.

The magic formulas are "old words, the inheritance of ancient time when the sap of man was strong and the tongues were powerful." They may also consist of apparently meaningless connected words dreamed by old men. They are handed down from generation to generation, and the single individual looks upon them as

26) The dead have been buried under stones only since the fourteenth century, when the Inuit migrated from Alaska to Inglefield Land. Previously they must have thrown their dead into the sea. The taboos concerning food, clothing, sexual relations, and behavior varied according to climate, circumstances (physiological state, wife, mourning), age, and sex. Amulets (serattit) had considerable powers; they were "spoken charms" expressed in a lost language that dated to the time when men could still speak to animals. They were chanted in low tones; each word that was repeated twice carried a tanqeq or intrinsic power; uttered without thought they immediately lost their power." (Knud Rasmussen) Names—of which more than a hundred have been inventoried from 1818 to 1950—are a sort of memory of the spiritual and intellectual forces of this small people, transmitted from generation to generation. But a man or a woman has several names, which act according to the powers associated with them. In point of fact, an Inuit is never alone but is accompanied by all the shadowy figures that surround him, the ancestors whose lives are carried forward through the living being who bears their name.

invaluable treasures which one must not give away until death draws near. They are impossible to translate, and would therefore be difficult to recount in this short summary, which merely purports to give what is absolutely necessary for the understanding of these strange people who will so often be mentioned in the following narrative.

The soul, which is immortal, exists outside the man and follows him as shadow follows sunshine. It is a spirit which looks exactly like a man. When the man is dead it rises to heaven or goes down into the sea, where it foregathers with the souls of the fathers. And both places are good to be in.

The body is the abode of the soul; it is mortal, as all misfortune and illness may strike it down. In death all that is evil remains in the body, wherefore one must observe the greatest care in dealing with the corpse.

The name also is a spirit to which a certain store of vital power and skill is attached. A man who is named after a deceased one inherits his qualities.

The death of Thorild Wulff, 1917

First we call a council, as we are accustomed to do in serious situations like the present. We all agree that our arrival on land means salvation, for on this very land where now we set our feet the inhabitants of Etah are hunting hares and reindeer every autumn. On the other hand, it is clear to us that the remaining 200 kilometres to Etah is a serious distance for men as exhausted as we are.

Dr. Wulff immediately declared that he cannot continue at once. Koch also is of the opinion that he requires a couple of days' rest before he will be able to undertake the long walk. But, on the other hand, various circumstances make it essential that we should reach men as speedily as possible. First of all we do not possess ammunition for a prolonged stay here. Secondly, because of the water, our clothes are so far gone that our lives will be endangered unless we fall in with people before the approach of the first cold of autumn.

So we agree that Ajako and I must go to Etah for relief; we are both of the opinion that we are able to set out for the long walk without a rest. Harrigan and Bosun remain in order to hunt for Wulff and Koch, who no longer have the strength to pursue game.

Ajako and I reckon that in this stony and cleft land, intersected by a number of great rivers, we shall hardly be able to make the journey in less than eight days, considering the bad weather. Then the relief sledges have to be fitted out, and this will take at least twenty-four hours. At this time of year people do not yet have their sledges ready for use, and these preparations require time, so that the relief sledges could hardly be here for twelve or fourteen days.

None of us consider it advisable to remain here for such a long period. The area will be quickly exhausted of game, so the best thing is to move camp toward Etah in short daily journeys. This arrangement is desirable for other reasons as well.

Ajako and I reckon on the probability of being so completely exhausted by the time we find people that neither of us will have strength enough to return with the relief sledges. Others would have great difficulty finding our comrades' camp. We must therefore agree upon a spot where those who are to be saved can be found without delay. There is no such place here; but behind Cape Russell, in the immediate vicinity of the inland-ice, there is a big lake known to Harrigan from previous reindeer hunts, and with which all the inhabitants of Etah are familiar. We decide that our comrades must move by short journeys to this spot. If the place is not reached by the time the relief sledges are expected to arrive, the two Greenlanders can easily be sent ahead to communicate with the relief party.

I advise my comrades not to take too long a rest; when, in our exhausted condition, one fails to keep the body in motion, the weariness with all its pains will be felt doubly when once more one has to continue the journey. The ammunition is distributed so that Dr. Wulff's party gets eighty cartridges of small shot and forty rifle cartridges, which should be sufficient for the period of waiting, while I myself take a Winchester and thirty cartridges. As soon as all the details are arranged the three Eskimos set out hunting while we others remain to arrange the baggage. . . .

Early in the morning of the 25th I go up into the mountains to look out for the hunters, and meet Ajako some distance inland with a first bag of five hares. The next few days again seem lighter to us. May Ajako and I have strength to get quickly into communication with people and get speedy relief for our comrades!

The fog has been lying thickly across the land since we arrived, but about six o'clock in the afternoon it clears up somewhat, and in order to make the most possible out of our opportunity to get a view of the land, which neither Ajako nor I know, we set out on our walk. We bring merely the strictly necessary things—our kamiks, my diaries, and nothing else.

We part from our comrades in the best of spirits after a feast of newly shot hares. The camp on the steep cliff seems like a fairy tale; the glacier rolls toward it like a frozen ocean, and we ourselves jump on the stones like shipwrecked men just flung on land. Dr. Wulff has made himself a com-

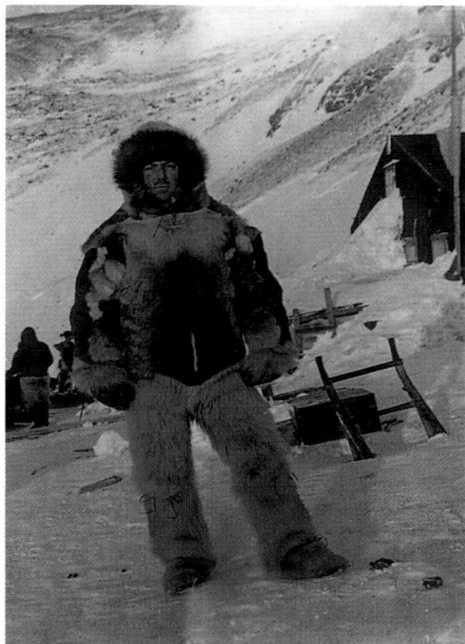

Thorild Wulff, a Swedish botanist, at Etah before the start of the Danish expedition of March 1917. Forty years old, he died of hunger six months later on the return trail. In the background, we catch a glimpse of the building at McMillan's base.

Thorild Wulff

The seven members of the tragic 1917 expedition. From left to right: Lauge Koch, Inukitsupaluk, Borseman, Ajako, Wulff, Hendrik Olsen, and Rasmussen. The photo was taken by an American near McMillan's base at Etah. Like Wulff, Hendrik Olsen would die during this expedition.

fortable little sleeping-place on a moss-clad shelf; smiling, he waves good-bye, calling to us: " Now don't forget to send some pancakes with the relief sledges!"

Harrigan and Bosun have not yet returned from their hunt, and this long absence is not merely a good proof of their stubborn endurance, it also gives us fresh hope that perhaps they have succeeded in shooting a reindeer; and reindeer tallow is the article of which we are most in need.

"Wulff is dead"

September 10th.—Wulff is dead. This evening the relief sledges returned with Koch, Harrigan, and Bosun. It was ordained, then, that after all he should not have the strength to continue, but must give up just as he had reached land and was not far from men. This last death takes me absolutely by surprise. I certainly know that he was exhausted, but so were we all; that death was approaching when Ajako and I departed I did not suspect.

What a tragic death, just as he had toiled through all dangers and seemed safe at last. I cannot understand it—I cannot understand it!

Yet it is true; the man with whom for a long time I have shared good and evil I shall see no more! Like his sledge comrade Hendrik, he has entered the great peace.

The report of Harrigan (Inukitsupaluk)

The following report which Harrigan gave after his arrival at Etah, and which I wrote down immediately from his dictation, is given as a supplement to Koch's report:

"On the day when Wulff gave up and sought a place where he could lie down to die, we were all exhausted and weary. We were very thin and suffered from anaemia. This was plainly visible from our veins, which almost disappeared, and made itself felt by sensations of giddiness; further, we had difficulty in keeping warm, especially our hands and feet.

"If we had been on the inland-ice or open ice, where we should have had a sledge, we would have tried to pull Wulff along, as we did occasionally during the last days on the inland-ice. But on this snow-bare land of cloughs it would be a matter either of carrying him—and none of us had the strength for this—or remaining with him; but as we should have to go a long distance before there was any game, this also proved impossible; it would be to seek death for ourselves without being able to help our dying comrade.

"And Wulff would eat nothing, at any rate no hare meat; of our last bag he tasted merely a mouthful of hare liver, although he might have eaten meat to repletion. We could do nothing for him.

"I believe he was ill, for during the last few nights he moaned often during his sleep.

"We had no alternative but to leave him behind, as he himself demanded. If we found reindeer in a place from which we could return whilst he was yet alive, we might still be able to save him. But this was the only possibility.

"We plucked grass and heather and made as soft and sheltered a bed for him as we could, and here he lay down when it was ready.

"As we arose to continue our journey he nodded a smiling farewell. And this smile from the poor man who had lain down to die was my last impression of Wulff. I believe that he would very quickly sleep into death."

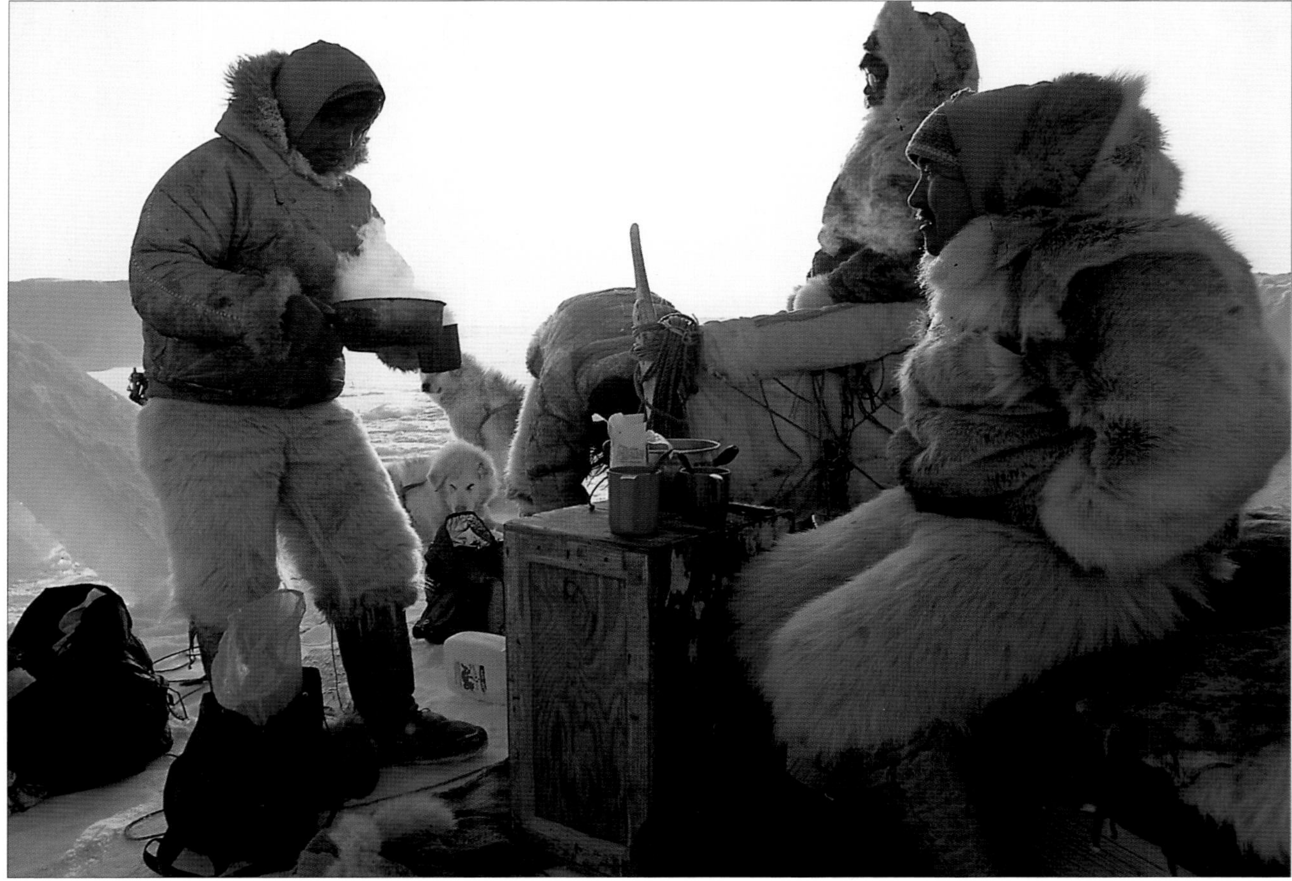

Bivouac on the white trail: "mugging up," the tea ritual, with the primus sheltered from the wind inside a crate (1990).

Piblokto: polar hysteria

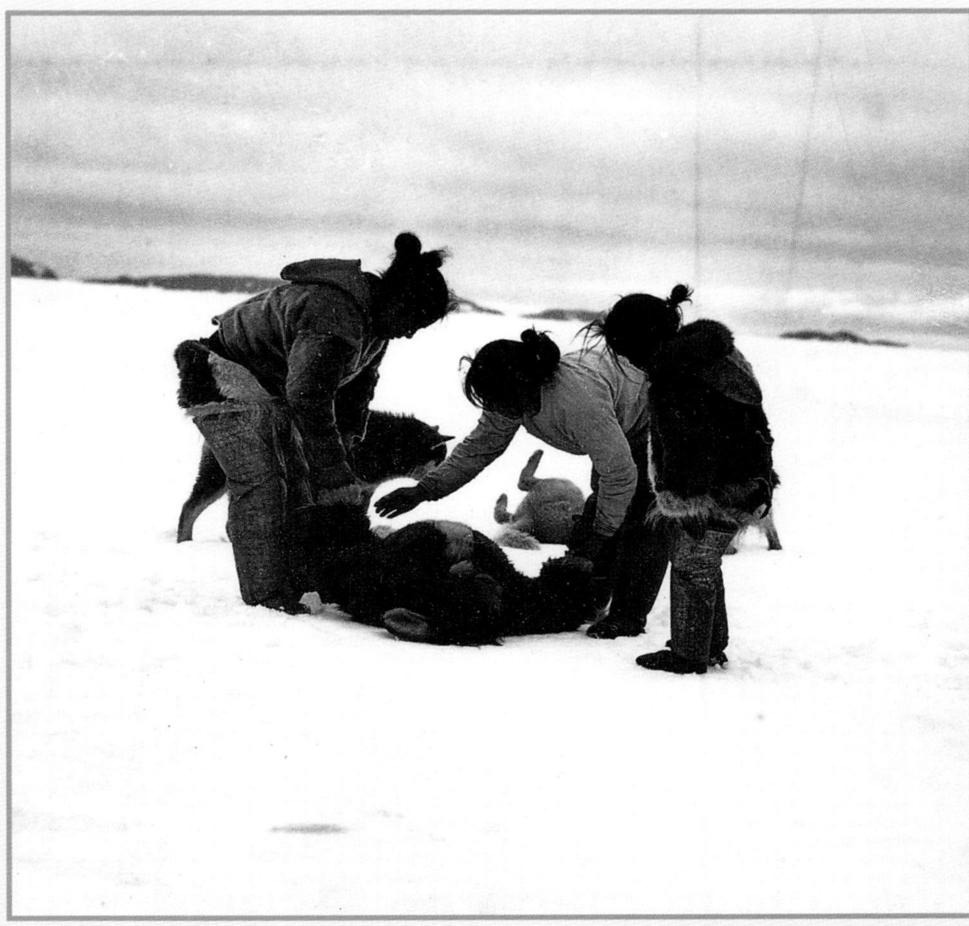

Etah 1914. Scenes from a fit of piblokto. The Eskimo woman Ivalu underwent the classic stages of this fit. Panting and muttering *ayaya* (traditional songs) and invective, she hit everything around her (including any people she came across) using a bone or a rock, smearing herself with dog droppings and even ingesting any she found in her path. Ivalu felt stifled (but not to the point of taking off her clothes, as often happens during fits of piblokto). Soon growing tired, she let herself slide off the little eminence onto which she had hoisted herself above the floe. Little by little she grew calm again, until she drifted off into a deep sleep. Only then did the Inuit intervene, speaking to her to calm her though she was unable to hear them. Finally, someone carried her back to her igloo. On waking up, Ivalu remembered nothing. "Her life was hurting her," as I once heard an Eskimo say. In 1950-1951 I saw truncated fits of piblokto in November, as though the primitive force and savagery had gone out of it. (See *The Last Kings of Thule*.)

The first Lutheran missionaries

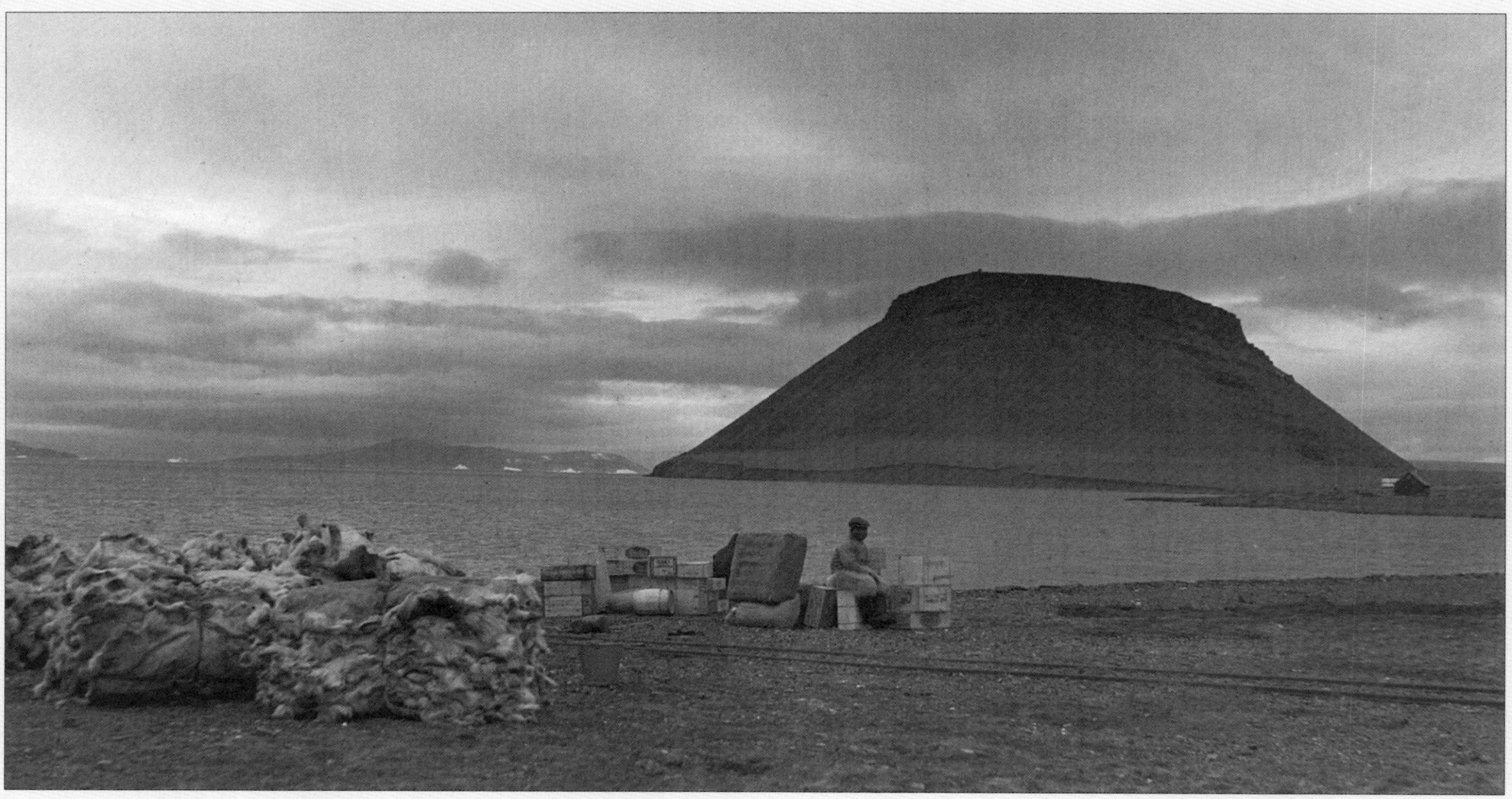

The unloading of wood, provisions, tools, and bundles of caribou skins from northern Scandinavia, July 1910. The caribou of the Thule region were decimated in 1890 and again in 1910, when a winter thaw was followed by a hard frost. The crust of the refrozen snow was so strong that the animals could not break through it with their hooves to graze on the lichens underneath. They died by the thousands, littering the shoreline with their carcasses, from Etah to Savissivik. A slight drop in temperature, a small anomaly in the seasons, can have immediate repercussions for the fauna of this northern region, always on the bare edge of survival. Ever since the migration of the Canadian Inuit in 1860, caribou skins had been used to make the *qulitsaq,* or winter vest. In the background is "Seal Heart" mountain, which protects the entrance of North Star Bay. The age-old Inuit site is to the right (northeast) of this butte, which is topped by a stratum of basalt.

North Star Bay (Wolstenholme Fjord), behind the peninsula, in August 1948, three years before its occupation by the American base. The traditional Inuit site is in front of this butte. The U.S. airbase was built in the valley of the Pitugfik River, whose sinuous outline is visible.

Gustav Olsen, South Greenlandic missionary to the Polar Eskimos (July 1909), who had Christian contempt for money and comfort. Under his guidance the Polar Eskimos helped to establish the new religion quickly on their territory—in particular its spirit of charity and sharing, and its attachment to the redeeming man-god Jesus Christ.
The first Polar Eskimo was baptized in 1912, the last in 1934.

Construction of the Lutheran mission at Uummannaq on North Star Bay, 25 July 1909. Rasmussen and Freuchen would rechristen Uummannaq with the name "Thule" in the following year.

The Christian mission and the first schools

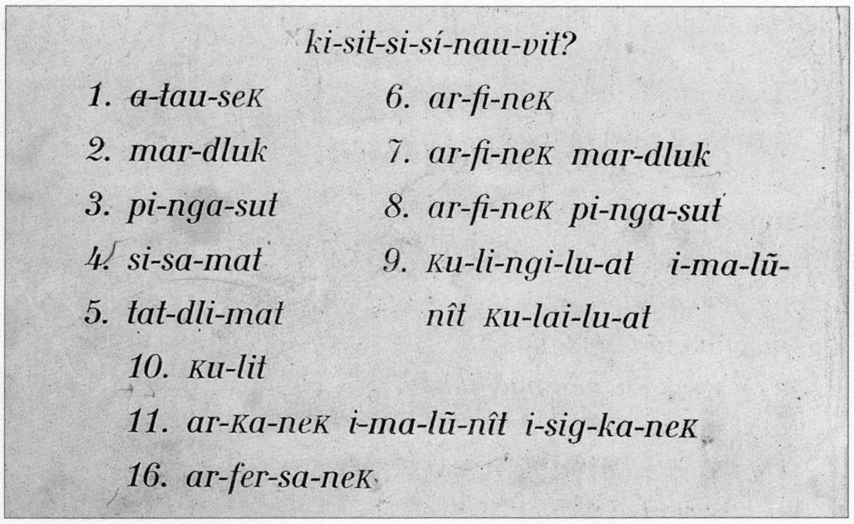

ki-sit-si-sí-nau-vit?

1. a-tau-seK
2. mar-dluk
3. pi-nga-sut
4. si-sa-mat
5. tat-dli-mat
6. ar-fi-neK
7. ar-fi-neK mar-dluk
8. ar-fi-neK pi-nga-sut
9. Ku-li-ngi-lu-at i-ma-lũ-nît Ku-lai-lu-at
10. Ku-lit
11. ar-Ka-neK i-ma-lũ-nît i-sig-ka-neK
16. ar-fer-sa-neK

A page from *ABD*, a reading primer for the Eskimos: "How to count?" The edition is dated 1933, and the language is South Greenlandic rather than the language of North Greenland. This is psychologically destabilizing to the Inughuit children. As of 2000, there was still no reading manual in North Greenlandic.

Baptism of my friends Nassapaluk and Sinarajuk, aged thirty-six and thirty-eight respectively, on the day of their wedding ((1931). The pastor is Jens Olsen (brother of Gustav), wearing his cassock and ruff. In the background, a painting showing Christ calling the (Inughuit) children to him—one, a little girl, is already in his lap.

Igloo

Near right, top:
Owluk-Ahningwaq in front of her rock and sod igloo (whose plan appears below). The *kataq*, or entry tunnel, beside which she stands is about three meters long. The igloo is lit by a single window made of gut (*erqut*) above the entry and consists of one room 4 meters long and 3.5 meters wide. Half of the area is taken up with a sleeping platform raised two feet off the ground. Ventilation is provided by a hole in the center of the roof, the igloo's "nose," or *qingaa*. (1914-1917)

Above,
different kinds of igloos made of stone slabs and sod. Drawing by Iggianguaq-Uutaaq (one of Uutaaq's sons), Qaanaaq, 1982.

Section of a traditional igloo with rock and sod walls. Imarasunguak's igloo. Drawing by Harald Moltke.

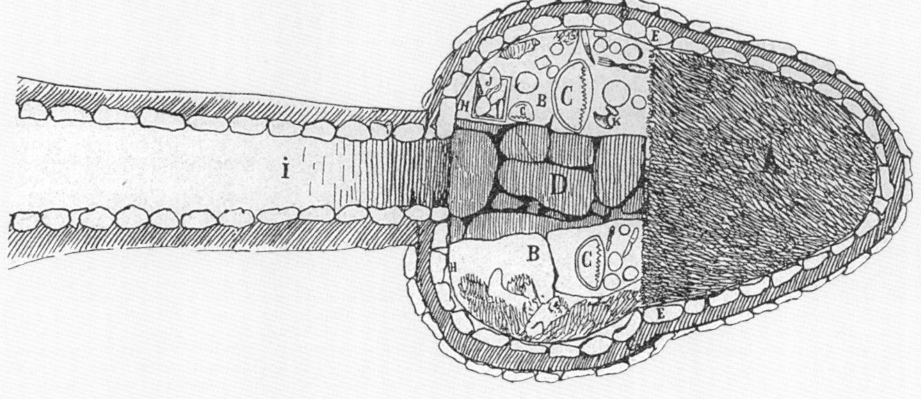

Winter igloo, built toward 1890 and photographed in 1909 in the Thule region. The vault rests on walls of stone and sod. The lateral pressure of the vault is contained by long, flat walrus bones, resting against the top of the wall and buttressed by large stones.

Opposite, **North shore** of Etah Fjord (across from Niaqornaq). An adolescent carrying the weapons for a walrus hunt. In his left hand, the harpoon with its detachable point (*tuukkaq*) and its seal skin lanyard some twenty meters in length. In his right hand, a lance.

Summer nomadism

Summer 1910. Four hunters and three women haul a walrus weighing a ton and a half and measuring 4.5 meters in length, using a hoist (traditional Eskimo technique). Although the objects are of foreign origin (pulley, rope, American hooks, canvas anoraks, caps and berets), the ancestral activities remain unchanged. Walrus are hunted from kayaks during the winter.

Below, **after a day's travel**, a summer camp, sheltered from the wind (circa 1910). The woman seated second from the right, who wears a hood and worn, patched boots, is under taboo.

Qaaqqutsiak, son of Eré and grandson of the sorcerer Uummannaq, in July 1909. He would be my proud and loyal companion during my geomorphological expedition to Inglefield, Washington, and Elllesmere lands (March-June 1951).

Upernak, the force of spring

Traditional rabbit trap, Etah, 1914. To make the leather loops more visible, the photographer, an American from the McMillan expedition, has placed a white sheet behind them. The expedition tried to find Crocker Land, an unknown land mass in the Arctic sea described by Peary. It does not exist.

Musk ox hunt on Ellesmere Island, April-May 1907-1908. The animal (*umingmak*) is being dragged back to camp on shore. In this anarcho-communist society, hunting is always communal.

A summer camp. Before a tent, an Eskimo woman and a Dane with his hands in his pockets look at five dogs attached by their leads to a piece of wood. Near them is a sled where Tukuminguark's son is playing. He holds a whip with a long lash that hangs backward. Drawing by Tukuminguark. Peary Collection.

"Our" Knud

Knud Rasmussen and his wife Dagmar took Eskimo orphans to live with them. According to Inuit tradition, these children were harshly treated.

Below, **Meqorsuaq,** one of the Eskimo immigrants from Baffin Island who arrived in northwest Greenland between 1860 and 1863. Born on the floe during one of his people's migrations, he was one-eyed and an *angakkuq* (shaman). His people reintroduced the kayak, the snow igloo, the bow drill, and the salmon spear to the Inughuit—technologies that brought unpredictable social upheaval. Himself a traditionalist, he mistrusted technological innovation. The legends and songs of the Inughuit were also greatly influenced by the immigrants from Igloolik.

Three Eskimos visiting Peter Freuchen, manager of the Thule trading post (1914-1917). From right to left: an unidentified native hunter; Asiajuk, wearing a *natseq* (seal skin jacket) with the traditional bear skin collar, breast piece, and cuffs; and on the left, Pualuna, born in 1873, a companion of Peary and Cook (and the central individual in the geneaology of the Polar Eskimos that I would draw up in 1950-1951 with his particular help).

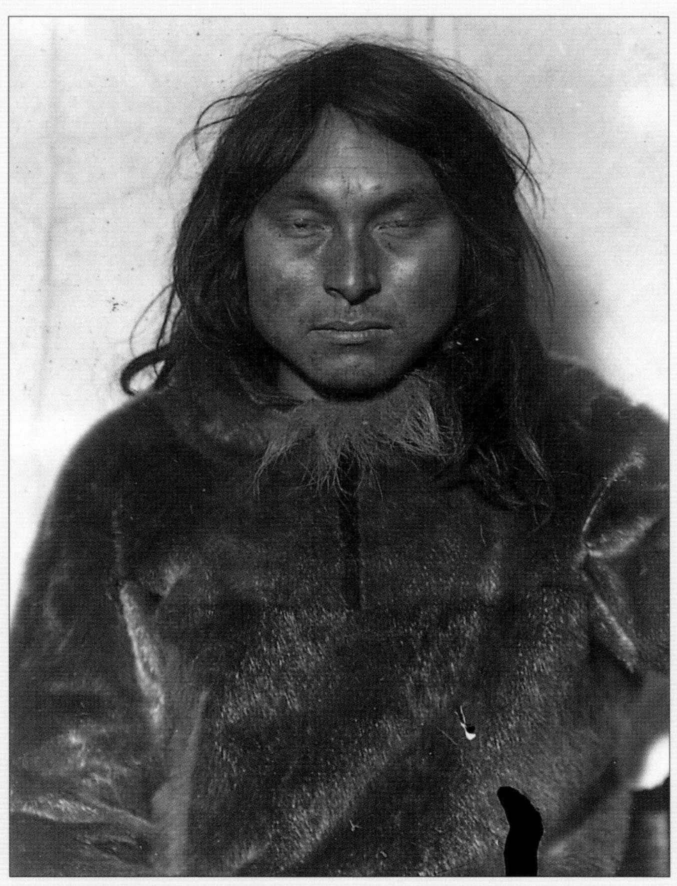

Left, **Uutaaq,** born in 1879, Peary's companion at the Pole in 1909. Known to be "difficult," he accepted Christian baptism only in 1925. He was the brother of Pualuna (my principal informer in 1950) and the father of Kutsikitsoq, my closest companion. One of the strongest characters in the group. I often met him in Uummannaq-Thule: he naturally spoke to me with passion about Piulissuaq, "The Great Peary." Photo taken in 1914-1917.

Top right, **Nasaitsordluarsuk,** 17 years old in 1901, nicknamed "Boadsman" or "Bosun" by the whites, who were unable to pronounce his Eskimo name. In February 1951, in Savissivik, he discreetly gave me his version of the tragic expedition of 1917. In the main, it corroborated the official version.

Right, **Miteq,** 20 years old, son of Masaitsoq and brother of Ittukusuk (1909).

Below, **men dressed as women** during a party given at Etah by the McMillan expedition (Etah, 1916).

KNUD RASMUSSEN, WRITER

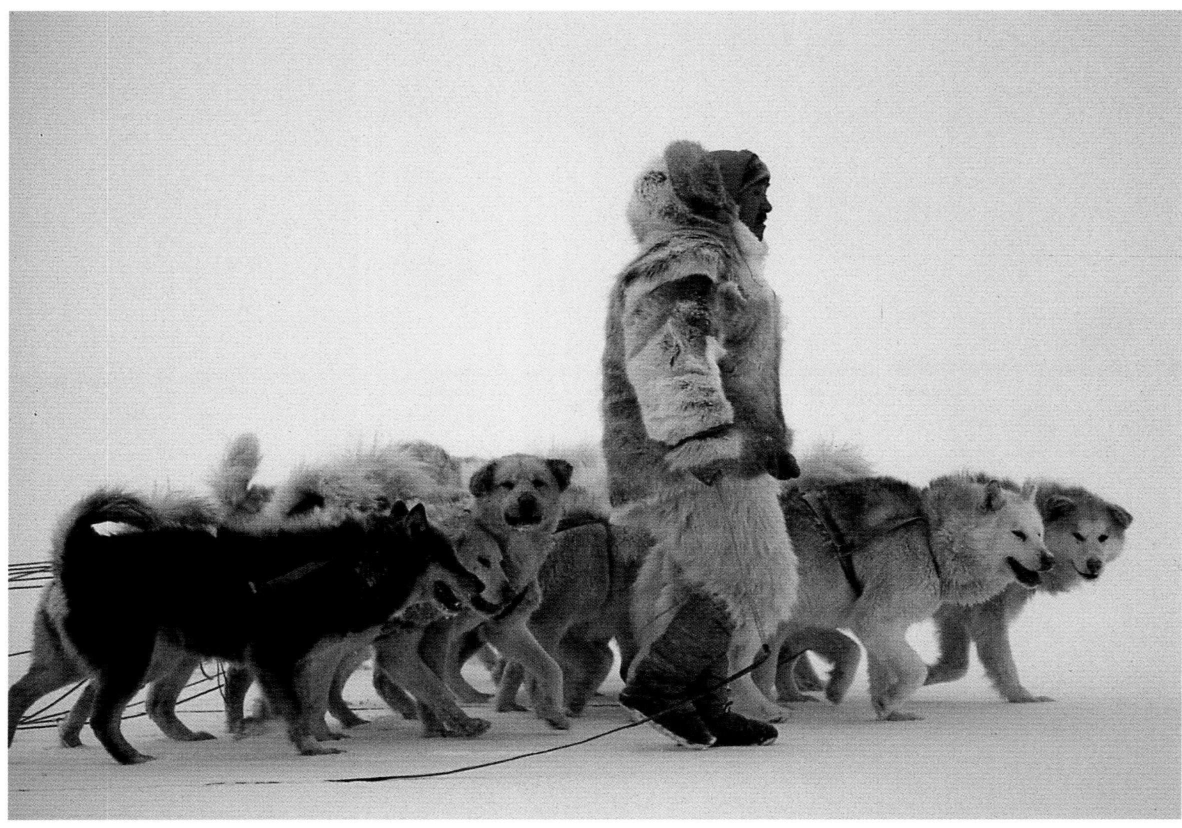

THE BEAR HUNT, *NANUQ!*

I have been asked to tell about the most exciting moment in my life and I shall try to do so, while admitting that there are plenty of elementary dangers to choose among.

I have fought starvation and been within an ace of perishing.

I have raced against drifting ice and reached land at the moment when everything behind me became a black, raging sea.

I have lost my way in a snowstorm that so overwhelmed me with cold and exhaustion that I was very near to losing my will to live.

And on a dark winter's night, half-naked and unarmed, I have fought a bitter and dramatic fight with an Eskimo who would have struck me down with a knife.

But are not all these adventures common in the lives of travelers?

No: if I am to tell about the strangest of all my adventures I have not the slightest hesitation in choosing a small episode from a hunt, when rapid and unforeseen events took such a course that I was to struggle for my life together with a polar bear.

Winter 1923. Rasmussen in the Danish base on a speck of land north of Southampton Island (Hudson Bay), during the Fifth Thule Expedition. Note the portrait of his wife Dagmar above his desk.

It took place in Melville Bay on a journey with the polar Eskimo Qolutanguaq, a celebrated great hunter from Cape York.

It was in the polar night; a week's gale had kept us inactive in a snow hut, and when at length the wind dropped we had used up our food supplies. We were a long way from people, the only game there could be any question of hunting at that time of year was bear, and we each had a team of dogs to procure food for us as rapidly as possible.

We started at dawn after having eaten our last meal. Our sledges were empty, and the same would soon be true of our stomachs. No wonder that we set off with every wish for a good hunt.

The storm had given the dogs a good rest and they took to the ice at a bound. With their tails raised like flying banners they dashed off with an energy which showed that their instinct told them this was no ordinary day of toil and labour but a hunt for food. They sniffed the air; their ears quivered as they strained them; and each time a breeze filled their nostrils with the smell of flesh from a seal's blow-hole they quickened their pace still further.

We were already a long way from our camping place without having seen a single fresh track. The daylight was giving way to dusk, and we were beginning to fear that the night would find us empty-handed. But close to a bank of pack ice the dogs suddenly gave such a tug at the traces that we toppled over backwards on the sledges. A strong, warm scent had crossed our path, and from now on the pace was so furious that the sledge often shot forward with one runner suspended in mid-air, just like a ship with one rail pressed down into the sea during a storm.

Both our teams consisted of trained bear dogs. They kept close alongside each other; it was a race, and we knew that only a bear could excite them like this. It was not long before we drove into fresh tracks: large, deep impressions in the soft snow. But the bear had already heard us; the tracks showed in long bounds the flight that had taken it in the direction of some icebergs which lay a couple of miles to the east of us, not far from the ice-cap.

When possible, hunted bears always seek safety at the top of a steep iceberg where the dogs cannot follow them. Even though the iceberg has vertical, slippery surfaces, bears can get a hold with their sharp claws. I have only once seen a bear lose its footing, near the top; in falling it broke a hind thigh, and yet was able to smash a hole in the ice and seek refuge under the iceberg.

It was essential that we should catch up with the bear as quickly as possible, while it was still on the level field ice.

At the moment of reaching the tracks the dogs paused and, trembling in every limb, sucked in the smell of the prey, as if to determine which side to run. Their red tongues protruded from their foaming jaws, and their nostrils were wide open to the wind. Now Qolutanguaq's dogs lost their heads from sheer excitement; they got flurried, and before he could prevent it they were following the track in the wrong direction.

Hungry dogs become wild beasts at the moment they smell bear. The old wolf instinct wakens in them; they throw off all discipline and no longer hear their drivers' shouts. So here: all twelve dogs flung themselves into the nearest ice packs, and soon they lay in one large heaving mass, kicking out in confusion, the traces hopelessly entangled in the clumps of ice.

I was malicious enough to laugh at this accident; for I was now sure of so much lead that this bear hunt could be all mine. And that was just what I wanted. All hunters are children at the sight of big game, and every bear hunt is a challenge between drivers. The aim is to be the first on the trail and the first to shoot. And now this was to be my bear. I whistled my bear's signal through my teeth, and the sledge was slung right into the air as twelve hungry and desperate dogs gave chase to their old mortal foe.

A fleeing bear tries to put as many obstacles as possible in the way of its pursuers. It makes for the edge of the ice, where it flings itself into the water with the agility of a marine animal returning to its element. But if this is too far it may be content with impassable pack ice, where sledge and dogs will stick fast. Fortunately, however, the dogs are faster and more agile and, what is even more important, have more stamina. And so as a rule it is overtaken.

The first thing I had to do now was to loose four of my best dogs. That was not easy at the whirling speed I was now making over the rough ice. I had my work cut out to ensure that I was not flung off the sledge. While having nothing to hold on to, I grasped the front leash which gathered the traces of all the dogs in a large knot of tangled reins and began to haul in the team, which was now running at a speed of some twenty miles an hour. I had my knife crosswise in my mouth, and as soon as I could reach the dog I wanted to release, I let go the traces with my right hand, snatched the knife from my mouth, and cut the trace. The released dog at once flew ahead, a bunch of liberated muscles visible for only a few short minutes before disappearing, whirled away by its own passion.

I imagine that the most thrilling situation in the life of any bear hunter is when he balances right out on the ends of the sledge crossbars, holding all his wild leaders in his left hand while with his right he swiftly cuts the traces. If you are thrown off you cannot help but fall in front of the sharp runners, and no shouting in the world can stop dogs that have smelt bear.

One, two, three, four quick slashes, and the knife was back in my mouth again as with both hands I once more let out the traces to their full length. The best dogs were now the advance pursuers, and even though they would not be able to stop an old bear entirely they would delay it enough for the rest of us to overtake it soon.

Bear dogs have their own tactics; they bury their teeth in Bruin's hind quarters. This may not hurt very much, but the bear finds the joke undignified, and sitting down on the part attacked whisks the impudent insulters off with his broad forepaws. Meanwhile the hunter gets nearer.

The great moment in all this breakneck hunt came when I had the bear in sight: a great yellow body dancing round in the white snow, the dogs swarming about it as if they had wings, and so aggressively that the bear could only make its way very slowly, with frequent stops, to the icebergs that we had now reached. For the last time I hauled in the front rein, and a single slash of my knife at the bunched traces let all the dogs loose. They were off in a pack, the sledge still speeding over the ice. I grasped my rifle and followed after.

It was necessary to fire at very close quarters so as not to hit one of the dogs. They had now quite surrounded the bear, and a bullet can sometimes go right through the bear and hit a dog into the bargain. The shot must be fatal; for as soon as the hunter appears, the bear knows that he and not the dogs is its true foe. Unless it is killed with one shot, it will fling the dogs aside and attack.

It was a young male, a regal wanderer of the wastes, resplendent in a long-haired, yellowish coat that sparkled in its freshgrown glory—a combat-trained, full-size giant come from the open sea of Baffin Bay, still with white, jingling icicles on the fine, waving belly hair. It was now on its way inland to hunt the fat fjord seals that inhabited the crevices opposite the great glaciers.

It was a handsome prey.

I was barely six yards from it when it observed me. Warm, steaming bodies flew around among one another, and I heard the rapid, puffing sound of working lungs. Vicious yelps accompanied each attack and were answered with a deep, rolling snarl. Twelve dogs were settling accounts with a mortal enemy. The scene was wild and magnificent.

At the moment of observing me the bear shook off the dogs and rose on its hind legs, even greater and handsomer than before as it stood there at its full height and stared at me. It remained standing for a few seconds until it had gathered all its

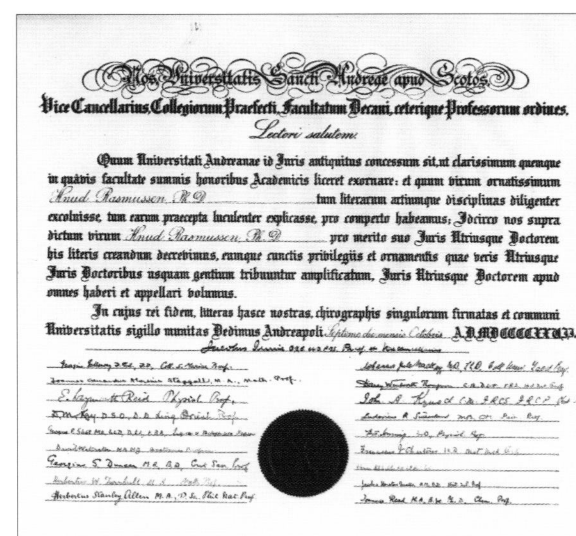

Nos Universitatis Sancti Andreae apud Scotos,
Vice Cancellarius, Collegiorum Praefecti, Facultatum Decani, ceterique Professorum ordines.
Lectori salutem:

Quum Universitati Andreanae id Juris antiquitus concessum sit, ut clarissimum quemque in quâvis facultate summis honoribus Academicis liceret exornare: et quum virum ornatissimum *Knud Rasmussen, Ph.D.* tum literarum artiumque disciplinas diligenter excoluisse, tum earum praecepta luculenter explicasse, pro comperto habeamus; Idcirco nos supra dictum virum *Knud Rasmussen, Ph.D.* pro merito suo Juris Utriusque Doctorem his literis creandum decrevimus, eumque cunctis privilegiis et ornamentis quae veris Utriusque Juris Doctoribus usquam gentium tribuuntur amplificatum, Juris Utriusque Doctorem apud omnes haberi et appellari volumus.

In cujus rei fidem, litteras hasce nostras, chirographis singulorum firmatas et communi Universitatis sigillo munitas Dedimus Andreapoli *Septimo die mensis Octobris* A.D. MDCCCCXXVII.

Honorary doctorate awarded to Rasmussen on 7 October 1927 by Saint Andrew's University in Scotland.

Portrait of Knud Rasmussen by Albert Engström, 1926.

breath, then it made a gigantic leap high above the dogs and dropped down on to the ice with all the weight of its body and all the strength of its tensed forepaws.

It performed all the favourite maneuvers of bears when they are on new ice. It wanted to break a hole, where it would be rid of me and rid of the dogs; for it knew that we had to keep to the firm foothold of the ice, while it had all the advantages of the water.

I fully realized what the bear was after; from former hunts I was so accustomed to the trick that I only enjoyed the beauty of this display of strength without heeding what would happen later. I knew that it would dive under the water like a seal and go well in below the ice to cool off; but it would not be long before it came back to breathe, and then would be the time for me to fire.

This time, however, everything was to take an entirely different course. The ice was thinner than I had thought, and a very strong current flowed here between the icebergs. The instant the bear smashed the ice beneath it, cracks spread in all directions, and before I could jump aside I was up to my neck in water.

In my first excitement I completely forgot the bear. My only thought was to get out again. With my rifle in my left hand, raised high above my head, I worked my way to the edge of the ice and tried to climb up. But the new ice was now wet and slippery and there was nothing I could hold on to; each time I thrust my chest up above the edge the ice broke under me.

I was wearing the usual winter dress of polar Eskimos: long boots and trousers of bearskin and a fur coat of reindeer skin; no sooner had the heavy, long-haired skins become soaked than I had difficulty holding my head above water. At the same time the strong current pressed me more and more under the ice.

To free both arms, so that I could manage to swim, I tried to throw my rifle across the ice; but my fingers were already so numb that the gun slipped from my hands and went to the bottom. For the first time my thoughts now turned to the bear, which was swimming about in the same confined pool as I was.

I was quite helpless, and all that I could do was to keep as far away from it as possible. To my relief I soon discovered that it was as afraid of me as I was of it. We were both caught in the same hole; the only difference between us was that the dogs had gathered in a knot around it but left me in peace.

Now that I had both hands free I again tried to clamber out, but with the only result that I broke off more and more ice and exhausted myself. At every movement I made I kept a close eye on the bear; I honestly admit that I was in mortal fear, expecting every minute that it would fly at me. It did not look pleasant, either; for each time I moved it ground its teeth and snarled, just as if it expected that I too would attack it.

My excitement did not last long, however; the cold water soon cooled my blood and a singular calm came over me. And without really being able to explain to myself why, I began attentively to study my strange companion. In spite of the dangerous position I was in I conceived a lively interest in it, and my brain worked quickly and soberly.

I, who had been accustomed only to kill, had never before known that a bear's eyes could be so expressive. At first I saw only fear and anger in them, but as it gradually accustomed itself to me in the same way as I had accustomed myself to it it stopped showing its teeth. I now regarded it even more attentively than before. And it struck me that I no longer looked upon it as a piece of big game to be killed, but as a thinking and intelligent creature that was in the same distress as I was. It was almost as if I could see its thoughts take shape. With its eyes alternately on the dogs and on me, it seemed to be wondering why I too had jumped into the water. It knew now that I meant it no harm. But what then? Possibly I too had taken to the ice hole in order to avoid the dogs? The bear could heave its body out of the water at a bound and throw itself well across the ice, if only it dared to do so for all the baying beasts that wanted to tear at its skin with their sharp teeth. And if I did not do so, was it not because we were both fighting the same fight against the same foes, the dogs?

Having got so far in my mind-reading, I almost had the feeling that the bear understood me and felt with me. But I went even further in my inferences. I saw that the bear noticed that while the dogs incessantly pestered it and snapped at its snout as often as they could get near enough, they kept away from me, exactly as

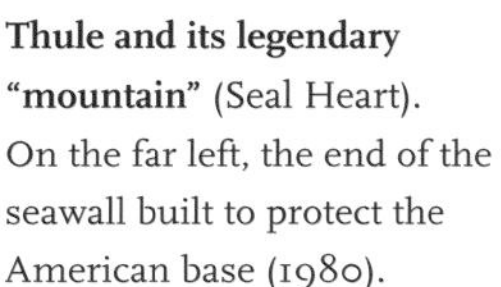

Thule and its legendary "mountain" (Seal Heart). On the far left, the end of the seawall built to protect the American base (1980).

if they were afraid of me. Could it be that I, more than it, was master of the situation; that I was stronger, more dangerous?

It now turned its head quite calmly toward me, and I could not help noticing that its expression was friendly. And to my great amazement it began quite slowly to work its way toward me in order to seek protection.

It was only a couple of yards from me; but though to some extent I felt safe from it, I suddenly became anxious again. The constant attacks of the dogs might so far unbalance it that it might vent a fit of rage on me. Acting on a sudden impulse, therefore, I shouted at the top of my lungs to the dogs, ordering them back. The hunt had now lasted so long they could once more sense that I had power over them; and though it took some time, they obeyed. Snarling with disappointment they drew further back on the ice and stood still at some distance.

For the first time since the hunt had begun, the bear was left to itself; and now something happened which I shall never forget. It understood that I had frightened its attackers away, and it turned its head toward me; this time I could not be mistaken: there was a look of gratitude in its eyes. It was the same expression I had so often seen in my dogs when I patted them or did something else that made them pleased.

It is not easy to describe the facial expression of a beast of prey, but nobody who is used to the company of animals will doubt that even wild creatures can show gratitude. This bear, which could have killed me, not only spared my life but approached me in the cold ice hole as a friend who helped it. It is no uncommon thing that men who fight a desperate struggle for their lives are filled in their impotence with good intentions and make promises they say they will keep if they are saved from death. That was what happened to me. I promised that if I escaped from this adventure with my life I would do all that was in my power to save the bear's life. My teeth chattering with cold, I promised myself that neither I nor anyone else should kill that bear; if it was left to me, it should be allowed to return to the great hunting grounds it had come from.

I had scarcely been in the water more than ten minutes; but it was ten degrees below zero and every minute seemed an eternity. I could not keep up very much longer, and if help did not come soon my arms would weaken and I would slip down under the ice.

I had almost given up hope when Qolutanguaq suddenly appeared from the pack ice a few hundred yards away. No sooner had he seen me almost shoulder to shoulder with the big bear, with the dogs at a distance, seemingly uninterested in the game, than he got so furious he emitted a loud roar, jumped off his sledge, and doubled his speed. I knew that I was saved. In a minute or two I should be out of the hole. Now was the time to think of my promise, and gathering all my strength I shouted to Qolutanguaq: "Don't shoot the bear—don't shoot the bear!"

My teeth were chattering to such an extent that the shout became an inarticulate yell. I had to repeat my words several times before he understood them. At first he was dumbfounded. He thought I had gone mad; but at length he seemed to guess my meaning and shouted back:

"No, of course—I'm going to help you first."

So saying, he let loose all his dogs, and while they rushed to the edge of the ice in order to fall on the bear, he seized a long harpoon line he had on the sledge, extended it with a whip, and threw it out to me; the line reached me and I grasped it. I turned away from the edge of the ice and hung on to it with the back of my neck, and thus having both hands free I tied the line round my waist. It was then only a matter of a moment before Qolutanguaq had hauled me up.

The last I saw of the bear was a bound which it made across the ice in order to keep the new enemy at a distance. But the dogs stopped it and it slipped back into the hole.

Scarcely was I out of the water before the cold hit me with such violence that I lost consciousness. I tried to speak, but the words died away on my lips in a whisper: "Don't shoot—don't shoot—" And then all around me was black.

When I came to again, my wet clothes lay frozen stiff on the ice beside me; I myself lay naked, but warm and full of life in my sleepingbag. The Eskimo stood smiling in front of me with a steaming cup of tea which he held to my lips.

My first thought was for the bear.

"But the bear—where's the bear?"

The Eskimo laughed heartily, tickled at the thought that the slayer of a bear is not always the man who is first on its track and the first to catch up with it.

"Never mind the bear," he teased, "I've already skinned it."

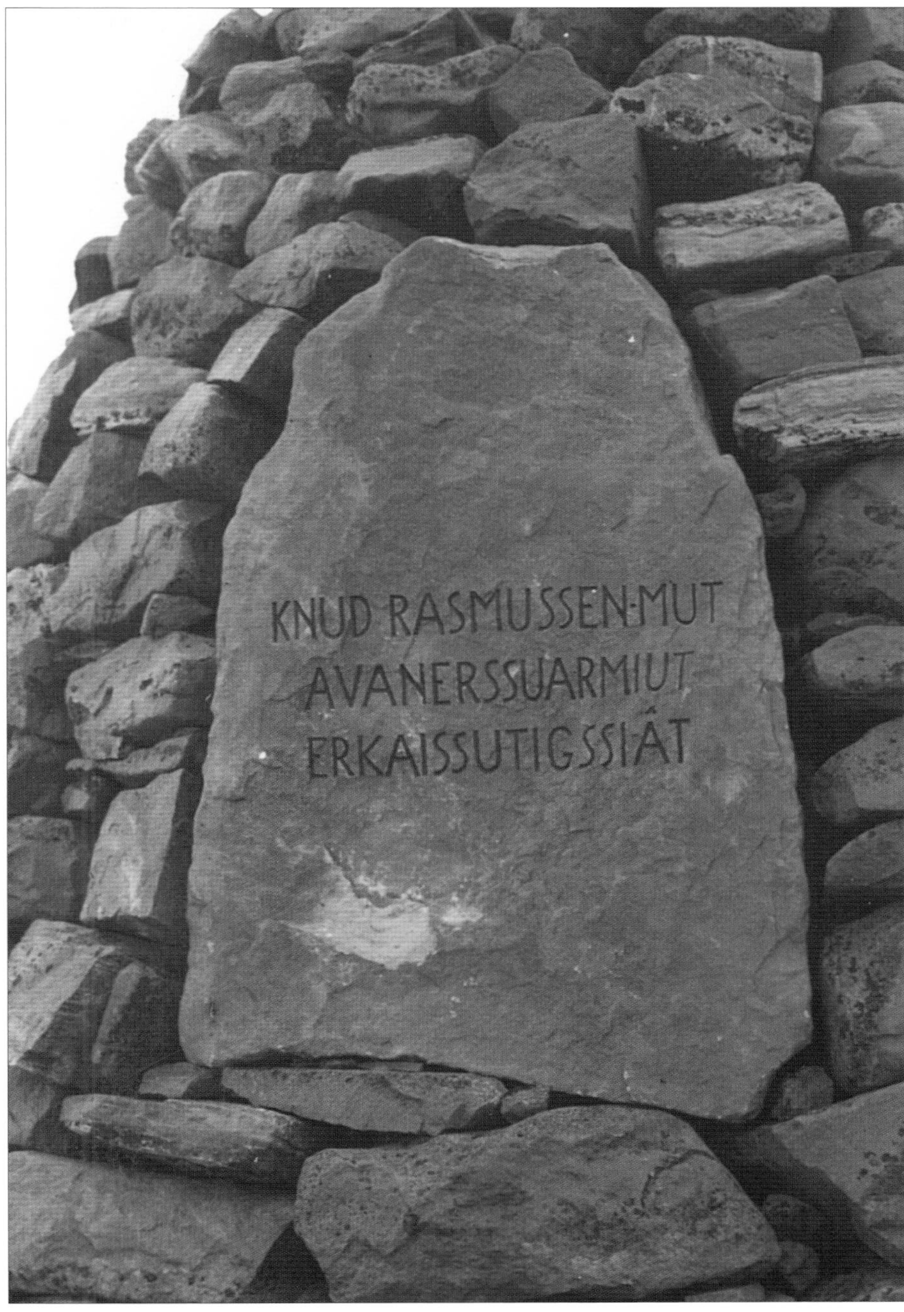

Stone erected at Thule by the Inughuit to honor Rasmussen for the work he did with and for them: "To Knud Rasmussen, the Men of the North, so that it will be remembered."

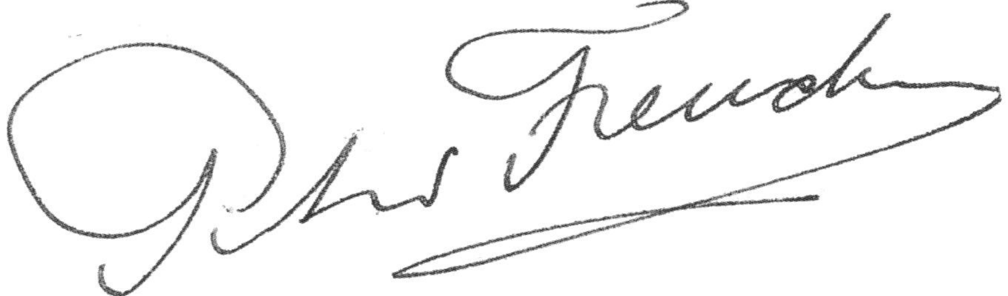

PETER FREUCHEN 1896-1957

THE FIRST TO HONOR THE INUIT PEOPLE BY MARRYING AN INUIT WOMAN

Tall, with the beard and stature of a Viking, Peter Freuchen merited the name of "Big Peter" given to him by the Polar Eskimos. A cofounder with Knud Rasmussen of the Thule trading post, he belongs among the more neglected characters in Arctic history.

In the circle of the Danish intelligentsia in Copenhagen, it was long fashionable to consider Freuchen as no more than a journalist and a writer. His many accounts are set apart by the fact that they relate actual experiences in strong and vivid language, though his writing has been declared facile and of little ethnographic interest. But his time in purgatory is now at an end, and Freuchen's reputation is being re-evaluated. He is now cited with a certain respect. [1] His fair-mindedness, his natural modesty, and his humor long obscured the originality of this privileged witness. Freuchen is now being republished and "read."

A geographer and explorer

Peter Freuchen was born into a modest Danish family in Nykoebing; his father was a grocer. In 1906, the young medical student decided to join the great Danish expedition to the northeast coast of Greenland as an assistant in geology and meteorology to the great German geophysicist Alfred Wegener. [2]

During this difficult expedition, on which Mylius-Erichsen (leader of the Danish Literary Expedition) died of hunger with his Eskimo companion, Peter Freuchen gave proof of the courage, endurance, and generosity that would be his trademark all through life.

Back in Copenhagen in 1908, Freuchen met Knud Rasmussen, then twenty-nine years old. The young Danish Greenlander was still under the spell of his first winter among the Polar Eskimos in 1903-1904, which decided his life's course.

With the enthusiasm and gift for friendship that characterized him, Rasmussen told Peter Freuchen of his intention to return to northwest Greenland and proposed that they join forces. He had decided to administer the region for Denmark and to found a private trading post there to

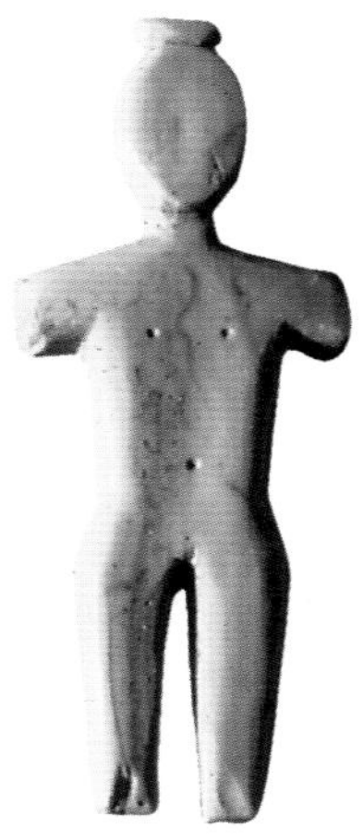

Thule culture woman (start of the Christian era, height 5 cm). Ellesmere Land, Skraeling Island. Schledermann expedition.

OPPOSITE, **Peter Freuchen** (on right) next to his friend and companion Knud Rasmussen (spring 1912). They were about to embark on the First Thule Expedition, a daring crossing of the ice-cap to Peary Land.

1) The Friends of Peter Freuchen Society was founded in Copenhagen. The president, an eminent Central Asian ethnologist, opens each meeting with the reading of a passage from Freuchen's work.

2) Wegener, the father of the theory of plate tectonics, would die on the Greenland ice-cap in November 1931, with his Greenlandic companion Rasmus, while returning to the central station (Eismitte).

Cerastium cerastoida, caryophyllacia family. Gravelly tundra, sun exposure.

free the Polar Eskimos from the dominating influence of Robert Peary and the state of dependence in which he kept them. Rasmussen believed they needed to be helped and protected. "I immediately told Knud that I would accompany him, and I have never regretted my decision," wrote Freuchen in his memoirs.

The decision would not only change his life but have major consequences for the future of the two hundred Polar Eskimos. The Thule trading post, created in 1909, gradually converted this primitive society to a market economy. If Rasmussen was the "creator" of Thule and the architect of this people's profound religious, moral, and intellectual revolution, Freuchen's influence during this critical juncture would be felt in his management of the post for the ten years from 1909 to 1919. After all, it is in everyday relations that bonds are established..

Co-founder of Thule and manager of the trading post

Freuchen shared Rasmussen's ideas on the role of the administrator in a northern territory. The trading post, conceived in the spirit of scientific research, was highly unusual in character—unique in colonial history, I believe, or at least in Arctic history. The profits were applied—apart from a salary paid to Rasmussen and Freuchen—to scientific expeditions and to research in which whites and Eskimos took part on equal terms. The point was not simply to illustrate the history of the Inuit people from Greenland to Siberia but also—and this was a profound innovation—to make this people a partner and sponsor in the study of its past. Thus would the Inuit be better prepared to meet their future.

Faithful friend and companion

Peter Freuchen's role, which was crucial to the scientific program, is still not given its proper value.

The First Thule Expedition in 1911 had only two members: Rasmussen, who was not a geographer and knew nothing of celestial navigation; and Freuchen, a navigator and cartographer. Though he had not finished his university studies, Freuchen learned a great deal during his apprenticeship to Wegener on the Mylius-Erichsen expedition. It was that expedition which carried out the first survey of Peary Land and corrected the serious mistakes made by the "Discoverer of the North Pole," Peary.

Freuchen's crowning achievement was his part in the Fifth Thule Expedition, a three-year voyage that brought Polar Eskimos from Canada (Danish Island, north of Southampton Island) to Siberia (Chukotka Peninsula) in 1922-1925. The expedition's geographer in Hudson Bay was Freuchen, and his work—though not of the first order—is of great value. He also paid heavily for his part in the work of scientific discovery, as his right leg froze in the Canadian Central Arctic and had to be amputated in the field.

His sincere friendship for Knud Rasmussen never wavered, especially during the conflict between Thule's founder and Lauge Koch after the tragic death of the Swedish botanist Thorild Wulff on the Second Thule Expedition (September 1917).

Ethnography as lived experience

Perhaps not wanting to enter into competition with Rasmussen, Freuchen never wrote an ethnographic work. In his numerous articles and his books, which are a mine of information on his life and the Eskimos' at the time of the expeditions, as well as on his relations with Rasmussen and the Polar Eskimos, Freuchen always put the emphasis on drawing an accurate picture, and on his talent as a writer. The observations that pepper his notes and novels, expressed without academic cant, are extremely perceptive. He was undoubtedly, along with

Expedition's return to Thule (after 1910).

Rasmussen, the explorer who knew the Polar Eskimos best. It is unfortunate that his *Journal* and *Unpublished Notes* have not been published. The ethnographer's role as a collector—some say voyeur—apparently did not suit his temperament. Extremely shrewd, and gifted with a subtle humor, Freuchen was in any case the first to analyze the observer-observed relation—this strange strategy of breaking in on another, a seduction in which both parties see double, each with an internal understanding of the other's reality and his imaginary world.

Freuchen was the first white man in the history of the Polar Eskimos who chose to live in Thule (in all, longer than Rasmussen) and who married and started a family there. His wife was Navarana, a Polar Eskimo woman to whom he gave his name and with whom he had two children. These circumstances clearly made for a special relationship between Freuchen and the Inughuit. One is rarely the ethnographer of one's own family!

The anti-authoritarian

Freuchen was harshly critical toward the civil servants in the Danish administration—who, for their part, feared him. He found them "bureaucratic and colonialist" in outlook. He felt a similar dislike for the missionaries, who converted the Eskimos in the name of their faith, despised the Eskimos' ancestral religion, and discouraged their "prattling on" about their beliefs, considering them morally unacceptable. Freuchen always expressed his opinion in strong terms whenever he thought it necessary. Thus from a young age he denounced Cook, both in the Danish newspapers and in his own books, saying that Cook was incapable of taking a celestial observation. Although he had reservations about Peary's brutal character (Peary and he never met, but he heard a great deal about him from the Inuit), he never publicly contested Peary's claims to have discovered the Pole.

The death of his wife Navarana marked him indelibly. She died in Upernavik in 1920 during the Spanish flu epidemic, and Freuchen then left Thule for the United States. His two children chose to return to his native country, Denmark, where his daughter Pipaluk still lives. His successor at the post was Hans Nielsen, Hansipaluk, whom I knew well in Godhavn during my stay there in 1949 and with whom I held useful discussions on organizing my geomorphological research in Skansen, south of Disko. [3]

After Rasmussen's death, when the Danish authorities definitively took over the Thule trading post in 1937, they awarded financial compensation to Peter Freuchen just as they did to Rasmussen's heirs.

At the end of his life, Freuchen became recognized by the international community of Arctic scientists as one of the Arctic's most original explorers. I always regretted that I did not meet the man. On my return to Thule in September 1951, I was traveling on a small Danish ship. We were trying to make a landing in Julianehab, a port on the south coast where Eric the Red landed in 966, founding the colony of Esterbygd which lasted for five hundred years. Peter Freuchen, half-visible in the evening mists, was on the quay. He and the seamen on our ship tried to hold a shouted conversation, but the distance was too great. I kept only the memory of his tall, slightly stiff silhouette, seen through my binoculars, and a sailor's cap perched over the generous face of a Viking.

When, as a budding scientist, I published the first Danish edition of *Last Kings of Thule*, Freuchen wrote a wonderfully generous preface for it, and his review of the book in the *New York Times* was full of praise.

He died in Alaska at the age of seventy-one. His ashes were scattered by an American airman over Thule's little mountain on North Star Bay, which lay at the heart of his life.

His memory has remained vivid in Greenland. "Piitarsuaq," the elders would say in speaking of him, "Big Peter." ■

Spring has arrived and a group of Inuit await the opening of the Thule trading post. They will exchange their fox skins for rifles, ammunition, knives, and wood. This house was first lived in by Rasmussen, then by Freuchen with his Eskimo family from 1910 to 1919.
It was here that the five scientific Thule expeditions were planned. This historic house still occupies its high and solitary place above North Star Bay.

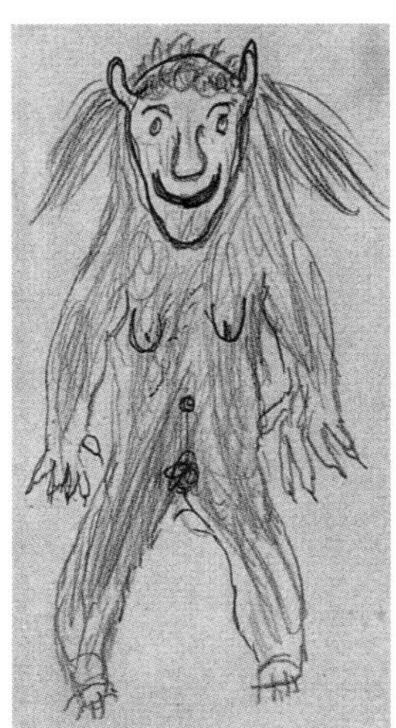

3) Cryoclasty of the rocks, hydrology of the rivers, surveying for a 1/25,000 map, a record of water turbidity at a particular time during the spring floods: 25g to the liter, with the flow increasing in a few weeks on a scale of 1 to 12, and in some years from 1 to 80.

The *Advance*, the *United States*, the *Polaris*, the *Alert*, the *Discovery*, and the *Roosevelt* were not only transport ships but also served as expedition headquarters. Because of the cramped space on these ships, life on board had a prison quality that the more rebellious expedition members did not readily accept.

Eskimo women who accompanied Peary's expedition, living on the *Roosevelt*. Photograph taken by Matthew Henson when the Peary expedition was at Cape Sheridan (82° 29 N., 61° 26' W.) in 1908.

Some aspects of the explorers' daily lives have never been publicly admitted. The logbooks of course mentioned theatrical productions, classes to teach unlettered seamen to read, and Sunday prayer sessions, but even the private diaries of the officers preserve silence about what is most central to human psychology, that is, their emotional and sexual lives. In the first place, the homosexuality that occurred in these confined spaces; and secondly the relations the explorers had during the winter months with Eskimo women. The homosexuality is hidden behind a veil of prudery. But the sexual relations with the Eskimos were real and visible. They occurred either on board or in the vicinity of the Advance, *the* United States, *and certainly aboard the* Roosevelt, *since Peary kept his Inuit wife Ally in his cabin, like a pasha. He even spoke of the situation with a certain cynicism, saying that one had to encourage these relations since "it makes the men more relaxed." Were these expeditions to a distant country a form of outlet for Anglo-Saxon Puritanism? The ethic, at any rate, was tinged with racism, as the children that issued from these liaisons were never recognized. Having drawn up the geneaology of 1400 Polar Eskimos over several generations, I had a chance to note paternity in some cases: Nassaapaluk, for example, was the son of an American mechanic. And there were many other instances of children conceived during a night of ardor who were then abandoned.*

In colonial history, the white man often cohabited with a young native woman as a normal part of life. These kinds of relations certainly had an effect on the Inuit. For them it no doubt offered a form of entertainment as a well as a way to obtain scarce material goods. They were also responding to a longstanding desire to avoid inbreeding, whose bad effects they plainly saw. New blood has always seemed desirable to them.

For the white man, these encounters were primarily a source of sexual gratification. The most powerful, whether in rank or physical prowess, quickly took the prettiest women for themselves, which sometimes evolved into cohabitation. Such was the case with Peary and Henson, as we have seen, both of whom kept the same woman during their eight expeditions from 1891 to 1909. For other women these encounters were no more than a form of prostitution. And what do the young of mixed blood who issued from these unions think? In 1950 they told me that they felt no resentment, but they were so manifestly different from the other Inuit that they kept a low profile.

With the whalers the sexual relations were brief, passing encounters. The ships would be traveling to the "North water" and therefore could only stop, depending on the movement of the ice, for a few days. No whalers overwintered at Cape York, unless one counts the North Star *(1849-1850), which was searching for Franklin. The military expeditions of Ross, Nares, and Greely were governed by rules that would seem to preclude any sexual relations with the Polar Eskimos, but the private expeditions of Kane, Hayes, and Peary practiced this form of "fraternization." Godfrey, a seaman on Kane's expedition, lived on intimate terms with the Eskimos at Etah—did he not say that the Eskimos fed him "mouth to mouth"? The shipwrecked party from the* Polaris *at Qallunaalik (1873-1874) lived intensely with the Etah Eskimos who came to help them, and it is reasonable to suppose, given the dissolute morals of the expedition (sponsored by the United States government) after Hall's death, that sexual relations with Eskimo women were not forbidden.*

After Peary, in July 1909, the first missionaries settled in North Star Bay, with Rasmussen's blessing. They gradually dinned into the Inuit the notion of the sins of the flesh. [4] *The subsequent expeditions were all scientific: those of Koch, Shackleton, Holtved, Van Hauen, and my own. To the Inuit, scientists were the ilisimatuut, learned men, and their research was of an entirely higher order than that of predecessors who sought the mythical Pole. The Inuit seemed almost to revere these men who made mapping surveys, studied rocks, investigated their earliest past, and studied their language—sublimating in the process their sexual desires.*

4) I can testify that this notion was still very superficial in 1950, not to say incomprehensible!

Portrait of Majaq,
by Harald Moltke
(Appat, 11 June 1903).

Peter Freuchen (on the left), wearing the traditional canvas anorak, with a South Greenlander. Note "Piitarsuaq's" gaze, which is full of humanity, yet sharp, because purged by modesty, humor, and selflessness during the harsh trials he experienced.

Ethnography as a lived experience

It was Knud Rasmussen's idea to go up there, appropriate land, and live in the northernmost inhabited section of the globe. And he proposed that I go with him.[5]

I thought about it for several days. I had myself to think of, and my own future. I realized that I had an opportunity to make a living in the civilized world. I might complete my studies and become a doctor. Or I could become a sailor. I might make a name for myself as a newspaperman. I might do any number of prosaic things.

But I decided against all these possibilities. The spirit of adventure was my heritage. My grandfather, somewhat of a roamer himself, had encouraged me to seek out the strange and the different.

I told Knud I would go with him—and I have never regretted my decision.

The qiviqtuq, *tormentor and captor of souls*

High up in the nunatak[6] we came upon old abandoned huts. Asayuk told me of desperate men who had run away from home and gone into the mountains. They became ghosts or were taken by the Inland people, the Eqidleet.[7] He told me from his own experience of one such person, a man who was driven mad by a woman.

It is funny, but it is told, he said—and Asayuk was known to speak only the truth—that there are men born who care for one particular woman and it takes them seven years to forget her. A certain young man had taken a girl from her family and lived with her at Inglefield Gulf. He made himself conspicuous by speaking of her when out hunting with other men. When they stayed out overnight and all slept together, he regretted that he could not be at home with his wife, and even mentioned her name without shame on several occasions. At last some of the dignified hunters remonstrated with him. It is well known that a man who reveals such dependence upon a woman is likely to offend the seals, as they do not care to be hunted by inferior persons. Therefore, he was told either to stay at home and sew and care for the lamps or employ his mouth for the talk of men.

But the poor boy persisted. Then one day a big hunter with many children to care for lost his wife. And while the hunter could have taken a widow experienced in housekeeping, he thought it would be amusing to take the young man's wife and see if he dared fight for her.

The frantic young husband did his best, but he was not permitted to kill the hunter, as that would have been too great a loss to the tribe. He was advised to use his arms and strength, or depend upon the speed of his dogs to recapture her. Instead, he did nothing but sit upon a stone for three days and cry like a baby. Even his wife said to the other women that he had left his dignity behind in the tent where they had lived.

When the young man saw her laugh and chide him for his weakness, he determined to live no longer with his people; he went inland and became a qivitoq—a ghost who may never return home.

He was seen once from a distance, but as those who saw him felt he was about to approach, they fled. He had not been heard of for many years until a hunter went up-country for caribou, and found his dead body in a small hut.

Asayuk had known the young man and told me that he was only a boy, but he remembered that the other men had kidded him because he was never willing to lend his wife or borrow other men's wives.

This is the story of a man who died because of his belief in one, and only one, woman! [8]

Ittusarssuk, a great lady

After we reached the house of Qolugtinguaq I learned more about the old woman, Itusarssuk, and why she was so fond of children. She was one of the great ladies of the community, a worthy soul, gentle and kind and meek. Realizing this, it came as a shock to me to discover that she had once killed four of her own children. [9]

A long time ago she had lived on Herbert Island alone with her former husband and their children. She suffered the terrible fate of watching him drown. He had been out in his kayak for many hours and had fallen asleep. Itusarssuk could see him, but he was so far out at sea that her voice could not reach him. Suddenly as she looked at him, a wave upset his tiny craft. She saw him threshing around in the water for a few minutes, and then drift away, face down. She was alone and could do nothing rescue him. She was left to provide for her five children.

The summer was not far advanced, and they had not brought their spring catch to the island, so she had little to eat. There are almost no auks on Herbert Island, and she had to kill and eat the dogs, hoping that some help would arrive. Once she saw a dead whale float by the island, but she had no way of getting to it. Another time she saw two bears on an ice pan, and in the far distance specks that were kayaks from other islands. But among them were no relatives of her husband, and they did not come to her.

She had to make her own house for the winter, and it was hard for her. The children cried for food, and when their eyes were not upon her, she cried too. Finally they ate their clothes made of animal skins, and when nothing more was at hand she knew that she had to end the pain for the small children, so she hanged them. The oldest girl, about twelve years age, helped her mother hang the younger ones. After three of them were dead, the eight-year-old boy refused to die. He said that to die looked very unpleasant, to judge by the expression in the children's eyes. And he said that he would look out for himself until he was ready to die.

After he had run away, the girl herself fastened the noose around her neck, and said that perhaps after a while she would not feel the hunger. Her mother tightened the line, and soon the girl's misery was ended.

Ituarssuk's strength was entirely gone, and she could not even cry any more. After a while she took the bodies down and buried them. The girl's hand was raised, and refused to allow the mother to place it alongside her body. This was because she had never been possessed by a man.

Iggianguaq was the boy. He lived the whole summer on grass and the excre-

From left to right, photographed on the shore of North Star Bay, 31 July 1909: Kaviak, Atangana, Qaaqqutsiaq (my companion in 1950-1951), Gutiten, Arnarulunguaq, Sinorajuk (the future wife of Nassapaluk, both of whom I met inn Etah in March 1951 and whose guest I was), Aleketsiaq (brother of my friend Inuterssuaq and of Navarana, Freuchen's wife).

5) Peter Freuchen was the co-founder, with Knud Rasmussen, of Thule (1909). This is too often forgotten in Copenhagen and elsewhere. As the post's first administrator, he was in direct contact with the Inughuit for the duration of his functions (1909-1919) during a critical period in their technological development and conversion to Christianity. It is through daily activities that a people assimilates new ideas and foreign technologies and expresses its own questions.

6) A nunatak is an isolated mass of rock rising through above the flow of a glacier.

7) The Eqidleet are foreigners and the enemies of the Inuit. Most often, the name is applied to Indians.

8) During Hayes's expedition, one of the Greenlandic hunters at Etah suddenly set off into the rockfall in the mountains to become a qiviqtuq. His life was "hurting him."

9) An instance of the heroism and dignity of this great race of Northerners. Their painful life allows them to appreciate that each day of life is a grace. Euthanasia is the outcome of extreme harshness (famine, widowhood, etc.). Necessity determines the law: one has to survive.

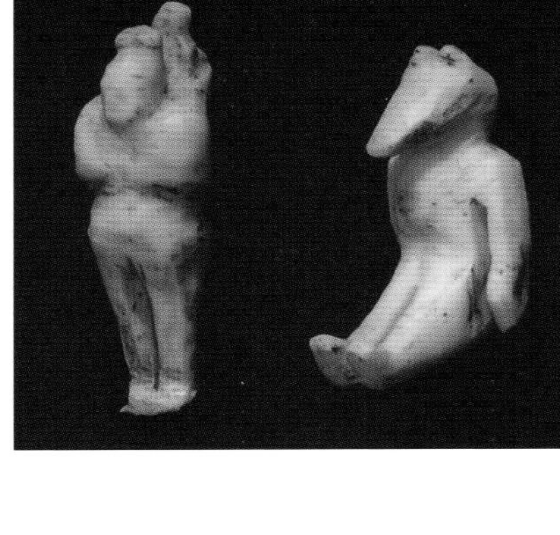

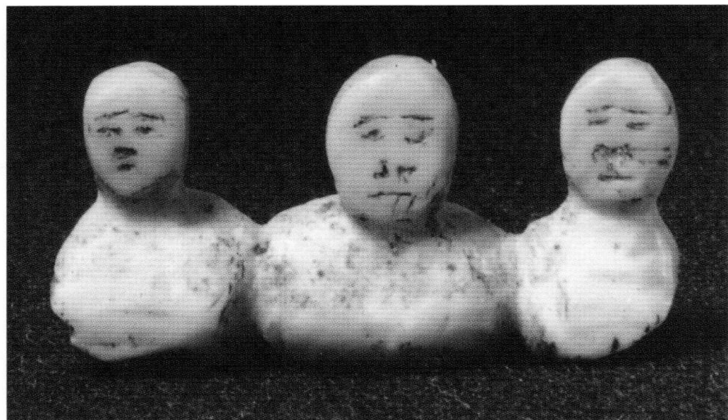

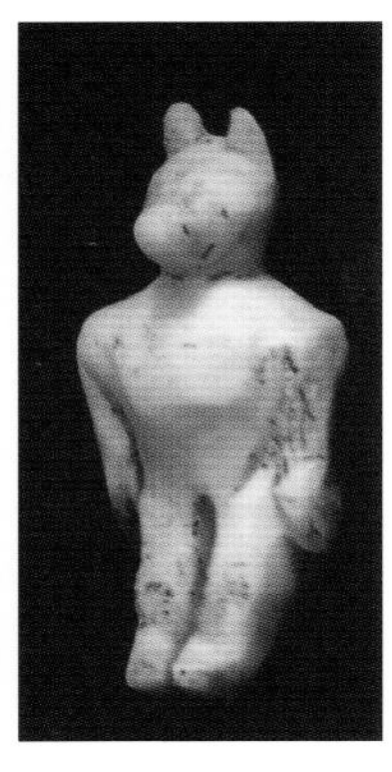

Walrus ivory carvings. From left to right: woman carrying her child in her hood (height, 3.2 cm); mythical figure with the head and "mouth" of a bird (height, 2.8 cm); busts of three mythical Inuit characters, a form of representation rare in Inuit art (height, 3.1 cm); man with the head of a dog, or anthropomorphic dog (height, 3.6 cm). Carving in ivory is reserved for men.

ment of rabbits. Occasionally he killed a young gull, and he and his mother both held on to life.

Minik, a good-for-nothing?

Minik was a great nuisance to all of us. He was an unhappy lad with a bad disposition. As a boy he, his father and others, had been taken to America. [10] All except Minik had been stricken with an epidemic in New York and died. He had been adopted by very decent people and been given every opportunity, but he was a born good-for-nothing. He felt that rules did not concern him, and laws were made for him to disobey. After countless attempts to get him interested in something—anything—he was given the opportunity to choose a profession. His choice was to steal money and run away. He was apprehended at the Canadian border, sent back to New York, and finally brought home to Greenland on one of Peary's relief ships. He returned to the North with no property or money—he had been given plenty in America but had spent it all during the trip for liquor and such. He was absolutely destitute when I first saw him. We had taken him into our house, and soon found that he did not remember a thing he had learned in America, and could barely read or write. At least he never did.

I do not tell this as a proof that it is impossible to educate Eskimos, for even in Greenland Minik was regarded as unintelligent and irresponsible. But he believed that the world had been bad for him and he blamed others for his lack of character. In America he had longed for Greenland, and now that he was in Greenland he wanted to be back in America.

Wife exchange

This so-called wife-trading among the Eskimos is an interesting custom. Most persons believe it results from a lack of morality, but this is decidedly untrue. I have never met a people with a more strict moral code, though it is a different code from that of the white race.

An Eskimo's love for his wife is quite separate from the urgencies of his sex life. If a man desires a woman and has no wife of his own, he may borrow another man's wife. It would be impossible for him, however, to go to a married woman and suggest that she sleep with him without first consulting her husband. [11]

There is also a purely practical and economical advantage in wife-trading for the hunter. If he goes alone, he must spend a great portion of his time building an igloo, cutting ice and melting it. At night he must return to a cold shelter, and he has no means of drying and tanning his skins. Instead, his evenings must be spent mending boots and drying clothes, and he must carry plenty of spare clothes with him. However, if he brings a woman along, all this is quite different. He builds her an igloo, and she takes care of everything else. She has the house warm when he returns, and his food steaming hot. His boots and mittens are dry and soft and mended, so that he need not cart along many changes. And while he is out hunting the woman dries the skins on a frame inside the igloo, scrapes them and removes all fat and meat, so that they can be folded together and he may return home with thirty or forty instead of the ten raw skins he would otherwise be able to haul. This is perhaps the greatest advantage in having a woman along—besides this, she can hunt rabbits and take care of the meat caches. Oh, there are many fine things about a woman.

Now, it may happen that a man needs skins, and his wife is unfit for travel. She may be ill, or pregnant, or caring for a tiny baby. How much better for him, then, that he arrange to leave her with a friend while he is away and, in exchange, take his friend's wife along with him.

The Eskimos believe that the human animal can be trusted in any relationship save the sexual one.

The rape of a society: conversion to Christianity

I never like to say too much concerning Christian missions among pagans. I have seen all manner of men and women missionaries, and many of them were unfit for the task they elected to perform. At home no one is able to judge whether or not these persons will make successful missionaries, and those who donate to the cause always believe in the benefits of carrying the word of God to the pagans—it is natural for anyone to assume that his charity is not wasted. [12]

Any fairly intelligent person can pick a man out of the street and teach him a set of rules to follow in accomplishing a given problem. But a missionary—who is supposed to teach a little of everything—should be a man of great culture, general knowledge, and sympathetic understanding. It is unfortunate that such a combination is

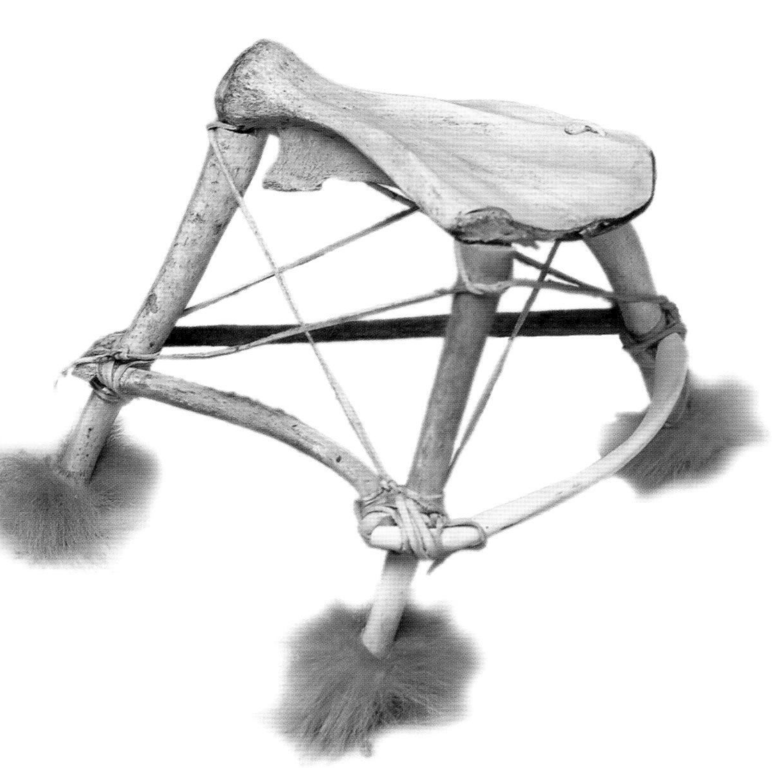

Nikurvautaq. Three-legged stool used in hunting seal, made of walrus and seal bone, with sealskin lashings. The feet are tipped with bear fur to keep the stool from crunching on the ice and alerting the seal. The hunter waits by a seal's breathing hole (*aqluq*), his harpoon in his right hand.

rare among missionaries. Usually all it takes for them to secure appointments is a burning desire to preach about their God, and everything else be damned!

We must realize that missionaries are going to violate all manner of racial rules and traditions, and even trample upon what the pagans have always believed to be decency. Such a program requires tact and infinite patience.

Usually they set to work on the question of sex. It is strange how sex has always interested the church. Of course, sex has always interested everybody, and if the church is able to control it, the church is immediately an important factor in the life of a people. But I have always been a little embarrassed for preachers, who seem to wield such small influence over their own flocks at home, daring to interfere with the ways of an alien race.

Freuchen weds Navarana: the marriage proposal

Finally one evening when she came Arnanguaq was absent, and I told Mequpaluk that she had better stay with me. She looked at me a moment and then remarked simply:

"I am unable to make any decisions, being merely a weak little girl. It is for you to decide that."

But her eyes were eloquent, and spoke the language every girl knows regardless of race or clime.

I only asked her to move from the opposite side of the ledge over to mine—that was all the wedding necessary in this land of the innocents.

Next day she wanted to know whether she was to return to her home or not, and when I said no, that was final. A few hours later one of her brothers came to ask why she had not come home. She said:

"Somebody is occupied by sewing for oneself in this house!"

The boy was startled but said nothing, and turned on his heel to race from house to house with the news. After a few hours sledges hurried north and south to tell what had happened and to hear firsthand the comments of the neighbors.[13]

Again I was amazed at the discretion of these wonderful people. Not one of them spoke a word to either of us that would indicate that the girl had not always lived in our house. Visitors came as usual, and talked as if she had been my wife for years and they had been her guest many times.

Many years later I heard the term "going native," but it did not occur to me then that that was what I was doing. I did know that my marriage to an Eskimo girl made a final breach with the world I had known as a young man, but I had already left that world far behind. Navarana was immediately accepted as my wife wherever we visited in Greenland, and no one worried over the duration of our union. Not until long afterward, after our two children were born, did any of the natives admit to me that they had not at first taken our marriage seriously. Even Navarana's mother had thought it but a casual arrangement, and that Navarana would soon be sent home.

Navarana's own life had been a bloodcurdling saga of the Arctic. As a small girl she had lived with her parents on Salve Island. One of those inexplicable epidemics that so pitifully ravage a primitive race struck the people, and on the island where they lived only Navarana, her mother, and her small brother were spared. They had no meat to eat and were forced to butcher their dogs for food. When this source of supply was exhausted they ate their clothes and dog traces and anything available. The little boy was about three years old and was still nursing. The mother soon had no milk left, and the child in a frenzy of hunger bit the nipple off her breast. Then, seeing no hope of keeping him alive, she hanged him while Navarana looked on. The mother's grief, Navarana told me, was worse than the sight of the dead child, and she swore to her mother that she did not want to die, no matter how hungry she was, but would remain to comfort her.

Navarana, 21 July 1919. Freuchen's young wife had another two years to live.

Navarana told me that she ate grass and the excrement of rabbits and chewed on the tatters of old skins and, with the fall ice, Uvdluriark arrived on his sledge and took them both to his house.

After a couple of years Navarana went to live with her grandfather and grandmother. Her grandfather, Mequsaq, was a veteran of great dignity and experience, and he lavished all his affection upon her. While living with Mequsaq she had the

Axe (Kroeber, 1890-1900).

10) In 1897, six Polar Eskimos were brought by Peary to New York, at the request of the American Museum of Natural History. Within six months, four of them had died of tuberculosis. Peary sold or donated their skeletons to the museum. (See the story of Minik in the chapter on Peary above.)

11) Other than its procreative function, spouse exchange serves to break the ties of reciprocal possession in marriage. In the Inughuit's primitive communitarianism, the greatest danger is the disaggregation of the group into large families, each claiming portions of their territory through marital alliances. One child out of three is given at a young age to another family, who may or may not be related, so as to partially break the bonds of natural descendence within the group.

12) The first missionaries were all South Greenlanders. They came from the southwest coast and disembarked in what would become the bay of Thule in summer 1909. They belonged to the Danish Lutheran mission. Poor, evangelical in spirit, and living as Eskimos, they left a memory of high-mindedness among the Inughuit. Enok Kristiansen, who lived in Siorapaluk in 1950-1951, was my neighbor. Originally from Disko Island, he had been selected by his childhood friend Knud Rasmussen. Kristiansen on occasion spoke of his early years as a catechist at Thule. Intransigeant about dogma, and inflexible on the score of shamanism, he had a neophyte's rigid faith. I regret now that I did not ask him questions on specifics, but questions of religion—though of crucial importance—then interested me fairly little. Also, I came under his supervision, and he would not have appreciated that a foreigner was stirring up trouble by asking pointed questions about these matters.

The first Eskimo accepted conversion in 1910. The last to be converted was Nukappiannguaq, father of Sakaeunnguaq, in 1934. I met him in Etah. His first wife was the daughter of the famous Hans Hendrik. The Polar Eskimos entertained a dual religion until about 1970. The shamans lost their power as the trading post gave the Inughuit increased security, thus freeing them from a closed mental universe of taboos. But primitive thought still subsists in all the Inuit, in their dreams and times of misfortune. And their legends (oqalualaat) retain their vigor.

13) Navarana was the sister of Inuterssuaq, who was one of my companions and informers in 1950-1951 and also on later visits. His grandfather, Meqorsuaq, came from Canada in 1863 and long resisted technological changes, refusing for instance to use a rifle. Inuterssuaq was the first Polar Eskimo to write a book, in 1982.

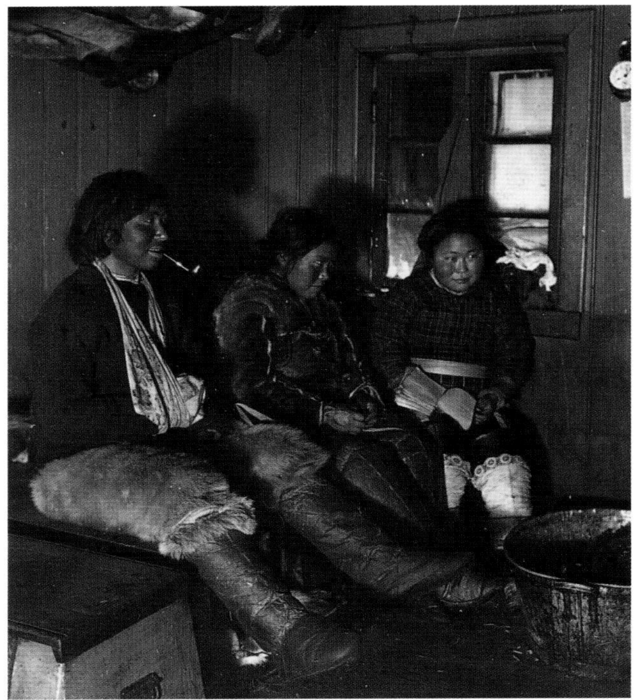

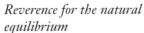

Two Polar Eskimos and a woman from South Greenland visiting the Thule post, which was the house of Knud Rasmussen and Peter Freuchen.

good fortune to escape a siege of starvation that wiped out thirteen others at Cape Alexander. This had occurred the year Mylius-Erichsen and Knud Rasmussen were there for the first time.

The old man and his wife and Navarana found only two others alive, Kullabak and her son, Kraungak. They took the boy along with them (there was not room on their sledge for Kullabak) and, when they reached the next community, left Navarana and Kraungak in a shelter while they went out to look for walrus. They got one, rescued old Kullabak and saved all their lives. Navarana told me that she remembered only one incident of this experience: while she and Kraungak waited for the old people to return, the boy, whose feet were frozen, cut off one of his little toes with a knife in order to impress her. He said it didn't hurt, but she could never forget it.

Papaver dahlanium. Buttercup, or *sungaartuaraq.*

Close-mouthed about what really matters

I had thought I was well acquainted with the people of Greenland, but now their lives became doubly rich for me. Navarana told me countless tales I would otherwise never have heard. The Eskimos, great gossips about surface matters, are remarkably close-mouthed and conservative concerning anything that really matters.

Reverence for the natural equilibrium

I remember that it was on the big glacier that we saw the sun for the first time, about February 22nd. The Eskimos with us all removed their mittens and hoods, and asked us to do likewise. I complied, but Wulff laughed and said he had no intention of humoring the natives in such a stupid fashion, and kept on. [14]

The break between Rasmussen and Lauge Koch

Knud and I believed that whenever a death, accidental or otherwise, occurred, there should be an official investigation. We felt that it would be very embarrassing if such an investigation should involve us in the Danish courts—there would always be a few persons who would censure Lauge Koch for deserting his companion.

Both of us knew the truth: there was nothing against him and, as he could not carry Wulff, it was his duty to save himself and we thought it might be better to see the action through in Greenland. There was a judge here, and it would be much simpler to hand his decision to journalists in Copenhagen than to drag the mess through the courts there. [15]

The inspector in the south was willing to hold the court we sought. But now Lauge Koch refused to submit to such a trial. He had visited the scientific station at Disko and the Danes there had advised him against it. What arguments they used on him I never knew; whatever they said I am sure they meant to be in his best interests.

But it was the beginning of a lifelong misunderstanding between those two big contemporary Arctic explorers—Knud Rasmussen and Lauge Koch. Many persons later tried in vain to bring them together again. After Knud Rasmussen's death it was most unfortunate that Lauge Koch published an article in the leading Danish paper denouncing his first companion and helper. It made Knud Rasmussen no smaller nor did it make Lauge Koch greater.

Navarana's death

Navarana was still very ill. It was difficult for her to walk, and we carried her in a boat from the harbor to the assistant's house, where we slept in our clothes—it was summer and one could drop down to sleep wherever it was most convenient.

It was apparent by now that Navarana had Spanish influenza, the same disease to which I had fallen victim the year before. I did not leave her side, and got our good friend, Fat Sofie, to help nurse her. Navarana was thankful that I could be with her, though she was torn with anxiety for her children. She would have liked me to go up to Thule and see that Mequsaq was being cared for properly.

"Now both the babies are away from us," she said, and asked me to tell her about little Pipaluk—how was she? what could she say? did she ever ask about her mother?

The next day Navarana was worse. There was no doctor in Upernivik at the time, and there was nothing more we could do for her. In the evening she asked me what I thought was the matter. Her head was buzzing with thoughts that came unsummoned, she said. It was ghastly to sit helpless and watch her fade away. I told her to try to sleep, but she could not.

After a while she began to talk about her visit to Denmark and the things she had seen there. That had been the high point in her life.

"But tell me the truth," she said. "Was that girl an angel? She danced like one and looked like the pictures the missionary showed us. I never could figure it out or get it right."

I told her again that it had only been a show, that she had not seen real angels.

"Then maybe one never has a chance to see them," she concluded.

I admitted this might very well be true, and she lay still for a long while. Then she took my hand in hers and told me how happy she had been in having a husband who would talk with her as an equal. And finally she said that she was very sleepy.

I went into the kitchen to brew tea for her. As I sat and watched the water it came over me how much I loved her, and how much she had developed since our marriage. I don't know why, but suddenly I regretted that my good friend Magdalene had not been in Denmark when Navarana was there, and that the two girls had never met.

Navarana was so quiet that I tiptoed in

14) This incident occurred in February 1917. On the Second Thule Expedition, in September 1917, Thorild Wulff was abandoned by the expedition and died of hunger in Inglefield Land.

15) This tragic event caused a rift between the two great Danish explorers, Knud Rasmussen, the expedition leader, and Lauge Koch. Koch reproached Rasmussen with leaving him in an impossible situation when he set off southward for relief. Freuchen had stayed behind in Thule, but it was he who, with Lauge Koch, returned to Etah, then to Inglefield Land in October 1917 to recover the expedition's crates and especially the body of the Swedish scientist, which was never found. I was the first foreign scientists to return to the site of the tragedy afterwards. There was no cairn or monument there, as though the incident needed to be expunged from memory.

16) Navarana left behind two children: a daughter, Pipaluk, who lives near Copenhagen, and a son, Meqqusaaq, who died. There was no doctor in Thule until 1925.

to look at her. As I watched, her lip just quivered. Then she was dead.[16]

A miserable little priest

The minister in Upernivik, an undersized, native imbecile, came to me with the statement that, since Navarana had died a pagan, she could not be buried in the graveyard. No bell might toll over her funeral and, he was sorry, he could not deliver a sermon.

It was relaxing for me to be so furious. I told him to go to hell with his bells and his sermon, but my wife would sleep in the cemetery and not be thrown to the dogs. Still, he said, he had already warned his congregation of the horrible consequences of dying without baptism, and this was his opportunity to offer them an example.

I am glad that I did not strike him. I had the good grace only to tell him to get out and let me manage the service.

It was the most pitiful funeral I have ever witnessed. The workers of the colony acted as pallbearers, and I was instructed to pay them each a kroner for the task. I remember that I was angry at the blacksmith because he smoked a cigar during the procession, if such a word as "procession" may be used, since there were only four of us—Aage Bistrup, the manager, and his young assistant, both Danes, and myself, and then Fat Sofie, who made the only gesture of gratitude. She had fashioned a sort of bouquet from gaily colored Christmas tree decorations, and it lay upon the coffin with a silly-looking Santa Claus peeping through the ornaments.

Hidden behind rocks and houses were the natives, terrified at the approach of this funeral procession that had not been solemnized by a minister or sanctioned by the tolling of bells from the church. They dared not follow such a pagan to her final resting place, my little Navarana who had fed and entertained them whenever they visited her or she came to their houses.

Now, a few days before I wrote this, I read the gracious book written by Mrs. Ruth Bryan Owen, American ambassador to Denmark. Mrs. Owen was in Upernivik in 1934, and laid a bouquet of red flowers upon Navarana's grave. It brought tears to my eyes to read of it, and reminded me of my rancor toward the church at that time.

I had a simple, beautiful stone carved to mark the grave, which is atop the cliff.

The texts by Peter Freuchen are excerpted from *Arctic Adventure: My Life in the Frozen North* (New York: Farrar & Rhinehart, 1935).

Communal trance, maintained with singing and drumming, during the winter. Moltke, 1903. *Ingmiqtuq.*

Summer 1910. Hunting for the barnacle goose, an Anatid of the extreme north, and for eider (whose down was used for winter clothes), at the foot of the coastal cliffs of pre-Cambrian sandstone. The Eskimos carried their loads on their back, with a tump line passing across their forehead. This technique, which leaves one's hands free, is common to all American Indians.

Daily Life

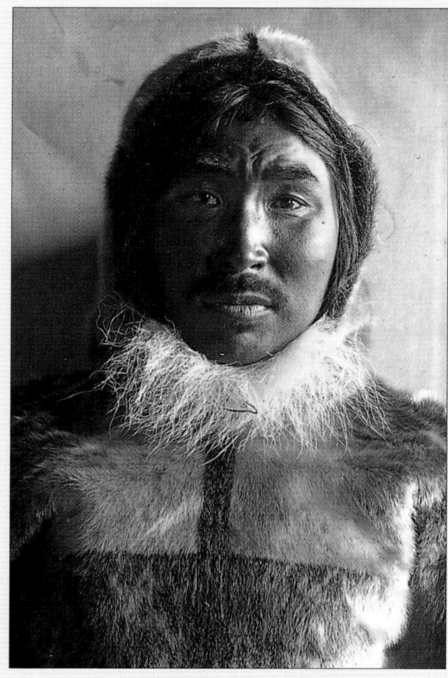

Ak-Pood-A-Shah-O, an Etah Eskimo, photographed by a member of the McMillan expedition (1916).

Daily life. On the left, a woman (with a child in her hood) defecates nearly standing in a snow shelter; the tethered dogs wait; a child runs. At the top, a woman checks the roof of a snow igloo, particularly its breathing hole (*qingaq*). Children sled down a snow slope. A mother delouses the hair of a neighbor, who sits on a *nikurvautaq*, or bone seat made without nails or mortises. Top right, hunting with a harpoon for a walrus or large seal, which is sleeping on the floe. Bottom right, hunting for seal at a breathing hole in the ice (note the shelter against the wind and the hunter's three-legged bone stool). (Drawing by a young Eskimo woman, Aninaq, Knud Rasmussen collection.)

Eating in the traditional Inuit fashion: the meat is held between the teeth and steadied with one hand while the other cuts it with a whaling knife held to the nose (Etah, 1914-1917). The young Inuk above, photographed in 1937 by Erik Holtved, performs the same traditional gesture.

An old woman softens a thread made of narwhal tendon by passing it back and forth between her teeth. She will then even it out by rolling it against her cheek. Her thimble is an import, not the traditional one of seal skin.

Summer 1917: this young Eskimo is holding a kind of sausage whose casing is made of seal intestine and which is stuffed with the yolks of eider eggs. The sausage is set out to dry during the summer for consumption in the winter (a preservation technique antedating 1860-1863).

This hunter is sucking the fat from the outturned skin of an auklet (*appaliarsuq*). The fat of this bird, which is eaten raw in the springtime, is one of the Eskimos' favorite foods. The head is broken with a sharp crunch of the jaw and the brain swallowed. Each family catches 250 to 300 auklets per year. Those that can't be eaten fresh are stuffed into a seal skin and left to ripen under a pile of rocks until the winter, when they are eaten soaked in their own grease (*kiviaq*).

The use of the bow drill, *nuin*, was reintroduced by the Eskimos who immigrated from Canada in 1860-1863. Miteq demonstrates the technique at Cape York in 1909. In his teeth, he clenches the mouth piece, holding the top of the long bone, which revolves freely as the bow (a seal rib with a seal skin thong) is moved back and forth by the right hand. The lower end of the long bone holds the metal drill bit, which pierces the object Miteq holds in his left hand. In 1950-1951, I saw several Eskimos use this ancient technique. Masaitsiaq, then seventy years old, was making a point for his harpoon with a bow drill while U.S. marines landed at North Star Bay.

Lauge Koch 1892-1964

"I DON'T WANT TO BE STABBED FROM BEHIND"

Tall in stature, with the sharp eyes of a bird of prey, Koch was curt in manner and somewhat distant. He was descended from an ancient Danish family, and many of his forebears had been bishops and pastors. He had immense pent-up vitality, and vast ambition.

The young Lauge Koch decided in adolescence to follow in the great tradition of his uncle, I. P. Koch, the first Dane to map and explore Greenland. He went on his first expedition in 1913. It was in Disko Bay, Koch was twenty, the season was summer. A happy and productive trip, it influenced Koch to make a lifelong commitment to studying the north and east of Greenland, little of whose geology was then known. And for generations, he would be the uncontested leader in that field. His matchless competence led him to solicit the directorship of the Danish Geological Service, a post he richly deserved.

An exceptional geologist and explorer

Koch's expeditions were models of courage, organization, and stubbornness—a trait he claimed to have inherited from his Austrian ancestors, who were peasants from the Setesdalen valley. Koch also chose to share the Eskimos' life fully, making them his collaborators and even his assistants in surveying. His faithful companion, Inuuteq, whom I knew well (he was my informant in November 1950 on socio-economic questions in Kangerluarsuk), told me of Koch's great skill as a teacher. This was confirmed to me by Inukitsupaluk (father of Iggiannguaq-Uutaaq's wife) during our frequent meetings in Thule while he was teaching me my first words of Polar Eskimo and correcting my South Greenland accent: "Koch? What energy! Early in the morning, once camp was broken, Koch would set out on foot ahead of the sledges to break the trail, while the Eskimos finished packing."

In 1930, Koch started to use aircraft, never thinking twice about flying in single-engine planes to areas without landing fields when his work required it. A surveyor of the first order, Koch is probably the foremost Danish explorer of northern Greenland. During World War II, cut off from Greenland, he wrote a seminal work on the freezing of the seas of Greenland and Iceland.

Regrettably, though, Koch had no interest in writing a book about his human experiences, despite being a privileged witness to the life of the Inuit. Did he not disappoint the hopes of the Inuit in this? They turned spontaneously to him, but did they not secretly hope that he would act as their spokesman? Who is to say? I questioned him on the subject. He gave me a long, silent look, as though asking himself that very question.

Part of Koch's reason for not writing about his coworkers was certainly his humility as a scientist. He felt unprepared to produce an ethnographic work of the kind so ably written by Thalbitzer and Boas. "I am only a geologist," he answered me when I questioned him on the

Opposite:
Lauge Koch in 1923, on the ice of northern Kane Basin and Kennedy Channel.

Thorild Wulff, the Swedish botanist, photographed in Disko (July 1916). He was abandoned, still alive, in the empty tundra of Inglefield Land (September 1917). His solitary death was one of the most tragic in arctic history.

matter a second time. But was his refusal not also explained by his scientific training, which made him consider an ethnographic account of the kind Rasmussen wrote too literary—in the most pejorative sense of the term? He said as much to me.

Wulff abandoned

But let us go back a bit. In 1917, Koch was only twenty-four years old. He had been selected for Rasmussen's Second Thule Expedition, scientific and multidisciplinary in conception, along with the Swede Thorild Wulff, three Polar Eskimos, [1] and a South Greenlander.

The expedition set out from Thule in April, and ended tragically in September. Six men were returning from distant Peary Land, exhausted and close to starvation on the barren plateau of Inglefield Land. Within a few days, the brilliant young Danish geologist would have to make the horrible decision to leave behind on the trail his older companion, the Swedish botanist Wulff. Having reached the end of his strength, Wulff deliberately lay down on a bed of grasses in a little valley in the tundra. He could not and would not walk any farther. He wanted to die. The two Eskimo hunters accompanying Koch, concerned that they too would die, were anxious to leave the area as quickly as possible for the more game-rich coast. Koch was obliged to follow them and leave the Swede to his fate. He never forgave Knud Rasmussen, the expedition's leader, for having left the main party to get help from the Eskimos and thus delegated to him the awful responsibility for Wulff. "It was his responsibility," he said to me, "to save us all, and Wulff in particular. For weeks, Wulff had been dragging on the trail." [2]

Although he had agreed with his leader's decision eight days earlier to set off for Etah to save his companions—only Rasmussen had the charisma to convince the Etah Eskimos to come and rescue them immediately—Koch never accepted the role he had been condemned to play. The young geologist did not have the temperament of a sacrificial goat. When he returned to the little Eskimo encampment at Etah, he confronted Rasmussen with his anger. The Eskimos who were present described the scene to me in precise terms thirty-five years later: Koch standing, towering like a statue, Rasmussen collapsed, sitting in a boat, devastated by the news he had just heard. Koch was deeply wounded, wounded in his soul and in his conscience, when he lashed out at Rasmussen.

And several months later, at Godhavn (Disko Island, Greenland), Koch refused to testify before the Danish representative of the Greenland police, as law required, and as Rasmussen wished. Rasmussen was afraid that poorly informed lawyers and judges would later pursue the matter. Koch requested a jury of honor, composed of eminent polar explorers who could study the sequence of events in their full context so as to establish the responsibility of each of the actors.

Such a jury was in fact never convened. Only the two great explorers Nordenskjöld and Nansen declared, on being consulted, that Koch's behavior was irreproachable—repeating the opinion of Rasmussen and Freuchen. But Koch announced that he was dissatisfied with the proceedings, and he would always remain so.

From that date on, Koch and Rasmussen drew farther and farther apart. The unlucky site of the tragedy, which I was the first foreign scientist to visit, traveling there by dog sled in May 1951, lies in a valley unmarked by any monument. And Wulff's body was never recovered. Koch subsequently formed his own sponsoring committee for scientific work and devoted himself to the study of the geology of North Greenland. Rasmussen, meantime, remained director of the Thule trading post (managed by Peter Freuchen) and organized his remarkable Fifth Thule Expedition, which traveled from Canada to Siberia (1922-1925).

Rasmussen became a national hero in Denmark and Greenland. Lauge Koch pursued his scientific work in the shadows, remembering the sad, perhaps accusing, smile of the abandoned Swede as he waved weakly one last time.

The cost of baseness

Was Koch irritated by the growing success of his former companion? In December 1933, during the Christmas holidays, while the people of Denmark and Greenland mourned the premature death of their beloved Knud Rasmussen, Koch perpetrated an act of villainy. He had been asked by the great Danish paper *Politiken* for an article, and he provided the editors—as he told me, grinning—with "the same broken record" that is usual in such circumstances. The editor of *Politiken* then called him on

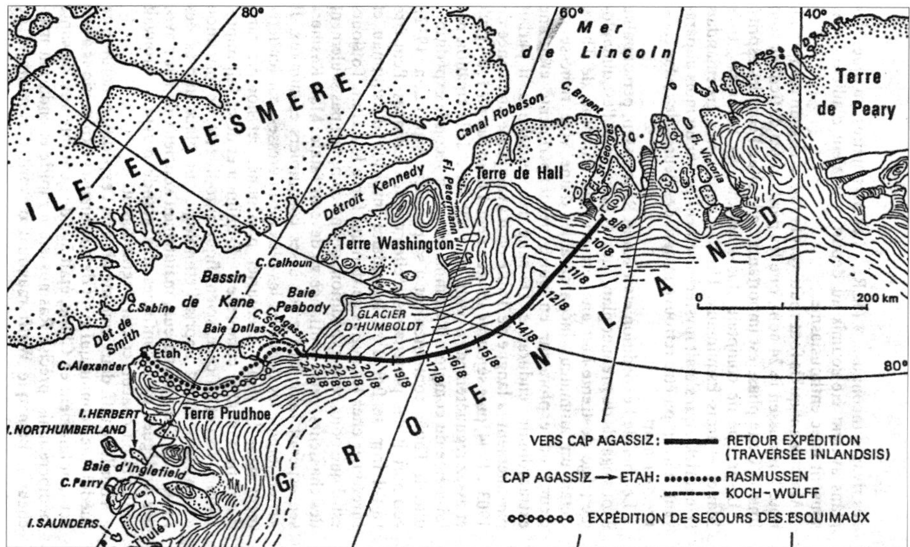

Inglefield Land, site of the tragedy in September 1917.

Lauge Koch, left, in 1921 on the slopes of Robertson Fjord (a few kilometers to the west of Siorapaluk), with a Danish companion and an Eskimo woman.

the telephone himself, saying: "Knud Rasmussen is part of Denmark's history, and so are you. Surely you have something more personal to say. After all, you were his companion, yet you have had no official dealings with him for a very long time. So what about it?"

And Koch, who had kept his peace for many years, took the journalist's bait. He spoke a few curt words, long held back: "Knud Rasmussen? A good dog sled driver who was certainly a better novelist than he was a rigorous scientist."

Denmark was dumbstruck. To what depths would a man not stoop! To try and maim the reputation of a national hero after he was dead and could no longer defend himself, and to do it to Knud Rasmussen, who had given the young Lauge Koch his start! When public opinion is outraged, it becomes implacable, and this is particularly true in cases of slander.

The academic world attacked Koch at the first opportunity. When his *Geology of Greenland* appeared, the geology faculty of the University of Copenhagen, headed by Dr. Alfred Rosenkrantz, accused him of "theft of intellectual property." Apparently he had used notes that were of uncertain provenance. A public hearing was held, and Koch, in order to defend himself before his peers, sold his library. "I was truly alone," he told me. The court rendered an ambivalent verdict, saying the case was not within its jurisdiction. The Thule Executive Committee, which administered the trading post, took this opportunity to attack Koch, subjecting him to police-like interrogation. "Those were the worst hours in my entire life," he told me. "Legally, I won, but in fact I lost everything."

The Danish academic world, which (along with the Danish Geological Service) was the summit of his aspirations, was closed to him forever. Henceforth he only worked as a consulting geologist to the Ministry of Greenland, on an annual contract. Such was his title and such were his functions when I knew him—-I still see the tiny office in the ministry building where he received me. Furthermore, no Dane ever wanted to participate again in his expeditions to Greenland's east coast, however well organized and richly endowed they were. Only the Germans and the Swiss agreed to accompany him.

"I would need eyes in the back of my head to keep from being stabbed from behind," he said one day to a journalist. Of course, Koch was internationally respected. It was through one of his expeditions to Greenland's east coast in 1945-1951 that the main lead and molybdenum mines in Mestervig were discovered. These were of great importance, as they long provided the Danish government with its primary source of income from Greenland. But public opinion has a long memory. Koch did not betray his companion, true, but he acted dishonorably.

Alone against all

"Alone against all" could well have been Koch's motto. Though he wrote in his journal that he had never been

1) I knew two of them well, and one of them, Borseman, confirmed to me the account he dictated to Knud Rasmussen.

2) For the detailed account of this tragedy, see my *Derniers rois de Thule*, 5th edition, 1989, pages 436-488.

Inuuteq, Koch's favorite companion, was also an excellent singer and drum player. Photographed here at 21 (1920-1923 expedition), he was my own informer at Kangerluarsuk in November-December 1951, at the age of 50.

Lauge Koch at his base in Illulorsuit, a few kilometers west of Siorapaluk, working on his cartographic surveys during the winter of 1920-1921.

Tupilak or tormenting spirit seen in a nightmare. Drawing by Iiggianguaq-Utaaq, born in 1919. Qaanaaq, 1982.

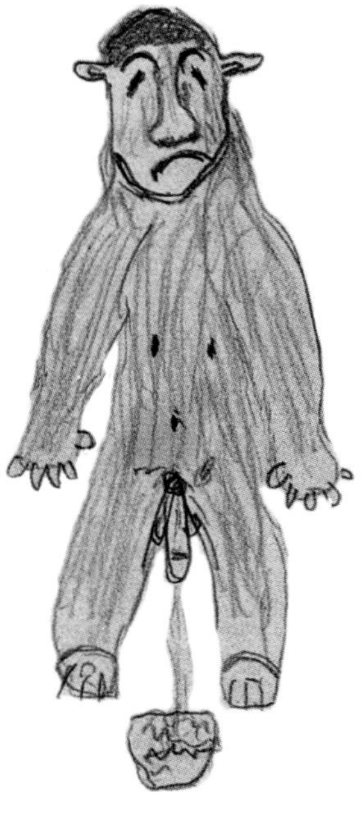

"Rasmussen's enemy," he reiterated some time later in the *Berlingske Tidende* what he had said in *Politiken* after the death of Greenland's national hero: "What I wrote at the time of Rasmussen's death about his scientific contributions was not, to my mind, a criticism but an impartial evaluation, and I stand squarely behind what I wrote."

Koch died on 6 June 1964 at the age of almost seventy-two, completely neglected. His funeral, I am told, was sparsely attended. I naturally sent a letter of condolence, and had I been in Copenhagen I would have attended the ceremony. I salute the eminent scientist. As to the man . . . I would not have chosen him as my friend. At the end of his life, Koch was unable to publish his late work—fundamental though it was—for lack of funds. His works (50 volumes, and 20,000 pages) represent a quarter of the *Meddelelser om Grønland* collection, which assembles the key scientific knowledge about the island of Greenland.

Lauge Koch spent approximately one third of his life in North Greenland (six winters, thirty-three summers) and is certainly its most eminent geologist. Can this title, which no one in the world may contest him, succeed in making the people of Greenland and Denmark forget the haughty and somewhat pathetic judgment he passed on his former leader and companion? The case serves to confirm André Malraux's epigram that "A man is nothing but a mass of little secrets."

The man I knew

I met Lauge Koch on several occasions; two of these meetings have remained particularly vivid in my memory. The first was in the spring of 1953 in Paris. While we both belonged to the same profession, Koch was a geologist interested in structures, and this was his first encounter with the dynamic morphological geology that I practiced. My methods and my program for a quantitative study of erosion, preceded and followed by geomorphological laboratory experiments and simulations, interested him vividly. We also had in common that, in our explorations, we had both crisscrossed the same area by dog sled, known the same men (Inuuteq in particular), and undergone many similar experiences. Thus ties developed between us. [3]

I questioned the older man about a few of the dramatic events in his life. A long monologue in English poured forth as we sat for some five hours in a restaurant on the Boulevard Saint-Germain. The main turning points in his life were described in detail: from his meeting with Rasmussen in 1917 to the latter's death in 1933; then his lawsuit against the Danish geologists. I have the memory of a man who was already old, trying to justify himself. Across the screen flashed the biography of a "geometer," in the sense Pascal gave that term. Lauge Koch was bitter, jealous, and revealed little-known details about Knud Rasmussen—I prefer not to say any more. Anger and sadness can make a man small, acrid, and venomous.

The other meeting, which was to be the last, took place in the winter of 1955, in Copenhagen. I visited him in his office at the ministry for Greenland. Koch had the flu and his eyes were feverish. He asked me to wait a few moments while he took some medication: "A massive dose, and I will be fit to talk to you!" He reappeared a quarter of an hour later, lucid and full of energy, his usual self.

After looking at my maps, my geological sections, my work in progress on the geodynamics of the North Greenland rockfall, and having examined specific questions about the structural geology and geomorphology, we suddenly found ourselves talking about Inglefield Land, where I had worked with Qaaqqutsiaq, brother of Ajaku, who had been one of Rasmussen's companions, and the tragedy of September 1917 suddenly arose between us in all its matter-of factness. Koch knew that I had been the first European to return to the place where he had abandoned Wulff alive and that no monument, cross, or cairn had been erected there by Rasmussen or him. And when, after searching for hours, I was unable to find the exact spot where my Danish predecessors (Freuchen and Koch) had also sought in vain for Wulff's remains, I did not feel entitled to erect a monument on an arbitrary spot. "The Eskimos, Borseman, Inukitsupaluk, they certainly told you . . . told you everything. They were there with me, half starving, in Inglefield

Illulorsuit, March 1921. Departure of the Jubilaeum Expedition toward Peary Land. Sixteen sledges are visible, along with a hundred or so dogs.

Land in September 1917. I see them, here in this room, as though it were yesterday. Ah! Let's talk of other things!"

I am quite certain that Lauge Koch was not trying to hide anything and even wanted in some way for "everything" to be discussed in detail, particularly as he knew that I was on the point of publishing a book where the subject was sure to be mentioned. He gave his version of the event again at length, often speaking aggressively, sometimes caustically, and always with great pain. But despite his attempt to maintain a scientific distance and not let his emotions get the upper hand, the suffering that I saw etched in his face has remained burned in my memory as providing the secret key to this powerful character. His suffering was sharp, undimmed after all those years.

And I thought back to the scene described to me by Dagmar Rasmussen, the explorer's wife, at one of our dinners: "A year after the tragedy, Knud and the members of the Second Expedition had gathered at Hunsted in our summer house. It was in September 1918, and suddenly a great black June bug flew into the room, buzzing. Everyone was quiet except Lauge Koch, who said, 'It's Wulff's ghost, come to pay us a visit,' in a voice that I still remember—low and hoarse. The others met this observation with silence."

These testimonies, and many others—particularly from the Thule Eskimos, some of whom were eyewitnesses of the event (and who have given me written testimony)—have led me to think about the fateful moments in the Second Thule Expedition. "Kukkok (Koch) was exceptionally brave during this expedition," Inukitsupaluk told me, "but he was so young and so strong and his eyes were so intense that sometimes at night when we were sleeping we Inuit were afraid that he would devour us. I can't tell you anymore about it tonight."

I have gone over the circumstances and the personalities of each of the expedition members, considering their varied and complex personalities. My reactions, my conclusions, have often oscillated in one direction or another. But with time, and having learned from long experience that in those latitudes and under those situations, decisions must be plucked from a tangle of elements and difficult choices made, I have kept from forming any judgment. The best is to maintain one's distance, as being the fairest course, and to salute each of these men and their great work with the respect that is due to men of exceptional destiny.

My final words, therefore, are: Honor to "Kukkok"! Honor to the unchallenged master of Greenland's geology! Honor to his courage and his solitary scientific obstinacy! Peace to those who have passed on! ■

Lauge Koch,
doctor honoris causa.

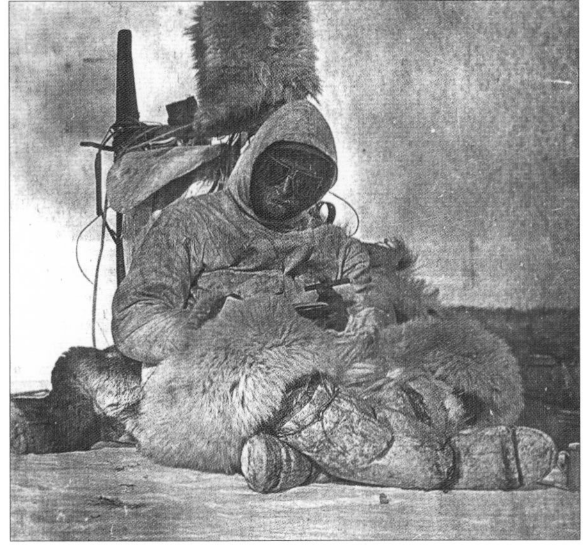

Lauge Koch during the Jubilaeum Expedition. Leaning against his sledge and smoking a cigar, the great geologist sits on the floe itself to draw up his notes. The photograph was taken by one of his companions in mid-June 1922. The personalities of Koch and Rasmussen, which were fundamentally different, could have been complementary. The tragedy of September 1917 caused an unhealthy rivalry to spring up between them. The heroes of arctic history too often harbor rages fed by implacable rivalries.

3) The first geologist of northern Greenland, he was meeting its first geomorphologist.

To the south, the crepuscular horizon, seen from Siorapaluk. Autumn, Kangek Point.

The first geologist in northern Greenland

The expedition journal of a mapmaker. Landmarks in memory.

Before me is a small pile of notebooks. They are worn and ragged, and exude a faint odor of rancid fat, gasoline, and animal blood. Some of the pages are yellow and spotted, others have remained clean, almost white and crisp. These are the pages used on the "inland ice," when we were fasting and therefore had every opportunity to stay clean. The notebooks are filled from the top to the bottom of their pages with figures, long columns of observations that would be turned into maps after the trip. Among the columns of figures are surveys of the terrain, sketches of cliffs (*fjeld*) and glaciers, and illustrations of geological profiles, drawn in colored pencils, with each color indicating a stratum of a different age. At the very beginning of the notebooks are a few lines that recount the events of the day. When I would come back to camp, almost always dead tired, often not having slept all night, sometimes even starving, I had first to go over these long columns of figures, then review the geological profiles, and, finally, when the Eskimos around me had long ago fallen asleep, I wrote down the events of the day. These were often expressed in telegraphic style. Sometimes I had the strength only to write a brief note: "Good day of traveling," or "Day from hell." When I look at these notebooks now and reflect on the first of them, written in 1913 (I was barely twenty years old), my first impressions of Greenland come flooding back to me. We were approaching the coast in driving snow when, all of a sudden, the snow stopped and the fog slowly lifted. I straightened up, looking into the air. A wall of rock emerged from the fog just ahead of us and rose higher and higher. For me, who had never seen cliffs before, it seemed as if these rocks were going to rise indefinitely. There are notes from my first summer in Greenland when I was learning to know the country and when my attention was focusing more and more on the north coast, whose geology was truly unknown. While the expedition was heading south and the cliffs of Greenland were disappearing on the horizon, I made my resolution: I would make a survey map of North Greenland and complete the provisional Danish reconnaissance of the country.

Inuit village: snow igloos and Inuit games, perhaps simulating the giants who were the legendary forerunners of the Inuit. In their period of overlap, the giants terrorized the Inuit and raped their women.

The first opportunity to do this presented itself three years later. On 1 April 1916, I embarked for Greenland once more with Knud Rasmussen as my expedition leader and the north coast as my goal. The entire voyage was supposed to last five months, but an unusually early spring kept us from carrying out our summer plans. We didn't want to return empty-handed, however, and the voyage lasted twenty-five months. But we accomplished the tasks we had set for ourselves. Melville Bay and part of the north coast were reconnoitered and surveyed.

But I had another, more important goal. There were still large expanses of land waiting for me in North Greenland. Each time we suffered from hunger, and saw our comrades die of hunger on the Second Thule Expedition, I asked myself how to make use of our bitter experiences so that the next voyage would be free from catastrophes.

Fort Conger, still standing in 1921

"Fort Conger" is situated in what appears to be a remarkably sheltered spot. It lay under a thick layer of snow that had never been exposed to the wind, from whatever quarter it blew. The snow undoubtedly covered many traces of the expeditions that have stopped here for longer or shorter periods. Despite the snow, it was easy to orient oneself. On the cliff, the monument erected by the Nares expedition still stood in good condition, and we had another memento of this expedition in the wooden panels raised in memory of the two sailors Hans and Poul, who died on the north coast of Greenland and were buried near Hall's grave. I was sorry to learn that one of my sled drivers, a very young Eskimo, took down these panels, whose importance he totally ignored. The fact was quickly noticed, however, and they were put back in place without suffering any damage. Little is left of Greely's house. The foundations are still well preserved, and many boxes can be seen nearby, their contents intact. Some coal from the nearby coal mine has been stacked on the foundations. Slightly to the northeast of this cabin, Peary and his Eskimos built their three huts. One is so tumbledown that it is no longer habitable. The second is almost entirely filled by the cache put there by Godfred Hansen for the Amundsen expedition. The third contains a camp cot and a large American stove. The roof leaks, but the house is still livable. The Eskimos call it "Peary's House." [4] The one that contains Amundsen's depot is supposed to have been built by Henson, Peary's black servant, while the tumbledown house is said to have sheltered the Eskimos.

In Peary's cabin there were still novels and magazines under the camp cot which had belonged to the Greely expedition and to Peary and his men.

Wulff, abandoned alive

At Cape Distant, I found the remains of Dr. Wulff's hunger camp [1917]. His botanical specimen box was there, as well as two books on botany, a small spade, a thermos, a moving picture camera, some undergarments, and many dog skulls, which more than anything else testified to the famine we experienced in those cruel days. While I inspected all this with great interest (I had often drunk tea out of the little abandoned thermos), an Eskimo went to the cliffs and killed six hares in a half hour.

"We are where the great Peary walked"

Nukappiannguaq, who had learned a great deal while traveling with the Americans and had a deep sense of the respect due when approaching one of these "Varde" [or cairns], asked for my permission to photograph me as I planted the flag there. He thought I could make a great sum of money from such an image when I returned to the land of the whites. Before searching the cairn, we raised our two flags on it and photographed each other at the foot of the "Varde" in more or less gracious poses. Whereupon we set to work making a careful search, moving a rock here or there in order to see better, scratching at the snow along the edges, but without turning up the least message, despite our meticulous examination. This was a great

Camp on Greenland's north coast (1921). In the center, an Eskimo (probably Inuuteq) plays the drum. To the right, the theodolite. The wheel on the back of the sledge activates a distance counter. The party will build a cairn here. The tradition in the Arctic is to remove any message found in the cairn and pass it on to the proper authorities, while leaving a new message in its place.

disappointment, and a great surprise, as the "Varde" was remarkably well preserved. I took out Peary's map and sat down to orient myself with the help of the terrain around us. Behind my back I could hear Nukappiannguaq pacing back and forth, taking big steps and coughing loudly and continuously. Startled, I turned to look at him, and he explained with a smile that he was imitating Peary. The long strides and the cough were peculiarities of Peary's in his last years of exploring. Nukappiannguaq quite proudly said to me: "We are the ones who are now walking where the great Peary once walked." [5]

The Eskimo as scientific assistant

Nukappiannguaq, the younger of my companions, was twenty-seven or twenty-eight years old—my age. As I have already mentioned, the Eskimo who was originally to have accompanied me to "Peary Land," which he knew well from having traveled there twice before, was obliged to return home, and Nukappiannguaq presented himself spontaneously. He barely had the necessary equipment. Yet despite his mediocre dog team, and though he had to wear clothes that had been made for his comrade, he nonetheless set off with the greatest enthusiasm. Unlike Inuteq, he somewhat overestimated the dangers and difficulties of the expedition, and he was ready to offer his maximum effort. The only expedition Nukappiannguaq had taken part in was MacMillan's expedition from Etah to "King Christian" Land on Ellesmere Island. Of my companions, he was certainly the one who best understood the expedition's scientific role, and he was always the easiest to persuade to give up the hunt for the sake of our survey. This is why, whenever I had to divide the expedition into two parties, one for hunting and one for scientific research, he always stayed with me. And several times along the way, he took advantage of his hunting forays to bring back little topographic sketches or panoramic drawings. He had a good eye for finding the best point of observation, and he performed valuably on mapping surveys, conscientiously studying the landscape we were to cross through the field glasses—he often pointed out details to me that might otherwise have escaped my notice. He learned quickly to break out and pack away the theodolite, and he performed this work with such care that I entrusted this task to him for the entire two years of our voyage together, during which there was never an accident. [6]

4) Fort Conger was built by Greely in July 1882 during the First International Polar Year (in the same site once used by the Discovery) and was reoccupied by Peary in 1896 during the winter when he lost several of his toes. Roald Amundsen had a cache of emergency supplies made there during his expedition to the magnetic pole and the Northwest Passage (1902).

5) Nukappiannguaq, whom I met for the first time at Etah in March 1951, was the father of my companion Sakaeunnguaq. Peary, the first white man to have impressed them, is still very much present in their minds. In 1950-1951, Imiina mimicked "the great Peary" in practically the same way: Peary's pacing back and forth, his throat clearing, and his coughing.

6) For Lauge Koch, for Erik Holtved, and for me, the Inuit proved so devoted and so intelligent at their scientific work that it would be impossible to praise them too highly.

Where Piulersuaq, the "Great Peary," walked.

The construction of the cabin that would be Lauge Koch's base at Illulorsuit (September 1920). No trace of it was left in 1950. In 1967 I gathered sod from these slopes in order to study the paleo-climate of this area.

Summer 1921. Lauge Koch is in the center.

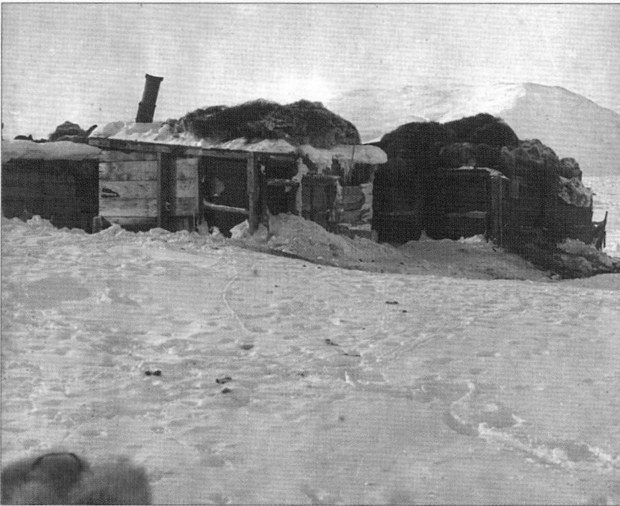

Fort Conger, Ellesmere Island, in April 1921. Koch, on his way to Peary Land during the Jubilaeum Expedition, visited the three cabins that Peary built for himself, for Matt Henson, and for the Inuit he employed. Not far away is the American station built by Greely in 1881-1883.

Two Eskimos inflate *avataq* (bladders) during the trip to Peary Land. On the right is Inuuteq (1921).

POST MORTEM, A KNIFE IN THE RIBS

ARTICLE BY DR. LAUGE KOCH, *POLITIKEN*, 22 DECEMBER 1933

With the death of Knud Rasmussen, one of the greatest figures of our time has disappeared. He was endowed with qualities and abilities that make a man a legendary hero, around whom stories and anecdotes are woven. With the passage of the years, he will no doubt be transformed, in the eyes of Danes and Greenlanders alike, into one of those great mythical figures whose existence he so often conjured up. His charm was such as to make him an immediate center of interest. He created a community of admirers around himself who did not always look at him with a critical spirit.

When *Politiken* asked me today to write about Knud, I did so gladly because I owe him a debt of gratitude. But I conceive the assignment as affording me the right to speak my own opinion, even where it differs on some points from the opinion of others. In a life as rich in events as Knud's, it is difficult to pick out the particular actions that stand above the rest and are likely to have lasting effect. First and foremost must be the creation of the trading post in the territory where Peary had worked for almost twenty years. Knud discovered this area on his first real expedition, the so-called Literary Expedition, and he returned there later as a young man and came to know the Eskimos. In 1910 he created the Thule Trading Post as a private enterprise, because the state felt unable to assume the responsibility. The first years were difficult, and Knud needed all his diplomacy and tact. A large, rich American expedition [D. B. MacMillan's] had taken up quarters at Etah during these years, and difficulties arose with the Americans and the Eskimos. Only after the war ended did Thule become a "good deal" from the financial point of view.

In the history of Greenland, the founding of the Thule station, thanks to which North and Northwest Greenland became Danish, is one of Knud Rasmussen's great exploits.

Then came the so-called Thule expeditions. The first voyage out and back across the inland ice with Peter Freuchen and two Eskimos was a brilliant use of the ancient Eskimo technique of travel and also a magnificent sporting accomplishment.

On the Second Thule Expedition to the north coast of Greenland, the Eskimo technique proved insufficient. We suffered from hunger all summer, and the Greenlander Hendrik Olsen died during the expedition, as well as Dr. Wulff. The outcome of this voyage was different than Knud had expected, and it sometimes discouraged him. But on these expeditions, he learned that the places that interested him most were those where the Eskimos had once lived. These early expeditions over the inland ice and to the extreme north of Greenland belonged, as he saw it, somewhat outside of his life's work. In the years that followed he focused his efforts more on the great voyages he had dreamed of in his youth, such as the voyage across Canada, where he visited practically all the Eskimo tribes living there today. This voyage was accomplished in 1921-1924 and made Knud our only polar explorer working on an international scale. His most important results were the Danish study of the Canadian tribes and the immense collections that will forever make Copenhagen the center of Eskimo research.

Knud Rasmussen, wearing the South Greenland cloth anorak.

When the problem of East Greenland cropped up, Knud was too active and alive a character not to take part in this work. He spent the summer of his last years on the coast of Greenland, especially between Julianehaab and Ammassalik as the leader of several multidisciplinary expeditions. But he also took part because of his love for this people he himself belonged to, because of the importance of this region as a hunting ground for the Eskimos, and because of the mythical universe of the East Greenlanders, a universe for which he felt a particular attachment.

Each of the four exploits I have just cited is enough on its own to make posterity retain this man's name. The founding of the Thule station, the Thule expeditions to the north of Greenland, the voyage to the Canadian Arctic, and the voyages to Southeast Greenland—this is what will remain of Knud after his death. Another activity that was less obvious but perhaps just as important was his commitment to creating one community out of Denmark and Greenland and fostering the sense of intimate collaboration and deep understanding that unites the Dane and the Greenlander, and the special feeling that characterizes relations between the two countries, however remarkable their differences. There also, Knud's contribution has to be accounted among the most significant.

If we consider Knud's literary production, we find it very uneven in value. The book that made his name, *Neue Mennesker* [The New People], is the best of them all. In it we find descriptions of nature, and a representation of life in Greenland—a constant thread running through his literary work, and a vein of writing in which he was unequaled. The myths are part of the natural scenery. Later, Knud's literary activity would be divided into a series of travel accounts, which were uneven, and a series of legends, which were very freely told, so that posterity will have a hard time separating the body of the tradition from the magnificent clothes contributed to it by Knud.

Knud Rasmussen and Peter Freuchen, friends from their youth, both became great writers. Knud wrote what he believed to be science, but which came to be the subject for novels. Freuchen called his books novels, but a large part consists of descriptions of reality. I am not alone in having some doubts as to the value of the collections of legends published by Knud Rasmussen. On this point he was not always well served. From childhood, Knud always felt great admiration and humility toward science, and he was very eager to serve it. Writing labels was intrinsically foreign to his nature, but I have been told that the collections he personally brought back from his voyages to Canada, where he visited the tribes in question, were labeled with care.

Still young, Knud was fully aware of his limits. To be awarded a doctorate *honoris causa* was the great dream of his life, and he hardly dared hope that it would come true. We may well ask whether such a title should have been conferred on him. He understood it as something other than it was, as more than a title; he had the impression that it was a seal of scientific legitimacy, and he interpreted it wrong.

Author's note: A single comment, which I borrow from Voltaire: "There are two monsters that ravage the Earth: intolerance and slander. I will fight them both until I die."

LORD SHACKLETON 1911-1994

AN ULTIMATUM FROM THE INUIT

The Oxford University Expedition was the first British expedition to the Arctic Ocean since George Strong Nares's valiant expedition on *Alert* and *Discovery* in 1875-1876.

The North Pole—or what passed for it—had been discovered by the American Peary (6 April 1909). The South Pole had been discovered by the Norwegian Roald Amundsen (14 December 1911), then the Briton Robert Scott (17 January 1912). The British public, which had supported and passionately followed the heroic exploits of its countrymen in the nineteenth century in search of the Northwest Passage, was disappointed not to see the Union Jack more honorably represented at high latitudes.

A group of young students at Oxford University, passionate explorers, understood this sentiment. Their expedition, under the aegis of the Explorers' Club at the university, benefited from the prestigious name of its organizer and moving force: Edward Shackleton, the son of Sir Ernest Shackleton. [1] But Edward was not simply the bearer of a famous name, he was already an accomplished explorer who had made an expedition to Borneo, and whose courage and spirit of conciliation would remain celebrated among the Inuit. [2]

The expedition's goal was Ellesmere Island. The largest island in the Canadian Arctic, it is as big as Great Britain. The earth sciences program promised to be of great interest: the island's vast expanses had only been cursorily explored by the American Isaac Israel Hayes (1854 and 1861). After visits by the Englishman George Strong Nares (1875-1876), the American Adolphus Washington Greely (1881-1884), the Norwegian Otto Sverdrup and his geologists (1898-1902), then by the Americans R. E. Peary and F. A. Cook, enormous tracts still remained to be discovered.

There were six Englishmen in the Oxford University

Edward Shackleton, 23 years old, a student at Magdalen College, where he organized the Oxford University Ellesmere Island Expedition (1934-1935) under the sponsorship of the Oxford Exploration Club. He had already led a remarkable exploration of Sarawak (Borneo).

1) Born in Kilkee, Ireland, Sir Ernest Shackleton (1874-1922) was one of the most extraordinary men in polar exploration. His name has become emblematic. Scott's rival, he reached to within 97 nautical miles of the South Pole on 9 January 1909. But his companions were exhausted, and he turned back. "I thought you might prefer a living ass to a dead lion," he wrote his wife.

2) I heard him spoken of with vivid sympathy, sixteen years after the fact, by four of my closest Inuit companions: Kutsikitsoq, Nukappiannguaq (father of my friend Sakaeunnguaq), Qaaqqutsiaq, and Inuterssuaq, all of them members of the British expedition with whom I lived or traveled. I met Sir Edward Shackleton quite late, in 1985. I was encouraged to do so by Inuutersuaq, who often said: "Go see him and give him my greetings. We write to each other occasionally; you will get along. And he must be a member of the royal family, or very nearly. He could be of help to you, and to us as well." The Order of the Garter, which Shackleton was awarded, thus made him a member of the royal family in the eyes of the Inuit!

Thanks to our mutual respect for the Eskimos, we formed a friendship that led to a common enterprise: the Second International Festival of Arctic Film, an event I founded at Dieppe in 1984. It was held at Rovaniemi in 1986 under Shackleton's chairmanship. Minister of the Royal Air Force (1964-1970), leader of the Labor opposition in the House of Lords (1975-1982), he directed that body's Private Committee for Science and Technology.

The expedition members on board the *Signal Horn*. From left to right: Winston Moore, photographer and biologist; Edward Shackleton, geographer; Robert Bentham, geologist; Dr. Noel Humphreys, physician, cartographer, and expedition leader; and Sergeant Stallworthy. Missing is David Haig-Thomas, ornithologist, who took the picture. August 1934.

The *Signal Horn*, a Norwegian sealer, en route to Smith Sound. The ship has put in at North Star Bay, at the foot of Thule's famous mountain (whose buttresses can be glimpsed), while the expedition settled administrative problems with the Danish authorities (August 1934).

Expedition. Despite being exceptionally organized by Shackleton, who sought advice and help from various sources including Knud Rasmussen, the expedition very quickly met with great difficulties, particularly in its logistics. The Norwegian ship *Signal Horn*, which left London on 17 July 1934, was in fact unable to reach Fort Conger or the Bache Peninsula (protected from the winds), owing to the extent of the ice. The expedition was forced to winter on the Greenland coast at Etah, in the very place where McMillan had established headquarters for four years on his Crocker Land Expedition (1914-1917). As McMillan had conducted numerous geological, meteorological, and ornithological studies in this sector, the Shackleton expedition's scientific program lost much of its interest.

Calendar and achievement

Let us go back over the dates: on 21 August the British disembarked in the little bay at Etah (78° 19' north) on the northwest coast of Foulke Fjord. The expedition took on a number of Eskimos, with the official consent of the Danish authorities. Unfortunately, some were "assigned" by the Danish representative, when it should be up to the expedition leader to choose his team members himself: the cohesion of the group depends on it. The Eskimo does not like to be "assigned" but chosen. The site very quickly proved execrable: the winds were strong and incessant (Etah is known as "the home of the blizzard"). Walrus and seal meat to supplement the dogs' diet had to be hunted several days' journey west of the fjord in the distant open waters of Smith Sound. And finally, an event occurred shortly after the expedition's arrival that could have been disastrous. For want of adequate facilities, a certain number of the dogs bought in Godhavn (Disko) and Jakobshavn (Disko Bay) were left to

themselves on a little island near Etah. Sixteen of the seventy-two dogs were devoured by the pack, while still others ran away on the early-autumn ice. During the winter, the winds howling down the north-south valley above Etah were so strong that the expedition did not leave its prefabricated hut (brought from England) except to make a few forays. A first attempt was made to visit the neighboring village of Siorapaluk by dog sled, but the sea ice was in bad condition and the attempt failed.

No ethnographic study of the Etah Eskimos was on the expedition's program. Its members were environmentalists, geologists, and geographers—there is a danger in specialization on expeditions to distant places, where the hazards of the weather and contingencies of every kind force you rather to be a generalist. In the spring, the expedition was ready to embark at all costs on the vast plan of geological exploration on Ellesmere Island, as originally conceived at Oxford. The heady planning stages far in the past, the British explorers hesitated to go forward. The capabilities of their expedition leader, Dr. Humphreys, as they had had every opportunity of judging during the long polar night, struck them as inadequate. Coming from Central Africa, Dr. Humphreys, an older man but a competent geologist, worried the others by his abruptness and paranoia. Tensions increased, as they can do in cramped quarters. Words flew back and forth, and an explosion threatened. Things might then have come to a head had it not been for the Inuit. They had been observing the young (and not so young) explorers and for several months had noticed a general uneasiness, though it was repressed by the imposed hierarchy. At this point the Inuit threatened to quit, waiting until the eve of the intended departure so as to avoid discussion. In this way they saved the expedition from catastrophe, without force, simply by opening the door to wisdom. The story of this singular business has never been told.

Lord Edward Shackleton, the last survivor, testifies

Yet in May 1986, at Magdalen College, Oxford, where Shackleton studied and where I was a visiting fellow, I heard the story of those days from him. We had both put on the black robes of the Oxford professor and were proceeding in single file into the thirteenth-century great hall of the college which serves as a refectory and where we were to be neighbors at the High Table. A hundred students rose to their feet as we entered. The president said grace, and the meal began. We greeted each other to right and left ceremoniously, then one after the other lifted a golden hanap to our lips, which a waiter respectfully presented to each of the guests of the High Table and which was filled with a brandy made from fruits grown on the grounds. Each in turn stood and spoke the ritual words: "*Jus tibi . . .*" evoking the inalienable rights of the fellows of the college, which had been trampled by the Catholic Charles II. Of partly Scots ancestry, I grew pensive. Suddenly, Shackleton took me aside and whispered in my ear: "Do you know . . . but surely you must, the Inuit would have told you . . ." Then a few minutes later: "I am going to tell you the whole truth." And so it was that, in this medieval hall, in fits and starts, interrupted by the shushing of our neighbors, I heard one of the most singular stories in Polar exploration.

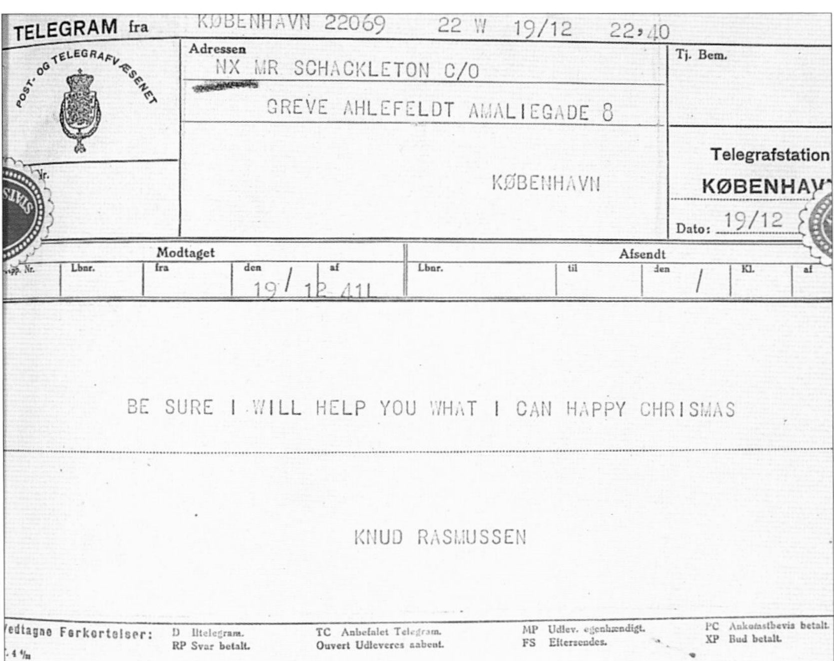
TELEGRAM fra KØBENHAVN 22069 22 W 19/12 22,40

Adressen: NX MR SCHACKLETON C/O GREVE AHLEFELDT AMALIEGADE 8 KØBENHAVN

Tj. Bem.

Telegrafstation KØBENHAVN

Dato: 19/12

Modtaget: Lbnr. fra den 19/12 af 411 — Afsendt: Lbnr. til den / Kl. af

BE SURE I WILL HELP YOU WHAT I CAN HAPPY CHRISMAS

KNUD RASMUSSEN

Vedtagne Forkortelser: D Iltelegram. RP Svar betalt. TC Anbefalet Telegram. Ouvert Udleveres aabent. MP Udlev. egenhændigt. FS Eftersendes. PC Ankomstbevis betalt. XP Bud betalt.

Telegram from Knud Rasmussen to Edward Shackleton.

"I have the right to tell you—are we not Polar Fellows?—facts known to no one else. My five companions are all now dead. I am the only survivor. Let me tell you what happened.

"Let us go back in our minds to Etah in September 1934. The expedition seemed to form a seamless whole, thanks to the attributes of its members. You know how important the group's cohesion is. I had seen to it personally, having devoted considerable time and attention to preparations. In 1932, I had taken part in the Oxford University Expedition to Sarawak (Borneo). Staff Sergeant Stallworthy, for example, whom I had chosen for our Ellesmere Island expedition, was a veteran of the Canadian Mounted Police. He had spent thirteen years in the Arctic. There were four other members, all young British students, good friends from Oxford, and very competent in their respective fields. Dr. Humphreys, who was to become the expedition leader, offered to join us. He was a biologist and a physician, fifty years old, who had acquired his experience in Africa, in the Ruwenzori, and nothing gave any indication that he was 'inclined to dark suspicions of others.' This horrible tendency only grew more pronounced as the winter progressed through the polar night, made all the more oppressive by the great gusts of wind battering us in the 'home of the blizzard.'

"The oppression grew as we brooked failure after fail-

Two Inuit dog sled teams traveling toward Grant Land (spring 1935). Nukapiangguak and Inuutaq were in charge of the expedition's Inuit support team.

ure. We were unable, in the first instance, to winter on Ellesmere Island as we had intended. Tensions mounted, and the expedition's future seemed in doubt. We played poker hour after idle hour, listened to the radio and the gramophone, all the while making plans for our spring expeditions. Our success would depend on how well we had prepared, on our equipment, but also on the dogs' food, the quantities of pemmican we had. . . and on the Eskimos, above all. But our fears about Dr. Humphreys were being confirmed: he grew more and more authoritarian, proposing plans that were truly unrealistic. The Inuit, who watched all this without a word, grew more circumspect, keeping their distance in the Asiatic way. A spirit of rebellion against Humphreys even started to spread among the other five of us, but British discipline is a strong force and appearances were maintained. Each took part in the preparations for the May-June expeditions without openly expressing his fears. At the end of March, while we were putting the finishing touches on the very heavy equipment we intended to take, one of the Eskimos—Nukappiannguaq or Borseman, I don't remember which—but one of the Eskimos who had spent the entire winter with us suddenly announced that 'The Inuit will not go with the whites. As far as the Inuit are concerned, the *naalagaq* (leader) is no good.' His abrupt manner showed just how upset he was. And they started to make preparations to leave right away, to abandon us. But without the Eskimos, the expedition was doomed to failure. Immediately, the five of us gathered—Dr. Humphreys was away. We discussed the situation briefly and found ourselves all in agreement. We decided to send the youngest of our number—Moore, with whom I had conceived the expedition at Oxford—to ask Dr. Humphreys to resign as expedition leader in the interests of all. Out of discretion, and because of my name, I held back. I didn't want to impose on the group and sink the entire enterprise.

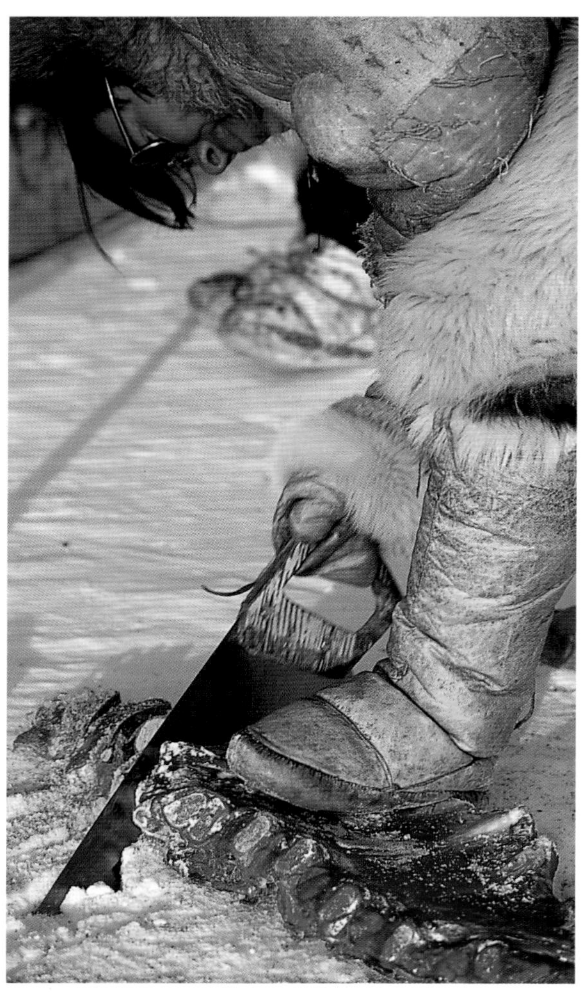

A hunter since the dawn of time, the Inuk remains a hunter, supplying 90% of his own food, consisting of meat, which he shares with his dogs.

"Moore took the assignment, thank God. It was a thankless role, but it represented our only chance. And Moore was the only one who could have carried it off. He set out on his embassy to Dr. Humphreys, who was coming and going on the floe. To kill time, some of my companions went and lay down on their bunks. I made myself a cup of tea. The tension was very great, and no one said a word. The Inuit were outside. To all appearances indifferent, they were going about their business as though they were independent of us and led a separate existence. They were busy with their sleds and their traces, as though preparing to go on a hunt or to leave us once and for all.

"After a time, Moore returned. We could hear his steps. He was with Humphreys. He opened the door cautiously. Without saying a word, he advanced into the center of the room. We watched him intently and tried to read his expression. Suddenly, he raised his thumb: 'It's "Yes,"' he said. There was a commotion. I told the Inuit of this immediately. Laconically, they said they would go with us to

Akilineq (Ellesmere Island) as planned. And they unharnessed their dogs. Humphreys had behaved gallantly."

Such was Lord Shackleton's tale.[3] What was one to make of it? The Inuit have not forgotten the misfortunes of earlier arctic expeditions, where the "folly" of the leader played a determining role: Hall and Bessels, Greely and Garlington, Krueger. . . . By giving an ultimatum, they saved the six Britons, helping them to come to a decision that was unprecedented in polar history. They provided these young white men, who were bound by their sense of discipline, an excuse to "depose" their leader. Dr. Humphreys's agreement to step down—which does him honor—was followed by a rapid reorganization of the expedition, which split into three independent parties, each responsible for its own decisions, collectively arrived at.[4] The leader's demotion was accompanied by an express condition: though he had renounced the expedition's leadership, all the expedition members were tacitly to continue to respect the initial hierarchy in their behavior and their written reports. In the historical record, Dr. Humphreys remained the official leader.

The official history and the reality

The *tuluit* (Englishmen) held to their gentlemen's agreement, until Shackleton revealed the story to me in the end. The Inuit who were present never said a word to me on this score. Their laconic account of the expedition, given our intimacy, had always somewhat surprised me.

Such are the facts. We must thank Lord Edward Shackleton for having provided, in the sole interest of truth, his irreplaceable testimony on this moment in arctic history, and for reminding us that in exploration there are always two stories: the one *ad usum delphini*, and the other, more secret, which is the expression of the most varied feelings. An expedition is a group bound by artificial ties, whose members are not heroes every day. The task at hand is to rewrite the history of polar exploration truly depicting the drives that animated each individual.

Shackleton's testimony, by revealing what had till then been obscured by official accounts, is precisely in line with the spirit of the present work. ■

3) The account, begun at Magdalen College, was completed in October 1988 when we met at the House of Lords for lunch. Our talk was continually interrupted by introductions and greetings as a procession of peers of the realm, ministers, bishops, and business men passed by.

4) Moore and Stallworthy produced a good geological study of the north of Grant Land (to 82° 25' N), revealing a mountain chain 3,300 meters in altitude. Two other sectors were also studied: western Grinnell Land, by Humphreys and Haig-Thomas (geology and archaeology); and Bache, Princess Mary, and Scoresby bays, by Shackleton and Bentham (geology and cartography). Excellent ornithological work was accomplished by David Haig-Thomas in Inglefield Fjord. Remembered fondly by the Inuit (Kutsikitsoq named one of his sons David), Haig-Thomas was killed in a Royal Air Force engagement in 1943. In July, facing difficulties, the expedition judged that it had accomplished its program. On 11 July the pack ice broke up, and the expedition reached Europe on 5 August 1935.

Angalahuq. On the trail of a hunting expedition. The steep ascent of Dodge Glacier makes it possible to reach Etah Fjord via the inland ice. The glaciers are travel routes, and the passes allow the Inuit to cross the peninsulas by the shortest path.

Lord Shackleton's secret

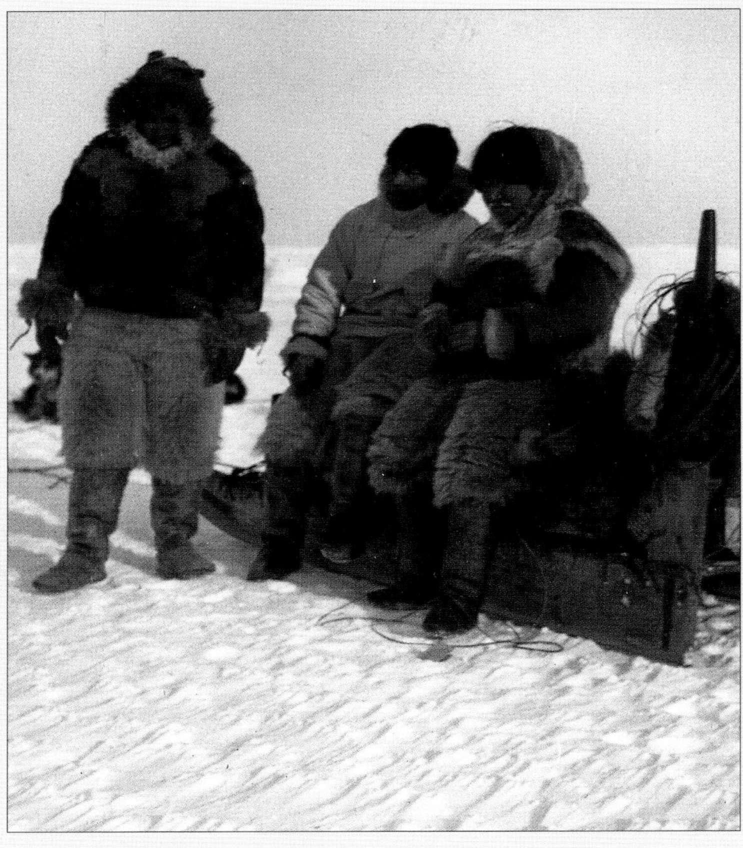

Three of the Inuit who, by their "defection," forced the Englishmen to take a painful but necessary decision when their expedition was in an untenable situation (spring 1935).

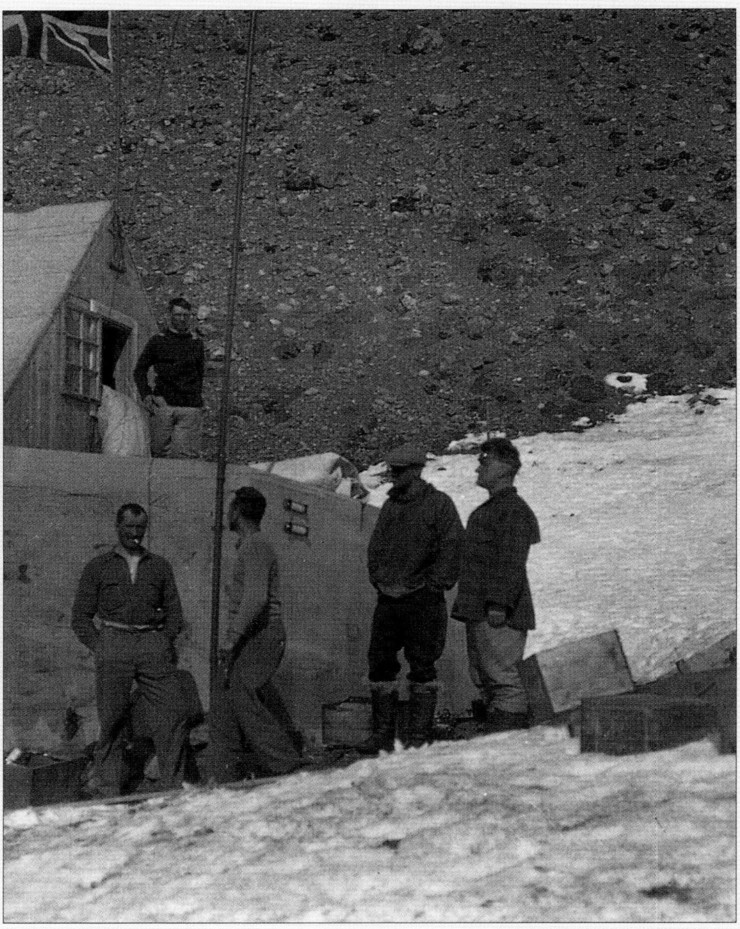

The expedition on the eve of its departure for Etah. Its reorganization had not yet occurred. 21March 1935.

Enserch House
8 St. James's Square
London SW1Y 4JU
01 930 1752
01 930 8697

7th November, 1986.

Monsieur Jean Malaurie,
Terre Humaine,
8 Rue Garanciere,
75285 Paris CEDEX 06.

My Dear Jean

Thank you very much for your letter together with the chapter dealing with the Oxford University Expedition to Ellesmere Island. I have a number of comments which I think it may be worth while using to amend.

I thought the section was very readable and can be amended without too much difficulty. Some of my comments are, of course, general.

On page one you state that the Oxford University expedition was the first to operate etc, "since the valiant and unfortunate expedition headed by Sir George Nares"... I do not think this is really accurate. Not only did Peary operate along the North coast of Greenland, but of course travelled far into Ellesmere Island, and especially on his various North Pole attempts. Nor would I have said the expedition of Sir George Nares was unfortunate. I would have thought it was a reasonably successful expedition which returned safely without loss of life (or with very little loss of life). Then of course MacMillan and others to whom you refer later did a lot of work in Ellesmere Island. The Greely expedition was the real disaster. Most of the members of the expedition died of starvation and certainly one or more were eaten by their fellow members. Also in the first paragraph where you refer to the leader of the expedition, I think I would suggest a form of words which reads something like: 'internal tension arising in part from the personality of the expedition leader'.

At the bottom of page one in the reference to myself, you are really too polite. You might wish to insert that before I went to the Arctic I had spent six months in Sarawak Borneo together with Winston Moore, where among many things I made the first descent of Mount Mulu, and it was following this that Moore and I decided to try exploring the Arctic.

- 2 -

On the third page referring to the winter, it is not strictly true to say that we were confined to the hut. Indeed, we did quite a lot of travel by moonlight in the vicinity, including one successful crossing over the ice-cap to Robertson Bay Siorapaluk (?). You also refer to the sea ice. The difficulty was that right throughout the winter the sea ice (outside the fjord) was breaking up and there was a good deal of open sea which made travel by sledge difficult, except of course over the ice-cap. There certainly were severe Katabatic winds.

In the reference to the incident with Humphreys, I do not think it is true to say he suffered from megalomania, but he was both obstinate and in a way inclined to dark suspicions of others to the point of being paranoid. I think this is a more accurate description than the reference to megalomania; and Sgt. Harry Stallworthy, an immensely experienced Arctic traveller with the Royal Canadian Mounted Police, who really understood both the Arctic and the Eskimoes, did not trust Humphreys' judgement.

On page 5, it was not Borsman, it was Inutuk who spoke to me. The reference to Moore I have already mentioned this earlier, but you may care to bring his Borneo background in at this point.

On page 6 in the dramatic description of Moore's return, he and Humphreys both came into the hut together. Moore could not speak at all at that moment but he did signal that he had succeeded. Perhaps we should add that Dr. Humphreys behaved very well and the harmony of the expedition was unaffected. This, in fact, coincides with what you have written.

Let me conclude by saying I think the description is as good an account as one could prepare of events long since past, and of course as the only survivor I cannot produce others to substantiate my story. I have no doubt, however, that it is accurate.

I hope this meets your wishes.

Regards

SHACKLETON

Letter from Edward Shackleton to Jean Malaurie, in which he moderates the characterization of Dr. Noel Humphreys as megalomaniacal, saying he was "inclined to dark suspicions of others to the point of being paranoid."

OPPOSITE,
Grant Land. Camp at the foot of a cliff (spring 1935).

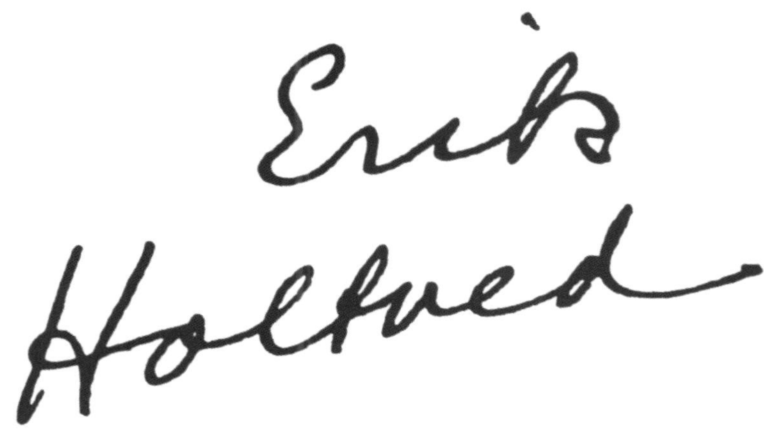

ERIK HOLTVED 1899-1981

THE FIRST ARCHAEOLOGIST IN THE HISTORY OF NORTH GREENLAND

Early in life, Holtved wanted to be a painter. But Knud Rasmussen picked him to be in charge of the archaeological program of the Sixth Thule Expedition to the southwest coast of Greenland, Lindenow Fjord, in the summer of 1931. This first contact with the Arctic would change his life.

A modest, meticulous man, who lived in great poverty while he was an artist, Erik Holtved was the first university-trained ethnologist to devote himself to the study of the Polar Eskimos. [1] He was also an archaeologist and a linguist.

During the summers of 1932, 1933, 1934, and after Rasmussen's death, Holtved pursued his archaeological research in Disko Bay and in Julianehaab Fjord. A research assistant on the expeditions he took part in, Holtved decided at the age of thirty-two to take a degree at the University of Copenhagen. There he quickly came under the notice of the great linguist and Eskimologist of Greenland's east coast, Thalbitzer, who took Holtved as his student. In 1935-1937, Holtved, accompanied by his wife, Joko, undertook the first Danish archaeological excavations at Thule and in Inglefield Land, which form the basis of our knowledge of the prehistory of the Inughuit. Extracting specimens from the frozen ground one by one, Holtved collected some twelve thousand artifacts, which he analyzed and dated.

It was on his return from this expedition that he acquired his university degrees: a master's degree in 1941, and a doctorate in 1944. After his philological expedition in 1946-1947, when he not only collected numerous ethnographic documents but also one hundred seventy-eight tales and legends, Holtved could rightly claim the title of foremost linguist of the Thule Inuit. In 1951, he would finally be named professor of Eskimology at the University of Copenhagen. The birthplace of the Polar Eskimos on Ellesmere Island (one hundred fifty prehistoric sites near Alexandra Fjord), where they lived for five thousand years, was only discovered in 1977 by my friend the Danish-Canadian archaeologist Peter Schledermann.

"Big Erik"

"Erissuaq" ("Big Erik"), as he was known in Thule, created a vast body of work. His accurate and carefully argued publications provide a foundation for the prehistory and

OPPOSITE:
Erik Holtved in the field in North Greenland, with the temperature at –10°C: tea time (Spring 1935).

1) We should however mention certain pioneers in the field: the folklorist Kroeber, though he worked from New York on objects and "living subjects" brought back by Peary for museums; the geographer Steensby, who wrote a substantial article on the material culture of the Inughuit after a short stay in the summer of 1910; and finally, of course, Knud Rasmussen, who wrote many books on folklore after his famous *Nye Mennesker* (*The People of the Polar North*, 1908). Strangely, he never wrote a scientific monograph on this people that he knew so well, though he was associated with noted anthropological studies of the Eskimos of Hudson Bay, the Canadian Central Arctic, and Alaska. Rasmussen was never on the faculty of a Danish university.

Kaalipaluk, Peary's only Eskimo son to survive to adulthood, born in 1906 aboard the *Roosevelt.* Seen here in summer 1935, he was accounted one of the ten best hunters among the seventy families. Sociologically communitarian and egalitarian, Inuit society is functionally aristocratic.

ethnography of the Inuit people; his cautious dating (using stratigraphy and comparative analysis) is authoritative in the field. He first established that an ancient Dorset people had inhabited Thule, prior to the maritime culture that we know today. Holtved then discovered remains at Inuarfissuaq of the so-called Punuk culture, with direct ties to Alaska, thus establishing a cultural link between Thule and Alaska in the fourteenth century. It was also through Holtved's digs that Viking objects—though few in number—were proven to have been known to the Polar Eskimos from the Middle Ages to the fourteenth century.

Erik Holtved recognized the enormous problems posed by the translation of tales and legends from a people as different as the Inuit. "Soul," "breath," "spirit": did these Western concepts correspond to the Inughuit idea represented in these texts? Holtved was very conscious of the problem, and basic work in semantics still remains to be done. Holtved was not a man to entertain theories; he was extremely cautious, and structuralist studies of myths left him cold, given how fragile the original materials were—which he was the first to appreciate. "Much remains to be done. I did my best, but it is only an introduction to so vast a field of knowledge." These Inuit texts come to us through successive filters: from Eskimo to Danish (Holtved was the translator); from Danish to English (through a Danish translator). It is to Holtved's enormous credit as a philologist and a folklorist that he insisted on publishing the tales word for word in the native language. And so as not to lose the intonations and pauses, Holtved had many of the legends recorded on disks.

Of course, Holtved arrived too early to make use of the filmed image, which would have allowed us to see the storyteller in all his glory: his gestures, carriage, the movement of his eyes . . . But Holtved was an able photographer and left images of great realism and significance, which provide exceptional documentation of the Inughuit. I have had the good fortune to consult this trove of images often, with its author's consent. Some of the photographs from it are published in the present book. That these photographs have not been collected in book form can only be explained by Holtved's natural modesty—and the world's general indifference.

A crucial meeting

"Erissuaq" is vividly remembered in Thule. Qaaqqutsiaq, who was Holtved's companion before he was mine, and Patdloq, his wife, and Amaanalik or Aama, who were our

Tumi. In pursuit of the bear.

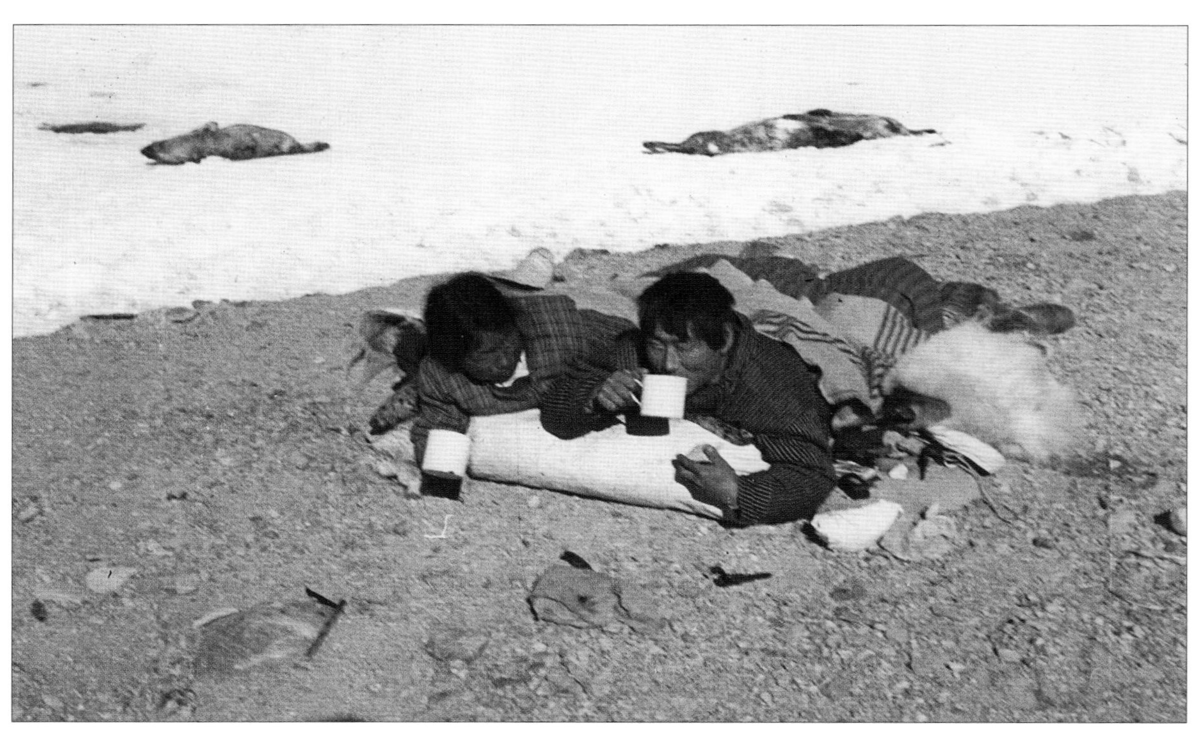

Patdloq and Qaaqqutsiaq taking their morning tea. Life is a gift: the Inuit can be hedonistic, and the quest for pleasure is always shared (March 1936, Inglefield Land).

common informants and friends, spoke to me often about his warm presence. He was discreet, and naturally aristocratic and scholarly.

Before my departure for Thule in 1950-1951, Holtved kindly agreed to meet with me. I was then a young geographer, and he told me how happy he was to see a foreigner also studying the Inughuit, particularly a Frenchman, as it would be the first time a French national had lived in those parts. He welcomed without a trace of jealousy that a colleague should work in his study area. In his office at the Museum of Ethnography in Copenhagen, we examined together the various research programs in demography and human geography that I had planned for the winter months.

When the first Danish edition of my *Last Kings of Thule* was being prepared for publication, he wrote a wonderfully elegant preface for it, and we subsequently corresponded regularly on various scientific problems, particularly concerning Eskimo names of people and places.

Erik Holtved honored me with his friendship, and we spent happy evenings together whenever I traveled to Copenhagen to do research at the National Archives or the Køgelige Bibliotek. The simple and cordial hospitality of his house on the outskirts of Copenhagen was charming. We would first speak of the scientific problems on which I wanted to consult him, then Joko, his dear and devoted wife, would set the table . . . We would then toast each other with the traditional "*Skol*," like Danish lords from another century. If necessary, we resumed our scholarly conversation later in the evening, Holtved smoking a pipe and Joko a cigar.

Free from academic pretension, Holtved would occasionally admit to his uncertainty about some aspect of the Eskimo language, which is extraordinarily complex. I can still see him climbing to the second floor of his house to check a word or phrase so that an important letter I was sending to Thule might be perfectly correct and comprehensible, or a translation I had been stuck on in Paris could be made perfectly clear.

We often, by the light of the two ritual candles on his table, spoke with melancholy passion about the "high period" of the Inuit people, who were already so dramatically threatened. And I can still see him lowering his eyes and changing the conversation whenever we touched on the problems caused by the administration's ill-considered attempts at "development."

When the subject turned to the terrible quarrels that existed between so many arctic heroes, he simply shook his head and sighed: "Is it possible that such 'great' men could so far have forgotten themselves? Let's turn to something else, my dear Malaurie, we have better things to do with our brief lives! To slander another is to dishonor oneself!"

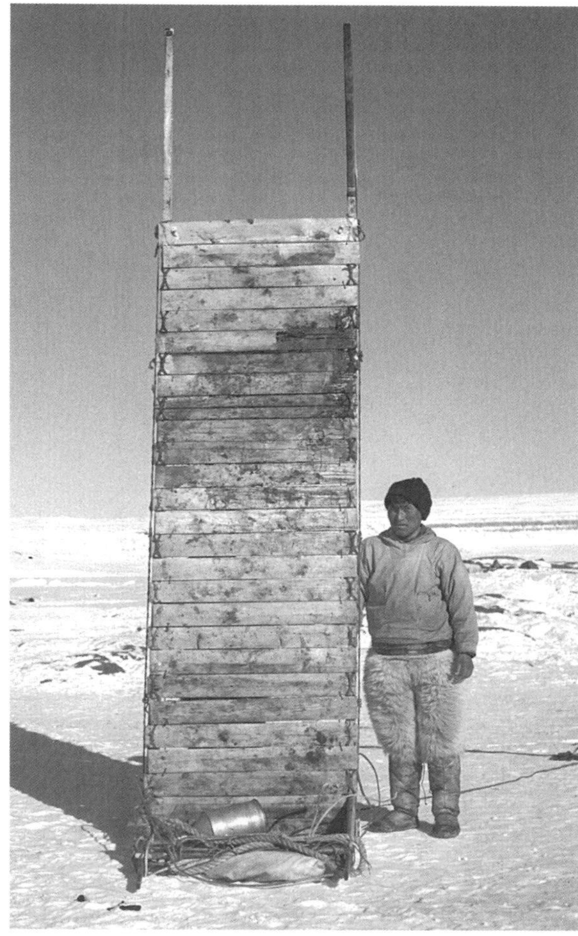

9 May 1936: Kutsikitsoq (born 1902) beside his upraised sled. Average in size for the period, this sled is 3.9 meters long, 0.915 meters wide, and 23 centimeters high. The *napuk* (cross slats) abut each other, which is a sign of wealth. Note the lashing, with seal skin thong, alternatively on the top and bottom of the slats. At the time of Erik Holtved's explorations, the largest sleds were 4.75 meters long and the shortest measured 2.87 meters. (A sled lasts a long time. It is perfectly possible that Kutsikitsoq used this same sled on our expedition together in 1950-1951.)

At the end of his life, Erik Holtved turned once more to painting. He died in Copenhagen on 24 May 1981 at the age of eighty-two. He had bequeathed his magnificent library to the new Institute of Eskimology at the university, and his photographs to the Arktisk Institut.

He was wise man and a noble soul. Undoubtedly he was among those, along with his old friend Knud Rasmussen, who most greatly honored the Eskimo people: the grandeur of its past, the pride of its present. ■

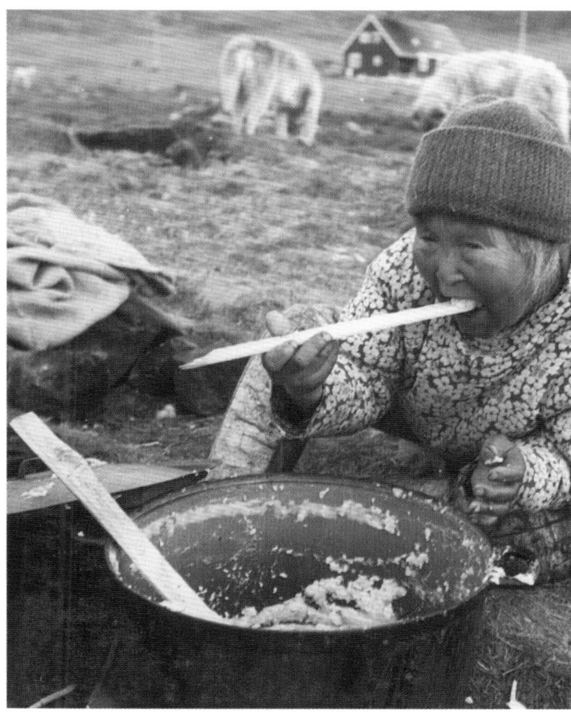

A delicacy: seal blubber. North Star Bay, summer 1936.

March 1990. Hunting for seal through its breathing hole in the ice (*agluq*). The hunter uses traditional equipment, except for the nylon rope, which would formerly have been made of seal skin.

Inuit civility

The day is ending, autumn has arrived (1938). Fishing for trout through a hole on a frozen lake. The fish is attracted by a *nakkartoun* (lure) of ivory or wood, which is jiggled up and down. The fish is then caught with the leister, or fish spear.

Aristocrats

During the hunting trip, I noticed that no one had spoken the words "tobacco" or "cigarettes," except to offer me some from their personal store. At our camp, they were not in the habit of hiding their wants, but outside, on their territory, I was their guest, and they played the part of hosts with tact and delicacy. [2]

The Thule trading post in 1936. Hans Nielsen, who was both the post manager and the administrator for South Greenland, succeeded Peter Freuchen in 1920. The trading post was intended for use by non-Eskimos, who would buy Eskimo products at a price that was both fixed and as high as possible. It then sold them, at artificially low prices, items they could not make themselves (guns, tools, household implements, wood), while avoiding all luxuries and unnecessary items.

Equality, fraternity, modesty

Qâvigarssuaq [Qaavigarssuaq], still very excited, continued his drum dance from Alaska, and in the glow of the lamps filled with seal blubber and turned down as far as possible, his wild and grotesque gesticulations started to produce their effect. The women started to shiver, but as soon as Qâvigarssuaq noticed their anxiety he started to smile and asked them if they were afraid—only to continue with redoubled violence. Inûteq, himself one of the greatest singers and drummers of Thule, had up till now looked on with a somewhat superior air; but when Qâvigarssuaq suddenly started to make fun of him and to parody his Thule dance, with its grimaces and convulsions, so different from the great style of his own Alaskan art, it was too much for Inûteq. He put off looking grave and burst into inextinguishable laughter. [3]

Names, carriers of the vital force

Now all of a sudden Qâvigarssuaq discovered that I was his uncle, owing to the fact that a man called Tiguaq had a son named Ere, just like me. But to my knowledge, Qâvigarssuaq was not related to Tiguaq, so that this kinship struck me as fairly inexplicable. Similarly, Joko became the sister of the children, and the nurse, whose name was pronounced Kullavak, had for a long time been considered the mother of old Pualorssuaq. I could not help taking this kinship lightly, and it was only later when I happened to wound my "nephew" Qâvigarssuaq severely that I discovered how strongly the Eskimos hold to their ancient conception of the importance of a name. [4]

The law of the group, the division of tasks

The heat of the room had a numbing effect on me after two days at sea, and I was going to put myself to bed when a messenger arrived from the pastor, our neighbor, inviting us to come and eat a walrus heart with him according to the ancient custom. It had been prepared Eskimo-style, which is to say that we sat on the floor around the dish of meat, which had been set on newspapers in the outer room so as to preserve the nice flooring. Afterwards we moved into the sitting room to drink coffee in the European style.

The next night, it was the manager's turn to offer us walrus heart, and on Monday morning the boats once more put to sea, but with new crews, so that everyone in turn could have a chance. Harpooning is also a right that falls to each in turn, so that every man may have the chance of getting the head with its long tusks, which are necessary for making certain Eskimo tools.[5]

The quiet strength of Aama

The women were very unhappy and had nothing to eat. One of them, a young girl, Ama [Aama], had left on Monday of the previous week—ten days before, according to what Moses understood—with no food or anything else, to cross the inland ice and reach Arfargdluarfik or Neqi in the hope of finding others who might help them.

Another young girl, Manumina, had followed her as far as the inland ice, then turned back, finding that it was useless to go further. Since then, no one had seen Ama. It was a reckless undertaking, since the ice had melted at Arfargdluarfik and its inhabitants must have gone south, so everyone believed that Ama was lost . . .

Avortungiak [Avoortungiaq] believed that even after ten days she could still be alive, if conditions were favorable, if she had really been able to reach the coast and hadn't perished in a snow storm on top of the inland ice . . . and I therefore offered to go there with two sleds to check . . . if necessary as far as Neqi. There was nothing else we could do . . .

Gradually it became more difficult to follow the tracks. The storm had been severe and the wind had swept the little blisters where Ama had trampled the snow. The older marks of the sleds were no more than thin rails of snow laid directly on the hard surface of the ice. We hardly dared think what this might mean for Ama . . .

Toward six in the morning, we finally stopped, the trail having petered out com-

Kapatak. Parka made from blue and white fox skins. Drawing by Aamma, born 1919. Qaanaaq, 1969.

Inside the igloo of Kaalipaluk (second from left) and his wife, Benina (right). In this single room measuring 150 square feet, visitors are always welcomed warmly. The sod wall is carpeted with seal skins. A coffee pot hangs from the ceiling, where gloves and boots are drying, warming over a (metallic) seal blubber lamp. A few porcelain cups are stored on the wall shelf above the sewing machine—rare signs of riches from the outside world. Photographed on 28 February 1935, in the middle of the polar night.

---

2) Code of civility. No people is more polite than a primitive people. The "barbarians," unfortunately, are too often ourselves. The jungle of our cities and daily relations reminds us of this.

The Inuit have an entire code of behaviors and gestures: of the father to his son or daughter; of the son to the uncle; of the daughter to the aunt; of the son-in-law or daughter-in-law to the mother-in-law or father-in-law; of the prepubescent girl to a male adolescent; of an orphan to a family; of the young to the old; of one group to another. The Inuit are acutely aware that their territory belongs to them and comes under the jurisdiction, if not of a nation, then of a people. Erik Holtved, as a white, was considered a stranger. They tried to remind him of this subtly while he was on their territory—of which the supreme instance was the hunting ground—by exhibiting a behavior devoid of any dependence on their part. In the neutral territory of the village, the laws of hospitality, that is, of exchange, prevail.

3) Ridicule can kill among the Inuit. Qaavigarssuaq was Rasmussen's companion on the Fifth Thule Expedition, which set off by dog sled from Hudson Bay and studied all the Eskimo groups it met on its way to the Bering Strait. In Alaska, the dances are broader and more theatrical than in Thule, where the songs and rhythms are more restrained. Dance is an inner relation, joining psychomotor and religious elements, between the Inuit and the natural environment. It harks back to the time when the hunter lived in symbiosis with the animals he believes himself to be descended from. Dance is psychically liberating but has a propitiatory function as well. The Inuit think as much with their legs, arms, and torsos as they do with their heads. When Qaavigarssuaq, who was valued and admired, though sometimes resented for being a mixed breed, gave his conceited exhibition, it succeeded in irritating his audience—but his skillful parody, performed with all the brio of the great Inuit dancers of Alaska, turned the situation around. Now Inuuteq could only join the general hilarity and give his approbation.

4) Kinship through names. Names create alliances and relations. The Inuit give a newborn the name of an important person who has died during the previous year. The baby inherits the qualities and faults of its namesake. All sorts of prohibitions and rules apply to names: one is not to say one's own name or the name of another, and one has to help anyone with the same name. Two Eskimos who have no blood relation but share the same name are apparit, that is, halves of an indivisible whole and therefore related and obliged to help each other. The Inuit have no family name.

5) The law of the group is not reductive. This egalitarian society obliges each man to surpass himself. During a walrus or a bear hunt, the roles are silently and naturally rotated in succession. The leading role—harpooning—is granted successively, that is, it passes to a different member of the group at each hunt, so that every man may surpass himself. Egalitarian Inuit society, when it is not degraded in spirit, aims at not reducing the group to its smallest common denominator, but making it reach the greatest possible, so that each can realize his personality to the full. The custom thus has the function of sparing a bad hunter the humiliation of being always considered second-string. It corrects a natural inequality.

Drum dances are performed mostly in summer, when taboos are fewer and less strict. They are not restricted to a single sex: in the photo on the right a woman is dancing. Psychologically (and sexually?) liberating, the drum dance can set off a sort of ecstasy that is related to *perlerorneq* (approximately translated as "polar hysteria"). The Eskimo drum is called *qilaun*. It measures 20 cm by 30 cm. The head (*isaa*) is made from the stomach of a dog.

pletely. We returned to the last place where we were still certain of the tracks and worked outward in wider and wider circles searching the ground. Suddenly, we heard a shout from Maigssánguaq: "Here!" Ama had finally turned back, but heading in a more easterly direction, toward the land . . .

We discovered that Ama had traveled through a terribly desolate area. The snow had hidden the accidents of the terrain, and I constantly stumbled, my feet getting caught between the stones at the bottom, so that finally I had to jump from rock to rock . . .

We now found ourselves in a stream bed, which would lead us without the slightest doubt directly to the coast, and it was obvious that Ama had followed the same path. The cliffs were sheer on either side. We could not go astray, but the snow had now become deep and soft, so that the dogs sank heavily into it and had to struggle to make any headway . . .

Not long after, a sled appeared in the distance. It was Angutdluk and Utuniak, who were returning to Inuarfigssuaq to celebrate Pentecost. They informed us that Ama had returned that very day "when the sun was there!" Given the direction they were pointing, it must have been before noon, and when I asked Angutdluk how she was, he answered that there was no "how" to report, so she must have been all right. She was only a little tired. During the past five days she had not had anything to eat, but then she did not herself know just how long she had been away . . . Little Ama, whom we had thought lost when she had tried a difficult crossing of the inland ice to bring help to her family that was starving! [6]

The drum song

People readily came to visit us once a day, either from curiosity or to see the walruses. One day, during one of these visits, I suddenly noticed that Qaaqutsiak, [7] lost in thought, was playing with a stone and drawing something on the surface of the rock. Gradually the stone moved more and more agitatedly, then he started forcefully to tap out an impetuous rhythm, singing in a very low voice, so quietly that even a few steps away he couldn't be heard. [8]

Moses, who was sitting next to him, was certainly aware of this occurrence, but he acted as though nothing were happening. After a time, Qaaqutsiak seemed to emerge from his trance and spoke again in a normal voice, but it was clear that he had had an "attack" of drum dancing, while everything around him remained perfectly calm.

Excerpts from *The Polar Eskimos: Language and Folklore* (Copenhagen: MOG, 1951).

The *ingmerneq*, or drum song. Two singers (Inuutersuaq and Inukitsorssuaq) stand facing each other. One holds the drum and sings, while the other, following him in silence, his eyes half closed as though "absent," holds a little piece of wood that he will twirl between his index fingers at the end of the song. Only then will he join in with the first singer, who will raise the drum in front of his face. Both will cry out "Ueye! Ueye!" in gradually accelerating rhythm. These codified songs (each has his own *pisia*, or individual style and tone) express the singers' joy at belonging to the group and reaffirm man's alliance with the invisible forces. January 1936.

6) I knew Aama in 1950-1951 and encountered her again in my later travels. She was still living in 1982. Her husband Piuaatsoq (the Peaceful) died at the end of the 1980s. When I questioned her on this again in 1982, Aama gave me the same answer: the adventure was of no importance to her.

7) Qaaqqutsiaq. My faithful and exemplary companion in 1950-1951.

8) Inuit song is not a mental construct or a ready-made item that one uses. It is the very expression of the inner, instinctual life. Each singer has his rhythm and his tone (psia), which are his very own. A song is the property of its author, and as long as the author is alive, no one else has the right to sing it. Many archaic terms are used, which the contemporary Eskimos do not always understand.

Animal skin . . .

A *nanoraq* (bear skin) dries in the sun and the wind. This work is performed exclusively by women: Avoortungiaq delicately removes the fat from the hide (summer 1936).

Patdloq, wife of Qaaqqutsiaq (and grand-daughter of Tornit, one of the immigrants from Canada in 1862), hangs seal skins from a tripod to dry them (summer 1936, Erik Holtved's archaeological expedition to Inglefield Land). Patdloq and Qaaqqutsiaq took an active part in my geomorphological expedition to Inglefield, Washington, and Ellesmere lands in 1950-1951.

Making a kayak. Six meters long and 60 centimeters wide, the kayak (which is strictly a personal object) has been used only since 1863-1870. It takes five or six fresh, dehaired seal skins to cover the kayak's frame. Here, the skins are sewn by the hunter's wife with a thread made from narwhal or beluga whale which she has made supple between her teeth. The needlework is of crucial importance: the watertightness of the kayak depends on it. Since 1892, the bone needle has been replaced by the metal needle. July 1936.

Preparing a seal to be cut up. Before a seal is butchered, it is laid on its back and its skin is scored in four places. Then the thorax and the flippers can be skinned. The animal is then turned over, the scores in the back are widened and the meat is cut up. The skin of the thorax from the head to the tail is used for making soles for boots, lanyards, and straps (see Erik Holtved, *MOG*, 1967).

RIGHT: **making a bladder** (*avataq*). The skin of a ringed seal is emptied entirely. The orifices and the harpoon wound are carefully sewn up or plugged with a wooden stopper. The skin is scraped of its hair with an *ulu* (woman's knife), then turned over and scraped of its fat after drying inside and out for a long time. Only then can it be inflated to serve as a bladder when hunting walrus or beluga whale, serving to tire the animal and keep it from diving into the depths. July 1936.

JEAN MALAURIE

FROM THE KINGDOM OF THULE TO INTERNATIONAL ACTION

1950 was the year of all-out confrontation. 1990 was the year of reconciliation : in the interest of objectivity, I asked Eva Rude, the Danish journalist and president of the Danish and Greenlander Women's Association, to interview me about my life and research in Northern Greenland. Here are some of the answers she elicited.

Q: Jean Malaurie, most Greenlanders are aware that you are an admirer of the Danish hero Knud Rasmussen, to whom your book* The Last Kings of Thule *was dedicated. It is my honor and pleasure to tell you that as far as we Danes are concerned,* The Last Kings *is a major classic. The childhood of Kunnunguaq—"our own Knud," as the Inuit call him, led to his choice of Thule as the focus of his international effort on behalf of the Arctic. How great a part did the experiences of your own childhood play in your researches?

A: My childhood was one of dreams and hibernation, and when I was a boy one of the books that made a strong impression on me was *Nils Holgersen.* I dreamed of flying like him across the vast frozen north on the back of a wild goose. Otherwise, two other texts entranced me: Stevenson's *Treasure Island,* and Dickens' *Oliver Twist.* In fact, I think *Oliver Twist* made me aware of the concept of humiliation, as part of the human condition. My first grievings as a child were over that book, and I owe it to Dickens that I then began to understand how alone I felt in the world, despite the presence of my sister and my two brothers. During my teens, the three writers who impressed me most were Chekhov, Gorky and Katherine Mansfield. The steppe, the world of the wanderer, the literature of the unwritten things and the silences that exist between men, the practical ABC of life's tremors, were already the most important things to me. Some people may find it odd that I don't mention Jules Verne, nor any book specifically about the polar regions, but there simply wasn't one that engaged me. Nevertheless for several months during the final stages of school I found myself riveted by the novels of James Fenimore Cooper. Then came James Oliver Curwood and Jack London, who were my first guides in the woods and snow. At the Lycée de Saint-Cloud, and later at the Lycée Condorcet in Paris, I lived in a kind of waking dream. I worked the soil in a corner of the big garden at our family house in Garches. I watched the flowering of humble primroses and honeysuckle with the keen interest of a naturalist. And in the woods nearby, which had the comical name of Saint-Cucufa, I felt the awakening of a lifelong attachment to trees. Trees are still a passion for me. Over the last few years I have planted 1500 of them in Normandy, and when they suffer in any way I suffer along with them.

It was purely by chance that I discovered the wide open spaces and the feats of the great explorers. I was at school

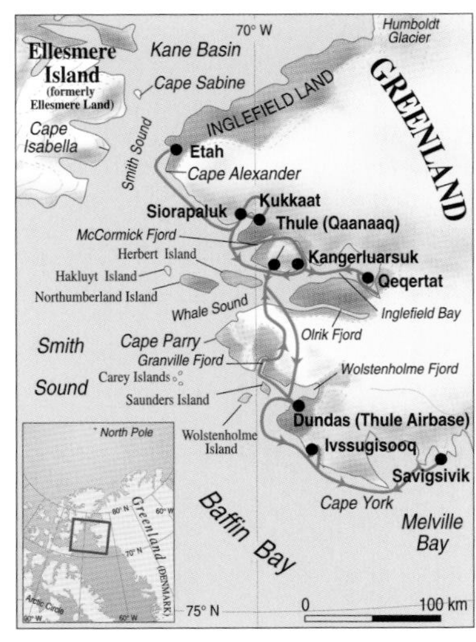

Jean Malaurie expedition (by dog sled). Winter 1950-1951 (November to March).

OPPOSITE:
Back from expedition in Inglefield, Washington, and Ellesmere lands. North Star Bay, Thule, 20 June 1951. (Photo by Sakaeunnguaq.)

My father and mother, Albert and Isabelle Malaurie, on their wedding day. Saint-Nazaire, 31 July 1912.

Center:
Jean Malaurie, Mayence (1928).

Right:
Monique Malaurie and Guillaume (Kutsikitsoq), my son, 1957.

at the Lycée Condorcet, near the Gare Saint-Lazare in Paris, and I often spent my lunch hours in the gigantic Citroën showroom looking at the cars my father didn't own—and never would own, just like his son after him. One afternoon, I saw a film that was showing round the clock on the showroom's small screen: it was called *La croisière jaune.* I can still see the roads in that film—and the half-track vehicles of George Hardt and Louis Audouin-Dubreuil struggling through the high mountains of Tibet. I never suspected as I drank in these images that I would see them again ten years after and talk about them with Pierre Teilhard de Chardin, one of the most illustrious savants of the Société Géologique de France. It was this great geologist who introduced me into the complexities of palaeo-anthropology in his modest rooms at the Rue Monsieur headquarters of the Jesuits.

Q: France, like Denmark, was brutally occupied by the German army. How did you react to this, as a teenager?

A: I was born into to what you might call the nationalist, Christian bourgeoisie. My father was a university professor and a patriot who had been seriously wounded in the first months of the 1914-18 war, after being the first French officer to enter Alsace. Thereafter he worked for the Deuxième Bureau at Belfort. The horror of the great European civil war persuaded him to join with Konrad Adenauer, the Mayor of Cologne, and above all with Dr Dorten, in an intellectual Franco-German reconciliation, within the framework of an autonomous Rhine-Palatinate. Poincaré, Barrès, the University of Strasbourg, my godfather Léonard Constant, the philosopher, friend and inspirer of Marc Sanguier (who founded the *Sillon,* the first Christian socialist movement), Jules-Albert Jaeger and Dr. Bucher, Alsatian patriots all, and all supporters and friends of my father, were likewise associated with the project. That was why I was born at Mayence, beside the River Rhine, where I spent eight years of my life and became deeply imbued with the legends and gods of the Teutonic pantheon.

Cutting up a hare for the first time in boy scout camp. March 1936.

My father died when I was seventeen, and my mother when I was twenty-one. I watched, like all my generation, with immeasurable sadness as France collapsed before the German onslaught, and the pride of our nation, the French army, was completely routed. After the fall of France, I witnessed the cowardice of my people: in 1941 I was one of the very few young students to attend the funeral of the great philosopher Henri Bergson at Garches, near Paris, where I lived. Three or four young men, and only a few rather mute officials, were the only people there! From that day forward I have maintained a vigorous mistrust for intellectuals, who tend as a class to be utterly pusillanimous in the face of peril. And I think that on the same occasion I acquired my absolute and enduring horror of racial persecution.

I joined the French Resistance in the most natural way possible. Since I belonged to a graduating class that had been sacrificed by the Laval government (1942) I immediately abandoned my studies (I was preparing for the exam for entry into the Ecole normale supérieure at the Lycée Henri IV in Paris) and went underground (June 1st, 1943). I only found out in the aftermath of the war how few of us there really were in the Resistance, when I received my *carte de réfractaire* (no.3730). The vast majority of the French bourgeoisie played the waiting game endorsed as a virtue by the elderly Marshal Pétain: but my deepest being rose up against this idea. Like my dear friend Marie-Madeleine Fourcade, the head of Europe's most extensive resistance network, the fight was all I cared about. In the history of a great nation, there are certain principles that brook no discussion.

Q: Which texts and personalities most influenced your thinking during your adolescence?

A: I have always instinctively rejected books about theories and systems that looked like they might smother my own creativity. Of course major works like those of Spinoza, Descartes, Kant and Nietsche were the basis of my first philosophical studies. But before long, categorical, closed systems began to make me uncomfortable and suspicious. This instinct is deeply rooted in me. Marxism and psychoanalysis and scientific anthropology, the pillars of contemporary thought, seemed inadequate on many counts to the specific conditions of the people of the polar north and the nomad civilizations of the world's deserts. And then I grasped the fact that the brilliance, talent and genius of these founding fathers of *soi-disant* universal ideology and theory, who wrote before the full inventory of all the organizational systems of the universe had been completed, were more than likely to stop me following my own ideas to their conclusion. Since studying philosophy, I have carefully pursued whatever was in harmony of rhythm and thought with my own inner quest—and then stretched it further. If you do anything else, you run the risk of merely dabbling. Proust constantly reminds us of the need always to go beyond research into the realm of creation [1]. Never forget: some great works have the power to kill.

Some of the adventurers who are closest to my heart—Giovanni Battista Vico, Michelet, the geologist Suess for his admirable *Antlitz der Erde* (The Face of the Earth), Rimbaud, Bernanos, Bachelard, Simone Weil and all the rest—what beacons of hope they were to me as I groped through the fog of my student youth! To their books, the friends of all my sleepless nights, I owe the happiness of having lived my true destiny. [2] At university I was a militant unionist and was president of the Paris Geography student's union for two years at a time of great uncertainty (1945-46). The lonely road of self-discovery can be a thankless one as well: when we are young we must avoid conventional reflexes and blood-instincts like the plague. But if we reach the final years of life and look at ourselves and feel that we have been loyal to the main lines of our original choice, then we can congratulate ourselves that at least we are not among those who, out of craven weakness, have surrendered to the rules of the group. Of dissatisfied people like these, their liberated brothers must beware. They are like the dog in the La Fontaine fable, whose neck was galled by his collar, but who nevertheless persisted with the forced smile of conformity—only to discover in secret, after many awful years, that he was the prisoner of no-one but himself. It infuriates such people to see rebels like me daring to live the life of their choice. My own freedom, previously acquired in dribs and drabs, was finally confirmed among the Inuit at the age of twenty-six. I owe my personal, joyous liberation to the Inuit. They are my true family.

Q: How did you recognize them as your family?

A: It wasn't so much the taste of a *madeleine* that did it, as the smell of the skin of an animal. This smell raised in me two very vivid memories. It was in November 1950: one evening I was driving my dog-sled through the polar dusk, by the milky light of the moon. I was heading through Whale Sound, on my way back to my base camp at Siorapaluk. I can pinpoint the location almost exactly—close to the sandstone cliffs of Qaanaaq, not far from Cape Tyrconnel. Everything around me was dark green. I was alone for the first time, alone with my own harness dogs. The Inuit hunters had stayed behind in their igloos at Kangerlussuaq. They were eating. I was racing onward, brimming with the joy of my new-found freedom in the polar desert after mastering the complexities of a man's relationship with his dog team. I was moving across a skin of ice a foot thick beneath which the sea was 500 fathoms deep. The Eskimos had advised me not to go near the capes, where the ice was thinner—but how was I to identify them in the moonlight? Crevasses might open in front of me at any moment: many men have lost their lives that way. Nevertheless I was happy and utterly at peace, so strong was my bond with my dogs. Nothing could hurt me; at the top of my voice I sang a Gregorian chant, then tried to remember the sequence of somber musical phrases that makes up the overture to *Don Giovanni*. In my nostrils was the pungent animal odor of my *qulittaq*, blended with the reek of my own perspiration. I closed my eyes, and in that instant saw myself at five years old lying on a rough bed in a chalet somewhere in the Black Forest, to which I had been carried after a terrible accident. I had been struck by a German car and brought there,

June 1943: I refused to be drafted for the shameful STO, the "Service du travail obligatoire," an obligatory two-year stint of work in Germany for all French citizens, ordered by the Vichy government in 1942.

Washington Land, near Cape Jackson and Kennedy Channel (80° 03' N, 67° 06' W). I was making a cartographic survey and a systematic study of the areas of rockfall.

1) "It is for [my mind] to discover the truth. But how? What an abyss of uncertainty whenever the mind feels that some part of it has strayed beyond its own borders; when it, the seeker, is at once the dark region through which it must go seeking, where all its equipment will avail it nothing. Seek? More than that: create. It is face to face with something which does not so far exist, to which it alone can give reality and substance, which it alone can bring into the light of day." *Swann's Way*, trans. Scott Moncrieff (New York: Random House, 1934), I, 35.

2) Think of the extraordinary effort made by certain adolescents of this lost generation, like me stamped by the rigid and stereotyped seal of their education, to eliminate and then reconstruct themselves.

1948-1949: geographer for the Paul-Emile Victor expeditions. The half-track vehicles had a difficult time in the area chosen for the Central Station. Some 50 miles across, 350 miles from the coast, and near the high point of the inland ice (at above 3000 meters), the site was chosen as a semi-permanent laboratory for meteorological, glaciological, and geophysical observations, staying in operation for several years.

barely conscious, injured in the left knee and with my arm in a sling. Sunlight was filtering through the shutters: it was spring. My bed was built roughly of broad planks and covered in dog skins. I could hear birdsong and the coughing of stags in the forest.

Later I had another Proustian experience: in February 1951, I found myself again on a sledge but this time side by side with my friend Kutsikitsoq. We were traveling towards Ummannaq, the tiny capital of the Inuit of Thule, in North Star Bay. The temperature was minus 45° C; far away to the south there was a glimmer of dawn, which sent its rays across the surface of the snow and bathed the vast ice floe in violet and pale pink. We had been moving at full speed for four hours. We were huddled in our furs, made of reindeer and bear skins, to keep out the cold. In the empty, crystalline air was the scent of sea salt. At that moment, in my mind's eye I saw myself walking on the Rhine, as I had done in my childhood, and felt very distinctly the soft pressure of my father's hand over mine. He led me out on the ice that covered the great river during that exceptionally cold winter, and together we crossed from one bank to the other. We were still living in Mainz; I was frightened and I cried. My fingers touched the tears on my face and found them turned to ice.

My father, a blue-eyed Viking, was a tall, slender man who taught his children the value of courage and achievement. He seemed an immense and lofty figure; yet this brilliant officer and history scholar could at times be wonderfully tender with me, despite his austere Jansenist manner. It is to my mother, however, that I owe any Scottish atavism, dry humor, and gaiety that I possess. I am reminded of her whenever I meet a kilted Highlander on the moors, or in a Dundee bar. My ancestors on my mother's side, the Carmichaels of Baiglie, were loyal to the Stuart dynasty: James Carmichael went into exile in France with Bonnie Prince Charlie after the Battle of Culloden, independent Scotland's equivalent of Waterloo. Who knows? Perhaps I remember these ancestors in the wave of emotion that engulfs me when I survey a Scottish landscape of lakes and hills, so akin to the polar horizon, or hear the near-human wail of bagpipes. Indeed it was probably my Scottish side that set me on the path I took in life.

Q: You were also a great lover of deserts. Apparently you were in the middle of the Sahara when you received the Danish government's permission to enter Thule. Why did you choose the cold desert over the hot one?

A: Perhaps because I wanted to help in the protection of what I consider to be the essential factor in my life. I mean the freedom of ideas which I have preferred to the study of the great philosophers. I wanted to find thoughts that were more universal, those of stones and of men of all conditions and all continents in all their humble daily truth. Inspired by Vico, I chose geography as my discipline of the mind: I resolved to follow the personalized courses which the grand master of physical geography, Emmanuel de Martonne, was imparting to a few students selected by him at the University of Paris' Institute of Geography. After that, wishing to go beyond Martonne's own *Traité de Géographie Physique (1910)*, which was beginning to appear outdated, I dedicated myself (with his blessing) to the quantitative and serial geodynamics of the earth's activity, which eventually led me to laboratory work on geocryology. In this way I came to specialize in the study of desert screes, those masses of rubble that lie around the bases of cliffs. The study of such screes offers precise evidence of erosion over time.

As a geomorphologist and analyst of rock forms, rock reliefs and their history, I became a specialist in the dynamic processes embodied by masses of homometric stone. I was drawn to the idea of determining the results of mechanical and chemical erosion in a given place and climate over a precise period of time: specifically, the post-glacial era in North Greenland, over eight thousand years. Another specialty of mine was the study of similar formations in the Sahara desert. Why the Sahara? Because to compare is to begin the process of rationalization. And why the desert? No doubt because of my love of solitude, but also because the spaces in arid zones are, for the geomorphologist, more bare and more readable in their geometric forms. I love constructed spaces. In the Arctic, plateaux and valleys are colorless in winter and spring, being uniformly covered with snow. After close examination, the vast horizon falls into a kind of order, built as it is by stages, like a drawing along the same lines of force that Inuit carvers express in ivory with such extraordinary accuracy. It was during my theoretical researches in geomorphology that I became smitten with the polar environment as a whole, and began reading about Roald Amundsen, Edward Peary, John Franklin and, above all, Ernest Shackleton.

Q: Of course—but nearer to you than any of these was Paul-Emile Victor, with whom you traveled as a geologist in 1948 . . .

A: I was present at the first informal meeting in 1946 of the Club Alpin Francais, a committee which included 'polar' adventurers from every walk of life. There were about twenty of us—scientists, travelers, missionaries, artists and enthusiasts. At the end of the table was Paul-Emile Victor, a French explorer, who in his skilful, modest way offered to place his private secretariat at the service of our somewhat confused medley of needs and wishes. This meeting and the co-ordination that was its sequel led to the creation of Missions Paul-Emile Victor, a private association for the promotion of French polar expeditions.

This organism was reinforced in 1947 by Edgar Faure's finance ministry with a credit of 40 million francs (he later became my friend)—and on behalf of the Académie des Sciences, Emmanuel de Martonne proposed me as official geographer to Paul-Emile Victor's first and second polar expeditions to Disko Bay in western Greenland (1947 and 1948). The principal goal of these expeditions was to build in the center of Greenland, 400 km from the coast, on the main glacier and at an altitude of 3000 meters, a French meteorological and glaciological station—to be known as Central Station. The exact spot had been baptized *Eismitte* (middle of the ice) by the German geophysicist Alfred Wegener during his heroic but tragic expedition in 1930.

Our team began by moving forty tons of material into place, building a road six kilometers long using iron bars and explosives, and devising a cable system for crossing a barrier of rocks. Thereafter my personal task was to continue my research on rockfalls, begun in the Hoggar region of the Algerian Sahara and in the south of Morocco. I believe that I was the first to tackle this fundamental problem in the north of Greenland. During the winters of 1949 and 1950, for the sake of comparison, I undertook solitary missions for the CNRS to study the transmission of temperature and rapid temperature changes (from freezing to over 70°C) in the dry rockfalls in the Hoggar, and around the sub-humid cliffs of Oued Draa in southern Morocco.

In late 1949 I decided to leave the French polar expedition and conduct my own more specific and personal researches of arid-zone geomorphology further to the north (76°-80°), outside the perimeter allocated by the Danish government to Paul-Emile Victor (69°-70°). The purpose was to study the anthropogeography of the northernmost people in Greenland. Again on behalf of the CNRS I made a solo expedition to visit the Inuit group at Thule, numbering 302 souls, before continuing onward through the desert tundras of Inglefield, Washington and Ellesmere, 10° farther north. This third mission was the subject of my book *The Last Kings of Thule,* which came out in 1955.

All of my subsequent expeditions (31 in all) were made for the CNRS, the EHESS, and the Center for Arctic Studies which I founded in 1957. For the most part, I traveled alone among the Inuit.

Q: Your focus changed from the study of stones to the study of human beings . . .

A: Let's talk about the stones before we go any further. The geomorphological analysis of the polar regions, on which I concentrated my researches for a period of 15 years, in my view yielded general information of the highest importance, both for the understanding of erosion processes in peri-glacial

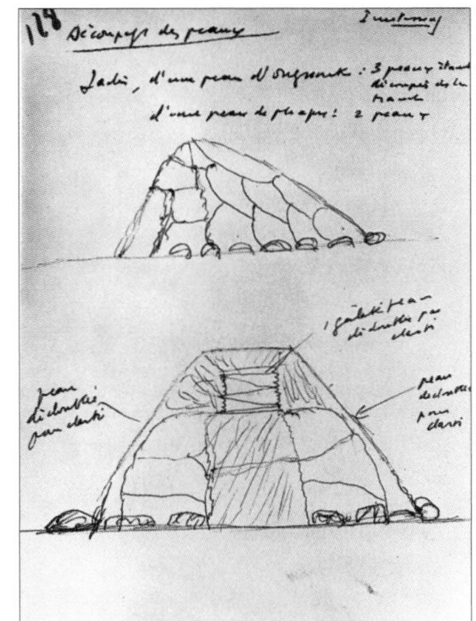

Tent used during the eight weeks of summer, made of seal skin. Half way up, the skins are cut into strands to allow light in. It also has a window of thinned hide. The stones at the base serve to anchor the skins. Inutersuaq, 1967.

Puffin.

The south coast of Washington Land, a few miles from the entrance to Kennedy Channel. This was the northernmost section surveyed between late March and early June, from Etah to Cape Jackson, to a depth of three miles in from shore. This territory, the furthest point reached by birds, is deserted. It is 150 miles from the nearest inhabited spot.

In Thule-Ummannaq, July 1950. The young academic between his silent Inuit teachers: on the left, Uutaaq, discoverer of the Pole with Peary in April 1909; on the right, Inukitsupaluk, the companion of Peary, Rasmussen (the tragic 1917 expedition), and Lauge Koch (the Jubilaeum Expedition, 1922-1923).

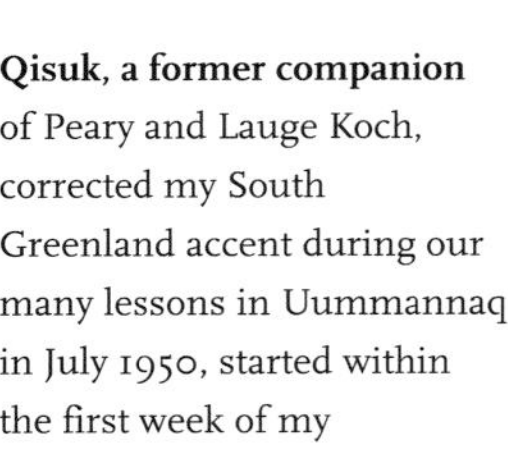

Qisuk, a former companion of Peary and Lauge Koch, corrected my South Greenland accent during our many lessons in Uummannaq in July 1950, started within the first week of my disembarking.

zones—where the phenomena of freezing and erosion were little understood in France, the Soviet Union and the USA—and for research into the paleomorphology of temperate zones, notably in France, the cradle of European prehistory. There have been dry climates, humid ones, cold ones, less cold ones, sub-arctic ones, arctic ones—who is to distinguish between them from a scientific standpoint, if not the geomorphologist? Only a detailed comparison between surfaces of stones, cross-sections of earth, rock lichens, profiles of gradients, and the deeper structures of European and Arctic screes can make it possible for us to judge and determine the significance, or otherwise, of a biotope. And the subsequent analyses of the social structures, ways of life and eating habits of Paleolithic and Mesolithic hunters, along with their religious and pictural outlook, will naturally be conditioned by an exact appreciation of the climates they had to face and the environments in which they lived. The least we can say is that those conducting French prehistoric studies just after the war were seriously ill-equipped and ill-prepared in the field of geomorphological research. And you can easily appreciate how important it was for the general study of European prehistory that there should be detailed analytical research in the highest latitudes such as I intended to carry out. My work began in 1948 and as I said before it quickly became focused on Arctic rockfalls. No-one had concentrated on this field before: it was a brand-new one. At the time, only a single American geologist had published a study on the rockfalls of the Rocky Mountains : this was Anastasia van Burkalow, writing in 1945. Accompanied by this ghostly, romantically-named colleague, and another, H. Behre, who wrote a short article on the screes of the Rockies, I began my lonely and mute dialog on the subject of the vast rock slopes of Greenland.

I was also fascinated by Cubist theories on the nature of landscape. I had read a treatise on landscape by the painter André Lhote and was intrigued by Marcel Duchamp's *Nude Descending a Staircase*, a static painting of movement. My own highly specialized, systematic work (there were only two or three others working on these problems at the time) was begun in humid sub-Arctic conditions (Disko Bay, which is frozen for seven months of the year) and continued from 1950 onwards on the northern coast of Greenland (where the sub-soil is frozen to a depth of 1500 feet, and where the sun is absent for three months of the year). It was at this time that I worked out the definitive methodological procedures that were to serve me constantly thereafter. [3]

I operated in the following way. On a sheet of ruled paper affixed to a board, I set out to find the hidden architecture of a given landscape, from outcrop to outcrop. Many of the plateaux I traveled through had never before been visited by 'white men.' After making my sightings from the ice floe, I climbed to the top of the plateau having set my aneroid barometer at zero, at sea level. With a pencil, I divided up the various masses and directional lines—shorelines, thalwegs, cliffs, stepped levels—and a hierarchy of volumes gradually emerged. Constructive lines of direction, angles, curves and straight lines distributed themselves through my sketch, as from valley to valley of the snow-clad landscape I hunted for the place around which the eye of the surveyor could give it some kind of order. [4]

I soon realized that the geodynamic interpretations that constituted the aim of my research were only valid when based on extremely precise—and therefore highly localized—data. Thereupon I set myself to make observations mostly backed up by figures and taken from a very few points. This procedure, given that physical geography had for so long been descriptive and typological in nature, was completely new. The Eskimo hunter who accompanied me remained with the dog teams and sledges in the ice floe; I climbed the rocks, which sloped from 27° to 35°, rising between 100 and 200 meters. Lying successively at the top, the middle and the bottom of the rockfall, I calculated with a plumb line and a protractor the ratio and shape of the incline (concave, convex etc.); used calipers to gauge the dimensions of the rocks (length, breadth and thickness) in areas squared off for reference; painted (at Disko) outlines that would serve my hy-

3) From a geomorphological point of view, the map of these barely weathered primeval strata of Inglefield and Washington lands was a blank. Peary had made no topographic surveys at this latitude, and Kane's were very rudimentary. Lauge Koch was the first geologist to provide a basic survey and a geological sketch of this shoreline. Proceeding methodically, I therefore undertook a mapping survey on a scale of 1:100,000 along 300 km of coast to a depth of 3 km inland, a recording notebook and an aneroid barometer in hand. The details—bare outcrops, raised beaches, snow cover, state of the floe at a given time (direction and density of the crevasses)—were checked and refined from raking aerial photographs. The results were published on two sheets at 1:200,000 by the Imprimerie nationale and honored by the French Academy of Sciences. My maps, thanks to my collaboration with the natives, employed native place names for the first time, names that I had scrupulously recorded from the native hunters. I even gave twelve new names, some French but most of them Inuit, belonging to those Eskimo heroes whom the Polar explorers always failed to honor: Uutaaq, Aaqqiaq …

4) These activities were carried out at extremely low temperatures (minus 20° C to minus 30° C), sometimes with the dry east wind off the ice cap blowing, or the damp southwest wind off the open North Water, both bitterly cruel, and I was forced to work fast. My Inuit companions helped me with the material elements: erasers, colored pencils with sharpened points, altimeter. They held them ready for me on demand. When the wind blew, they protected me with their bodies. Thus I reconstructed day by day, as we slowly progressed by dog sled from south to north, from Etah to Cape Jackson in Washington Land, the external structure of this great plateau.

5) One thousand five hundred measurements were thus recorded in my notebooks. They con-

pothetical successors in measuring how rockfalls evolved over time; dug trenches with the help of the Inuit, to examine soil structures.[5] On the spot I made precise observations of wind speed, humidity, temperature and snow thickness, since on my return to Paris I intended to reconstruct these phenomena at the CNRS and at the city of Paris material resistance laboratory. The laboratory taught me humility, showing that microdata within this complex interface had been obliterated by both my predecessors and myself—a lesson in experimental method which I never forgot.[6]

Q: Perhaps it was on account of the small-scale, thoroughly manual nature of your research that you became more engrossed in ethnology, the study of man.

A: Absolutely. It is only when you examine the tiny details that a system shows itself to be operational or inexact. This truism has stayed with me ever since that time. Indeed the social sciences have always appeared to me somewhat cobbled together: the sooner they accept the fact that they are by nature inexact, the sooner research will make real progress. The time for building universal systems and theories has not yet come. In the fields of psychoanalysis and micro-economy there are gaping holes in our knowledge of peoples such as the Inuit. There has been insufficient research. Our theories of primitive economy, Inuit social psychology, and pre-logical systems of religious thought look to me like so many completely provisional mental constructions. The complete picture, backed by sound logic, cannot be arrived at until every one of the pieces has been identified. Such is not the case at present.

I am no structuralist. We are still at the inventory stage. I have confirmed this to my own satisfaction, on the spot, by attempting unconventional approaches to the subject, such as factor analyses of micro-economies (Igloolik, Hudson Bay; Back River, Central Arctic; Savoonga, Bering Strait), along with the first Rorschach tests and attention-span tests in Inuit society and the first nominative genealogy of the people.

Going back to the rocks, a patch of scree tends to take the form of its age; with time, it puts on flesh. At its foot, the processes of freezing and unfreezing give it dynamism. Debris, shards shattered away by the cold, coarse gravels and fine sandy clays of various sizes penetrate it and come to rest on the skin of the permafrost. Ice deposits take shape and exact unequal pressures—pressures that create further imbalances, within masses that are teetering anyway and capable of setting a whole sector in motion. Rock to rock, the entire bank can be affected. Stone is very much living matter. I have a fist-sized lump of red sandy limestone, which I picked up in the screes of Etah; as part of the scree, it was set in motion by a protective ecosystem. Its size and shape are characteristic of the mechanical resistance that is specific to its petrographic makeup. In terms of the destruction process it has been through over thousands and thousands of years, this stone represents a threshold of equilibrium, an authentic ecosystem. This is a conclusion that I have reached, or at least identified.

As I drove my team along the thalwegs and clambered up the slopes of scree, I recited aloud a passage of Francis Jammes that I had learned by heart: "Plants, as much as animals and stones, cast over my childhood a spell of mystery. When I was four, I would gaze at the pebbles from smashed mountains, lying in little heaps beside the roads. Knocked together they made sparks in the dusk. Rubbed against one another, they gave off a smell of burning. I picked up one of marble, which seemed heavy with water concealed within it. Streaks of mica in granite aroused in me an insatiable fas-

September 1950. Last months of light-heartedness in Thule before the American invasion. The Inuit hunt narwhal in Wolstenholme Fjord. Uummannaq (Seal Heart), Thule's little mountain, is emblematic of this area central to the Inuit. Drawing by Kiutika Dunek, born 1932. Qaanaaq, 1991.

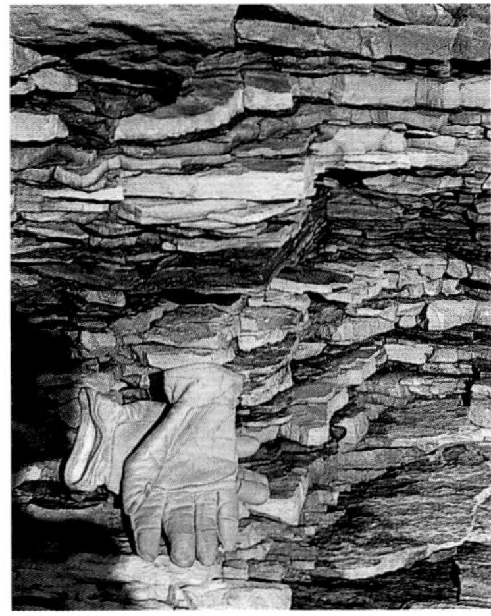

The effect of frosts and thaws (during the eight weeks of the annual thaw) repeated over the eight thousand years of the present interglacial. Cracks and breaks in the calcareous sandstone.

cerned the different rock substrate (granite, gneiss, limestone, basalt), climatic zones (high-latitude sub-humid zone along the shore, dry in the interior of Inglefield Land and Washington Land, 79° N; medium latitude sub-humid and sub-arctic in Disko Bay, west central Greenland.)

6) The experiments in geo-cryology with samples from Greenland using simulated conditions (dry, sub-humid, or humid cold, with varying winds) gave unexpected results, and for each kind of rock and level of precision in measuring raised more questions than it was possible too find answers, given the state of cryology. In the area of "shapes" I was more fortunate and was able to arrive at geodynamic certainties.

Two observations, which have become general rules: there exists one and only one shape for a given rock type and a given set of climatic conditions below which accumulated material will no longer move of its own weight. And rocks that measure similarly in terms of geology and climate develop a set of fairly constant measurements, as they detach from the outcrop in successive blocks and gradually fragment. Therefore, for each rock type there exists a relative equilibrial state, in a given climate. This equilibrium represents a balance between the resistance of the rock, freezing, and humidity.

As the weeks passed, and as we progressed from sector to sector, the physical ecosystems I was representing in my tables gained increasing meaning. I became so familiar with the figures, and the figures became so predictable, that from a distance on the floe I could tell from my sled just by looking at the shape and inclination of a draping of rocks below a cliff what rock type I would find when I later went to examine it, rock hammer in hand.

The dogs at rest after the dangerous crossing from Greenland to Canada (3 June 1951). I bivouacked in Alexandra Fjord, within sight of Skraeling Island, a few miles west of Cape Sabine, where nineteen young Americans died of hunger seventy-seven years earlier during the same season.

cination. I sensed there was something here that nobody knew how to explain, and that something was the life of stones . . ."

The four Inuit—Kutsiqitsoq and his wife, Natuk, Qaaqqutsiaq and Patdloq—whose life I shared, eating, hunting, dreaming, sleeping side by side, body against body, half naked in the night so our clothes could dry out, could hear me talking to myself. They saw me, so close to them, writing, drawing with my pencil, making maps, reflecting on the poetry of space. At the end of the "white night" they told me their dreams of the night before. In the total intimacy of our lives together, because I was the focal point of the group my dialectic had to be shared with them. They wanted to know why I came and went, here and there across the plateaux, why I lay down on the scree in my bearskin trousers and *qulittaq* of reindeer pelts with my hood up against the fierce cold; why I took such care to bring back stones that showed visible signs of change, which to them looked merely worn. At each halt, at their request I demonstrated the intense life within such and such a humble frozen stone. It aroused their curiosity. The stone was passed from hand to hand, as we tore at half-cooked lumps of seal meat. With my mouth full of fat and blood, I did my best to simplify complex phenomena with explanations that often seemed at odds with one another.

I saw doubt in their faces. How could this white man, devoid of skill with a dog whip, with nothing but a ruler, a hammer, calipers, thermometers and barometer (instruments they had already seen on whaling ships and aboard the *Roosevelt*), how could such a man know what was going on inside these *ujaraks* (rocks)? The notes I took with such difficulty on page after page of my book did not impress them. The Eskimo is so made that he will accept nothing as truth that he has not verified with his own eyes. This is the foundation of his dignity. They did not grudge me their esteem, because for very little reward they were willing to face appalling dangers and were ready to share my difficult mission purely as an adventure. This they did out of a kind of affectionate intuition. But as far as they were concerned white men's science was not to be relied upon.

When we were alone on our sleds, whose flexibility and responsiveness to our efforts sprang from the supple sealskin thongs that bound their wooden parts together, with the Eskimo in front facing the dogs and myself behind facing out, our dialogue was more confident. One or other of them would question me, [7] as if following his own solitary line of thought; the flood, which they had seen proved to their satisfaction by seashells found at 200 meters above sea level and whose truth I reconfirmed at every estuary with samples carefully taken from the beach, was the most frequent subject of their questions. *Nuna*: the Earth. *Nunavut*: our Earth. "Good for the Eskimo" they told me when they saw me spreading out the map I was making. For them, cartography was born of a shamanic procedure: flattening the planet with straight lines and curves, with spot heights and the chart oriented north, *Nunap*. It was thus, according to them, that you could view the universe vertically, from the earth to the moon and the sun, with nature integrated into a cosmic order with a top and a bottom, the earth suspended between.

Q: Would you say there is a congruity between your area of specialization and your attachment to the Inuit people?

A: For me, geomorphological work is not an open-and-shut branch of science, but an Ariadne's thread leading to the intelligent systems of a strictly ordered world in stone. The genetic psychology of the environment is an outward expression of this. The Inuit are not children of men, but of Nature. There is no other race in existence whose imagination is more free-ranging and fantastical than that of the

Greenland's climate as recorded in the sod, to 1950: my data and conclusions.

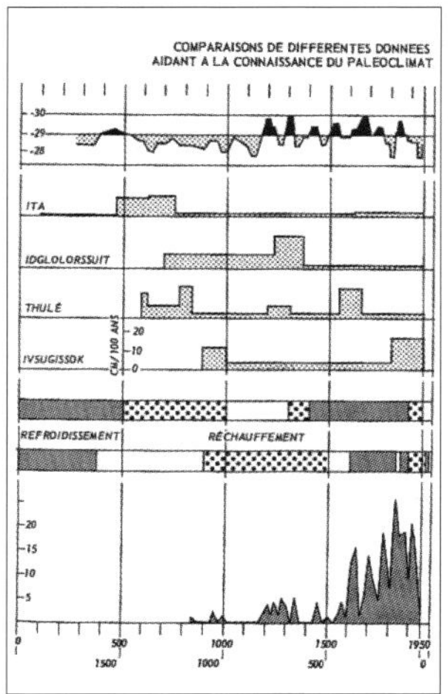

THE FOURTEEN SOD SITES
NORTHWEST COAST

Carbon-14 and paleontological analysis

Start of warming	8000-6000 B.P. to 3300 B.P.
Opening of the fjords	4500-2500 B.P. (according to Fredskild)
Most favorable period of warming	4000-3300 B.P.
Cold period	3300-1500 B.P.
Warm period	A.D. 500-1000
Warm period	A.D. 1300-1400
Cold period	A.D. 1400-1860
Warm period	A.D.1860-1950

Inuit. In their shamanic visions (some had made maps long before the Eskimos were discovered by the white man) they also constructed a personalized universe proceeding from their inner selves—and it was thus that nature, animals and stones became what Jacques Brosse [8] has so happily called an introduction to the world and a cosmic drama. This reading is a surrealistic one. For the Inuk, seeing is dreaming; surrounded by his dead ancestors, who lie buried on a promontory at the north end of the bay, he allows himself to be penetrated by their shades. He strives at all times to hear the voices and opinions of the dead, for an Eskimo is never alone. In his grand book of nature, every outcrop that resembles a man or an animal becomes a particle of memory and a dream-object.

I packed my numbered samples in small canvas sacks. The Inuit watched me with detachment, their black eyes darting. The stone is a fundamental element of their history, an expression of creation with powers of its own. What I was doing was a violation of their ancestral taboos. Holm relates that in 1864 a shaman on the east coast of Greenland, having abstained from food and sex for several months on top of a mountain near a crevasse, positioned himself to face southward and achieve communication with the forces of the earth. For days on end he revolved two stones round and round each other in his hand until a transfer of thought could be established. At this moment he saw a familiar spirit in the form of a monster approaching him, who advised him on the way to refine his young shaman's vision in the future. By a process of mutation, the Inuit becomes stone. It is a refuge for him. Qiituuarssuk, a frustrated young orphan who could not have a wife, was pursued for crushing to death in their igloo a young married couples who were making love with too much joyous abandon. He took refuge in a huge stone. His pursuers were unable to get at him, though they could hear that there were two beings within. Which is how, having turned into a huge rock, the fugitive affirmed his identity as Qiituuarssuk, and was shown to me in his place near a glacier. [9]

I have spoken of stones; I might just as easily have spoken of animals. The prehistoric Inuit learned exactly how to hunt the seal by observing the bears that lived on the tundra before they did. There is the same long wait beside the breathing hole dug by the seal in the frozen sea ice, the same smashing blow of the forefoot (the ancestor of the harpoon) to the body of the prey as it bursts up to gulp the air. The Eskimo also learned from the bear how to construct his igloo out of snow. The era when men and animals spoke together is still only yesterday in Eskimo terms of intemporal thought: indeed man continues to speak to his dogs, and to hear what they tell him. The legends recounted every evening by my companions constantly brought this home to me. They all knew I loved hearing the tale of Iquimarasugsugssuaq, the Eskimo Bluebeard. The details were far more realistic than those supplied by Perrault, and my friends who had adopted me the previous winter during the period of polar night told it to me over and over again during their long visits to my solitary cabin, intoning the words in a way that has haunted me ever since. "Tell it again", I would say sleepily of some favorite passage, before dropping off at last . . . and they would placidly take up the thread of the tale again. Sometimes we would be up until three in the morning.

ABOVE: **cairn built on Ellesmere Island,** Alexandra Fjord (3 June 1951). BELOW, a cairn in Washington Land. Above it, the metal box where, in a metallic sleeve, I put a message giving my past and projected itineraries, and the state of the party, in the polar tradition of leaving word under a cairn in a visible location. I would write the message in English, and my companions would give our position in Eskimo so as to guide a rescue party should we not return by autumn. The Inuit themselves considered my expedition to Inglefield and Washington lands and Ellesmere Island very adventurous. The tragedy of the German geologist H. K. E. Krüger was still fresh in people's minds. He crossed from Neqi, near Siorapaluk, and was lost without a trace somewhere on Ellesmere Island. My cairn was found by Peter Schledermann in 1977, and the message in it discovered (below, near image).

Through my intimacy with these men, who lived at such a pitch of surreal osmosis with their environment, I moved insensibly from the study of rocks to the study of man. As a geomorphologist, I continued to study screes, which collapsed from time to time as a result of climatic changes. [10] How could I remain unaware that my eyes were seeing the men around me as part of the same cosmic-dramatic vision? Metaphorically, the history of their society resembled an accumulation of rocks at the base of a cliff; it was an attempt to preserve the balance of a collection of in-

19th of August 95

On board the Icebreaker Kapitan Khlebnikov, Memorial Mission of Once again visiting my cairn erected on the 4th of June 1951 during the "first French geomorphological expedition" to North Greenland (Inglefield – Washington South, Ellesmere) I was then accompanied by my excellent Inuit partners Kutsikitsoq, Qaaqutsiaq, Etah, Patdlag and Nasaitsuk their wives.

Today, I am joined by my daughter Eleonore (Ikuma) and Dr Peter Schledermann, Jonathan Pridie, the pilot of the helicopter of the Russian ship, and Gilles Gamond —

However, I was not able to find my last message (June 1951) found in August 1977 by Dr Peter Schledermann.

Jean Malaurie
19th of August 95 —

7) During our discussions, the women would stay wordlessly off to the side, eight or ten feet from our group. Invited to take part in the scientific and hunting expedition (an unusual occurrence), they had decided not to take part orally in our debates. But silent, with lowered heads, they were physically present, as witnesses and judges of the group as a whole, and in that sense my allies.

8) Jacques Brosse, *L'Ordre des choses* (Paris: Julliard, 1989).

9) I also saw at Anoritooq, north of Cape Inglefield, a petrified Inuit woman. Her head with two eyes and a mouth could be clearly seen. Lower down there was a slightly blackened hole: her pudenda. Who does not know her story? After adopting a bear cub to take the place of her only son, Anoritooq (as this woman was called) taught it to hunt for her. And so that her cub would not be killed by men, she daubed one whole side of his body in soot, telling everyone not to kill a two-colored bear cub. Unfortunately, he was killed by a careless hunter. Anoritooq climbed to a high place, where she called another bear to come to her aid, and while she was waiting for the bear to arrive turned herself into stone. She has remained petrified ever since. It is traditional to bow to this stone before going on a bear hunt, and to feed it by coating the mouth and pudenda with fat. I was careful to do this in April 1951. Several weeks later, in point of fact, a bear came to be eaten by the four of us.

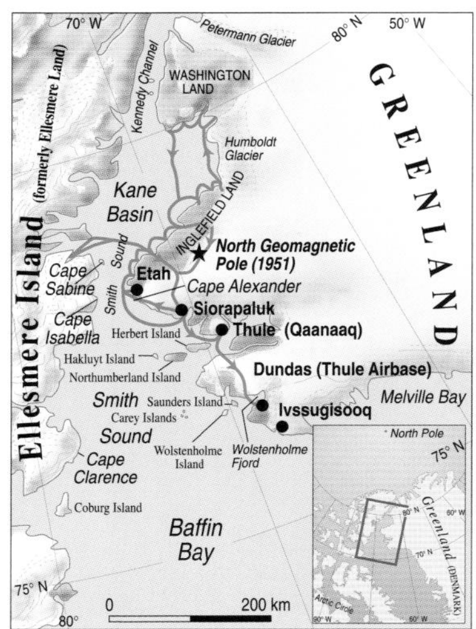

French geomorphological expedition (by dog sled), led by Jean Malaurie in Inglefield and Washington lands and Ellesmere Island (March-June 1951).

dependent-minded men, structured like tiles on a roof with systems more anarcho-communist than anything else. The society formed by the thirty to seventy odd families of Thule hunters, between 1818 and 1950, was indeed a fragile ecosystem of itself, given that its members owed their survival solely to their own experience and courage. Their egalitarian framework was so precarious that social tensions due to such things as falling birthrates, family quarrels, vendettas caused by crimes of passion and famines, could wreck it at a stroke. Like a scree destabilized by the shifting of one or two rocks or by a leakage of the sand-clay ballast between them, the group strives, year after year, to preserve its equilibrium and to maintain its peace. A group is not static, nor is an archaic society one that lacks a history. It is only our own blindness which make us think such peoples are inert. The Polar Eskimos have experienced a series of crises in their history: for example, in 1850 they were nearly wiped out, whereas in our Middle Ages the abundance of game in their region saw them expanding their geographical reach far beyond its former limits. [11] Like all expressions of life, the Inuit group must struggle for existence. But for

Goodbye to the last ship of the year. Siorapaluk, August 1950.

every generation, the overriding task and duty is to transmit, in a messianic perspective, as much as it has itself been able to add to the sum of technical and spiritual body of knowledge. The future is viewed by the Inuit, not as a chronological concept but as an eschatological one. "We, the Inuit!" they say proudly.

In my own insistent desire to achieve a more intimate relationship with this geo-analytical order of the universe, my second mission to Thule in 1967 was undertaken in a spirit of paleo-climatic research. I thus found myself confronted head on by the anthropo-geographical, socio-climatic relationships maintained over eons by the people of the Arctic with their environment; and it was by pressing forward on this naturalist's path that I came upon the phenomenon of men and history in harmony.

I have never felt more strongly the sensation at the root of Arctic anthropo-geography, which I taught for thirty years in my seminars at the Institut des Hautes Etudes, than I did one morning in March 1969. I had gone on a four-week trek by dog sled with the hunters Qaaqqutsiaq and Sakaeunnguaq, heading in the direction of Inssugissoq, north of Savissivik. The name of the place implied that this deserted bay (which had been visited briefly by Nordenskjöld's *Sofia* in 1884) had deposits of peat somewhere in its back country. But where? This was the question. After two days of travel in bitterly cold conditions, having fortunately crossed, with our twenty dogs, two sea inlets and a glacier rising to 3000 feet, we found ourselves overlooking the bay. It was surrounded by high walls of red sandstone. We halted at the edge of the floe; the harnessed dogs settled their rumps in the snow and looked at us questioningly. Before us lay a flat landscape of snow and ice, while to the east gleamed the enormous glacier of Sermersuaq.

The Eskimos watched as if they expected me to conjure the mystery we were searching for straight from this empty space. I walked up and down the shore through a thin powdering of snow, scanning the tops of the banks for signs of tundra-edge. With the toe of my sealskin boot I probed the snow layer, computing and thinking. I adopted an attitude of scientific detachment, then jabbed my spade into the slope. I took a few steps forward, then stopped again. By now the wait had already gone on too long for the Inuit. I could feel their eyes boring into me. With their whips in their hands, they stood still and silent beside the two sleds. Unblinkingly skeptical, they were evaluating the scientist "Illisimator" I purported to be. They had brought me here;

PRECEDING PAGE, BELOW: **19 August 1995, Alexandra Fjord,** I rediscovered the cairn. We were on the Russian ice-breaker Kapitan Khlebnikov, with Peter Schledermann and my daughter Ikuma (Little Flame). I left a new message in a bottle.

10) Nature abhors chaos. Accompanied day after day by these men whose sensibility and mythology became part of my consciousness, I was led little by little to look on them as human screes. I analyzed their society as an ecosystem, convinced that living in osmosis with their ice and stone environment, unconsciously, they had built on the slopes of their history over the course of generation systems of organization inspired by nature, whose parameters fit together according to the circumstances.

11) In defiance of everything, the Eskimos have always tried to maintain or recover the equilibrium of their primitive communism, in a closed society with little capacity for innovation. An isolated population is reductive. The Inuit are repetitive, as though aware they have no alternative. In their way, they explained to me that they wanted to be cautious and maintain tradition because they knew that if the group became too rich it would fall into a despised class system, with the stronger crushing the weaker; and if it became too poor, it could explode, giving way to a suicidal "every man for himself" ethos. They live on the razor's edge.

12) In these regions of extreme conditions, what is true at A is no longer true at B. These south-facing slopes are several degrees warmer than these north-facing ones; these black rocks absorb more heat. The observations made on the on the coast of Inglefield Land, by a floe with 10% crevasses and a certain humidity, will be entirely unlike those I might make three miles to the east in the middle of the dry plateau, and even less like those from five or six miles further east on the much more humid edge of the glacier. The same is true of men. Each arctic society has its own geography and individual history; just as each man has, beyond his destiny within the egalitarian group, his hard and secret core which confers on him his true identity.

While this observation is a universal one, the margins are smaller, the structures more differentiated and opposite. The Caribou Eskimos, though they closely share socio-religious structures with the maritime Eskimos, have highly contrasting conceptions and ways of life—to the point where they try and avoid each other. The Back River Eskimos, among whom I lived briefly in 1963, had no caribou but maintained a prohibition against hunting seal, even to feed their dogs, and had no wish to meet their seal-hunting neighbors. Their own life was centered on fish (Salmonids), which they fished in coastal streams.

their mission was accomplished, and now I had to accomplish mine. This was the moment when, as a geomorphologist and historian, I had to make the place speak, and that immediately: I had to justify the reality of my knowledge. The pressure of the surrounding emptiness suddenly told on me, and I resolved to gamble. Turning resolutely to my comrades I suggested in a low voice brimming with false conviction that if indeed there was peat in the area, it could only be . . . over there, in that direction. Their eyes lit up, and with a relieved murmur of "*ieh!*" they told me this was exactly their opinion . . . they must know the place, I thought. The heaviness of the moment had passed. At the same time I reminded myself that Eskimos hate having different ideas than those of their close companions.

At the base of a slope which I judged would be covered in thick grass in summer, we searched with shovels, picks and ice-axes. The goddess Gaia was with us—the site was indeed rich in peat. We set up a small tent covering an area of three square yards, and kneeling in it, scratched away at the frozen ground with ice-axes and knife. Flake by flake, to a depth of five feet, we unearthed eleven centuries of history. The hole was cone-shaped; the peat, frozen to a stony hardness, was brown in color with traces of purple and tiny white veins running through it. "This *issoq* looks like high walrus meat at the end of winter," panted Sakaeunnguaq, his face pouring with sweat just like my own, despite the temperature of 20° below zero. We were both spattered with brown by small shards of frozen peat that had melted on our skin. It was hard work, encased as we were in our caribou jackets and bearskin trousers. We couldn't use the motorized sample drill: the gases it emitted might alter the makeup of the peat and make carbon dating much more difficult. Using our knife blades, we detached fragments five centimeters thick encasing 1.61 cm of vegetation per century approximating to recent times, and 11 cm per century to ancient times, as diluted by the nearby glacier. On another site (Saunders Island) the past could be traced back through the peat for nearly 5000 years. I passed the samples one by one to my companion, who carefully packed them in plastic bags. To avoid any possibility of error, I identified each bag myself with a felt pen: and so we worked on for ten hours without stopping.

The fourteen sites we found and investigated were all between sea-level and an altitude of 300 feet. Thus they can only have evolved after the third millennium before Christ, whereas the shrinking of the ice cap began 8000 years ago. I began to invest the place with drama, seeing in my mind's eye flashes of what might have been its human history. Perhaps there was a ruined igloo here—harpoons, arrows, skeletons—perhaps even a skull with a powerful jawbone. It is by questing and thinking with our hands that we become historians of mankind and nature. This search for lost time in the frozen earth was for me a lesson in methodology; I learned that the human landscape only reveals itself to whoever takes the time to listen to it and look at it.

Thule-Qaanaaq (Whale Sound). A Danish-style city has been built (September 1982).

Young Polar Eskimo woman of the modern era, met during my dog sled expedition. I was extracting samples of sod frozen to a foot in thickness. Savissivik, April 1969.

Back in Paris, I had my peat samples carbon-dated at the CNRS. At Ulu, in Finland, pollen traces of *cassiope, salix, betula* and *dryopteris* were found set into the peat by my friend Vasare, the botanist. These determined the temperature and humidity of the territory over successive periods, from 5000 years before Christ through to 1950.

All in all, three initial observations suggested themselves. First of all, there was little sense in generalizing at these latitudes. This was made clear to me day after day: everything changes completely within a few miles.[12] Secondly, we have a tendency to believe that the "hard" sciences lead to definitive conclusions. We deceive ourselves. For example, we have little knowledge of the limits of resistance of wild plant species, given that the aging of a plant can keep it alive against all the odds in an environment that is no longer its own. Such limitations can hardly be characteristic of a biotope, and our reasoning has to be made relative in consequence. Lastly, in very high latitudes geodynamic processes have a preservative effect. For lack of water (only 40 millimeters of snowfall annually, much of which is va-

1990: interior of a Scandinavian-style house. The Inuit are still hunters: seals and bears are still welcomed after the hunt as guests in the house . . . after having been "invited" there.

Bering Strait. Nome. In the early morning, I begin a pastel of the dramatically colored sky. Photograph taken by Bruce Jackson, October 1997.

porized at the beginning of the thaw, or else swept away by the great anti-cyclonic wind off the inland ice), geodynamic processes are very slow. For example, I am convinced that my own footprints in the sand and the soil will be virtually intact 100 years from now. [13]

Q: Which of the explorers mentioned in your book had the greatest influence on you? Which of them do you most admire?

A: Without a shadow of a doubt, the work which made the deepest impression on me was that of Captain John Ross, the great Scottish explorer, who in my view has not yet been given his full due by his British compatriots. I am repeatedly staggered by the precision and excellence of naval officers like Ross, as well as by the honesty of their interrelated observations, which were always made under conditions of intense danger on ships forced to navigate under sail through uncharted ice floes. The Admiralty was a superb school for men, as military history demonstrates over and over; likewise the entire history of exploration reminds us of this fact, in book after book.

Another who fascinates me is the delightful Elisha Kent Kane, a North American medical doctor and an aristocrat of the masonic tradition. I have visited and mapped the deserted Rensselaer Bay, where he abandoned his ship in 1855. This place was the focus of my thoughts for some time, since I had selected it as the site for my main depot of food and supplies. For Kane, it was a place of intense geophysical and climatic observation over two winters, as well as the backdrop for the appalling drama of an expedition by white men that was ill-conceived from every possible angle. Kane's private journals taught me the value of one outstanding quality in a man, which he himself showed again and again in Rensselaer Bay by his dogged persistence in the face of all the difficulties besetting his marooned expedition, ravaged as it was by jealousy and violence.

But it was from the example of Knud Rasmussen that I learned to organize my expeditions like commando raids. Thanks to the Eskimos I was able to move easily and happily across zones that by their own admission cost several of my predecessors unspeakable suffering. I knew Rasmussen not only from his books but also from the objective descriptions of him left by his companions. I have spent many an evening talking to Qaavigarsuaq, a hunter from Thule who was with Rasmussen on his great dogsled expedition through Canada and Alaska (1923-1925). I could also mention my conversations with my Siorapaluk neighbor, Inuk. Inuk was the first missionary to come from Jakobshavn in 1910, in order to convert the polar Eskimos who at that time were still completely pagan. I also knew Rasmussen's wife, Dagmar, who in 1958 donated all of her husband's works to the Library of the Center of Arctic Studies, then in its infancy, so that he would remain present among us. Finally, there was Erik Holtved, Rasmussen's modest friend and an eminent professor. I first met Erik in Copenhagen in 1950; together, he and I projected a new program of anthropological study in the territory. Our French-Danish scientific collaboration, conducted in a spirit of real friendship, made it possible for me to carry out demographic and microeconomic research that had never before been attempted.

Q: It is a striking fact that most of your missions were undertaken alone. Why?

A: I took part as a geographer in the glaciological and meteorological expeditions led by Paul-Emile Victor in 1948 and 1949. These were exceptions to the general rule in my life. We were about thirty men in all, of whom ten were scientists. I shall never forget my debt to the founder of the EPF (Expéditions Polaires Françaises), which breathed new life into French Arctic and Antarctic research after the war under the direction of Robert Gessain, the ethnologist, and Raymond Latarjet, the head of the Radium Institute at the University of Paris. It was Paul-Emile Victor who gave me my first opportunity . . . but in general you are quite right, the experience of those unwieldy expeditions convinced me that in the end they were little different to those of Kane and Hall in the nineteenth century, which were exclusively made up of white men, with no Eskimos contributing whatever. It was this certainty that convinced me to work alone with Eskimos from 1950 onwards. Big expeditions don't fit my temperament.

My need to conduct my research alone became more acute the older I became. I think I made an instinctive decision to take part in no more western expeditions, because I wanted to avoid the problems arising from personal rela-

13) The Algonquian gneiss and granite peneplain I trod day after day in Inglefield Land in April and May was so little altered by the glacial age four million years ago or the more recent glaciation that it can still be considered Algonquian. This observation ran totally counter to the prevalent views of the day, which considered the glacial agents (frost, water) such powerful erosive forces that a note read at the *Académie des sciences* by one of my colleagues actually spoke of "glacial obliteration." This scientist had jumped to conclusions: frost is selective.

tionships—which under conditions of isolation will always absorb much of your attention, not only imposing handicaps on your work schedule, but also affecting the quality of your inspiration.

Q: The problems you mention, didn't you come across a few of them later on when you were leading your own expeditions?

A: Life is full of such detours . . . naturalists and anthropologists tend to be solitary people. I had many difficulties, for example during the filming of my series *Les Derniers Rois de Thule* and *Inuit*. There were nine films in all, which I had to direct with four different teams of French and foreign filmmakers in Greenland, Alaska, Canada and Siberia. There were problems for me at every level. First there was the savage cold, to which everyone and everything was subjected, not least the cameras. In Alaska and Siberia we were often filming at 50° below. Then there were our relations with one another and more importantly with the natives. The scenarios dealt among other things with the questions of ethnic minorities and their defense—thereby touching on highly sensitive political issues, both for the Eskimos and for the government authorities, which kept a close eye on my activities. Finally I had to learn all about directing films, and how to reconcile camera crews and actors—both groups being extremely nervous for different reasons. Not to mention the political problems I had to grapple with, particularly in North-Eastern Siberia, where two representatives of the Soviet government accompanied me at all times while I was directing a Soviet TV crew composed of wildly different nationalities and temperaments (Georgians, Jews, Russians and Yakuts). On top of that, it was November and we had only three hours of daylight a day, under conditions of terribly dry cold.

Q: Your researches on the Polar Eskimos have demonstrated the structured nature of their demography, which according to you shows a Malthusian type pre-planning of births and deaths. You have also defined, through a micro-economic analysis of their society, what you call a state of "anarcho-communism."

A: The social history of these people is tied to a climatic context which alters very little. This was the subject matter of the research you mention. These people, as I have said before, are in osmosis with the stones, the flora and the fauna by which they are surrounded. Using their five senses, their hunters are capable of reading a world that remains unknown to us. The Eskimo is constantly listening to nature and has developed an exceptional sensory memory. The vibrant pitch of his senses provides him with all manner of information; he is constantly watchful and alert, sniffing the wind, observing the clouds, smelling the odor of the earth, which steams in the summer; he knows how to read the crackling sounds made by the ice, and the muffled ones made by the snow; he can interpret the moods of animals, the state of their innards, the halo surrounding the moon. Whenever they meet, Eskimo hunters exchange

ABOVE: **expedition** to the area of the North Geomagnetic Pole, at 78° 29' north and 68° 54' west. I traveled with Kutsikitsoq and two dog sleds across the inland ice (left). I was unquestionably the first Frenchman to voyage in this sector, without intending to be (29 May 1951).

the information they have gathered, and their collective awareness reinterprets the sum of each man's contribution like a kind of central computer.

And this is how these tiny, apparently aimless Paleolithic groups have perfected, over thousands of years, a social structure that is sociologically egalitarian and functionally élitist: whereby the earth, the hunting ground, the sea, and the igloos belong to the group, which remains the supreme arbiter. Their inheritance is limited to the handing down of strictly personal effects—those, that is, that are not sacrificed close to the tomb of the deceased. Eskimo society is the inveterate enemy of profit; it insists on the immediate sharing out of everything it kills, shares being determined according to the role and talents of each participant. Each member of the group exercises his particle of authority. Every three to five years the Inuit change their place of residence in order to avoid the *de facto* appropriation of a given hunting ground. Their codified sexual promiscuity is intended, within strict rules of family relationship, to correct any hint of alienation that may arise as a result of a couple's reciprocal possession of one another. By the ritualized exchange of men and women, the Eskimos mean to break, from time to time, any spirit of exclusive ownership that a woman may have for a man, or vice versa. The same goes for family ties: one child out of three is given for adoption to an unrelated family, so that the child can avoid the sentiment of belonging to a fixed family which is in reality only a provisional structure (significantly these societies have no family names). Thus the group is able to head off any danger of degenerating into an association of rural families. The group, in fact, is a collection of people

Aamma, 63 years old. Qeqertarsuaq, August 1982.

Volunteer teacher at the Inuit settlement of Clyde River (Baffin Island), 600 miles southwest of Thule (May 1987).

Are the minds of these little Siberian Eskimos elsewhere, dreaming of the sea ice, living the great myths of their history with their tutelary bears, whales, and ravens? Will their teacher know how to follow them there? Chukotka Peninsula, 1930.

each of whom has one name only, that of the person in the group who died most recently before his or her birth. Thus the spirit-name is perpetuated from one generation to the next, and the group is much more than an assembly of families—it is an association of the living and the dead.

Q: You have repudiated standard academic methods by showing that micro-encounters can exercise a decisive influence on the dynamics of Eskimo society, because they affect the thoughts and emotions of a population.

A: The Polar Eskimos suffered one of the heaviest blows in their long history in June 1951, when the Americans built their ultra-secret airbase at Thule during the first months of the Korean War, which proved so disastrous for the US Army. At that time the whole world was living under the imminent threat of a third world war.

I was the only foreign scientist present at the time among the 302 Polar Eskimos, 70 families scattered over an area of 500 km^2. Their territory was suddenly invaded by 1000 men who arrived by air, with no authorization whatever from its inhabitants or their native local representatives. This advance force was followed on July 9 by a fleet of 100 ships. Rarely can such an encounter have been so badly prepared. All of this was of the deepest significance for the future, but in *Ultima Thule* I have wanted to carry the debate to another level. Wherever civilizations meet in this way, over time mini-encounters occur and accrue until their effects are every bit as important as technical revolutions and sudden, out-of-the ordinary events, such as the introduction of guns or the shock of a brand new military base.

During the months spent by my predecessors in winter quarters, words, sensations, repulsions and attractions spread a kind of sediment, what one might call a heavy deposit, in the deep recesses of personality of every Inuit. These endured, being added to the collective unconscious of the group. We are dealing here with the phenomenon of the integral preservation of memory, which Freud analyzed at the individual level. These memories, hitherto pushed into the background, may resurface at unexpected moments, independent of the natural course of each person's thought. Because dormant collective thought has no purity, its parallel realities are part and parcel of individual thought, which for that reason flows in contrary channels.

These mini-factors, which have such significant consequences, are the main subject of my book. From the first moment they were discovered by the outside world on August 10, 1818, the Inuit people began to change. This is why it is so important for historians to analyze every word that

was uttered at that encounter, and set down in the various publications of Captain John Ross and his officers. Everything that the Eskimos present saw and heard reverberated outwards through the minds of the twenty to forty families of the scattered Inuit community. Through the process of comparison and questioning, their isolation began its traditional protective process of drawing in, of crowding together like musk oxen facing danger. And it all proved entirely futile, because the germ of the outside world had already penetrated their society, and was already homeopathically active among them.

What proof do I have of this? No written document tells of the secret hopes and fears of these illiterate Inuit, nor of the mute dialogs with the Eskimos, the barterings and rapes carried out by the whale hunters (the *upernaallit*, men of the springtime) who were also illiterate and put in regularly at Cape York, the main port of call in the area. In all the expeditions that ensued, sharing moments of extreme danger in tents and in dogsleds, the last confidences of starving, desperate men were exchanged without the slightest racial complex. In their reports and private journals, the white explorers seemed to register these changes with no special display of interest, as though they were not themselves responsible for them. From this point of view, there is no question that Peary was the one who most deeply changed the Inuits' material and mental landscape. Indeed it was the daily association between Americans and Inuit during his advance to the Pole which laid the groundwork for the most decisive changes.

For example, there was the relationship between men and women. The Eskimo custom of exchanging women—which was coded, seasonal and egalitarian in spirit—was degraded under the influence of Peary and his brutal sailors, who took the most beautiful or accessible Eskimo women in the group in exchange for material rewards. The blood of Peary himself, as well as that of whale fishermen and other anonymous whites, was mixed with that of the Eskimos and had its effect on the way the natives viewed our civilization. This practice, with its colonialist and racist undertones, also changed the way the Inuit looked at their own women. While the latter remained a source of union, in certain cases they had become a source of profit.

In December 1950, the Eskimos were anxious that a wife should be found for me—largely out of friendship, since in the Arctic celibacy is inconceivable and every man must have his female companion. It isn't good for anyone to be alone in their igloo. It was a generous gesture on their part, to wish me united with a woman according to their tradition; but the Peary precedent rendered their offer ambiguous, to say the least. This ambiguity was the reason behind my refusal—along with the lessons learned during my previous short experience in the Sahara, which had turned me against any hint of colonial morality. I was adamant that no doubtful motive should mar the trust between me, a young white man, and the Inuit. In any event, my companions, and especially the women, had already felt a deep intuition that I was to be the last witness of their happy, egalitarian society before the great events they knew were coming. Their concern that I should record every trace of the life they knew was threatened led them to give me their complete confidence, to respect my decisions, and to encourage me to note the smallest details in my books. "Good for the Inuit," they all told me. I was then so eager to acquire an intimate knowledge of Eskimo society that I was unwilling to risk taking a woman accomplice and fathering a child who would be an orphan in his own country or a rootless person in mine (as some explorers and ethnologists, indeed some of the greatest of them, did not hesitate to do). Such an act would make our relationship an unnatural one. Would I follow the example of Peter Freuchen, the only Polar explorer to take an Eskimo as his lawful wife and treat her as his full equal, instead of a temporary plaything from an inferior race? But my decision was already made. I would marry in my own country, like Knud Rasmussen.

One of my ethnographic notebooks, with daily notes.

Q: In your books you say that the Inuit encouraged your tendency to follow your intuition.

A: I have always mistrusted my impulses, being cautious by nature. Faced with a given problem—such as the one posed by a negotiation in 1988 with a Soviet research organism—I tend to examine it in great detail, as equably as I can but with as much vigilance as I can muster. I then take outside advice before I make my final decision.

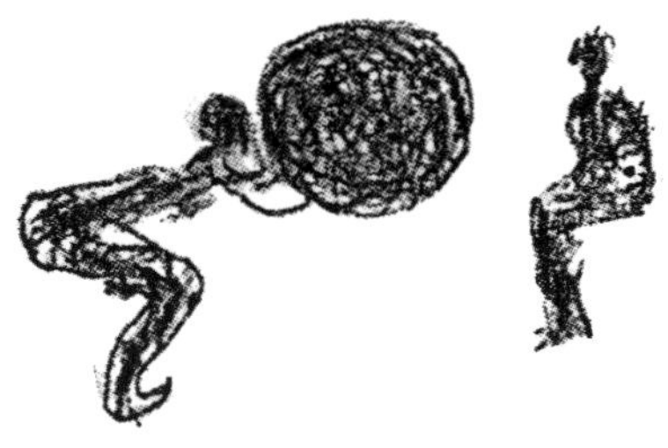
1990: Inuit converts practice a Christianity that fuses with their former pantheism. The sacred drum keeps a forbidden shamanism alive.

On the other hand, it sometimes happens that I have a firm intuition when faced with a choice, and I have never lost sight of this. In July 1950, I decided within minutes to spend the winter on the spot in Thule, though I had no food and no special equipment for winter, my initial authorization and my accreditation having been for four weeks in summer only. On the ice of Kane Basin, one morning in May 1951, I resolved to make the Greenland-Canada crossing in the manner of a commando raid without taking food supplies, at a critical moment before the thawing of the pack ice in early June. This was a major risk. I would be cut off from my base, living on the empty island of Ellesmere for 11 months. I sincerely believe that I was so changed by the Inuit, who think as they act, that when I got married in Paris it was to a young woman I had only known for a few days. This happened on my return from Thule in December 1951; my wife was the daughter of one of the greatest physicists of our generation. I remember that before I was even introduced to her, the timbre of her voice heard through a door had settled the matter.

Q: Were the Inuit influenced by men they personally trusted, more than by others?

A: Someone once called the Inuit "affable savages"; they have always been an eminently curious people, open and

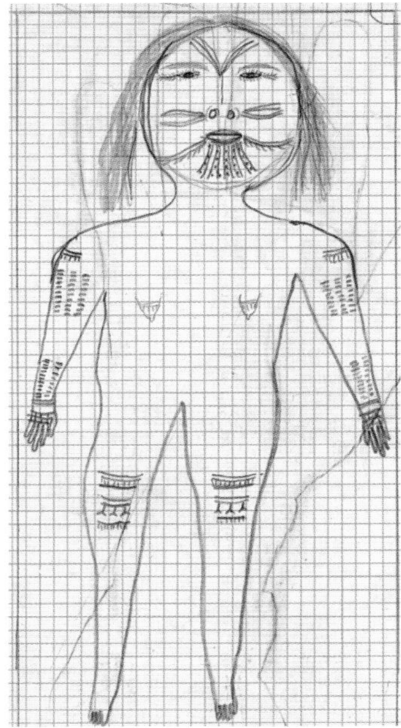

Tattoos of a woman born in 1910 on Boothia Peninsula. The Inughuit of North Greenland, since their discovery in 1818, have never used tattoos, despite the influx of immigrants from the Canadian Arctic in 1863.

adventurous, and they were obviously intrigued by the Christian South Greenlander Hans Hendrik. Hendrik was a master of technical innovations they knew nothing about, such as the kayak, the bow and the gun. Similarly, they questioned me very closely about my geomorphological work, and my methods in genealogy and cartography. They also wanted to know the reasons for my silences and my delight in landscapes and the hunt, and were inquisitive about my various, occasionally contradictory thoughts about things. My stories about the war, the Nazis, the French Resistance and the atom bomb were listened to with close attention, as were my nuanced views about the Common Market, to which they were offered to join because of their integration in Denmark. They feel closer however to Canada as their Inuit cousins live on Baffin Island.

Societies like the Inuit are commonly said to cut off from the world. "We are alone on the earth," they declared to John Saccheus in 1818. The great French historian Lucien Febvre, who analyzed the effects of repetition on the closed societies of the Middle Ages in France, wrote to me at Thule in September 1950 to ask me to make a very careful study of how an archaic isolation managed to survive, both during the two centuries of the Little Ice Age (1600-1800) and during the period up to 1950, given that the Danish administration forbade all communication with Greenlanders south of Melville Bay and imposed very strict immigration controls. As a result I discovered that this *soi-disant* closed society was actually highly porous, having received a regular input from abroad in the manner of a blood transfusion.

I can offer three examples of this, which show how the Eskimos actively looked for such transfusions and were subsequently apt to retain traces of them.

The author with Jacques Lacarrière (left) and Wilfrid Thesiger (right), the great British explorer and author of *Arabian Sands.*

The first concerns a singular legend recounted by Knud Rasmussen in 1904, which suggests that the Inuit saw William Baffin's ship the *Discovery* in 1616 and retained a folk memory of the event.

Second, in May 1950 my four companions and I were on a sandstone shore on the south side of Washington Land, 300 km north of any human habitation. We were eating our daily ration of half-boiled seal, some of us standing, the rest squatting on our haunches. Our aluminum stew pot was standing in the snow, cooling fast, and we were helping ourselves with our fingers, using knives and teeth to tear up the blackish meat. Bit by bit we gulped down the swill of blood and flesh. I happened to be telling them about the Buchenwald concentration camp, describing the horrors endured by the cadaverous inmates in their black and white striped canvas smocks and trousers. I described how they were beaten, tortured, and condemned to slow starvation on a daily diet of thin gruel, which they fought over like dogs. They were horrified. "What you tell us, we have heard already. The Whites are *alineq* (bad men)." They knew—and yet at that time the Eskimos of Siorapaluk had no local newspaper and the echoes reaching them from the outside world were few and very far between.

Third: In September 1972, Inuterssuaq told me in his cabin: "You must meet with the *Tulussuaq* (The Great Englishman). He was a friend to the Inuit at Etah; he will be your friend. This could help you and us too. He has something . . . the Inuit do not know quite what . . . with the King of England: perhaps he is his cousin . . ."

In October 1988, in London, I reported these words to Lord Shackleton—who, thanks to the Polar Eskimos, was to become my friend. Shackleton was the *Tulussuaq*, the Great Englishman. We were having lunch together in the Gothic dining room of the House of Lords, and Shackleton—who was as keen as I was to understand more about the Eskimos—was delighted. "The Inuit are quite wonderful," he said. "Do you know that I was given the Order of the Garter a few years ago, ages after I visited them, and I've never been back, sad to say. Those men will never cease to amaze me. They know everything, really. I'm obviously not exactly the Queen's cousin, but it's quite true that the Order of the Garter is the highest honor in the Queen's gift." [14]

Clearly, we must be extremely careful about classifying collective behavior as "authentic" or "primitive". We must also beware of philosophical, psychological and psychoanalytical conclusions that claim to define the essence of a people's thought without taking account of their history . . . quite apart from the fact that their responses are often geared to what their questioner wants to hear. *Ask no questions. Listen.* I myself have known first-, second- and third-generation Eskimo Pearys, and if I think specifically of the beautiful

Mikissuk, who featured strongly in my film *The Last Kings of Thule*, I can testify to her originality, as well as to the depth and complexity of her character.

Q: What of the future? We Danes are very worried about this. It looks very black to us.

A: For the Polar Eskimo, the occupation of a fifth of their territory by American forces in June 1951 was as important an event as August 1818, the date of their discovery. The highly respectable Danish protectorate fell apart at the first hint of American pressure. I witnessed it all first hand: there was no question of consultation with the natives. It was evident that Copenhagen, in the interest of its own security, had abandoned the territory of Thule to an economic and military future which had little or no relation to the principles that had initially governed the Danish protectorate.

"Little or no relation" is actually putting it mildly. The Eskimos, whether they liked it or not, were placed in the front line of America's military defense strategy. In *The Last Kings of Thule* I described the consequences of this occupation, which I openly denounced, even though it was ultra-secret. The rape was completed in 1953, when the Eskimos of Thule were expelled from their capital and dispossessed of a fifth of their territory, leaving behind them their past and their dead when they were deported to a fjord farther north. At that time the Inuit had to endure the most difficult challenge of their history—a battle with progress and money, waged against themselves.

Without any doubt, one or two generations were sacrificed, but those who have survived have learned much, finding in their own traditions the memory of the draconian solutions to which their ancestors occasionally had to resort. I was officially consulted in July-August 1967 by the communal council at the request of the Ministry of Greenland (Claus Borneman) and I offered the Danish government a detailed plan of economic and social development. This was only partially adopted, but nevertheless I can see a number of positive signs today. The first is that the population is on the increase (302 Polar Eskimos in 1951, 789 in 1985, only 8% being Danish immigrants divided among six localities, as opposed to ten in 1951). Second, there has been a total ban on snowmobiles, which are used elsewhere all over the Arctic and which pollute the atmosphere and ruin the native economy. This has been all to the advantage of the Greenland dog, which has played such a crucial part in Inuit history. [15] I described this development in the fifth edition of *The Last Kings of Thule*, in a lengthy afterword.

A Japanese engineer from Tokyo decided to make his home at Siorapaluk, north of Thule, and to marry an Eskimo woman. He had read *The Last Kings* in Japanese. "I immediately wanted to live with these people and be just like them. Your book changed my life," he told me, at our first meeting on the Qaanaaq coast in August 1982. This alliance with a man from the Land of the Rising Sun is a symbolic one. A distant relative from Asia, whence the Inuit themselves came some ten thousand years ago, has shown them something of the way forward. In the fog of progress into which they must march, everyone knows that they need to hold fast to their identity papers and their baggage. Japan, which has learned the hard way to live with its past as well as its future, brings to the Inuit of the year 2000 a proof that everything is still possible at Thule.

Q: Listening to what you have to say, it would seem that luck has always been on your side. Nevertheless you must have had times of real hardship and difficulty . . .

A: My answer to that is especially for the young people

The author with Admiral Ivan D. Papanine, leader of the drift expedition to the "Pole of inaccessibility" (1937), at the Presidium of the Soviet Academy of Sciences in Moscow, where I showed my film *The Inuit, from Greenland to Siberia* in July1980.

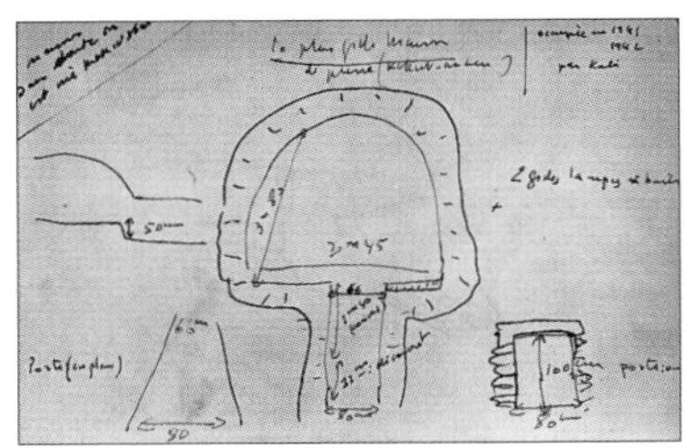

Stone and sod igloo where I filmed the interior scenes for *Last Kings of Thule* in May 1969. This igloo was occupied by Kalipaluk (Peary's son) in 1940, then by Sorqaq. Qeqertarsuaq, 1967.

14) These facts eloquently show how so isolated a society registers even the slightest detail. Imagine the sum of knowledge they have assimilated since their discovery in 1818, what was said to them by Kane and his companions, by Hayes, by the refugees from the *Polaris*, by Peary, Cook, and Rasmussen. In those 132 years, they have integrated every fact, every remark, every shock to their unconscious and their thinking minds, but this incorporation will forever be hidden from us. Their memory, in point of fact, is so selective that their myths are singularly silent about all these explorers. This extremely cautious reaction is all the more rigidly adhered to for their knowing—one might say from the "inside"—what and who they are talking about. Their behavior and their inner world are no longer purely Inuit but mixed, like their blood. There is some whaler in them, some American, some Danish, and even some Black, and since the time of their discovery what they have mistrusted and obscured is a new part of themselves. We should also mention certain "benefits" that come from moral hybridization, and the influence of certain white "virtues" that were so patent in some of the great heroes of the Arctic . . . Who is to say in this context what part is purely native? The "Eskimo" dignity and greatness of soul (inseparable from a severity that can sometimes become cruelty), of which I myself have largely benefited, to what extent are they due to the impact of a Ross, a Kane, or a Rasmussen? I saw that the Inuit, who were so distant toward Hayes, had the same confidence in me, a penniless scientist, that they had for Knud Rasmussen, also penniless in 1903 and 1910, but whom they respected for his ideals.

15) Furthermore, negotiations have started between the community of Thule and the military base, so that the base—which is obsolete in this era of missiles—may return to the Inuit. A court review conducted by the Danish Ministry of Justice in 1989—to which I was convoked on 5 November 1989 to speak before the court of appeals (5 hours of testimony!)—was aimed at re-examining in minute detail the authoritarian conditions under which the Thule Eskimos were displaced to Qaanaaq 60 miles farther north.

The polar night.
Qaanaaq, 1990.

who may read this. Life offers its truest blessings when you are faced with a seemingly impossible task, when you are alone, and when you are filled with doubt. I have had to face many difficulties—desperate shortages of money, the blindness and deafness of technocrats. Somehow I have found the vitality to carry on like a sleepwalker, taking the risks I have to take with the energy of despair: and I am not speaking of physical risks. In my heart of hearts I have always been certain that I would achieve my ends, which I knew were morally worthwhile. I navigate alone and surrounded by mist, according to my own personal geography.

I am a geographer. For the last forty years I have witnessed not so much the crisis of geography as the crisis of geographers who never cease to ask questions of themselves concerning the specificity of their discipline and the ways in which it connects to other disciplines. They are free to do as they like. I am inspired by such great naturalists and philosophers as Buffon, Humboldt, Rousseau, Goëthe, who consider the history of man without ever forgetting his ecological dimension. When I chose to make the Arctic region my field of study, there was no chair of polar geography in France's institutes of advanced study because France had never colonized the cold regions. I deliberately chose my direction without any certainty that it would lead to any kind of career. That was the right way to do it. *You should go straight to the point where research is breaking new ground.* My lucky break was my encounter with the visionary mind of Fernand Braudel, who created the Ecole des Hautes Etudes en Sciences Sociales. When I was elected its youngest member at the age of thirty-five, I was given the first and only chair of Polar Studies in the history of French university.

But my troubles were far from over. Little by little I made the Eskimos my special field of study. But the French academic system then refused to entertain—and continues still to neglect—the study of people whom it considers "residual." The general view was that such peoples belonged in museums of anthropology. When I defended my thesis at the Sorbonne on April 9, 1962, I had to resort to the man-nature dialectics of Marx, Michelet and Bachelard; later I had to struggle with my tutelary authorities to win acceptance of the fact that, in a Center of Arctic Studies, research in the social sciences (scandalously described as "soft sciences") is of equal interest in a fundamental area as research in the exact sciences ("hard sciences"). This debate took place at the highest level of the CNRS. And here I must salute the contribution of Professor Francois Kornilovsky, the director-general of the CNRS, who as a biologist has always supported my interdisciplinary outlook.

I also had to defend the idea that the unschooled thought of a primary nomad people could be just as complex as that of our own agriculture-based societies. Cultural racism is a deep and widespread phenomenon. There are advanced, pioneering peoples (Anglo-Saxons, Nordics); there are others, who may be decadent or vanquished (Old Europe for example) ; there are also underdeveloped peoples such as Africans, natives living on reserves, people who require help within the evolutionary framework. A third cause for which I have fought is the continued use of French as a scientific language. Here and there I detect a certain acceptance of defeat on this front, which reminds me unpleasantly of Vichy.

Q: Is it true that people on the political right call you a leftist?

A: Yes—and on the left they call me a man of the right. Left and right are no more than convenient labels for politicians and the media machinery that feeds them. We know perfectly well that our real problems are global and are addressed by a jet set of financiers and powerful economic forces. All I know is that I loathe and despise totalitarianism in all its forms, whether overt (as in the case of Stalinism and Nazism) or hidden (money and the power of money). I also loathe all mafias. I belong to no political party because I cannot resign myself to having my views dictated to me by any faction, whatever it may be. I know all the inconveniences of steering a middle course and they are frequently greater than the advantages. Believe me, when it comes to problems and controversies, we must all go forward alone without a safety net—no party, whatever its color, will be there to help.

Q: How much of your time is taken up by your role as director of the Terre Humaine collection?

A: I created *Terre Humaine* in 1954 when I wrote *The Last Kings of Thule*. The CNRS hailed the book as an act of resistance, and gave its blessing to the collection. At the same time I was reprimanded for the anti-scientific procedure of publishing a mass-market work before I had completed my doctoral thesis (1962). But I felt that it was my clear duty to do so. As the sole witness to a people in dire peril as a result of the construction of an ultra secret nuclear base, I considered it my duty to go straight to the heart of the matter and to pay on the spot my debt to their endangered society. My book, by alerting public opinion—especially in Denmark—to what was going on, brought about a dialog between the Inuit and the administration. As I conceived it, *Terre Humaine* involved research that paralleled my own in the Arctic, with the aim of recreating that "literature of the real" which the naturalists called for during the nineteenth century. It was inspired by the all-inclusive intellectual approach of Lucien Febvre and Fernand Braudel; I even dare say that I put into action the spirit of the famous *Annales* review the most respected historical movement in the world between the two wars and the Ecole des Hautes Etudes en Science Sociales. I hope that *Terre Humaine* stands for their line of thought, which calls for an association of man with the place in which he lives, and for enlarging this idea to include the entire planet.

Glenn Gould, talking about the art of the fugue, once said: "I have come round to the idea that a work is more rigorous in its unity when it is made up of disparate segments placed end to end under a single interpretative hat." The *Terre Humaine* collection began with the Inuit of Thule; it developed into a movement of original ideas that has left its mark on the intellectual and literary life of France over the last forty-five years, and we owe this fact to the Eskimos.

Q: Going back to your battles in the Arctic—there being no French territories in the region, how did you make France's voice heard by the two superpowers, the USA and the Soviet Union?

A: With the support of Fernand Braudel, my first president at the Institute of Advanced Studies (Sorbonne) who became a good friend, I was able to negotiate agreements with British, Canadian and Scandinavian institutions, as well as with the Academy of Science and the Institute of Arctic and Antarctic Research in the Soviet Union. By then I had been nominated to the Ecole des Hautes Etudes en Science Sociales as well as being director of the brand new Centre d'Etudes Arctiques. I had a certain weight. But any cooperation with the Soviet Union, even in the scientific field, was a source of passion and conflict at that time. For the communists, the issue was unconditional adherence to a system; for their opponents, the Soviet Union itself was a monstrous lie and to collaborate with its researchers was treasonous. Both authorities left me cold. As I saw it, 60% of the Arctic was Siberian, and the duty of a researcher was to go where the problems were to be found.

The Americans have always viewed France's role in the Arctic as thoroughly baroque. It was no surprise that their research organisms, which anyway had little or no time for research in the French language, were distinctly cool to the prospect of a French presence within the framework of their own accords with the USSR. At the international Arctic Congress (Leningrad, December 12-15 1988), which was organized by the USSR around the iron premise that only countries near the Arctic had any right to discuss its destiny, there were only two Frenchmen present: one for the Arctic (myself) and another for the Antarctic. Other great powers (Great Britain, Japan and West Germany) were given only two representatives; the rest of the world was dispensed with entirely. Facing us were 150 Americans and two hundred Soviets.

This approach was preposterously archaic. In my speech I said as much, making clear my view that the Arctic could

I finish writing *The Last Kings of Thule*, Vézelay, 1953.

The silver medal of the Paris Geographical Society is awarded to Iggianguak, in honor of his father Uutaaq, one of the four Inuit discoverers of the Pole on 6 April 1909. November 1983.

The first international congress on arctic petroleum was held at Le Havre on 2-5 May 1973. It brought together Inuit delegates and world experts on petroleum. The forum was organized by the Center for Arctic Studies and the French Foundation for Nordic Studies, under the aegis of Jacques Le Goff, president of EHESS.

only be "scientifically" developed according to the spirit of UNESCO, meaning between powers on an equal footing, whatever their latitude. It is high time that exclusive chauvinism of this kind was permanently banned. The International Polar Congress on Siberian Development in December 1988, which was held at the Leningrad Academy of Science, came on the heels of a historic speech made by President Gorbachev in Murmansk (2 October 1987), whereby the Siberian Arctic was opened to international scientific and economic cooperation within the framework of the de-nuclearization of Northern Europe and the inauguration of a new approach to "shared European space." At this congress I made the point as vigorously as I could that the Arctic Siberian peoples were not democratically represented among us. At this crucial and historic moment the inalienable rights of native peoples were being utterly ignored. Consequently, as a French scientist, I took it upon myself to suspend France's adherence to the International Arctic Science Project. I was supported by my old friend Dr. Terence Amstrong.[16]

Research expeditions by Jean Malaurie to study ancient climatic conditions and Inuit anthropology in 1967, 1969, 1972, 1982.

Q: Was your life as a researcher made easier by collaboration between the CNRS and the Soviet Academy of Sciences?

A: Indeed it was. The Center for Arctic Studies pioneered a richly productive scientific collaboration with the ethnographic Institute of the Soviet Academy of Science, from 1958 onwards, for shared study of the peoples of the Arctic Circle. There were four bilateral seminars and co-publications on given themes, but what was always lacking was work in the field with robust discussion of concrete realities, meaning a Franco-Soviet mission to Northern Siberia in the spirit of the Jesup Pacific Expedition, in 1904-1909, which made it possible for Americans and Russians to collaborate in a friendly way across the ocean—cradle of an immense and varied history. Alas, despite thirty years of patient negotiations, the Soviet authorities continued to refuse me and all other Westerners all access to Chukotka Peninsula, the only region where Asian Eskimos still survived.

Thirty years! I have always viewed this as an intellectual scandal and absurdity: what else but free dialog between opposing views can express the true greatness of a nation? My friend and colleague, the great Soviet historian Lev N. Gumilov,[17] was sentenced to 14 years in the gulag: this was no way to build a modern state. For this reason I adamantly refused to publish my socio-economic observations on other northern Siberian regions, which I have visited four times, for as long as I was refused permission to go to this important sector and pursue my studies there.

After the Leningrad Congress in 1988, I finally met with the academician Dimitri Likashov, an advisor to President Gorbachev. He told me that over the years I had adopted the right course of action. "We were wrong to stop you going to the North. Now we mean to make amends, by appointing you as scientific director of a joint Soviet-French expedition to the Chukotka region. This will be the first international expedition of its kind in this Asian Eskimo territory. Your role will be to appraise the policy on the Arctic minorities which has been applied by us for the last sev-

16) West Germany, Great Britain, and the Netherlands also refused to join this organization, whose founding was postponed indefinitely. This action naturally stirred up comment, and had political repercussions as far away as Moscow.

17) A specialist in the civilization of the Central Asian steppes, he is the only son of Anna Akhmatova.

enty years. All Party files, even the most confidential ones, will be made available to you; and when your mission is complete, if you so desire we would like you to remain as our advisor on these problems, within the framework of Gosplan and the Culture Fund."

Accordingly in August and September 1990 I led the first Franco-Soviet expedition to Chukotka since the October Revolution. There were fifteen of us in all. In my socio-political report on the condition of the 1600 Siberian Eskimos and maritime Chukchees, I was highly critical but also constructive in my observations. The entire affair is described in detail in *Hummocks 2 (1999)*. At my insistent request, which was backed up by the scientific community of St Petersburg, this report led to the creation in 1991 of a school for cadres of the Native Northern peoples at St Petersburg, which I agreed to direct, under the patronage of the ENA in Paris. This became the State Polar Academy in 1997, and now has 1000 boarding pupils, including the sons of herdsmen, hunters and apparatchiks. By January 2000, we had trained 150 high officials, all of whom are now in place and at work. They represent the Siberia of the future. The French language is one of their two obligatory foreign languages (the other being English). Our first list of graduates in 2000 was named after General de Gaulle.

The Center for Arctic Studies, the Ecole des Hautes Etudes en sciences Sociales, and the Danish authorities all lent contractual support to this program. The next problem was to invent specific teaching procedures for 26 separate peoples whose literature was exclusively oral. We also set out to preserve the best aspects of their heritage, including their shamanism and their political structures. Their ambition must be to develop their territory while absolutely respecting its threatened ecology.

The Canadian Inuit authorities at Nunavik, personified by Charlie Watt, the Inuit senator in Ottawa, then asked me to cooperate with them in the preparation of a shared program of instruction and exchange for the Canadian Inuit élites. The Greenland authorities have confirmed their eagerness to participate in this.

Q: It was you who coined the phrase Northern Third World. Do you still think it applies to populations that are dependent on the world's industrial superpowers?

A: In capitalist as well as socialist countries, most policies framed to deal with minorities have failed, for one reason or another. There is one shining exception: the economic and industrial policies of Greenland up till 1953.

I have criticized the absence of audiovisual facilities for peoples whose literature is oral, and who think in terms of images, and I deplore the assimilatory approaches of schools in Alaska, Canada and Siberia, which I saw from the inside while working as a volunteer teacher in several schools in 1987 and 1990. We know only too well how destructive welfare plans can be. Before we drown the Arctic peoples in pseudo-development projects costing millions of dollars and Danish kroner, we should realize that all societies need to develop from the top down, by the formation of an élite. A native "Oxford" for Inuit administrators is sorely lacking. "Less but better" should always be the golden rule.

Finally, I would like to say that in all my battles I have relied on public opinion, which I kept steadfastly on the alert through the press, radio and TV. As a university academic, I am well aware that my peers frequently take a dim view of my behavior. Nevertheless I am quite sure that beyond my seminars at the Ecole des Hautes Etudes en sciences Sociales (EHESS) there exists a far greater university, the university of public opinion. We must always trust the intelligence that rules that university.

Knud Rasmussen, in his exemplary work at Thule, leaned heavily for support on the wisdom of the Danish people, which he solicited through the press. For my own part, to see my own thought through to its logical conclusion I need the renewed assent of the popular conscience, which can be as severe in its judgment as it is generous. If he has that assent, no warrior, whoever he is, need ever feel that he is fighting alone. ■

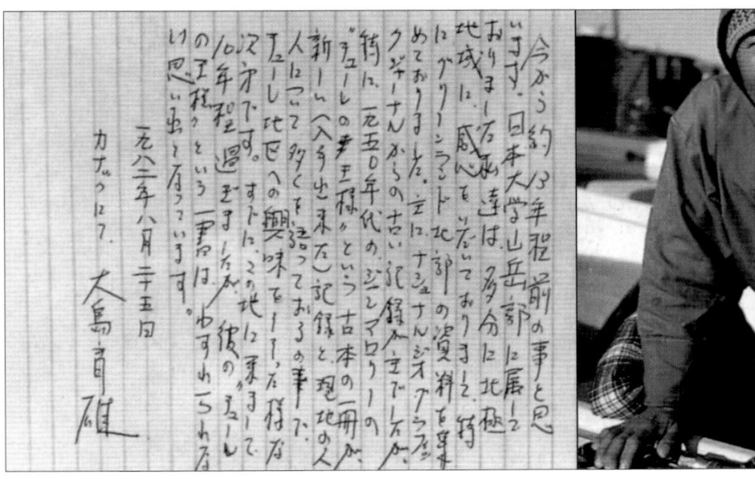

今から約13年程前の事と思
います。日本大学山岳部に居り
おりました私達は多分に北極
地域に感心をいだいており、特
にグリーンランド北部の資料を集
めておりました。主にナショナルジオグラフィッ
クマガジンからの古い記録が主でしたが、
偶然に一九五〇年代の終りマロリーの
「チューレの最后の王様」という古本の一冊が
新しい(入手出来た)記録と现地の人
人について多くを語っておる事で
チューレ北極への興味を一層かき立てられたのが
10年程前です。そしてこの地に来まして
10年程過ぎましたが、彼の「チューレ
の王様」という一冊は、わすれられない
思い出と成っています。

一九八二年八月二十五日

カナックにて

大島育雄

TO JEAN MALAURIE

It happened fourteen years ago, I believe. I belonged to a group of mountain climbers at Nippon University (in Tokyo). We had a keen interest in the Arctic regions, and we were looking for works relating to North Greenland; for the most part, we had old accounts from *National Geographic Magazine*. Then, by an extraordinary stroke, I discovered a used book in Tokyo published in the 1950s, *The Last Kings of Thule*, by Jean Malaurie. This book provided us with new and key information and spoke eloquently of the people who inhabited this region, awakening a deep attachment in me for the northern land of Thule. . . . Ten years have passed since I have come to Siorapaluk—the village in the book—and reading *Last Kings of Thule* will remain an unforgettable experience for me.

Oshima Ikao

Qaanaaq, 25 August 1982

I land at Thule-Uummannaq on 23 July 1950 and am adopted by the family of Qisuk.

The first geomorphological expedition to the north of Greenland

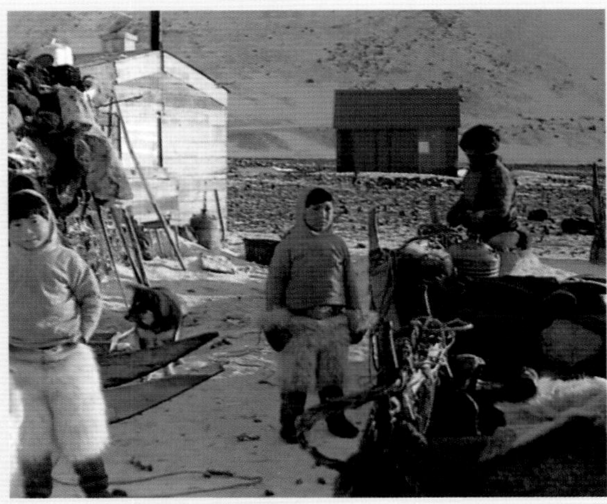

31 March 1951: After a winter of great scarcity, there was no food (pemmican) in this village for my 43 dogs, and reserves of walrus meat were low. My expedition to Inglefield Land therefore faced considerable dangers.
My companions and I decided to hunt every day in order to continue with our projects.

THE FUTURE, OVERCOMING WINTER

"The individual who thinks against a sleeping society," wrote Alain, "it is forever the same story, and the spring will always have the same winter to overcome." It is more than ever necessary to overcome the winter, to call forth those who would awaken conscience and go against the times.

It is fashionable to rebel against the conservatism of French society, calling it a "blocked" society. In fact we are experiencing a silent revolution through the reversal of established hierarchies. Power slips into the hands of technocratic groups that are gradually becoming multinational, in which the fact of having marginal ideas and expressing them is reason enough to be disqualified.

And this technocracy by no means acts responsibly! The third world alone is the subject of 14,000 colloquia per year. The group of consultants for the UN, for UNESCO, and for the many organizations providing international development aid constitutes in itself a restricted number of international officials who run a prosperous "colloquium" economy. These experts are all the less efficient for having no real responsibility, their careers depending entirely on the organizations or governments who employ them. Is it any wonder that the third world—three quarters of mankind, part of which is dying of hunger— is sinking into poverty despite the billions of dollars invested? But the thinkers who discuss at great length the pluralism of cultures and intercommunication do nothing but "speechify" about the people without being in solidarity with them or sharing in their hard life. The people, for their part, constantly remind us that to think is good, but to live is better.

What is needed is knowledge of the other, not voyeurism. Understanding can only arise from shared joys and pains. Culture is only a reflection of life—but it first has to be lived. Such is the price for grasping a civilization's destiny. We must urgently awaken the nomad each of us carries within. This is the historian's duty, and the ethnographer's, and the philosopher's, to be done with the time for colloquia, to emerge from the libraries, to help man discover another self among those "true" voyages that underlie his imaginative faculty.

***Terre humaine* bulletin, February 1985.**

Areas of rockfall, which are accumulations of rock at the foot of cliffs, are a consequence of erosion. For fifteen years I studied them systematically in hot and cold deserts; in their depths as well as on their surfaces, they were explored, measured, and mapped. My companion, far off on the floe, keeps a watch on me. At each camp, our party of three sleds would split into two groups. Alternating duties, one group would go off and hunt seal and hare while the other, taking me on the sled, would retrace our earlier path. At each thalweg I would climb unaccompanied to the plateau. From there, alone and on foot, mapping as I went, I would return to the sled. North Inglefield Land, near Cape Agassiz, May 1951.

Inglefield and Washington lands, and Ellesmere Island

Polarpunga: a young woman visits us in our snow igloo.

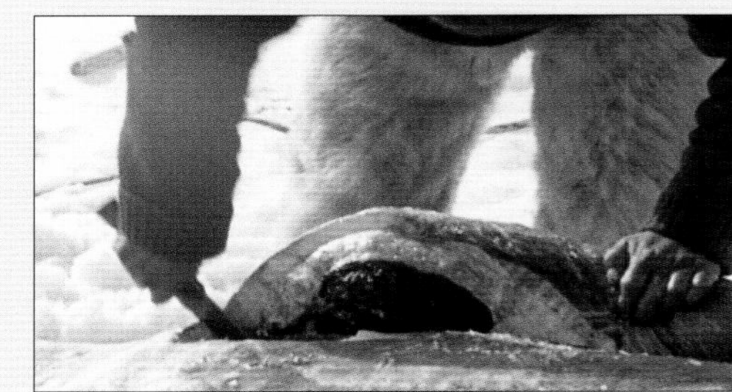

First cut into the skin and blubber of a harpooned walrus.

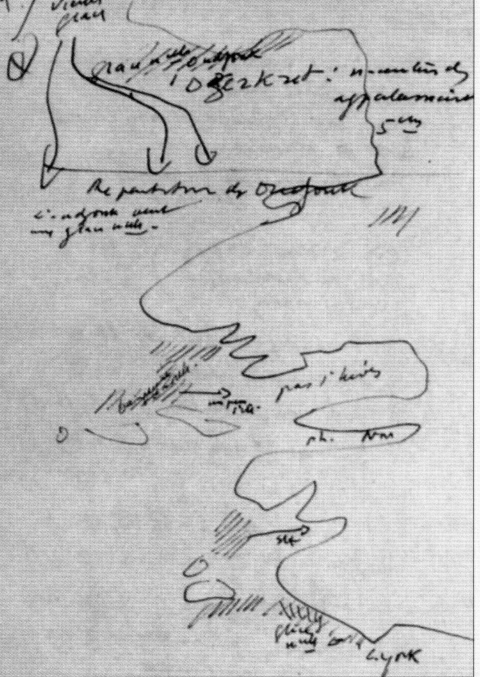

Pages from some of my twenty notebooks (these are from 1967). My four expeditions among the Polar Eskimos included work in geomorphology (1951), paleoclimatology (1967 and 1969), the demography and genealogy of this isolated population of 1400 people over four generations, the study of the subsistence micro-economy at different dates, the making of an atlas of animal and human ecology, the ethnohistory of the Inughuit from its discovery in 1818 to 1989, the description of the process of acculturation and the birth of a new people since 1967. These notes were written daily while observations were fresh. I also kept an expedition journal, more personal and private in nature, on a regular basis.

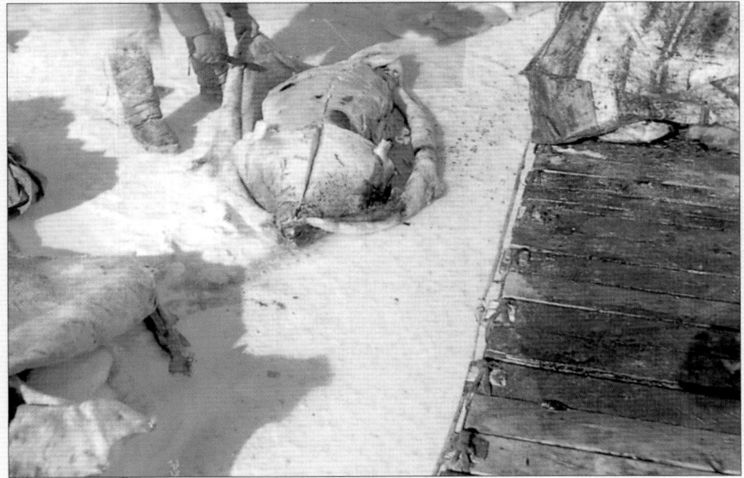

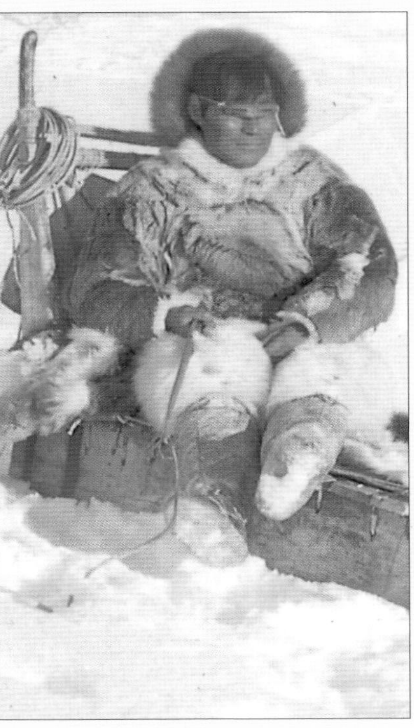

Kutsikitsoq, born in 1903, was my companion on all my expeditions. His father, Uutaaq, Peary's famous companion, first brought us together. Kutsikitsoq helped me in the winter of 1950 when I was traveling from group to group during the polar night gathering information for my genealogical study. He also came with me when I set out on my dangerous geomorphological expedition, in which I traveled 900 miles across Inglefield and Washington lands and Ellesmere Island. Kutsikitsoq asked me to give his name to my firstborn if it was a boy—which it was. His face has become the emblem of *The Last Kings of Thule,* the first volume in the "Terre humaine" collection. Inglefield Land, May 1951.

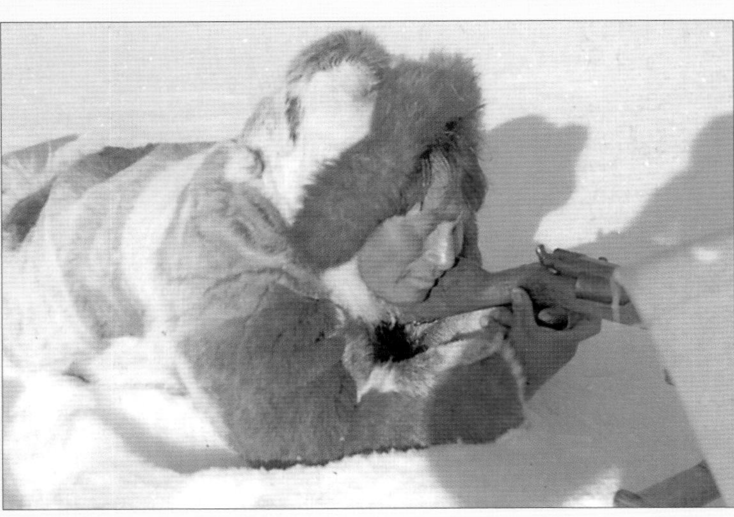

Kutsikitsoq, stalking our daily seal at Inuarfissuaq (Marshall Bay) in April 1951. Hunting for survival, March-June 1951. Without pemmican, the dogs had to be fed fresh meat every day. The seal was hunted at the mouth of his *agluq*, from the end of March to the beginning of April, at times of intense cold. In the beginning of May, the seal hauls himself onto the ice through his breathing hole in order to bask in the sun. Kutsikitsoq creeps up on the seal behind a screen of white cloth stretched in front of the sled. The seal must be hit between the eyes to kill him instantly. If he is only wounded, the hunter must run up to finish him off before he slips back into the *agluq*, from which he never strays far.

Precambrian cliffs some 1300 feet high near Aannartoq, in Rensselaer Bay, where Kane wintered in 1853-1855. Our expedition was traveling north on ice ten feet thick. In the lead, pulled by nineteen dogs, is Kutsikitsoq's sled, on which his wife Natuk is seated. Behind were my own sled and the sled of Qaaqqutsiaq and Patdloq. April 1951.

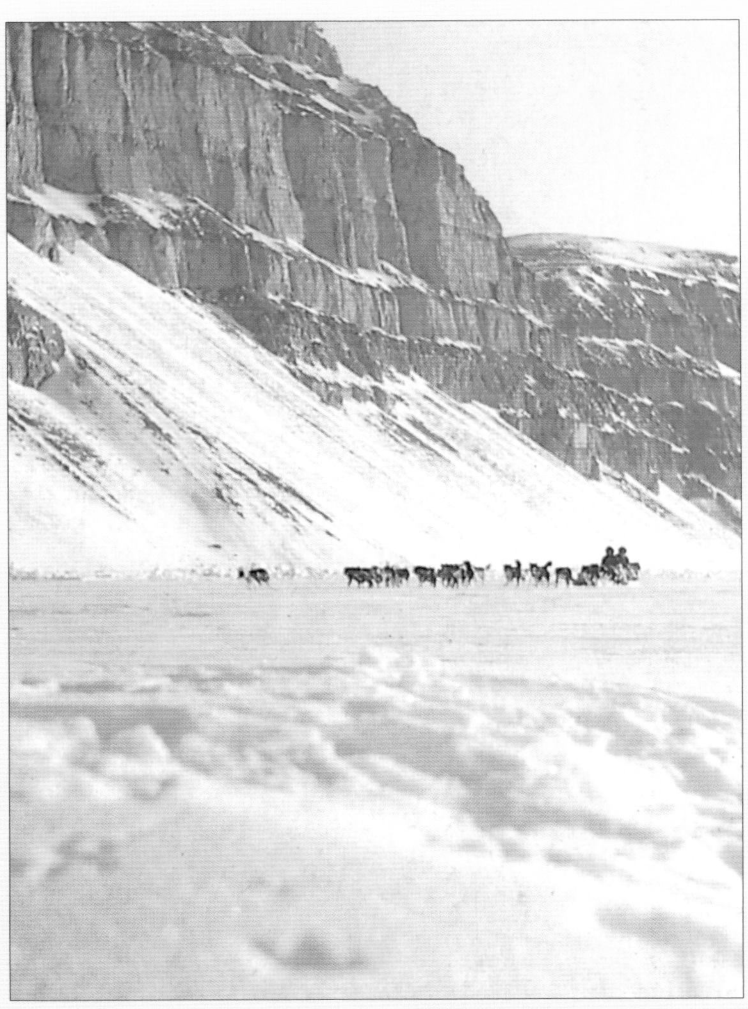

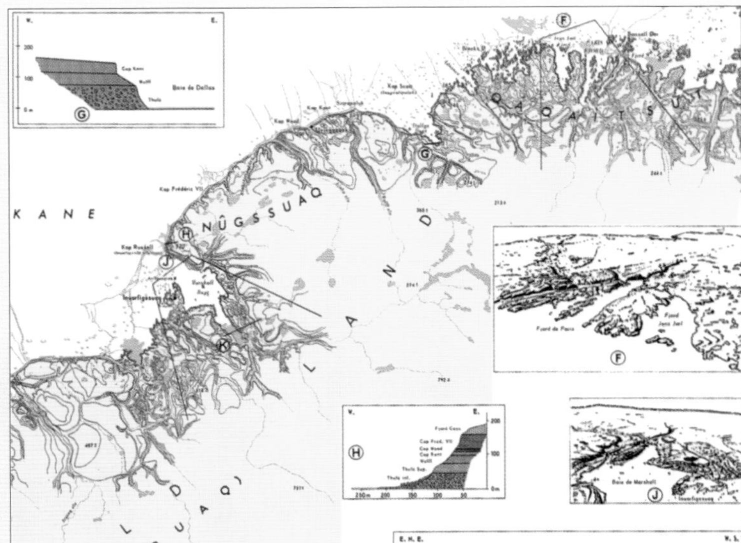

Section of the 1:100,000 map of south Washington Land and Inglefield Land (French Geographic Mission to Thule, 1950-1951), established by Jean Malaurie to a depth of 3 kilometers inland, from Etah (Smith Sound) to Cape Jackson (Kennedy Channel), and published on a scale of 1:200,000.

My team and I

In November 1950, Paapaaq, the unquestioned *naalagaq* (team leader), finally demonstrated after three months that he wished—despite my clumsiness—to be my friend.

To prove that I acknowledged him as such, when I fed the dogs their daily ration of walrus or seal I threw the meat to Paapaaq last. I could see by the far-off look in his eye, and his indifferent way of sitting on his haunches, that he liked to be distinguished from the others in this way.

It was a while before he showed his gratitude. One winter's morning near Etah in late March 1951, with the temperature at thirty below, I made my way across to my sled where the dogs were carefully attached by their traces to a knife stuck in the ice. At the delicate moment when my finger was hooked in the seal leather loop holding all the traces, and I was just about to hitch it to the sled, all eight dogs suddenly rose from the snow, arched their backs and—believing they were hauling the *qaamutit* [sled]—began to pull with all their might on my finger, which was trapped between the leather and the ice. The more my finger resisted, the more they pulled. Five, ten minutes passed; in my pain and desperation I reached for my knife with the wild intention of slicing off my own second finger. At this moment, Paapaaq turned his head, saw what had happened and made the team back up, releasing me. But now the dogs were loose, and this was a wide fjord. Having made it round to the far side of the icy water lapping against the cliff face, Papaaq sat down and stared back at me; the breakout had lasted long enough, he seemed to be thinking. I stood stock still, silently holding my useless whip in one hand; not quite helpless, but inwardly screaming for help. Paapaaq scrutinized me for a few seconds, then cantered back, followed chaotically by the rest of the pack.

June 1951

Since our return from the excursion to Ellesmere Land, the team and I have become inseparable. The pace is fast; after 1500 km the dogs can sense the joy I feel. Our yelling, super-human and super-canine efforts among the tangled fifteen-foot hummocks are forgotten now. Crouched on my sled, I let my thoughts drift, rocked by the gentle rhythm of the team, lulled by the hiss of the whip-thong slipping through the snow. The dogs have begun to walk at a different, ambling pace, slower and more regular; they are aware of the well-being which has stolen over me. They sense that I am in another world, dreaming as though drugged. I am in a kind of visionary trance which is much prized by the Eskimos, but which only their dogs can trigger. A brief moment of ecstasy, filled with the smell of my sweat and the skins that I wear, the muffled sound of the sledge, the sun, the light.

It lasts for only a few seconds, but even so the dogs let me know that they feel it too: without turning to face me they wag their tails and rotate their small triangular ears. They have done me great honor today . . .

It is no longer snowing: it is raining. The ice around is greenish, with intermittent white streaks. The dogs are moving forward up to their shoulders in fresh water that has accumulated on the ice floe, when they are suddenly swallowed up in a crevasse spotted just too late. Only a trained eye can distinguish the deep black of the sea from the clearer band of fresh water running along this yawning cavity, which opens to a sea 3000 feet deep right below the ice floe.

The dogs fall in bunches; I am stranded on the 12 foot long, 300-kilo sled which sits bridge-like athwart the crevasse. The sea is choppy, and the two lips are gradually drawing apart. The animals are desperate—Paapaaq, with his light brown eyes, tries to swim as close to me as possible. I grab the scruff of his neck, haul him out of the water, and—kneeling foursquare on top of my fossil boxes—hurl him towards the ice floe a few yards away with all the energy my arms can muster. I do the same with four more dogs, but have no strength left for the remaining three. With his four mates, Paapaaq waits for my order, then, digging their claws into the thawing ice and arching their backs with the effort, they manage to get a purchase on the heavy sled, which by now has tilted 30 degrees with its rear end submerged. Finally the front drops with a dull thud, and I use a billhook to drag the three remaining dogs from the freezing sea.

Old friends, how can I ever forget you? As I write these lines, 39 years later, I can still smell your coats and your warm breath; my fingers probe your heavy underfur as I straddle your backs to harness you in the morning; between my thumb and forefinger, I recall the rough black skin of your feet and the cracks from which I prized the slivers of June ice with the point of my knife, at the risk of stripping the living flesh away. I remember your peculiar passion for the excrement of men; curiously, the Inuit myths say that men came from the union of a dog and a woman in the recess of a shit-filled bowel. I can still hear your joyous cries around the bear brought to bay after a silent chase; your snuffles in the early morning when I found you, the eight of you, Paapaaq, Alineq, Pikali . . . poking your heads from the mantle of snow that covered you in the night, shaking it spasmodically from your necks, with your noses stuck out straight, shrewdly gauging not so much the weather as the mood of this man, me, your master and accomplice in all things.

J.M., 15 January 1990

Living Eskimo-style

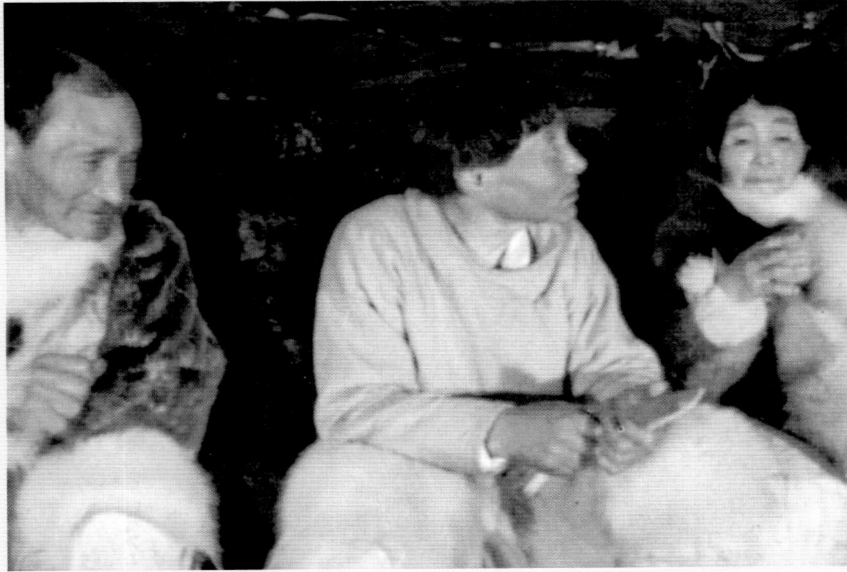

Night activities in the igloo, Qeqertarssuaq. From left to right, Sorqaq, sitting on the sleeping platform of stone covered with skins; Piuaitsoq, scraping a tusk to make a harpoon point; and Aama, his wife, tending the modern cookpot hanging over the blubber lamp resting on its stone base. Pieces of a walrus killed in the preceding days are warming in a blood broth. On the sandstone slabs that form the igloo's floor, in the foreground, lies a partridge, serving as a napkin for wiping one's lips and hands. Still image from *Last Kings of Thule*, shot in April-May 1969 with a French television crew, and directed by me. (INA Archives)

The blubber lamp. After the hunt, in which two walruses were harpooned, the hunters spend the night in a stone igloo. This woman is trimming the wick of the lamp, where seal and walrus blubber is burning. Stills from *Last Kings of Thule*.

The isolated population of Thule.

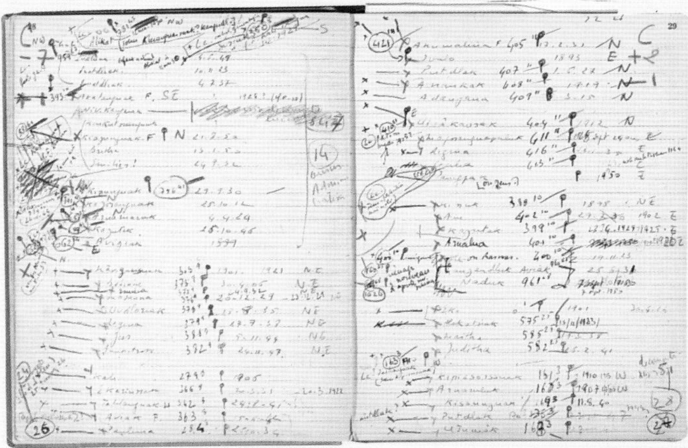

My genealogical survey, family by family. The first census of the seventy families dispersed in ten villages (302 Inuit) over 300 miles. The work was accomplished on dog sled journeys during the polar night.

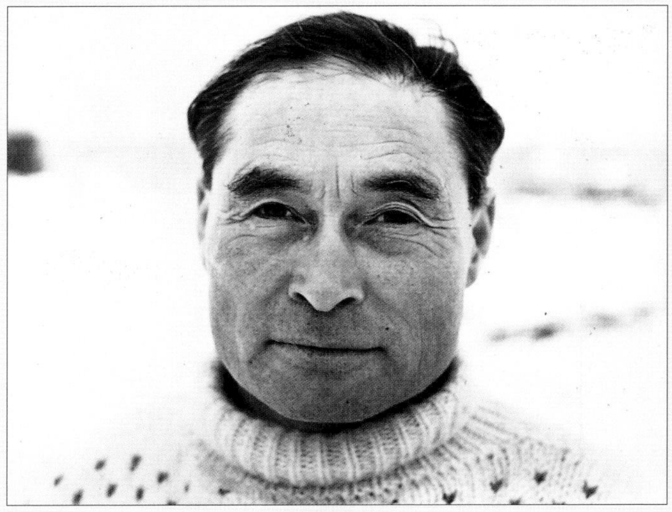

Kaalipaluk, born in 1906. Peary's Eskimo son, his mother was Aleqasina. Cautious, modest, and a capable hunter, he established himself as a pre-eminent figure among the Inuit. Qeqertarsuaq, 1967.

A native hunter died in 1993. This child from Siorapaluk, born in the same year, was given his name. The spirit of the deceased lives on in him. His young mother is presenting him to me.

Uutaaq, born in 1877, was 74 years old when this photograph was taken in Uummannaq in 1951. Peary's companion at the Pole, he was an unquestioned authority among all the Polar Eskimos. Baptized only on 25 October 1925, he is descended from one of the fourteen Eskimos who immigrated from Igloolik, Canada in 1863.

The future: children at school in Qaanaaq.

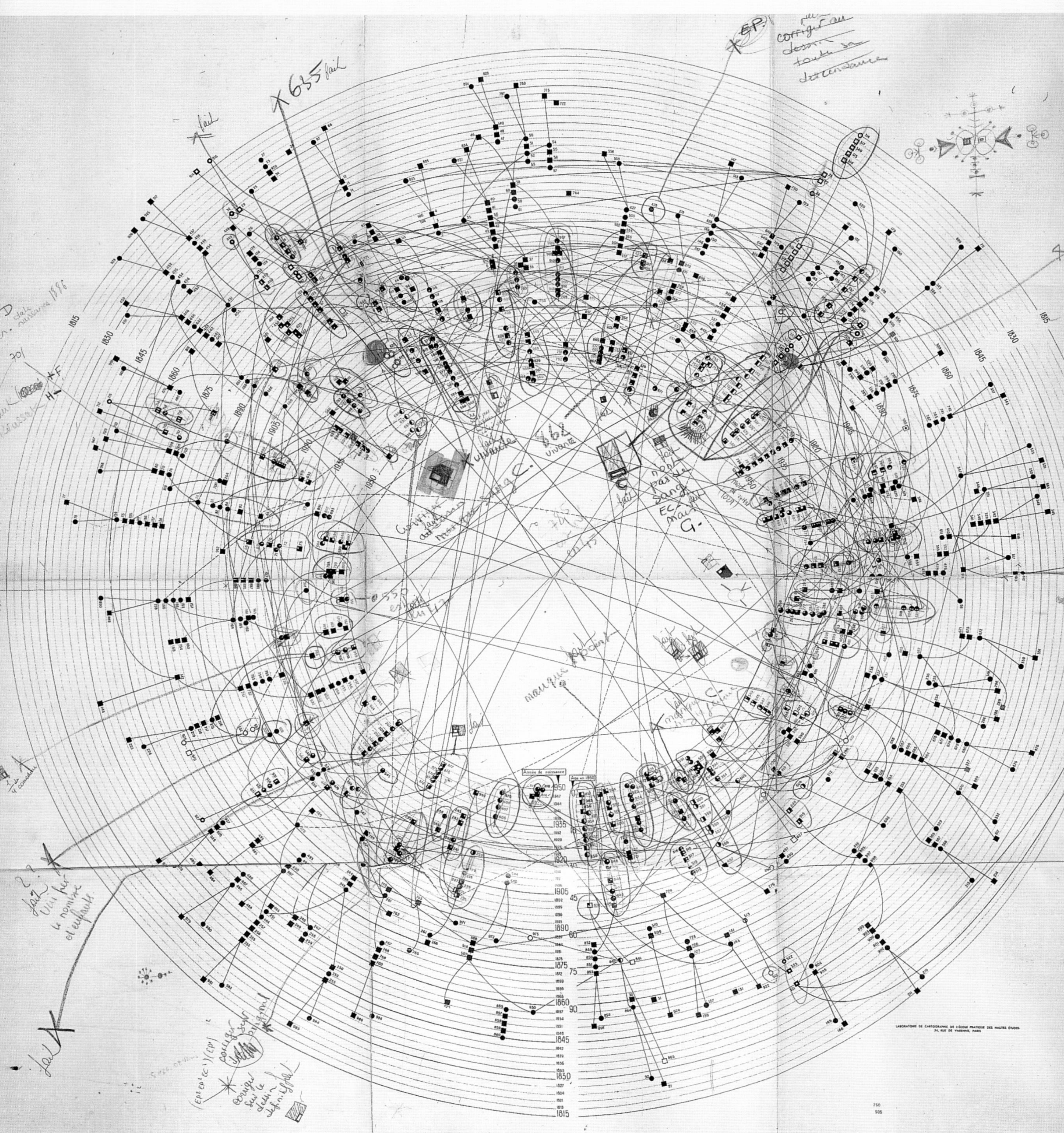

Graphic representation of the first genealogy of the Polar Eskimos of northwest Greenland. I made this survey, individual by individual, during the winter of 1951. The genealogy was drawn up, after a second expedition in 1967, at the National Institute of Demographic Research in Paris with Léon Tabah and the geneticist Jean Sutter. From 25 to 40 families of these most northerly Eskimos in the world survived in isolation for two centuries (1600-1818). In 1855-1880, the group numbered from 150 to 200 individuals, and in my census of 31 December 1950 they numbered 302 men and women. Their survival depended on planned marriages, what Claude Lévi-Strauss has called the elementary structures of kinship. To avoid the dangers of inbreeding, the Inuit forbade the marriage of men and women related up to the fifth degree. A computer study of this genealogical chart has confirmed the practice. In order to master its own destiny, this primitive people makes and follows plans. This is also true in the ecological realm. Relying as they do on hunting, they take care not to put undue pressure on the animal populations by overhunting them. Rules and taboos prevent the Inuit from doing this.

Young Inuit learning meteorology. They now hold posts of responsibility in this and other fields, replacing Danish civil servants.

The cemetery at Siorapaluk, August 1995.

Below,
young hunters of the year 2000 perpetuate their people's traditions. Against all odds, they insist on hunting in the old style. They refuse to use snowmobiles, feeling a bond to their dogs and to tradition.

Opposite,
Qaanaaq, 2000. "Oh Whites! What have you done to my people?"

15 June 1951. On the trail toward Thule, near the summit of the glacier, Sakaeunnguaq senses forthcoming disaster. He asks that we stop our three sleds and, for lack of a sacred drum, accompanies his ritual *ayaya* by beating out the time with a knife on the rim of a metal box lid. (See also page 380.)

A dangerous rescue

April 1969. Whale Sound. The filming expedition is in danger: they must cross the rotten pack ice on foot.

Ululik got up at six o'clock in the morning. Bent double, he assessed the overcast sky. The wind had dropped. Horrors, the temperature was rising; already a thick fog had mantled the horizon. Somewhere behind it were our companions.

The boat could no longer be seen. Under his breath, Ululik murmured to no-one in particular that they must be out of tobacco out there. It was an early morning in April. The air carried specks of sleet and the cloud cover was very low; a dusting of snow had fallen in the night which covered our heads, our shoulders and our equipment with its soft down. Ululik's hair had gone white, and no doubt I looked just the same to him, prematurely aged and shrunken. He came to my side and sat down. We waited together, motionless; with his brown face bent forward, Ululik was thinking hard, from time to time clenching his gnarled fingers and grinning mirthlessly. Then he spoke to me in low tones, laying stress on the latter part of each phrase. I glanced at the muscular backs of his hands. The fingers were pudgy, the nails broken and blackened. Something was troubling him deeply; he stood up, paced forward with short steps, then came back to sit beside me. There was another long silence, broken again when he went to lean against the *napariaq* of the sled we shared as a bed. He continued to gaze intently at the skyline, as the dawn gradually came up, pallid and frosty.

All at once two young hunters lurched out of the mist, wild-eyed, having taken shocking risks to reach us from the boat. We rose to meet them. They stood stiffly upright, facing us at the extreme edge of the ice floe. We had little time to ask questions: tense as they were, they could barely look at us. They wanted to go back as soon as they could, once a rescue effort had been organized with me. They reassured us in our conviction, already silently reached, that we had to go, *massarkut! assut*! immediately, to where we were needed. Not a moment could be lost: the younger Inuit were losing their nerve. The drift of the ice had placed the six men aboard the boat in serious danger—four Eskimos and two Frenchmen who had put their trust in me. I would never forgive myself if I failed to take charge of a situation that was my responsibility alone. What could we do once we arrived? I didn't know yet; to go was the priority.

The four of us quickly made ready to leave the floe.[19] For the two Frenchmen I carried changes of clothes and European food. We said nothing: before us, beyond the hard edge of the firm, six-foot-thick ice, lay an impassable channel ten yards wide edged by a far more treacherous surface. This expanse of floating ice, intersected by zones of black water, appeared vast and strange to me. In Indian file, four to five yards apart and unroped, we moved gingerly along, searching northwards for a passage across the first channel. Ululik took the lead; I followed, carrying a six foot Inuit lance, with Masaannaa and Asiajuk at my heels. The horrible surface was more shattered than I had imagined: where I was placing my feet there was sheet ice, as well as oscillating plaques like frozen lily pads and dislocated, pancake ice that tilted underfoot and looked grayish and rotting—though it was shot through with jade-colored veins when it was sound. The Inuit took short, quick steps, their stocky torsos bent over, acutely alert: they moved in silence, with the utmost care, placing their small feet regularly one in front of the other in the rhythm of a universe whose balance they utterly understood.

As the going grew more perilous, the pace suddenly increased. We had to move fast, hopping from block to floating block, to avoid bearing them down. Beneath us the sea was infinitely threatening—3000 feet deep. I imitated Ululik's dancing, scuttling run, watching his least movement, choosing the same path but remembering

April 1969. Whale Sound.

19) Among my companions was Kutsikitsoq's son, Masaannaa, whom I knew well in childhood. He immediately told me in his hoarse voice that he wanted to be at my side during this chancy affair, as his father would have been.

The sled carrying the two Frenchmen sinks into the rotten ice.

with every stride that I weighed a lot more than he did. He moved forward remorselessly. *"Assut! Assut! Malaurie!"* Faster, Faster, "*Pissortut Inuk*!" (Like an Inuk!) The hunters following me, who were pulling a bare sled, encouraged me with joy in their voices–'Quicker. Quicker! Just like us.' The harsh cries of Masaanna, chiming with those of Ululik and Asiajuk in front and behind, literally raised me up and carried me onward. Suddenly I turned my head: Asiajuk, with his tufted hair, his silky white bearskin breeches and his elegant fox fur *kapatak* with blue and white trimmings, was ten yards back. I had never seen such an eye as his, gleaming with the absolute pride of an Inuk moving in majesty across the shifting, treacherous ice, though it sank and yawed under his feet in disjointed blocks. Through the mist he looked like a man walking miraculously on water. He favored me with a quick, knowing glance: and in that fraction of a second I learned more about his mysterious people, now bound to us for better or for worse, than in all the books I have ever read. Ah, Inughuit! How I loved you, every one of you, in your wilderness.

Q'aalassoq (the Navel). A great bear hunter, he is Ululik's brother.

We approached a small iceberg, floating like a shattered crystal tower, and I slowed my pace a little, perhaps from overconfidence. My face was pouring with sweat, my sodden hair was glued to my face–and for a moment I raised my eyes, which had hitherto been fixed on an area half a meter around my boots. In the moment it took me to draw breath, my lagging feet dislodged a shard of ice and I began to slip. Before I knew it I was in the water up to my groin; instinctively I arched forward and grasped a providential spur of the iceberg, hauled myself out and scurried onward. Neither of my boots, thank God, had shipped any water. The figures on the boat ahead watched our approach, all of them grave, some clearly petrified with fear. They were wrapped in thick furs, their brown faces tightly encased in double hoods of anorak material and caribou skin (*qulitsaq*); huddled together like shipwrecked mariners, they stared at us from the rail of the boat, which in consequence was listing sideways. They all knew it would soon be their turn to brave the ice, if they didn't want to drift for weeks in this uncertain season.

At the last moment, just when I thought I had made it, I failed to notice that the boat's swaying had smashed the thin night-freeze around it, and I nearly went under a second time. But strong arms pulled me aboard, to meet the distraught eyes of the younger men. Our resolution overruled their doubts; a few words were enough to convince them that they had to abandon ship immediately, before the nervous energy that had carried us thus far had time to subside.

The two Frenchmen, aghast at the predicament into which I had led them –they had only been in Greenland for a week, if I remember rightly–goggled at me as though I was from another planet. But one of them said a gracious thing: "You shouldn't have come. It was a mad act–but thank you."

It was clear that the only course open to us, however dangerous, was to place them on the small sled hauled by the two Inuit in my wake. The heavier of the two Europeans would sit behind, and the other would squat in front, moving forward or backward to maintain a balance according to the orders of Ululik or Masaanna, translated by me.

"They have to stay on the sled, whatever happens," I was told to say. That was all.

We spent a few more minutes aboard, just time to catch our breath. A milky light bathed the scene. I scanned the way back, the channels of black water, the rotting icepack. It seemed there was nothing but water ahead of us. One of the young hunters tossed a piece of walrus meat on the ice and watched gloomily as it vanished in the slush. I felt my heart sink. "Luck won't be on your side this time," said a cold voice within me. What if we should wait till nightfall, as originally planned? The air's freezing, the sea might do the same and make a safer surface. But the Inuit sensed what I was thinking, and they knew we would be paralyzed if it was expressed. They immediately caught me up in faster action. They were only too aware that if we stopped to think like that we would never get back–ever.

Three Eskimos went ahead, with me to translate their directions into French to my compatriots on the sled. The two other Inuit brought up the rear. I left my lance aboard the boat. Together we pushed and pulled the sled-cum-raft along–at least it was made lighter by the addition of a sealskin bladder on one side. Steadied as it crossed the broader pieces of ice, carried forward by a momentum which we had to keep going at all costs, often it literally floated on slush as we sped along. It was nine feet long and built of wooden pieces lashed together with sealskin thongs. For fear that it might begin to sink along with its two passengers, the Inuit skillfully sought out the broadest, safest ice plaques so as to shore up the front or the back of it as required. A moment came when we were traveling too fast and too confidently, missed an adjustment, and watched aghast as the front rose tragically into the air. But we righted the contraption and plunged onward, keeping the pace fast and furious as our instinct for survival took over. In the blur of the mist, we rushed through a chaos of ice and water. Ahead we began to distinguish the outlines first of the solid floe ahead, and then of our tiny base camp, a greenish canvas tent covered in blotches of seal fat. We continued to haul and push with all our might. The directions passed along by the Inuit were short and incisive, always complementing one another whoever they came from.

The last two Inuit, who had been on the boat and who had left it immediately after us, had chosen a different but no less perilous route. They were pulling a sealskin cable and a nylon extension which they had lashed to the stem of the launch; their intention was to bring the other end of it to solid ground.

The final ten yards consisted of ice so dissolved that we had to change our tactics. The sled was hauled across by Sakeuunguaq and Inuutersuaq, the two Eskimos who had remained in camp, the former organizing the maneuver. We were evacuated one by one: first the French sound man, then the cameraman, then me, then the five Inuit. The ice sagged like jelly but held firm for as long as it took to bundle the sled across.

At last! With my feet on solid ice, I realized the extent of our unbelievable luck. Without stopping for breath or changing our clothes, Ululik and I immediately assembled the forty huskies and harnessed them to the cable. Men and dogs then set to and hauled the launch in, yard by yard. *Qorfaa! Aroo! Aroo! Assut!* We yelled like madmen; the dogs lapped at the tin coating of snow that had fallen in the night, set their claws into the ice, doubled up and pulled for all they were worth, barking spasmodically. Their efforts were timed by staccato strokes of a whip-handle on the taut cable. The boat itself weighed at least a ton, and it contained another half a ton of walrus meat and fat in addition to our big TV camera and the footage that had been so bravely filmed in the course of our unfortunate hunt. Yet little by little all this was drawn across the slushy ice, following the path we had taken. The ghostly ease with which it seemed to travel reminded us all too graphically of the risks we had taken, on foot, not an hour earlier. The cable vibrated with extreme tension; we feared it would part from rubbing against the sharp projection of ice; but somehow it did not, and at last it was right in front of us. With a final effort, we dragged it across the last few yards and heard the dull thud as its metal-covered keel struck the solid bank.

We stopped to draw breath, then addressed the task of beaching the launch. The hull teetered forward, back–then with a collective rush and wild shout from the Inuit, it was torn from the cruel sea. Today I can see on screen these final scenes; our gallant cameraman and soundman, as soon as they set foot on the floe, had the presence of mind to use our Bell-Howell backup camera to record the end of a desperate adventure that might have ended in disaster had we made the smallest mistake.[20]

Unguaq, one of the hunters who had been on the boat, was a man who wielded a certain quiet authority over the others. Now he came slowly up to me, swaying slightly. Staring deep into my eyes, he wordlessly shook my hand.

April 1969. Whale Sound.

So ended the maddest and most dangerous operation I have ever undertaken. I could not be sure of its outcome. Instinct guided me throughout and gave me, drawing on some strange inner violence, the strength and self-command that I needed. Having survived this, I was physically able to comprehend what the winter had taught me unawares–how a group of Inuit, having involved their own destiny with your own, can bring you to surpass yourself. The moment I made my decision, the Inuit silently devised among themselves a complex strategy involving their own participation, the sled, the liaison role I would play and the cable to warp in the boat. For my benefit, they had planned out the only course open to us, despite the appalling risk to their own lives.

I think often of that extraordinary time, which remains so alive in me. I see it sequence by sequence. It was the certainty of pure instinct that made me stay behind in camp, in readiness for anything that might happen. During the day and night I spent reflecting with Ululik, it was not over the decision or the principle involved in the rescue attempt that I hesitated, but on how the operation was to be accomplished. I had to do it; but I couldn't manage without the Inuit. Without a word, without a moment's pause, they applied their method. It was they who assimilated me and did the job, strictly in response to my silent request.

I had entered their group, which was already constituted as such, because I was with them. Once in it, I was carried along by it. On the boat, I behaved with my two compatriots not like a Frenchman, but like a member of my Inuit group, living with its strength and conviction, grasping in a few seconds that there was no alternative to racing home across the rotting ice, something that would otherwise have been deemed total folly for a foreigner. Again, it was the group which, by imposing its own solution on me with such force, obliged us immediately to go back the way we had come.

In the snow igloo with the Inuit, after the ordeal.

In dangerous situations, I instinctively blended into the spirit of the Inuit tribe, to such an extent that I sometimes did things that astound me in retrospect. Integrated as I was into an Eskimo group, it was occasionally I who took an initiative that was tacitly followed by all. I was a free and active element within the team. I never followed it or led it; I was merely of it, and sometimes called upon to contribute certain decisions for the success and survival of all.

J.M.

20) I commend the cool courage of these two Frenchmen, so suddenly thrust into danger, and the confidence they unfailingly showed me during the rescue operation. Had I not been there, they would no doubt have had trouble agreeing to evacuate the boat and run this terrible risk themselves.

The fantasy world of the Inuit

THE BEAR HUNTER REMOVES HIS SKIN TO KILL A SKINNED BEAR

The ancestors one of them went to hunt bear. When he was out hunting, they say, he saw this bear that was skinned. Without any skin, they say, skinning himself, stripping his own skin off, he killed him. He made his little boy sleep, thinking it would scare him to death, they say. When he'd killed him, the bear, he put on his skin. When he was wearing it, he woke up his little boy. They went home and the little boy told it like that making a story. Because they were the great ancestors and so they spoke of it.

NUTIK (the Crevasse)

Nutik, they say, was married to a human. The great Nutik, they say, was married to a human. So in this way he had her for a real wife, Nutik. From the country of his big crevasse, he took a human for his wife, he had her as his wife, there. He often went hunting, always taking a lot of game, the great Nutik; during the hunting expeditions he always took fresh game, always like that, always hunting. So when he went hunting, whenever he came back to the house after taking fresh game, then he went to bed without any clothes, so he went to bed, went to bed, went to bed. So the people, these people they didn't know him at all, always in bed and eating.

He was always away hunting in this way always taking game, going to bed when he returned to the house. Finally one day his wife became pregnant. Again as always after going out hunting and coming back to the house he now went to bed again, and he went to bed. Finally, they say, the mother of his wife came in. She came in, they say. And then, they say, when she came, seeing him like that she said: "Your father-of-the-house, how does he usually eat, his excrements does he usually eat?" she asked her daughter. And then, they say, she said: "Your father-of-the-house, how does he usually drink, his urine does he drink?" When she had spoken, his mother-in-law, finally he, the great Nutik, spoke thus, his face nothing but crevasses in his shame, he who always went to bed, spoke thus: "I am not at home among humans, let me go out, my mittens, where are they?" His wife, they say, his mittens gave to him. Then, they say, he went out like that saying only that, because he was ashamed. When he went out, they say, he stayed out, he became a crevasse, because he was a crevasse. And so, they say, he stayed there afterward. And now, they say, she lived poorly! As long as he stays far away I say this. So the mother of his wife spoke, they say. Finally, they say, there she was now, now that she had no husband, she had her daughter. She gave birth to a son, they say, his wife gave birth to a very skillful son. The animals that he hunted too, he brought them down alone, as he often went hunting, becoming the one who always caught something, his little hunting expeditions always bringing in fresh game, the son of the great Nutik . . .

TWO STARS (Agssuk)

An old woman, they say, a child would come and visit her, not having a mother but a grandmother only. To the old woman he was in the habit of making visits the old woman she spoke to him like this: "Of your mother the hind flipper (or tail bone?) go gnaw on it!" Thus she spoke to him, because she had a flap of a coat (?), they say, of seal, always she would speak to him like that during his visits. To his grandmother finally he said: "The old lady always she says to me: 'Of your mother the flipper (tail bone?) go gnaw on it!'" His grandmother said to him like this: "Say to her like this: 'Your daughter-in-law in a crevasse far from land killing her did you shut her up?' Speak to her like that when you go to visit her." When he went to visit her, the old woman she said to him: "Of your mother the flipper (tail bone) go gnaw on it!" Coming in finally the child said to the old woman this: "Your daughter-in-law in a crevasse far off there killing her did you shut her up?" The old woman got really angry. Finally the child when he left, the old woman chased after him, her stick taking it she chased after him, the house all around for him. Finally they rose up in the air, becoming stars (points); here there is that one the big one that one the little one.

HUNGER

The ancestors, they say, again when they started to be short of food, their companions they ate them, turning them into dried meat.. Finally, when they had eaten them all, to another place they went, one of them, a woman only trying to leave the place. She followed them stumbling, she was completely starving. When they stopped on the way, she caught up with them. Finally, going off, to a place with sea ice they arrived. They (two) tried to hunt. One of them took (a seal). From that moment they took lots of seals. When summer came, the walruses their bones collecting they made kayaks.

When they had kayaks they started to take beluga whales, when winter came they encountered them. They started to try and take bears. Finally with one that fell into a trap, they had a bear. Their house (with) meat quarters after placing them around, they left, wanting to see human beings. Toward the human beings they tried to go, with bones building sledges. Toward the human beings they started to go, toward the human beings, when they arrived (they) being starving, their companions (that they had made of them) dried meat. So they told them. A woman, since he did not have a wife, she wanted him very much for a husband, only her husband refusing. She took him for a husband. He being very able her husband (with) another woman simply got married.

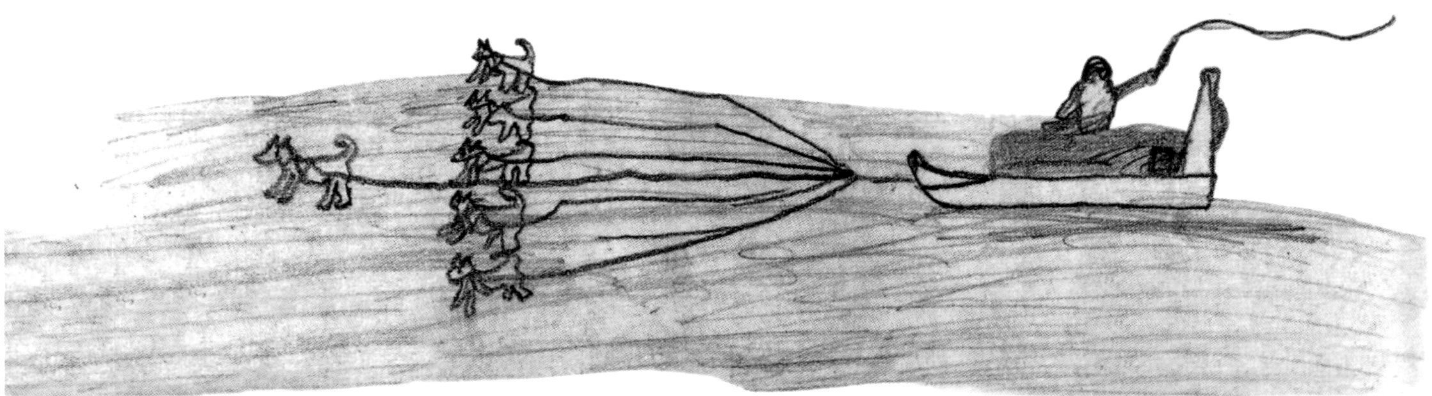

THE GIANT AND THE DWARF

A giant, they say, he took him so as to have a human companion with him. When he had him to watch over him, he spoke to him like this: "The mites don't bother them." Little foxes, they say, he called them mites. Having a companion, they say, (with) a dwarf, he, they say, the giant's dwarf (his) human companion, he planned to kill him. The giant, they say, his little human companion he spoke to him like this: "Teeth two! Call him like that!" In truth the dwarf, he said to him: "The human, him, I want to kill him, good!"

The giant, they say, he being very strong, they fought, his little human companion in the eyelet of his *kamik* putting him. The dwarf, as he found it easy (to get the better of him) the giant his little human companion, he kept him from being killed, the dwarf, though he still wanted to kill him.

The giant, they say, the bears he called them foxes. Of the giant, they say, his little human companion he shook him, the giant hitting him (with a stone) because he had said ordering him to hit him (that he hit him). When he had shaken him, they say, he said: "A bear, look over there!" when he had entered the access tunnel of the house. When he was awake, they say, the giant he said: "A fox, look over there!" Bears, they say, he called them foxes. Thus, they say, humans say this about them, the giant and the dwarf.

THE ABANDONED WOMAN PUTTING A SPELL ON FOXES SO THAT THEY WILL COME TO HER

An old woman, they say, and her grandson, they having been abandoned, when they started to suffer from hunger, she spoke like this: "Wandering foxes, let them come in, the wandering ones only those I ask to come!"

A reindeer, they say, though he came, she did not let him enter, they say. So, they say, finally she said: "Those that taste good" she said, "only those I ask them to come!" The reindeer as she did not like it.

A bear the reindeer came after. "This," they say, "I don't want!" being afraid of it. And then, they say, foxes started to come in. These, they say, she started to kill in great numbers, her little fox house on the point of being full, so that there no more room to put anything. The side platform when it was filled, and the place where they slept when it was filled, they say, her grandson she said to him: "Let that be enough, someone is saying!" When they continued to come, finally they say, she just sent (them) away "Sysssss!"

WHY BOWS AND ARROWS FELL OUT OF USE

The ancestors those who lived in ancient times, when they still had arrowheads made of stone, they being out hunting caribou, his companion killed him tricking him, pretending that a caribou he was going to shoot at.

When he had killed him, his companion, he would have no more arrows.

CRAZY ABOUT WOMEN

He started to put patches on the soles, they say, he started to put patches on the soles, of the women when they started to desire them. He put patches under the soles, he put patches under the soles, several one on top of another, many one on top of another. Really so as to couple with the women finally they went away. They went away far, so without getting any sleep they went to bed with the women, they went to bed with the women, "hamar-aa! hamar-aa!" They were accustomed to kicking her in the stomach the poor woman who bled (menstruation), they kicked her wanting constantly to couple with her, trying to make her bleed, wanting very much to couple like a dog so; not stopping, not sleeping, they were always in bed with the women, like dogs that looked like humans. I don't know any more after that; let them stay like that!

The boats, they over there calling them. They left, they say, then the boats they drove them. They camped there.* When they had camped, they say, so when these men had camped, those who were rowing in the boats it started to blow a storm. Those over there who had taken in a trap a bunting being shipwrecked, being shipwrecked, the bunting because he had put a spell on them.

*Not necessarily on land, although the literal sense is: going toward the shore.

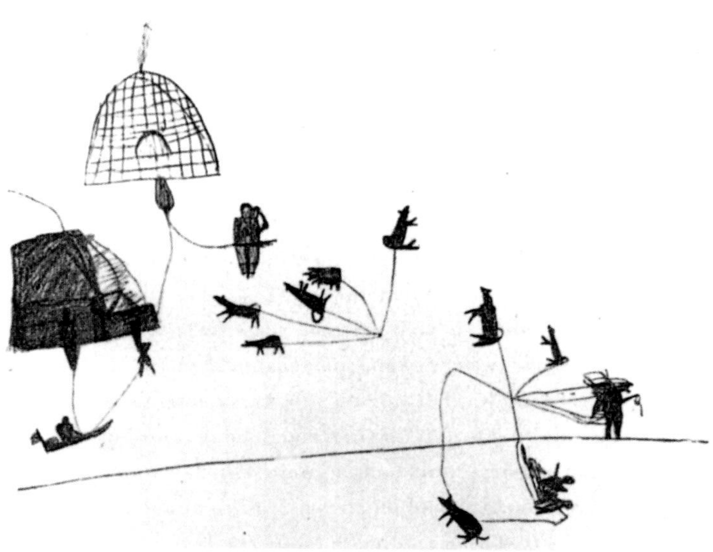

THE LAMENT OF THE SNOW BUNTING

So, they say, over there, they say, boats, they say that they live them, two snow buntings who always came to watch over their little ones, to watch over them there, they being good to eat, snow buntings. The two who always came to see always acted like this (coming and going in the air), then again some who were rowing in a boat caught sight of them. When they caught sight, they said, one of them he was going to set a trap to take them, with his hair he set a trap to take them. Her little husband, they say, her children, when he came to watch over them, so he was trapped there in this trap. When he was trapped, then they took him only, and his young pissing on them and (they) went away. So she, they say, about his wife, of the buntings, she saw her little ones that he had pissed on them the human, that and then taking in a trap her little husband. So, they say, the boats, they say, the last when it passed, she started to sing the little snow bunting:

"My husband, my husband, my husband, the humans so, because they are more powerful because they are stronger, with the cruel (trap) whale bone so trapping him they took him. Qalumina (with) urine drinking burst. People with houses not reaching them you must make camp this night!"

Legends collected by Erik Holtved,
from The Polar Eskimos, Language and Folklore,
MOG (Copenhagen, 1947).

THE GIRL WHO WAS CHANGED TO STONE AND HER SEWING KIT OF AUKLETS

She did not want any man. She, who did not want to marry, they came to fetch her: "Qautsupaluk, someone is saying, he would like to have you for a wife!" She did not want to at all. (Saying) twice he said to her: "Prepare yourself, someone is saying, Qautsupaluk, he is coming to take you!" "I don't want to, and it has been said!" "She doesn't want to, she has said it!" "Well then, let us move away from shore!"

So they traveled over the water. When they had left the shore, she followed them along the shore, she got ready (to leave). "No, we say, no, we say."

So she followed them: "Come here, you! Come here, you! My big toes are turning into stones. Come, you, come here, you!"

She followed them. She felt that she was changing into stone, the soles of her feet, they were starting to make a hard sound. Finally she fell, she fell. When she fell, her little kit, they say, it started to roll. The girl started to sing: "Ty—tyyty, ty-ty-ty . . . tyyq ty ty-ty-ty . . ." they becoming birds, before the little auks all of them, she was turned to stone. So here I am going to stop, because I don't know any more.

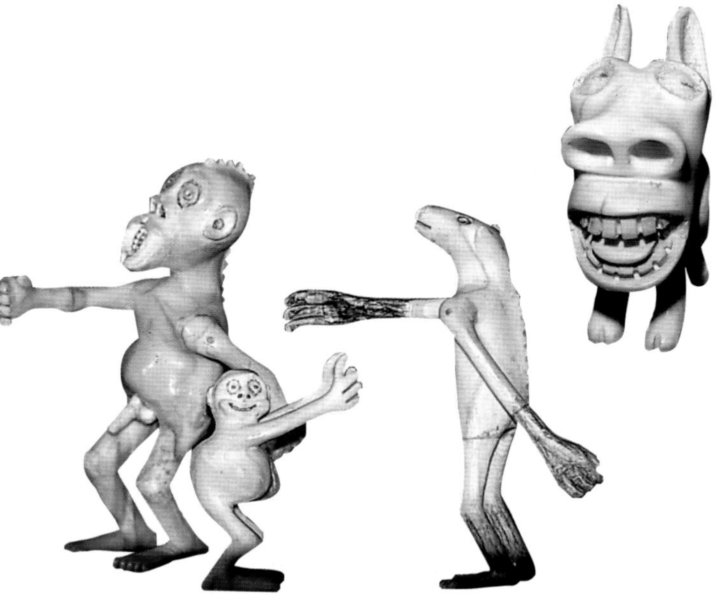

Fantasy at one's fingertips.

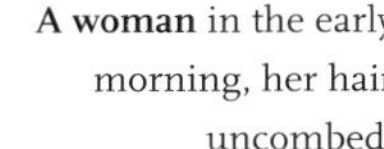

A woman in the early morning, her hair uncombed.

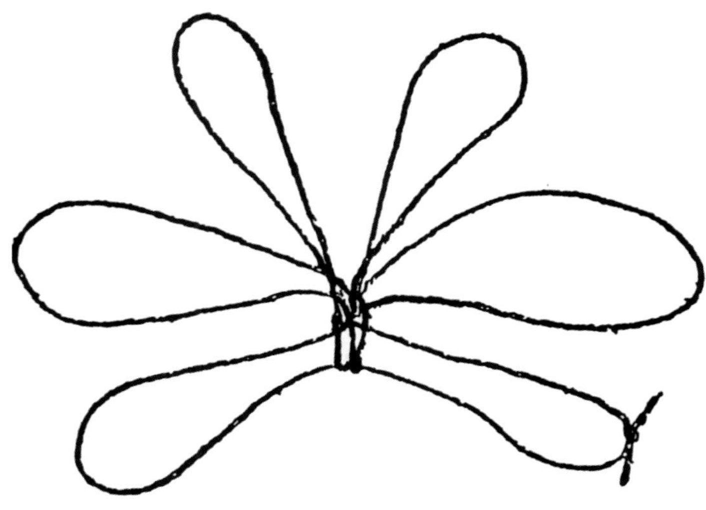

Natuk was very skilled at *ajurraarurit* (string games). Here, she has brought to life a caribou between her fingers. The "string" is either a thin cord or, more traditionally, a leather lanyard about a yard in length, whose loops are slid over the outspread fingers to make the most varied figures. Some players can make dozens of figures in this way. Children start to play from the age of five or six. By tradition, the game is only played during the polar night, lest the hunters tangle their dogs' traces or their harpoon lines. 1937.

A woman's mons.

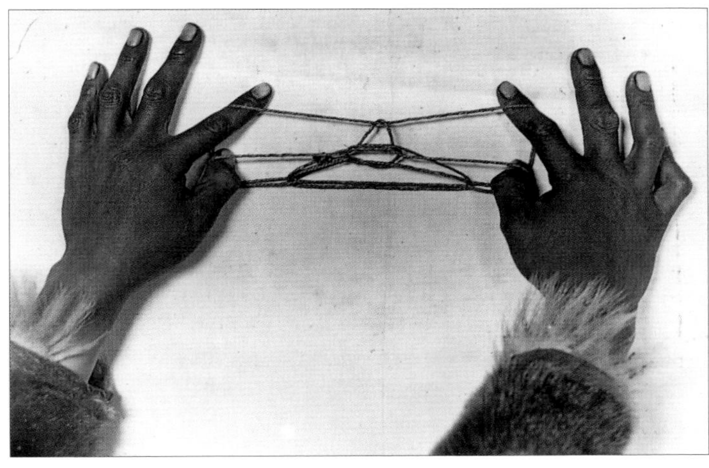

Ajurrarurit representing a small sled with its back upstanders raised. (1914-1917)

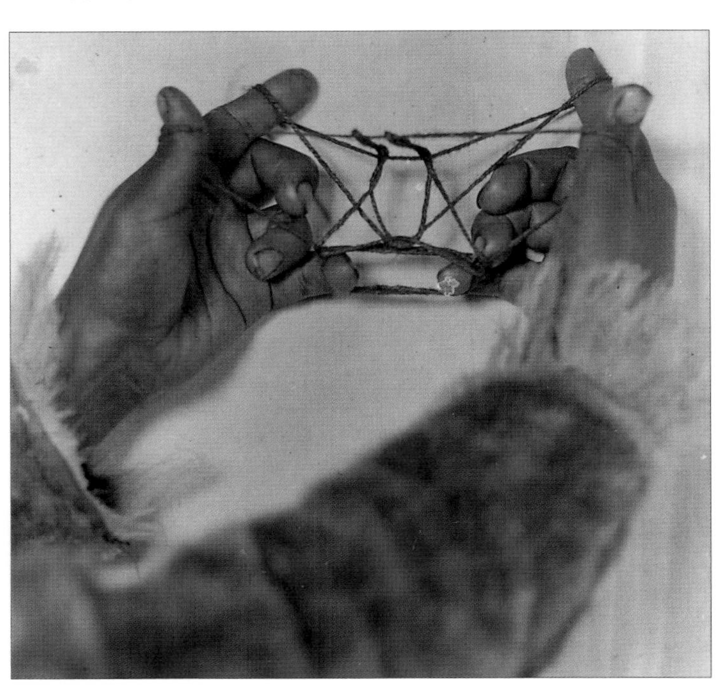

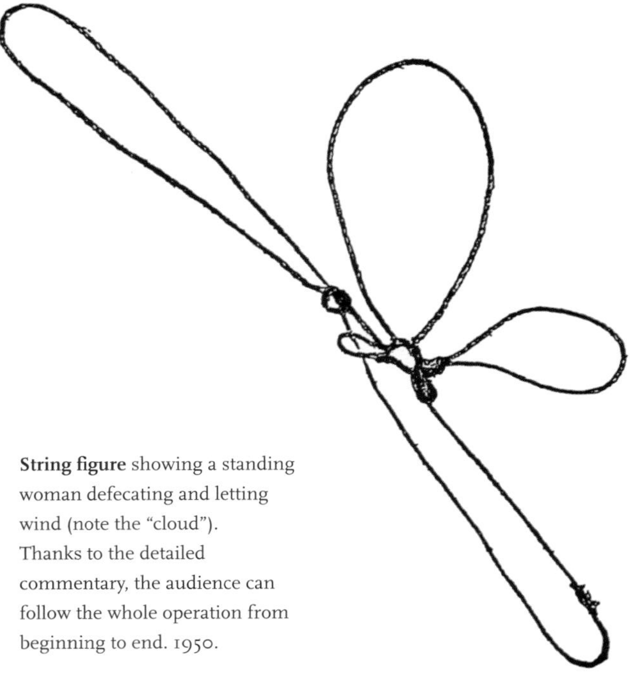

String figure showing a standing woman defecating and letting wind (note the "cloud"). Thanks to the detailed commentary, the audience can follow the whole operation from beginning to end. 1950.

THULE 2000

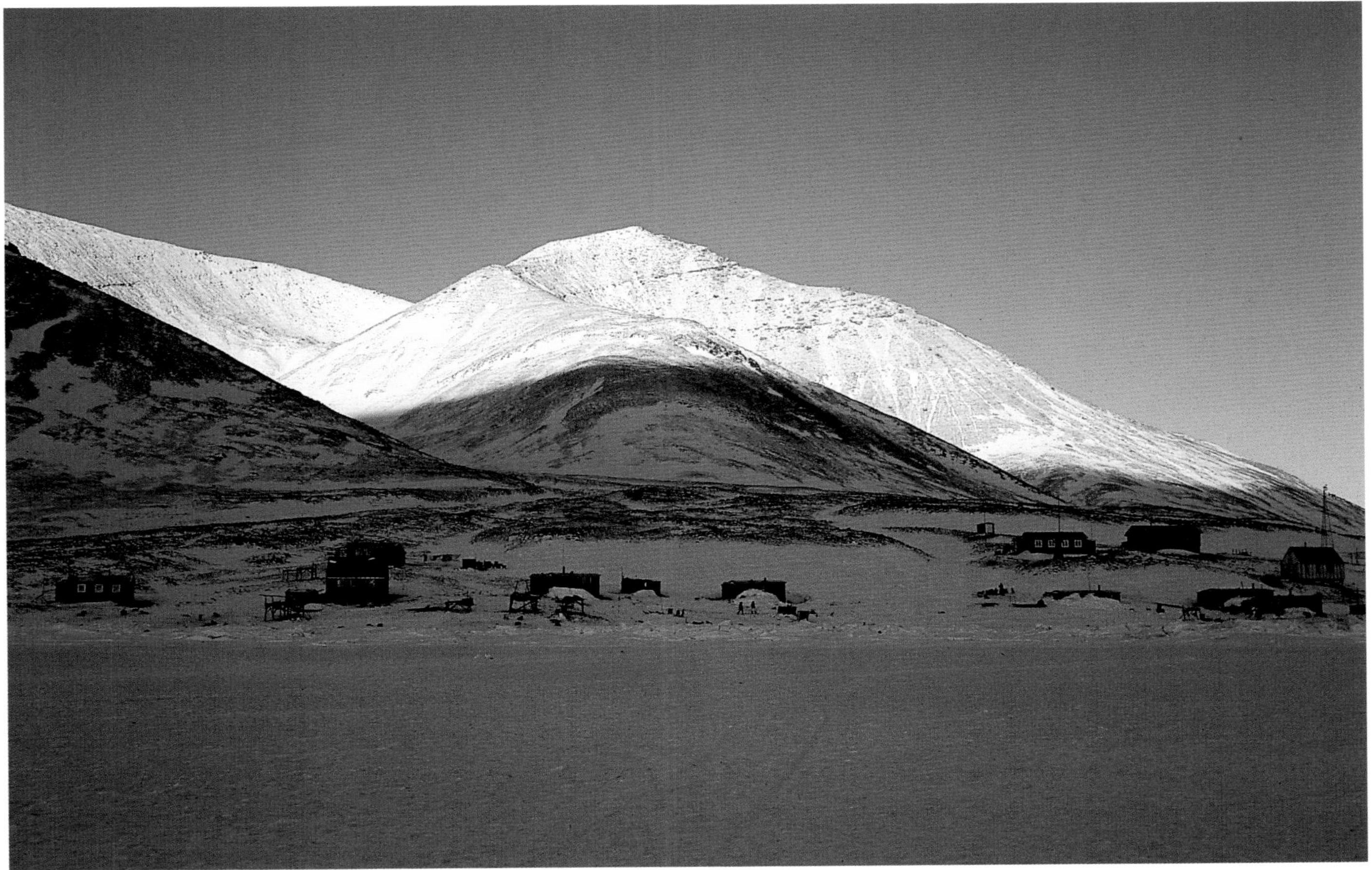

ABOVE, **Siorapaluk.** Daybreak over the most northerly Inuit village in Greenland, which lies at the foot of a cliff with the continental ice immediately beyond. 69 Inuit. 1998.
OPPOSITE, **High holy place** of Inuit shamanism: the Alley of the Whales. This is the birthplace of the Eskimos of Asia, north of Cape Chaplino, Arakamchechen and Yttigran islands. The Yupik civilization of the Bering Strait, through its knowledge of the power of primitive numbers and (perhaps!) Feng Shui, has inspired Inuit shamanism from Siberia to Greenland. (See page 377)

THE INNOCENCE OF A FIRST NATION: THE INUGHUIT

Siorapaluk: The sky reapers

August 3, 1950, Siorapaluk, in the extreme north of Greenland

I have arrived. The vastness of the space around me takes my breath away. The emptiness of pure air magnetized by billions of microparticles. Static electricity. A strong smell of virgin soil. By the cliffs, there is a modulated din of birds, which echoes off the mountainside. The sky there is thick with little auks, [1] black and white, with thick, short, stubby beaks, shiny black, darting back and forth between the sea and the tall cliffs, cackling and snapping their wings.

They dive with a kind of black flip to seize a crustacean or mollusk. After 30 seconds, as long as they can hold their breath, the clown heads poke out again, with their small round black intense eyes. Ten seconds to fill their lungs and again they plunge. At unexpected intervals, they take heavily to the air, their throats bulging with the crustaceans they have eaten, their dripping feet tucked under their wings. Flocks of 500 to 1000 males intermittently return to feed the auk chicks born in July among the rocks. The incubation period of these birds is between 28 and 35 days, with the parents taking turns to warm a single egg. Twenty days after they are hatched, the chicks go down to the sea and three weeks later they start learning to fly, flapping like novices. Night and day the parents dart to and fro along the sandstone cliffs, describe broad circles 1000 feet above the fjord, going back and forth in a kind of joyous dance; responding to some obscure signal, they swoop to the cliff's edge, then rise again steeply to continue their evolutions with all the greater freedom. The flocks sway forward and back with an elliptical motion, taking short intervals of repose on rocks projecting from the general scree. They move in a spiral like a great breathing lung suspended in the air.

I see men behind walls of stone, wielding long-handled landing nets. They are dressed in double-rumped bearskin breeches, some of them worn bare, and poncho jackets made of sealskin (*natseq*). They stand on tiptoe among the rocks, trying to net the birds as they hurtle by. Their eyes are intensely focused on the whistling flight of two to five hundred dovekies, which swoop about at different altitudes above them. The Inughuit have round heads, shorn on the bevel, long broad torsos and stocky legs. They leap from rock to rock, climbing after the stricken auks. A man lays his net on a rock, extricates an *appaliarsuq* from the mesh in a welter of feathers, crosses its wings over its back, presses on its heart with gnarled thumbs. Then he lays the little body gently at his feet.

1) *Alle alle*: some 10 inches long, with a black back and head; the throat and front of the neck, along with the lower parts, are immaculately white. Wingspan: about 20 inches; weight: 4.5 to 6 oz. Large pale yellow egg, slightly blue, with spots. The nestling sucks a regurgitated pap of plankton from the throat of its father and mother.

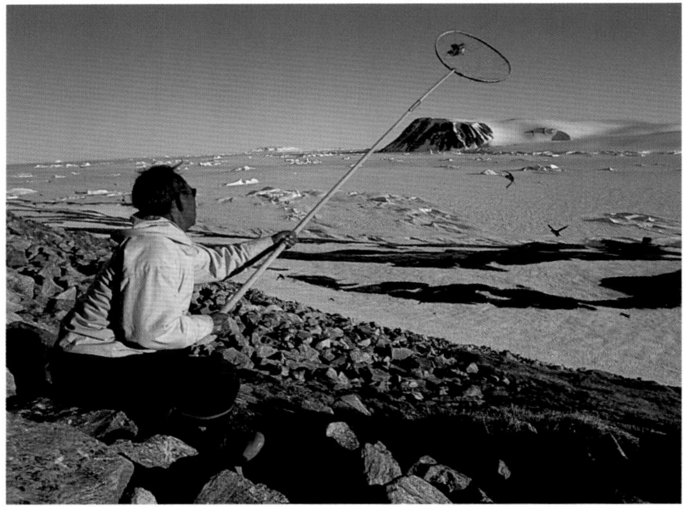

Savigssivik. Hunting for small auks in July. In the background, Cape York.

From time to time these kings of Thule rip open the birds and eat the red-brown meat on the spot. No sooner have their sweat-streaked faces registered the ecstasy of this than they resume their sky-reaping, the blood trickling down their chins. Every spring tens of thousands of dovekies fly up from Virginia on America's western seaboard, to keep the rendezvous with their cousins the Inughuit and be eaten just after the long polar night has drawn to a close. This wild banquet, the sight of which I shall never forget, is the expression of a proud, free people; masters of their destiny, the Inughuit know themselves to be in accord with the eternal balance of nature.

The polar night

"I sing of Night, Mother of Gods and Men. Orpheus calls her the origin of creation: for us, she is Venus!"

"*Taaq!*" It is dark. The short summer has ended. The shadows of night are lengthening. The great sand and limestone counterforts, the ice-floe with its now indeterminate hues, are gradually fading into the gloom. Sounds are muffled and the dry air freezes. "*Kapirlaktuq.*" The winter night has come.

This period, which lasts for three months at Thule, is far from the death-shroud one might imagine. On the contrary, its embrace is that of a mother: warm, humid, fecund. Little by little, snuggling in its bosom, we return to the original matrix. [2] It is when the sun returns, in February, that the cold is bitterest. In the night, the moon (*Anninga*) plays a vital role; it is curiously masculine; the long-awaited sun (*Siqiniq*) is feminine in nature.

There is a universal myth of the Inuit, told from Chukotka to Greenland, which explains this. Once there was an incestuous union of a certain brother and sister, during the ritual exchanges of women in a pitch-dark igloo (the seal oil lamps are always extinguished at this time). The brother and sister lay together; but the girl, in her anger at the illicit coupling, displayed herself by lighting a torch, so all could see. Then the pair rose into the sky together, circling higher and higher. In the firmament of the stars, they share the same igloo, only it is a double one; the warm and shining girl became the sun, while her cold, shadowy brother became the moon. During the summer months, the sun comes out of the girl's house. The weather is warm and clear, there is no more night time and the moon stays secluded out of sight. But in the winter, the sun stays at home and the moon comes outside; he only absents himself when he goes to find animals for men to hunt. Thus when the Inuit see the first quarter of the moon lighting their way through the heavy darkness, they cry out: "Thank you, Thank you! You have brought us game!" [3]

The Inuit love the night. They look forward to it. It is in this season that you hear their infectious laughter most often; they go visiting, sit together, embrace each other in the igloos of their ten small villages, so widely scattered across the land. Their seventy families, because they are united, feel themselves stronger and more resolute in their confrontation with a pitiless, crushing environment. "Oh Nature, who in holiness made men!" wrote Rimbaud in *Le Mal*. "Chthonian night, oracular night, night that tameth gods and mortals." [4] It is amid such darkness that we know the peace of the elemental, structuring forces of the earth, the shudder of the ice, the hum of stones, the intimate interlocking architecture of equilibrium. Listening, we hear a sound of breathing—and what we hear is the force of the earth, the living energy of the cosmos.

"In the beginning, there was chaos and night," said the ancient Inuit in their *oqaaluktuara*. [5] Murmuring these, the Inuit are one with the colossal universe, which they see as a cathedral whose roof is lost in infinity. Like all other men, in the time of their genesis their eyes were turned to heaven. They asked questions of it, understanding that the terrestrial universe with its vast black firmament may be read like a sacred text. Among the stars, the constellations (*ulluriat*), the planets (*ulluriatqjuat*) and the rings around the moon, they singled out *aagssuk* (Aquila), *pituaq* (Cassiopeia), *qilugtuussat* (the Pleiades) and *tuqtuhuit* (the Great Bear), who announces the return of the sun. [6] In the clear night, they find their way by known points along their shores. I myself never did anything else: traveling meant going from landmark to landmark. But when a man is in danger, when a blizzard is blowing, the stars become his friends. They guide him; they are the *ulluriat* which tremble above him, or are suddenly obscured by clouds. Some appear close, others are veiled by gases and stellar dust. Shooting stars race across the firmament in blazing trails; *ignirujait*, a flame. "Pftt, Pftt; that is the star's message to us, showing its gratitude that we have remembered it," Ara once told Knud Rasmussen in 1923.

One reason why Thule is such an important site in the Arctic is because it lies at the center of the Northern Lights zone. Savigssivik, by contrast, is an important sector of meteorite attraction. Hundreds, perhaps thousands of years ago, a cluster of three meteorites tumbled to earth here, a gift from heaven. In addition, for a thousand years Savigssivik was the sole source of iron for the Inuit, who otherwise possessed neither wood nor metal. 'The Woman, the Dog and the Tent,' say the Inuit, projecting their dreams and legends in describing the forms the meteors take. From time immemorial, at the Iron Island of Savigssivik, 'The Woman' had been the sole source of metal.

"*Miagguuqtuq!*" At unexpected moments, the dogs begin to howl. Their muzzles are raised to the moon and their eyes are haunted. Their first desolate wail fades across the snow. They are calling on their ancestors, the wolves. Other teams take up the cry, until the whole pack is keening dismally. It is a cry of the earth, as if the dogs, the progenitors of the Inughuit, of all the Inuit, are summoning the god of chaos. It goes on for three minutes at a burst, then is repeated two or three times more before ceasing abruptly, as if silence had been imposed by an invisible magician.

Glenn Gould felt a deep empathy with the mystical North. He dreamed of hearing Johann Sebastian Bach's prayer sung in the depths of the polar night; near to the wolves, but also to the Inuit, who can invoke hidden powers with their sacred drums. "For years I have dreamed of spending at least one entire winter north of the Arctic Circle . . . truly I would love to do this, and I tell you that one day I will." Glenn Gould was a voyant, and when he said he was convinced of his need to travel to the solitude of the Arctic, it was because for him the North was sacred. Alas, the Canadian government failed to give him a chance to do so, in 1967, the centenary year of the Confederation. The conductor Leonard Bernstein, a close friend, later tried to explain what Gould was looking for. "He felt he was on a cosmic quest; he had a near-magic, spiritual dimension, which was linked in some way to the magnetic pole."

The Inuit are our brothers, much closer to us than we allow. They possess a wisdom that the world has never needed so badly as it does today. The West has no inkling of the way the Inuit, who have been bound body and soul for thousands of years to this sacred area of the world, are transported with joy at the coming of each new spring, and share the trembling ecstasy of nature's re-awakening. Is such happiness a utopian dream for the rest of us? Alas, yes: but can the wisdom of the Inuit rightly be called a Utopia, when we know the extreme conditions under which it has been tried and tested? "These insignificant, incapable *miserabilis personae*, who appear unable to do anything for themselves, can in reality do much for the world. They have in them a mystery of recognized power, a hidden treasure; they can tap the deepest wellsprings of nature. We have called them barbarians, savages, children . . . yet the greatest sorrow of all is that their instinct is unknown to us, and they themselves cannot make us understand it." All those who spend their lives fighting on behalf of minorities will sympathize with this remark by Sydney Possuelo, a defender of the Amazon Indians in the heroic mold of the Villas Boas brothers. What is the use of such people? Here is the answer: "When I say they must be kept isolated, I mean we need to play for time—time for ourselves. Time will not change them, but perhaps it will change us. I hope that given time, our society will become a little more human . . ."

The pantheism of the Inuit is not only a collection of hunters' rituals aimed at creating a dialog with their dead through sorcery. It is also a philosophy; and we can grasp its height and depth when we make the pilgrimage to the Alley of the Whales in Chukotka, the cradle of the Inuit people. On Yttygran Island, the pantheist influence was so strong that it provoked Inuit migrations to Eastern Greenland, 5000 miles from the Bering Strait. Since 1976 we have known that male initiates visited the sacred island of Yttygran/Arakamchechen in Chukotka every year since the thirteenth century, right up to the time of the Soviet persecution. There they practiced an arcane science based on the use of sacred numbers. A sanctuary in the area, which is still in place, was revered by the Inuit; I went there myself in 1990, to meditate before a hearth in which a fire of whalebones had once glowed. The Alley of the Whales—where thirty-four whale jawbones, 15 feet tall, point to the sky in a line 400 meters long; these are aligned with 47 whale skulls on the island of Arakemchechen opposite, each of which weighs a ton and a half, with the noses turned toward the frozen land behind, and the occiputs facing skyward. The skulls are distributed along the Yttygran shoreline, by odd and even numbers. From beyond the divinatory water flowing down the Seniavine Channel, they send vague echoes of the I-Ching, of the thought of Lao-Tzu perhaps, or even of an ancient Heraclitic vision of the universe. [7]

March-June 1951: a nomad university

There were five of us, with three sleds and 43 dogs. My geomorphological and cartographic mission to the tragic lands of Inglefield and Washington in northern Kane Basin had at last begun. We left Siorapaluk on 30 March 1951, intending to cover 900 miles in one another's company, our party consisting of Qaaquutsiak (48 years old); his wife, Patdloq (40); Kutsikitsoq (48); his wife Natuk (40), and myself (28). We took no radio transmitter, wishing to remain resolutely alone. Nor did we carry any food save coffee, sugar and tea. Along the way we hunted seal and bear, whose meat was vital both to ourselves and to our dogs. In the course of this scientific expedition, to which the Inuit became more attached every day, I made a systematic map of 300 kilometers of coastline, on a scale of 1/100,000, including 3 kilometers inland. [8] I filled in cape after cape, bay after bay, torrent after torrent with the Inuit nomenclature transmitted to me by my companions, and in all I added ten French names (among them 'Paris Fjord' and 'Martonne Fjord' in honor of my master) and three Inuit proper names (among them Uutaaq, the father of Kutsikitsoq, who was with Peary when he reached the "Pole" on April 6, 1909). Thereafter my companions began to open their hearts to me. Because I was gradually integrating myself into this land with its icy covering, into the subterranean life of stones and plants, and into the secrets of their own labyrinthine thought and dim, tumultuous history, the Inuit told me their gratitude and displayed their growing delight.

On May 29 1951, I reached the Geomagnetic North Pole in company with Kutsikitsoq. Our three other companions had stayed on the ice floe to hunt seal, and I had forced the pace. Our two groups had elected to rendezvous within a certain time on a precise sector of the shore.

The Geomagnetic North Pole? It had been a day of pea-soup fog, I recall; an ugly east wind howled along the edge of the glacier, and snow flakes had been fluttering around us since our departure. Thousands of snow-threads began twisting through the air around us; they grew steadily more frantic, while to the southward the mist was lit by a thin gleam just above the line of the horizon. We advanced steadily, heading

2) What's more, the dark depths of the sea are ruled by a young girl, Nirrivik, the great regulator of the waters.

3) Jean Malaurie, *Les Derniers Rois de Thulé, Avec les Esquimaux polaires face à leur destin*, 5th edition (Paris: Plon, Terre humaine, 1989).

4) *Iliad*, 14th canto, verses 258-261.

5) Literally "they story-tell." The telling of the great myths.

6) John Macdonald, *The Arctic Sky: Inuit Astronomy, Star Lore, and Legend* (Royal Ontario Museum / Nunavut Research Institute, 1998). A remarkable work, written in close and intelligent collaboration with the Inuit of Igloolik.

7) Jean Malaurie, *Hummocks II*, see chapter 3, "Journal privé pendant la Première expédition soviéto-française en Tchoukotka, 1990," pp. 335-528 (Paris: Plon, Terre humaine, 1999).

8) Jean Malaurie, *Thèmes de recherche géomorphologique dans le nord-ouest du Groenland* (Paris: Editions du CNRS: Mémoires et documents, 1968).

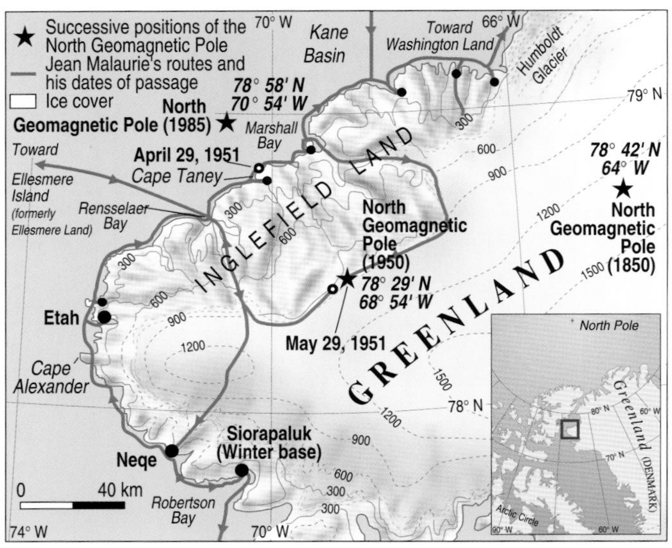

The North Geomagnetic Pole, reached on 29 May 1951. Route of Jean Malaurie.

southwest from the 79th to the 78th parallel. We had climbed, with considerable difficulty, the western side of the North Greenland ice cap. On the steep ice slope, our sleds yawed crazily to the right. The constant tension was telling on our nerves: visibility was down to a few yards—but why dramatize things in advance, the fact is that danger is only overcome when you choose to confront it. To talk about it is childish. I was keeping a close eye on the altimeter, which was hovering around 3000 feet. Given the barometric variations we had seen since our departure, I obviously wasn't sure if this reading was correct, but I did know we needed to hold our direction with great precision in this sector of Greenland, which at that time was still unmapped or only very vaguely mapped. At 1800-1200 feet, the continental ice had dangerous clefts in it, because of the proximity of a disquieting and unbroken rampart of ice cliffs. I made my calculations according to the position of the sun, our speed, the orientation of the isotypes and above all the line of the icy, snow-choked ravines which I crossed by approaching them crabwise, thus ensuring that our course would remain parallel to the edges of the dreaded cliffs.

I summed up our situation as we went along, without reining in the team. Provisions for the dogs and ourselves amounted to a reserve of seal fat and ribs that would last four days. The compass was unusable, because the needle wouldn't settle in this latitude. I repeat we were in a major geomagnetic sector. We had no radio transmitter and were completely alone. We bivouacked at 78° 50', sleeping on the big sleds run together side by side. By the heat of our oil-burning primus stove we used stout needles to sew up our long-sleeved reindeer skin hoods *(qulitsaq)*, bearskin breeches *(nano)* and boots *(kamik)*.

We advanced silently, in single file, along the rough edges of the glacier. On May 29, in the late morning, we unintentionally reached a significant abstract site—the Geomagnetic North Pole (78° 29' N, 68° 54' W). Actually my goal had been to observe the Inglefield plateau (whose shoreline I was then charting) from above, and to study the point at which the base of the continental ice and the pre-Cambrian plateau came together (collecting sand, clay and rocks from the border). I presumed that this northern ice cap was "dry"—i.e., without moraine—and had been in some way superimposed on the bedrock without "rasping" it. This would be the converse of what I had observed in June and September 1948, as geographer for Paul-Emile Victor's expeditions around Disko Bay on the 69th parallel. The ice cap to the south rested on a humid mass whose existence had been confirmed by geophysical soundings. The terminal moraine in this zone was a major one, which explained the jaggedness of the relief freed there when the ice receded.

Our overriding objective was to get back to the coast to the north of us, and not to miss, in its angle at the edge of the continental ice, the mysterious pass or declivity along the cliff line that would lead us out of this howling desert of ice and snow and bring us back to our shore base, where our three Inuit companions awaited us with reserve stores. The ice cap, I should add, takes the form of a peninsula, which points toward Cape Alexander: the Whites call it Prudhoe Land. For how many days could two men and twenty-seven dogs survive in this place without eating? We could devour the dogs, of course: they were our last resort. But in reality such an idea was out of the question.

On May 30, in a milky late-afternoon fog, we finally stumbled on the trail to safety. The towering wall of ice was cleft for a distance of about one kilometer, with a soft, snowy ramp running down. Blessed be the sacred names of all the Inuit gods! And blessed be the name of my personal guardian spirit, my *tuurngaq*, sculpted for me out of walrus tusk by Pualana, Kutsikitsoq's uncle, in December 1950. This figurine was in my pocket at all times, where I could feel it and invoke it with my fingertips. In a squall of wind, we plunged with our teams down the side of the drift, enveloped in powdery snow. When we reached the rocky plateau below, we turned to look back: the ice precipice behind us was all too real and, in retrospect, absolutely terrifying. Like an animal, I scraped with my foot the ancient gneissic floor of the longed-for Inglefield Land. Through the sealskin soles of my boots, the ten toes of my feet caressed the mineral, primordial, solid ground. I blessed the sterile rock of Inglefield—and even now I can remember the touch of it. Thereafter I proceeded, along the edge of the ice cap with its complete absence of terminal moraine, to construct a detailed cartographical and geomorphological survey, just as I had intended. The glacier was indeed "dry" and receding. I made precise observations, then took samples. After this, our eyes fringed with frost and bodies hunched, we resumed our journey with shouts of "*Hak! Hak! Huughuaq!*" as walked ahead of the dogs.

With the butt of his whip Kuksikitsoq pointed out an almost imperceptible point in the distance. A needle-like block of moraine could just be descried on the far horizon. From stone to stone we followed the line of the longest slope of a thalweg running south-north, on its way to the ice floe and the bountiful sea. We drove rapidly down a snow-filled valley 25 kilometers in length. By the morning of May 31, the iced-over sea of Rensselaer Bay (*Aunguartoq*), where Kane wintered on the *Advance* a hundred years ago, was well in sight. The breathing holes of seals seemed to be steaming before us in the frozen air, as our imaginations ran riot; such holes would be our salvation, providing us with fresh, red, healthy, firm, bloody meat. At ten that morning, we at last came up with our three dear companions at the agreed rendez-vous.

June 1, 1951. We headed immediately westward with our sleds and our 43 reunited dogs. Our goal was to cross the 100-kilometer ice-bound strait separating Greenland from Canada. Carried along by our sense of brotherhood and the exaltation of absolute freedom, we felt ourselves capable of anything. We had embarked on a test of endurance, from Greenland to the deserted island of Ellesmere, without our precious reserves of seal meat and fat, without special winter equipment, without rubber dinghy or kayak, alas! [9] All we had was ammunition enough for ten months, three rifles, our harpoons and our lances. We were traveling commando-style, that is with the minimum of weight so our sleds could cross snow hummocks from 9 to 21 feet in height. There was a risk we would break the sleds on these hummocks and under Qaaqutsiak's supervision I practiced cutting out "steps" in them with my axe. Our scientific objective was to determine the respective heights of the beaches above sea level and to take samples of fossils that could be carbon-tested for age, and thereby to estimate the volume of ice on the relatively small Ellesmere Isand (Canada) and compare its rhythms of deglaciation with those of the massive icecap Inglefield (Greenland) over the last ten thousand years.

This was one of the most daring adventures of my life, and the Inuit and I had silently agreed to undertake it together, with no more than a glance at one another, on our return from the mission to the Geomagnetic North Pole. In this period of late spring thaw, we were all five of us aware that once we reached Ellesmere we faced being cut off from Greenland, and our one and only small reserve of seal meat and equipment at Aungnartoq in Rensselaer Bay, by a sudden drift of the ice pack in the strait: in which case we would be forced to spend the winter in a stone igloo on a totally deserted island, after hastily amassing a new and completely hypothetical store of seal meat.

Every day the runnels of water on the slopes and rocks and the melting sea ice breaking off the southern edge of Kane Basin reminded us that spring was already well under way. But no matter!

My companions and I were fully aware of the tragic events that had accompanied the discovery of this part of the world. In 1863, the first 14 immigrants from Canada arrived at Etah, farther south. Attempting to make their way back to the land of their ancestors at Igloolik, they endured appalling hunger at Cape Sabine, and Tornge, Patdloq's grandfather, only survived by cannibalism. Later, the German expedition led by H. K. E. Krueger vanished without trace here in April-May 1933; the wife of the excellent Eskimo hunter Ajaku, who was one of the three men lost, had told me all about it (the full story is told in "*Hummocks 1*"). Now I myself was heading straight for Cape Sabine where 19 Americans in Greely's ill-fated expedition died of hunger one after the other, some of the living eating the bodies of the dead, in April, May and June of 1844.

The appalling effort and peril that I was asking my Inuit companions to share with me, without any question of renegotiating the modest fee we had agreed upon, was consistent with their natural taste for adventure. This was *Angalavagoq*! Adventure with a capital A, the one thing that ennobled life and gave it real meaning.

From Greenland to Canada (deserted Ellesmere Island), expedition of 1-6 June 1951. Smith Sound was partially cleared of the thawing pack ice. Our three sleds travel through the hummocks. In the lead is Kutsikitsoq, then Qaaqutsiaq, and finally my sled. A detailed sketch, which the communal memory allowed Giutika-Dunek, born in 1932, to draw in 1990.

And why this particular adventure? Because I was a man of science—*ilihamahuq* [10]—working with them *and for them*.

To open a future for the Inuit, in company with a white savant whom they had educated as an Inuit, in whom they had confidence, and over whose actions they had control, was exactly what they wanted. The cracking of the ice was disquieting to me. "Take your time. Do what you believe you must do," the four Inuit kept telling me. Padtloq, who was perhaps the most venturesome of their number, favored going further south-east, as far as Igloolik 1100 kilometers away in Canadian territory, beyond Jones and Lancaster sounds. Her own ancestors had made their way up from there. "Let's visit the descendents of our ancestors, those great beloved ones," she whispered to me. "Yes, Yes!" But on 5 June, alas, I made the decision to return eastward. I had taken the measurements I needed and I was unwilling to take any further risks. By 6 June, having miraculously retraced the original path we had cut through the hummocks, despite the drift of the icepack, we were back in Inglefield Land, in Rensselaer Bay.

Why were these people attached to me as they were? Because they had perfectly grasped, without a word needing to be said, that they were the glue that held my authority together. I owed it entirely to them, such as it was. They had delegated to me any power I had. Even better, they gave me the strength and the means to achieve my ends, because they had sensed in advance—the women perhaps even more than the men—that this *piqatigiit* ("being together") which we personified was something more than the customary hunting group. They had understood that, as in the time of Knud Rasmussen [11] ("Our Knud," *Kunoki*, they called him) we were building a future for their children al-

9) We had mistakenly omitted to bring any. Mistakenly? At least in the case of the kayak, we chose not to carry one over the hummocked sea ice, where it was likely to break.

10) Literally "knowing," seeing farther and knowing better.

11) The Fifth Thule Expedition, an innovative exploration in the Canadian Central Arctic and Alaska (1922-1925) in which two Inuit from North Greenland took part, had an enormous subterranean influence on the mindset of the Thule Inughuit. The Inuit were no longer "objects of study" or "guides and dog sled drivers" as in Peary's time but full partners of the Danish ethnologists, archaeologists, and geographers. Their expedition contract, drawn up by Rasmussen in 1917, stated this explicitly. And Rasmussen saw to it that the writings of the seven Thule expeditions were distributed at mission's end to the Inughuit people by his expedition partners: Ajaku (brother of Qaaqutsiaq) and Kravianguak (whom I knew and who showed them to me). It then belonged to the educators (Lutherans) to capitalize on this extraordinary window into the Inuit and North American worlds and complete this evolution in outlook. Regrettably, they did not do this. But the Inuit were aware, as they leafed through these pages—which they could not understand as they were written in English, but whose photographs, sketches, and maps they examined—that they had played a major role in this discovery. The first push had been given, which it now behooves us to follow up.

Thule, July 1951. The U.S. Air Force arrived in June 1951 to construct a secret military base, then the Navy disembarked on 9 July: 5,000 to 10,000 men have been stationed there at a time, according to political circumstances. The base is still active.

most unawares. We prepared a new society by day as we made our maps, and we pondered the outlines of a new destiny for the Inuit when evening came. In short, my friends felt themselves to be the pioneers of a new era, one that would be opened by the nomad university we symbolized as we traveled outward with our dogs and our three modest sleds. As they performed such calculated acts of daring, these free men, to whom alcohol and violence were unknown, were fully aware of the implications of what they were doing. They were also inspired by a lofty ideal.

So with this I pay homage to the 302 Inuit whose joys and sorrows I shared in absolute intimacy for a whole year of my life. If I am writing these pages, fifty years after the unforgettable adventure we shared together, it is because they have remained in my heart ever since: even as they slowly prepare—at their own determined rhythm and in their utter solitude at the top of the world—to enter the third millennium.

THE COMING OF THE AMERICANS —15 JUNE 1951

A forced march from Rensselaer Bay across Inglefield Land to Siorapaluk. We crossed the ice cap and regained our winter base camp, which we finally abandoned on 12 June. Heavily laden as we were with fossils and various other items of evidence, we traversed the fjords and bays with the utmost difficulty. We had the three teams, those of Qaalaasoq (*"the Navel"*) and Sakaeunnguaq (who had taken over from Qaaqqutsiaq and Kutsikisoq at Siorapaluk) and my own. My team and Sakaeunnguaq's had almost been lost in a crevasse after we failed to identify it in the fog. It was raining, and the heavily fissured ice-floe was thawing at a great rate everywhere except on the shoreline, which forced us to make long and dangerous detours. We divided the boxes of fossils and the sacks of notebooks, sketches and photos that constituted my harvest of results and placed them atop the baggage where they wouldn't get wet. The heavy rains had turned the floe into a lake nearly 15 inches deep.

Now we were at an altitude of about 3600 feet. Traveling round the clock, we had been able to reach the great glacier by a new route and

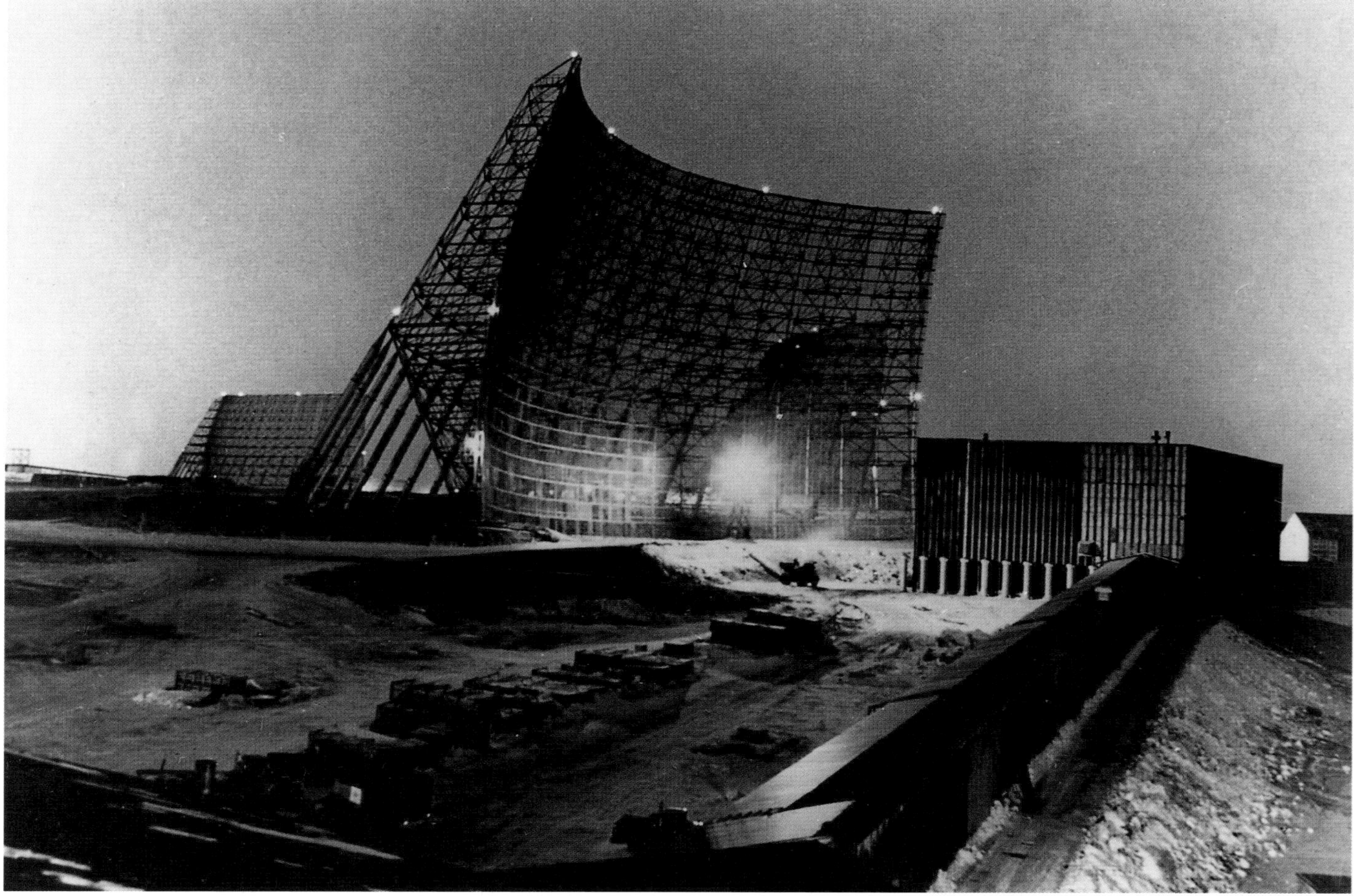

One of the radars for the 70 satellites that the Thule airbase tracks night and day. Thule is an essential base for the Pentagon for all military operations conducted in the northern hemisphere.

were now moving south-southeast. On June 15, we completed the long, steep climb onto the ice cap on our way to the legendary North Star Bay and the immemorial capital of Thule, where the Danish supply ship put in once yearly, when all of a sudden Sakaeunnguaq stopped dead in his tracks, cupped his hand to his ear and listened. Sakaeunnguaq was a shaman. It was a moment of prescience. With agony in his eyes, he was hearing some dreadful murmur in the distance. Immediately he reached for a metal box lid and drummed out an improvised *iingerneq*, a song to conjure up the spirits and the forces of the nether world. His eyes were ecstatic, his soul elsewhere. He had sensed that an immense and terrible misfortune was about to befall his people. It was in absolute silence and foreboding that we continued on our way.

The invasion

We reached the summit at last. The great southward vista lay stretched before us . . . and the air seemed to be filled with Martians. In fact what we were seeing was the airplanes of the US Air Force, which, at a rate of one giant transport every 30 minutes, were swooping in to land with materials for building a giant military base on the south side of Wolstenholme Fjord.

The base swelled quickly from 4000 to 10,000 men. A port was constructed; on July 9, icebreakers led in an armada of sixty-three ships that had been held up in Melville Bay throughout May and June. From this first convoy, 300,000 tons of cargo were brought ashore. I was present on the beach when the first marines disembarked on the 9th, waist deep in the surf, with fixed bayonets. I thought we were on the eve of a Third World War.

This is what had happened. On 25 June 1950, five North Korean divisions occupied Seoul. On 27 June, President Harry Truman ordered US forces to force the invaders back to the 35th parallel, in support of the South Korean army. The United Nations approved this action. Of the 59 member nations, 53 supported the United States, and 42 contributed to the war effort, of whom 16 (including France) contributed military forces. On 27 November, China intervened in the conflict, retaking Seoul. After a general retreat of the United Nations troops, the front stabilized on the 38th parallel. General Douglas MacArthur, commander-in-chief of the UN forces, was recalled on 11 April 1951, having threatened Manchuria, North Korea and if necessary China with atomic retaliation. In July 1951, negotiations for an armistice began at Kaesong. Broken off at the end of August, these talks resumed later at Panmunjom. And it was at this dire juncture that the Pentagon decided, during the winter of 1951 when I was in Inglefield Land without a radio transmitter and totally cut off from the outside world, to construct a gigantic air base at Thule. At the time Moscow had a considerable advantage in terms of long-range missiles, and Soviet military intervention appeared imminent. Stalin had told Mao Tse Tung that he wished to intervene before the alliance between the US and Japan had time to solidify. "The moment has come to strike at capitalism. Great Britain has demobilized, so has France; Germany's military has been annihilated and America is retreating into isolationism. It is time to crush the evil. If we wait any longer, it will be too late," was the substance of what he wrote in secret documents preserved by the Russian presidency that were shown to me in Moscow in 1989. In other words, Stalin was ready

The American map of the Thule airbase and its environs. One can make out North Star Bay, the port, the roads, the watch towers, the reservoirs . . . The scale is 1:250,000.

to engage the Red Army if Mao would send more Chinese divisions. By refusing to do so, Mao prevented a Third World War.

The base at Thule (codenamed "Blue Jay") was ultra-secret and remained so for three years. I was the only foreign observer on the spot, and my presence was a deep embarrassment to the first American authorities I encountered, notably the US Air Force general who ran the base during its construction phase and with whom I immediately demanded an interview. "You are released," he told me curtly on June 18. I remembered Diderot's words in his *Supplement au voyage de Bougainville*: "And thou, chief brigand to whom the others owe obedience, steer your vessel away from our shores without delay: for we are innocent and happy, and you can only spoil our happiness. We follow the pure instinct of nature and you have tried to eradicate it from our souls. Here, everything belongs to everybody, and you have preached upon us I know not what distinction betwixt *thine* and *mine*.'

Diplomacy

I came and went along the beach at North Star Bay, still thinking of the *oqaaluktuara* of Nirrivik and the amorous bear; I questioned myself and I questioned the Inuit. Mentally and emotionally, I stood with their community and its destiny. I besieged the young Danish administrator Torben Krogh, pressing him to convene the Inughuit Parliament immediately (this was the *Fangerad* of Thule, originally created by Knud Rasmussen on 7 June 1930) so it could send a written protest against the shattering invasion of Inuit territory without their authorization. I would be the irrefutable witness to this. He refused to do so. I insisted. An Inuit "no" in June-July 1951 would have considerably strengthened the 1955 diplomatic dossier instituted by the Greenland Prime Minister (Greenland having finally won its autonomy) when he spoke out against the secret activity of this foreign base and its very presence in his country.

Why did the young Danish administrator refuse, in July 1951, to convene the Fangerad? Because he had clear instructions from Copenhagen not to do anything that might obstruct the actions of NATO. This was admitted to me 20 years later. On 27 March 1951, secret negotiations were begun in Copenhagen aimed at a new program of defense cooperation, within the framework of NATO. Why had

Thule, in Northern Greenland, been singled out in preference to deserted Ellesmere, from which I had just come, or Baffin Land, both of which were in Canadian territory and had plenty of deserted fjords that were eminently suitable? The reasons were diplomatic. Ottawa was allied at the time with Washington, but remained highly circumspect in regard to the cold war, which was just getting under way in the most alarming fashion. The American wartime bases of Goose Bay, Frobisher and Baker Lake had caused a raft of trouble for the Canadian authorities. Power in these military bases in sovereign Canadian territory was never equitably shared during the cold war years. I was able to confirm this at Igloolik (Hall Beach, Hudson Bay) in July 1960, while on an official mission on behalf of the federal government in Ottawa. Nor did London support Washington's determination with any greater commitment; Great Britain preferred to maintain its traditional role of appeasement to maintain the balance of power.

As NATO's cold war grew more intense, Copenhagen came under strong pressure to cede part of the territory that was emblematic of the Polar Eskimos—and the cession was to be absolute. Thule was to become an exclusive military site; yet the central axiom of the Danish policy of Greenland for the Greenlanders, which had been so successful for half a century in the spirit of the venerated Knud Rasmussen, was precisely that the people of North Greenland should be left *strictly isolated* from all harmful outside contact. I myself was subjected to this enlightened policy of protection and insulation. In March 1950, it required a strong personal petition from the French Ambassador Gérard de Charbonnières to obtain the Danish government's agreement for my expedition to live for a few weeks in summer among the Polar Eskimos. Permission for the winter I spent there was negotiated on the spot. At that time the only whites in the entire Eskimo territory were an administrator, a doctor and radio operator, all with their families, and myself. The only other presence was an outpost of the very small American Weather Bureau at Pitugfik, near Thule, which was rigorously isolated from the Danes and the Inuit.

The showdown: 302 Inuit and a base of 5,000 military personnel.

In 1951 there were, in total, 302 Inuit, all of whom had been kept insulated from free markets and the industrial world.

They now faced a brutal confrontation with Western civilization. The vast American garbage heaps became their new frames of reference. Boxes, cans, wood, tent canvas, plastic, tools, empty cans of food and the carcasses of wrecked cars and planes accumulated in mountains of what for the Eskimos was treasure. In August 1818, a nail, a barrel hoop or a plank were unimaginable wealth. In 1900, a knife or a gun might be the reward for a full years' work. In 1950, a gun was still the fruit of savings made over several months' hunting. Now a young hunter would never again agree to earn in one year what a soldier or a laborer earned in one month. My own micro-economic studies carried out in 1967 (see appendix at the end of this book) demonstrated all too clearly that the social condition of the hunter quickly degenerated. My friend Kenn Harper, who for years was a teacher at Thule and won fame with his book on Minik, one of the Eskimos taken by Peary to New York, [12] lived at Iqaluit, the capital of Nunavut; in September 2000 he confirmed to me for the purposes of this afterword that the future for hunters was just as doubtful in Thule as it was in Nunavut. Young Inuit today are discontented, and why wouldn't they be? The fur market has become severely restricted as a consequence of Western ecologists' campaigns. If the hunters still continue to hunt, it is thanks to the artificial prices so generously maintained by the Greenlanders and the Inuit governments of Nunavik and Nunavut; seal and walrus fat are now considered to be contaminated, and pregnant women in Canada are advised not to eat it on a regular basis. They are told instead to eat imported canned food.

Thule-US, a completely unreal place, never ceases to surprise us. On this site mankind has truly created something born of the imagination of Jules Verne—a subterranean city beneath the ice. At Camp Century (opened in 1959, then closed again in 1967), 250 km east of Thule, a futuristic ice-town was built 180 feet below the surface. As its entrance, 63 tunnels fanned out leading to residential quarters, research laboratories and stores. Heating was supplied by a small nuclear power station, which also solved the problem of fresh water supply; the surplus heat was recovered and recycled. A hole was dug alongside the glacier to create a reserve of fresh water.

I lived among the Inughuit before the coming of alcohol. All my books bear witness to their *joie de vivre*; in their geographic isolation, they had achieved a balance in their social existence; they had organized their demography with the utmost foresight, rejecting intermarriage to the fifth degree in order to avoid the risks of too-close consanguinity. Their economic wisdom was such that, despite a certain financial austerity (about $60 per family per year), they managed to invest a third of their revenue from sales of fox pelts in new equipment. Lastly, the territory of Thule benefited with its hunters' council of the Fangerad from a privileged regime that strictly protected its peoples' customs and usages, and at the same time initiated the Inuit to the ways of democracy. But all this came to an end with the coming of the American base, which projected everyone into a period of deep difficulty.

When I returned to Thule in 1967 I saw the lethal results of liberalism, which is sometimes foolishly described as a "spur to initiative." It was an unqualified disaster: it had led (to take only one example among many) to the highest rate of tobacco consumption on the planet. Not for nothing do the Eskimos call cigarette smoking "the pastime of boredom."

My companion of the night on the ice-floe stops me in front of the shop: his mouth is dry. At first familiar, then bullying, he invites me to drink with him. Everyone knows my loathing for alcohol, that I forbid my companions to drink while on mission. He insists, repeating over and over, "I am great hunter . . ." His lips are coated with white spittle. His jacket is grimy. He talks incoherently for three hours, drinking his way through eight cans of Danish beer. Suddenly, he goes into spasm: his whole body is wracked. I leave him. The same night he tries to meet up again, with four more cans of beer in his pockets. After a friendly word, I close the door on him. He goes to cry at his mother's door, whining like a dog in the muck.

Why do they drink? Why do their children sniff glue and turpentine essence, at the risk of destroying themselves? The sociologist's reply is that the alcoholic is an unhappy person. This unhappiness is betrayed by an ever-increasing suicide rate, by hanging, or by leaping into the icy

The visible part of the Thule military base, looking west.

sea, or by blowing their brains out. This last is the surest way. Sometimes, young people in the Canadian Arctic make suicide pacts and keep them[13]. Along with illnesses like bulimia, schizophrenia, paranoia, manic depression, debility, cardiovascular disease and alcohol poisoning, the epidemic of suicides has decimated every one of the Arctic communities in Greenland, North America, Canada and Siberia. Prisons and psychiatric hospitals, the proud symbols of civilization, are waiting in the wings.

But all is not lost. Cornelius Remie tells me that at Qaanaaq—New Thule—150km north of North Star Bay, a "Blue League" of resistance groups has formed, uniting all those who wish to free the region of such horrors. They are in a minority, alas; but who knows but the action of time, improved education, and an awareness of what is truly at stake will bring about a radical change of heart and instill a new sense of mission for the future.

JANUARY 21: NUCLEAR DISASTER

The 15th of June 1951 was a determining date in my life. I understood on that day that I could not be a scientist working with a people and refuse to defend them in a time of danger. For that reason I wrote *The Last Kings of Thule*, which appeared in 1955. *The Last Kings* was the first work in the *Terre Humaine* collection, which I created and which, with 80 titles, now represents one of the major currents in French thought in the late twentieth century (as Pierre Aurégan has written) in narrative anthropology and social literature. [14] The book appeared in Copenhagen in 1957 and caused an immediate sensation. With a preface by the philologist and eminent Eskimo scholar Erik Holtved, it created shock waves among Danish citizens who for years had willingly made considerable sacrifices to finance two-thirds of Greenland's budget. They now discovered that the people most closely associated with the Danish national hero, Knud Rasmussen, were in wretched straits. Public opinion in the noble state of Denmark showed its gratitude to me, a foreigner, for standing up to defend the Inughuit. Not a single article appeared in the Danish press expressing the remotest irritation that a Frenchman was putting out views that were critical, as well as encouraging and favorable.

Disinformation and passive attitudes in the media

Yet ordinary people have a certain lingering innocence, and they are still inclined to believe what their governments tell them. What was the essence that filtered through the communiqués put out by the Danish administration? It left little room for doubt. "Within the framework of the agreements binding us to NATO, we have agreed that a military base should be created at Thule. This American base of the Air Defense Wing, [15] we can assure you, is a *defensive* installation." This summed up official Denmark's reasoning on the matter. Word for word, the following is the resolution passed by the Danish Parliament in 1968. "At Thule, there exists no nuclear weapon. No nuclear weapon exists on the soil of Greenland." This statement calmed public opinion, which was thereupon convinced that the authorities would do whatever was necessary for the common weal.

Alas, the damage to the Inuit had already been done.

As far as I was concerned, having watched the construction and

12) Kenn Harper, *Give Me My Father's Body* (Frobisher Bay: Blacklead Books, 1986)

13. Cornelius Remie, ed., *Facing the Future: Inughuit Youth of Qaanaaq*, Report of the '98 University of Nijmegen Student Expedition to Qaanaaq (Nijmegen University Press). A remarkable investigation, which boldly probed the real problems, sharply and prudently.

14) Pierre Aurégan, *Terre humaine, un des courants de pensée de la fin du XXè siècle*, with a preface by Henri Mitterand (Editions Nathan, Références, 2001).

15) The bombers under the command of the Strategic Air Command (SAC) that carried nuclear weapons were not authorized to fly over Thule or to land there. Thule came under the Air Defense Wing and not SAC, in diplomatic terms. But what do principles count in the face of absolute necessity, which only the military authority can judge?

development of the base from its earliest foundation, I was perfectly aware that it was not merely defensive but offensive too. From the start, offensive bombers had been parked on the tarmac there, and these had to be carrying nuclear bombs at the height of the Cold War in June-July 1951. Otherwise, what earthly use were they? Like anyone else with any sense living at Thule I dreaded the moment of truth. Sally Schnell, co-founder of the Thule Association created at Copenhagen to protest against this obscure and shameful deception, testified to this effect at the World Uranium hearings in 1992.

The crash of the B-52

On 21 January 1968, in the middle of the polar night and two years after the nuclear accident at an American base in Palomares, Spain, a B-52G on a secret reconnaissance mission crashed on the ice floe 8-12 km west of the Thule airbase. Aboard, the crew had struggled vainly to contain a raging fire which cut off all the aircraft's electrical control systems. Six of the seven crew members were able to eject; the aircraft flew low over the base and struck the North Star Bay ice floe at 900 km/h rather close to the Thule base. The B-52 disintegrated on impact, causing its 132,500 liters of fuel and the conventional explosives accompanying three of its four nuclear bombs to detonate. Thus three bombs along with their payload of plutonium, uranium, americium and tritium, were blown apart across an area of 15 to 20 square kilometers; a section of the ice floe measuring 305 meters wide by 610 meters long was melted by the intense heat at impact. The fourth nuclear bomb vanished intact into the ocean depths. The fire and the explosions lasted for twenty minutes, and a red cloud enveloped the region. An entire sector, known as the "black snow" area, was contaminated, along with the Inuit village of Moriussaq, 30 km to the north. The fourth bomb posed a serious problem: it was supposed to have been recovered by American submarines in 1979, but there are still serious doubts about this claim, and it has never been officially proven. The first to arrive and help one of the American pilots was an Eskimo I knew well from Moriussaq, who naturally ignored the danger of radiation. I met this man and filmed him describing what happened; I recorded his voice on my tape recorder [16] and took down his remarks in my notebooks, along with the declarations of some of his companions, who had helped to clear away the contaminated ice and the wreckage of the aircraft and its bombs.

In April 1969, I went out to direct a crew of French filmmakers to record the points of view of the Eskimos who were employed in the most scandalous way to assist in the decontamination operation. This film, made by French TV (ORTF), was banned by Danish and Greenland TV, despite the repeated requests of my Danish publisher. [17] I had touched a raw nerve in a government which saw itself as besieged by leftist parties and ecologists, even though it had declared through a joint Danish-American committee that the thermonuclear contamination of Thule in February 1968 represented no present or future danger whatsoever either for human beings or for the biological environment.

The Danish press is concerned: what happened to the fourth bomb, and what effects will it have on the population? Drawing by Julius, *Fyns Amts Avis*, 16 August 2000.

The cleanup operations, meanwhile, went ahead in a climate of extreme secrecy. Over seven hundred specialists from America and Denmark, representing on the American side some seventy government agencies, participated in the decontamination effort; the climatic conditions were extremely difficult, with winds of 137 km/h, temperatures sinking to 33° below zero and chill factors of up to 57° below. According to official reports, and given the urgency of the work, the equipment of the workers was highly inappropriate for such icy temperatures. Everyone was driven by the need to finish the task before the spring thaw. Ten thousand five hundred tons of snow, ice, and debris of all descriptions were packed into sealed containers and sent by sea to the Savannah River Plant in the USA. One hundred fifty Danish workers took part; nearly three kilograms of plutonium fragments were recovered from the three exploded bombs, while an unknown quantity vanished into the sea and into the columns of smoke that had risen hundreds of feet into the air on the plane's impact. About 500 grams of Pu-239 dispersed in tiny particles was found in seaweed and on the sea bottom during radio-ecological studies conducted during the summer of 1968. They would have disappeared into the undersea sediment, becoming part of the food chain going right up to seals, walruses and whales. The aircraft parts (fuselage and jet engines) were sent to Oak Ridge (USA) to be buried underground in the appropriate conditions. In May 1969 I myself took marine and submarine samples of all kinds, which I transmitted to the French nuclear center at Saclay. The conclusion was always the same: no contamination. It was uncannily like the response of the French authorities to the radio-active dust cloud emitted by the explosion at Chernobyl: "Naturally, it stopped at the blue line running through the Vosges."

Twenty years after the Thule accident, a group of men who had been among the 500 Danish workers on the base reported a rash of very serious health problems: cancer, sterility and severe physiological symptoms. The cause was clearly traceable to the work they had done on the ice floe in February 1968 and after, during the decontamination effort. According to them, they had worn no protective clothing against radiation; masks were mostly put aside, since they made breathing difficult in the terrible weather conditions; the teams, which to begin with were exclusively American and later included Danes as well, cleared up much of the debris by hand. US Air Force personnel were given the job of collecting the contaminated snow and ice, while Danish volunteers filled the massive containers and barrels. This was the official story. But I know through my Greenlander contacts and recorded interviews that the Inuit also took part in the cleanup, wearing their ordinary bearskin hunters' clothing right from the first days of pain, confusion and hurry. They must have caused a problem because one of their number, Ullulik, complained to me that his bearskin breeches had been taken away for tests, and were never returned. Today Ullulik is dead. To save time, nasal secretions were tested instead of urine samples, and as one Air Force doctor pointed out to me, in these wintry temperatures men's noses dripped abundantly, so one could only have strong reservations about such tests.

In the succeeding years, in-depth tests were made on 300 of the Danes engaged in the decontamination program, 98 of whom were found to have contracted cancer of one kind or another. In December 1986, Paul Schlueter, the Prime Minister of Denmark, declared that it would be necessary for the Thule workers to be re-examined by radiologists and specialists; no doubt the same was true for the Inuit concerned, but I fear that most of them were already dead by that time. Eleven months later, the Danish institute of clinical epidemiology declared that the Thule workers who had taken part in these operations showed a cancer rate 40 times higher than that of the three thousand workers who were at the base before and then after the accident; and that in any event their cancer rate was 50% above the national average. By late 1987, nearly 200 Danish workers, to head off foreclosure by the American authorities, sued the US government. During the subsequent investigation, hundreds of previously secret documents were made public. In particular, it was revealed that the personnel employed by the US Air Force at Thule, who had worked side by side with the Danes, had no training in how to protect themselves against radiation. How much less fortunate, then, were the Inuit.

To this day, the Air Force has refused to divulge any information about the inventory of toxic and radiation contamination caused by the bombs on the crashed B-52. Consequently this information has been very difficult to establish, but what nobody can deny is that a good part of the radioactive residue was dissolved in the pristine sea at Thule during the spring thaw. All the experts devoutly hope that the melt actually diluted the radiation to acceptable levels. For the record, plutonium 239 has a radioactive lifespan of 24,400 years; uranium 238, 4.5 billion years; Americum 243, 7,400 years.

The silence of the intelligentsia

I would like at this point to pay homage to those Danish leagues which have defended the Inuit. The Danish lawyers Christian Harlenge and Henri Karl Nielsen have vigorously presented the case of the 150 unfortunate Eskimos who were so roughly expelled [18] from Thule in the spring of 1953, and on whose behalf I vainly spoke in September 1989.

I must also express my admiration for Sally Schnell and Hannah Danielson, the cofounders in Denmark of the Thule Association. "From 1972 onwards, my husband, who worked at the base in 1968, was the victim of serious health problems. He died of cancer on April 30, 1987. Whenever anyone mentioned Thule, he became very aggressive indeed."

I also salute Per Walsoe, the Copenhagen advocate of the Commune of Thule (1989-1991), who assisted me during the court hearings which I attended, along with the journalist and writer Eva Rude, a peerless defender of Greenlanders' rights. Eva Rude is the founder president of

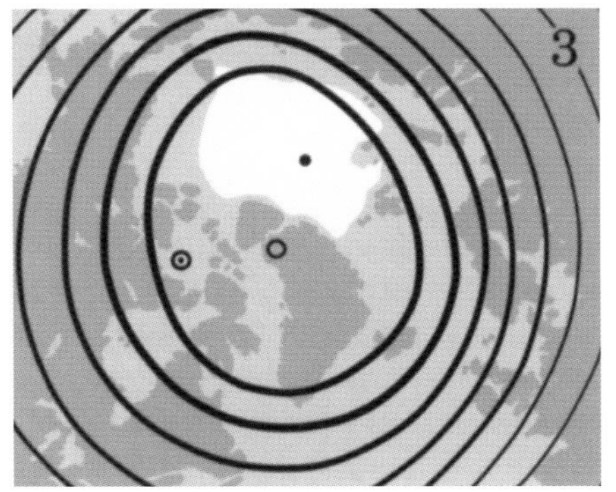

The site of the US airbase in Thule was not chosen at random. This large radar headquarters is at the center of the region of the aurora borealis in a major geomagnetic and magnetic sector.

- • Geographic North Pole
- ○ Qaanaaq
- ⊙ North Magnetic Pole

(from *Kalaaliit Nunaat*, Greenland, Pilersuiffik, 1990)

the Danish and Greenlander Women's Association.

Next, I must render a special homage to Professor Cornelius Remie, of the University of Nijmegen, who in 1998, during a multidisciplinary expedition in the district of Qaanaaq, made such inquiries into the condition of the Inughuit, as well as their social situation (alcoholism and suicide rate), and the contamination of the air in the zone they inhabited (study of lichens).

The people of Denmark, who have been passionately attached to Greenland for two and a half centuries, have been utterly appalled by this affair. They were convinced that the Thule base was purely defensive in its function, as their government had told them. There were massive, violently anti-American demonstrations at Copenhagen and in Greenland after the crash in January 1968. Although the complaint of the Danish workers was late in coming, it was a brave one: these days it takes a lot of courage for anyone to take on an employer as formidable as the United States Government.

And how can we forget the Inuit who ran to the aid of the stricken American pilots, and took part in the subsequent decontamination process? The wholehearted cooperation of those Eskimo hunters, completely bare of protective clothing against radiation, is seldom mentioned. But we live in a world where everything is all too rapidly stifled . . . those people whose minds are conditioned by television have become peoples devoid of memory.

Denmark, despite the actions of its Prime Minister, has never recovered its authority over the base at Thule, which remains strictly American. The effects of the wise Danish policy so rigorously applied from 1910 to 1951, whose objective was to keep this legendary people insulated from the outside world, have been completely and shockingly annihilated.

But the reader will conclude, what are five hundred or a thousand Eskimos, when the fate of the free world depends on the existence of military bases? In 1998 I learned that an anonymous American expert in social science had declared in an interview with *Paris Match* (*Le sentinelle extreme de l'Occident*, p 99), "At Thule we established a presence on which the security of several hundred million people depends today. Despite that, we have been vilified by everyone, and principally

16) In *The Last Kings of Thule* (1989), there is even a sketch by this hunter of the area of "black snow." It was he who picked up one of the pilots' hats. See p. 578, drawing by Ungak Kugaukitsoq, 20 June 1969: "Airplane's fall. Big light at 4:30. Visible from Moriussaq. Leaves immediately by sled . . . Picks up a pilot's hat off the ice . . . No moon, no wind, then a little wind from the south and flurries." (Excerpts from J.M. notebooks, 1969)

17) It was shown to the Greenland population of Qaanaaq only in April-May 2000 (thirty two years later !) by a group of young French cineastes. The reactions of the audience were filmed. The Inughuit's silence and the strong emotion on their faces are highly moving. Most of the Inughuit participants in *Last Kings of Thule*—two color films of 55 minutes each, "The Hunter Eskimo" and "The Unpredictable Welfare Eskimo"—were dead. This film, which I directed, is in the *Institut national de l'audiovisuel* collection (INA, 1969).

18) One hundred fifty Inughuit were evicted in the course of a few days. They were to travel 100 miles north of Thule by dog sled to northeastern Whale Sound, to the stretch of shore across from Herbert Island where the artificial town of Qaanaaq was to be built. The native population was evacuated at short notice. The American military base had decided to expand and deploy anti-aircraft guns. All of the Inughuit left by dog sled—the adults, the elderly, the children, and even the sick. Qaanaaq had not yet been built. At first they lived in tents.

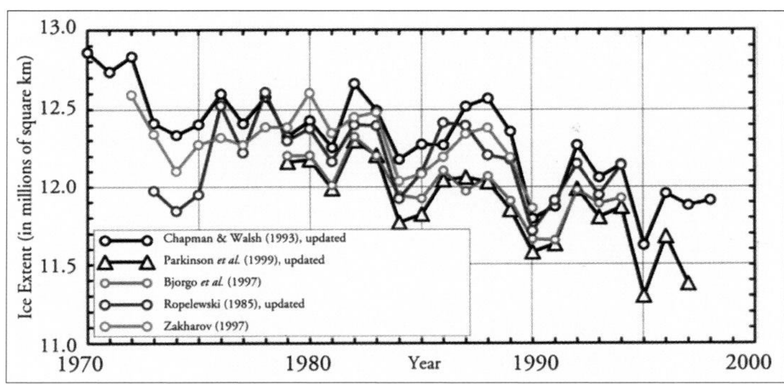

Five studies have shown that the extent of the ice has diminished in the northern hemisphere in the last 25 years. (From Vinnikov et al., *In Witness of the Arctic*, NSF, Spring 2000, vol. 8, no. 1.)

by French ethnologists." My book, *The Last Kings of Thule* was published all over the world—and it was particularly noticed and appreciated in the United States. Nevertheless I received this negative message loud and clear. It is my duty as a scholar to face powerful interests in such serious circumstances. "They" will always find some lackey or other who will act as their agent in an attempt to destabilize you. The American and Danish newspapers have always respected and honored my battle on behalf of the Thule Inuit. The leading newspapers in Paris, concerned that they might be perceived as anti-American, held their fire. At that time the US was suffering reverse after reverse in Vietnam; the daily papers, all except for one, had refused my text with excuses, or else had accepted it with deep cuts which I myself would not allow. Only one was prepared to publish the full, unabridged text; this was *Le Figaro Littéraire*, with the backing of Marcel Jullian, who was then the head of the TV channel Antenne 2. In this world of ours where the rights of man are invoked at the drop of a hat, may we not with equal force evoke the rights of native people who are poorer than the poorest Danish laborer?

Is it possible, I ask publicly, that a great democratic power should place as hostages, in a forward base of the Western world that serves as the first line of military defense, indigenous populations whose society is still heavily traditional?

The Arctic is vast, and the American army could easily have chosen another site on its own territory where there were no people. It was highly imprudent to violate symbols so vital to man's history: the victims at Thule, after all, were the people of the Unicorn, the Hyperboreans of Friedrich Nietsche. In modern times when colonialism has in theory been abolished, tutelary powers still appear to negotiate military agreements more or less as they like, which determine the destinies of the native peoples for which they are responsible before the United Nations.

This is true not only of Greenland but also of the Amazon, Aboriginal Australia, French Polynesia (up to January 1996), Okinawa, Tibet, and Arctic Russia, which has been so hideously polluted by the Red Army's nuclear test program.

Would it not be simply *right* that these native peoples, who never asked to be protected by anyone, and certainly not by the imperialist powers, should be fully informed of the fate proposed for them, and of the risks they would run if military bases or 'research centers' were built on their territory; and that then they should be asked, through a properly-conducted referendum, whether or not they agree to such? I think that is the least we can expect.

On 12 October 1995, the Prime Minister of Greenland presented a special declaration to the Greenland Parliament concerning the American base at Thule. In his speech he asserted that the displacement of the Inuit population of Thule in 1953 had been, beyond any shadow of doubt, a forced and coercive enterprise. This declaration represents real progress in the light of the hearings I attended at Copenhagen, [19] when the three commissioners nominated by the government questioned me gravely as to whether the population of 150 Eskimos at Thule had been *invited* to leave (willingly, consentingly, after persuasion?), whereas in June 1951 the Inuit were in a face-off with the US Air Force in Thule and had obviously been constrained to pack their sleds and leave their beloved igloos and the tombs of their ancestors with only a few days' notice. [20]

Who didn't know this at Thule and Qaanaaq ? Moses Olsen, in a remarkable speech reprinted here, insists that what occurred was nothing less than a "deportation". It was completely unacceptable.

The Prime Minister of Greenland also demanded that the Government of Greenland be given full access to every detail of the affair, as well as complete information about what was happening inside the US facility. Later, a number of complaints submitted through the Qaanaaq municipal council were presented to the Danish government, with a view to compensation for the *de facto* prejudice caused by the creation of the base in 1951, the forced deportation of 1953, and the illegal presence of nuclear bombs at least since 1960, which resulted in the catastrophe described earlier.

The American response came back in 1997. The NSF (National Science Foundation) arraigned to itself all the logistics of the base at Thule, in order to carry out studies of conditions in these high latitudes, both in winter and in summer.

SOS NORTH POLE

The Arctic is now in serious crisis. For twenty years, it has been warming at an unprecedented rate, and specialists have so far been unable to say why, due to the horrible complexity of the long-term climatic process. [21] Nevertheless, it is a reality: from 1958-1976 and 1993-1997, the thickness of the ice pack at the end of the season of melt was abnormally diminished in the greater part of the deep water section of the Arctic Ocean. The ice pack has lost 40% of its volume in less than thirty years, reducing from a thickness of 10 feet to 6 feet. Over two decades (1978-1998) the ice pack shrank at a rate of 37,000 square kilometers per year, according to the American weekly review *Science*.

The floating Arctic ice pack in winter covers 14 million square kilometers. The melt has accelerated since 1990. Since 1993 the Greenland glacier has thinned by more than one meter a year at its southern and eastern edges. And the glacier in the North of Greenland is 'dry,' according to observations made by me during my geomorphological expeditions; thus its balance is highly unstable, given that its maintenance depends on the glacier to the south which preserves the climate in which it functions. The greenhouse effect is a scientific certainty and its causes are CO_2 emissions from the industrialized areas of Western Europe, North America, Siberia, China and India, among many others. This warming of the Arctic can rise to 5° at the North Pole, at worst; if it does, the geophysical consequences for the rest of the planet will be extremely serious, including earthquakes, cyclones, forest fires, and viral and parasite-borne illnesses due to changes in insect biology. At the moment a hundred million men and women are directly threatened by drought in twenty-three countries in Africa, Central Asia and the Middle East. In temperate areas like France, the warming of the Arctic will cause disturbances in the currents of the ocean (notably the Gulf Stream) which will make for a cooler, unstable climate, with alternating heavy rainfall and periods of extreme drought. Meanwhile the seas will rise to significantly higher levels in consequence of the melting ice-cap.

On top of all this, there is pollution.

We are on red alert and the light is flashing. The Polar region has become a dump for all our refuse. The contaminants now present in the Arctic are mainly agricultural and industrial in origin, being carried on the wind from the south. Organochlorines reach the Arctic directly via an endlessly repeated cycle of evaporation, movement through the air and condensation. Heavy metal particles and radio-nuclei, on the other hand, move on the winds from the source emission to the area of deposit. Contaminants are present in all the Arctic regions, and levels of pollution of Arctic fauna and flora are often very high indeed. The principal contaminants are organo-chloric pesticides like toxaphene and chlordane, DDT and DDE, and industrial chemicals like polychlorinated diphenyls and PCB. Concentrations of these are now being found in the fat of marine mammals.

The principal heavy metals now present in the Arctic food chain are lead, cadmium and mercury. Significant levels of these exist, again, in marine mammals, as well as in caribou flesh, especially the livers and kidneys.

At Qaanaq (Thule), unexpected levels of pollutants generated locally, unknown to the inhabitants, were registered in the report of Cornelius Remie. [22] The Canadian polar bear, which symbolized the Arctic, has developed reproductive problems on account of chemical products that damage its endocrine system. Men, at the top of the food chain, should be seriously alarmed by this.

On 31 July 1998, in its final session, the ICC (Inuit Circumpolar Conference), under the presidency of Aqqaluk Lynge, expressed its anxiety over levels of contamination in Arctic animals, provoked by pollutants from industrial regions in the south. But however worrying the situation may be, we should be prudent in assessing it. The Canadian health authorities estimate that whatever the alternative, " . . .the risks posed by the non-consumption by native inhabitants of their traditional foods are far higher." The vitamins contained in the local game are so essential to the human organism in these high latitudes that this diet simply must be maintained. On the other hand, "it is advisable to limit the consumption of marine mammal fats, and to grill or boil the meat before consuming it."

The effect of such threats on the minds of Inuit hunters may easily be imagined. They mean that the pure, untouched Arctic is a thing of the past, and the sea is no longer a mother, but an image of menace.

In Northern Siberia, the situation is much more alarming, and in some parts it is quite simply tragic. Chukotka, [23] the cradle of the Inuit, faces an appalling medical crisis. Valery Trufakin, of the Siberian Institute of Physiology, stresses the disastrous effects on the tundra wrought by the nuclear tests at Novaya Zemlya carried out by the Red Army between 1955 and 1962. The Nenets population now suffers from an abnormally high rate of infant mortality and their adults routinely develop a wide variety of cancers. Only a quarter of the population can be said to be in good health. The Kola peninsula, adjoining the Barents Sea—which is the richest fishing ground in the Northern Hemisphere—is (according to the experts) a "slow-motion Chernobyl." Constant sulfur dioxide emissions from the Zapolyamy nickel mine, nuclear pollution from the Red Army's nuclear weapons tests carried out between 1956 and 1980, and the scuttling in the sea of superannuated nuclear submarines and nuclear waste, have all contributed to this.

If we look at the problem on a planetary scale, the picture looks even blacker. In less than 30 years, 10% of the world's natural forests were destroyed and more than half its original forests were gone by the year 2000. Many species became extinct. Today, the hot deserts are expanding. The sands are creeping outward in the Sahara. Sixty thousand square kilometers return to the desert every year. The vital signs analyzed and recorded each year by Lester R. Brown and his remarkable team all warn of impending catastrophe, amid a climate of general indifference.

An unprecedented social crisis

For over forty years, enlightened scientists have been denouncing the brutal treatment of first nations—Indians, Inuit, Northern Siberians, Sami—by the all-conquering West. Paternalistic and colonialist policies have been the rule for far too long.

Primary school teaching among these peoples has been scrutinized recently by Professor Cornelius Remie's special commission. It has been shown to be wildly inappropriate: for example, the local language of North Greenland is not the one used in the primary schools there. The South Greenland language is used instead, since this is the tongue spoken by government-employed teachers throughout the island, from north to south. As a result the northern children who continue to speak the language of their fathers [24] are destabilized. Inughuit language teachers need to be trained and brought into service; at the moment there are none. Furthermore, standards in the schools are mediocre, according to the report of the University of Nijmegen.

We should never forget that the children we are discussing here come from traditional societies in which culture, heritage and values

19) See above, page 385, notes 17 and 18, and page 386.
20) The survivors and their families were individually compensated by the Greenland authorities, though only much later. I do not know the sums they received. In fact, the right questions weren't asked ; why the people of Thule were not consulted in June 1951 about the issue of a base on their territory ?.
21) In Thule-Qaanaaq, temperatures have been dropping steadily, as can be seen from the temperature graphs. Long-term trends in air movement patterns are subject to local anomalies and exceptions.
22) Remie, *Facing the Future*.
23) *Tchoukotka, 1990*, the eight scientific reports of the first French-Soviet expedition to Chukotka, under the direction of Jean Malaurie (Paris: EHESS-Economica, 2001). And Jean Malaurie, *Hummocks II* (Alaska-Siberian Chukotka) (Paris: Editions Plon, "Terre humaine," 1999).
24) See Remie, *Facing the Future*.
25) Cécile Beizmann, Jean Malaurie, Hélène Trouche-Simon, Nina Rausch de Traubenberg, "Twelve Rorschach-method tests on Inuit Eskimos in northern Greenland (1950–1951): mission Jean Malaurie," *Internord 18*, Paris, CNRS, 1987, p. 191–223; René Zazzo; Jean Malaurie, Hélène Trouche-Simon, "Psychomotor tests of *Deux Barrages* on polar Eskimos (northwest Greenland), mission Jean Malaurie, 1950–1951, second psychological study." *Internord 19*, Paris, CNRS, 1990, p. 301–319.
26) Marc Tadié and Jean-Yves Tadié, *Le Sens de la mémoire* (Paris: Gallimard, 1999), page 368.

are all handed down orally. Deprived of their own culture, such children find it very difficult to integrate into an alien written culture, though Rorschach tests and my own tests on attentiveness (in 1951) gave ample proof of the wealth of their imaginative powers and the acuteness of their observation.

The situation is not uniformly dire. The push, as always, must come from behind; it has to begin with the people themselves, and especially with the women, who have become noticeably empowered among the Inuit. Greenland, whose government's autonomy is growing with every year that passes, now has a high percentage of female mayors. The Inuit language is alive and well and used officially in Greenland, at Nunavik and Nunavut; it is also widely spoken among the Inupiats and Yupiks of southern Alaska, as well as in the islands of the Bering Sea.

Another encouraging factor is the growth of the Inuit population. In 1992, 127,000 Inuit were recorded in the polar regions as a whole; likewise Inughuit numbers are on the increase, from 302 in 70 families in December 1950, to 830 in 1998 (all of these are Inughuit born in Greenland, with 608 unfortunately concentrated in the town of Qaanaaq and 222 in four villages elsewhere). There is, without question, a vitality in mankind which transcends misfortune.

This population is one whose senses are hyper acute, another huge advantage. We know, through the work of Marc Tadié, [26] that in first nations there exists a special level of neuronal plasticity, ensuring that the development of dendrites is stimulated by cravings. The hunter, ever on the watch for game, knows many cravings. Likewise, affectivity and perception are sharpened. A strong emotion can provoke a nosebleed. A word can kill a man. These people's neurons, stimulated by nervous flux, are highly developed; those which are not go into apoptosis, whereupon the cells wither and die. We also know that neurons possess long-term knowledge. When a situation provokes a strong emotion, it is recorded. If an event of the same kind reoccurs, neuronal memory is triggered, as Proust's memory was triggered by the taste of his *madeleine*. The Inuit, continually subjected to stress, were historically prey in the fall season to the crises of hysteria which I described in 1951. They are constantly on the watch, looking, observing. These men, on account of their environment, their emotivity, and the collective lives they live in which everyone derives encouragement from observing and judging himself, possess extrasensory powers that are far more developed than those of white men. This means that the phenomena of telepathy, telegenesis and perception of the invisible are perfectly possible in the context of shamanism, and are more developed generally among traditional peoples than among Westerners. Again, this explains their great artistic gifts—as demonstrated in their sculpted masks and ivories—and their openness to religion.

For over 150 years the Inughuit of North Greenland have been learning to understand us, ever since their first meeting with Captain John Ross in August 1818. They acknowledged our courage and our technical inventiveness, but also our cynicism, egotism and murderous violence. Yet it would be wrong for any reader of *Ultima Thule* to conclude that Western progress has brought the Inuit nothing but grief. History feeds on constant contact and change, and isolation means atrophy and death in the long term. Until now, Inuit in every region of the Pole have contrived at various times to adapt remarkably well. We should remember that they moved adroitly from the lance, to the bow and arrow, to the rifle, from stone traps to steel traps, from dog sleds to snowmobiles, from snow igloos to spacious wooden houses; they have also become experts in the use of computers and the Internet. At the dawn of the third millennium, young Inuit aspire to extraordinary and radical change. Whilst their elders remain conservative and cautious, the young are deeply involved in their own revolution. The sacred drum seems to be forgotten; rock music is now a part of their culture. We should be under no illusions about this; the civilization that Americans, Europeans and Asiatics have evolved with such effort, suffering, and ingenuity, is only available to the Inuit in its virtual form. When we observe the actual shifts of power that have taken place, we note with sorrow that the process of empowering the Inuit has been agonizingly slow. Teaching in their schools is so ill-adapted that there is a lack of co-ordination between the reality on the ground and the substantial means offered by negotiated autonomies like Nunavik, Nunavut and Greenland. The young, who in every culture have their wits about them, understand quite well that all this has been put together far too hastily; they have been betrayed, and this explains their despair.

The future looks bleak to the new generation of Inuit. Hunting, fishing, and services are no longer their nation's only callings. And these young people are just as much in the dark as we are. What is to be done? I asked myself this question when I was a volunteer teacher on Baffin Island, at Clyde River (Kangiqsugaapik) in April-May 1987. [27] Vacant jobs for dentists, doctors, lawyers, nurses, physicians, astronomer, computer scientists, ecologists, biologists, historians, and ethnologists are seldom filled by Inuit. Alcoholism and drug addiction are rampant among them. They no longer have the superb health they once had. [28] The corollaries to these evils—battered women, sexual abuses, violence—are realities that nobody can deny. An international study has shown that the incidence of lung and throat cancers in Greenland is among the highest in the world. In 1950, cancer was unknown among the Inuit on account of their diet; [29] today it stems from their very high consumption of tobacco and alcohol. AIDS is also a problem in Greenland. [30] The suicide rate, I repeat, is alarming, too: in 1962-66, out of a population of 56,000, there were 19.4 suicides per 100,000; in 1972-76, there were 53.9; in 1982, 114.1. And these suicides (1977-1986) were principally males (81%; 62% unmarried, 27% married). They tended to be unemployed (569/100,000)—though hunters and fishermen were also affected, because of their low incomes and status (277/100,000). Even students at technical schools were affected (195/100,000). In Greenland the suicide rate has stabilized since 1990, though it is still very high. The causes have not been addressed. At Kuujjuaq in the Nunavik region, 1800 km north of Montreal, where the native population controls its own destiny by managing economic life through its Makavik cooperative, there has been a recent suicide rate of 211/100,000, contrasting with the Canadian national rate of 14/100,000.

In fact suicide is not merely an act of despair. It is also a *political act.* It sends a message to the effect that the society in place does not concern itself with the suicide. This implies a failure of western administrations, universities, banks, and state investments, which have cobbled together a "future" for the great Inuit civilization much too hastily, with very little hard sociological backup.

The same goes for the churches, which have not always been up to the task of preaching a brighter tomorrow. At this decisive moment in Inuit history the churches are in full retreat, facing so many lawsuits that they have turned to the government for financial aid. There have been 5,800 personal suits and four collective ones against church organizations in Canada, pertaining to 100 native schools in which 160,000 natives, Indians, and Inuit were boarders between 1800 and 1970—at which time they were closed down by the Federal Government. In these schools, set up by the government in Ottawa, the use of native languages was forbidden, as was traditional shamanism. Sexual abuses were rife, a scandal which deeply affected the minds of young Inuit so hungry for thing sacred and so confident in their priests.

The Inuit, thrown on their own resources, have "Inuitized" the message of Christ, with the support of Pentecostalists and Baptists. The Inuit want more than schoolmasters and psychologists; they want visionaries who can help them preserve their status as hunters while opening up to the new world. They will accept anyone of good will; left to themselves they can sort the good from the bad very quickly.

The Inuit are a people who used to experience the hunt as a mystical activity inspired by their own shamanic vision of the Universe. They are groping now for a perspective that can take in their own heritage as well as the technological world of the West. For them this time of profound change is a dream coupled with a nightmare. Their post-colonial era, despite certain bright areas of progress, has been mostly bungled by the emissaries of the West.

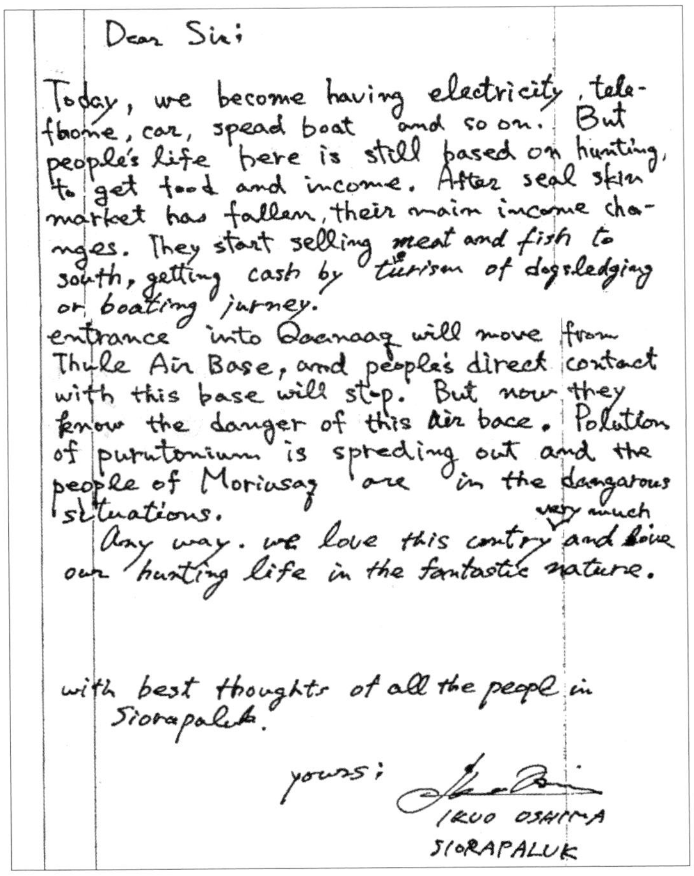

Dear Sir:

Today, we become having electricity, tele-fhone, car, spead boat and so on. But people's life here is still based on hunting, to get food and income. After seal skin market has fallen, their main income changes. They start selling meat and fish to south, getting cash by turism of dogsledging or boating jurney.
entrance into Qaanaaq will move from Thule Air Base, and people's direct contact with this base will stop. But now they know the danger of this Air bace. Polution of purutonium is spreding out and the people of Moriusaq are in the dangarous situations.
Any way. we love this contry very much and live our hunting life in the fantastic nature.

with best thoughts of all the people in Siorapaluk.

yours; [signature]
IKUO OSHIMA
SIORAPALUK

LETTER FROM OSHIMA IKAO TO JEAN MALAURIE

(sent from Siorapaluk to the Center for Arctic Studies by fax, 7 July 2000)

Dear Sir:
Today, we become having electricity, telephone, car, speed boat, and so on. But people's life here is still based on hunting to get food and income. After seal skin market has fallen, their main income changes. They start selling meat and fish to south, getting cash by tourism of dog sledding and boating journey.
Entrance into Qaanaaq will move from Thule Air Base, and people's direct contact with this base will stop. But now they know the danger of this airbase. Pollution of plutonium is spreading out and the people of Moriusaq are in the dangerous situations.
Anyway, we love this country very much and live our hunting life in the fantastic nature.
With best thoughts of all the people in Siorapaluk.

Yours,
Ikuo Oshima

Ongoing disinformation

The facts laid out above are routinely censored by the Western media: they seldom surface. The televisions of the world report the Arctic as though it had signed some kind of contract with the ecotourism industry, describing only the "immaculate snows" and "virgin spaces" of autonomous territories that are actually moving decisively into a new political era. Occasionally there is a dismissive reference to the tendency toward alcoholism of a few wretched people on the fringes who are unable to face their altered destiny. It goes unsaid that these problems are the responsibility of the Westerners and scientists who have remained silent for altogether too long.

"*Nunavut*! Our land!" was the watchword of the Inuit league (Inuit Circumpolar Conference), for which the Rouen Congress was the first real platform. The ICC was created at Point Barrow (Alaska) in 1977; I was one of the few white scientists invited to attend by the Inuit authorities. The same slogan was repeated there, day after day: *"Eskimo power!"*

Alas, in Greenland and Alaska it was only very late in the day that the Inuit were given the right to administer themselves. Alaska acquired this right in 1971, Greenland in 1979, Nunavik in 1986 and Nunavut in 1999. In Siberia, Soviet policy held only to a kind of muddled, atheistic russification, amid a maelstrom of contradictory initiatives.

"Modernization," writes Péguy, "is a blessing confined to men of the world. Liberty, by contrast, is a poor man's virtue." In *Notre Jeunesse*, he adds: "Everything begins with the mystical and ends with politics. Everything begins with the mystical, with something mystical, with that which is mystical of itself; and everything ends with politics."

The Inuit actually have no choice. If they are not to be gradually swallowed up by the rest of the shapeless world, they must not only redis-

27) Jean Malaurie, *Hummocks I* (Paris: Editions Plon, Collection "Terre humaine," 1999), chapter 6, pages 434-467.
28) André Nenna, "Avis d'un utilisateur sur l'information médicale, automatisation," in *Arctica*, 1978, Seventh International Congress of Northern Libraries, CNRS, under the direction of Jean Malaurie (Paris: Editions du CNRS, 1982), pages 345-346.
29) See Hugh Sinclair, "Evolution des Esquimaux: de la santé d'autrefois à la santé d'aujourd'hui," in Sylvie Devers ed., *Pour Jean Malaurie, 102 témoignages en hommage à quarante ans d'études arctiques* (Paris: Editions Plon, 1990), pages 529-535.
30) Thorslund Jorgen, *Ungdomsselvmord og modernisering-sproblemer blandt Inuit* (Doctoral dissertation, Roskilde University, 1992).
31) Jean Malaurie ed., *Le peuple esquimau aujourd'hui et demain; The Eskimo People Today and Tomorrow*, 4th International Congress of the Centre d'études arctiques, EHESS, Bibliothèque arctique et antarctique, volume 4 (Paris and The Hague: Editions Mouton, 1973.

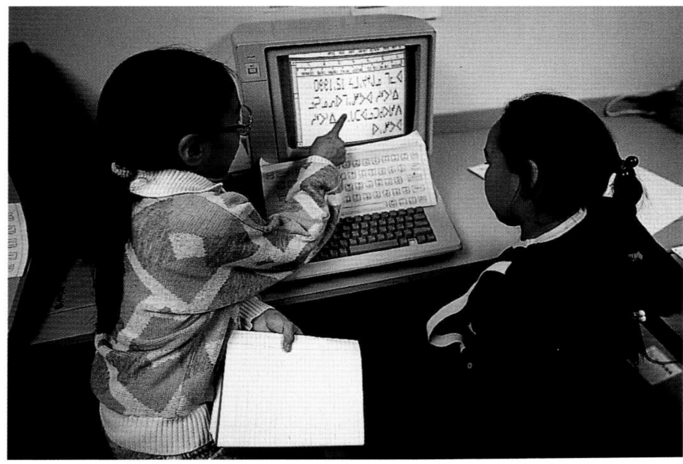

The Inuit children of Greenland connect to the Internet.

cover the grandeur of their past but also establish beyond doubt that their civilization is a vibrant and creative one. They have to convince themselves that their Pantheist civilization has the advantage of the treasure of freedom. We who aspire to retire at age sixty, in our spiritual obscurity, need the enlightenment of Inuit thought. The present generation must run the gauntlet of all the dangers: they will have to show real character. Their schools and museums must teach them to make use of their history, not as something to fall back upon, but as a means of inventing a new way of thinking and a new economy for their territory, which is otherwise so rich and so coveted by the great empires. *"We were once a great civilization,"* say the Inuit. Now the hour has come to prove this, at a time when the West has never been more cynical. *"The three most enormous private fortunes in the world represent a total which is equal to the total GNP of all the world's most backward nations, with a total population of six hundred million people."* (Extract from a speech delivered at the Elysée Palace by President Jacques Chirac, 14 July 2000.)

The Inuit react

With a verve and modernity of spirit that takes in the most advanced methods (computers, Internet, cooperatives, tourism 100% controlled by the Inuit), the Inuit and Indian authorities are fighting back. Among many others, I can single out the names of Charlie Watt, the Inuit Senator in Ottawa—one of the fathers of Nunavik, in the north of the province of Quebec; Jonathan Hunt, the Inuit senator of Nunavut; Jonathan Motzveldt, Prime Minister of Greenland; and Moses Olsen, the former Greenland Minister of Culture. The Greenland authorities are perhaps more politically comfortable with their autonomy than the Canadians, on account of the long experience of self-government given them over the years by the Danish administration. And who knows? The leading men of Nunavik and Nunavut may perhaps be called upon, in the near future, to create a single Inuit geopolitical region. Whether or not this is mere speculation, Nunavik, Nunavut and Greenland are already in constant contact; there is a direct air link between Nuuk (the Greenland capital) and Iqaluit (capital of Nunavut). Geography inspires history, but what history : that of the movement of a new people in synchresis.

Furthermore, there are the young people, whose numbers are increasing but whose future (as I have said before) appears confused. Oshima Ikao, a Japanese who became a naturalized Eskimo, is married to an Eskimo woman of Siorapaluk; he has four children and he worries about their future, though for thirty years he has been one of the more prominent Inuit in his territory. I made contact with him at Qaanaaq by email, and then spoke to him on the telephone. From Siorapaluk he sent me the letter included here, before leaving for the traditional bird hunt, to which he invited me. Also included (facing page) is a message sent to me by Moses Olsen.

The kernel of the problem is that in this delicate business of coexisting cultures, nobody has a fully satisfactory answer. Everyone agrees that policies involving compulsory reserves and physical isolation have been discredited since June 1951—my own book's potent title[32] was chosen to reflect this. It has become a matter of urgency for us to educate the world about the vital issues at stake in the Arctic. This is happening—the successes in recent negotiations are a proof of it—but there must be a constructive follow-up, for which the creation at Thule of a major research center could be a major opportunity. A decision has already been taken to found an advanced hunting school at Qaanaaq, a highly laudable move. The future of Inuit hunters needs to be made secure by guaranteeing, through subsidies, a much higher income for them. But—quite understandably—many of the younger generation have other ambitions. I deeply regret, and I say so openly to my American friends, that the Thule base—where at least one and probably several new radar complexes have recently been installed—was not returned to the Greenland government[33] when Greenland was given her autonomy in 1979. Tourism is certainly an advantage for the Inuit but in our short sightedness we have to make sure that the Inuit Arctic does not become a victim of mercantile tourism. The recent acquisition by the National Science Foundation (NSF) of the equipment and buildings on the base will provide a logistical center of the highest importance to American scientists, who now plan to make an in-depth study the High Arctic.

I used to know the kings of Thule, but that was another era. We have to be realistic. It is from the top down that a people gets stronger and rights itself. I devoutly hope that the NSF, whose generous spirit is well known, will provide job opportunities for young Inughuit technicians, scientists and creative spirits, many of whom are astonishingly gifted in the disciplines of mathematics, biology and ecology. Side by side with European and American scientists, they can become part of the complement of space engineers and ecologists working on the base, so that ultimately it can be an Inuit International Academy worthy of the name. The base offers an extraordinary opportunity to create, at Thule, an open university for all the Inuit, to reconquer, little by little, their territory, to defend the threatened ecosystems of the world's high latitudes. What a symbol this would be! An academy that would train, to the highest level, an intellectual nucleus of Inuit inventors working with the most modern techniques. One might hope that between five and ten major figures might emerge from such an institution within a few short years. What a source of pride this would be for the population of 1000 Inughuit sprinkled over 500 km in the camps and villages of North Greenland, whose numbers would be swelled by an influx of young Inuit scientists from South Greenland, Canada, Alaska and Siberia. Such an initiative would go a long way toward obliterating the memory of the dark years.

A young Inughuit from Thule might thus find himself with a choice of careers: the life of a full-time highly paid hunter, or the life of a scientific researcher on the spot, who could spend his leisure hours hunting in the traditional manner. On the other hand, if the U.S. allows this opportunity to slip away, the Thule of advanced American science will appear to the wider world as the agency that bullied the Inughuit into a kind of civilizational apartheid.

A new destiny for the Inuit

We can only fight despair in a people if they are willing to have faith in themselves. The confrontation of the means available to the West, and those available to the Inuit civilization, has created inferiority complexes that every page of this book must show to be transparently groundless. The era of hunting and isolation is gone today: for most Inuit the old mythical dimension of wild creatures has vanished forever, and as I have said, there must be work for those young Inuit who want to stay in their ancestral home, but do something new and different. The base at Thule, against which I have fought a long and solitary struggle, now represents the future of the Inughuit in stark, uncompromising terms. It is there to stay.

The Inuit must be both outside it, and inside it as well. It is my ardent hope, despite my full awareness of the dangers of assimilation, that very soon there will be modern institutions throughout the Arctic that are capable of awakening the energies of the Northern peoples, just as Nuuk and Ottawa have been doing. Recently I had a series of highly constructive meetings in Ottawa with the Inuit senator of Nunavik, Charlie Watt, in which we discussed a European-Canadian program of cooperation in this regard (May 2000).

Another project I support wholeheartedly is that of establishing a CD-ROM teaching program accompanied by textbooks and films, both on the Internet and directly in schools. The languages would be Inuit, English and French; the program would demonstrate the broad lines of archeological, historical, anthropological, medical and ecological knowledge, to which the ancestors of today's Inuit contributed without ever being informed of their results. The style of the program should be adapted to their outlook, hence it should be both specific to Inuit and open to modern life. This was the method of Knud Rasmussen, who brought his own work in history, anthropology and film to fruition through a permanent collaboration with the Inuit. It was they, after all, who did the most to refine his thought as a Dane and an Eskimo.

When Kleinschmidt founded his newspaper *Atuaglitutit* in the late eighteenth century at the request of Heinrich Rink, the Danish administrator who wanted to build a "Greenland for the Greenlanders," he had no other goal in mind than that. But today we must go further. We need to do more than open the Inuit to the world and to politics; we need to help them discover their own world, studying side by side with their fathers and grandfathers.

We will never win the cooperation of the young unless their élite can be made aware that the explorer whites did not carry out their expeditions alone, and indeed that most of these expeditions were enterprises shared with the Inuit. I have seen this happen at the State Polar Academy of St. Petersburg, where every year we train one thousand sons of shepherds, hunters, herdsmen and administrators. In educational texts, we need to draw a distinction between the whites who collaborated mentally or directly with the Inuit, in their best interest (for example Knud Rasmussen, Peter Freuchen, and, in our own time, John McDonald at Igloolik), and those who cynically exploited the Inuit to further their own careers.

Tourism, too, is an option—of sorts. The Arctic is vast and noble, with immense mystical power. Specific charters with the Inuit communities concerned are currently being prepared; an interactive form of tourism needs to be devised, and without delay. The Inuit should not be condemned to stand and smile while hundreds of zombies queue to take their photographs. I am told that in Canada, the Inuit have to be paid to grin at their voyeur-visitors, so fed up are they, like the people of Central America, with greeting them politely. Obviously tourism can generate revenue. But we all know the sequence: first come the small, wealthy groups guided by tour operators, whose organizers work very well with the local population; then, as profits rise, these operators are bought out by powerful companies specializing in mass tourism. Thereafter, the fragile social and physical ecosystem is increasingly at risk.

The State Polar Academy at St. Petersburg was founded in 1994

MOSES OLSEN TESTIFIES

Nuuk, Greenland, 3 June 2000. Written statement for *Ultima Thule*.

I believe that the Thule region has evolved in a positive way since 1992. The region has attracted the attention of the central authorities thanks to local initiatives. Primarily, the population fought to be compensated by the Danish government for its deportation from Qaanaaaq in 1953. This initiative received the support of Greenland's domestic council, and through the "Hingitaq 53" and the Danish judicial system, the people received damages, though to a lesser extent than requested. But the important thing was that the Danish government finally had to admit that there had truly been a case of deportation. This is good. And from the political point of view, it opens new political possibilities in our struggle for the right of ownership over the whole of our country, which has been colonized since 1722 by Denmark without our having asked for it. The colonial towns were often founded on spots that were chosen at random, to suit the economic interests of the colonial power of the time, and not on the basis of the Greenlander's instinctive knowledge of the best-adapted sites. These choices were very destructive and still pose problems today. As far as the fauna is concerned, the animals that are hunted or fished, the population of Thule still stands apart from the rest of Greenland in that their exploitation of the living resources is not based on greed but on the needs of daily life. Thus they still live in harmony with nature and not regardless of it.

My vision for the Inuit of Ultima Thule

Even if the Inuit can no longer isolate themselves from the rest of Greenland, we must recognize that they still live at the outer limits of the possibility of human life in the extreme north. This is why any development must continue to rely on the judgment and discernment of the local population, on its experience of surviving for thousand years in extreme conditions. Other than by offering technical assistance, the central authorities will have to keep from interfering in any way in the Inuit's mode of daily life or its traditions. We must at all costs avoid the old saying: "Our land is composed of small parts called states or colonies. The former have a civilization, which they impose on the latter until they have done away with them."

The original Greenlandic civilization is doing very well in the far north, and let us leave it alone, if we wish to pursue our original mode of life.

MOSES OLSEN

Former minister of culture to Greenland

President of the Society of Salaried Workers of Greenland

32) Malaurie, *Last Kings of Thule*. 33) To facilitate tourism, the young Greenland government has had to build a special airport at Qaanaaq to provide shuttle service to the American base. 34) Saint-Vaast La Hougue, Département of Manche. 35) Jules Michelet, *Le Peuple de Paris*, 1974, pages 194-195.

with the objective of creating an intellectual nucleus for the North; and I have the honor to be one of its founders and its president.[36] This school provides education for one thousand native students and administrators belonging to the forty-five ethnic groups of Northern Russia and Central Siberia; its rector is Mrs. Azurguet Tarbaevna Chaoukenbaeva, and its objective is to train regional authorities to be wary of the West as well as of themselves, while at the same time embracing the technologies of the future. The French and English languages are both obligatory. France has made a significant contribution within the framework of the *Centre d'etudes arctiques*; Denmark is also associated with the project. The students are all sons of shepherds and hunters destined one day to become school headmasters, and advisers to the political leaders of their territories. They are the future backbone of Northern Siberia. Of course not everything is perfect in St. Petersburg, but at least the movement has been launched. I hope with all my heart that the Kings of Thule will find their way forward from exactly where they are, like Oshima Ikao and Moses Olsen, but we must also be inventive. The time for perfectly isolated societies is past.

Ilisumatusarfik (the University of Nuuk, in Greenland); the Hunting Institute at Qaanaaq; Arataq (the Canadian Inuit Cultural Institute run by Robert Watt, Charlie Watt's son), and Scandinavian bodies such as the Sami schools are now up and fighting against the destructive influences of the West. I think, as many of my colleagues do, that there should be an *international* Inuit hunting school at Qaanaaq and an advanced scientific Inuit school at the American Base at Thule, as soon as possible. They would be the logical, ethical outcome of the thirteen courageous expeditions to the North Pole, recounted in *Ultima Thule*.

The duty of any Polar scholar, in addition to scientific research, must be to serve the peoples of the North who are currently in such imminent danger. This responsibility was acknowledged by Knud Rasmussen in 1910, when he created a trading post for the Polar Eskimos and gave the name of Thule to Uumaannaq. This is what I have been trying to achieve for most of my life, in tandem with basic research, just like so many of my American, Canadian, Danish, and Russian colleagues.

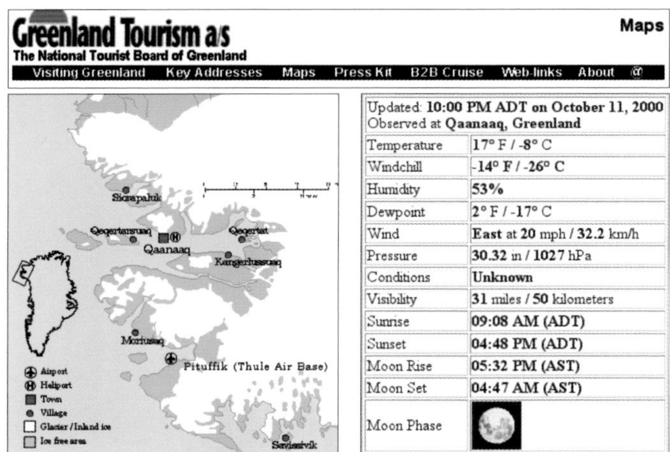

Greenland Tourism a/s
The National Tourist Board of Greenland
Maps
Visiting Greenland
Key Addresses
Maps
Press Kit
B2B Cruise
Web-links
About
Siorapaluk
Qeqertarsuaq
Qaanaaq
Qeqertat
Kangerlussuaq
Moriusaq
Pituffik (Thule Air Base)
Savissivik
Airport
Heliport
Town
Village
Glacier /Inland ice
Ice free area
Updated 10:00 PM ADT on October 11, 2000
Observed at Qaanaaq, Greenland
Temperature 17° F / -8° C
Windchill -14° F / -26° C
Humidity 53%
Dewpoint 2° F / -17° C
Wind East at 20 mph / 32.2 km/h
Pressure 30.32 in / 1027 hPa
Conditions Unknown
Visibility 31 miles / 50 kilometers
Sunrise 09:08 AM (ADT)
Sunset 04:48 PM (ADT)
Moon Rise 05:32 PM (AST)
Moon Set 04:47 AM (AST)
Moon Phase

Tourism, the foremost source of revenue for native hunters.

OPPOSITE:
The future of the Arctic and the Inuit people is represented by this hunter's adventurous progress over the ice.

REACTIONS OF THE DANISH PRESS

The Danish people are passionately attached to Greenland. The Danish press was buzzing in July, August, and September 2000 over new rumors concerning the effects of the B-52 crash in Thule. Is the fourth bomb lying under the water? The Inuit would like the report stating that the bomb was found and neutralized to be confirmed, and they are not satisfied with the typical stonewalling of the military authorities. The Danish minister of foreign affairs, Nils Helveg Petersen, declared (*Politiken*, 17 August 2000): "There is no bomb."

The Danish press is also concerned about the expansion of the Thule base and the fact that exclusively American authorities run it.

One man's career counts for little beside this great cause. The most pressing task is to train among the Inuit, Sami, Indians and other first nations leaders who are proud of their nations' past. Then we shall have men and women who are Eskimos and proud of it. A Nelson Mandela, a Gandhi, will surely one day emerge from this new nation of people. Of their heritage, let them retain what is still alive and functional; but let us at the same time build an Inuit Arctic with strong economic, sociological, intellectual perspectives. If we do not, the higher latitudes will be economically colonized by the South within the span of a generation. The oil companies and mining concerns, with their thousands of workers, are already poised to move in.

We must preserve these people from the mortal danger of the "reservation." Moreover the suicide rate among young Inuit remains a major challenge. We must fight side by side, the peoples of the Arctic and scientists who work with them, so that this region at the top of the world can again become a paragon of man's respect for the immutable laws of nature. A Thule base on which Inuit, Europeans and Americans can work together to prepare a new world, would be a wondrous symbol of this respect, in the purest tradition of Jules Verne.

The West needs to learn from the wisdom of the Inuit and their like, who are among the chosen guardians of the planet. Their tragic fate in recent times has starkly revealed our own incapacity to manage the world, despite our pretensions to superiority as a civilization. We are destroying what we have inherited, little by little, with our blindness and obstinacy. If there had been no Inuit standing in our way, the destruction of the polar ecosystems would be much more advanced than it is now. In 2000, the Prime Minister of Greenland turned down a request to enlarge the American base at Thule, which he intends to "Greenlandize" as soon as possible. David is challenging Goliath at last. Let us give the Inuit authority, complete authority, to prevent an ecological catastrophe in their region. What will be our legacy to our children, a hundred years from now? The Pole is the roof of our world, the birthplace of our climate conditions, and the earth is not eternal. Men of science, like men of state, have a duty imposed by ethics. The Earth is a living thing; it can and will avenge itself; already there are portents. The Earth has no time left for men's ignorance, arrogance, sophistry, and madness.

Jean Malaurie

36) Jean Malaurie, *Hummocks II* (Paris: Editions Plon, Collection Terre Humaine, 1999).

SALIENT POINTS IN THE HISTORY OF THE POLAR ESKIMOS, 1616 TO 1999

BEFORE 1818

Warming: 1000-1600

Exploration
5 July 1616: *Discovery*, 57 tons, R. Bylot commander, W. Baffin pilot, in sight of Cape Alexander. No landing. Perhaps seen by the Eskimos, according to the legend by "the Gull." Jones Sound, 10 July; Lancaster Sound, 12 July.

Little Ice Age: 1600-1800

IN 1818

Events

Discovery on 9 August 1818 of 8 Eskimo hunters by John Ross (2 ships, 94 officers and men) after two centuries of isolation. "Ross and his men were, without the slightest doubt, the first strangers that this group had encountered." (Bessels)
18 Eskimo visitors aboard these ships. They believe themselves superior and are in any case very independent-minded. Women and children have fled to safety inland. Thievery on the ships (nails). Saccheus teaches them to bare their heads before the English out of respect and good will, which they do. Firing of muskets on 12 August, the Inuit dwellings being 6 or 7 miles from the ships.
"Though his face expressed good humour, one could also read there a mix of ignorance and, if I may say so, of savagery characteristic of uncivilized peoples." (John Ross)

The white man's report

First words exchanged: 10 August 1818. Saccheus: *"Kahkeite!"* (Come closer!) Polar Eskimos: *"Naakrie, naakrie ai plaite!"* (No, no, go away! and also: Don't kill us!) *"Eigh-yaw,"* pleasure and surprise. *"Aamnah ajah. Weehee weehee,"* song, final sounds of song.
Names (the first recorded): Ervick, first Eskimo met and the oldest. Names of two nephews of Ervick: Marshuick and Otooniah. Two Eskimos from the second group: Meigack, adult; Kaweigack, son.
"Arctic Highlanders." (John Ross)

Demographics

Eight hunters at Cape York: "We are many," pointing to the north (Ross, 1818).
Minimum number: 20 to 30 families, or 100 to 150 Eskimos (?).

Technology and material culture

Half-buried stoned igloo; walls of sod; 45 to 90 sq. ft.; *katak* or entrance tunnel 3 to 4 meters long. No seat in the igloo. No wood, no iron except meteoric iron (4 meteorites known). Use of skins, bone (walrus, bear, seal), and stone (flint, basalt, soapstone). No kayak, bow drill, bow, or snow igloo.
Bird darts, ax (bone and stone), bird nets. Narwhal ivory: lance, harpoon. Bladder (emptied and inflated seal skin). Knife: flakes of meteorite obtained by striking the meteorite with a volcanic stone. 10,000 rocks (from 1 to 10 kg) serving as hammers around the site of one meteorite (Ahnighito). From 2 to 7 flakes flattened by hammering, set with fish glue (?) into a groove in a handle of bone or stone. A few knives of European iron (nails on driftwood) (?), trade with the Vikings through Disko Bay or Upernavik (?). Sporadic trade with Greenlanders from Upernavik. No pottery.
Sledge: walrus or seal bone and slats of narwhal ivory. Distances of 50 or 60 miles traveled in a day.
Dogs: chest harness 2 inches wide or collar (problem unresolved). One family (or more?) migrated from the Upernavik region by *umiaq* at the end of the eighteenth or beginning of the nineteenth century, according to a tradition collected in Upernavik (not substantiated by the Polar Eskimos).
Traces: nine feet long.
Fire: by striking iron pyrites against flint to light a cottony willow catkin.
Containers made of greased seal skin. Soapstone lamp, crescent-shaped, sometimes made from the shoulder blade of a walrus; wick of lichen or moss soaked in oil (blubber of seal or walrus).

Clothing

Jacket-poncho, or *attili*: 500 bird skins; seal, fox; tab in front and behind. Fox fur hood. Seal skin tunic lined in bird skins.
Qulitsaq: bear, musk ox. Fox skin jacket (woman) or *kapatak*.
Pants of bear or dog (men) to the top of the thighs and above the knees. Fox skin pants (women). Boots lined with seal skin, fur inward (unisex). Rabbit lining (men). Thread: narwhal sinew. Needle: bone.

Food

Birds (auks) raw or lightly cooked. *Kiviaq* in winter: main food. Seal, sometimes walrus, and narwhal. Meat eaten raw, frozen in winter. Meat preserved in a hole dug into the frozen ground. Shellfish and seaweed. *Qajoq* or meat broth. Eggs and a very few vegetables. Taboos against salmon, caribou, and, in certain cases, hare and partridge, depending on age and sex. Pure water sipped through a bone tube from a seal skin bucket.
10 August 1818:
They spit out the biscuits they are offered, as well as the salt meat. Disgust for wine and strong liquor.

Social structure

First observations: (1818).
Primitive communism: (land and water) communal. Sharing of all game. Sharing of all gifts (present of a board divided into small portions for general distribution, 1818).
Hypothesis: rotation of houses for periods of time; adoption of one child in three (?) to break family bonds.
Monogamy: divorce if woman is sterile. Parental choice of marriage partner?
Population control: sexual taboos, infanticide of little girls to three and infants when mother dies. Abandonment of elderly.

Religions and legends

Legends, drum songs, dances, taboos. No tattooing or engraved art. No memory of the active maritime culture known in these parts by their ancestors before 1600 (start of Little Ice Age). Were they thoroughly questioned on this point?
Long hair for men and women. "They ignored the existence in the world of other people than themselves." (Captain Sabine) Bad translation or failure to communicate? Hazy tradition of earlier, stronger people. Myth of Sun and Moon. Shamanic religion with *angakkuq*. No apparent sensitivity to English music (violin). No name for salmon or caribou. Name for whale. Unfamiliar with the words *kayak* and *tuktin* (caribou). (Sabine) Yet the handle of a knife given to Ross was of antler. Count only to 10.

Physiology and health

Ervick's height: 5'1" (1.67 meters).
Winter amenorrhea (?). Births seasonal (winter) (?). Three-year birth cycle (?). Polar hysteria (?). Nosebleeds among the young. Excellent teeth, but front teeth ground down at a young age due to use as auxiliary tools. No deformed or mishapen Eskimos. "They do not seem to be subject to illness." (Ross)

Economic level

Archaic society (stone and bone). Six dogs per team: 8 August 1818, Melville Bay; dogs that have lost an eye from the whip. Groups settled in areas of bird cliffs, Savissivik, Uummannaq, Wolstenholme Sound, Herbert and Hakluyt islands, Siorapaluk coast at Etah (?). Small villages of 2 to 5 families (?).
No hunting at sea for marine mammals (no kayak), except from floating floes. No salmon fishing, no caribou.
"They appeared happy and satisfied; their clothes were in good repair." (J. Ross)
Absolute refusal to give Europeans a dog, though they traded knives (at least 3 from 8 hunters) and a harpoon with an iron point (from driftwood?).

Administrative system

None.

Warming: 1818-1852

FROM 1818 TO 1860

Events

Brief layovers (south only): Cape York and Carey Island; whalers come from south, then head to Baffin Island. Attract Inuit (trade) and terrorize them.
Whalers in North Water: 100; whalers 1820: 10 to 50 per year. Shipwrecks, but no accounts of whalers living among the Polar Eskimos.
First overwintering of whaler *North Star* in Uummannaq, 1853-1855; bay later renamed "North Star Bay."
South Greenlander Hans Hendrik deserts and lives for 6 years with the Polar Eskimos (provider of cultural and technological information: 1853-1861).
A Polar Eskimo is taken to Newfoundland (Erasmus York) by the explorers Austin and Penny; dies in Newfoundland, after conversion (1856).

The white man's report

"The human animal who answers to the name of Eskimo." "His positive inconsistency as a social creature." (Hayes)
"The natives among whom I lived managed to satisfy all their desires and live happily." (H. Hendrik)
"Each man is seated on the platform with a bowl rich in grease between his knees and a piece of frozen liver beside him. Eating antiscorbutic meats, they laugh, as though the ice and water did not oppose them." (Kane)
"You have done us good. We are not hungry. We will not steal from you. You have done us good. We want to help you. You are our friends." (Eskimo speaking to Kane in the last days before his departure)

Demographics

Approximate census (Kane) 1852-1855: 140 natives, 8 villages, from Cape York to Etah.
1860-1861: 100 (Hayes).
Severe famine in 1855 (period of cooling).
High infant mortality. Female infanticide in cases of famine and death of mother. "Families of 3 and 4 children are exceptional." (Hayes)
1855-1860 (Hayes): 9 births, 34 deaths (hunting accidents, falls into crevasses, floating away on floes, murders—rivalry over women).
Probable interbreeding with the whalers whose layovers at Cape York were brief.
"Our people have only a few suns left to live," says a Polar Eskimo to Kane (1855).

Technology and material culture

Culture is conservative, faced with onslaught of technology in successive expeditions.
Material culture unchanged 1818-1860: Igloos same; 1 igloo per family: 100 sq. ft., pear-shaped; *katak*: 4 m. long. "They have no wood," (Kane, 1855). Knife with iron blade rare; none in the northernmost territory. And yet they know about iron: harpoon head given to Ross in 1818. "They have neither wood nor iron," (Hayes, 1861) because they are anchored in a stone culture. Traded wood rare (harpoon and lance handles of narwhal tusks). The whalers often burned their abandoned ships. Wrecks must still have remained . . . Indifference?
1855-1860: stay of South Greenlander Hans Hendrik, deserter from Kane expedition. Hendrik teaches, but Polar Eskimos refuse to introduce the kayak, bow drill, and bow, to abolish their dietary taboos, or to seek iron.
Blubber lamp: 6 inches by 8 inches (Hayes).
Sledges: runner of ivory covered with a film of frozen water during the hard winter frosts.
Hot rocks used for heating and cooking in soapstone pots.

Social structure

8 villages 1853-1855: communal house (?); house for the young (?); the elderly definitely abandoned.

Religion and legends

Shamanism and burial of the dead (Kane, Hayes).
Fear of the brutal and greedy whalers. No Eskimos enlisted on whaling ships.
Society shaken from within by Hans Hendrik's recitals (Christianity, use of iron, power of the rifle) but no text exists. Mixing of South Greenland and North Greenland legends(?); influence of South Greenland music (?).

Physiology and health

Sleep naked in their igloos. Epidemics at Cape York: 1853-1855, 1860-1861. Infanticide of young girls up to age 10 who have lost their mothers (Kane). Girl punished, buried alive under pile of rocks (Kane). Hysteria or *piblokto* of dogs.

Economic level

Dog teams, according to Osborn, of 5 dogs (1851). Misery and conflict during winters of great cold (cf. Kane).
Contradiction (1864):
Kane's account (describing this society as starving and on the decline). Kane also reported honestly the ironic reaction of Kalutunah to this pessimistic picture: "He smiled . . . and laughed." Kane unaware of this group's ability to contract and dilate, threatened as it has been for centuries.
"The household goods of these nomads of the Arctic are not bulky. The entire load of the sledge: 2 packets of bear skins, the family's bedding, half a dozen seal skins for the tent, 2 lances and 2 harpoons, a few good harpoons lines, a couple of soapstone pots and lamps, various tools and materials for repairing the sledge, a small seal skin sack for sewing, a roll of dry grass for their boots, some dry moss for the lamps." Hayes, 1861) Also: knife, flint, bird net.

Administrative system

None.
First treaty between the Inuit and the Whites: 1854. "We, Americans, promise that we will not visit you with death. . . . You, Eskimos, will be welcome on board . . ." Communal discussion and observation of the treaty by the Inuit.

Cold Period: 1852-1860

IN 1863

Events

Migration from Canada: 14 Canadian Eskimos migrate from Baffin Island. Last migration in Inuit history. They live and intermarry with the Polar Eskimos for six years. 1867 (?): migration of an *umiaq* and 5 kayaks from Canada with bows and a tattooed woman; according to Davis (Etah, Polar Eskimos), in 1873.
Revolutions in technology, outlook; native music influenced by Igloolik rhythms; demographic isolation ended.

Demographics

Interbreeding with Canadian Eskimos. 1950-1951: 15% of population of Canadian descent, from genealogical evidence (J.M.).
Start of population expansion from 1850-1895 (150 to 253). Though Kane's numbers err on the low side, the group is expanding overall.

Technology and material culture

Rediscovery and gradual use of: bow, salmon spear, bow drill (for fire and drilling), snow igloo with entrance tunnel better designed for ventilation. They are encouraged to it by learning that their Eskimo "cousins" from Canada have used these techniques from time immemorial, though they appear revolutionary to a Polar Eskimo (and though Hans Hendrik had discussed them in 1855-1860).

Clothing

Widespread use of caribou skin for the *qulitsaq*. It is lighter than bear or musk ox skin. It is little used, however, for bedding or for the sledge (where dog skin is preferred).

Food

Taboos about salmon and caribou are abandoned.
More abundant and balanced diet.

Religion and legends

Incorporation and combining of legends of Baffin Island Eskimos. Two thirds of legends derived from Canadian legends.
Partial obliteration of native heritage likely; influence also of South Greenland. Burial of native hunter witnessed by *Polaris* expedition (1873). Body wrapped in skin, placed on sledge with all equipment. Behind the hill, on the top, body put seated in snow hole, facing west. Women present with dried grasses in left nostril, men in right nostril. Widow kills her 6-month-old baby.

Economic level

Dog teams larger. Hunting territory more extensive.
1872: a sledge of Etah Eskimos visits the *Polaris* expedition with 9 dogs.

FROM 1863 TO 1909

Warming: 1860-1930

Events

Stays in Inuit territory:
1872-1873, tumultuous wintering of a party of Americans and Germans from *Polaris* expedition, north of Etah. The Polar Eskimos see white men drunk and quarreling.
Rescue expeditions for Greely: 1882-1884; depot of food and equipment on the coast of the Cape York district at Littleton Island. Food and equipment probably looted by Eskimo groups.
7 Peary expeditions (1891-1909). Cook's expedition (1907-1908). Danish Literary Expedition (1903-1904). Peary's material power (*Roosevelt*: 1500 tons) impresses Eskimos, as does his tenacity and boldness. He is "Peary the great."

The white man's report

"These natives are truly to be pitied and the establishment of a Missionary Station among the savages would be a good work. If we could deport them to somewhere in the south of Greenland . . . I am certain that the American government and also the Danish government would approve of it." (Davis, ed., Report of the *Polaris* expedition, 1873.)
"This poor, ignorant people." (Josephine Peary, 1893) "A quasi-abject situation." (Peary, 1891) "My Eskimos." (Peary, 1909) "In 1894, R. E. Peary looked on the Arctic world as his fiefdom, and the Eskimo people as his vassals." (F. A. Cook) "The Eskimos are of good character and make themselves useful and agreeable to those who treat them with kindness." (Davis, ed., *Polaris* report) "In his bearing Peary has all the appearance of a conqueror." (Steensby) "Peary a great tormentor." (Steensby) "People with a good and loyal heart . . . A simple but intelligent people and capable of controlling its fate with certain success." (Cook)
"The Eskimos are unquestionably impressed by our firearms." (Josephine Peary)

Demographics

1873: 150 (*Polaris*, Davis). Bessels (also on *Polaris*): 102 Eskimos seen (estimate: 110-112).
First count by Peary (1895): 253 (140 males, 113 females).
Population growth, 1855-1895: 80.7%.
Annual growth, 1855-1895: 2.01%.
Peary census, 1894: 234.
K. Rasmussen census, 1903: 195 (110 m, 77 f).

Peary census, 1906: 207 (119 m, 85 f, 3 children unknown). Even if Kane and Davis undercounted by 30%, we see a rise in births linked to abandonment of sexual and dietary taboos in 1863-1865, before Peary's arrival.

Technology and material culture

Igloo 1908: pear-shaped, *katak* 3m. Fire: bow drill: wooden shaft set vertically into cavity in wooden board and rotated rapidly. Tinder: vegetable fibers, including moss.
1872-1873: work for wages on the *Polaris* expedition, use of modern equipment (wood, rifles, etc.). "Jimmy killed two seals with a navy pistol." (May 1873)
First rifle used by the Eskimos toward 1873. Sharp modernization of methods.
Selective technological adaptation: wood (widely used, but sledges in 1909 of 5 to 7 pieces of wood), iron, tools (knife, axe, saw, file, needle), a few rifles: "They manufacture their bullets themselves of stone or of bone." (Isachsen, Sverdrup expedition to Ellesmere). Steel traps (Peary). Dual society: rifle if Peary in residence; traditional tools of stone and bone, narwhal lance, ivory harpoon when he is gone. "Rifles were not in demand, as the Polar Eskimos were uncertain of being resupplied with powder and shot." (Steensby, 1909)
In 1883 (*Sofia*) at Ivsugissoq, Cape York region: no kayaks or boats. "Few men have kayaks." (Peary 1895)
Refusal of a few "conservative" adults (shamans) to adopt new technologies (Sorqaq).

Clothing

Occasional canvas anorak for summer use (10% of group?): lighter and holds fewer fleas.

Food

99%: native food.
Discovery of alcohol in 1872-1873 with *Polaris* expedition. Occasional coffee, tea, tobacco, and oat flakes for the very poorest. Alcohol prohibited by Peary and Cook. Food discovered with whalers: unknown. Tobacco: "Immoderately fond of tobacco ... invariably take the nicotine-impregnated feathers I throw away and suck on them." (Whitney, 1908-1909)

Social structure

1903: 8 villages, 39 families and igloos, or 5 persons per family and per igloo (Rasmussen census).
First wage-work (in kind) with *Polaris* expedition (winter 1872-1873 in Inglefield Land). Inuit given nicknames: Jimmy, Sharkey, etc. Wage-work (in kind) for half of the men in the population with Peary and Cook expeditions. Amounts given: unknown.

History, outlook / Religion and legends

Deportation of 6 Polar Eskimos to New York (5 die), skeletons in the American Museum of Natural History (New York). One Eskimo comes back from trip to New York (Minik). He talks. Believed to be simple-minded (by Freuchen and some Inuit). Fear of Whites with massive means. Discovery of phonograph and Western music (Peary and McMillan). Ethnography ignorant and contemptuous: "In art, science, culture, and other manifestations of civilization, the Polar Eskimos know nothing."
"The Eskimos have no religion." (Peary) No missionaries until 1909. Shamanism.

Physiology and health

Mortality: famine, murders, accidents (drifting floes, crevasses, falls from bird cliffs), infanticide. Epidemics noted here and there. 1883: 4 igloos; 4 to 5 corpses of epidemic victims per igloo, north of Cape York. 1895-1896, Cape Sabine: little information. 1895-1896: "flu" epidemics with 20% decrease in population. Cases of gonorrhea (1906) but resorbed naturally (information from Uutaq).
Height of men: 5' 0"; of women: 4' 10".

Economic level

1891: each village has its hunting territory. Also, "common" areas. Teams of 5 to 6 dogs. Individual capital (Cook survey, 1891): 1 family at Kiatak, Herbert Island, 13 members): "Each family owned 1 kayak, 1 harpoon, 1 lance, 1 bird net, and two families owned bows and arrows."
Toward a trapping society that trades with the whites. Expansion of hunting grounds thanks to Cook: discovery of musk ox range in Ellesmere Island, called "Umingmiung" Island.
7 Peary expeditions: 20 to 30 families employed full time for 12 to 24 months. Payment: radical modernization of technology. Gradual improvement: rifles, steel traps, wood, tools, boats.
Removal by Peary (without compensation) of 3 meteorites, sold for $40,000 in New York. Peary's accounts of his business dealings not published. "Peary made a fortune buying the precious production of the tribe: fox and bear." (Steensby) Profits from 400 export-quality furs per year, ivory, and ethnographic collections. Trading rates: $100 fur for 10-cent knife; pewter cup (9 cents) for ivory tusk ($ 90). From 1891 to 1909: one million dollars (in 1989 dollars) over 7 expedition.

Administrative system

None. In 1910, Peary asks Congress to annex North Greenland to the United States. Congress refuses, ceding to Denmark all claims owed to the United States' for its first exploration of North Greenland in return for rights to the Dutch Antilles.

FROM 1910 TO 1938

Height of warming trend: 1930

Events

Thule, July 1909: resident Lutheran mission.
1910: Uummannaq is named "Thule" by Knud Rasmussen and Peter Freuchen.
1911: End of whaling (Thule: 2 whalers).
Thule trading post, supporting with its profits the 7 Thule expeditions (1911-1933).
Polar Eskimos collaborate on scientific program from financial side (profits from trading post) and by participating in the first five expeditions. Knud Rasmussen's respect: ethnology to the fore. Local scrip: 1915. From barter to the concept of money.
1914-1917, 1923-1924, 1925, massive McMillan expedition to Etah region and farther north. Relief expeditions blocked by ice at Thule due to incompetence of captains: 1917, rescue by Captain Bartlett aboard the *Neptune*. First Byrd flight: 1923. Lauge Koch expedition: 1920-1923. Mapping of North Greenland, from Melville Bay to Peary Land.
Hans Island, under Danish rule (contested by Canadians in 1980 when petroleum found), is mapped for the first time by Lauge Koch in 1932. 1929-1930: Krueger Expedition to Ellesmere Island. 1932: Peary monument, Cape York. 1934-1935: Oxford Expedition to Ellesmere.

The white man's report

"The natives knew what they wanted and obtained it all on their own." (P. Freuchen, 1914)
"The happiest people in the world ... a well organized and conflictless society where no one enquired into what didn't concern them." (P. Freuchen) "During the past year (1903-1904), there was well-being everywhere ... It was the general rule: a spontaneous joy in life." (K. Rasmussen, 1905)

Demographics

Sporadic famine: 13 deaths, Cape Alexander (P. Freuchen), 1910.
K. Rasmussen censuses. 1918: 235; 1923: 251; 1930: 250; 1932: 239 (129 m, 110 f); 1933: 240 (128 m, 112 f); 1934: 244 (130 m, 114 f); 1935: 251 (135 m, 116 f); 1936: 249 (133 m, 116 f); 1937: 245 (131 m, 124 f); 1941: 269.

Technology and material culture

Igloo: start of rectangular shape.
1914-1919: matches very occasional. Containers: a few rare pots. Fuel containers salvaged from expeditions.
1910: establishment of a private trading post by Knud Rasmussen and Peter Freuchen. Regular sale, with local scrip, of guns, ammunition, wood, iron, tools, matches, cloth, basic foods (coffee, tea, sugar, oat flakes, flour), enameled pots and bowls. Scarcity of goods in 1914-1918: no ammunition or matches. Regular shipments from Denmark interrupted.
Competition with McMillan's American station (Etah) 1914-1917, 1923-1924. Wooden sledges with iron runners, gradually. 1900-1909: 5 to 6 dogs per sledge (Steensby).
Sledges: 98 (1933), 91 (1938). Dogs: 778 (1933); 857 (1938). Cloth tents: 61 (1933), 66 (1938). Boats: 3 (1938). Kayaks: 69 (1933), 73 (1938). Rifles: 113 (1933), 113 (1938). Shotguns: 24 (1933), 25 (1938).

Clothing

Growing use of cloth anorak in summer and cotton undergarment; in winter, a few sweaters seen. Skin mittens. Men continue to wear their bear skin pants in summer. Seal skin pants rare.

Food

95% native food. Tea, coffee, sugar; oat flakes in times of dearth. Tobacco; alcohol known, in summer when Danish ships visit trading post and American ships come on expedition.

Social structure

Barter economy between Polar Eskimos, alongside trapping and market economy.
Division of hunting by sexes: small game (hare, partridge) by women; large game (seal, walrus, narwhal, bear) by men.
Last instance of eliminating a crippled group member (strangulation, 1919); infanticide still exists (but hidden). 1923: 251 inhabitants, 12 villages. 1935-1936: 54 families and igloos (Holtved census), or 4.5 residents per house. (Average in S.W. Greenland: 1835: 4.5 res./house). 13 villages.

Religion and legends

1909: Lutheran missionary station. First official Danish ethnographic study: Steensby. 1910: end of long hair. Translation into Greenlandic and distribution of Rasmussen's book on Thule. 1925: 1 doctor, 1 hospital with 4 beds. 1930: inauguration of church at Uummanaq. Young learn to read. 1934: baptism of last adults.

Physiology and health

Height 1909: 8 men from 5'1" to 5'5" (152cm to 163 cm); 10 women from 4'9" to 5'0" (142 cm to 150 cm).
Major fatal illnesses: pulmonary tuberculosis, flu, infant diseases (bronchitis). Common illnesses: bronchitis, rheumatism. Cases of hysteria (men and women).

Economic level

1852-1855: 8 villages. 1903: 7 villages.
No records for smaller settlements.
1923: 12 villages; 1933: 12 villages; 1941: 12 villages; 1943: 7 villages.
1950: 10 villages.
Houses in 1905: 16 sq. ft. to 140 sq. ft.; 5 residents per house.
1919-1930: 800 fox skins per year (blue and white).
1910-1911: 208 blue fox; 141 white fox.
1926-1927: 944 blue fox; 927 white fox.
1938-1939: 884 blue fox; 312 white fox.
1947-1948: 722 blue fox; 212 white fox;
Price per skin:
1901: 36 Kr (blue), 10 Kr (white); 1920: 275 Kr (blue), 194 Kr (white); 1939: 118 Kr (blue), 37 Kr (white).
Sales 1912: 200 fox skins. Copenhagen: 12,000 Kr (Freuchen).
1913: 4th meteorite (*samik*) acquired by Rasmussen for cost of a rifle (Qilagtoq).
1933: 49 houses (wooden, one-room, single-family igloos with sod insulation of 160 sq. ft. to 215 sq. ft.). 113 rifles, 69 kayaks, 98 sledges, 2 wooden boats, 778 dogs, 47 seal nets, 33 skin tents, 28 cloth tents, 24 shotguns, 1 communal motor boat.
Typical individual capital: 1 sledge, 7 adult dogs, 1 rifle, 2 harpoons (winter, summer), seal skin lanyards, tools (file, hammer, saw), bow drill, cup, and 2 pots. Value (1950): 300 Kr.

Administrative system

Knud Rasmussen's private company under Danish rule. Administrators: Danish rule but privately administrated (officially after 1922). Peter Freuchen: 1910-1922. Hans Nielsen (from South Greenland): 1922-1930, able administrator.
Native council established by referendum among the Inuit (12 August 1929) and Law of Thule based on customs. 7 June 1930, local council of hunters; first Inuit government in history. Men and women vote, women not eligible for office.
1929: Fangerraad. Law of Thule (1930) codifying customs of local administration; men and women vote to elect Inuit deputies to Council.
Local scrip: 1915 (30,000 coins). Considerable profits on part of Thule Trading Company (1909-1936, accounts not made public).
1931: Rasmussen represents the Danish state.

FROM 1938 TO 1951

Events

21 December 1933, Copenhagen: death of Knud Rasmussen, administrator of Thule.
Regular administration by Danish government starting in 1937.
Special status awarded (specified in 1929), strict legal isolation of the group. No admission for Danes or foreigners without special permission, which is very difficult to obtain.
Danish administrator Torben Krogh, starting in 1949. Danish doctor present since 1925. School run by pastor. Separate administration.
Expeditions: E. Holtved: 1935-1937, 1946-1947.
1939-1941: Van Hauen's Danish expedition (Neqi), with Rasmussen's son as photographer.
1950-1951: French geographic expedition to Thule: Jean Malaurie.
Since 1818, 14 expeditions have preceded Jean Malaurie (J. M.) in this district: Britons, Americans, Danes, Norwegians, and Germans.
June-July 1951: landing of 5000 Americans at Thule. Combined operation: air (early June) and sea (9 July). Establishment of the Thule Blue Jay Airbase. Ultrasecret operation. Danish authorities given several months' advance notice. The local administrator protested that he received no instructions from Copenhagen to prepare the population (confidential messages). Request made 15-20 June 1951 by J. M. to local Danish authorities for immediate convening of the Fangerraade (Native Council) to protest and negotiate a treaty directly, but in vain. (See *Last Kings of Thule*)

The white man's and the Inuit's report

"The Polar Eskimos are still a primitive people ... They know that within the frame of their existence, they are superior to all strangers; when they feel that you are treating them as equals, you will nowhere find a better collaborator." (Holtved, 1942)
"All that," they say, waving a finger at the American base, "all that is not for us. Nothing good will come of it!" (the Thule Eskimos, 1 July 1951, quoted by J. M., 1955)
Jean Malaurie: "The Polar Eskimos are an extraordinary symbol. For its tutelary unicorn, its status as a high holy place, its anarcho-communalism, Thule forces one to a higher level. A northern aristocracy survives there, within the mental sphere of the mythic Hyperboreans, within the Apollonian idea of regeneration in the North."

Demographics

1937 census: 245 (131 m, 124 f). 1938: 245 (126 m, 119 f). 1939: 262 (139 m, 123 f). Parish censuses (1937-1942). 1940: 267 (138 m, 129 f). 1941: 269 (142 m, 127 f). 1942: 271 (139 m, 132 f). J. M. census: 302 living (31 December 1950) (156 m, 146 f). J. M. deducted Danish and Greenland immigrants. Annual increase 1895-1950: 0.8%. Interval between births: 28 months. Time between onset of puberty and parturition: 4 to 6 years. Higher female mortality. Average life expectancy: 27 years for males, 22 years for females. Average age of women at birth of first child: 20 years. Minimum age of puberty: 13/14 years. 16% of women of childbearing age are sterile due to inbreeding.
1940-1950: 116 births: 63 m, 49 f, 4 stillborn. Rate of fecundity 173‰. Births seasonal. Spring (return of sun): months of conception. Higher female mortality.
J. M. genealogical census: 1200 individuals.

Technology and material culture

1950: house with inner structure of wood and sod cladding. Single room. 190 sq. ft. to 215 sq. ft. Rectangular. *Katak* or entrance tunnel of igloo, 2 meters. Use of charcoal.
Harpoon head: walrus ivory. Harpoon shaft: wood with iron point. Lance: wood and iron point. No bows.
Harness: 1/4 canvas. Traps: steel. Bow drill: wood and seal skin.
Heavy rifle for bear and walrus owned by every hunter (70); seal gun (.30-30 or .22) owned by 40 hunters.
Wooden sledges: 2 upstanders of oak: pine slats; runner: iron and film of frozen water in January-March. Length 4 m, width 90 cm, height 23 cm, upstanders 85 cm. 70 sledges.
Blubber lamp: soapstone. Length 35.5 cm, width 20 cm, depth 3 cm: 1/4 households. Gas lamp widespread. Primus stove used on trail. Canvas tent (80%). 2 tents of seal skin.
Spoons (1 to 2 per family) but no forks. 1 family in 4 has one or two plates. Still eat squatting and with fingers. Cylindrical metal cup in general use.

Clothing

1950: same, with bear skin pants summer and winter, cloth anorak commonly used in summer. No female undergarments (bra, panties), exceptionally boxer shorts; male undergarments: cotton long johns universal and some 20 of 70 hunters wear sweaters. No special night time clothes. 1 to 2 seal skin boots in reserve. No rubber boots.

Food

1950: 95% native food (seal, walrus, birds). Tea, coffee, sugar. Oat flakes in times of distress. Tobacco (pipes in 3/4 cases). Alcohol forbidden and not sought (social taboo).

Social structure

1950-1951: 64 families and igloos, in 10 villages. 4.7 residents/house.
Anarcho-communism of 1818 + "common house" (school) and 1 young singles' house per village. Structure of family and igloo change very slowly. 1903: 5 persons.
Parental structures: marriage rule over 3 generations: 6th degree of kinship (J. M.).
Trapping and market economy regulated by K. G. H. monopoly: buying prices for skins and ivory low but constant. Sale of utilitarian items at very low price: guns, wood (at trading post). European products not widely available so as to maintain specificity of population.
Population starts to concentrate in the large villages (Uummannaq: 1/3 of group) and slow abandonment of small hamlets (10 hamlets and villages, that is, fewer than in 1923 (12), more than in 1853-1855 (8)).
No savings except for 5 hunters who have small deposits (200 Kr) in local bank.
Protests of Eskimos on Native Council: slow awareness of colonial socio-political structures. "It is unjust that others should make great sums of money from the product of our work." (Jess, 1953)
Slow inflow of foreigners: 1936: 31 resident Greenlanders and Danes, or 12% of population. 1950: 30 resident Greenlanders and Danes, or 10% of population. Thule-Uummannaq: 3 families, 1 Danish administrator and his family, 1 radio engineer and his family, 1 Danish doctor (1 annual trip in district). No contact between populations (South Greenland and Polar Eskimo). 9 July 1951: 5000 Americans and 302 Polar Eskimos.

Religions and legends

1950: totally Christianized traditional society; South Greenland pastor. Traditional drum song, 3 or 4 times per year. In times of great danger, individual acts of shamanism in secret. Slow and subterranean syncretism of traditional shamanist thought and Christian ideals.
1 radio per village in house of storekeeper. No book ownership, other than Lutheran hymnal. Three individu-

als have visited Denmark, three the American Arctic, and three South Greenland.
Very rudimentary knowledge (school) of history, geography, and literature. Elders: illiterate; adults know how to read but don't, except for hymns. Writing is difficult. Oral literature. Knowledge of English or Danish: 0 individuals.

Physiology and health

Hospital: 8 beds, 1 doctor.
Births seasonal (winter), though less so. No contraception or abortion. *Coitus interruptus* unknown. Homosexuality unknown. Modesty. Hysteria rare: truncated hysteria: 3 or 4 cases per year (autumn). No venereal disease or gonorrhea. 10% wear glasses. 0% wear prostheses. 1950: no taking of pharmaceutical drugs. No razors (hair is removed). No sanitary napkins. Soap: 1 family in 4. Toothbrushes: unknown. General increase in height: 2 inches (5 cm) since last census.

Economic level

7 dogs per sledge. 101 sledges.
1948: 60 single-family houses, stone, wood, and sod cladding, 42 rifles, 109 shotguns, 70 kayaks, 5 boats (1 with a communally-owned motor), 803 dogs, 19 seal nets, 4 skin tents, 52 canvas tents, 700 to 893 steel traps. Estimated value of total means of production, in Kr: 66,363 Kr. Hunting grounds of village of Siorapaluk (1950: 21 sq. km; 8,484 seals hunted, or 29 seals per person. 934 foxes. Total: 27,028 Kr, of which 80% from foxes).
Total income in Kr: 49,702, or 153 Kr per person per year.
Self-sufficient society of traditional hunters, with small investment in capital goods, and highly profitable production.
Cash revenue: 500 Kr per year (1950) per family (1 Kr = 14 cents in 1950 dollars).
Individual capital: same, but greater number of dogs per sledge. From 6 dogs (1818) to 10 (1950). 1950: primus stove, hurricane lamp, kerosene lamp, sewing machine (1 family in 3), accordeon (1 family in 5).
No European jewelry.
Pensions in 1951: 7 individuals (120 to 200 Kr per year: old, infirm).
Reference prices: 1951-1952: 1 dog: 20 Kr (1950). 1 sledge: 600 Kr (1950). 1 .22 rifle: 60 Kr (1 rifle 1989: 80 Kr). 1 knife: 3 Kr. 1 bear skin: 155 Kr. 1 blue fox pelt: 42 Kr. White fox: 35 Kr. 1 seal skin: 4 Kr. 1 kg tea: 11 Kr. 1 kg coffee: 9 Kr. 1 kg sugar: 0.90 Kr.
Danish profit in Thule 1938: purchase of furs (fox and seal) 27,028 Kr. Sale of furs (fox) by the monopoly in Copenhagen: 111,000 Kr.
Spending at the trading post:
Polar Eskimos: 288 Kr/year/person. Danes: 804 Kr/year/person. Breakdown of purchases: Siorapaluk post 1940-1941: food 38%; cloth 21%; firearms 18%; tobacco 8%; fuel, hardware 9%; miscellaneous 6%.
Discovery in 1963 by Buchwald of an eighth meteorite, in the one place they have been discovered in Greenland, at Cape York, North Greenland, Agpalilik (20.14 tons). No compensation made, that we know, to the Eskimos community of Qaanaaq.

Administrative system

Danish rule, administration by the K.G.H. monopoly.
NATO accord (1949) for US bases in Greenland.

FROM 1952 TO 1989

Events

1953: despoliation of 25% of the hunting grounds of the Polar Eskimos (Uummannaq and the surrounding area, Wolstenholme Sound and the area around Saunders Island), without compensation. The Eskimos are expulsed from their capital: creation of Qaanaaq-Thule, 60 miles north (facing Whale Sound).
1953: agreement on Native Council in Thule. Jess demands firmly and repeatedly for equal treatment of Eskimos, Danes, Americans, and South Greenlanders: "Copenhagen has only granted Greenland autonomy after authorizing a massive Danish immigration and installing irreversible social and economic structures." (J.M., 1965, *Last Kings of Thule*). "*Qallunaat ayorpok!*" (The Whites are no good!): statement often made by the young, Qaanaaq, 1982. Building of primitive low-cost houses at Qaanaaq for the deportees. "House good for dogs. Our houses stolen. Our dead in Uummannaq." Statements by elders.
The ancestral cemetery of Thule-Uummannaq is inaccessible to the Inuit. It is on the airbase.
Minister for Greenland (C. Bornemann) consults J.M.: 1967 expedition. Written report to ministry recommending self management and territorial autonomy. Request for immediate compensation, with lease payments for airbase sector going directly to the "Territorial Community of Polar Eskimos." The report was tabled.
Sakeus affair (*Last Kings of Thule*, 1965): claim for fair compensation made to Canadian Mounted Police, who employed him and his father, the famous Nukapianguak, on Ellesmere Island. Matter tabled by Copenhagen and Ottawa.
Complete set of Inuit names on survey map by J.M.: Inglefield Land and Washington Land (south coast). The names of Uutaq and other Eskimo figures given to capes and bays of Inglefield Land (1958), which Peary had never done. Shortly after, for the first time, the Danish government decided also to honor Uutaq, giving his name to the northernmost island of Greenland, north of Peary Land (83° 41' N, 30° 40' W).
7-10 November 1983: Iggianguaq Uutaq invited to International Congress on the North Pole in Paris, chaired by J.M. Statement by Iggiannguaq-Uutaaq, half brother of Kutsikitsoq: "Peary went to the North Pole with my father." For the first time in Inuit history, Uutaaq, a Polar Eskimo and his companions are considered Peary's equals, discoverers of the Pole. The *Société géographique de Paris* awards a silver medal to Iggiannguaq-Uutaaq, the same one awarded to other conquerors of the Pole, in honor of his father. First scientific medal received by a Polar Eskimo for the Pole.
1985: Two young Danish Eskimologists, Jens Brøsted and Mads Faegteborg, publish *Thule: Fangerfolk og Militaeranlaeg*. Uproar in Copenhagen.
1976: First book published by a Polar Eskimo in Greenlandic (Inuterssuaq), translated into Danish (1985).

Demographics

1985: Census. The Polar Eskimo population stands at 789, divided between six villages, the northernmost sites having been abandoned. Savissivik: 127 inhabitants, 125 of them born in Greenland. Moriussak: 87 inhabitants, 84 of them born in Greenland. Thule-Qaanaaq: 449 inhabitants, 396 born in Greenland. Qeqertarsuaq: 28 inhabitants, 27 of them born in Greenland. Qeqertaq: 39 inhabitants: all born in Greenland. Siorapaluk: 59 inhabitants, 57 of them born in Greenland.
The American military base at Thule-Uummannaq houses 2000 to 3000 Danes and Americans. The grounds are off limits to the Polar Eskimos. They come onto it, once they have received permission, to take the SAS plane to Denmark.
In 1950-1951, the population was 302 inhabitants, divided between ten villages, from Savissivik to Etah, all of them Inuit. Siorapaluk had 1 white man (me), and Thule had 8 Danes, otherwise the villages were 100% Inuit.
Economic situation: overequipment. Breakdown of the hunting economy. No alternative work. Social welfare and service economy.

Study of Siorapaluk:

1950: 7 hunters; production exceeds consumption. 1 wage earner.
1967: 13 hunters. Production = 1/4 of consumption. 6 wage earners. 62 of 98 individuals receive subsidies: family assistance (31); aid to young mothers (10); old-age pensions (11); partial or total disability (4). Collapse of market for narwhal and seal. A hunter earns 1/3 the salary of a broom-pusher or shop clerk earns, 1/6 that of an unskilled Danish worker on the American base (who also receives room, board, and clothing), 1/9 that of a skilled worker on the base (taxi driver, for example), 1/14 that of a mechanic or foreman on the base, 1/20 that of a faculty member at a French university.
A hunter working 1000 hours per year, making an investment of 40,000 Kr, securing a return of 5% in the best of circumstances, earns a monthly income of 600 to 800 Kr, with most earning half of this amount.
Monthly salary of an Eskimo employee in the store (8 hours per day and weekends off): 1100 Kr (1 Danish Kr in 1988 = 0.20 US dollars).

The hunter's capital investment

1967: the hunter's equipment requires considerable financial investment, both for the cost of the materials and for the time involved. A set of clothes for the hunter (coat, caribou or bear skin pants, boots) costs 600 to 1000 Kr. It must be replaced every two to five years. Cost of a sled: 400 Kr; of a dog: 40 Kr (for a team of 10 dogs: 800 Kr in all); of a kayak: 500 Kr; of a motor boat: 30,000 Kr (loans at 2% for thirty-three years are available, but though the rate is favorable the cost is still very high given that the boat can be operated only three months of the year, during the breakup). Fuel: 12 hours: 40 Kr. Cost of seal net: 25 Kr., or 125 Kr for five nets, a minimum; 20 traps at 5 Kr each, or 100 Kr; 2 guns: 200 Kr; annual expenditure of 500 rounds of ammunition for walrus, 1000 .22 rounds for seal, foxes, and hares, and 200 shotgun shells. Total cost for long-term materials and equipment: 32,825 Kr, or approximately 33,000 Kr.

The hunter's income

1967: 600 to 800 Kr per month per hunter, or 7,200 to 9,600 Kr per year, for a hunter's catch of approximately: 50 seals, 20 to 30 foxes (hunted more or less intensively according to price for pelts), 2 walrus, 1 beluga whale, 2 *kiviaq* of birds, 100 to 200 salmon, eight days' food from eider eggs, eight days' food from birds, eight to fifteen days' work for whites as a stevedore or guide. These figures apply to an active hunter.

Consequences

Hunting: a survival economy, as the sale of seal and fox skins is no longer profitable. Seal, walrus, and beluga are hunted to feed the dog team and the hunter's family (70% self-sufficient in food). The hunter without a second line of work in the family is poor. As hunters congregate in greater numbers in a single place, and because of overhunting, the distance the hunter must travel to his hunting grounds is always increasing. From August to November: 18-hour round trip once a week. Winter: twice a month, 30 to 50 miles (walrus); once a week: 20 to 25 miles (trapline for foxes).
Work time is greater, profitability is less. The equipment is in part bought and not built by the hunter. The profession is low-status.
Working two jobs: employee of the Danish and Greenland administration (town services, construction, store) in a junior positions, for want of adequate training, or guide on polar expeditions. The hunter is no longer a free man; his hunting culture is on the way out.
Making souvenirs: about 25% of the income in certain families. Quality decreasing.
Welfare: Pensions, retirement benefits, social aid. Same system as in Denmark, widespread social security. The old become a source of social benefits.

Individual equipment

Clothes:
Men's everyday summer, 80% Danish or American origin. Leather or rubber boots, leather shoes. Pants of canvas or corduroy, underwear and undergarments of cotton, sweater, down or synthetic vest, outerwear. Gloves of lined leather. For winter hunting: traditional clothes, generally.
Women's everyday summer, 90% Danish in origin. Traditional on Sunday.
Food: Danish imports, increasingly.

Transportation and hunting

Traditional wood sledge: nylon lashings, plastic runners. Motor boat in general use, replacing kayak. It is expensive, and the propeller disturbs the fauna (seal). The young are not trained to the kayak and are afraid of it.
Snowmobile: community-wide prohibition (unique in the Arctic), but several Danish civil servants own them. Rifles: with scope; very modern binoculars. Traditional equipment: harpoon, lance ...
Housing: renewal since 1988 of houses built in 1960-1970. Lease and sale of comfortable two-story wood houses (650 to 1000 sq. ft.), built with prefabricated materials on a native design.
Household equipment: similar to that of a well-paid European middle manager: electric range, refrigerator, washing machine, individual beds and blankets, tables and chairs. (The convivial sleeping platform is gone.)

Schedule

Many do not hunt; occasional communal hunting, to the extent dog teams available; hunting no longer the main activity. People stay in the villages, especially if there is electricity, and therefore TV and video player, day and night sometimes. Thule-Qaanaaq has 50% of the total population.
Increasing concentration of population. Alcoholism, teen suicide at unpredictable moments. Mediocre success of Blue Cross (anti-alcoholism).
Recruitment of the young: many of the young no longer know how to hunt or paddle a kayak.

Community equipment

School: primary school in each village, the teachers are from South Greenland. Secondary school in the administrative capital, Qaanaaq-Thule; students board, and teachers are Danes and South Greenlanders.
Hospital in Qaanaaq enlarged. Church in Qaanaaq enlarged. Arctic museum in Knud Rasmussen house moved from Thule-Dundas (North Star Bay). Link by Danish helicopter with base. Community boat service between villages. Electric plant at Qaanaaq-Thule (1953), Savigssivik (1987), Siorapaluk (1991). Running water for Danish houses and some Inuit houses in Qaanaaq-Thule. Communal bath house and lavatory at Savissivik. Private telephone in all villages.

Culture

Young are bilingual: Danish and Greenlandic. Greenlandic books: many titles. Native press. Thule-Qaanaaq newspaper: *Hainang* (since 1956). Little interest in reading, with rare exceptions. TV and radio. Video player: brings news of the world, also pornography and violence. Dance: modern music. Folklore is left to the elderly.
A new people is coming into being, in the midst of a moral and social crisis. Primary role of education.

Migratory flow

2 to 5% toward Denmark and South Greenland. 2 to 5% immigration from Upernavik area too Savissivik. South-Greenlandization of Savissivik (M. Søby study). 1 Japanese married to an Eskimo woman (Siorapaluk). 1 American married to an Eskimo woman (Savissivik).

External events and nuclear accident

1953: Greenland becomes an integral part of Denmark.
1 May 1979: autonomous Greenland government; the Territorial Community of Thule loses its separate identity. The general laws of Greenland apply. Free movement from South to North Greenland and vice versa.
1968: on 21 January, a B-52 carrying 4 hydrogen bombs crashed a few miles from the Thule base in Greenland's extreme north. Thirty years after the accident, some twenty Danish and Inuit workers who took part in the "cleanup" of the contaminated ice floe brought suit. Fifty thousand tons of snow and ice were contaminated, and the crash site extended for several hundred yards and was partially melted under the impact of the submerged bomber. Pollution 10 miles from the point of impact.
The suit was late in being brought: the plaintiffs' legal rights with respect to the US Air Force, their employer, expired on 25 January 1988. The international public was stunned to learn that 98 Danes out of the 1200 men employed by the American base for the cleanup died within a year of the accident—a mortality rate, according to the Danish health authorities, 40% above normal. And the Inuit?
2000: the National Science Foundation of the United States takes over the logistics of the base in 1997. Rumor has it that the base is being equipped with new radars. Concern on the part of the Thule Inuit, certain experts, and the Danish press. Where is the fourth H-bomb? Did it remain underwater, creating a potential hazard?

Politics

Thule District, called Avanersuaq: 65,000 sq. mi. 10 January 1984: general elections.
Distribution of votes: Atassut: 134 votes. Siumut: 139 votes. Inuit Atagatgit: 34 votes. Various: 7 votes. Total: 314 votes, or 62.9% of voters. 10 May 1988, general elections: Atassut: 84 votes. Siumut: 146 votes. Inuit Atagatgit: 60 votes. Various: 7. Total: 304 votes, or 51.3% of voters.
(Atassut: collaboration with Denmark. Siumut: autonomy. Inuit Atagatgit: independence and closure of the Thule airbase.)
Creation in 1989 by the Danish authorities of an Investigatory Committee on the events in Thule between June 1951 and August 1953, date of the displacement of the Thule Inuit to Qaanaaq. The committee held hearings at the Court of Appeals in Copenhagen. J.M. testified for five hours. 80 witnesses heard. Report submitted to the government for a decision in 1990.

INDEX

INDEX OF NAMES
Page numbers in roman refer to the main text, numbers in italics refer to photo captions.

INDEX OF BOATS
Page numbers in roman refer to main text, numbers in italics refer to photo captions.

INDEX OF PLACES
Page numbers in roman refer to main text, numbers in italics refer to photo captions.

GLOSSARY

CAIRN: Pyramid of stones raised by seamen and explorers as a landmark or sign of their passage. Messages are sometimes left in cairns. The Inuit refer to cairns as *inugsuk*.
CHUKOTKA: Farthest east point of Asia in northeast Siberia. Cradle of the Eskimos. The people of Chukotka are called the Yuit.
CRYOLOGY: Study of the action of freezing on rocks.
ESKIMO: Word of Indian (Algonquian) origin meaning "eater of raw flesh." The native word is *Inuit*, and *Inughuit* for the Polar Eskimos of North Greenland.
GEOMORPHOLOGY: Branch of physical geography. The analytic study of the form and history of the earth's topography.
HUMMOCKS: Ice barriers from ten to twenty feet in height caused by the pressure exerted on the ice by winds and currents.
HYPERBOREANS: Imaginary people of the high latitudes.
ICEBERG: Floating mass of ice from an arctic glacier that calves into the sea. The iceberg is a store of fresh water for the Inuit.
IGLOO: Generic term for a house of stones and sod. In North Greenland, snow igloos are temporary structures.
INLAND ICE: Vast continental glacier, ice cap.
INUGHUIT: Specific designation for the Polar Eskimos of North Greenland. For a long time they were known as the Avanerssuamiut.
INUIT: In political terms, designates all the native peoples from northeast Siberia to the east coast of Greenland: Chukotka; southern, western, and northern Alaska; northern Canada; and Greenland–in all, 120,000 souls. Properly speaking, only the Canadian Eskimos are Inuit.
INUKTITUT: The Inuit language.
INUPIAQ: Language spoken by the Eskimos of northwestern Alaska.
KALAALIT: Designates the peoples of Greenland.
METEORITE: Fragment of a celestial body that passes through the atmosphere leaving a luminous path. South of Thule, at Savigssivik (Cape York), is an area that has received many meteorites: 9 fragments have been found, weighing a total of 58 tons. This was the Inughuit's only source of metal.
PACK: Sea ice floating over a wide expanse. Pack ice is made from salt water.
POLAR HYSTERIA (or *PIBLOKTO*): Psychic disturbances specific to the Inuit at the start of the polar night. Not a neurosis of the kind studied by Charcot.
POLE: There are three poles: the geographic pole, the magnetic pole, and the geomagnetic pole.
POLYNYA: Large, semi-permanent area of open water in the midst of pack ice, due to currents on the surface and at depth. The so-called North Water at the top of Melville Bay is a polynya, which explains the presence of many right whales there.
SHAMANISM: Traditional religion characterized by an awareness of the order of nature, and the power of beneficent and malefic spirits. The shaman is endowed with certain powers and is known by the name *angakkuq* among the Inughuit. Shamanism a scribes to a pantheistic vision of the cosmos.
TUPILAK: A spirit, often an evil one. A fantastic figure of the Inuit's nightmares.
YUPIK: Language spoken by the Eskimos of southwest Alaska and Siberia.

ACKNOWEDGMENTS

The author wishes to thank Henri Frossard, whose distinguished collaboration on the work leading to this book has been invaluable, Sylvie Devers, Annie Serbonnet, Huguette Joffre, Élisabeth Cardin, and Ariette Fraysse of the Centre d'Etudes Arctiques (CNRS), Paul Adam, National Museet, Copenhagen, Henri Bancaud, François Bellec, Vagn F. Buchwald, Thérèse Davet, Hélène Cook-Vetter, Robert Keith Headland, archivist at the Scott Polar Research Institute (Cambridge), David S. Henderson, conservator of the Broughty Castle Museum (Dundee, Scotland), Sir Wally Herbert, Alfred McLaren, Commander U.S. Navy, George Michanowsky of the Explorers Club of New York, Mme Gertrude Nobile, Monique Pelletier, Map Department (Bibliothèque Nationale), Eva Rude, Peter Schledermann, Regitze Margrethe Søby, Commander Ed. Stafford-Peary, Dr. Peter Wadhams, Wilcomb E. Washburn, Alison Wilson, Center for Polar Archives (National Archives, Washington). Arktisk Institut, Copenhagen; Avanersuup Kommunia, Qaanaaq Thule; Dalhem Museum, Berlin; Geodaetisk Institute, Copenhagen; Smithsonian Inst. Washington; Magdalen College, Oxford. My friends at the Dundee Museum. The Hakodate Trappist monastery (Hokkaido, Japan). Among my many Inuit friends in Thule Qaanaaq, Siorapaluk, and Qeqertarsuaq, who, in looking at the proofs of this book, have added unrecorded historical facts, provided many ethnographic commentaries to the illustrations, and identified deceased individuals, I thank: Inuterssuaq, Imina, Sakaeunnguaq, Qaaqqutsiaq, Kalipaluk-Peary, Aama, and Pallo. For this second edition, published by the Éditions du Chêne, I offer warm thanks to the team at Éditions du Chêne. My friend the Danish photographer Ivars Silis and the photographers Francis Vernhet and Jocelyne Leveau, as well as the photographer Francis Parel, and Kenn Harper, and also my colleague and friend Bruce Jackson. I send cordial and faithful greetings to Oshima Ikao (Siorapaluk) and Moses Olsen (Nuuk), former Minister of Culture of Greenland.

BIBLIOGRAPHY

Arctic. Calgary, since 1950.

Arctica 1978, Proceedings of the 7th Northern Libraries Colloquy (under the direction of Jean Malaurie). Paris: Éditions du Centre National de la Recherche Scientifique, 1982. 580 pages. Thematic bibliographies, Arctic libraries, Arctic museums, filmology of the Arctic.

Den Grønlandske Lods Vest Grønland. Copenhagen, 1966.

Grønland. Copenhagen.

Inter-Nord, an international review of arctic studies. Paris, CNRS, since 1960 (19 volumes).

Polar Record. Cambridge, since 1920.

Back, George. *Narrative of an Expedition in Terror*. London: 1838.

Bartlett, Robert A. *The Log of Bob Bartlett*. New York: 1928.

Beizmann, Cécile, Jean Malaurie, Hélène Trouche-Simon, and Nina Rausch de Traubenberg. "Douze tests de Rorschach d'Esquimaux polaires, Inuit du nord du Groenland 1950- 1951 . Mission Jean Malaurie." *Inter-Nord* 18 (1987).

Bessels, Emil. *Einige Worte uber die Innuit*. Braunschweig: 1875.

Borup, George. *A Tenderfoot with Peary*. New York: 1911.

Bradley, John R. "My Knowledge of Dr Cook's Polar Expedition." *The Independent*, 16 September 1909.

Brøsted, Jens, Mads Faegteborg, *Thule —Fangerfolk og militaeranlaeg*, Jurist og Økonomforbundets Forlag. Copenhagen, 1985.

Buchwald, Vagn F. "Meteorites in Greenland." *Inter-Nord* 19 (1990).

Cook, F. A. *My Attainment of the Pole*. New York: 1911.

——. *Return from the Pole*. New York: 1951.

Davis, C. H., ed. *Narrative of the North Pole Expedition . . . USS Polaris*. Washington: 1876.

Devers, S., ed. *Pour Jean Malaurie, 102 témoignages en hommage à 40 ans d'études arctiques*. Paris: 1990.

Eames, Hugh. *Winner Loses All*. Boston: 1973.

Fisher, Alexander. *A Journal of a Voyage of Discovery to the Arctic Regions in His Majesty's Ships Hecla and Griper*. London: 1821.

Fox, Margaret. *The Love-Life of Dr Kane, Containing the Correspondance and a History of the Acquaintance, Engagement and Secret Marriage between Elisha Kent Kane and Margaret Fox*. New York: 1865.

Freuchen, Peter. *Arctic Adventure*. New York: 1935.

Gibbons, Russel W. "F. A. Cook 1865-1940 (Centenary of his birth)." *Inter Nord* 10 (1968): 309-316.

Rolf Gilberg, *Polar Eskimo Bibliography*. Copenhagen: Meddelelser om Grønland, 1976.

Godfrey, William C. *Godfrey's Narrative of the Last Grinnell Arctic Exploring Expedition*. Philadelphia: 1857.

Greely, Adolphus W. *Report on the Proceedings of the United States Expedition to Lady Franklin Bay*. Washington, 1888.

—— *Three Years of Arctic Service*. New York: 1886.

—— "Dr. Cook's North Polar Discoveries." *The Independent*, 16 September 1909.

Gussov, Zachary. "Some Responses of West Greenland Eskimos to a Naturalistic Situation of Perceptual Deprivation, With an Appendix of 60 Case Histories Collected by Dr. Alfred Bertelsen in 1902-1903." *Inter-Nord* 11 (1970): 227-263.

Hall, Thomas F. *Has the Pole Been Discovered?* Boston: 1917.

Harper, Kenn. *Give Me My Father's Body*. Frobisher Bay: Blacklead Books, 1986.

Remie, Cornelius, ed. *Facing the Future: Inughuit Youth of Qaanaaq. Report of the '98 University of Nijmegen Student Expedition to Qaanaaq*. Nijmegen University Press.

Hayes, Isaac Israel. *The Open Polar Sea*. New York: 1867

——. *An Arctic Boat Journey*. Boston: 1869.

Hendrik, Hans. *Memoirs of Hans Hendrik, the Arctic Traveller, Serving under Kane, Hayes, Hall and Nares, 1853-1876*. London: 1876.

Henson, Matthew. *A Black Explorer at the North Pole*. New York: 1969.

——. "The Negro at the North Pole." *World's Work*, April 1910.

Herbert, Wally. *The Noose of Laurels, Robert E. Peary and the Race to the North Pole*. London: 1989.

——. "Commander Peary–Did He Reach the Pole?" *National Geographic*, September 1988.

Holtved, Erik. *The Polar Eskimos: Language and Folklore*. Copenhagen: Meddelelser om Grønland, 1951

——. *Contributions to Polar Eskimo Ethnography*. Copenhagen: Meddelelser om Grønland, 1967.

Hrdlicka, Ales. "Contribution to the Anthropology of Central and Smith Sound Eskimo." *Anthropological Papers of the American Museum of Natural History* (1910), vol. 5: 175-280.

Imbert, Bertrand. *Le Grand Défi des Pôles*. Paris: 1987.

Inglefield, E. A. *A Summer Search for Sir John Franklin*. London: 1853.

Ulloriaq, Inuterssuaq. *Beretningen Om Qillarsuac*. Copenhagen: 1985.

Kane, Elisha Kent. *The U.S. Grinnell Expedition in Search of Sir John Franklin: A Personal Narrative*. New York: 1854.

——. *Arctic Explorations: The Second Grinnell Expedition in Search of Sir John Franklin, 1853, 1854, 1855*. Philadelphia: 1856.

——. *Journal* (Stanford University Library).

Koch, Lauge. *Au nord du Groenland*. Paris: 1928.

Kroeber, A. L. "Tales of the Smith Sound Eskimo." *Journal of American Folklore* (1899), vol. XII, Nos. 44,46.

Loomis, Chauncey. *Weird and Tragic Shores*. New York: 1971.

Lopez, Barry. *Arctic Dreams*. New York: 1986.

McMillan, D. B. *Four Years in the White North*. New York: 1918.

——. *Etah and Beyond*. Boston: 1927.

Malaurie, Jean. *Thèmes de recherche géomorphologique sur la côte nord-ouest du Groenland*. Paris: Ed. du CNRS, 1968.

——. "Les Civilisations esquimaudes." In *Encyclopédie de la Pléiade*,

Ethnologie II. Paris: Gallimard, 1979.

——. "New Information Concerning Captain John Ross's Ethnographical Collection following the Isabelle and the Alexander's Expedition along Greenland's North West Coast in August 1818." *Inter-Nord* 18 (1987).

——. "Polar Eskimo Bibliography (II), A Complementary List of 600 References." *Inter Nord* 18 (1987).

——. *Les Derniers Rois de Thulé*. Fifth edition. Paris: Éditions Plon, collection "Terre humaine," 1989. *The Last Kings of Thule*. New York: E. P. Dutton, 1982.

——. Jean Sutter, and Léon Tabah. "L'Isolat esquimau de Thulé (Groenland)." *Population* 4 (1952).

——. Jean Sutter, and Léon Tabah. "Méthode mécanographique pour établir la généalogie d'une population. Application à l'étude des Esquimaux polaires." *Population* 8 (1956).

——, ed. *The Eskimo People Today and Tomorrow, IVth International Congress of the Centre d'études arctiques*. Paris: Mouton, 1973.

——, ed. *Pôle nord 1983, Histoire de sa conquête et problèmes contemporains de navigation maritime et aérienne, Xe Colloque international du Centre d'études arctiques*. Paris: CNRS, 1987.

Markham, A. H. *The Great Frozen Sea: A Personal Narrative of the Voyage of the "Alert" during the Arctic Expedition of 1875-1876*. London: 1878.

Markham, Clements. "The Arctic Expedition of 1875-1876." Royal Geographical Proceedings 21, no. 6, 1877.

Martin Miller, J. *The Discovery of the North Pole*. New York: 1909.

Mylius-Erichsen, L., Harald Moltke. *Grønland*. Copenhagen: 1906.

Murray Smith, D. *Arctic Expeditions*. Edinburgh: 1875.

Nares, George Strong. *Narrative of a Voyage to the Polar Sea during 1875-1876 in HM Ships Alert and Discovery*. London: 1878.

Ollivier-Henry, Jocelyne. *Sila Naalagaavoq. Avec les Inuit du Nord Groenland*. Éd. Diabase, 1998.

Peary, Josephine, *My Arctic Journal*. London: 1893.

Peary, R. E. *Northward over the Great Ice: A Narrative of Life and Work along the Shores and upon the Interior Ice-cap of Northern Greenland in the Years 1886 and 1891-1897*. New York: 1898.

——. *Nearest the Pole: A Narrative of the Polar Expedition of the Peary Arctic Club in the S.S. Roosevelt, 1905-1906*. New York: 1907.

——. *The North Pole, its Discovery in 1909 under the Auspices of the Peary Arctic Club*. New York: 1910.

Plaisted, Ralph. "How I Reached the North Pole on a Snowmobile." *Popular Science*, September 1968.

Rasmussen, Knud. *Nye Mennesker*. Copenhagen: 1906.

——. *The People of the Polar North*. London: 1908.

——. *Avangarnisalersârutit*. Copenhagen: 1909.

——. *Grønland Langs Polhavet*, Copenhagen: 1919.

Rawlins, D. *Peary at the Pole: Fact or Fiction?* Washington: 1973.

Rosing, O. ABD. Nuuk: 1946.

Ross, John. *A Voyage of Discovery*. London: 1819.

Ross, W. Gillies. *Arctic Whalers, Icy Seas: Narratives of the Davis Strait Whale Fishery*. Toronto: 1985.

Sabine, Edward. *Remarks on the Account of the Late Voyage of Discovery to Baffin's Bay*. London: 1819.

Schley, Winfield S. *The Rescue of Greely*. New York: 1885.

Shackleton, Edward. *Arctic Journeys*. London: 1936.

Slaedespor, Nye. *Dagbogsblade fra den litteraere Grønlands ekspedition, 1902-1904*. Copenhagen: 1984.

Søby, Regitze Margrethe. "Savigsivik Westgreenlandic Influence on a Settlement in Thule." *Inter-Nord* 17 (1983).

Steensby, H. P. *Contributions to the Ethnology and Anthropogeography of the Polar Eskimos*. Copenhagen: Meddelelser om Grønland, 1910.

Det Grønlandske Selskabs Skrifter XXVII. Copenhagen: 1985.

Vanstone, James W. "The First Peary Collection of Polar Eskimo Material Culture." *Fieldiana Anthropology*, vol. 64, no. 2, 1972.

Whitney, H. *Hunting with the Eskimos*. New York: 1911.

Wright, Theon. *The Big Nail*. New York: 1970.

Zazzo, René, Jean Malaurie, and Hélène Trouche-Simon. "Tests psycho-moteurs des Deux Barrages René Zazzo sur les esquimaux polaires. Mission Jean Malaurie." *Inter-Nord* 19 (1990).

FILMOGRAPHY

Peary's Race for the North Pole. Wollper prod. Libr. Catal. Film inc. 52mm, Wilmete, 1974.

Race for the Pole. CBS/ITT Production, 1984.

Herbert, Wally. *Across the Top of the World*. London: BBC, 1970.

Julen, Stefan and Ylva Julen. *Inughuit*. Stockholm: 1985. 16 mm color, 85 min.

Jean Malaurie. *Les Derniers rois de Thulé*. Part one: *L'Esquimau polaire, le chasseur*. Part two: *L'Esquimau chômeur et imprévisible*. 16mm color, 125 minutes. Filmed in Thule, April-May 1969. Paris: ORTF, 1970

——. *Inuit*. 16mm color series, filmed in 1974 and 1976 from Greenland to Siberia. Paris: Antenne 2, 1980. I. *Inuit, le cri universel du peuple esquimau*, 90 min. II. *Les Groenlandais et le Danemark: Nunarput (Nortre Terre)*. 55 min. III. *Les Groenlandais et le Danemark: le Groenland se lève*: 16 mm, 55 min.

Compact disk, compiled Jean Malaurie: *Chants et tambours inuit: de Thulé au détroit de Béring*. Paris: OCORA, 1987. 72'30".

CD-ROM, Jean Malaurie. *Inuit*. Paris: Éditions Montparnasse, 1995.

BY THE SAME AUTHOR

Le Hoggar, Journal d'une exploration dans le massif de l'Ahaggar et avec les Touaregs. Paris: Editions Fernand Nathan, 1954.

Thèmes de recherche géomorphologique dans le nordouest du Groenland. Paris: Editions du CNRS, 1968.

Les Derniers Rois de Thulé. Avec les Esquimaux Polaires face à leur destin. Paris: Editions Plon, collection "Terre humaine," 1955.

Ultima Thulé. Paris: Editions Bordas, 1990.

Hummocks I (Nord Groenland–Arctique central canadien). Paris: Editions Plon, collection "Terre humaine," 1999.

Hummocks 2 (Alaska - Tchoukotka sibérienne). Paris: Éd. Plon, collection "Terre humaine," 1999.

WORKS ABOUT THE AUTHOR

Pour Jean Malaurie. En hommage à quarante ans de recherche arctique. Paris: Éditions Plon, 1989.

Bogiolo-Bruna, Galia, ed. *Per Jean Malaurie. Alla ricerca della quadrature del circolo polare*. Il Polo Fermo, 1999.

ILLUSTRATION CREDITS

Abbreviations t: top, m: middle, b: bottom, r: right, l: left, neg. negative. Private collection: refers to documents taken from books belonging to the author. Collection Jean Malaurie: refers to documents and photographs belonging to the author. 2-3: Private collection–Photo Philippe Harvey © Chêne. 6: National Museum of Denmark, Copenhagen. Photo © J. Meldgaard, National Museum 8: Collection Jean Malaurie. 9: Scott Polar Research Institute, Cambridge–Photo © SPRI. 10-11: Collection Jean Malaurie. 12: National Museum of Denmark, Copenhagen–Photo © J. Meldgaard, National Museum 13: DR. 14: Collection Jean Malaurie. 15l: Northwest Territories Legislative Assembly, Yellowknife. 15r: Collection Jean Malaurie. 17: National Museum of Denmark, Copenhagen–Photo © J. Meldgaard, National Museum. 18: Photo © P. Schledermann, Arctic Inst. of N. America, Calgary. 19: National Museum of Denmark, Copenhagen–Photo © National Museum 20: National Maritime Museum, London, Greenwich, Hospital collection–Photo © National Maritime Museum, London. 22t: Private collection–Photo Jeanbor © Photeb. 22b: The British Library, London–Photo © Photeb. 23: Private collection–Photo P. Harvey © Chêne. 24t and b: Collection Jean Malaurie. 24m: Private collection–Photo Jeanbor © Photeb. 25: Collection Jean Malaurie. 26t: Private collection–Photo Jeanbor © Photeb. 26b: British Museum, London–Photo © courtesy Trustees of the Museum. 27t: Private collection–Photo Jeanbor © Photeb. 28-29: Collection Jean Malaurie. 30: Private collection–Photo Jeanbor © Photeb. 31 Private collection–Photo Jeanbor © Photeb. 32t and m: National Galleries of Scotland–Photo NGS Picture Library. 32b: Scott Polar Research Institute, Cambridge–Photo © SPRI. 33: Hull City Museums–Town Docks Museum–Photo © Hull City Museums. 34t: The National Maritime Museum, London–Photo © Picture Library. 34b: Private collection–Photo P. Harvey © Chêne. 35 t, m, and bl: Royal Geographical Society Archives, London–Photo © Royal Geographical Society Archives. 35br: Scott Polar Research Institute, Cambridge–Photo © SPRI. 36tl and b: Private collection–Photo Jeanbor © Photeb. 36tr: Scott Polar Research Institute, Cambridge–Photo © SPRI. 38t: The British Museum, London–Photo © courtesy Trustees of the Museum. 38b: Photo © Ivars Silis. 39: Collection Jean Malaurie. 40: Private collection–Photo P. Harvey © Chêne. 41tl and b: Scott Polar Research Institute, Cambridge–Photo © SPRI. 41tr: Photo © Mary Evans Picture Library. 42 and 43b and tr: The British Museum, London–Photo © courtesy Trustees of the Museum. 43tl: Private collection–Photo © Docent VF Buchwald, Copenhagen. 44t and br: Private collection–Photo P. Harvey © Chêne. 44bl: Collection Jean Malaurie. 45b: Private collection–Photo Jeanbor © Photeb. 46-47: Photo © F. Vernhet. 48: Scott Polar Research Institute–Photo © SPRI. 49: National Portrait Gallery London–Photo © courtesy the National Portrait Gallery. 50: Private collection–Photo Jeanbor © Photeb. 51: National Portrait Gallery London–Photo © courtesy National Portrait Gallery. 52-53: Collection Jean Malaurie. 54bl: Private collection–Photo P. Harvey © Chêne. 54br: Private collection–Photo Jeanbor © Photeb. 55: Photo © F. Vernhet 56t: Scott Polar Research Institute, Cambridge–Photo © SPRI. 57tr: Scott Polar Research Institute, Cambridge–Photo © SPRI. 57m: DR. 57bl: The British library, London–Photo © British Library. 57br: Photo © Owen Beattie, University of Alberta, Edmonton, DR. 58: DR. 59: Scott Polar Research Institute, Cambridge–Photo © SPRI. 60: Private collection–Photo P. Harvey © Chêne. 62-63: Collection Jean Malaurie. 64, 65, 66b, 67tr: Private collection–Photo P. Harvey © Chêne. 67b: © Dundee Art and Heritage: McManus Galleries. 68t and m: © Dundee Art and Heritage: McManus Galleries. 68b: Hull City Museums–Town Docks Museum–Photo © Hull City Museums. 69, 70, 71: © Dundee Art and Herritage: McManus Galleries. 72,73: Photo © Francis Parel. 74: U.S. Naval Academy Museum Collection, Gift of Bayard Kane and C. Carey–Photo © Naval Historical Foundation. 76, 77, 78, 79, 80: Private collection–Photo P. Harvey © Chêne. 81t: American Museum of Natural History, New York–Photo D.B. MacMillan © AMNH, neg. 232588. 81b: Private collection–Photo P. Harvey © Chêne. 82, 83, 84: Private collection–Photo P. Harvey © Chêne. 85t: Photo © Ivars Silis. 85b: Private collection–Photo P. Harvey © Chêne. 86, 87: Private collection–Photo P. Harvey © Chêne. 88, 89: Smithsonian Institution, Washington, Dept. of Anthropology–Photo Smithsonian Institution, neg. 8112058, 823397, 823398, 823399. 90: Private collection–Photo P. Harvey © Chêne. 91: Photo © F. Vernhet. 92, 93tr and b: Private collection–Photo P. Harvey © Chêne. 93tl: National Archives, Washington–Photo National Archives. 94: Collection of the New York Historical Society–Photo © NY Historical Society. 96, 97: Private collection–Photo P. Harvey © Chêne. 98t: American Museum of Natural History New York © AMNH, neg. 231568. 98b: Photo © Francis Parel. 99t: The New York Historical Society–Photo © N.Y Historical Society. 99b: Private collection–Photo P. Harvey © Chêne. 100-101: Photo © Ivars Silis. 102t and m: Private collection–Photo P. Harvey © Chêne. 102b: Photo © Ivars Silis. 103t: Photo © F. Vernhet. 103b: Private collection–Photo P. Harvey © Chêne. 104: Private collection–Photo P. Harvey © Chêne. 105t: Photo © Jocelyne Leveau. 105b: Private collection–Photo P. Harvey © Chêne. 106 National Geographic Society, New York–Photo © National Geographic Society, neg. 938214-021162964. 107l and m: Field Museum of Natural History, Chicago–Photo © Field Museum, neg. 102233. 107r: American Museum of Natural History–Photo © AMNH, neg. 230920. 108t: Arktisk Institut, Copenhagen–Photo © Danish Polar Center. 108b: National Archives, Washington–Photo © National Archives. 109: National Geographic Society, New York–Photo © National Geographic Society, neg. 938215-021164690. 110 Private collection–Photo © C. C. Loomis. 112 and 113m: Private collection–Photo P. Harvey © Chêne. 113b: Smithsonian Institution, Washingon–Photo © Smithsonian Institution, neg. 8112059. 114- 115: Private collection–Photo P. Harvey © Chêne. 116: National Archives, Washington–Photo © National Archives. 117-118: Private collection–Photo P. Harvey © Chêne. 119t: Photo © Ivars Silis. 119b: Photo © Francis Parel. 120-121: Collection Jean Malaurie. 122: National Archives, Washington–Photo © National Archives. 123t: DR. 123bl: National Archives, Washington–Photo © National Archives. 123br: Photo © C. C. Loomis. 124-125: Photo © F. Vernhet. 126: Private collection–Photo P. Harvey © Chêne. 127t: National Archives, Washington–Photo © National Archives. 127b: Photo © Jocelyne Leveau. 128, 129, 130, 131: Private collection–Photo P. Harvey © Chêne. 132: Photo © F. Vernhet. 133: Photo © Jocelyne Leveau. 134, 135, 136: Private collection–Photo P. Harvey © Chêne. 137t: Scott Polar Research Institute, Cambridge © SPRI. 137b: Private collection–Photo P. Harvey © Chêne. 138: Private collection–Photo P. Harvey © Chêne. 139t: Photo Thomas Mitchell, George White © Coll. National Archives Canada, Ottawa-C5249. 139m and b: British Museum, London–Photo © courtesy Trustees of the Museum, neg. 000382-001355-001343-097402-097401. 140: National Archives, Washington–Photo © National Archives. 142-143: Private collection–Photo P. Harvey © Chêne. 144: Photo © Francis Parel. 145-146 Private collection–Photo P. Harvey © Chêne. 147: Photo Thomas Mitchell, George White © Coll. National Archives Canada, Ottawa-C52497. 148: Photo © Ivars Silis. 149: US Naval Historical Center, Washington–Photo © Dava Still Media Depository. 150: Smithsonian Institution, Washington–Photo © Smithsonian Institution, neg. 8112056. 151: Collection Jean Malaurie. 152: Private collection–Photo P. Harvey © Chêne. 153t: © The Royal Swedish Academy of Sciences, Stockholm. 154: Coll. M. Ray Spear, U S Naval Historical Center, Washington–Photo © Navy Center. 156, 157, 158, 159, 160, 161l: Private collection–Photo P. Harvey © Chêne. 161r: National Archives, Washington © National Archives. 162, 163t: Private collection–Photo P. Harvey © Chêne. 163b: Photo © E1éonore Malaurie. 164: Private collection–Photo P. Harvey © Chêne. 165: National Archives, Washington–Photo © National Archives. 166t: Private collection–Photo P. Harvey © Chêne. 166b: National Archives, Washington–Photo © National Archives. 167: National Archives, Washington–Photo © National Archives. 168t: Private collection–Photo P. Harvey © Chêne. 168b: National Archives, Washington–Photo © National Archives. 169t: U.S. Naval Historical Center, Washington–Photo © Dava Still Media Depository. 170: National Archives, Washington–Photo © National Archives. 170-171: Photo © Francis Parel. 172tl: Private collection–Photo P. Harvey © Chêne. 172tr: Scott Polar Research Institute Cambridge–Photo © SPRI. 172m and b: © P. Schledermann, Arctic Inst. of N. America, Calgary. 173tl: National Archives, Washington–Photo © National Archives. 173tr: U.S. Naval Historical Center, Washington–Photo © Dava Still Media Depository. 173b: Photo © Francis Parel. 174 American Museum of Natural History, New York–Photo © AMNH, neg. 272315. 175: Collection Jean Malaurie. 176t: American Museum of Natural History, New York–Photo © AMNH, neg. 2A9577, 2A9579. 176b: Private collection–Photo P. Harvey © Chêne. 177t: Collection Jean Malaurie. 177m: National Museum of Denmark, Copenhagen–Photo © Nat. Museum, neg. L 212. 177b: Arktisk Institut, Copenhagen–Photo © Danish Polar Center. 178t: Photo © Hulton-Deutsch Collection. 178b: Photo © The Bettmann Archive. 179t: Private collection–Photo P. Harvey © Chêne. 179b: Explorers Club, New York–Photo © Explorers Club Archive. 180t: Photo © Francis Parel. 180b: Photo © The Bettmann Archive. 181t and bl: Private collection–DR. 181br: National Archives, Washington–Photo © National Archives. 182t: American Museum of Natural History, New York–Photo © AMNH, neg. 117604. 182m: Collection Jean Malaurie. 182b: Private collection–Photo P. Harvey © Chêne. 183t: Collection Jean Malaurie. 183b: Smithsonian Institution, Washington–Photo © Smithsonian Institution, neg. 7810878. 184t: DR. 184b: Private collection–Photo P. Harvey © Chêne. 185t: DR. 185b: Photo © Ivars Silis. 186: DR 187: National Archives, Washington–Photo © National Archives. 188: Arktisk Institut, Copenhagen–Photo © Danish Polar Center. 189: National Museum of Denmark, Copenhagen–Photo © Nat. Museum, neg. FN 13. 190: National Archives, Washington–Photo © National Archives. 190t: Collection Jean Malaurie. 190bl: Photo © The Mansell Collection–D.R. 190br: American Museum of Natural History New York–Photo © AMNH, neg. 103633. 192tr: National Archives, Washington–Photo © National Archives. 192b: Private collection–Photo R. E. Peary © DR. 193: National Archives, Washington–Photo © National Archives. 194t: Private collection–Photo P. Harvey © Chêne. 194b: National Archives, Washington–Photo © National Archives. 195: Collection Jean Malaurie. 196: Photo © The Bettmann Archive. 197t: American Museum of Natural History, New York–Photo © AMNH, neg. 272318. 197b: DR. 198tl: National Archives, Washington–Photo © National Archives. 198tr: Photo © Hulton-Deutsch Collection. 198b: Photo © Frank Hermann-Wally Herbert. 199: National Archives, Washington–Photo © National Archives. 200: Photo © F. Vernhet. 201t: Collection Jean Malaurie. 201b: Photo © Francis Parel. 202: American Museum of Natural History, New York–Photo © AMNH, neg. 329140. 203t and m: National Archives, Washington–Photo © National Archives. 203b: Private collection–Photo P. Harvey © Chêne. 204 and 205t: National Archives, Washington–Photo © National Archives. 205b: Private collection–Photo P. Harvey © Chêne. 206l: National Archives, Washington–Photo © National Archives. 206r: Private collection–Photo © DR. 207t: Private collection–Photo P. Harvey © Chêne. 207b: National Archives, Washington–Photo © National Archives. 208t: Arktisk Institut, Copenhagen–Photo © Danish Polar Center. 208b: National Archives, Washington–Photo © National Archives. 209t: National Museum of Denmark, Copenhagen–Photo © National Museum, neg. 1.74. 210t: Arktisk Institut, Copenhagen–Photo A Bertelsen © Danish Polar Center. 210b: National Archives Washington–Photo © National Archives. 211: National Museum of Denmark, Copenhagen–Photo © National Museum. 212-213: Photo © F. Vernhet. 214 from l to r: (6 objects.) Field Museum of Natural History, Chicago–Photo © Field Museum, neg. 102238. (2 objects) The British Museum, London–Photo © courtesy Trustees of the Museum. 215 from l to r: (2 objects) Field Museum of Natural History Chicago–Photo © Field Museum, neg. 102244 ; 102239. (2 objects) The British Museum, London–Photo © courtesy Trustees of the Museum. 216 from t to b: (2 objects) Field Museum of Natural History Chicago–Photo © Field Museum, neg. 102240. (1 object) DR. (1 object) Field Museum of Natural History, Chicago–Photo © Field Museum, neg. 102242. (1 object) DR. 217t: (4 objects) Field Museum of Natural History, Chicago–Photo © Field Museum, neg. 102242. 214m: National Museum of Denmark, Copenhagen–Photo © National Musem. 214b: The British Museum, London–Photo © courtesy Trustees of the Museum. 218t: Private collection–Photo P. Harvey © Chêne. 218ml: The British Museum, London–Photo © courtesy Trustees of the Museum. 218ml and b: American Museum of Natural History, New York–Photo © AMNH, neg. 231652, 231214. 219tl: Field Museum of Natural History Chicago–Photo © Field Museum, neg. 102236. 219tr: The British Museum, London–Photo © courtesy Trustees of the Museum. 219mr: Field Museum of Natural History Chicago–Photo © Field Museum, neg. 102235. 219b: American Museum of Natural History New York–Photo © AMNH, neg. 110605 ; 231652. 220: Photo © courtesy George Michanowsky–Explorers Club Archive. 222: Photo © Gibson-Private collection–Photo © DR. 223t: The Royal Library Copenhagen–Photo © Royal Library. 223b: Collection Jean Malaurie. 224: Private collection–Photo P. Harvey © Chêne. 225t: Photo © Hulton Deutsch Collection. 225b: Collection Jean Malaurie. 226: Private collection–Photo P. Harvey © Chêne. 227t: Private collection–Photo © DR. 227b: Photo © Francis Parel. 228: Arktisk Institut, Copenhagen–Photo © Danish Polar Center. 229t: DR. 229b: Photo © The Bettmann Archive. 230-231: Photo © Ivars Silis. 232t: Arktisk Institut, Copenhagen–Photo © Danish Polar Center. 232b: The Royal Library, Copenhagen–Photo © Royal Library. 233-234: Private collection–Photo P. Harvey © Chêne. 234m: Collection Jean Malaurie. 234b: DR. 235t: DR. 235b: Collection Jean Malaurie. 236: National Archives, Washington–Photo © National Archives. 237: DR. 238t: National Archives, Washington–Photo © National Archives. 238b: Photo © Ivars Silis. 239: Photo © Ivars Silis. 240 DR. 241: Arktisk Institut, Copenhagen © Danish Polar Center. 242: Arktisk Institut, Copenhagen–Photo © Danish Polar Center. 244: DR. 245t: National Archives, Washington–Photo © National Archives. 245b: Private collection © DR. 246, 247, 248, 249: Arktisk Institut, Copenhagen © Danish Polar Center. 250l: National Museum of Denmark, Copenhagen–Photo © National Museum. 250r: Arktisk Institut, Copenhagen–Photo © Danish Polar Center. 251t and bl: Arktisk Institut, Copenhagen–Photo © Danish Polar Center. 251m and br: Private collection–Photo P. Harvey © Chêne. 252-253: Photo © Ivars Silis. 254: Arktisk Institut, Copenhagen–Photo © Danish Polar Center. 255: Private collection–Photo © DR. 256t: Collection Jean Malaurie. 256b: National Museum of Denmark, Copenhagen–Photo P. Freuchen © National Museum. 257t: Arktisk Institut, Copenhagen–Photo © Danish Polar Center. 257b: The Royal Library, Copenhagen–Photo © Royal Library. 258t: The Royal Library, Copenhagen–Photo © Royal Library. 258b: American Museum of Natural History, New York–Photo © AMNH, neg. 231217. 259: The Royal Library Copenhagen–Photo © Royal Library, neg. 88646 ; 33191. 260t: Private collection–Photo © DR. 260b: Photo © Ivars Silis. 261t and b: American Museum of Natural History, New York–Photo © AMNH, neg. 23154. 261m: Private collection–Photo P. Harvey © Chêne. 262-263: Photo © Ivars Silis. 264t: American Museum of Natural History, New York–Photo © AMNH, neg. 231041. 264m: The Royal Library Copenhagen–Photo © Royal Library, neg. 32527. 264b: American Museum of Natural History, New York–Photo © AMNH, neg. 123055. 265t: Arktisk Institut, Copenhagen © Danish Polar Center. 265b: Royal Geographical Society, London–Photo © Royal Geographical Society Archives. 266t: National Museum of Denmark, Copenhagen–Photo © National Museum, neg 1.1231. 266b: Collection Jean Malaurie. 267t: The Royal Library, Copenhagen–Photo © Royal Library, neg. 33189. 267b: Collection Jean Malaurie. 268: American Museum of Natural History–Photo © AMNH, neg. 232148; 231248, 31246. 269t: The Royal Library, Copenhagen–Photo © DR 269b: National Museum of Denmark, Copenhagen–Photo P. Freuchen © National Museum, neg. L.1336. 270: Arktisk Institut, Copenhagen–Photo © Danish Polar Center. 271: American Museum of Natural History, New York Photo © AMNH, neg. 231007; 231242. 272: Photo © Ivars Silis. 273: American Museum of Natural History, New York–Photo D. B. MacMillan © AMNH, neg. 232192; 232198, 232197, 232189, 232188, 232205, 232190, 233743 ; 231541, 230555. 274t and mr: Arktisk Institut, Copenhagen–Photo © Danish Polar Center. 274bl: Photo © Geodaetisk Institute of Denmark, Copenhagen. 274br: National Museum of Denmark, Copenhagen–Photo © National Museum, neg. L.199. 275t: Private collection–Photo P. Harvey © Chêne. 275b: Arktisk Institut, Copenhagen–Photo © Danish Polar Center. 276tl: Collection Jean Malaurie. 276tr: American Museum of Natural History, New York–Photo E. O. Hovey © AMNH, neg 234331. 276m: National Museum of Denmark, Copenhagen–(t) Photo Th. Thomsen © National Museum, neg. 1.82–(b) Photo © National Museum, neg. 1.2090. 276b: Arktisk Institut, Copenhagen–Photo © Danish Polar Center. 277: American Museum of Natural History, New York–Photo D. B. MacMillan © AMNH, neg. 231658. 278tl: National Museum of Denmark, Copenhagen–Photo P. Freuchen © National Museum. 278tr: National Museum of Denmark, Copenhagen–Photo Th. Krabbe © National Museum, neg. L207. 278b: National Museum of Denmark, Copenhagen–Photo Th. Thomsen © National Museum, neg. 1.71. 279t: American Museum of Natural History, New York–Photo © AMNH, neg. 231671. 279m and b: Private collection–Photo P. Harvey © Chêne. 280t: Arktisk Institut, © Danish Polar Center. 270b: National Museum of Denmark, Copenhagen–(l) Photo P. Freuchen © National Museum, neg. 1851; (r) Photo © National Museum, neg 1.1138. 281tl and b: American Museum of Natural History, New York–Photo © AMNH, neg. 231080, 231235. 281tr: National Museum of Denmark, Copenhagen–Photo P. Freuchen © National Museum. 281mr: Arktisk Institut, Copenhagen–Photo © Danish Polar Center. 282t: Photo © Ivars Silis. 282b: The Royal Library, Copenhagen–Photo © Royal Library. 283: The Royal Library Copenhagen–Photo © Royal Library. 284t: Private collection–Photo P. Harvey © Chêne. 284b: Photo © Francis Parel. 285-286: Arktisk Institut, Copenhagen–Photo © Danish Polar Center. 288t: :F. Vernhet. 288b: National Museum of Denmark, Copenhagen–Photo P. Freuchen © National Museum, neg 1.1069. 289t: The Royal Library, Copenhagen–Photo © Royal Library neg. 28787. 289b: Collection Jean Malaurie. 290: American Museum of Natural History, New York–Photo M. Henson © AMNH, neg. 2A10258. 291: Private collection–Photo DR. 292-293: Arktisk Institut, Copenhagen–Photo © Danish Polar Center. 294t: National Museum of Denmark, Copenhagen–Photo © National Museum, neg. L7331, L8393, L4280. 294b: Collection Jean Malaurie. 295t: Arktisk Institut, Copenhagen–Photo © Danish Polar Center. 295b: Private collection–Photo P. Harvey © Chêne. 296t: National Museum of Denmark, Copenhagen–Photo © National Museum, neg. 1.1066. 296b: Photo © F. Vernhet. 297t: Photo © DR. 297b: National Museum of Denmark, Copenhagen–Photo P. Freuchen © National Museum, neg. L.751. 298tl and bl: American Museum of Natural History, New York–Photo © AMNH, neg. 231030, 232071. 298tr: Private collection–Photo P. Harvey © Chêne. 298br: Arktisk Institut, Copenhagen–Photo © Danish Polar Center. 299tl and br: American Museum of Natural History, New York–Photo © AMNH, neg. 232122, 231643. 299tr and bl: National Museum of Denmark, Copenhagen Th. Jomsen © National Museum, neg. 1.738, 1.80. 300-301: Photo © Ivars Silis. 302, 304, 305t: Arktisk Institut, Copenhagen–Photo © Danish Polar Center. 305b: National Museum of Denmark, Copenhagen–Photo P. Freuchen © National Museum, neg. L.1769. 306t: Arktisk Institut, Copenhagen–Photo © Danish Polar Center. 306b: Collection Jean Malaurie. 307: Arktisk Institut, Copenhagen–Photo © Danish Polar Center. 308-309: Photo © Francis Parel. 310-311-312-313: Arktisk Institut, Copenhagen–Photo © Danish Polar Center. 314-316-317-318t-320t-321: Scott Polar Research Institute, Cambridge–Photo © SPRI. 318b, 319: Photo © Ivars Silis. 320b: Collection Jean Malaurie. 322-324-325-328-329b-330t and b-331: Arktisk Institut, Copenhagen–Photo © Danish Polar Center. 326-327: Photo © Francis Parel. 329t-330m: Collection Jean Malaurie. 332-334-335-337t-338-339t-340t and b: Collection Jean Malaurie. 336: Coll. EPF–Photo © DR. 337b: Geodaetisk Institute, Copenhagen–Photo © DR. 339b: Exp. Paul-Emile Victor–Photo © D.R. 340m: Photo © Francis Parel. 341t, mt and b: Collection Jean Malaurie. 340mb: Photo © Peter Schledermann. 342-343t-344b-345: Collection Jean Malaurie. 343b: Photo © Ivars Silis. 344t: Photo © Bruce Jackson. 346t and m: Collection Jean Malaurie. 346b: Arctic and Antarctic Museum, Saint Petersburg–Photo © D. 347t and m: Collection Jean Malaurie. 347b: Photo © Ivars Silis. 348t: Collection Jean Malaurie. 348b: Photo © Editions Plon. 349t: Presidium of the Academy of Sciences, Moscow–Photo © DR. 349b: Collection Jean Malaurie. 350: Photos © Ivars Silis. 351t: Collection Jean Malaurie. 351b: Photo © Therese Davet. 352: Le Havre Presse–Photo © DR. 353-354-355-356b-357: Collection Jean Malaurie. 356t and m, 359: INA, Paris–Photo © DR. 358: Photo © Francis Parel. 360tl and m: Collection Jean Malaurie. 360tr © US Army. 360bl: Photo © Eléonore Malaurie. 360br: Photo © Francis Parel. 361: Collection Jean Malaurie. 362tl: Photo © B&C Alexander/Cosmos. 362tr: Photo © Eléonore Malaurie. 362m and b: Photos © Ivars Silis. 363: Photo © Ivars Silis. 364: Photo © E1éonore Malaurie. 365-366t-367: INA, Paris–Photo © DR. 366t: Collection Jean Malaurie. 368-369: Photo © Ivars Silis. 370tr-371-372: Collection Jean Malaurie. 370 (hare, bird) American Museum of Natural History, New York–Photo © AMNH. 373tl: Arktisk Institut, Copenhagen–Photo J. Bang © Danish Polar Center. 373tr and br: Collection Jean Malaurie. 373m et bl: American Museum of Natural History, New York–Photo © AMNH, neg. 231275, 231273. 374: Collection Jean Malaurie. 75: Dr. 376: B & C Alexander/Cosmos. 378: DR. 379: Collection Jean Malaurie. 380t: Photo © DITE-USIS. 380b: Photo © Th. Etévé. Coll. Research Consortium of US. 389: Collection Jean Malaurie. 390: Photo © B& C Alexander/Cosmos. 393: : Photo © B& C Alexander/Cosmos.

Illustrations : Euresys, Inc., in Baisieux, France
Printed in Italy: Editoriale Lloyd
Legal depot : 4974, November 2000
ISBN : 2.84277295.4
34/1457/0 - 01